Modern Art in Africa, Asia, and Latin America

An Introduction to Global Modernisms

Edited by

Elaine O'Brien
Everlyn Nicodemus
Melissa Chiu
Benjamin Genocchio
Mary K. Coffey
Roberto Tejada

WILEY-BLACKWELL

A John Wiley & Sons, Ltd., Publication

This edition first published 2013

Blackwell Publishing was acquired by John Wiley & Sons in February 2007. Blackwell's publishing program has been merged with Wiley's global Scientific, Technical, and Medical business to form Wiley-Blackwell.

Registered Office
John Wiley & Sons, Ltd, The Atrium, Southern Gate, Chichester, West Sussex, PO19 8SQ, UK

Editorial Offices
350 Main Street, Malden, MA 02148-5020, USA
9600 Garsington Road, Oxford, OX4 2DQ, UK
The Atrium, Southern Gate, Chichester, West Sussex, PO19 8SQ, UK

For details of our global editorial offices, for customer services, and for information about how to apply for permission to reuse the copyright material in this book please see our website at www.wiley.com/wiley-blackwell.

Library of Congress Cataloging-in-Publication Data

Modern art in Africa, Asia and Latin America : an introduction to global modernisms / edited by Elaine O'Brien... [et al.].
p. cm.
Includes bibliographical references and index.
ISBN 978-1-4443-3229-2 (hardback) – ISBN 978-1-4443-3230-8 (paperback) 1. Art, Modern–21st century.
2. Art movements–Africa–History–21st century. 3. Art movements–Asia–History–21st century.
4. Art movements–Latin America–History–21st century. I. O'Brien, Elaine, 1945–
N6497.M635 2012
709.04–dc23

2012023204

A catalogue record for this book is available from the British Library.

From top: Rhod Rothfuss, detail from *Cuadrilongo Amarillo*, Colección Patricia Phelps de Cisneros; Pang Xunqin, detail from *Such Is Paris*, 1931, courtesy of James D. Chang; Gerard Sekoto, detail from *The Song of the Pick*, © Sekoto Foundation. BHP Billiton Art Collection.

Cover design by Simon Levy Associates.

Set in 11/13pt Dante by SPi Publisher Services, Pondicherry, India

Printed in Singapore by Ho Printing Singapore Pte Ltd

1 2013

Contents

List of Figures

Acknowledgments

The editors of this book want to thank first of all the authors, translators, and copyright-holders who allowed us to reproduce the texts and images included here. That no one refused our requests means that not only does this book reflect our true intentions, but also its re-mapping of modern art history is widely welcomed. We are perhaps equally indebted to our students, who read and discussed these and many other texts considered for this volume in seminars on global modernism and courses in African, Asian, and Latin American modern art. Special thanks go to students Paula Bossa, Susie Kuo, Christina Maradik, Tatiana Reinoza, Leticia Rodriguez, and Lisa Young for their thoughtful dedication to this book in the early stages of the editorial process; and to Kristian Romare for his insightful contributions to the African modern art section. The support of the College of Fine Arts at the University of Texas, Austin, and California State University, Sacramento made it possible to advance the work and is thankfully acknowledged. Jayne Fargnoli at Wiley-Blackwell embraced this project and patiently guided it over several years. We are grateful to her and to Wiley-Blackwell's entire editorial and production team, whose masterly skills and gracious professionalism made every step sure and pleasurable. Finally, the editors of this volume, who have worked together across continents and oceans for several years, feel they owe much to each other for the opportunity they have had to recalculate the many geographies of modern art.

General Introduction
The Location of Modern Art

Elaine O'Brien

I have said School of the South: because, in fact, our North looks South. For us there must not be a North, except in opposition to the South ... This correction was necessary; because of it we know where we are.

Joaquín Torres García

For Joaquín Torres García of Montevideo, as we see from his remark above and his inverted map of South America, modern art like his from the "School of the South" required a reoriented view of the world. To Torres García, as to cosmopolitan moderns everywhere, location had to be imagined differently for them to "know where we are." For what they created to be truly theirs and seen for what it is, the mental map of modern art would have to be redrawn and its histories realigned. *African, Asian, and Latin American Modern Art: An Introduction to Global Modernism* takes up the project of remapping modern art that Torres García proposed in 1943, but it does so from multiple locations and world perspectives rather than any one place, "north" or "south," "east" or "west."

This book brings together critical art histories and documents of modern art produced approximately between 1890 and 1970. Dates for modern art are here as everywhere imprecise and flexible, and for this volume they can vary significantly depending on each situation and the point of view of each author and editor, but the inclusive "when" of modern art we present coincides with the last century of the Age of Europe: the final sweep of the great half-millennium wave of European expansionism that was emblematically set into motion with the seismic 1492 Encounter on Hispaniola, rose high across four centuries, then surged and receded while the art in this book was being made.

Modern Art in Africa, Asia, and Latin America: An Introduction to Global Modernisms, First Edition.
Edited by Elaine O'Brien, Everlyn Nicodemus, Melissa Chiu, Benjamin Genocchio, Mary K. Coffey, and Roberto Tejada.

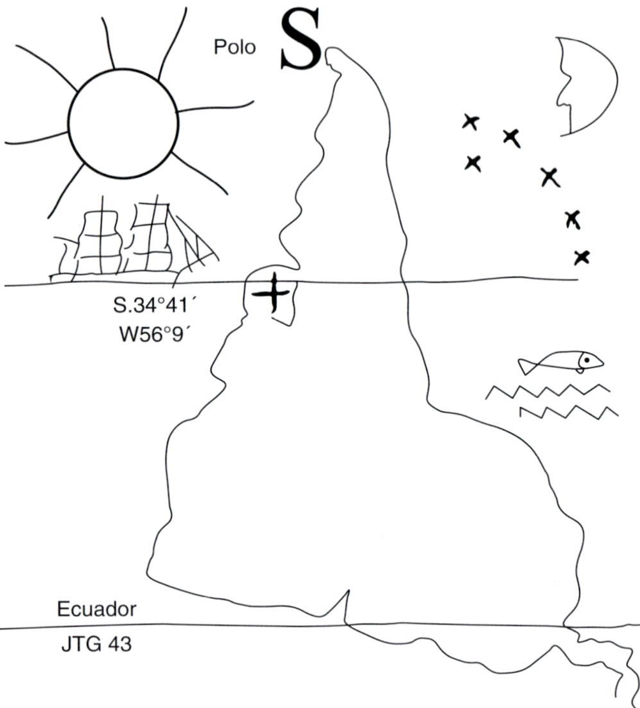

Figure GI.1 Joaquín Torres-García, *Inverted Map*, 1943, courtesy of Cecilia de Torres, New York, © DACS 2011.

To locate modern art geographically we take a planetary perspective, look past the borders of nations, continents, and bounded cultures[1] to the movement of individual artists and objects of visual culture along the imperial trade routes of the Age of Europe: the network of commerce that wrapped the globe and linked cosmopolitan cities like Paris, São Paulo, Shanghai, and Lagos. A complete mapping of modern art would include every world city on the routes of modernity, which is not the case for this volume. The controlled scope of *African, Asian, and Latin American Modern Art* allows us to trace vital exchanges among the world's modern artists and begin to see a larger and truer picture of why modern art looks as it does, so wholly different from what came before. The reader draws extra-regional connections from an anthology that organizes the production of African, Asian, and Latin American artists in three self-contained sections edited by area specialists.

The book is assembled from local points of view: national, continental, and regional; but national approaches are the primary source for most of the scholarship involved here. The national perspective dominates not only because it is the standard for art historiography, but also more substantively because the nation and nationalism held a central place in the political and cultural unconscious of most modern artists; and as a governing construct of modernity, the nation effectively determined the shape of modern identity, politics, and official culture. Chika Okeke asserts, for example, in an essay included here, that modernism did not arrive on the continent of Africa until the "independence decade" (1955–65) and the rise of nation states. Colonized status, Okeke maintains, precludes the freedom of expression requisite to modern art. Only "the increasing nationalist fervor in many countries," he writes, "strengthened the resolve of artists to seek out aspects of their cultures discredited by the logic of colonialism." Indian art critic Geeta Kapur makes much the same argument for the temporal location of modern art in India. While she acknowledges that cosmopolitan artists such as Rabindranath Tagore (1861–1941) and Amrita Sher-Gil (1913–41) participated in international modernist discourse and produced signature works early in the twentieth century, Kapur contends that modernism inside India's troubled borders began only decades later with the nationalist struggle for independence from British colonial rule.

The idea of the nation is central to modernity and essential to our story, but the vertical point of view is nonetheless inadequate as it fails to comprehend the vital extraterritorial dynamics of global modernism that are inimical to binary (inside–outside) boundaries. Only a satellite view can make it apparent that national borders, which protected and disciplined heterogeneous, often antagonistic, populations, were ever porous and mutating. More importantly for the history of modern art, border crossing was the essential catalyst of invention.

What becomes evident is that modern art's trademark mongrel innovation was cultivated not in nations but in the world's most open, artist-dense cities, where internationalism, long considered "the main merit and sign of modernism," flourished (McFarlane 1976: 78). In world cities, intersections of artistic encounter, cultural traditions co-existed and cross-fertilized through the agency of individual artists, writers, and musicians who exchanged ideas across the arts. Old ways and new ways, our ways and their ways met, mixed, and remixed there in ever-multiplying translations, ever-original hybrids. What prevailed in the liminal urban spaces of modern art was a translocal exile consciousness that denaturalized the norms of both home cultures and adopted ones.

Within each cosmopolitan center were districts where the concentration of peripatetic culture makers was highest and contact constant. The northern Manhattan neighborhood of Harlem in the 1920s and early 1930s is one such catalytic zone, or "third space," apart from mainstream nationalist culture. With the Great Migration, African Americans flowed into Harlem from the rural south; veterans returned there from Europe after World War I; other migrants came from the West Indies and some from Africa. The daring freedom and invention of Harlem in the interwar period, so evident in its famous music and nightlife, was a magnet as well to artists, musicians, poets, and intellectuals of downtown Manhattan bohemias. Up from the Village flocked young artistic émigrés from every point of origin, of varied races and ethnicities. Harlem then is described as "the epicenter of cool" before "cool" was coined: "an orgy of painters, intellectuals, punks, whores, studs, gentlemen, writers, hipsters, sculptors, swingers, fags, queens, niggers, heroes, poets, piano rollers, and all-night parties … Harlem knew no fear" (Amos 2000: 5). The world capital of black modernism, Harlem gave its name to the Harlem Renaissance, presented in this volume by Michael Harris on the visual art of the African diaspora. As with every contact zone on the circuits of modernity, the influence of Harlem was centrifugal and planetary. Artists nurtured there were cosmopolitans who traveled to other centers on the imperial circuit, notably the metropoles of Europe where black modernism, literary, and visual art, but especially jazz – the very name of the age – was avidly appropriated as it was itself transformed through creative encounters. "Harlem," Paul Gilroy notes of the music,

> became an imaginary repository of transgressive feeling to many far-flung affiliates of the avant-garde … As the musics travelled, they registered the processes of dissemination in their own attenuated forms … European critics began to write about the music seriously and respectfully but without always appreciating its historic ties to black America. (Gilroy 1997)

At the same time, on the other side of the world from Harlem, the so-called golden age of Chinese modernism (ca. 1919–45) had arrived in one of the most cosmopolitan centers on the trade routes of modernity: Shanghai, from the perspective of Chinese leftist and communist writers, "a bastion of evil, of wanton debauchery and rampant imperialism" (Lee 1999: 4). A 1934 Shanghai University Press guide to the city describes a location tense with the vibrant contradictions of modernity: "Cosmopolitan Shanghai, city of amazing paradoxes and fantastic contrasts; Shanghai the beautiful, bawdy, and gaudy, contradiction of manners and morals; a vast brilliantly hued cycloramic, panoramic mural of the best and the worst of Orient and Occident."[2]

Great Britain had forced China to open its ports to direct trade with the West after the First Opium War (1839–42) and the defeat of the Qing navy. Vital seaport districts of Shanghai were surrendered to Western colonial rule as part of the unequal Treaty of Nanjing. Surging economic opportunity and political and social freedom in Shanghai's new Westernized zones drew foreigners from everywhere and ignited

> the fastest urban growth in East Asia of its day and … [b]y the first decade of the twentieth century Shanghai's foreign community in the colonized districts included Chinese, British, French, and United States citizens, nationals of Japan, Russia, Germany, Portugal, Italy, Spain, Poland, and Greece in addition to those from India, Indochina, and other colonial possessions of the British and French empires. (Yeh 2010: 12)

Massive migrations from inside China further enriched Shanghai cosmopolitanism. Unending anti-imperialist wars, internal rebellions, floods, and famines that would eventually bring down the Qing dynasty sent thousands to the city seeking refuge. Shanghai modernism was thus spun out of the center of a world vortex. The foreign districts formed a contact zone whose commercial wealth, clamoring cultural diversity, and freedom drew many artists, like Xu Beihong, a young provincial from Yixing who arrived in 1915 to pursue a career as a painter. The story of Xu Beihong's engagements with global modernism in Shanghai, Tokyo, Peking, Paris, and Nanjing – his and other artists' appropriations and re-appropriations in a shared, competitive quest for an "authentic" Chinese modernism – are told in the Asian section of this book by Eugene Y. Wang, Ralph Croizier, Zheng Dongtian, and by Ni Yide, Pang Xunqing, and the other members of the Shanghai avant-garde group, The Storm Society, in their 1932 manifesto.

In world cities, besides artists, there were also traveling objects of art on view from every historic and living world tradition: exotic works that astonished viewers and inspired levels of invention unsurpassed in the history of art. Exposure to them and to copies made for commercial trade occurred on the streets, in markets and in shops. But perhaps the most significant place of encounter was in modernity's new metropolitan museums of art and (colonial) anthropology: institutions that served as principal sites of appropriation in the nineteenth and twentieth centuries. All the marvelous objects of Europe's formal and informal empires were brought to its imperial metropoles like booty: influential expropriations from Africa and Oceania joined collections of objects taken in previous centuries from conquered indigenous cultures of the Americas and elsewhere. Cut loose from intended meaning and social function, many found their way, with works (and copies) of classical and European art, to provincial and colonial museums around the world. The awesome treasures of empire were also presented at "universal" expositions: trademark displays of modernity, nationalist spectacles of industrial and cultural power.

London's 1851 Great Exhibition of the Works of Industry of all Nations, first and exemplary of a century of such world fairs, was seen by six million visitors. With its global reach as a trade extravaganza, its unbridled display – over 100,000 products and 14,000 exhibitors – London's Great Exhibition proclaimed the triumph of Western Europe's commodity culture and was as prophetic of the century to follow as was the Crystal Palace of prefabricated iron and glass that housed it. The impact of such foreign spectacles on artists and the globalization of culture that world expositions signaled is a defining story of modern visual culture. Wherever they were encountered in modernity's systems of propagation, foreign works (regardless of the maker's intention) were reimagined as "art" in the modern sense of a product of individual expression meant for individual secular contemplation. En route they acquired often radically alien value as portable, collectable commodities destined for the art market, private collection, and art museum. What did not travel was made available to avid eyes everywhere in photographs.

"As soon as there was photography there was travel photography" (Osborne 2000: 3). Just eight weeks after the daguerreotype process was revealed in Paris in 1839, Frenchman Pierre-Gustave Joly de Lotbinière was taking pictures of the Athenian Parthenon. Countless photographs followed of art and architecture from distant times and places, and as photographic reproduction processes developed over the next decades, copies became abundant and were readily at hand for urban moderns. All had access to the world's visual cultures past and present in the vast new photographic "museum without walls" that unfixed meanings and the boundaries of art.

The photographic arts were, like every art, complicit with the best and worst of the Eurocentric order, but it is fair to say that photography and film were manipulated and censored more by commercial and political powers-that-be than any other visual media. In this anthology, Joe Takeba, for example, tells of the silencing of avant-garde photographers by Japan's military regime from the 1930s through World War II. Free of excessive restraint, however, this newest and most populist vehicle of expression gave proof that worthy subjects and ways of seeing them are abundant. The multiple and contradictory individual manifestations of reality captured in photographs had the power to throw stereotypes and conventions into doubt. This is true of Mario de Andrade's (1893–1945) "errant" photographs, presented here by Esther Gabara, which give us a subjective and undefinable Brazilian landscape – landscape as existential question – radically different from the Brazil that traditional painting or tourist photographs portray. Authentic identity is the challenge taken up by other modern photographers in these pages. This can be seen in the dialogue between two celebrated cinematographers of African life, Senegalese Ousmane Sembène (1923–2007) and French ethnographer Jean Rouch (1917–2004). Sembène accuses Rouch: "You look at us as if we were insects!" While the European may reply that his outsider representations of Africa are necessary because, as he sees it, they are objective, for the African, not only is his own insider's view uniquely authentic, but it is more ethical, since it equalizes the power of the filmmaker and the filmed.

Ongoing creative dialogue took place in modernity's contact zones among individual artist strangers, travelers, and exiles, each one a bearer of local traditions and attitudes. Modern artists in this book originate from equal and unequal regions of the world, but all are comparable as artist agents of cultural translation. Inequalities of regional power and opportunity in the modern era, as well as the Eurocentrism of art historiography, have made too little of the parity of artistic intercourse at the individual level of creative friendship and exchange in the world's alternative "third" spaces. Each artist conceived unique hybrids and carried newly invented forms and ideas everywhere he or she traveled: to other urban centers and back home, where he or she often stayed to produce and teach. Their influence and works spread modern art to smaller cities linked to the global network by ever-modernizing transportation and communication technologies. Thus an avant-garde little magazine like *Boletin Titikaka* (1926–30), published in the town of Orkopata, Peru, could be and was read in cosmopolitan Mexico City, Buenos Aires, and Paris (Hedrick 2003: 66–7).

Demographically, the African, Asian, and Latin American artists in this book are almost all men of at least adequate means and education, most of whom emerged from the middle classes and chose membership in what can be seen as a class apart, the international avant-garde, sharing values and alternative lifestyles outside or in opposition to the conventions of the dominant middle social classes of their origins. From the global perspective, the class identity of modern artists is complicated by the multiplicity of social systems around the world and how thoroughly issues of socioeconomic class are entangled in the biases and inequities of the age, especially in colonized regions. In Latin America, for example, where decolonization began in the early nineteenth century, Eurocentric hierarchies of race closely tied to economic and social privileges of class persisted through the modern era. For black and native Latin Americans it was rarely a personal choice to be déclassé, rare to be shown on the world stage, and rare to have the chance to achieve it. Race is a subtext for many authors in this volume. Robert Stam, for one, takes it as his subject in "Carmen Miranda, Grande Otelo, and the *Chanchada*, 1929–1949," an excerpt included here from Stam's book on race in Brazilian cinema and culture. The bohemian "starving artist" – the heroic anti-bourgeois persona like the banker révolté, Paul Gauguin – was not an option for black artists in Africa either. In Steven Sack's "From Country to City: The Development of an Urban Art" we read about black township artists of apartheid-era South Africa, like John Koenakeefe

Mohl, Helen Sebidi, Dumile Feni, and Gerard Sekoto, for whom poverty was the inescapable situation they shared with all township residents.

Regardless of socioeconomic class, few women artists appear in these pages because women, from anywhere in the world, were not often included in writings on art history, not even in regional histories of African, Asian, and Latin American modern art before the last decades of the twentieth century when our study ends. No matter how closely we peer into the sea of time where our dead sisters' thoughts, feelings, and artistic genius vanished, we can see little. To date, the recent field of global feminist art history has concentrated on contemporary artists and not their modern precursors. As you will read in Everlyn Nicodemus's introduction to the African section, this is especially true of African art history. There is much historiographical work to be done.

No amount of art historical research, however, can retrieve a never-created masterpiece. The hardest fact of why there is scarce record of modern experience as seen through the eyes of women is much less the blindness of art historiography than the real historical situations of women worldwide in the modern era, regardless of social class. Though individual situations varied depending on context, nowhere in this period were women routinely offered equal opportunity for a modern kind of artistic education, let alone freedom for independent travel or migration to cosmopolitan cities to mix with worldly strangers. This was especially unimaginable in the bohemian, sexually liberated neighborhoods typical of avant-garde modernism. Even in imperial metropoles, female creativity occurred almost exclusively within the private spaces of femininity. Women everywhere were kept from creative intercourse by walls of societal stereotypes upheld by nearly all men and women of the time, including the most sophisticated social critics. Even enlightened modernist circles were conventionally and nearly universally patriarchal and homosocial. Domestic arts associated with the typology of the good woman varied, but all versions were antithetical to the type of the modern vanguard artist who paradigmatically rejected conventional domestic roles for alternative lifestyles and identities that allowed freedom for encounters with strangers and the development of creative liaisons in the public, masculine spaces of world cities.

The artists in this book participated in the creation of the first truly global visual culture, avant-garde modernism. Culture makers from Africa, Asia, and Latin America, like all modernists, produced art from inside the era's profound axiological shift from tradition to futurity. With the future ever present, to be relevant meant to be of one's time and to share a utopian impulse toward the creation of a better society, even when that meant returning to a pre-modern past or turning inward to investigations of subjective consciousness. Understood as an oppositional, alienated, or autonomous posture toward the status quo of establishment culture and society, the historical avant-garde is associated with groups of young artists and writers who stood together as individuals to transform the given. Independent vanguard magazines formed to publish their poetry, cultural commentary, and signature manifestos such as those included in this anthology:

Takahashi Shinkichi's "Assertion is Dadaist" (1923, Tokyo); "The Storm Society Manifesto," signed by Ni Yide, Pang Xunqin, *et al.* (1932, Shanghai); Oswald de Andrade's "Cannibalist Manifesto" (1928, São Paulo); and Uche Okeke's "Natural Synthesis" (1960, Zaria, Nigeria). Roughly synonymous with the "cutting edge" of a modernity presumed to be advancing, that edge that cut countless ways was honed on hope and a shared belief in the power of art and the ethical role of the artist in society. Since each artist was by definition experimental and individualist, since each vision and situation was unique, the question of what it means to be avant-garde has drawn a range of responses across time and place.

"Avant-garde" originated as a French military term for an advance guard sent out ahead of the army. It carried connotations of perilous exploration, youthful camaraderie, duty, and courage. French utopian socialist Henri de Saint-Simon (1760–1825) is credited with first appropriating the term to refer to an elite class of artists whose superior imaginations and expressive skills would show the way to a new and better world. Saint-Simon's conviction that the creative individual can (and should) innovate ways to improve the human lot was a foundation of vanguard modernism. In the Western tradition, such ideas go back at least to Plato and continue through the Renaissance and Enlightenment. But the catalyst for the nineteenth-century Saint-Simonian precept that the artist has the prophetic vision and obligation to serve society as witness and critic of modernity was revolution.

Social, political, industrial, scientific, and technological revolution erupted ceaselessly during the Age of Europe. Positioned after 1492 at the crossroads of knowledge from all corners of the world, Europe was the innovative center that over the next centuries fostered the extraordinary achievements of the Scientific Revolution. By the last Europe-centered century, the epoch of this book, the great advances of science had instilled in many moderns a deep faith in progress in all aspects of human endeavor. Imperial expansion took that conviction to every population of the world; all were affected, overwhelmed by the implacable combined forces of capitalism and modernization, seduced and inspired by the emancipatory potential of humanist utopianism. Reason for hope, yet at the same time those very ideologies of scientific rationalism and teleological progress served as instruments of imperial governance by which global majorities were mismeasured and managed. At once inside and outside this ideological double bind, avant-gardism thus took on different layers of paradoxical complexity in each contact zone and for each artistic encounter. However singular, every creative interaction was located in the era's universal agon between past and present in pursuit of the future. This is evident throughout this collection.

One example is a discussion of Indonesian modern art in which Jakarta-based critic Jim Supangkat underlines the differences he sees between Indonesian and Western modernism but notes that the progressivism of Indonesian modernism in the 1930s

> reflected idealism … As in the West, Indonesian modernists rejected conventional values and academic art, stood up for individual freedom, and focused on subjects

> that had their roots in social reality … [E]mergent modernism was an important sign of a rejection of feudal elitist values in independent (modern) Indonesia. (Chapter 13, this volume, p. 112)

Similarly, Argentine art historian, Andrea Giunta, presents Latin American modernism in these pages as a range of tactics deployed by artists interacting with particular social, political, and cultural situations. She sketches out the "strategies of modernity" of key modernists, including constructive Universalist Joaquín Torres García (1874–1949). A protagonist of avant-garde circles in Barcelona, Madrid, New York, and Paris before returning home to Montevideo in 1934, Giunta wrote,

> Torres's aesthetic programme … would acquire [in Montevideo] a new dimension from its confrontation with a diverse reality in which currents of Latin Americanist thought circulated intensely … [I]t was in the country to which he returned that his proposals to integrate art with life … were received and accepted. (Chapter 29, this volume, p. 310)

In Jakarta and Montevideo, as in every contact zone on the trade routes of modernity, avant-gardes recast the liberated syntax and palette of modern art to co-create a living language of both local and global address and inspiration.

An avant-garde attitude, then, unites global modernists, but it was a unity of difference. Besides the infinite range of contexts, each modern artist's stance was unique and complex. More than that, within every artist's lifetime situations and strategies changed. Certainly the politicized Saint-Simonian position was not of a piece nor was it ever the only one considered avant-garde. The avant-garde concept has had a notably eclectic history up to today's so-called post- or neo-avant-garde art world where it continues to be redefined for the past as well as the present. The majority of the modern artists presented in this collection have been received by art history as members of an avant-garde of formal invention. Their art was of its time, but seldom has it been interpreted as a didactic, overt response to specific sociopolitical conditions. Rather, the modern artists you will meet here are credited with reinventing the language of art by creating unique syntheses drawn from multicultural forms, Western and non-Western, elite and popular, mimetic and nonrepresentational. In doing so they liberated the abstract elements of art (form, line, shape, color, texture, space, value, composition, materials) from conventional applications to say something that had not been said and could not have been said in that way by anyone else. For avant-garde modernism, the *new*, as in "the tradition of the new" and "the shock of the new," refers to the nearly endless individual variations of a fusion culture created by artists consciously engaged in one way or another with the conditions of modernity that shaped each of their lives differently. Engagement determined the historical relevance of modern art, and in revolutionary times engagement required the invention of new forms that could hold permanence and change in dynamic tension.

Today's twenty-first century attitudes toward progress and the possibility that the artist can lead the way to a better future are characterized rather more by skepticism than by faith, but we can easily recognize the modernist confrontation of old and new as a continuing crisis in our own times. By referring to modernity in the present tense as he points to its essential character, intellectual historian Marshall Berman underlines the continuity of the modern experience into the present:

> Modern environments and experiences cut across all boundaries of geography and ethnicity, of class and nationality, of religion and ideology: in this sense, modernity can be said to unite all mankind. But it is a paradoxical unity, a unity of disunity: it pours us all into a maelstrom of perpetual disintegration and renewal, of struggle and contradiction, of ambiguity and anguish. To be modern is to be part of a universe in which, as Marx said, "all that is solid melts into air." (Berman 1982: 15)

Berman's view of modernism as an ongoing project supports a planetary perspective on modern art historiography. Because today's artists are caught up in the same borderless dynamics, the same "maelstrom of perpetual disintegration and renewal," as the artists in this book, global modernism continues in the bloodstream of contemporary art in a way that a hermetic Western modernism cannot. The expanded lineage of modern art strengthens it, moreover, because of the time lag of opportunity between the modern and the contemporary; the inclusion today of new streams of world artists who would have been excluded in the past by racism and sexism has kept avant-garde idealism flowing into the present.

From the global perspective of this book, what emerges as the unifying strategy behind the creation of modernisms everywhere is the transformative act of appropriation, understood here to subsume all cross-cultural artistic exchange: Primitivist, Orientalist, and Occidentalist (i.e., both non-Western and Western).[3] Appropriation was not invented by the moderns, but under nineteenth and twentieth-century conditions of mass urbanization and the modernization of travel and communication, distances shrank and cross-culture encounters with foreign artists and objects of art greatly increased to become everyday matters in contact zones. On all sides, artist-agents of modernism stole for their own art the power they saw in alien traditions, vastly expanding the concept, vocabulary, and expressive potential of art. Strong misreadings were the normal, necessary lubricants of modern art making, and conservative art forms from one culture functioned in quite radical ways in transferred cultures. In the first years of the twentieth century, for example, while Pablo Picasso (1881–1973), a Spaniard in Paris, was appropriating the formal language of traditional African art, Aina Onabolu (1882–1963) of Lagos was appropriating the mimetic illusionism of the academic European tradition. Although Picasso and Onabolu (who would study in Paris and London only after developing his Occidental style) probably never met, they were equally and simultaneously vehicles of African–European cross-fertilization.

"In the African context," writes Everlyn Nicodemus in this volume, "the young [Onabolu's] appropriation was a revolution: 'modern' in that it was a clear break with the past. Aina Onabolu's choice of easel painting and academic realism was also deeply political." The artist's Occidentalism, his appropriation of the very methods of Western-style academic painting that the European avant-garde rejected, was for the African a way to steal the fire – the all-too-evident power – of Europe. Onabolu's Occidentalism was not unique in the global context. Academies of art founded in Europe's colonies, former colonies, and areas of influence during the Age of Europe trained artists worldwide in European-style naturalism and established the normative frame for the Eurocentric view of world art. European and European-trained artists traveled to art academies throughout the empire to teach, for example, at the Academia de San Carlos in Mexico City, the first academy of art in the Americas, which opened in 1781. On the Indian subcontinent during the British Raj (1858–1947), Western-style institutions supplanted the traditional schools of miniature painting; and in Meiji Japan (1868–1912), representational oil painting was officially embraced as the sign of modernization and Western might. In the context of Onabolu's colonial Nigeria where Western art was not taught until the artist himself introduced it, and where European "scientific" racism justified the flagrant control and exploitation of his people, the artist's mastery of mimesis was self-determined and strategic, political first of all as proof of black–white racial equality.

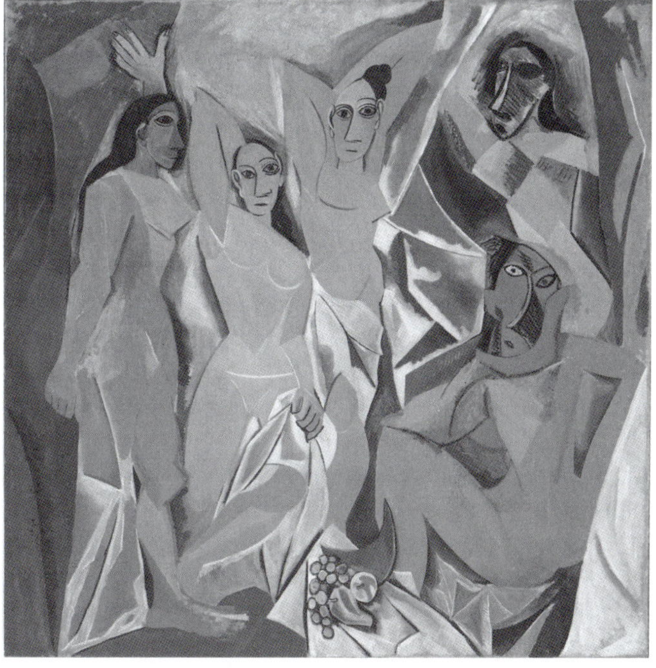

Figure GI.2 Pablo Picasso, *Les Demoiselles d'Avignon*, 1907, New York, Museum of Modern Art (MoMA), oil on canvas. Acquired through the Lillie P. Bliss Bequest. 333.1939, © 2011. Digital image, the Museum of Modern Art, New York/Scala, Florence, © Succession Picasso/DACS, London 2011.

On the Parisian side of the cultural exchange – an often-told story – the young Picasso encountered galleries of expropriated sculptures from French African and Oceanic colonies in the Musée d'Ethnographie du Trocadéro and later testified to their transformative affect. He told André Malraux years after his epiphany,

> The masks weren't just like any other pieces of sculpture. Not at all. They were magic things … *Les Demoiselles d'Avignon* [1907] must have come to me that very day, not at all because of the forms; because it was my first exorcism painting – yes absolutely! (Picasso, quoted by Malraux [trans. Guicarnaud] in Leighten 1990: 625)

Picasso scholar Patricia Leighten notes that

> at the very least we can say that Picasso's interest in African art lay as much in what he imagined to be their function as ritual objects as in their forms, whose very abstraction encoded the mystical power he wanted to appropriate. (Leighten 1990[4])

Against what were to him the enervated traditions of Western art, Picasso would incorporate the liberated syntax of African sculpture into his art. What he took from the Musée d'Ethnographie would infuse his painting with the power that rocked the artist in those dusky galleries. His paintings would acquire the expanded vocabulary needed to "exorcize" personal and cultural psychosexual anxieties and the establishment values and exploitative practices of Europe so scorned by his countercultural circle. In both Lagos and Paris, then, appropriation had relational, politicized artistic intent for modern artists. The syncretic art of Onabolu and Picasso responded in equal measure to the conditions of modernity. Their art was not specifically African or European but both at once and more than that: its themes, techniques, and styles transcended bounded locations of time, place, and ideology to produce something new.

For many global modernists, appropriation and the ever-new hybridized vocabulary of modern art were the means of creating a self-determined modern identity out of the dynamics of tradition and change specific to their experience. Efforts by modern artists to counter given orders of identity punctuate numerous stories told in this book. Many readings offer evidence of this deconstructive/reconstructive purpose for global modernisms, but perhaps most explicit are those by Partha Mitter in "The Formalist Prelude," Jim Supangkat in "Multiculturalism/Multimodernism," Uche Okeke in the 1960 manifesto *Natural Synthesis*, Andrea Giunta in "Strategies of Modernity in Latin America," and Oswald de Andrade in the 1928 "Cannibalist Manifesto" (Manifesto Antropófago). In this last text, "cannibalism" – the eating of other cultures – is a strategically chosen synonym for appropriation. Andrade affirms the centrality of cultural cannibalism to Brazilian, Latin American, and global culture in the first lines of his manifesto: "Cannibalism alone unites us. Socially. Economically. Philosophically. The world's single law. Disguised expression of all individualism, of all collectivisms. Of all religions. Of all peace treaties." Translator Leslie Bary underlines this point in her introduction to the text:

> In the ["Cannibalist Manifesto"], Oswald subversively appropriates the colonizer's inscription of America as a savage territory … the cannibal metaphor permits the Brazilian subject to forge his specular colonial identity into an autonomous and original (as opposed to dependent, derivative) national culture. (see Chapter 39, this volume)

The aim of *An Introduction to Global Modernism* is to relocate modern art production on the world map so as to see it as a relational, transcultural enterprise: a conceptual shift that changes everything. By proposing an interactive, extraterritorial paradigm that integrates narratives of vanguard production by African, Asian, and Latin American artists, this anthology expands and decenters the historiography of modern art. The stories offered in these pages make sense of the mongrel global culture that avant-garde modernism was, but as importantly, they give contemporary global art production its missing history. It is because the transcultural world reach of modern art has been ignored that today's cosmopolitan artists and their artworks are so often presented thematically, as if they had no histories or precursors. Among the texts in every section of *An Introduction to Global Modernism* are those that address neglected topics in modern art that are especially relevant to contemporary art, such as art and artists in diaspora; international avant-garde exhibitions and magazines; and local differences in art worlds and situations for artists. Introductions with leading questions frame each part and chapter to situate every historical narrative in its relevant contexts, link it to other histories in the book, supply clarifying background, and guide the reader through key theoretical positions and debates.

Finally, *An Introduction to Global Modernism* has been made for twenty-first century readers accustomed to thinking in terms of global–local creative tensions and dynamics like those behind the art in these pages. Over recent decades, the disintegration of the European empire and its structures of knowledge have distanced us from the moderns. But what remains are global modernism's cosmopolitan network, the transcultural appropriative processes of its artists, and (however sobered and transformed) the international avant-garde's purpose and adversarial, interrogative, or autonomous attitudes toward the given. This book locates modern artists on very nearly the same planetary routes taken by today's jet artists and expatriates. For both the past and the present, then, relational lines can be drawn connecting artists and places where radical new forms of visual culture are conceived. With such a map in hand, the large picture of how new art comes into being can also restore the relevance of the artistic past to the present as it continues its headlong rush to the future.

Notes

1 Terms for bordered regions are entangled in a cartographic history associated with global empire and the management of it. Benedict Anderson's 1983 *Imagined Communities: Reflections on the Origin and Spread of Nationalism* historicized the idea of the nation as a modern identity construct that spread throughout the world; see the revised edition (Anderson 2006). See also V. Y. Mudimbe (1988).

2 Unknown author, *All About Shanghai and Environs: A Standard Guidebook*, Shanghai: Shanghai University Press, 1934, quoted by Nancy Berliner (2010: 25).

3 On primitivizing as a universal strategy of global modernisms, see Mitter (1994, especially Part One: "The Phenomenon: Occidental Orientation," pp. 1–25), Lemke (1998), and Pan (2001).

4 On the political significance of the appropriation of African art by Pablo Picasso and his circle, see Leighten (1990: 609–30). For key texts on Western Primitivism, see Leighten (1990: 609, n.2) and Flam and Deutsch (2003).

References

Amos, Shawn (2000) "Notes from a Wanna-be Harlemite." In *Rhapsodies in Black: Music and words from the Harlem Renaissance*. Los Angeles, CA: Rhino Entertainment Company.

Anderson, Benedict (2006) *Imagined Communities: Reflections on the Origin and Spread of Nationalism* (rev. edn). New York, NY: Verso.

Berliner, Nancy (2010) "Reaching to Heaven: Shanghai Architecture and Interiors." In *Shanghai: Art of the City* (pp. 25–31). San Francisco, CA: Asian Art Museum of San Francisco.

Berman, Marshall (1982) *All That is Solid Melts Into Air: The Experience of Modernity*. New York, NY: Simon & Schuster.

Flam, Jack and Deutsch, Miriam (eds) (2003) *Primitivism and Twentieth-Century Art: A Documentary History*. Berkeley: University of California Press.

Gilroy, Paul (1997) "Modern Tones." In *Rhapsodies in Black: Art of the Harlem Renaissance* (pp. 102–9). Berkeley: University of California Press.

Hedrick, Tace (2003) *Mestizo Modernism: Race, Nation, and Identity in Latin American Culture, 1900–1940*. New Brunswick, NJ: Rutgers University Press.

Lee, Leo Ou-fan (1999) *Shanghai Modern: The Flowering of a New Urban Culture in China, 1930–1945*. Cambridge, MA: Harvard University Press.

Leighten, Patricia (1990) "The White Peril and L'art negre: Picasso, primitivism, and anticolonialism." *Art Bulletin* (December): 609–30.

Lemke, Sieglinde (1998) *Primitivist Modernism: Black Culture and the Origins of Transatlantic Modernism*. Oxford, England: Oxford University Press.

McFarlane, James (1976) "The Mind of Modernism." In M. Bradbury and J. McFarlane (eds), *Modernism 1890–1930* (pp. 71–94). Atlantic Highlands, NJ: Humanities Press.

Mitter, Partha (1994) *Art and Nationalism in Colonial India, 1850–1922: Occidental Orientations*. Cambridge, England: Cambridge University Press.

Mudimbe, V. Y. (1988) *The Invention of Africa*. Indianapolis: Indiana University Press.

Osborne, Peter D. (2000) *Travelling Light: Photography, Travel and Visual Culture*. Manchester, England: Manchester University Press.

Pan, David (2001) *Primitive Renaissance: Rethinking German Expressionism*. Lincoln: University of Nebraska Press.

Yeh, Wen-hsin (2010) "A tale of three cities: Shanghai from 1850 to the present." In *Shanghai: Art of the City* (pp. 11–13). San Francisco, CA: Asian Art Museum of San Francisco.

Part I

African Modern Art

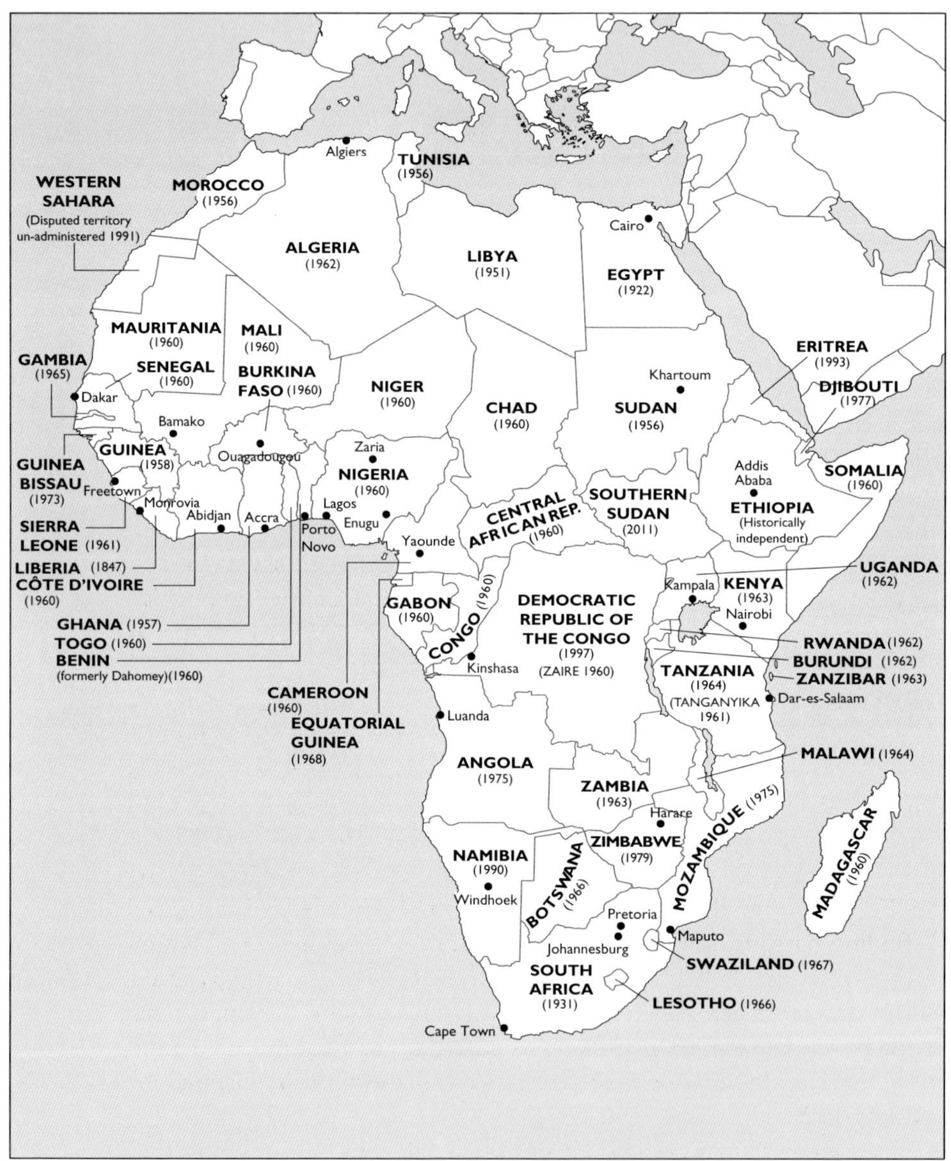

Map 1 Locations of Modern Art in Africa.

Introduction
African Modern Art: An Ongoing Project

EVERLYN NICODEMUS

In the year 1900, Aina Onabolu (1882–1963), a young man in the British colonially ruled city of Lagos in what is today Nigeria, began a career as a self-taught portrait painter. Fascinated from childhood by reproductions of European paintings in foreign magazines, Onabolu became notorious in school as the only black African to make images like the whites. The European painting that he copied was academic realism, which, with its exact likenesses of individuals, objects, and landscapes, presented something starkly different from the religiously functioning carved idols and masks that constituted the main tradition of African visual culture with which Onabolu had grown up. In the African context, the young artist's appropriation was a revolution: "modern" in that it was a clear break with the past.[1]

Aina Onabolu's choice of easel painting and academic realism was also deeply political, an act of defiance against the bigotry that oppressed all Africans. This was a period in the colonial history of African–European relations when so-called scientific racism flourished in Europe, branding black Africans as subhumans and hardening the colonizers' attitudes against them. Indigenous Africans, according to the "science" of Europe at this time, were not intellectually capable of producing fine art in the Western sense; they were fit only for craft. Acknowledged as a gifted professional, finding patrons among Lagos' population of educated black immigrants, freed slaves returning from America and Europe, Onabolu managed to have art lessons introduced in black schools and initiated the training of professional artists in Nigeria by the 1920s. Less attention has been paid to what this revolution meant than to the simultaneous change in European modernism inspired by premodern African art.[2]

The case of Onabolu is typical and exceptional. Exceptional by being that early; typical because the difficulties he faced were those that have challenged all

Modern Art in Africa, Asia, and Latin America: An Introduction to Global Modernisms, First Edition.
Edited by Elaine O'Brien, Everlyn Nicodemus, Melissa Chiu, Benjamin Genocchio,
Mary K. Coffey, and Roberto Tejada.

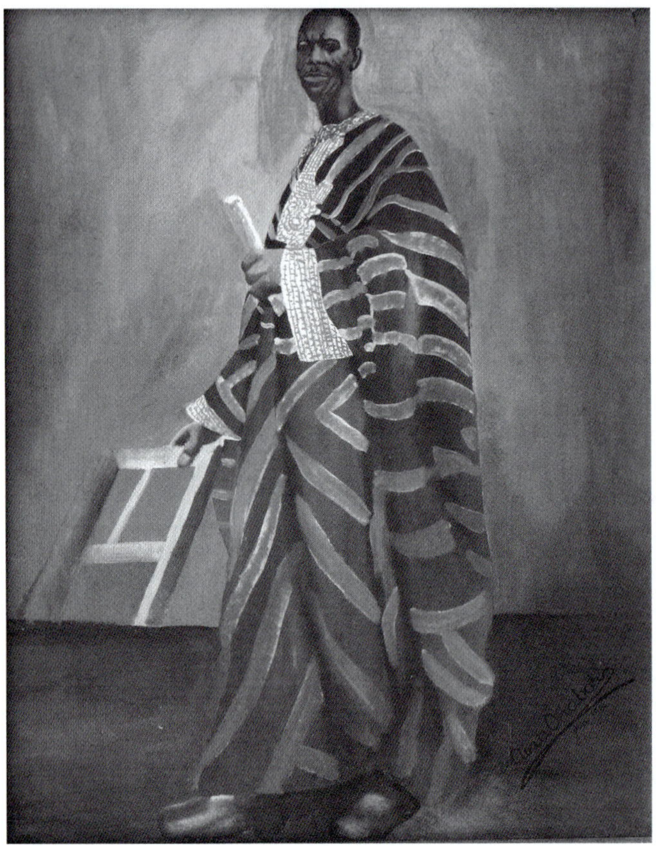

Figure I.1 Aina Onabolu, *Portrait of a Man*, 1955, 48.5 × 38.5 cm/19 × 15 inches, watercolor on board. Omooba Yemisi Adedoyin Shyllon Art Foundation (OYSAF).

black African artists at every step towards an African modernism here conceived as an ongoing project.

As in most formerly colonized parts of the world, the time frame of modern art in Africa differs considerably from that of modern art in Europe and the United States where modernism chronologically coincides with the era of colonialism. What is considered modernism's *terminus* in the West with World War II and decolonization corresponds to the definitive establishment of modern art in Africa. To further complicate periodization within the African continent, some countries like Nigeria and South Africa came early to modern art while other countries are still in the preliminary phase. Yet, however one negotiates the chronology of global modern art and the link between colonialism and modernism, what is indisputable is that in Africa modern art responds to colonial relations from the opposite side, the side of the colonized. This gives it a politico-philosophical distinction ultimately linked to the notion of the black African identity: a difference that is something more than hybridization.

When talking about African history, there is another time aspect to keep in mind: historiography itself. On the rather flimsy ground that handing over knowledge about the past has traditionally occurred in African societies through oral tradition and rarely through written documents, the West has declared Africa a continent without history. "The central myth," stated Kwame Nkrumah (1909–72), the first president of independent Ghana, "is the denial that we are a historical people."[3] Western anthropologists and ethnological Africanists, who long functioned as the dominant authorities on African cultures, preferred to treat African cultures as if they existed in an unchangeable "present past," preserving some mythical primeval origin. The order of the day was the West's passion for the "primitive."

Africa as the "heart of darkness," an isolated "dark continent," is a Eurocentric myth. Exchanging and adopting new ways and ideas were always part of the pattern of African life. Africa was never the changeless continent Western explorers and colonizers depicted. On the eastern side of the African continent, for example, long before the Portuguese discovered sailing routes around the Cape of Good

Hope in the fifteenth century, Africa was an active part of world trade networks with Asia, including China and India.[4] All the while, other routes of trade had been crossing into the interior of the African continent. Traveling Arab historians collected a vast knowledge of its cultures and history of which Europe long remained mainly uninformed.[5]

Providing the surrounding world with gold and ivory and at an early stage exporting high-quality iron to the East, Africans had been active as merchants from ancient times and the continent had been crisscrossed by traders from outside with the introduction of new religions, mainly Islam, following in their footsteps. The trans-Saharan trade intensified when North Africa was Arabized and big parts of sub-Saharan Africa were culturally integrated into the Muslim world with intellectual capitals like Timbuktu. The African slave trade, initiated by the Arabs some six hundred years before the Europeans, was dramatically accelerated by the demand for labor in the New World. The Euro-American transatlantic slave trade (1601–1870) was to have a paradoxical double impact, mainly brutalizing and draining many parts of the continent of human resources, but also globalizing African culture. In the century leading up to Europe's rapacious scramble for Africa instigated at the Berlin Conference of 1884–5, the modern technological revolution in the West enabled an intensified Atlantic trade. Shipping increased economic and cultural exchange between African regions and the West, and between African and European individuals. Nonetheless, the West's deep and widespread belief in Africa as a primordial land with no history grew in popularity. The blind and pervasive force of the myth of primitive peoples can only be understood as a necessary illusion: the rationale for a massive and otherwise morally inconceivable crime against humanity.

For a long time, the adventure of developing African modernism was carried through by a few rather isolated individuals, daring and obsessed like Onabolu. Some went to study in Europe, some art schools were established in African countries, practicing modern art spread. But it was not until the years after World War II with the struggle for freedom from colonial rule, which for the majority of African countries was acquired in the 1960s, that modern art production became a regular part of African culture. Not until independence could deeply rooted aspirations blossom out as the expression of the self-esteem of an Africa that had shaken off the colonial yoke. The two things that all the countries and all the peoples in Africa with few exceptions have in common are the trauma of colonization and the relief of acquiring independence. As Marshall Berman observed in 1982 about postcolonial modernisms, "When the lid is blown off, the modernist spirit is one of the first things to come out: it is the return of the repressed" (Berman 1982: 125). Africa's explosive postcolonial modernization was stressed by Marshall W. Mount in the preface to his groundbreaking book on African modern art. "Africa," Mount observed in 1973, "is currently undergoing transformation at a speed unequaled in the history of civilization" (Mount 1989). Independence era modernization is the universal context for the rise of modern art in Africa.

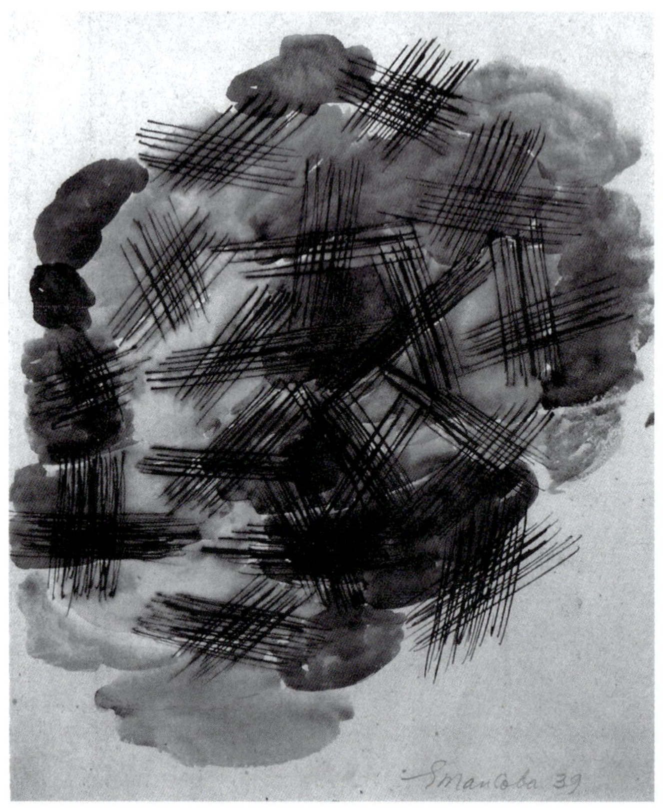

Figure I.2 Ernest Mancoba, *Drawing*, 1939, ink and watercolor on paper, 26.7 × 20.5 cm / 10 × 8 inches. Silkeborg Kunstmuseum, Denmark, photo Lars Bay, © Wonga Mancoba.

Newly independent African countries realized the symbolic power of modern visual art as a sign of progress and participation in the modern world. Art academies were established and artists were given official commissions. This occurred in the cities. But the newly awakened spirit of public investment in modern art could not conceal how formidable the changeover was and how alien to the approximately eighty percent of the population who still lived in villages in rural Africa. In the traditional system, which was gradually becoming defunct, ritual objects had been integrated as tools in collective social practices. In the new system, artists were supposed to produce works for an art market and an initiated audience. But building domestic art markets and developing supporting audiences was a very slow process, even in the cities.

African modern artists, those who have not gone abroad, have worked within limited and weak cultural structures and mostly been obliged to rely on benevolent foreign expatriates and embassy personnel as their patrons. The astounding thing is the swiftness with which modern art in Africa developed original aesthetic solutions and a vitality of its own despite underdeveloped infrastructures for promotion, distribution, and preservation of art. In a parallel Latin American context, García Canclini (1995) has pointed out that a developed capitalistic economy and a sufficiently high level of general literacy are prerequisites for a consistent modernism. Most African countries have been left lacking in both aspects. Where a cultural infrastructure and an art market did develop, as in Nigeria, the heterogeneity of the audience is often reflected in the production of artists. The Nigerian modernist pioneer Erhabor Emokpae (1934–84), for instance, alternated between painting huge figurative battle scenes in a conservative academic style and modernist nonfigurative compositions that express the artist's own philosophical reflections.

Despite the unity ascribed to Africa by the West and Africa's relations with the West, in the end it is questionable if one can talk at all about an "African" modern art or even about "Africa" as a defined entity. The continent is five times the size of the United States. It contains today more than fifty countries. Several of the countries, the borders of which were drawn with a ruler by the colonizing powers, count internally a great many different tribal languages and cultures, in some cases hundreds of them. Nigeria has for instance more than two hundred and fifty ethnic groups; my own native country, Tanzania, has one hundred and twenty. And before being colonized, the continent contained multiple kingdoms and trade centers with prominent trade languages and cultural institutions. To what do we then specifically refer when we mention "Africa"?

"Africa," the histories of the continent as well as the history of African art and its modern chapter, are stories containing within them multiple different stories, each with its own temporal trajectory and unique relations and exchanges with the outer world, predominantly with the West. If I here have chosen to speak about "Africa" referring to what is mainly called "black Africa" or Africa south of the Sahara, it should not be seen to diminish this paradox of a broadly generalized multiplicity, which makes the continent a model for perceiving the many contradictions of local and global transaction in other parts of the world.

Modern Art in Africa: Selected Readings

The chapters in this part of the volume present African modern art from a particular point of view. The selections reflect the fact that I am a black African woman, an artist, and independent scholar who participates in an African-diasporic intellectual culture that is transnational. A critical choice was to focus mainly on black Africa and much less on the north of the continent, where the art could be discussed, with no less relevancy, in a Middle East geopolitical context. To give a comprehensive and composite picture of African visual creativity within different arts during the modernist era, I have as far as possible given priority to texts written by black African, African American, and black diaspora authors dealing with black artists. And in order to indicate parallels with modern African literature, I have among the limited number of images selected Uche Okeke's illustration to Chinua Achebe's seminal novel *Things Fall Apart*, a book which gives an impressive account of how a traditional African society is confronted by the colonizers. Some artists, art writers, and patrons within white minorities, mainly in South Africa, can be said to have contributed beyond their own communities. But to me the principal story to tell has been that of black Africa finding its way to modernism.

The authors of the selected essays also assume various postures on defining characteristics of African modernism. Chika Okeke in his essay "Modern African Art" has surveyed modernism within the African continent as a whole, including the Maghreb in the north. This approach enables him to broaden the picture of how modernism first emerged on African soil. From this larger perspective, Aina Onabolu in Nigeria was not alone in his early demands for modern art education. In 1908 a member of the Egyptian National Party, Prince Yusef Kamal, established in Cairo the first school of fine arts on the continent. Art schools followed in countries like Ghana (1936), Uganda (1939), Sudan (1946), and Nigeria (1953 and 1955). Some of them, like the School of Fine Arts at Makerere University College in Kampala, Uganda, became sites for vital cultural and political Pan-African interaction. At one of the early Nigerian art academies, in Zaria, a group of students, the so-called Zaria Rebels, took it upon themselves to formulate guiding principles for a modern art in independent Nigeria. See the chapter "Natural Synthesis" by Uche Okeke, the leading theoretician among them. Similar rebellions by black African art school students empowering themselves occurred at the Makerere art school in Kampala, where students like the sculptor Gregory Maloba and the painter Sam Ntiro took over as teachers, and in South Africa at the Polly Street Art Center in Johannesburg with Sidney Kumalo and Ezrom Legae.

While Chika Okeke deals with the wide, continental perspectives of African modernism, Steven Sack has written "From Country to City: The Development of an Urban Art" from a closely informed view of the devastating conditions of the black South African artists during apartheid. The history of black modern art in South Africa calls for special attention. Decolonization, which in most of Africa represented the moment that freed black creative power, did not occur in the same way in South Africa. Independence from Britain was here an agreement between whites, between Britain and British and Dutch minorities in South Africa, and it had hardly any impact on the situation of the black majority. On the other side, the existence of a white community of South African artists and liberal patrons facilitated in some cases exchange and interracial initiatives. The most important example is the Polly Street Art Center, mentioned above, and the case of the South African woman artist Gladys Mgudlandlu (1925–79) as told by Elza Miles in "Nomfanekiso Who Paints at Night: The Art of Gladys Mgudlandlu." Mgudlandlu is exceptional because of the press exposure and success she experienced despite increasing apartheid and because black professional modern women artists are extremely rare.

In fact, a first question during my research was always, where are the black women artists and where can I find texts written on them by black women authors? They exist, but I have had to resign myself to the fact that two patriarchal systems, the African one and that of the colonizing West, delayed black women's contribution to the production of modern art and the critical discourse surrounding it. This is specifically valid for the modern period. Black African women artists were in some countries accepted into professional art schools, but they were rarely encouraged and supported. Still, there exists in many traditional African societies a practice of painting that is a women's prerogative, namely the making of ritual decorations on the walls of houses and huts. In South Africa Gladys Mgudlandlu as well as Helen Sebidi are among the rare examples of women painters who managed to proceed to professional careers as fine artists from having grown up practicing within this tradition.

Photography as a modern technological medium played an important role in modernizing the pictorial tradition in Africa. As an art medium in the hands of black Africans it had an early chapter mainly in West Africa and predominantly in the form of studio portrait photography. Mama Casset in Senegal started to take such photographs in the 1920s, and Seydou Keita in Mali opened his portrait studio in 1948. In general terms their portraits represent descriptions of individuals as much as they are inscriptions of social identities, write Okwui Enwezor and Octavio Zaya in "Negritude, Pan-Africanism, and Postcolonial African Identity: African Portrait Photography." In the period of transformation leading to independence the photographs are instilled with euphoria and disappointment, pride and insecurity, confidence and contradictions. The photographs are modern, the authors point out, in the sense of implicitly diverging from a retrogressive side of Negritude that internalized primitivism; instead they manifest a "reluctance to be confined to … a natural-history or ethnographic setting."

Portrait photography addressed the private sphere. On the contrary, as Okwui Enwezor writes in "A Critical Presence: *Drum Magazine* in Context," *Drum Magazine* in South Africa introduced a vital form of socially and culturally investigative photography beyond the documentary. The magazine had a Pan-African readership outside South Africa through editions published in several parts of Africa. It contributed significantly to a developing modern African identity and self-esteem. In my childhood, *Drum* could be found at the coffee table in many middle-class families. The Pan-Africanism evident in the international popularity of *Drum Magazine* is a universal of African modernism. The roots of Pan-Africanism go back to the Atlantic slave trade and to a shared African history of diaspora, the transnational space within which black artists had long traveled and worked, as Paul Gilroy describes in *The Black Atlantic: Modernity and Double Consciousness* (1992).

Between the early sixteenth century and the second half of the nineteenth century around fourteen million Africans arrived on the other side of the Atlantic, kidnapped and shipped as slaves. They had been forced to leave their material culture behind and were forbidden most of their cultural practices. But they carried inside them creative patterns and interpretations of life. The essay by Cuban Gerardo Mosquera, "Africa in the Art of Latin America," in the Latin American part of this volume can be read in this context. In this part, Michael Harris begins his essay "Art of the African Diaspora"[6] by reminding us of the history of the black Atlantic. In the United States, the African heritage lived on mainly within popular arts, but in the twentieth century emancipated African American artists emerged with new self-confidence. In what is known as the Harlem Renaissance, black American artists in the 1920s drew inspiration from precolonial African prototypes to celebrate black African identity. In this they followed the primitivist example of European Cubists and Expressionists. For African American artists, however, the African sculpture that revolutionized Western art was their own ancestral heritage.

The African diaspora played an important role in developing modern African art. In the 1930s Paris became another diasporic center of activity. Some of the pioneering black artists who emerged in Africa during Europe's interwar period and who laid the foundation for modern art in Africa contributed after World War II to Pan-African activity centered around the Paris-based magazine, *Présence Africaine* (African presence), which also organized international conferences on black African literature and art. In Paris, black avant-garde writers, preeminently Aimé Césaire and Léopold Senghor from Francophone Caribbean and continental

Africa, worked out Pan-African theories of black African aesthetics, particularly Negritude, while the Caribbean psychiatrist and political thinker Frantz Fanon established a critical analysis of colonial and postcolonial culture in Africa. See the selections in this part volume from Césaire's *Discourse on Colonialism* (1955) and from Fanon's seminal *The Wretched of the Earth* (1961).

In architect Hassan Fathy's 1969 text, "Chorale: Man, Society, and Technology: An Experiment in Rural Egypt," we meet a committed and lively modernist voice from the African continent. It stands here for a category of production, indigenous modern African architecture, the more successful establishment of which is still in its initial stages in most parts of Africa. While the Egyptian Fathy achieved world recognition, few black African architects have so far managed to be awarded major domestic designs. Although large-scale urban modernization projects have been achieved in postcolonial Africa, for instance the new capitals of Nigeria and Tanzania, the architects chosen to design them have all been foreign.

Fathy was skeptical about international style modern architecture, at least when applied outside big cities in Africa. When commissioned in the 1940s to build New Gourna, a village close to the ancient site of the Valley of the Kings in Egypt, he chose an approach fundamentally opposed to that of Western architectural modernists. Instead of applying an abstract and anonymous international style, he modernized traditional Muslim forms and ancient techniques that still existed in that region of Egypt but were less and less held in esteem by the population.

We meet a similarly wide modernization of deep-rooted African traditions in Nwachukwu Frank Ukadike's chapter "Oral Traditions and the Aesthetics of Black African Cinema." He writes that modern black African cinema shares a sociocultural structure, a system of ideas and images of which oral performances, dance, music, singing, artisan crafts, metaphors, and proverbs are all integral parts. And this structure, typical of the oral traditions in most parts of Africa, has given rise to a new cinematographic language. The core of this system, the oral tradition, is a specifically vital African tradition of communicating by telling stories and tales. In the center of the performance is the so-called griot, the traditional storyteller who functions as an oral historian responsible for handing down from generation to generation a collective memory.

Ukadike's text tells us about a specifically African attitude among modern professional producers towards living traditions of popular arts, traditions that are characterized by powerful rhythms, colorful performances and intense bodily expressions. It is an attitude of mind which comprises respect and identification and which strongly differs from Western ethnographic interpretations of African folklore. See the dialogue between a prominent French ethnographic filmmaker and a pioneering modern African cineaste in this volume under the significant title "A Historic Confrontation between Jean Rouch and Ousmane Sembène in 1965: You Look at Us as if We Were Insects."

There can be no doubt that modern African art, produced in the inspiring vicinity of a uniquely vital popular culture, has drawn deeply from the inexhaustible watering holes of oral tradition and, as in the case of the Nigerian pioneering modernist Ben Enwonwu, from ritual masquerades (Ogbechie 2008).[7] If one could speak here about an internally African search for authenticity, then this symbiosis of modern experimentation and popular lore gives us yet another answer to how African modern art, diverse, local, and individual as it may be, manifests itself beyond Africa's modern experience of slavery, colonialism, independence, and diaspora as a uniquely and universally "African" modern art.

Notes

1 The biographical facts about Aina Onabolu are from Oloidi (1989) and from the obituary published by his son Dapo Onabolu (1963).

2 More or less simultaneously in the first decade of the twentieth century, when Aina Onabolu appropriated academic realism from Europe, initiating a new art system in Africa, Pablo Picasso and Georges Braque appropriated the geometric idiom and spatial forms of Cubism from the premodern African art objects they bought in curio shops in Paris.

3 In a speech at the Congress of Africanists in Accra, Ghana, in 1962.

4 Regarding the world trade on the Indian Ocean, see the exemplary history of textile trade by the Japanese scholar Yuko Tanaka (1995), which goes back to medieval time and mentions the East African trade ports Kilwa and Malindi.

5 For the history of Ibn Battuta, Leo Africanus, and other Muslim travelers to Africa see Oliver (1977).

6 While "African diaspora" generally refers to the movements of Africans and their descendants throughout the world, Michael Harris has in his essay chosen to focus mainly on African American art.

7 The thoroughly researched monograph throws light upon the dialogue between local traditions, Western training and international experiences typical of African modernist artists during the colonial period.

References

Berman, Marshall (1982) *All That is Solid Melts into Air: The Experience of Modernity*. New York, NY: Simon & Schuster.

García Canclini, Néstor (1995) "Modernity After Postmodernity." In Gerardo Mosquera (ed.) *Beyond the Fantastic: Contemporary Art Criticism from Latin America*. London, England: Institute of International Visual Arts.

Gilroy, Paul (1992) *The Black Atlantic: Modernity and Double Consciousness*. Cambridge, MA: Harvard University Press.

Mount, Marshall W. (1989) *African Art: The Years since 1920*. New York, NY: Da Capo Press.

Ogbechie, Sylvester (2008) *Ben Enwonwu: The Making of an African Modernist*. Rochester, NY: University of Rochester Press.

Oliver, Roland (ed.) (1977) *The Cambridge History of Africa: Volume 3*. Cambridge, England: Cambridge University Press.

Oloidi, Ola (1989) "Art and Nationalism in Colonial Nigeria." *Nsukka Journal of History* 1: 92–110.

Onabolu, Dapo (1963) "Aina Onabolu." *Nigeria Magazine* 79 (December).

Tanaka, Yuko (1995) "A Comparative Study of Textile Production and Trading from the Beginning of the 16th century to the End of the 19th century." *The Hosei University Bulletin* (February).

1

Modern African Art

Chika Okeke*

> *African modernism cannot be broached merely by invoking European modernism, for it is not, as some historians have claimed, simply an African manifestation of twentieth-century European art.*
>
> Chika Okeke

This essay by Chika Okeke establishes a conceptual and historical foundation for the texts that follow. It reverses the hegemonic Eurocentric viewpoint of art historiography and offers an authoritative history of African modern art from an African perspective. Okeke views modernism as essentially "a project of subject formation," an idea he links to the rise of modernity on the African continent. His story of modern art begins with the colonial period and translates key value terms of Western modernism – progress, originality, artistic freedom, individualism, alienation, paradox – for application to African art. He gives us a picture of modern art in Africa as a fusion of many sources, an amalgam the author appreciates as postmodern *avant la lettre*. For the larger project of understanding modern art from multiple global perspectives, such local viewpoints will add up to an overall revaluation of values: a radical expansion and restructuring of modernist epistemology.

Questions for reading: How does Okeke explain the debates around critical modernist concepts? According to the author, what is the fundamental paradox of this history? How, when, and where does he say modernity and modernism emerged on the continent? What part did Paris and cosmopolitan expatriation play, and what three factors brought African artists and intellectuals together, especially on the continent, during the independence decade (1955–65)?

* Chika Okeke (2001) "Modern African Art." In Okwui Enwezor (ed.) *The Short Century: Independence and Liberation Movements in Africa 1945–1994* (pp. 29–36). Munich, Germany: Prestel.

Modern Art in Africa, Asia, and Latin America: An Introduction to Global Modernisms, First Edition.
Edited by Elaine O'Brien, Everlyn Nicodemus, Melissa Chiu, Benjamin Genocchio, Mary K. Coffey, and Roberto Tejada.

Further Readings

Harney, Elizabeth (2004) *In Senghor's Shadow: Art, Politics, and the Avant-Garde in Senegal, 1960–1995*. Durham, NC: Duke University Press.
Mount, Marshall W. (1989[1973]) *African Art. The Years Since 1920* (with a new introduction by the author) New York, NY: Da Capo Press.
Ogbechie, Sylvester (2008) *Ben Enwonwu: The Making of an African Modernist*. Rochester, NY: University of Rochester Press.

African modern art has been an anomaly on the map of twentieth-century artistic modernity. It has been with us from modernism's inception, and yet, in a kind of cyclical ritual, it time and time again has seemed to need validation within the study of twentieth-century art. [...]

Whether or not colonialism unwittingly planted the seeds of African modern art, the extent to which that art remains accountable to European methodologies remains a subject of intense debate. [...]

The view of colonial education as the agent of African modern art's emergence faces a number of contradictions and a paradox. First, although the introduction of European art education in non-Islamic parts of the continent brought about a change in the attitude of colonized to colonizer, the colonial mission was by no means the main agent of artistic output there. In fact it initially paid no attention to the visual arts, being mainly concerned with fulfilling the colonial powers' need for low-level manpower – for clerks, for example, in the civil service. Wherever art did feature in the colonial curriculum, it was restricted to the notion of craft. The inclusion of art in the syllabus began only when educated Africans demanded it.

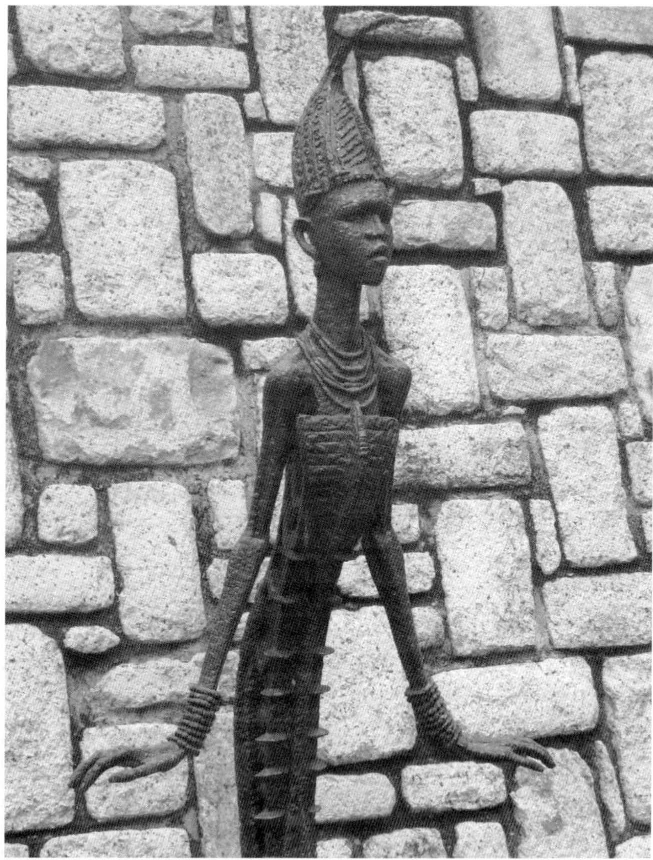

Figure 1.1 Ben Enwonwu Anyanwu, bronze (detail), 1954–5. National Museum, Lagos, © Ben Enwonwu Foundation. Photo Sylvester Ogbechie.

Therein lies one contradiction; another is the existence during the colonial period of a large body of sculptural and performance practices that engaged the colonial project with trenchant critique, humor, and empathy, exploring above all what the modern condition implied for Africans in terms of alienation. This alienation was double, existing first on the level of subject matter: a whole category of performance genres examined the figure of the colonialist, often parodying his presumption of control over African subjective productions. A second alienation emerged through the alteration of the traditional canon within which this critical insertion took place. What made these local interventions into the colonial space powerfully poignant and modern was their construction of a field in which a dialectical discourse on power relations was played out, with the audience immediately recognizing what the colonial caricature meant within a classical African corpus. And here the colonial officer experienced a deeper alienation, for he was barely able to decipher the critical codes of actions in which he was sometimes a guest of honor.

This brings me to the paradox within which modern African art operates. Contemporary Western scholars and artists generally acknowledge that one of the sparks for European art's paradigmatic change in direction in the twentieth century occurred as Western artists encountered African and Oceanic "ethnographic" objects and recognized the possibilities they offered for formal shifts in European painting and sculpture. From Cubism to Surrealism, from Pablo Picasso to Paul Klee, Georges Braque, Constantin Brancusi, Henry Moore, Alberto Giacometti, Amedeo Modigliani, Julio González, Wifredo Lam, and so on, the case has been sufficiently made. But the obverse of this discovery by Western artists was the discovery of European art by African artists born in the same period. In southern Nigeria, for instance, the Christian missions that were established in the mid-nineteenth century eschewed art education completely. It was not until the first decade of the twentieth century that the region's first modern artist, Aina Onabolu (1882–1963), began his lone crusade to convince the colonial administration in Lagos to establish an art course in secondary schools. Similarly, although many Western artists visited Islamic North Africa in the nineteenth century, especially during the Romantic era (after Napoleon's invasion of Egypt in 1798 had opened the region to European colonialist expansion), and although a number of these artists settled in Algeria, Egypt, and Morocco, French and British colonial administrations did not encourage the establishment of art training in the Maghreb. It was Prince Yusef Kamal – a member of the Egyptian National Party, which advocated independence from Britain – who established the first art school in colonial Egypt: The School of Fine Arts, Cairo, which opened in 1908.

It appears, then, that modern African art became a reality not so much because of Western-style education as because of a few individuals to whom art as an autonomous practice became a medium for expressing their subjectivity and coming to terms with their sociopolitical circumstances – with their own emergent modernities. If the development of modern art in colonial Africa seems to have been rather slow (that is, if we ignore some of the indigenous sculptural and performance practices mentioned above), this may be because modern artistic subjectivity is linked to political independence. The notion of artistic freedom was antithetical to the ethos of colonialism. Predictably, the first, clear, sustained modernist art in Africa appeared in Egypt, which experienced an early political independence and established a nationalist discourse before World War I.[1] For the rest of the continent, and despite the pioneering efforts of a few individuals, it would take the aftermath of World War II to set the stage for modern art. As imperial Europe, debilitated by war, counted its losses, and as its prospects of retaining its colonies dimmed, African artists and intellectuals sought to challenge the idea of progress inherent in modernism's conception of its mission (an idea not just formal but political, as can be seen in the cases of the Mexican muralists and of the avant-garde of the Russian revolution). Reflecting upon the emergent postcolonial condition, they engaged the issues of what it meant to be individuals and artists in societies experiencing dramatic social, political, and cultural change.

So how, one might ask, did these artists respond to their contact with Europe? The fanciful notion of mimesis, or mimicry, comes to mind. [...] The concept of mimesis found easy expression in anthropology, but its implications have also percolated in Western scholarship's view of African modern art. In 1964, for instance, William Fagg and Margaret Plass described a "'contemporary' African art which for all its merit is an extension of European art by a kind of involuntary cultural colonialism."[2] The argument of Fagg and Plass – and of generations of art historians worried by what they see as a lack of "authenticity" in modern and contemporary African art – is quite pernicious, for it denies any possibility of agency on the African artist's part. It assumes that because Africans have appropriated techniques or expressive media often associated with European art, they cannot create anything different or original. Nor can they even be involved in the aesthetic debates taking place in other far-flung outposts of the European imperial process.

Artists are not alone: similar arguments have been made about the literature of Negritude. For Fagg and Plass, "the suppositious philosophy of *négritude* ... is a product of Parisian existentialism and has no roots in Africa, for which reason we should prefer to call it *blanchitude*."[3] Many other critics, especially Anglophone Africans, including Wole Soyinka, have echoed this assessment. Yet for young, Paris-based African intellectuals from the French colonies in the 1930s and '40s, Negritude was an expression of their dissatisfaction with colonialism, its emasculation of their culture, and its deferment of their freedom. In a strategy that signaled the beginnings of a modern postcolonial subjectivity, the poets of Negritude, on a quest for a critical voice, adopted aspects of French Surrealism and rhetorical strategies from France's political and intellectual left. Yet their cultural and political agendas obviously differed from those of the French; they were, so to speak, cotravelers, in a parallel time, heading to different destinations.[4] For Europeans the enemies were fascism and reason gone amok; for African and Caribbean writers the enemy was unquestionably colonialism. Thus the poets of Negritude, despite loose alliances with Surrealism and the Paris left, created a literature quite distinct from the work of their French counterparts. Viewing Negritude as a mimicry of European literary forms, Fagg and Plass fail to appreciate the subtleties of its poetics and politics. They also fail to see that artistic modernity is rooted in a reordering process of quotation, and that Negritude is a product of this process – as becomes especially clear when we pay attention to its strategy of mixing tropes of otherness and "foreign" methodologies, its ordering of complex (and, as Soyinka has argued, sometimes conflicting) ideological and aesthetic propositions founded on the appropriation of fantasies of Africanness, and its anticipation of the hybridity of today's postmodern ethos.

Negritude extended beyond literature. A philosophy of black consciousness, it sought expression in all spheres of artistic production. What is the *Nègre* in Negritude if not the principle of making Africanness (whatever that may entail) part of the repertory of modern art? A conference organized by Alioune Diop, the founder of the literary journal *Présence Africaine*, in 1956 in Paris called on "negro" writers and artists to embrace such notions in their work. That the artists and writers gathered there almost a half-century ago are today considered some of the most important practitioners in their field suggests how successful Negritude became as a model of self-conscious repetition.

Given this history, and the more dominant history of European modernism, how can we discuss art from Africa, which has always been perceived as outside the scope of modernist aesthetics? What does modernism mean in the context of twentieth-century African art? First, modernism here is tied to the rise of modernity in the African continent, which is in turn connected to the colonial experience. In other words, as colonialism made European material culture and ideas more available, artists from the colonies invented new artistic expressions that reflected Africa's encounter with Europe, and also with the rest of the globe. Whether through an essentialist nativism or a supposedly progressive adoption of patently European aesthetic styles and propositions, the resulting work bore the unmistakable mark of the artists' *twentieth-centuryness*. Much as in the heyday of Paris in the early twentieth century, artists from all corners of the world converged in the French capital in the interwar period to share philosophies and aesthetic positions. In the climate of an art and intellectual world peopled by émigrés (Picasso, James Joyce, Gertrude Stein, Samuel Beckett, Aimé Césaire, Léopold Sédar Senghor, Fanon), the work evolved out of diverse colonial conditions, past the ravages of colonialism, and finally through the dramatic experience of decolonization. African modernism is defined by the conflation – rather than by any single one – of these episodes, and by the art forms and aesthetic ideas associated with them. The obvious implication is that African modern art does not propose a particular narrative of modernism, as the triumphalist European version did. In Africa one can even speak of a range of modernisms specific to the continent's different countries. In other words, African modernism cannot be broached merely by invoking European modernism, for it is not, as some historians have claimed, simply an African manifestation of twentieth-century European art – even though we will certainly find many instances of artists consciously adopting, adapting, quoting, decomposing, critiquing, and even transgressing European avant-garde strategies, creating work that dramatizes the restless intellectual encounters of artists engaged in a continuously evolving project of subject formation.

[...]

The Art of Independence

At the Pan-African Congress of 1945, in Manchester, England, the assembled representatives of the colonies sanctioned African anticolonial movements, marking the end of Europe's imperial age. The postwar period was also significant in African art history, for it witnessed an intensified migration of artists to European metropolises. Colonial administrations in most parts of Africa had been reluctant to establish a system of art education, but a few artists had traveled to Europe for training, often with private sponsorship. In Egypt and South Africa, art academies had been established before the start of the war, but racial conditions in South Africa foreclosed any possibility of black artists benefiting from the institutional structures available to their white counterparts. If they wanted to escape the artistic Bantustan to which they had been banished, emigration was the only choice. Some of South Africa's pioneering black artists, including Ernest Mancoba (born 1904 [died 2002]) and later his friend Gerard Sekoto (1913–93), were forced to emigrate to Europe.

Mancoba left for Paris in 1938. There he met the Danish artist Sonja Ferlov, who introduced him to her circle, including Giacometti. During World War II, interned by the German army (he carried a British passport), Mancoba married Ferlov, and after the war he moved to Denmark. In 1948 he participated in the *Høst* exhibition, the inaugural show of the emergent *COBRA* group, led by Asger Jorn, Karel Appel, Corneille, and Constant. Although his work is often omitted from *COBRA* literature, he brought the group in contact with African ethnographic material, and gave them guided tours of the Trocadero museum – an experience that would have a far-reaching impact on the work of Jorn and Ejler Bille.[5] Furthermore, Ferlov's and Erik Thommesen's sculpture seems to have been directly influenced by Mancoba's own early wood sculpture, which has a primal, monumental simplicity. His association with *COBRA* may in turn have helped shape his abstract style, his palette, and, in his drawings, his exploration of what Elza Miles calls "the relationship between the autonomy of an image and the power associated with it."[6]

Like Mancoba, Sekoto began his career in South Africa but recognized the impossibility of furthering his art beyond the limits set by the system for black artists. The creation of townships for black migrant workers, and the laws curbing the movement of black people, created pseudo-urbanized spaces marked by prisoncamp-type layouts, but there was a thriving black culture here, and the simple yet powerful portraits of blacks and "coloreds" that Sekoto produced before his 1948 emigration to Paris document life in the squalid streets of Sophiatown and District Six (townships in Johannesburg and Cape Town respectively). Although he never returned to South Africa, he continued to paint pictures of the townships as he remembered them.

On his way to Paris Sekoto stopped in London, where Peter Abrahams, a South African novelist also self-exiled, introduced him to the Nigerian artist Ben Enwonwu (1918–94).[7] Enwonwu was a student of the British art teacher and museologist

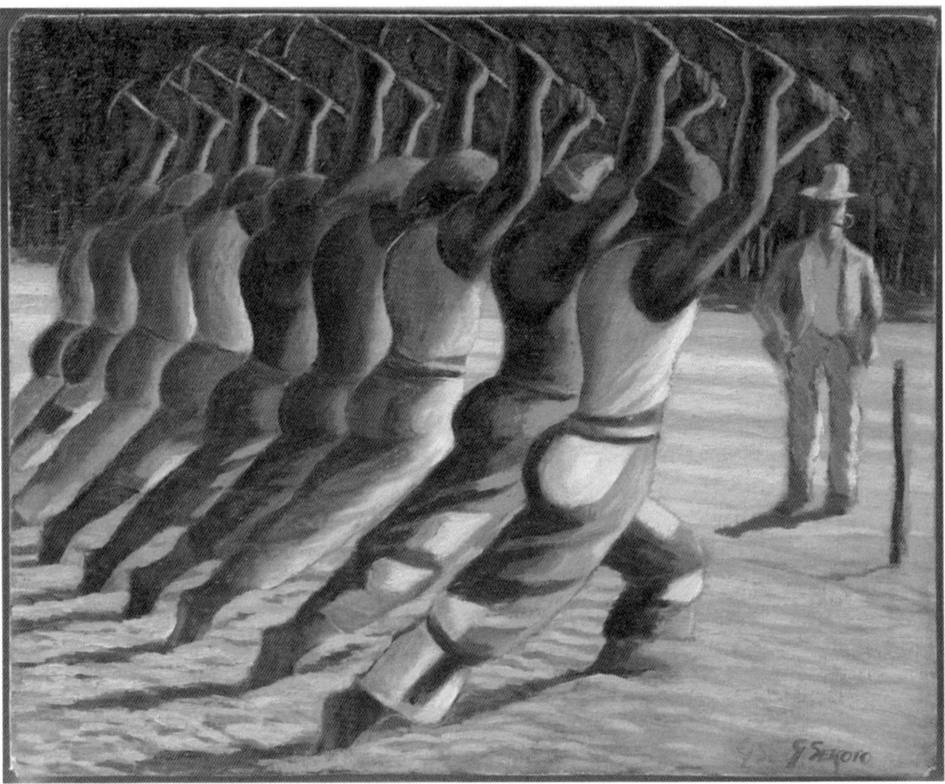

Figure 1.2 Gerard Sekoto, *The Song of the Pick*, 1946–7, oil on canvas, 49 × 59.9 cm / 19 × 24 inches, © The Gerard Sekoto Foundation.

Kenneth Murray, who, in 1927, had been invited by the colonial government to teach art in Nigerian secondary schools.[8] In 1944, a year before his younger compatriot Uzo Egonu (1932–94). Enwonwu had left for England with a joint scholarship from the Nigerian government and Shell Petroleum. His career was unprecedented: after graduating from the Slade School of Fine Art and Goldsmiths College, as well as attending Oxford, he became, at least in the popular press, "Africa's most famous artist." In 1957 Queen Elizabeth visited his studio, to sit for a controversial portrait statue commissioned by the colonial government. Many of Enwonwu's pictures from the early 1950s depict contemporary Nigerians engaged in social activities or participating in cultural ceremonies. He was in touch with debates on colonialism and African independence, and participated in the Congress of Negro Writers and Artists at the Sorbonne, organized by Présence Africaine in 1956, and, with Sekoto and Sam Ntiro (born 1923 [died 1993]) of Tanzania, in the 1959 Rome Conference, for which Sekoto designed the poster.

Enwonwu's reputation in London was matched in Paris by that of the Ivory Coast sculptor Christian Lattier (1928–78).[9] At the age of ten, Lattier had left for France, where he had joined the order of Marist Brothers. Leaving the order in 1945, he entered art studies at the Ecole des Beaux-Arts, Saint-Etienne, the following year. In 1947 he transferred to the Ecole des Beaux-Arts in Paris, where, departing from the academic tradition of modeling in plaster, he began experimenting with woven wire sculptures, for which he won the Chenavard Prize in 1954. His first experiments with wire seem to resonate with the copper-wire reliquary sculptures of the Bakota. He later employed woven fibers, recalling the basketry and other fiber arts found in many African cultures.

Sekoto and Mancoba never went back to South Africa to live, but many others returned to their home countries after training in Europe. This should not surprise us. Conditions in South Africa under apartheid made the return of its black artists ill-advised,[10] but artists elsewhere often went home to work as art advisors or teachers in their respective countries, whether colonial or postcolonial. Enwonwu, for example, served as federal art advisor in Nigeria; Kofi Antubam (1922–64) was special assistant on cultural affairs to Kwame Nkrumah in Ghana; Ntiro became the Tanzanian high commissioner to Great Britain; and Iba Ndiaye (born 1928), who had gone to Paris to study architecture in 1949, was invited by the Senegalese government to organize the painting section of the Maison des Arts du Senegal, later renamed the Institute National des Arts du Senegal. Unlike his colleague Papa Ibra Tall (born 1935 [died 2008]), who was more favorably disposed to Senghor's Negritude aesthetic, Ndiaye adopted a painterly expressiveness reflecting his association with the Groupe de la Ruche, a group of young postwar Parisian artists bound by a distaste for abstraction.

Egyptian artists too were drawn to the European capitals, but under different circumstances. Most of the country's pioneering artists trained at Cairo's School of Fine Arts, with a few then traveling to Paris or London for higher studies. Such was the case with Mahmoud Mukhtar (1891–1934), Egypt's first modern artist, who graduated from the School of Fine Arts before enrolling in the Paris Ecole des Beaux-Arts. His sculpture *Egypt's Awakening* (1919–23) predated his country's independence in 1923: pan-African and proto-Negritude, the work shares qualities with the Harlem Renaissance sculptor Meta Vaux Warrick Fuller's allegorical *Awakening of Ethiopia* (c. 1914), a work that the art historian Judith Wilson links to the Pan-Africanist novel *Ethiopia Unbound* (1911), by the Gold Coast nationalist J.E. Casely Hayford.[11] (The Gold Coast is today's Ghana.) *Egypt's Awakening* would become the signal artwork of Egypt's emerging aesthetic, and even of its political nationalism. Perhaps more than those of any other African country, artists in Egypt responded to political events both at home and in Europe during the mid-century. In 1937, a year after the end of the British Mandate and popular demands for free elections, Kamil Tilmissani (1917–70) published a statement calling for a new art founded on ancient Egyptian and folk art traditions, and initiated the Group of Contemporary Art to advance his ideas. In 1939, artists protesting fascism in Europe founded the Group of Art and Freedom. They also rejected orientalism, aligning themselves with the Surrealist movement instead.

Gazbia Sirry (born 1925), a third-generation modern Egyptian artist, chose not to begin her art training in Europe, taking her first degree at the High Institute of Fine Arts for Girls, Cairo, in 1948. Then, in the mid-1950s, she proceeded to

London and the Slade. Early in her career she was associated with Egypt's Group of Modern Art, which favored a post-Cézannean European-style modernism, but in the early 1950s she turned to the Group of Contemporary Art, creating work that was patently Egyptian in character. Then, in the late 1950s, her work began to reflect the political anxieties that had set in after the initial euphoria of Gamal Nasser's revolution.

It might seem paradoxical that African artists were flocking to European capitals while the Manchester Congress was urging decolonization. But, given the realities of colonial rule, this seems less a capitulation to the ingestive power of empire than a necessary process on the part of artists coming to terms with the full meaning of a selfhood defined largely by the encounter between Africa and Europe.

The Independence Decade and Beyond

The independence decade of 1955–65 saw increased interaction among African artists, especially within the continent. Several factors made these contacts possible, but the three most significant were the founding of art schools, which began to turn out more artists; the work of some expatriates; and the political and cultural awareness heightened by the apostles of Pan-Africanism, Pan-Arabism, and Negritude.

With the exceptions of Sudan and Ghana, only Egypt and South Africa had serious art schools, but this would change with changing attitudes in colonial education.[12] With the founding of art schools in Kumasi, in present-day Ghana (1936), Khartoum, Sudan (1946), Makerere, Uganda, and Ibadan and Zaria, Nigeria (1953 and 1955), African artists could finally train in their own countries (although many still went to Europe for further studies, especially during the colonial period). Most of the schools began with curricula fashioned after European prototypes, but nevertheless became sites for interaction among artists, writers, and political activists. At the Nigerian College of Arts, Science and Technology, Zaria, a group of students formed the Art Society, which, led by Uche Okeke (born 1933) and Demas Nwoko (born 1935) and guided by what Okeke called "Natural Synthesis," was dedicated to a pragmatic acknowledgment and fusion of inherited and acquired art traditions. These were often European, but the heritage of many African societies also included Islamic art, and the society's artists embarked on an aggressive recovery of traditional Nigerian art forms in all their historical variants. Combining media and techniques learned in art school, they encouraged less reliance on European subject matter and formal tropes. They were also concerned with the role of the artist in a culture in transition. [...]

Other African artists besides those in the Zaria Art Society took an interest in indigenous art traditions, which was hardly surprising given the political mood of the period. In Negritude, in Nkrumah's concept of African Personality, and in Nasser's Pan-Arabism, rhetorics of revalorized blackness were emerging, and the increasing nationalist fervor in many countries strengthened the resolve of artists to seek out aspects of their cultures discredited by the logic of colonialism. Thus the Sudanese painter Ibrahim El-Salahi (born 1930) and the Ethiopian Skunder Boghossian (born 1937 [died 2003]), after training at home and in Europe, turned respectively to Sudanese and Ethiopian art forms for inspiration. To reestablish links to his Sudanese identity, Salahi studied Islamic calligraphic forms and techniques, as well as graphic designs from Sudanese folk art. The symbolism of his lyrical drawings and paintings goes beyond a specifically Islamic heritage. Boghossian for his part has seen art by Lam, Matta, and Klee in Paris, and was especially fascinated by what he called Matta's "cosmic coordination in space and time and his metallic rhythm."[13] But he also drew on the symbolic and formal repertory of Coptic art, to which his intricate compositions owe much. Given the hallucinatory quality of some of his early work, his practice has been read – erroneously, one must add – as an African manifestation of Surrealism, but his position is actually quite different from that of an artist like the painter and poet Gebre Kristos Desta (1932–81). Attending a Cologne art school on a government scholarship, Desta was influenced by Wassily Kandinsky's abstraction and by the gestural techniques of Abstract Expressionism, and even after returning to Ethiopia he argued that an Ethiopian modernism contingent upon recuperating local traditions bordered on the retrogressive.[14]

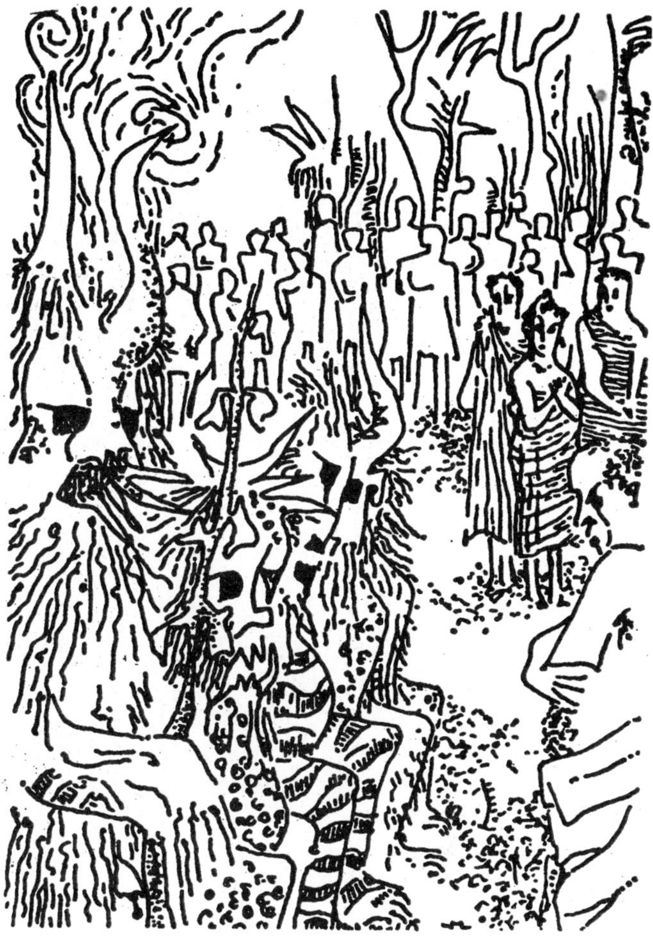

Figure 1.3 Uche Okeke, *Illustration of Things Fall Apart*, 1960–2, pen and ink on white paper, © Uche Okeke.

The Moroccan painter Ahmed Cherkaoui (1934–67), a descendant of a famous Sufi, became a student of the Koran and a calligraphic master at a very young age. In 1956, however – the year of Moroccan independence – he chose not to study at either of the two Moroccan academies (both of them steeped in orientalist and naïve painting styles, and desperately needing curricular revision) and left for Paris to study graphics at the Ecole des Métiers d'Art. There he met and exhibited with his compatriot Farid Belkahia (born 1934), as well as with other North African artists. Like Boghossian, Cherkaoui admired the work of Klee, and also of Roger Bissière. But his increasing interest in Berber art (his mother was a Berber), and especially in their tattoo and pottery marks, soon eclipsed Klee's influence,

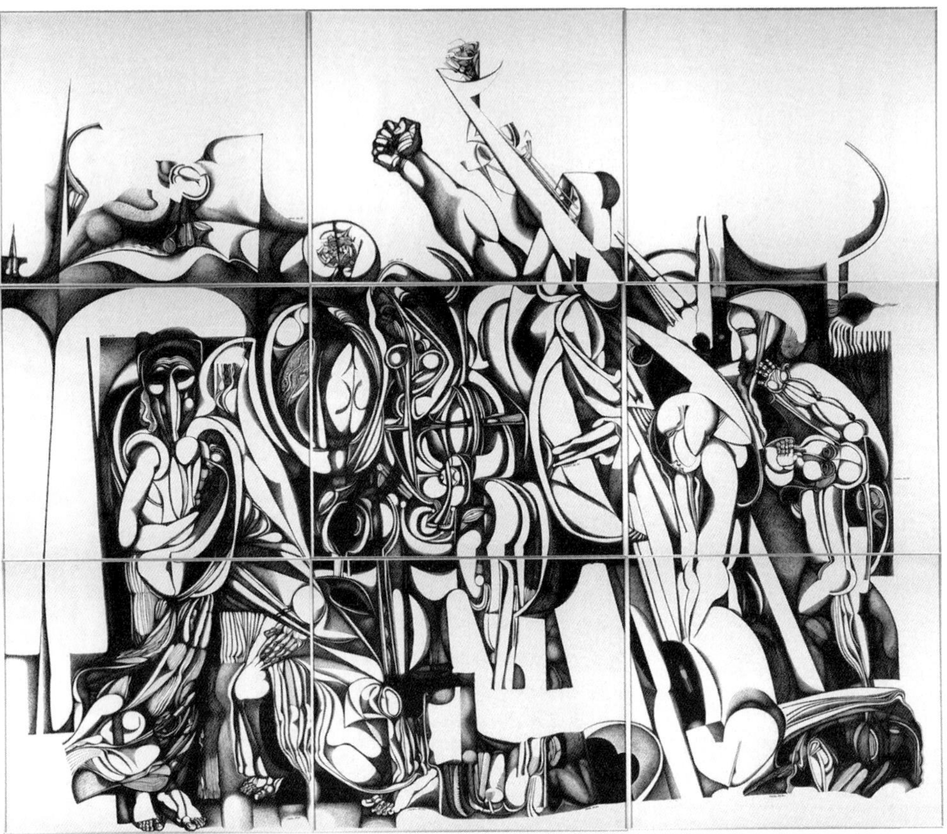

Figure 1.4 Ibrahim El Salahi, *The Inevitable*, 1984–5, India ink. Acquired through the African Art Purchase Fund, and through the David M. Solinger, Class of 1926, Purchase Fund. Photography courtesy of the Herbert F. Johnson Museum of Art, Cornell University, © Ibrahim El-Salahi. All rights reserved, DACS 2011.

enriching his work in the process. As for Belkahia, after taking over the directorship of Casablanca's Ecole des Beaux-Arts, in 1964, he incorporated calligraphy and the study of Moroccan handicrafts into the curriculum, and had an immediately palpable influence on Moroccan art. Thus Cherkaoui and Belkahia redefined Morocco's postindependence avant-garde project.

The independence decade also witnessed the emergence of artists from workshops mostly set up by expatriate culture workers and critics, or, in South Africa, by the white establishment. In Mozambique there was Malangatana Ngwenya (born 1936 [died 2011]); in Zimbabwe Thomas Mukarobgwa (1924–99); in Nigeria Twins Seven-Seven (born 1944 [died 2011]); in South Africa Sydney Kumalo (1935–88) and John Muafangejo (1943–87) from Namibia. Ngwenya's early work – encouraged by the Portuguese architect Amancio Guedes, who organized informal workshops for young artists in what was then Lourenço Marques – was vividly realistic and covered a wide range of subject matter, from religion to violent conflict to witchcraft. [...] Seven-Seven trained in the informal workshops organized by Ulli Beier in Oshogbo, Nigeria, in the early 1960s. His drawings and prints teem with bestial, floral, and human forms, and he often draws subject matter from Yoruba folklore or from his own personal mythologies. [...]

Seven-Seven's career was in many ways set on its path by Georgina Beier (born 1938), who ran the Oshogbo workshops in the mid-1960s. Disenchanted with formal art training in England, Beier turned away from European artistic trends, although her prints show stylistic affinities with early twentieth-century German Expressionism. Her encounter with Yoruba culture profoundly affected her work, and her practice raises questions about common assumptions of what constitutes modern African art. This is even more true of the work of Susanne Wenger (born 1915 [died 2009]), who has formulated new visual archetypes for Yoruba deities in architectural monuments and in narratives painted on fabric. [...]

If, in Nigeria, informal workshops provided alternative learning spaces, in Southern Africa they were black artists' only option. The most significant of the early South African workshops was the Polly Street Art Centre, established in 1948 in Johannesburg as an art and recreation facility for the black townships. In 1952, Cecil Skotnes (born 1926 [died 2009]), a fine-arts graduate of the University of Witwatersrand, became the center's director, and soon attracted a group of young artists who would become some of the most accomplished on the continent, including Sydney Kumalo, Ben Macala, Durant Sihlali (born 1935 [died 2004]), Louis Maqhubela (born 1939), Lucas Sithole (born 1931 [died 1994]), and Helen Sebidi (born 1943).

[...] Skotnes encouraged his students, many of whom he had earlier introduced to modern European art, to look to Central and West African sculpture for its expressive and formal sophistication and as a way to assert their Africanness – and this at a time when being African in South Africa was an existential burden. Kumalo's work both reflects on classical African sculpture and appropriates tropes of modern European sculpture. [...] At Johannesburg's Jubilee Art Centre in the mid-1960s, Skotnes became involved with Mslaba Dumile Feni (1942–91), an autodidact whose powerful charcoal drawings speak of the dehumanizing pall cast on South Africa by apartheid.

As the white government increasingly came to doubt apartheid's long-term viability, its mounting desperation caused it to adopt more violent tactics of suppression. Artists were involved in the liberation struggle in a number of ways. At a conference at the University of Cape Town in 1979 – two years after the charismatic black leader Steve Biko was murdered – South African artists resolved not to represent the nation abroad until black artists had equal access to state-funded art institutions. Many artists commented on the oppressive sociopolitical climate of the 1970s and 80s in their work, producing art often known as "resistance art": some of this work was polemical while some was subtle, allusive, and circumspect, yet both were potent gestures of resistance to the apartheid ethos. The screenprints of Gavin Jantjes (born 1948) take the former approach, clearly enunciating a conceptualist critique of power; the sculptures of Jane Alexander (born 1959), which suggest a bizarre experiment gone awry, and the multimedia works of Sue Williamson (born 1941) are examples of the latter approach. These works collectively speak of the darkest moments in South Africa's political history.

[...]

Notes

1 South Africa's independence in 1910 preceded Egypt's, but its peculiar political history led to a unique artistic development that has virtually no African parallel. Whereas the white minority population never completely lost contact with Europe, especially in the preapartheid era, the first black artists emerged about the same time as their counterparts from other parts of Africa.

2 William Fagg and Margaret Plass, *African Sculpture* (London: Studio Vista Limited, 1964), p. 6.

3 Ibid., p. 7.

4 Alioune Diop and Frantz Fanon, for instance, saw Jean-Paul Sartre's attempt to equate the condition of blacks under colonialism with that of European proletariats as distorting and mistaken. See Bennetta Jules-Rosette, "Conjugating Cultural Realities: Présence Africaine," in V.Y. Mudimbe, ed., *Présence Africaine and the Politics of Otherness 1947–1987* (Chicago IL: University of Chicago Press, 1992), pp. 14–44.

5 See Willemijn Stokvis, *Cobra 3 Dimensions* (London: Lund Humphries Publishers, 1999), p. 16.

6 According to Stokvis, the historian of the *COBRA* group, Ernest Mancoba's work had scarcely anything in common with that of his fellow artists, but this opinion comes as no surprise, for Stokvis was more interested in Mancoba's earlier figurative sculpture, which "showed his African origins." See Stokvis, *Cobra* (Amsterdam: De Bezige Bij, 1974), p. 356. See also Elza Miles, *Lifeline Out of Africa: The Art of Ernest Mancoba* (Cape Town: Human and Rousseau, 1994), p. 36.

7 Most of the literature on Ben Enwonwu states that he was born in 1921. Research by the art historian Sylvester Ogbechie, however, dates his birth to 1918. Since public servants during the colonial era often had official ages younger than their real ones, and since Ogbechie's attribution is confirmed by Enwonwu's family, I will keep the 1918 date. See Sylvester Ogbechie, "Ben Enwonwu in the Art Historical Account of Modern Nigerian Art," BA thesis, University of Nigeria, 1988.

8 Kenneth Murray's appointment had been secured by Aina Onabolu, who officially introduced formal art teaching upon his return from England in 1922. See Ola Oloidi, "Art and Nationalism in Colonial Nigeria," in Clementine Deliss, ed., *Seven Stories about Modern Art in Africa* (Paris: Flammarion, 1995), pp. 192–4.

9 See Yacouba Konaté, *Christian Lattier: Le Sculpteur aux mains nues* (Saint-Maur: Edition Sépia, 1993), p. 27.

10 The South African government staved off potential embarrassment by encouraging Mancoba and Feriov not to return to South Africa. See Miles, p. 41.

11 See Richard Powell, *Black Art and Culture in the Twentieth Century* (London: Thames and Hudson, 1997), p. 36.

12 Algeria's Ecole des Beaux-Arts was founded in 1920, Morocco's Escuela de Bellas Artes, Tetouan, in 1945. But both, for decades, were colonial institutions catering to the expatriate populations. On the other hand, the School of Fine Art, Makerere, Uganda, was founded in 1939, but graduated its first four-year diplomas only in 1957. See Marshall Mount, *African Art: The Years since 1920* (Bloomington: Indiana University Press, 1973), p. 95.

13 Skunder Boghossian, quoted in Louise Atcheson, "Skunder Boghossian," *Transition* (June 1963): 43.

14 See Sydney W. Head, "A Conversation with Gebre Kristos Desta," *African Arts* 2, no. 4 (1969): 20–5.

2

From Country to City

The Development of an Urban Art

Steven Sack*

> *... a fascinating exhibition, a feast which confirms one's sense of all the creative potential that has been lost, damaged or stunted by social inequality.*
>
> E. Heyns, editor, *South African Journal of Cultural and Art History*, July 1989

This selection from a 1989 catalogue essay by Steven Sack, at the time a lecturer in the Department of Fine Arts at the University of South Africa, highlights the stark difference between the social conditions out of which European modernism emerged and the situation for black South African artists under apartheid: the system of racism instituted by the federal parliament and legally enforced between 1948 and 1994. In every area of life, apartheid law strictly segregated Whites from non-Whites: Blacks (indigenous Africans), Indians (Asians), and Coloreds (mixed race). The black African artists presented here did not live in traditional agricultural villages as most southern Africans had done until the 1930s when the growth of industrialized cities drew the rural population to them as laborers. Sack tells of artists' efforts to represent African identity in transition between country and city, tradition and modernity. He begins in the 1930s and 1940s and takes us through the apartheid era when non-white urban workers were forced to live in new townships created exclusively for them by the government. Located near white cities like Johannesburg, South African townships were underdeveloped shack ghettos that lacked normal social and cultural amenities. Soweto, for example, with a population of over a million in the 1970s, had only one movie house, one nightclub, one hotel, and two sport stadiums. Artists were cut off from nearly every opportunity to develop their talents. How did they learn Western art

* Steven Sack (1989) "From Country to City: The Development of an Urban Art." In Anitra Nettleton and David Hammond-Tooke (eds) *Ten Years of Collecting* (pp. 54–7). Johannesburg, South Africa: University of the Witwatersrand, Art Galleries.

Modern Art in Africa, Asia, and Latin America: An Introduction to Global Modernisms, First Edition.
Edited by Elaine O'Brien, Everlyn Nicodemus, Melissa Chiu, Benjamin Genocchio,
Mary K. Coffey, and Roberto Tejada.

idioms and produce their own modern art under such circumstances? "Nomfanekiso Who Paints at Night: The Art of Gladys Mgudlandlu" by Elza Miles, which follows in this volume, focuses on one of the township artists mentioned by Sack; and Okwui Enwezor's "A Critical Presence: *Drum* Magazine in Context," presents another point of view on township culture in the 1950s and 1960s, one that stresses its vibrant richness.

Further Readings

Miles, Elza (1994) *Lifeline out of Africa: The Art of Ernest Mancoba.* Cape Town, South Africa: Human and Rousseau.

Peffer, John (2009) *Art and the End of Apartheid.* Minneapolis: University of Minnesota Press.

Spiro, Leslie (1989) *Gerard Sekoto: Unsevered Ties (catalog).* Johannesburg, South Africa: Johannesburg Art Gallery.

Many of the most talented of the black artists in South Africa have either died young and tragic deaths or have chosen to live in exile. This adds innumerable difficulties in the writing of this history. Andrew Motjuoadi (1935–68) died as the result of a stroke, Julian Motau (1948–68) was murdered in Alex township, Ephraim Ngatane (1938–71) died of TB, Cyprian Shilakoe (1946–72) was killed in a motor accident, Ruben Xulu (1952–85) was murdered, Thami Mnyele (1948–85) was killed by the SADF in Gaborone, John Muafangejo (1943–87) died from a heart attack, Nelson Mukhuba (1925–87) commited suicide, Mandla Nkosi (1962–87) fell to his death. Ernest Mancoba, Gerard Sekoto, Dumile, Louise Maqhubela and Azaria Mbatha all chose exile. Dikobe Martins, who is primarily known as a poet, is currently [at time of writing, 1989] in jail for political activities. It is remarkable that during the run of "The Neglected Tradition" exhibition at the Johannesburg Art Gallery (November 1988–January 1989) two of the participating artists died. Sydney Kumalo (1935–88) from an abdominal haemorrhage and Stanley Nkosi (1945–88) from a head injury.

Undoubtedly there have been many different contributing factors in the premature deaths of so many of the artists but the impact of apartheid and the inferior living conditions inflicted on black people are a major contributing factor.

During the 19th century most Africans in southern Africa lived in independent chiefdoms divided along ethnic lines. The vast majority of African people were dependent on the land for their survival; but with the discovery and harnessing of the mineral wealth of southern Africa "the very nature of work changed."[1] By the 1930s the forces of industrialisation had led to widespread urbanisation and the erosion of ethnic identities. Living conditions were transformed and many social and cultural practices underwent enormous changes. And so capitalism, largely in the hands of the white settlers, which transformed the nature of existence, also led to the development of new artistic practices. The activity of fine art needs to be understood in terms of the newly evolving capitalist economy. The very fact that the greatest part of the wealth being generated was in the hands of the white community made it essential for the newly emerging black artists to look to the white middle class for their patronage.

The new art that was produced during the 1930s illustrated the competing forces that were moulding the lives of urban Africans. Traditionalism, Christianity and the environment of the townships all influenced a new generation of artists who adopted western artmaking techniques and began to explore the iconography that arose from these contexts. Gerard Bhengu and Jabulani Ntuli produced innumerable studies of traditional life and custom; Ernest Mancoba undertook a number of ecclesiastical commissions; and John Koenakeefe Mohl and Gerard Sekoto began to portray the new urban environment.

At this early stage there were artists working in the Transvaal, Eastern Cape and Natal.[2] It is interesting to note that the Transvaal artists John Koenakeefe Mohl, Ernest Mancoba and Gerard Sekoto, like their fellow artists from the Eastern Cape, George Pemba and Gladys Mgudlandlu, were all trained as teachers at mission colleges.

There are distinctive differences between the work produced in Natal and that from the Transvaal, during the 1930s and 1940s. Natal/Zululand artists such as Simon Mnguni, Jabulani Ntuli, Arthur Butelezi and Gerard Bhengu were almost exclusively producing images of traditional life. Some of these were historical recreations of cultural and social practices that were dying out (as in the topographical and figurative work of Ntuli); others involved the portrayal of living people in traditional dress involved in traditional customs and practices (such as numerous studies of witchdoctors by Simon Mnguni). Apart from Bhengu, who appears to have received a certain amount of informal training, none of the other Natal artists mentioned received much art education. This contrasts quite dramatically with the Transvaal artists such as Mohl, Mancoba, and to a lesser extent Sekoto (as far as art training is concerned), who were all formally educated. Mohl remains one of the few African artists in the entire history of the South African fine art tradition to have received intensive academic art training. His work differs from most of the Natal artists both in terms of subject matter and medium. However, there are a number of similarities between him and Bhengu, particularly in their choice of landscape and their perspectival use of space. Mohl was one of the few artists who, at this early stage, had learnt oil painting technique and claims to have introduced both Sekoto and Pemba to oil painting.

The process of urbanisation took place differently in different parts of the country, particularly where the rural homestead was in closer proximity to the urban place of work. The 1913 Land Act, while greatly limiting the right of ownership to land on the part of black people, nonetheless ensured that the rural homestead remained the base of most black families. This dual existence of most Africans suited the needs of capitalism and the 1913 Land Act entrenched this. The notion and development of an art by black urban artists is informed by this constant interchange between rural and urban life. This phenomenon needs to be distinguished from the revivalist intentions of a number of artists working in the late 1950s and 1960s at the Polly Street Art Centre.[3] Their need to identify with traditional African culture had little to do with a personal connection with any rural homestead. They looked to the sculptural traditions of west and central Africa, as well as the modernist European translations of the same African sources.

From the 1930s until the 1980s the dualities of the city and the country, the traditional and the modern, were evident in the work of many artists. The works of John Koenakeefe Mohl, Andrew Motjuoadi and Helen Sebidi serve to illustrate this point. Unlike Gerard Sekoto, who concentrated virtually exclusively on township scenes,[4] Mohl painted rural and urban scenes. Mohl's work, more than that of any other artist, illustrates the conditions of life in the townships of the 1930s and the interplay between city and countryside. Mohl's paintings document his life in these two environments between which he regularly travelled, and captures the duality that was characteristic of the lives of migrant workers. Mohl maintained a close attachment to nature (he attempted to create a feeling of the wild in his garden in Soweto by planting indigenous cacti). He believed in the need to return to the rural homestead and encouraged his pupil, Helen Sebidi, to return to her rural home in order to rediscover her roots. However, Mohl was also involved in the township milieu and painted innumerable township scenes, often choosing dramatic moments such as thunderstorms and always making use of strong light and shadow contrasts. [...]

In a much later period of fine art produced by African artists, Helen Sebidi has produced work that, in terms of different artistic languages, address the dual experience of town and country. In her case the focus is far more on the figure itself, whereas Mohl gives greater attention to specific details that define locality.

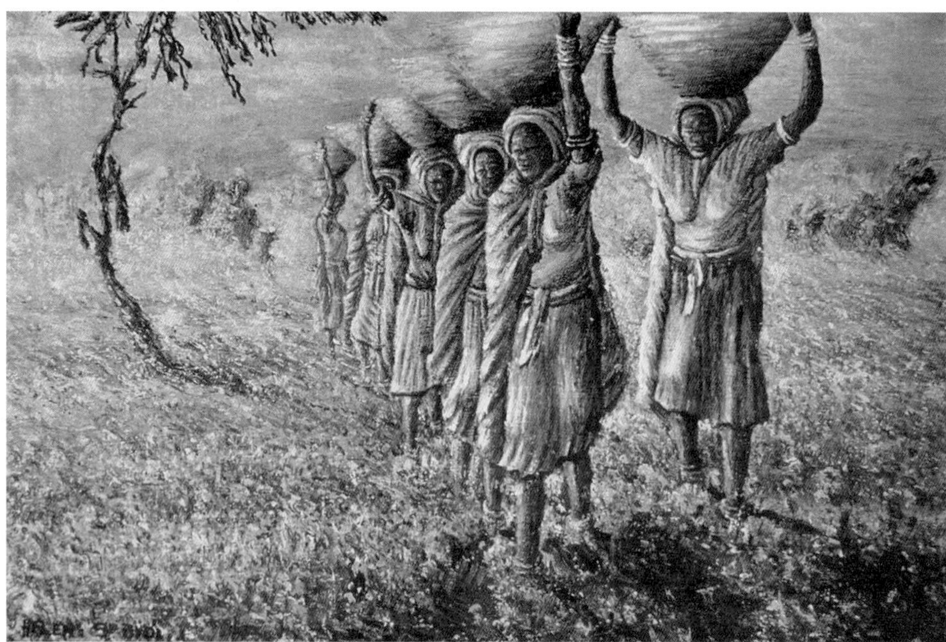

Figure 2.1 Helen Sebidi, *From the Lands, Carrying Food*, c.1979, oil on canvas, © Helen Sebidi.

In fact, Mohl differs markedly from Sebidi in his treatment of the figure. The dichotomy between urban and rural, which in Mohl's work has been indicated in literal reproductions of locality, is no longer conveyed through depiction of specific place, but through an attitude of mind (resulting from the exposure to modernism in art). Although both of Sebidi's paintings illustrated here [*Mother Earth* and *From the Lands Carrying Food*] talk of womanhood, they do so in quite different ways. The one talks of women's labour in a fairly literal way, using perspectival conventions that serve to create a real world, and women's labour in the lands is portrayed. The world portrayed in *Mother Africa*, however, is more symbolic and the title suggests a metaphoric and mythologising intent. It is not clear where these figures are. Sebidi completely eliminates locality in her works produced in the 1980s, resulting in images that are wholly constructed out of human figures and fragments of figures.

[…]

The paintings of township scenes that both Mohl and Sekoto were producing in the 1930s and 1940s were often a form of documentary reportage: portrayals of the mundane daily lives of the black inhabitants of the townships. Mohl's work was more attentive to particularised details, whereas Sekoto worked in an impressionistic style with a strong emphasis on painterly technique. There were no professional black photographers working at this time, and the earliest street photographers were engaged in "snapping away at pedestrians in couples,"[5] a practice that appears to have begun in the late 1940s. It was only in the 1950s that black photographers such as Bob Gosani and Peter Magubane began to document the township environment. It was left to the paintings of Mohl and Sekoto to capture in visual form some of the quality of township life in the 1930s and 1940s. Another interesting dimension to the phenomenon of township depictions had to do with the fact that the townships became less and less accessible to white South Africans. Whereas Sophiatown was, for a time, a place where all people could meet, the new townships built in the 1950s could only be entered by whites with a permit. Hence the scenes of townships painted by black artists, to be sold almost exclusively to a white audience, take on another kind of significance. These paintings conveyed images of an environment unknown to

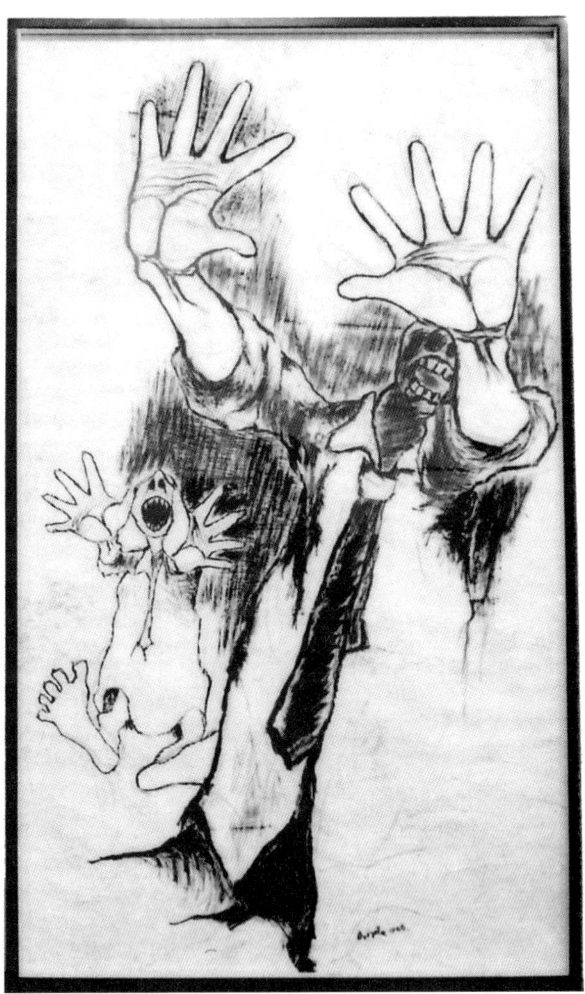

Figure 2.2 Dumile Feni, *Fear*, charcoal on paper, 131 × 77 cm/51 × 30 inches, Dumile Feni Family Trust, Pretoria Art Museum.

the white audience, and they therefore carried an enormous responsibility in communicating the nature and quality of life in the townships. It was simply not possible for the artists of the townships to paint quaint and picturesque broken-down houses. The environment in which they lived contained far too much violence. It has been suggested that the harsh reality of township life was largely ignored by the township artists. Undoubtedly many self-pitying and sentimental images were produced, to satisfy the demands of the commercial fine art market, and it is this kind of work that was to draw harsh criticism from the proponents of Black Consciousness. But the work of artists such as Dumile and Motau[6] attest to the enormous anguish and torment and the need to talk of the violence that surrounded them and that, in many instances, destroyed them.

[...]

Notes

1 J. Callinicos, *Working Life 1886–1940: A People's History of South Africa*, vol. 2 (Johannesburg: Ravan Press, 1987) p. 7.

2 Rural Transvaal, Eastern Cape, and Natal were provinces of South Africa until the end of the apartheid regime in 1994 when provinces and homelands were reorganized.

3 The Polly Street Art Centre in Johannesburg was an urban community center and the first art school where black artists, excluded from white art institutions, could get education, career assistance, and exhibitions. Cecil Skotnes (English, b. 1926 [d. 2009]) one of the leading artists in South Africa, became its director in 1952 and had over 40 students by the end of 1954.

4 B. Lindop, *Gerard Sekoto* (Randburg: Dictum Publishing, 1988), p. 20.

5 J. Schadenberg, *The Finest Photos from the Old Drum: A Bailey's African Photo Archives*, Penguin Books, 1987), p. 50.

6 Dumile Feni (1942–1991), the "Goya of the Townships," whose large expressionist drawings reveal the dark truths of Township life, immigrated to the US in 1968. Julian Motau (1948–68) was strongly influenced by Dumile.

3

Nomfanekiso Who Paints at Night

The Art of Gladys Mgudlandlu

Elza Miles*

> *I think I can claim to be the first African woman in the country to hold an exhibition.*
>
> Gladys Mgudlandlu, 1962

South African painter Gladys Nomfanekiso Mgudlandlu (1923–78), born twenty years before Helen Sebidi, the only other female artist mentioned in Steven Sack's "From Country to City: The Development of an Urban Art," was perhaps the most celebrated black township artist of the 1960s. A 1961 exhibition of her gouaches at the Liberal Party offices in Cape Town made Mgudlandlu the first African woman in South Africa to have a solo exhibition. While township painters were sometimes criticized for selling black misery to a white audience, her art seems to have been appreciated for its rich imagination. The artist's saturated color and expressive brushstroke describe landscapes, plants, animals, and scenes of southern African village and township life. Vivid, magical narratives shaped by Xhosa folklore, the paintings were, remarkably, made at night by the light of a paraffin lamp. There was no electricity in Nyanga, the township where she lived and worked as a primary school teacher. Admired by the white liberal art gallerists and patrons of Cape Town who exhibited and collected her work, Mgudlandlu has been criticized for pleasing them by not showing the harsh inequities suffered under apartheid.

Questions for reading: How would you otherwise account for and measure Mgudlandlu's rare artistic achievement and art world success? Did her affirmative imagination, however much it failed to confront real conditions, nevertheless help redefine African identity and artistic expression for modern times? What were her aesthetic sources?

* Elza Miles (2002) *Nomfanekiso Who Paints at Night: The Art of Gladys Mgudlandlu*. Vlaeberg, South Africa: Fernwood Press.

Modern Art in Africa, Asia, and Latin America: An Introduction to Global Modernisms, First Edition.
Edited by Elaine O'Brien, Everlyn Nicodemus, Melissa Chiu, Benjamin Genocchio, Mary K. Coffey, and Roberto Tejada.

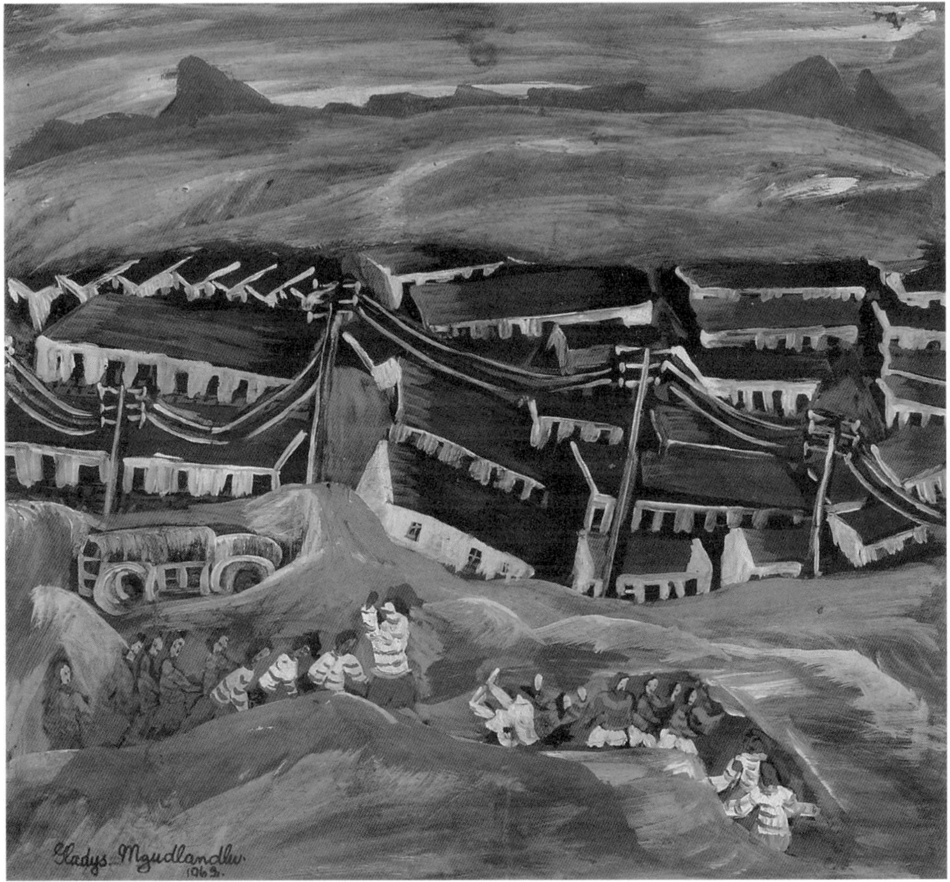

Figure 3.1 Gladys Mgdudlandlu, *Nyanga Landscape,* 1963, gouache on board, 57 × 60 cm / 22 × 24 inches. Bruce Campbell Smith Collection.

Gladys [Nomfanekiso] Mgudlandlu achieved success as a professional artist from the start of her career. Her rise was phenomenal and newspaper headlines announced: 'SA art record for Africa';[1] 'Even critics buy her work',[2] 'Stampede to buy African's pictures',[3] 'Native artist's success',[4] 'African artist scores a hit – may paint in US',[5] 'R105[6] work by Gladys sells in 3 minutes'[7] and 'Gladys Mgudlandlu's work fetches R1,000'.[8] Yet, her death on 17 February 1979 went unnoticed, as did her funeral on 3 March. Months later, artist Eduard Ladan paid tribute to her in *The Cape Times*: 'Black artist's death leaves a void in Cape art scene'.[9]

[…]

At a time when apartheid permeated every aspect of South African life, Gladys Mgudlandlu, known by the people of Nyanga[10] as 'the African queen', appeared on the Cape Town art scene. She held her first exhibition in the offices of the Liberal Party in 1961.

[...]

For eleven years, from September 1961 to January 1972, Mgudlandlu's vibrant personality and pristine form of expressionism enchanted journalists, artists and art lovers. Art critics not only reviewed her exhibitions, they also bought her paintings. Paging through newspaper cuttings, it is evident that, from her début to her last solo exhibition in 1972, she was, with the exception of 1969 and 1970, in the news every year. Her work fell into oblivion because she stopped painting and exhibiting her works during the last eight years of her life. In 1971, she suffered severe injuries in a car accident while she was on her way to the school where she taught.

[...]

[...] Mgudlandlu's work does not lend itself to pigeonholing. She is primarily an expressionist [...] [whose] expressionism evolved by drawing on indigenous sources, independent observation and the guidance of fellow artists and critics.

[...]

[Her] initiation into the art of mural painting as a child influenced her profoundly. Her Fingo[11] grandmother taught her the rudiments of this art form. When requested by the South African Association of Arts, for biographical purposes, to name her most important commission, Mgudlandlu replied: 'The painting of the murals on my hutment.'[12]

[...]

Mgudlandlu emphasized detail and textual differences in her early work, evoking the rich textile surfaces of tapestries and embroideries. Over the years, her brushwork became broader, to conjure up broad, simple planes and shapes. Her emphasis shifted from pictorial storytelling to scenes of documentary expression.

[...]

[The artist] was autodidactic in terms of Western painting techniques, but her experience of indigenous mural painting filtered through in her application of paint. She said the use of 'thick, opaque colours' in her paintings probably resulted from 'making designs in different coloured clays when she was a little girl.'[13]

[...]

[Her] first attempts at fine art were painting in watercolour and gouache. She recalls: 'One day I went to a shop in Cape Town and asked for watercolours ... I asked the shop assistant how to use them. Since then I have painted.' [As one Cape Town art critic] aptly noted: 'In the first and last instances, her creations are in paint.'[14]

[...]

Notes

1 *Eastern Province Herald*, 27 August 1962.
2 *The Cape Times*, 31 August 1962.
3 *Eastern Province Herald*, 13 November 1963.
4 *The Cape Argus*, 19 November 1963.
5 *Eastern Province Herald*, 4 December 1963.
6 South African Rand in 1970 was valued at R1.39 against the US Dollar.
7 *The Cape Argus*, 14 November 1963.
8 *The Cape Argus*, 16 August 1967.
9 E. Laden, *The Cape Times*, 26 June 1979.

10 Nyanga is a black township on the outskirts of Cape Town, South Africa. Such townships were artificial creations of the Group Areas Act of 1950 (repealed in 1991) created under the apartheid government of South Africa that assigned races to different and extremely unequal residential and business sections in urban areas.

11 Fingo or Mfengu people of the Eastern Cape in South Africa and the Xhosa/Bantu language group.

12 *The Daily Dispatch*, 19 January 1972.

13 *Eastern Province Herald*, 7 November 1962.

14 C.A. Bücher, "Aardse eenvoud hou haar by waarheid," *Die Burger*, 22 August 1962.

4

Negritude, Pan-Africanism, and Postcolonial African Identity

African Portrait Photography

OKWUI ENWEZOR AND OCTAVIO ZAYA*

The subjects of these photographs are the electorate who would cast the decisive vote for independence and initiate the radical break with colonialism.

Enwezor and Zaya

Until the 1996 exhibition, *In/sight: African Photographers, 1940 to the Present*, opened in New York City, most Westerners had never seen photographs of African subjects taken by African photographers for African audiences. Photographs by Western photographers for European and North American audiences, on the other hand, have been ubiquitous, and they helped ingrain the heart-of-darkness stereotype of Africa as primal, violent, erotic, and tragic. This reading, selected from the *In/sight* catalogue, undoes such primitivist conventions.

Here exhibition curators Okwui Enwezor and Octavio Zaya consider the significance of African commercial portrait photography of the 1940s to 1960s: crucial decades leading to liberation. Within the struggle for freedom from European powers and Eurocentric values, modern African identity was being shaped. The selection begins with a sketch of negritude, the leading identity theory of the era and one of the founding movements of African modernism, which held that what is essentially African is to be found in the continent's precolonial traditions. *Africanité* – what is "authentically African" on the continent and among the millions of Africans dispersed

* Okwui Enwezor and Octavio Zaya (1996) "Negritude, Pan-Africanism, and Postcolonial African Identity: African Portrait Photography." Selection from "Colonial Imaginary, Tropes of Disruption: History, Culture, and Representation in the Works of African Photographers." In Clare Bell, Okwui Enwezor, Danielle Tilkin, and Octavio Zaya (eds) *In / sight: African Photographers, 1940 to the Present* (pp. 17–47). New York, NY: The Solomon R. Guggenheim Foundation and Harry Abrams.

Modern Art in Africa, Asia, and Latin America: An Introduction to Global Modernisms, First Edition.
Edited by Elaine O'Brien, Everlyn Nicodemus, Melissa Chiu, Benjamin Genocchio, Mary K. Coffey, and Roberto Tejada.

worldwide – must be re-esteemed and restored. "Black" signified racial and cultural distinction. Influential theorists of negritude introduced in this piece are the francophone poets and public intellectuals Léopold Senghor (1906–2001), the first president of Senegal (1960–80), and Aimé Césaire (1913–2008) of Martinique. The prominent alternative postures of anglophone statesman Kwame Nkrumah (1909–72), the founder and first president of Ghana (1957–60) and major proponent of Pan-Africanism, which called for the unity of all people of African heritage worldwide, and the Nigerian author, Nobel laureate Wole Soyinka (b. 1934), are noted as Enwezor and Zaya locate photo-portraitists in the era's identity debates.

The authors want you to see that portraits taken by Mama Casset (1908–92) and Salla Casset (1910–74), Seydou Keita (1921–2001) of Mali, and other commercial studio photographers of the pre-liberation era are themselves strong visual arguments against the essentialist doctrines of Senghor's negritude. The African identity apparent in the pose, dress, and props shows us modern individualists – not generic "Africans." These are portraits of people who are already embracing modernity: individuals creating unique, knowing fusions of traditional and modern aesthetics and values.

Questions for reading: What conditions account for the difference between the photo-portraits featured in this article and the usual representations of Africans in anthropological, tourist, and news photos taken by Western photographers? How can a direct gaze and other attributes of a photo-portrait noted by Enwezor and Zaya convey an attitude toward modern identity and experience?

Suggested Readings

Anthology of African Photography [Anthologie de la photographie africaine et de l'océan Indien] (1998). New York: DAP.

Bajorek, Jennifer (2009) "(Dis)locating Freedom: The Photographic Portraiture of Seydou Keita." *Critical Interventions: Journal of African Art History and Visual Culture* 3–4: 100–13.

The emergence of the concept of negritude [occurred] in the late 1930s, in particular as a dialectical framework in the development of African and Caribbean postcolonial literary discourse. [...] The first appearance of the term *négritude* was in the startling epic poem by the great poet Aimé Césaire of Martinique. In "Cahier d'un retour au pays natal" ("Notebook of a Return to the Native Land"), published in 1939, Césaire set down the psychic and temporal order that would come to define this very important branch of modernism. He writes simultaneously out of righteous scorn and penetrating irony:

oh friendly light
oh fresh source of light
those who have invented neither powder nor compass
those who could harness neither steam nor electricity

those who explored neither the seas nor the sky but those
without whom the earth would not be the earth
gibbosity all the more beneficent as the bare earth even more earth
silo where that which is earthiest about earth ferments and ripens
my negritude is not a stone, its deafness hurled against the clamor of the day
my negritude is not a leukoma of dead liquid over the earth's dead eye
my negritude is neither tower nor cathedral
it takes root in the red flesh of the soil
it takes root in the ardent flesh of the sky
it breaks through the opaque prostration with its upright patience[1]

Though Césaire originated the word, its conceptualization and subsequent growth as a cultural movement were not his alone. The Senegalese statesman, poet, and essayist Léopold Sédar Senghor was [...] giving negritude its stamp and urgency. [...] Senghor's beliefs [...] were rooted in a kind of archaic revisionism. [...]

As negritude's tenets were taking hold, [...] the irreversible changes that would eventually inaugurate the struggle for the end of colonialism were being forged by the Pan-African ideology of Nkrumah and the "scientific socialism" supported by Anglophone intellectuals who rejected Senghor's negritude and Africanité as essentialist particularism, both emotional and regressive. At a writer's conference in 1962 in Kampala, Uganda, the young Wole Soyinka (who in 1986 was named Nobel laureate in literature) of Nigeria retorted with disdain, while discussing negritude, that "a tiger does not go about asserting its tigritude." [...] The points of these attacks are to be found in Senghor's unshifting position vis-à-vis Africanité, negritude, and the past. Often, his beliefs seem dangerously close to the ideas of nineteenth-century scientific anthropology, which privileged notions of originary essence. [...] Senghor emphasized the past at the expense of the present. [...]

Negritude's rejection by many African intellectuals on the grounds that it was revisionist and regressive seems to be confirmed in the photographs made by Joseph Moïse Agbojelou, Mama Casset, Salla Casset, Meïssa Gaye, and Keita in the same period. Nowhere in their works do we detect the sitters' desires to live in that so-called Negro-African museum. In fact, what we see is their reluctance to be confined in such a natural-history or ethnographic setting. [...]

The interpretation we may draw from this vehement cultural and ideological dispute is that the African self-image in the late 1930s and the 1940s was already being radically transformed. The subjects of these photographs are the electorate who would cast the decisive vote for independence and initiate the radical break with colonialism. [...] Their subjectivities and desires in a modern and modernizing Africa conflict with the Senghorian interpretation of an originary African essence. For if, as he argued, tradition was the mother of the primal essence, then technology no doubt should have represented its antithesis and negation. [...] But technology in the modern world was never the antithesis or negation of tradition. What simply happened, as James Clifford notes, was that "after the Second World War, colonial relations would be pervasively contested. ... Peoples long spoken for by Western ethnographers,

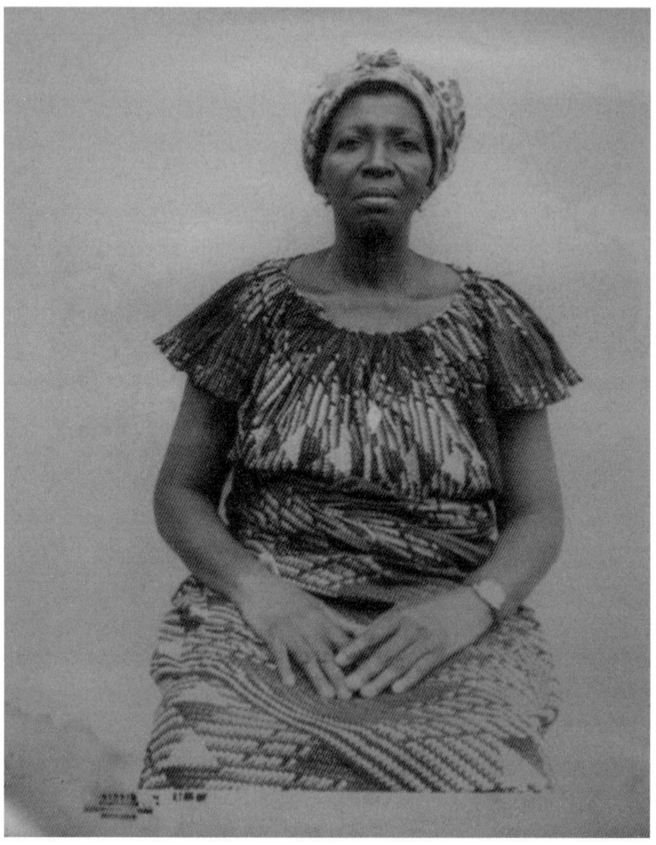

Figure 4.1 Joseph Moïse Agbojelou, *Portrait of a Woman*, © Leonce Agbojelou. Courtesy Frank Ogou, Patrimoine Africain, Benin.

administrators, and missionaries began to speak and act more powerfully for themselves on a global stage. It was increasingly difficult to keep them in their (traditional) places. Distinct ways of life once destined to merge into 'the modern world' reasserted their difference, in novel ways.[2]

Before World War II interfered with the drive for self-governance, Africa's sense of itself was changing. Like James VanDerZee in Harlem, New York and Richard Samuel Roberts in South Carolina, Mama Casset, Salla Casset, and Gaye had already established studios in Dakar and Saint-Louis, Senegal that catered to the elite and common folk of those cities. They methodically documented an important milieu in that negotiated space bridging the gap between colonial and postcolonial identity, between the self and the other, between modernity and tradition. Keita set up a studio in Bamako, Mali at the end of the 1940s, largely continuing the same kind of portrait work, but with a lyrical, modernist sensibility that is as fresh today as when his photographs were made. [...]

The existence of photographs of the 1940s provides us with an insight into the diverse and complex sensibilities that made up the face of Africa as it entered a new era. The images give us access to vivid, but by no means complete, visual records of a continent gripped by, yet emerging from, the political, economic, social, and cultural structures imposed by colonialism.

[...]

Portraiture, Reality, and Representation

Prior to the period of independence, those representations of Africa's social reality available in the West were the work of European photographers. The ubiquity of these photographs produced in mass numbers as souvenirs obscures the existence and availability of work by African photographers who were active in the colonies as early as the 1860s. A. C. Gomes, for instance, established a studio in Zanzibar in 1868 and opened a branch in Dar es Salaam later on; N. Walwin Holm started his business in Accra in 1883 and was, in 1897, the first African photographer inducted as a member into the Royal Photographic Society of Great Britain. Other photographers active during the later part of the nineteenth century were George S. A. Da Costa (in Lagos from 1895), E. C. Dias (in Zanzibar in the 1890s), and F. R. C. Lutterodt (of Ghana, who worked in Accra, Cameroon, Gabon, and Fernando Po in the 1890s). Many other names are currently lost to history.

The material available on these photographers suggests that they were not (either thematically or historically) linked to the decline and the disintegration of European colonial dominance. Nor could we say that they were involved in any way in the destructuring of European hegemony in African existence. Since very little early photography by Africans is available publicly, it would be difficult to claim their production as the embodiment of some counterdiscursive "native" sensibility in an insurgent photographic practice that could have overthrown the imperialist mechanisms of European invincibility and superiority. Within artistic practice, the reclamation of African subjectivity, in any kind of considered manner, existed within the practice of painting, in what Olu Oguibe identifies as a reverse appropriation in the work of the Nigerian painter Aina Onabolu, who was working in Lagos during the early 1900s and in Paris in the 1920s.[3] Kobena Mercer identifies the same process at work in Mama Casset's portraits of the 1920s and 1930s. He writes:

> Whereas the depiction of Africans in prevailing idioms of photo-journalism tends to imply a vertical axis which literally looks down upon the subject, thereby cast into a condition of pathos and abjection, Mama Casset's portraits are often set on a diagonal whereby the women he portrays seem to lean out of the frame to look straight out to the viewer, with a self-assured bearing that evidences an interaction conducted on equal footing.[4]

This positioning and sense of confrontation coincide with the reflective discourses advanced by the African liberation struggle, discourses that affected the work of the portraitists. [...] Thus, the period of independence, which began roughly at the end of World War II and ended in the early 1970s, was not a period of amnesia, tabula rasa, and newborn Africanity, but a time of sociopolitical resurrection, reassessment, and transformation. The temptation to search for some sort of "natural" or "pure" state of African photography emerging from this period is great. To proceed from such an assumption, which anticipates an allegedly original photography and an "other" photography, would overlook and mar the very existence and repercussions of the colonial enterprise. On the other hand, it conforms to the idea of an imagined "difference" that marks borders around those "other" cultural practices, isolating and fetishizing them. This kind of paternalistic identification thus separates the viewer from African cultural production and from the social conditions that have shaped its forms. At the same time, it reaffirms the imaginary unity of Western photography and the myth of its own distinctiveness, authenticity, and superiority.

Likewise, in assuming the illusion of an allegedly universal photographic language, we may be reinforcing the systematic process and hegemonic position of Western projection, identification, and appropriation. Too often, many Western critics, curators, and scholars, instructed and trained within the theoretical frame of Western photography, seem predisposed to applying their presuppositions to non-European photographers or artists, thus ignoring or dismissing specific sociocultural situations and ideological conditions that inform artistic practice in other regions of the world.

Kwame Anthony Appiah discusses an instance of Western projection in his revealing *In My Father's House: Africa in the Philosophy of Culture*: "The French colonial project, by contrast with the British, entailed the evolution of francophone Africans; its aim was to produce a more homogeneous francophone elite. Schools did not teach in 'native' languages, and the French did not assign substantial powers to revamped precolonial administrations. You might suppose, therefore, that the French project of creating a class of black 'evolués' had laid firmer foundations for the postcolonial state." Appiah also asserts that "the majority of French colonies have chosen to stay connected to France, and all but Guinée ... have accepted varying degrees of 'neocolonial' supervision by the metropole," either culturally, militarily, or economically. And, in most cases, the colonial languages of the British, French, and Portuguese remained the languages of government after independence, according to Appiah, "for the obvious reason that the choice of any other indigenous language would have favored a single linguistic group."[5] [...]

Ironically, in this period that promised African independence from Europe, the liberation struggle was formulated through many visions and schemes that were ideologically, culturally, and politically articulated within European history and philosophical traditions. Both Senghor's Africanité and Nkrumah's "scientific socialism" were nothing more than Eurocentric ideas projected and presented either as Africa's own self-conception (in the case of the former), or as a universal and globalized paradigm that unequivocally occluded African historicity and its concrete political and cultural existence (in the latter). If the former internalized and ontologized racism, as Tsenay Serequeberhan pointedly evidences [...] in his book *The Hermeneutics of African Philosophy: Horizon and Discourse*, the latter, by employing the abstract and universalizing language of Marxist-Leninist idealism, subordinates African existence to the terrain of a homogenized historicity determined by the "historical logic" of the international hegemonic power of the Western proletariat and of European modernity.

Other writers, statesmen, and intellectuals associated with the African liberation struggle, such as Césaire, Amilcar Cabral, and Fanon, focused instead on establishing an African political tradition grounded in African historicity. They articulated a critique exposing the contrast between the unfulfilled promises and ideals of African "independence" and the political realities of the new states. Aware that newly independent African countries were still connected to colonial attitudes and values, they enunciated a notion of liberation as a process of reclaiming African history. The "return to the source" established by Cabral as the basic direction for the movement he directed in the 1960s in Guinea-Bissau is not, however, a return to tradition in stasis; nor is it engaged, as Serequeberhan explains, "in an antiquarian quest for an already existing authentic past." On the contrary, in "returning," the

"Westernized native" brings with him "the European cultural baggage that constitutes his person," absorbing the European values into a "new synthesis." Serequeberhan elucidates, "In this dialectic European culture/history is recognized as a particular and *specific* disclosure of existence, aspects of which are retained or rejected in terms of the lived historicity and the practical requirements of the history that is being reclaimed."[6]

The works of photographers like Agbojelou (working in what is now Benin), Augustt (Côte d'Ivoire), Mama Casset (Senegal), Salla Casset (Senegal), Gaye (Senegal), Keita (Mali), Moumoune Koné (Mali), Boufjala Kouyaté (Mali), and Youssouf Traoré (Mali) are instilled with the euphoria and the disappointment, the pride and the insecurity, the confidence and the contradictions of this period of transformation. Even if none of these photographers directly problematized cultural, political, and social issues of colonialism and postcolonialism, they employed narrative means that contribute to unraveling the issues under discussion and to situating them within the specific historical and ideological framework of the African experience of this period. Taken as a collection of disparate images and aspects of traditional and modern forms and effects, these photographs reveal African societies in flux. Even Agbojelou's traditional and more luxurious portraits of weddings and other political, cultural, and religious ceremonies offer tradition as something alive, not sealed in the antiquity of a "reconstructed" culture.

In general terms, the portraits by these photographers are descriptions of individuals as much as they are inscriptions of social identities. Although most of them are frontal poses of individuals and groups in the photographers' studios, the portraits expose as much as they hide from view through the complexity and sophistication of representation. Set as they are within a historical model of photographic configuration, these portraits are not necessarily telling any "truth" about their subjects, but, as products of signification, they are claiming a specific presence in representation. Portrait photography, in general, creates the illusion of fixed, immutable presences in images rendered as real bodies. When we pose, we either imagine what people see when they look at us and then try to act out this image, or we want to look like someone else and imitate that appearance. We imitate what we think the observer sees, or what we see in someone else, or what we wish to see in ourselves. This process of reconfiguration and acting out of an ideal is what is so fascinating in the character studies of African studio portraiture. It evidences not only a social transformation but a structural and ideological one, in which the complex negotiations of individual desires and identities are mapped and conceptualized.

[...] As is the case with all portraits, those by these African photographers vacillate between glamorizing the sitters and uncritically reflecting their projections and desires. These portraits do not only render reality; they penetrate and evaluate it. These portraits are archetypes, models for the way their sitters wanted to appear. The portrait is, therefore, the outcome of an elaborate constitutive process. [...]

While reminiscing on that transitional period of the late 1940s, Keita comments that, by then, "men in town began to dress in European style. They were influenced by France. But not everybody had the means to dress like that. In the studio I had three different European outfits, with tie, shirt, shoes, and hat … everything. And also accessories – fountain pen, plastic flowers, radio, telephone – which I had available for the clients." Most of Keita's pictures depict individuals in traditional African clothing, but the variety, elegance, or origin of these clothes (already cultural inscriptions in themselves) is not precisely what these portraits emphasize; what they reveal is their own sociocultural value as signifiers of status and their functional role in the construction and transformation of identity.

Keita also recognizes that he helped his models to find ways to look their best. In his studio, he displayed samples of his photographs so customers could choose how they wanted to look. "I suggested a position which was better suited to them, and in effect I determined the good position," Keita admits. His clients were as conscious of their poses as of their dress and accessories. All elements amount to the construction of solemn images composed as signs of wealth, beauty, and elegance, which act – with the complicity of the photographer – as surrogates for the essences of their subjects.

The clients and subjects of portraiture by Salla Casset, Gaye, and Keita are primarily family members and friends, civil servants, bureaucrats, society ladies, and well-to-do people. Confirming his own position as a sought-after photographer, Keita comments, "Even our first president of the Republic [of Mali] came."[7] Most of the photographs, whether taken inside or outside the studio, place the models against plain or patterned backgrounds. In most cases, the backgrounds isolate the model with accessories and props; particularly in Keita's majestic photographs, they may blend with the subject's clothes, emphasizing the faces. Despite the realism and purported individuality and particularities of these portraits, the generic solid or decorative backgrounds and the props give them an abstract quality. Certainly, Casset, Gaye, and Keita were not trying to create or document a taxonomy of social types, but the generic character of such elements seems to counteract the subjectivity of individual models.

Portraiture in Africa recorded how models wanted to be remembered, or inventoried their past; sitters could then witness their own (or somebody else's) transformation as well as the disappearance over time of customs and cultural symbols. While the portrait, as a memento mori, could suggest a pathos to the model in its reminder of mortality, it could also be put to societal uses. Much of the most stimulating work of Augustt, for instance, consists of portraits made for identity cards in the mid-1960s. They are technically as sharp and clear as Keita's, but stylistically straightforward and uncomplicated. Augustt's portraits, of the poor, workers, job-seeking rural people, and others, make up a much broader social sampling than Keita's. The head-on-stare of Augustt's models evokes a cross between the mug shot, documentary photo, and old-fashioned studio portrait, although the portraits themselves assert an unusually modern quality.

Portraits also have religious functions in different African cultures. In a continent where technology is always narrated as being at loggerheads with tradition, photography – from the moment it was conscripted into service to create funerary objects – has been renovating and supplementing an existing tradition. Within this context, the portrait, in addition to being a presence in the world, carries great symbolic value, for it is said to represent the spirit of the subject, as an index, a pure trace of the body. In various African cultures, photographic portraits have been appropriated so that the images are perceived, almost literally, as surrogates for the body. Families cherish them. They protect and guard them against evil spells and ill will. Their codes and meanings, their aspect of liminality between the realms of the seen and the imagined, are invested, almost, with the potency of magic. Christian Metz writes about photography having the character of death. Photography, he notes, "is a cut inside the referent, it cuts off a piece of it, a fragment, a part object, for a long immobile travel of no return."[8] While this scenario essays photography as a fascinating outtake of immobility, we would argue the opposite, that the portrait as the object of an elaborate funerary enterprise exists in a rather complex metaphysical location, where it is subsumed within many traditional codes. Rather than being fixed in the immobility of death, the deceased's portrait is rescued from that still ether of abjection by the performative surrogacy enacted by the synecdoche of metaphysical transference.

Thus in various contexts, the portrait's meaning in Africa possesses its own distinct codes, its own play of signifiers. It enters into the service of myth and fetishism when its perceived opticality is turned into a rich and complex field of signs invested with ritualistic meaning.

[...]

Notes

1 Aimé Césaire, "Notebook of a Return to the Native Land," in *The Collected Poetry*, trans. Clayton Eshleman and Annette Smith (Berkeley: University of California Press, 1983), p. 69.

2 James Clifford, *The Predicament of Culture: Twentieth-Century Ethnography, Literature, and Art* (Cambridge, MA: Harvard University Press, 1988), p. 6.

3 Olu Oguibe, "Reverse Appropriation as Nationalism in Early Modern African Art," unpublished paper, presented on April 27, 1996 at the conference Cultural Responses to Colonialism, Reynolda House, Museum of American Art, Winston-Salem, NC.

4 Kobena Mercer, "Home from Home: Portraits from Places In Between," in *Self Evident*, exh. cat. (Birmingham, England: Ikon Gallery, 1995).

5 Kwame Anthony Appiah, *In My Father's House: Africa in the Philosophy of Culture* (New York: Oxford University Press, 1992), p. 166.

6 Serequeberhan, *The Hermeneutics of African Philosophy*, pp. 108–9.

7 All quotations from Seydou Keita, "Seydou Keita (Portfolio)" (interview with André Magnin), *African Arts* (Los Angeles) 28, no. 4 (fall 1995), pp. 90–5.

8 Christian Metz, "Photography and Fetish," in Carol Squiers, ed., *The Critical Image: Essays on Contemporary Photography* (London: Lawrence and Wishart, 1990), p. 158.

5

A Critical Presence
Drum *Magazine in Context*

Okwui Enwezor*

Drum magazine began publication in South Africa in 1951 just as apartheid laws went into force. This essay looks at the monthly's first decade when, with the support of a large cosmopolitan readership throughout the continent and against sometimes violent censorship and incarceration, *Drum* photographers reported on the full range of black African urban life: hard, but irrepressibly vital, optimistic, and modern. Okwui Enwezor argues from both local and global perspectives for the aesthetic and social power of *Drum* photography. Documenting the life around them from an insider's perspective, the photographs did much to subvert debilitating colonialist stereotypes.

Questions for reading: How does Enwezor see *Drum* magazine's part in modernizing Africa? With its regional editions in several African countries, how did *Drum* contribute a local, everyday content to Pan-African thinking?

[...]

From the time the Dutch arrived and established a trading post for the Dutch East India Company in 1652 in Cape of Good Hope, the story of South Africa has been one of occupation, colonial pillage, and contested territories, histories and identities. The introduction of apartheid in 1948, after the electoral triumph of the Afrikaner National Party, gave birth to a succession of laws including the Population Registration Act (1950), which allowed the government to classify people on the basis of race and color, and the Group Areas Act (1950), which authorized the forced removal and physical separation of people along racial lines. The Native

* Okwui Enwezor (1996) "A Critical Presence: *Drum* Magazine in Context." In Clare Bell, Okwui Enwezor, Danielle Tilkin, and Octavio Zaya (eds) *In/sight: African Photographers, 1940 to the Present* (pp. 179–91). New York, NY: The Solomon R. Guggenheim Foundation and Harry Abrams.

Modern Art in Africa, Asia, and Latin America: An Introduction to Global Modernisms, First Edition.
Edited by Elaine O'Brien, Everlyn Nicodemus, Melissa Chiu, Benjamin Genocchio,
Mary K. Coffey, and Roberto Tejada.

Laws Amendment Act (1952) ushered in the notorious pass laws, which curtailed and controlled the movement of Africans within South Africa. [...] These laws, which always carried the threat of violence, beleaguered any notion of a shared and representative national culture or identity, which inevitably led to a protracted, internecine struggle for freedom.[1]

In a sense, the long struggle against apartheid forced South Africa to bear the greatest burden among all the "modern" nations in qualifying for that designation. Simply put, it was an outlaw country. Everything in its rancorous history of well over three centuries pointed out the anomalousness of its status as a "modern" nation.

[...]

Beyond Renaissance and Awakening: 1950s South Africa and *Drum*

Difficult and unfathomable as it might seem, given the bleak prospects of existence under apartheid's hegemony, life was nonetheless lived with relish in many townships, precipitating a rare period that, today, many remember wistfully. It is almost as if the millions who later would be railroaded and systematically destroyed by the pernicious apartheid policy anticipated that the decades ahead would be devoted solely to the struggle to assert and reclaim the validity of their rights as empowered human beings and citizens. Jürgen Schadeberg, the first picture editor of *Drum* magazine and a highly respected photographer, who documented many of the memorable moments of the decade with sharp clarity and great compositional skill, notes, "The 1950s were exciting years. The ideas, the ideals, and the achievements of that time should not be forgotten."[2] Peter Magubane, who brought an intimate humanism to his photographs and with equal ardor left a legacy of great images from the period, spoke to me about how unbelievable that period was in the now-vanished Sophiatown, then known as the Paris of Johannesburg. He recalled its hedonism, joy, romance, and sense of place.[3]

[...]

When *Drum*'s first edition was published in Cape Town in March 1951 under the name *The African Drum*, its first editor and cofounder, Robert Crisp, with typical white South African attitudes toward Africans, envisioned it as an entertainment magazine dealing with aspects of "tribal" life, even though its target was an urban audience. Not perceiving themselves in the stereotypical and racist light under which Crisp attempted to cast them, the African populace at whom the magazine was directed roundly rejected its message. *The African Drum* was a failure, a vital lesson its subsequent owner would heed. After three issues were produced, Jim Bailey, the son of a mining magnate, took over the magazine as its sole proprietor, a role he would play until he sold the publication in 1984. Bailey changed its name to *Drum*, restructured its editorial direction, and moved its offices to Johannesburg. In order to ensure its survival, he had to radically reformulate the magazine's image as a forum for Crisp's condescending, imagined ideas of African "tribal" life to a sophisticated outlet for young journalists, writers, and photographers. [...] Added in succession were editions in Nigeria (1953), Ghana (1954), East Africa (1957), and Central Africa (1966) to fulfill [a] pan-African determination.

At the height of its popularity, *Drum* enjoyed enormous readership. Even a North American and West Indian edition was distributed. The magazine's circulation per issue stood at 450,000 copies, reaching far into many literate, cosmopolitan areas of Africa. But more than anything else, it was *Drum*'s keen insight into Africa's popular culture, contemporary life, and emergent sense of modernity that garnered wide devotion among this urban audience. With equal vigor – as well as measured discretion, for *Drum* could easily be banned like so many other publications presenting anything antagonistic toward apartheid – *Drum* also confronted serious sociopolitical issues within its pages. The magazine was witness to the worsening political and economic conditions in South Africa, and the independence and liberation struggles in Central, East, and West Africa. [...]

Writers like Peter Abrahams, Ayi Kwei Armah, Nadine Gordimer, Alex La Guma, and Lewis Nkosi contributed essays and stories to the magazine. It was also in *Drum* that Alan Paton's bestselling novel *Cry, the Beloved Country* was first serialized. Of its staff writers in the 1950s, Arthur Maimane; Casey Motsisi; Ezekiel Mphahlele; Henry Nxumalo, known as Mr. Drum for his ability to take on very difficult assignments; and Can Themba stand out like beacons. Their stories gave enormous texture and shape to the mood of the period, examining its politics, fun, culture, aspirations, even its petty crimes and capturing in words the fast-paced and changing lifestyles of various communities, such as Alexandra, Orlando, and Sophiatown, some of which would disappear forever.

Drum's photographers gave visual substance and glamour to the lives that comprised the intimate portraits of those stories. With equal scrutiny and attention to their diverse subjects, be they celebrities, hoodlums, or politicians, the photographers took pictures in the segregated, teeming, vibrant slums of South Africa's townships. Their nuanced images display an expressive freshness and energy borne out of an irrepressible hope and optimism. The photographers looked for their images in the most unexpected places. They donned disguises and had themselves arrested, whatever it took to obtain images to illustrate important stories.[4] [...]

By casting a critical gaze at territories that existed beyond the margins, the work of the *Drum* photographers transcends the prosaic. Offhandedly charming or accusatively caustic, the photographs are more like sociological excavations than purely documentary artifacts. By defying the conventions of traditional documentary photography, these pictures ably penetrate the surface of appearances to probe the psychological states of their subjects as well as their environments. Envisioning the circumstances of their production, we are struck by their deep implication. There is never a dull moment in the stories the photographs tell. For example, Ian Berry's intimate and revealing view of life in the capacious but subterranean world of the Moffies' male homosexuals drag culture, shot at the famous Madam Costello's Ball in Cape Town, poignantly captures that group's racial intermixture and its air of camp, sadness, and joie de vivre.

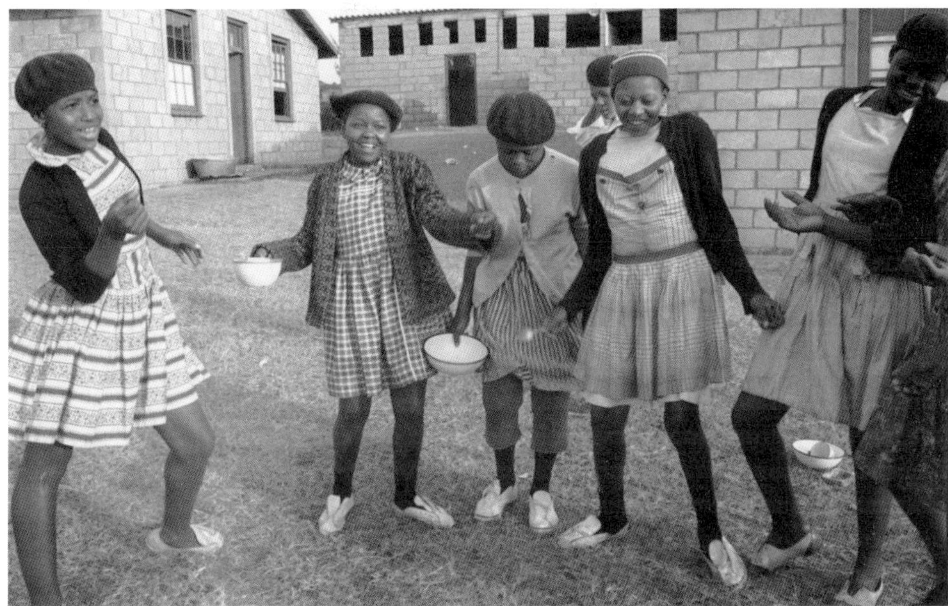

Figure 5.1 *First Sight of the Sea,* photo by G. R. Naidoo, August 1960. Bailey's African History Archive (BAHA).

[...]

Drum represents more than a mere publication in the minds of many people. It was a window into their aspirations and desires, and, in many ways, it was an eyewitness to those events defining the course of South Africa's political and social landscape in the years following World War II. It fulfilled an important role as a documenter and a disseminator, especially if we consider the magazine's importance in the African context.

[...]

In many ways, the work of the *Drum* photographers exists beyond the realm of the visual and assumes an important ideological function. [...] [Charles] Merewether, in contrasting the manner in which photojournalism is embedded in the activities of the public sphere with that of photographic portraiture's tendency to address the private sphere, notes that "the difference between the two is not simply a matter of genre and style, but the way photography transgresses and redefines the subject of taboo, that is, notions of the sacred, of intimacy and the private sphere."[5] We can access the full meaning and importance of *Drum's* photography through such transgression and defiance, which in many instances came with serious repercussions. Thus, with penetrating authority, the seductive, albeit compelling, images from *Drum* name "through an accumulation or excess of memory" the divided and irradiated space of desanctified memory. As such, the publication of *Drum* in the 1950s and 1960s remains vital and provides a key platform disturbing the various hedges erected by a repressive political order. It also provides real grounds for discursive narratives involving issues of desire, identity, and community as we map different cultural moments in Africa. [...]

Notes

1 On June 26, 1955, three thousand delegates from a variety of political organizations, including the African National Congress, South African Colored People's Organization, South African Indian Congress, and Congress of Democrats, assembled in opposition to apartheid. At the conclusion of the meeting, the groups drafted a document known as the Freedom Charter. Advocating a multiracial and equal society in a democratic South Africa, it was subsequently adopted by the ANC and for almost forty years remained the key ideology through which the party pressed for the end of apartheid.

2 Jürgen Schadeberg, "Taking Pictures in the 1950s," in *Sof'town Blues: Images from the Black '50s* (Pinegowrie, South Africa: Jürgen Schadeberg, 1994), p. 19.

3 Peter Magubane's comments on Sophiatown and *Drum* were made during an interview I had with him at his home in Johannesburg in January 1996. He also talked in detail about his work and colleagues at *Drum*, speaking with particular fondness and respect for Bob Gosani and Schadeberg, the latter with whom he has had a few public disagreements about the authorship of particular images published in *Drum* during their tenures as staff photographers.

4 As with most dictatorships, mere suspicion of hostility toward the apartheid regime was met with brutal force. No form of media frightened the regime more than photography did, with its powerful testimony that could be used to expose and counteract the sanitized, propagandistic images working in the government's favor, or to fashion an oppositional artistic practice of self-representation. Magubane, for example, was incarcerated, spending nearly six hundred days in solitary confinement, and was banned by the government for five years, during which he was not permitted to practice photography.

5 Charles Merewether, "Naming Violence in the Work of Doris Salcedo," *Third Text* 24, fall 1993, p. 35.

6

Art of the African Diaspora

MICHAEL D. HARRIS*

With the American Negro his new internationalism is primarily an effort to recapture contact with the scattered peoples of African derivation.

Alain Locke, "Enter the New Negro," 1925

Long before modern art appeared on the African continent it had been produced by artists of African descent in the Americas. This essay by African American art historian Michael Harris tells the story of African American art, focusing on United States artists and modern art centered in the New York City neighborhood of Harlem in the 1920s and 1930s. But the art of the African diaspora reaches much farther geographically and chronologically, with dates that correspond to the half-millennium age of Europe and the wholesale European colonization of the Americas. Less than a decade after the 1492 Encounter on Hispaniola, the Atlantic slave trade began to take uncounted millions of people out of Africa to forced labor in the Americas. The Atlantic trade in slaves lasted around four centuries, ending in the third quarter of the nineteenth century. Throughout the American hemisphere during the *age of Europe*, African, Indigenous, European, and Asian cultures cross-fertilized – despite epic destruction of traditions and inequalities of power – to form the world-influential "American" hybrids of global modernisms. For the influence of African diaspora cultures on Latin American modern art, see "Africa in the Art of Latin America" by Gerardo Mosquera in this volume.

* Michael Harris (2001) "Art of the African Diaspora." In Monica Blackmun Visonà, Robin Poynor, Herbert M. Cole, and Michael D. Harris (eds) *A History of Art in Africa* (pp. 500–14). New York, NY: Harry N. Abrams.

Modern Art in Africa, Asia, and Latin America: An Introduction to Global Modernisms, First Edition.
Edited by Elaine O'Brien, Everlyn Nicodemus, Melissa Chiu, Benjamin Genocchio,
Mary K. Coffey, and Roberto Tejada.

As you read this selection by Michael Harris, keep in mind the astonishing reversal behind the art of the African diaspora. Robert Scott Duncanson, for instance, who began an international career as a Romantic landscape painter as early as the mid-nineteenth century, was the grandson of a slave. From an utterly degraded identity as members of a race of slaves, African American intellectuals, writers, and artists contributing to the so-called Harlem Renaissance invented a race of culture bearers, "progenitors of the great art traditions of Africa." What made this possible?

Among many factors, perhaps the first is that most artists of the African diaspora and Harlem Renaissance were educated cosmopolitans, internationalists who spent time in Paris and other global contact centers. They discovered African art and the racial pride that went with it through exposure to Western collections of traditional African art. Artist Hale Woodruff (1900–80), for example, the last to be considered in this selection, testified that his first encounter with African sculpture was in an art book "written up in German, a language I didn't understand! Yet published with beautiful photographs and treated with great seriousness and respect! Plainly sculptures of black people, my people, they were considered very beautiful by these German experts! The whole idea that this could be so was like an explosion in me." The book that filled him with enthusiasm, Carl Einstein's *Negerplastik* (1915), was in fact the first in which premodern African art, previously looked upon as ethnographic objects, was recognized as art.

A second reason is that primitivism – avant-garde modern art inspired by long-established visual culture traditions – especially valorized traditional African sculpture, which was newly available by 1910 for re-appropriation by African diaspora artists who sought an "authentic African" identity. The quest for the self-untainted by urban modernity inspired them. In this way, Afro-Asian-Cuban Wifredo Lam (1902–82) appropriated traditional African forms much like Picasso and Surrealist artists of the School of Paris. Such artwork has been considered a visual counterpart to the writings of Aimé Césaire (1913–2008). Modernist "European" values are internalized in such works, but questioned from different artistic perspectives and forming unique modern syntheses.

Questions for reading: Considering information from other essays in Part I, how do the circumstances and attitudes of African diaspora artists compare with those of modern African artists on the continent itself? Why did modern art on the African continent not appear in earnest until the independence era following World War II? In what ways does the globalism of African diaspora art prefigure twenty-first century art?

Further Readings

Bearden, Romare and Henderson, Harry (1993) *A History of African-American Artists: From 1792 to the Present*. New York, NY: Pantheon Books.

Locke, Alain (1925) "Art of the Ancestors (Harlem Number)." *Survey Graphic* (March).

Nadell, Martha Jane (2004) *Enter the New Negroes: Images of Race in American Culture*. Cambridge, MA: Harvard University Press.

Perry, Regenia A. (1992) *Free Within Ourselves: African-American Artists in the Collection of the National Museum of American Art.* Washington, DC: Smithsonian Institution.
Schmidt Campbell, Mary (1987) *Harlem Renaissance: Art of Black America* (Studio Museum in Harlem). New York, NY: Harry N. Abrams.

Africans were taken into slavery and shipped across the Atlantic from early in the sixteenth century until the second half of the nineteenth century, with nearly half being transported during the eighteenth century. Approximately 14 million Africans survived the Atlantic crossing and, though they left their material culture behind, they were cultural beings who carried inside them various ways of approaching and interpreting life. Congregated in the New World, they formed communities and developed new means of meeting the same expressive and artistic needs they had felt in Africa. In some cases, Africans speaking the same language from the same cultural group were gathered together on plantations, especially in the Caribbean and in Brazil, and recognizable cultural practices from their homeland were revived and continued. Often cultural influences from several areas of Africa melded together. The Haitian religious practices known as Vodou, for example, combine Yoruba, Kongo, and Dahomean elements. In the United States, slaveowners, fearing rebellions, made an effort to group together Africans of varying cultural and linguistic backgrounds in order to suppress communication and collaboration. Still, Africans found what was most common among them and expressed themselves in ways reminiscent of their home cultural practices, though perhaps in more general ways.

[…]

After slavery was abolished, the continued existence of racism affected the aspirations, status, and consciousness of black people. The social restrictions and obstacles they faced affected the production of art, and it is useful to consider these social and historical factors when looking at the work of African American artists. The making and appreciating of fine art in European contexts was a middle- or upper-class activity. The social and economic oppression faced by blacks made it difficult to pursue this kind of art as a career prior to the second half of the twentieth century. Folk expression, however, was less encumbered by racism, and in fact may have flourished in part because segregation left black communities more intact socially to develop as subcultures.

[…]

[…]

Speaking Through New Forms

[…]

One of the first accomplished African American painters was Robert Duncanson (1823–72), a man of mixed race who resided for most of his adult life in the

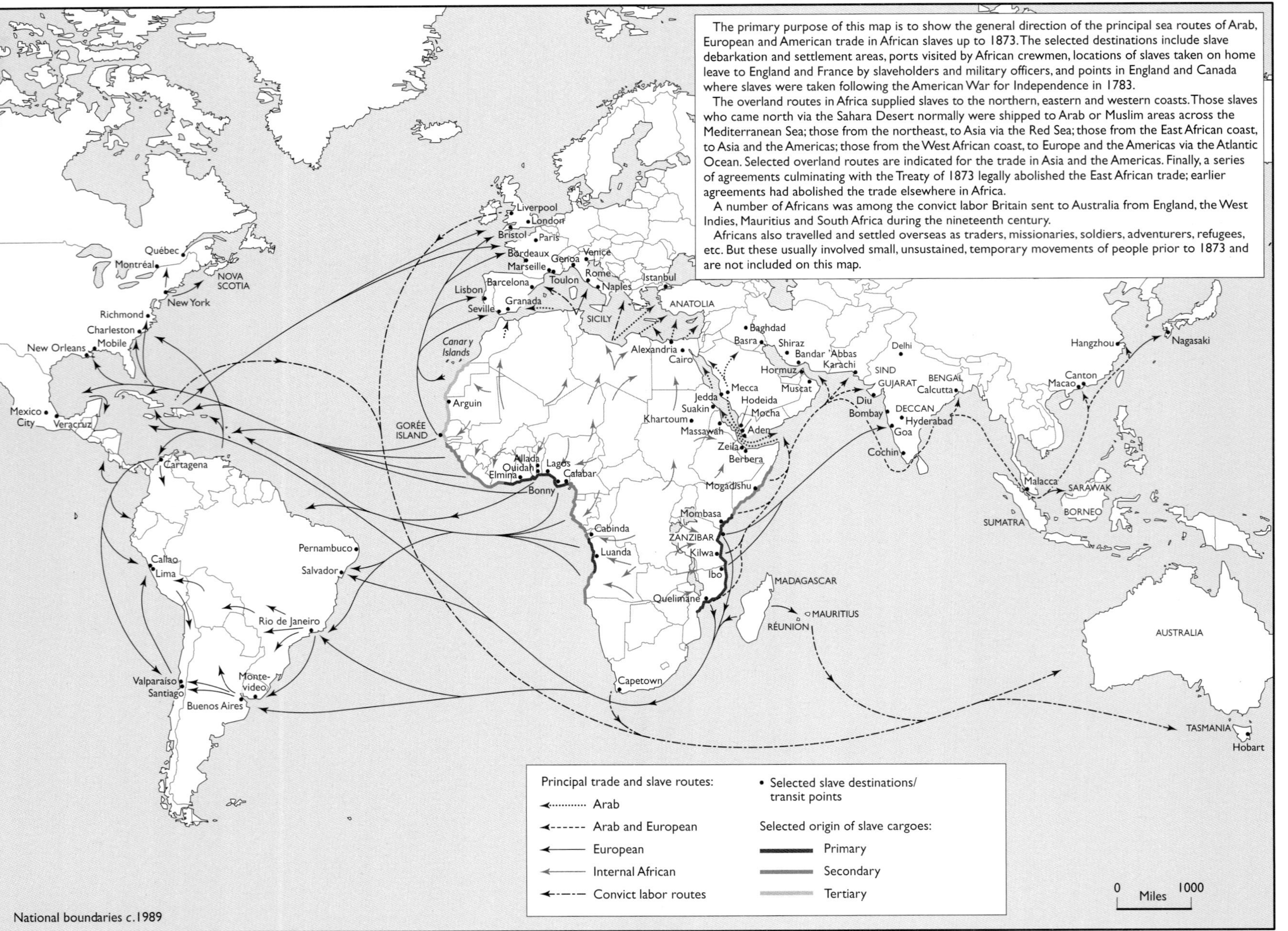

Figure 6.1 Africa Diaspora map. Courtesy of Doctor Joseph E. Harris.

Cincinnati area. Duncanson exhibited the broad range of atmospheric and emotional elements in his work typical of the style of American landscape painting known as the Hudson River school, but few of his works included African American subjects.

[...]

It is difficult to say how much Duncanson identified with his African heritage, but he lived during a time when there had been several riots in Cincinnati in which whites attacked blacks, and pro-slavery advocates had a strong presence there despite the fact that Ohio was not a slave state. Most indications are that he acknowledged his racial designation but chose not to address issues around that identity in his work other than in one painting, *Tom and Little Eva*, inspired by Harriet Beecher Stowe's abolitionist novel *Uncle Tom's Cabin*.

Edmonia Lewis (c. 1843–1909) was the first woman artist of African descent to gain prominence in the United States. Details about her life are sketchy, but she was born to African American and Chippewa parents. Lewis attended Oberlin College for a while before being forced to leave after a highly publicized trial in which she was accused of poisoning two of her roommates, and subsequent accusations that she had stolen art supplies.

[...] She settled in Rome in 1866 and developed her academic Neoclassical style there. One of her most notable works in this mode, and one of the few that survive, is *Hagar*. Lewis dealt with racial themes and subjects in her work more directly than most nineteenth-century artists of African descent, and *Hagar* illustrates how she pursued these themes with subtlety and allusion.

[...] Hagar is an African woman (despite the Neoclassical mode of presentation), a slave, and she was victimized by sexual liaisons with her master; a string of circumstances which directly related to the plight of many black women in the New World. The work was created at a time when blacks were being re-enslaved by the collapse of Reconstruction in the American South, and black women still were vulnerable to sexual exploitation due to disparities in power between whites and blacks. In Brazil, where the great majority of Africans taken in the Atlantic slave trade had been sent, the end of slavery was still over a decade away. Lewis's imagery was not black, but clearly her subject matter related to the experiences of many black women.

In 1893, at the same time as the World's Columbian Exposition in Chicago, blacks from Africa, the Caribbean, and the United States convened the Congress on Africa, possibly the first pan-African meeting. In attendance was Henry O. Tanner (1858–1937), the most accomplished and prominent African American artist of his time. That same year, Tanner completed one of the few genre paintings of his career, *The Banjo Lesson*. [...]

The Banjo Lesson presents a tender exchange between an elder and a youth, alluding to an educational tradition of inter-generational exchange in which lore and lessons were handed down. [...]

The sculpture *Ethiopia Awakening* by Meta Warrick Fuller (1877–1968) can be seen as an extension of Tanner's painting. Fuller's work allegorically depicts a

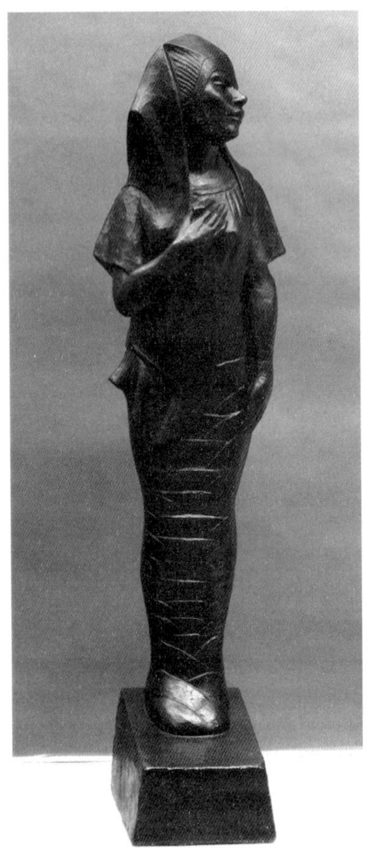

Figure 6.2 Meta Warrick Fuller, *Ethiopia Awakening*, c.1910, bronze, 170 × 40 × 25 cm/67 × 16 × 10 inches. Schomburg Center for Research in Black Culture, The New York Public Library, Astor, Lenox and Tilden Foundations.

woman emerging from a deep, mummified sleep into lively animation. The lower portion of her body is still wrapped as if entombed, but the upper torso has begun turning and waking from a metaphorical sleep. The work also suggests a butterfly forcing its way out of a cocoon into a new life. Ethiopia – from an ancient Greek word meaning the land of the "sun-burnt people" – was a term that embraced a variety of African peoples found in Egypt, Libya, Nubia, or Kush, down into the region of the present-day nation-state of Ethiopia. The term had long been applied to signify things African or black in American parlance – minstrel performances often were called Ethiopian operas – and Fuller uses it in this way here.

Fuller, who like many prominent African American artists of the era studied in Europe, worked in a narrative style. Her work, like that of Edmonia Lewis, suggested African themes and used Egypt as a synonym for Africa. With *Ethiopia Awakening*, however, the focus of Fuller's work moved beyond slave or plantation references toward a pan-African imagination. She linked the growing self-consciousness and self-confidence of African Americans with global trends, and her implication that racial identity was the equivalent of national identity as a means for unity in a common cause reflected the ideas of W. E. B. Du Bois (1868–1963), an eminent African American intellectual and one of the co-founders of the National Association for the Advancement of Colored People (NAACP).

Reclaiming Africa

The last decade of the nineteenth century and the first several of the twentieth century witnessed a number of significant events and trends which radically affected African consciousness for the remainder of the twentieth century. The 1893 Chicago Congress on Africa was followed by the formation of the African Association by Trinidadian Henry Sylvester Williams in England in 1897, and a Pan-African Congress in 1900 in England. The sacking of Benin by the British Punitive Expedition in 1897 led to thousands of African art objects appearing on the market. German ethnographer Leo Frobenius stumbled upon the Ife heads during the first decade of the twentieth century, and their naturalism challenged erroneous assumptions that African art was unintentionally abstract because of an inherent African inability to produce naturalistic work. The growing interest in African art as art shown by European avant-garde artists contributed to an increased scrutiny in the West of things African and a growing appreciation of African aesthetics. In the 1920s dancer and performer Josephine Baker, a black woman from St. Louis who moved to Paris, highlighted the fascination among the French with black cultural expression. W. E. B. Du Bois helped organize several pan-African conferences beginning in 1919, and the Marcus Garvey movement energized masses of blacks in the Americas and Europe with increased interest in Africa and their links to the continent.

Image and idea

Africa became a part of the cultural imagination of many artists in the late 1920s and 1930s. People of African descent in the diaspora had reached the second and third generations of the post-slavery period, and various migrations had moved many people from harsh, impoverished conditions in rural settings to the crowded urban settings of Chicago, New York, and smaller Midwestern and West Coast cities. Many people emigrated to the United States from Caribbean communities as well in search of economic opportunity. In the minds of most whites their African heritage linked them with African Americans as Negroes, and their shared experience of being black encouraged some pan-African ideas and sentiment. However, few of the artists of diasporan communities had actually been to Africa, and so the image and idea of Africa that inspired them, though important, was of necessity an imaginary one.

In 1925 Alain Locke published his important essay "Legacy of the Ancestral Arts" in the March issue of *Survey Graphic* magazine that he edited about Harlem, the neighborhood where most African Americans in New York lived. In this essay, reprinted later that same year in his significant book *The New Negro*, Locke implored African American artists to look to Africa for inspiration and aesthetic ideas just as European modernists such as Picasso, Braque, and Modigliani had done during the previous two decades. He also addressed the need to overcome the visual stereotypes of the nineteenth century, which had codified a distorted view of the physical features of people of African descent. Locke's challenge to African American artists was made during a period when artists and intellectuals were approaching their African cultural heritage from a perspective of self-discovery.

Many artists and poets of the astonishing flowering of literary, musical, and artistic talent known as the Harlem Renaissance created imaginary African settings or people in their work. [...] In the United States, this translated into an idea of the Negro "soul." The poet Langston Hughes connected African Americans with the Congo, Nile, and Mississippi rivers in his famous poem "I've Known Rivers," and Countee Cullen asked, "What is Africa to me?" in his 1925 poem "Heritage."

[...]

Lois Mailou Jones (1906–98) revisited the sense of Egypt/Ethiopia as a metaphor for an exalted African past in the black imagination with her 1932 painting *The Ascent of Ethiopia*. In this work she visually links contemporary African American creativity with the culture of ancient Egypt, represented by pyramids and the large pharaonic profile that dominates the foreground, suggesting a continuum of African achievement. Drama, music, and visual art are highlighted within concentric circles that organize and energize the composition. References to the arts emerge from behind skyscrapers just above the pharaoh's head, and each discipline is performed symbolically by black silhouettes. Art and civilization are linked graphically, mirroring the philosophical ideas of Locke, Du Bois, and other intellectuals of the period who felt that artistic and cultural achievement would help facilitate black acceptance into Western societies. [...]

On the West Coast, Sargent Johnson (1887–1967) explored an interest in the physiognomy of African Americans in his sculpture. "It is the pure American Negro I am concerned with," he said in a statement published in 1935, "aiming to show the natural beauty and dignity in that characteristic lip and characteristic hair, bearing and manner; and I wish to show that beauty not so much to the White man as to the Negro himself." The 1933 sculpture *Forever Free* reveals Johnson's interest in color, form, and understated social statement. The sculpture depicts a dignified mother protecting her two children at her side. The frontality of the work, its closed form, and the stylization of and emphasis upon the head link it stylistically with some freestanding African sculpture, yet its simplified form gives it abstract qualities that also invoke modernism and the work of Johnson's European contemporaries such as Brancusi or Henry Moore.

[...]

Cuban artist Wifredo Lam (1902–82) brought a somewhat different perspective to his career. He grew up in Cuba the son of a Chinese father and a mother of Congo descent, and his godmother was a priestess of Lucumí, also known as Santería, a religion that developed in Cuba from Yoruba belief. He moved to Europe at age twenty, living first in Spain, then in Paris, where he came under the artistic influence of Picasso and Cubism and also of André Breton and the Surrealists. In 1941, at the beginning of the Second World War, Lam returned to Cuba. There he combined the diverse cultural and artistic influences of his life in works such as *The Jungle*.

Painted in 1943, *The Jungle* reveals Lam's use of the geometry and multiple simultaneous views of Cubism, the juxtaposition of images in sometimes surprising configurations found in Surrealism, and the iconography and meaning found in Afro-Cuban religious practices. Figures that combine human, animal, and vegetative elements suggest humankind's oneness with nature.

[...]

New York artist Romare Bearden (1911–88) explored a variety of techniques and themes during his career, but he is most known for his collages portraying African American life in the South and in Harlem. Bearden became prominent as an artist during the Civil Rights era in the United States and was part of a group called Spiral. Inspired by the Civil Rights movement of Martin Luther King, Jr. and the 1963 March on Washington, Spiral organized an exhibition in 1964 called Black and White. [...]

From Bearden's discussions with Spiral grew an interest in devising photomontage collages, including a series drawn from his experiences growing up in North Carolina. [...] A 1964 collage, *The Prevalence of Ritual: Baptism*, combines Bearden's interest in and study of modern art stylistic movements such as Cubism, Surrealism, and Abstract Expressionism with African and African American cultural references.

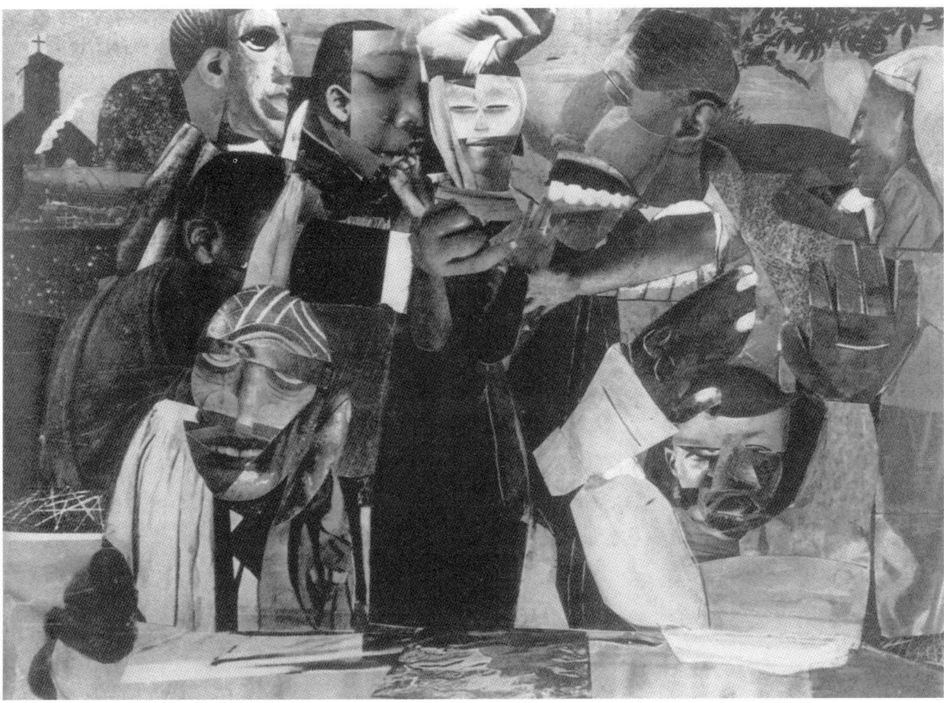

Figure 6.3 Romare Bearden, *The Prevalence of Ritual: Baptism*, 1968, 22.9 × 30.4 cm/9 × 12 inches. Baptism (projection), © Romare Bearden Foundation/DACS, London/VAGA.

The title of the work links baptism rituals in the black church with older African religious and social rituals, which is emphasized by the figure to the lower left with a mask-like face. The top of the face is drawn from African mask imagery, but the lower portion of the mouth and chin are collaged from photographs. This juxtaposition of the old with the new speaks of the effort made by many artists in the African diaspora to reconcile their heritage with their current circumstances.

[...]

Hale Woodruff (1900–80) commemorated the centennial of the 1839 Amistad mutiny – a celebrated incident when Mende captives took over a slave ship off the coast of Cuba to free themselves – with a series of murals at Talladega College in Alabama. In their form and inspirational character the works show the influence of the Mexican muralists David Rivera, José Orozco, and David Siquierios, whom Woodruff had met during a Mexican sojourn. The subject of the murals served to connect African Americans with Africans in the historical struggle for freedom. [...]

Woodruff completed several important mural projects after moving to New York, but by the mid-1950s he had abandoned social realism in favor of abstraction. His 1969 painting *Celestial Gate* shows how he eventually turned to African design for subject matter in his later abstract work. Painted in the expressive, painterly style of Abstract Expressionism, the work's underlying motif is a Dogon granary door decorated with images based upon Asante gold weights. Woodruff said, "I have tried to study African art in order to assimilate it into my being, not to copy but to seek the essence of it, its spirit and quality as art." He combined elements from two different African societies to make what can be interpreted as a pan-Africanist statement calling for unity among various peoples of African descent.

Getting behind the mask: transAtlantic dialogues

[...] During the 1960s, black nationalism, the Black Arts movement, the revitalization of pan-Africanism, and the optimism spawned by the increasing number of African nations throwing off the yoke of colonialism contributed to more aggressive explorations of African art and culture by younger African American artists, writers, and intellectuals. Many traveled to Africa for varying lengths of time, and the pan-African ideas of Kwame Nkrumah, Ghana's first leader after colonial independence, were inspirational to many in the diaspora. [...] This kind of direct experience allowed many in the African diaspora to gain a fuller understanding of African cultures, to develop relationships with people and artists living in Africa, and to confront their similarities to and differences from Africans. The romantic projections of Africa under the generic terms of Ethiopia, Egypt, or Congo gave way to more specific images. Artists began to penetrate the facade of form in African art. They began to get behind the mask.

[...]

7

Chorale: Man, Society, and Technology

An Experiment in Rural Egypt

Hassan Fathy*

There must be neither faked tradition nor faked modernity, but an architecture that will be the visible and permanent expression of the character of a community. But this would mean nothing less than a whole new architecture.

Hassan Fathy

This reading by modern Egyptian architect Hassan Fathy (1900–89) is from his internationally popular 1969 book, *Architecture for the Poor: An Experiment in Rural Egypt,* which offered an alternative to international style public housing that was the legacy of colonialism in Africa and many parts of the world. Here Fathy recalls his commission from Egypt's Department of Antiquities more than twenty years earlier. He had been asked to design and oversee the construction of mass housing for a settlement of 7,000 people: New Gourna, partially completed between 1945 and 1948. The new village would replace Gourna, built on the archeological Pharaonic sites of Upper Egypt's western shore near Luxor where makeshift dwellings sat over passageways to tombs, facilitating robbery that partly supported the households. Fathy's New Gourna was thus not purely a public welfare project; it was also imposed by the government as a way to protect Egypt's heritage.

Hassan Fathy's focus on culturally specific rural rather than urban international-style public housing, his revival of Nubian vernacular construction techniques such as mud brick vaulting, and his use of traditional Islamic forms made of low-tech, sustainable materials suited to local conditions amount to a strong critique of the global

* Hassan Fathy (1973 [1969]) "Chorale: Man, Society, and Technology: An Experiment in Rural Egypt." In *Architecture for the Poor: An Experiment in Rural Egypt* (pp. 24–6, 37–8, 43–5). Chicago, IL: University of Chicago Press.

Modern Art in Africa, Asia, and Latin America: An Introduction to Global Modernisms, First Edition.
Edited by Elaine O'Brien, Everlyn Nicodemus, Melissa Chiu, Benjamin Genocchio,
Mary K. Coffey, and Roberto Tejada.

dominance of Western modernism's machine aesthetic for low-cost mass housing. Fathy was among the first non-Western architects to move away from imported forms and materials towards a synthesis of indigenous and international architecture. *Architecture for the Poor* can thus be said to have globalized the "postmodern" critique of modernist architecture and urban planning advanced by other landmark books of the period, such as Jane Jacobs's 1961 *Death and Life of Great American Cities* and the 1972 *Learning from Las Vegas* by Robert Venturi, Denise Scott Brown, and Steven Izenour.

Fathy's narrative here will doubtless persuade you of his success in constructing a new architecture for the postcolonial era on the African continent, but it is not the end of the New Gourna story. Like so many other modernist public housing projects worldwide, it failed to satisfy the people for whom it was built. New Gourna's residents resisted for several reasons the theoretically ideal village Fathy had designed to fit their lives, location, and history; and in many cases they refused to move into the new village. The project was discontinued, and several main public buildings and more than one hundred of the dwellings remained empty for years. Fathy was mystified by the Gournis' reaction, but a contributing clue to their defiance might be that the "traditional" architecture he reconstructed from different prototypes was as unfamiliar to them as would have been a village in international modernist style. Fathy was not exempt from his own period-based paternalism: the trademark of the modernist celebrity architect that *Architecture for the Poor* strove to displace. For us, New Gourna remains as significant for the questions it raises as it is for the innovation of its syncretic forms. To compare other attitudes and issues around the globalization of modernist architecture, see in this volume James Holston and Clarice Lispector on Brasilia and Jonathan M. Reynolds on the history of Western-style modern architecture in Japan.

Further Readings

Hamid, Ahmad (2010) *Hassan Fathy and Continuity in Islamic Arts and Architecture.* Cairo, Egypt: American University in Cairo Press, 2010.

Pyla, Panayiota (2009) "The Many Lives of New Gourna: Alternative Histories of a Model Community and their Current Significance." *Journal of Architecture* 14(6): 715–30.

Steele, James (1997) *An Architecture for the People: Complete Works of Hassan Fathy.* London, England: Thames & Hudson.

Tradition's Role

Tradition is the social analogy of personal habit, and in art has the same effect, of releasing the artist from distracting and inessential decisions so that he can give his whole attention to the vital ones. Once an artistic decision has been made, no matter when or by whom, it cannot profitably be made again; better that it should pass into the common store of habit and not bother us further.

Tradition is not necessarily old-fashioned and is not synonymous with stagnation. Furthermore, a tradition need not date from long ago but may have begun quite recently. As soon as a workman meets a new problem and decides how to overcome it, the first step has been taken in the establishment of a tradition. When another workman has decided to adopt the same solution, the tradition is moving, and by the time a third man has followed the first two and added his contribution, the tradition is fairly established. Some problems are easy to solve; a man may decide in a few minutes what to do. Others need time, perhaps a day, perhaps a year, perhaps a whole lifetime; in each case the solution may be the work of one man.

[...]

Tradition among the peasants is the only safeguard of their culture. They cannot discriminate between unfamiliar styles, and if they run off the rails of tradition they will inevitably meet disaster. Willfully to break a tradition in a basically traditional society like a peasant one is a kind of cultural murder, and the architect must respect the tradition he is invading. What he does in the city is another matter; there the public and the surroundings can take care of themselves.

[...]

When the architect is presented with a clear tradition to work in, as in a village built by peasants, then he has no right to break this tradition with his own personal whims. What may go in a cosmopolitan city like Paris, London, or Cairo, will kill a village.

[...]

The Use of Mud Brick an Economic Necessity

We are fortunate in being compelled to use mud brick for large-scale rural housing; poverty forces us to use mud brick and to adopt the vault and dome for roofing, while the natural weakness of mud limits the size of vault and dome. All our buildings must consist of the same elements, slightly varied in shape and size, arranged in different combinations, but all to the human scale, all recognizably of a kind and making a harmony with one another. The situation imposes its own solution, which is – perhaps fortunately, perhaps inevitably – a beautiful one.

[...]

In Gourna a thousand families were going to take this step of getting a new house. Each family deserved the chance to make its house as efficient and beautiful as possible, and each family deserved to have a say in the design of the house. Because each family differs from all others, it would be necessary to design each house individually.

[...]

However, when we came to the actual building, I found that even the working drawings lost much of the importance they usually have. The masons were master craftsmen to whom every detail of the work had become familiar over many years, for it was their own technique. They knew by heart the proportions of the various rooms and, given the height of a dome or vault, could tell immediately where to begin the springing. In fact, they would even watch me while I was drawing, and tell me not to bother with these dimensions.

[…]

Change with Constancy

At all costs I wanted to avoid the attitude too often adopted by professional architects and planners when confronted with a peasant community, the attitude that the peasant community has nothing worth the professionals' consideration, that all its problems can be solved by the importation of the sophisticated urban approach to building. If possible I wanted to bridge the gulf that separates folk architecture from architect's architecture. I wanted to provide some solid and visible link between these two architectures in the shape of features, common to both, in which the villagers could find a familiar point of reference from which to enlarge their understanding of the new, and which the architect could use to test his own work's truth to the people and the place.

An architect is in a unique position to revive the peasant's faith in his own culture. If, as an authoritative critic, he shows what is admirable in local forms, and even goes so far as to use them himself, then the peasants at once begin to look on their own products with pride. What was formerly ignored or even despised becomes suddenly something to boast about, and moreover, something that the villager can boast about knowingly. Thus the village craftsman is stimulated to use and develop the traditional local forms, simply because he sees them respected by a real architect, while the ordinary villager, the client, is once more in a position to understand and appreciate the craftsman's work.

Yet, to arrive at a positive decision on the kind of architecture for the new village, further investigation was necessary.

Besides the man-made environment of Gourna, with which the new village would have to harmonize, there is the natural environment of landscape, flora, and fauna. A traditional architecture would have accommodated itself to this natural environment, both visually and practically, over many centuries. The new village would have to tone with this environment from the very beginning, and its buildings must look as if they were the product of centuries of tradition. I had to try to give my new designs that appearance of having grown out of the landscape that the trees of the district have. They should look as much at home in the fields as the date-palm and the dom-palm. Their inhabitants should live in them as naturally as they wore their clothes. But it was a very heavy task for one man; could I think myself into the experience of generations of village masons, or conceive in my mind all the slow modifications caused by climate and environment?

Yet we can seek the help of our elders to obtain such knowledge. The Ancient Egyptians had penetrated the soul of this land and had represented its character with an honesty that carries across to us over the intervening millennia. In their drawings – simple lines painted on the walls of the tombs – they convey more of the essential character of nature than do the most elaborate confections of color and light and shade by the most celebrated exponents of modern European-style painting.

As an architect's plans are all line drawings, I thought that I could place against my designs drawings of the flora and fauna of the district, done simply, like Ancient Egyptian drawings, and I was certain that these pictures of palm tree or cow as seen in the Tombs of the Nobles would set off the honesty or show up the falsity of the buildings. I did all my renderings of the test designs like this; carefully avoiding the professional slickness of many architects' plans, which often distort natural forms in order to make the setting match the buildings, I did not try to produce effects of depth, nor bring in convenient oak trees to balance a massing, but executed my drawings in plain lines and set about them sketches of the animals and trees and natural features of Gourna. These were: the hill above Gourna, which, with its natural pyramid on top, has always been a sacred rock; the cow, for the cow-goddess Hathor was the protectress of the cemetery of Gourna, and Gourna was in a district where there were many cows and where the ubiquitous buffalo of Egypt was not seen; the two trees, the date-palm and the dom-palm, for these are the trees of Upper Egypt; a certain character shown in the massing of some of the houses in old Gourna, with their loggias on top.

All these shapes I put against my first tentative, exploratory rendering, to act as a standard of comparison. I felt that in Gourna it was our duty to build a village

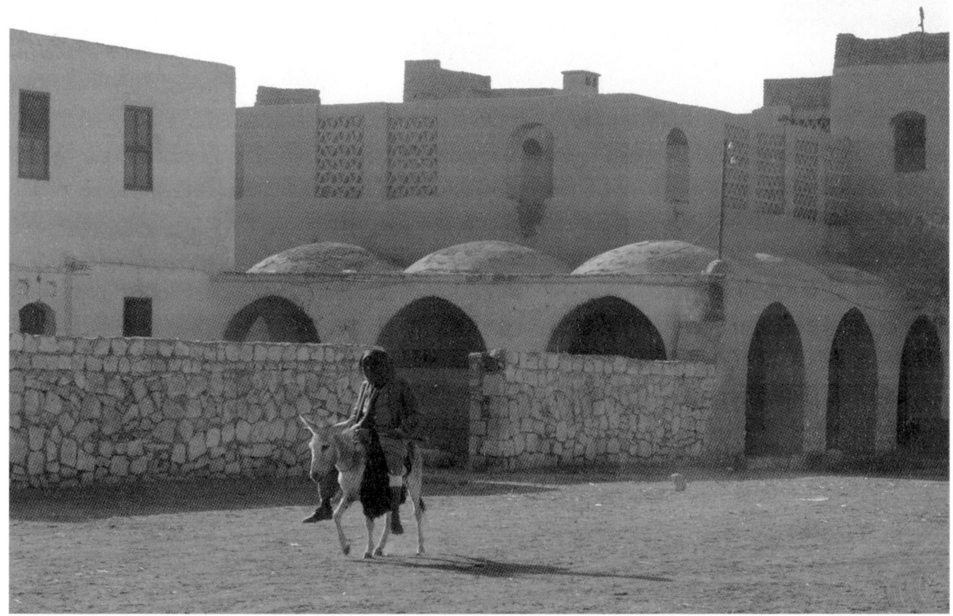

Figure 7.1 Hassan Fathy, *New Gourna*. Photo, © Christopher Little.

that should not be false to Egypt. The people's style had to be rediscovered; or, rather, refelt from the sparse evidence of local crafts and local temperament. We had a technique from Nubia; we could not build Nubian houses here. Being faithful to a style, in the way I mean it, does not mean the reverent reproduction of other people's creation. It is not enough to copy even the very best buildings of another generation or another locality. The method of building may be used, but you must strip from this method all the substance of particular character and detail, and drive out from your mind the picture of the houses that so beautifully fulfilled your desires. You must start right from the beginning, letting your new buildings grow from the daily lives of the people who will live in them, shaping the houses to the measure of the people's songs, weaving the pattern of a village as if on the village looms, mindful of the trees and the crops that will grow there, respectful to the skyline and humble before the seasons. There must be neither faked tradition nor faked modernity, but an architecture that will be the visible and permanent expression of the character of a community. But this would mean nothing less than a whole new architecture. Change would certainly come to Gourna anyway, for change is a condition of life. The peasants themselves wanted to change, but they did not know how to. Exposed as they were to the influence of the meretricious buildings in the provincial towns round about, they would probably follow these bad examples. If they could not be saved, if they could not be persuaded to change for the architecturally better, they would change for the worse.

I hoped that Gourna might just hint at a way to begin a revived tradition of building, that others might later take up the experiment, extend it, and eventually establish a cultural barricade to stop the slide into false and meaningless architecture that was gathering speed in Egypt. The new village could show how an architecture made one with the people was possible in Egypt.

[...]

8

Oral Tradition and the Aesthetics of Black African Cinema

Nwachukwu Frank Ukadike*

This tremendous fund of African imagery, ritual-spiritual language, music, dance, metaphor and proverbs, the mythic components and poetic resonances of the oral traditions, when adopted to filmic codes, would produce film aesthetics that are African.

Nwachukwu Frank Ukadike

In his celebrated 1994 book, *Black African Cinema*, from which this text is selected, Nwachukwu Frank Ukadike, a Nigerian film scholar, presents an insider's perspective on films by black Africans: films, he explains, that best represent authentic African culture, history, and experience. Such films counter and correct the extreme misrepresentations of Africa in Western films, which have done more to spread and entrench Eurocentric stereotypes than art in any other medium. Of countless examples, one has only to recall Hollywood's *Tarzan* films to understand the mandate of black African filmmakers. Despite the harm such movies have done, however, in this reading the author makes a strong case for film as the privileged vehicle for authentic African expression. Ukadike underlines what he and many cultural historians consider the essential, shared element of African culture: its oral tradition, the tradition of the griot, the storyteller. "In the oral tradition," writes Ukadike, comparing it with film, "the griot is endowed with multiple functions, as musician, dancer, and storyteller; he is the storehouse of oral tradition." The prestige and potential of film, then, for black African filmmakers, critics, and their global same/other audiences, is in cinema's griot-like ability to simultaneously employ verbal expression, visual language, and the

* Nwachukwu Frank Ukadike (1994) "Oral Tradition and the Aesthetics of Black African Cinema." In *Black African Cinema* (pp. 70–2, 201–16). Berkeley, CA: University of California Press.

Modern Art in Africa, Asia, and Latin America: An Introduction to Global Modernisms, First Edition.
Edited by Elaine O'Brien, Everlyn Nicodemus, Melissa Chiu, Benjamin Genocchio, Mary K. Coffey, and Roberto Tejada.

performative: music, dance, and theater. Cinema's message may be understood in any language and potentially bridges differences. Like other writers in this volume, Ukadike defines modernism as a synthesis of Western modernism and indigenous traditions. The author asks us to consider this question: "How has African cinema imbued the dominant film structure with oral tradition to penetrate the African condition and bring to the surface African facts to inform the public?"

Further Readings

Bakari, Imruth and Cham, Mbye (eds) (1996) *African Experiences of Cinema*. London, England: BFI Publishing.

Malkmus, Lisbeth and Armes, Roy (1992) *Arab and African Film Making*. London, England: Zed Books.

Pfaff, Françoise (2004) *Focus on African Film*. Bloomington: Indiana University Press.

[...]

France's interest in the development of cinema in most of its West African ex-colonies – Gabon, Congo, Niger, Mali, Senegal, Benin, Madagascar, Cameroon, and Burkina Faso – is certainly linked to the educational and cultural patterns that it adopted in colonial days, otherwise known as the policy of assimilation. This policy sought to "detribalize" the Africans by bringing them to the threshold of French culture. The French government, rather than regarding Africans as colonized people, preferred to call them "overseas Frenchmen."[1] However, since the French did not recognize or respect local African cultures, and since they considered culture the basis on which French citizenship was determined, they resolutely embarked on a program of turning the elite of their African wards into Frenchmen. The historical impetus for discrediting the African way of life, in other words, lay in the ideology of imperialism, enshrined in this case in the principles of assimilation. Thus assimilation resulted in the creation of an elitist class of Africans crowned with what Bernard Magubane aptly termed "the accoutrements of Western civilization."[2] This class of a few selected Africans was accorded certain privileges enjoyed by French citizens. More than any other benefit, their French education alienated them from their own culture.

Although directing films was one such privilege, some of the assimilated pioneers of African cinema did not cooperate with this policy,[3] demonstrating that cinema in Africa transcends the ideological motivations rooted in a specific dogmatic interest [...]

Between 1962 and the end of 1980, a great majority of films made in the francophone region were partially financed through the assistance programs provided by the Coopération. Some of the first directors who benefitted from this scheme between 1962 and 1970 were the following: Niger's Mustapha Alassane, *Aouré, La bague du roi Koda* (King Koda's ring, 1964), *Le retour de l'aventurier* (The adventurer's return, 1966), and Oumarou Ganda, *Cabascado* (1969); Senegal's Ousmane Sembene, *Borom Sarret* (1963), *Niaye* (1964), *La noire de ...* (Black girl, 1966), and

Mahama Johnson Traoré *Diankha-bi* (The young girl, 1969); Côte d'Ivoire's Timité Bassori, *Sur la dune de la solitude* (On the dune of solitude, 1966), *La femme au couteau* (The woman with a knife, 1968), and Désiré Ecaré, *Concerto pour un exil* (Concerto for an exile, 1967); and Cameroon's Urbain Dia Mokouri, *Point de vue* (Point of view, 1965).

The best known among the French-aided films are Ousmane Sembene's *Borom Sarret* and *Black Girl*. With the release of *Borom Sarret*, the impact of a serious indigenous African film production was felt. When it was exhibited at the 1963 Tours International Festival in France, it not only made history as the first black African film seen internationally by a paying audience but it also made an impression on the international scene by winning a prize – the second African film to do so after *Aouré*. Since then, recognition has accorded it the status of the first professional film ever made by a black African. Shot in Dakar, *Borom Sarret*, only nineteen minutes long, is unquestionably an African masterpiece. It dealt, in embryonic form, with important issues that later became dominant themes of black African cinema and which Sembene and other filmmakers since then have emphasized in greater detail. In the filmic treatment of microcosmic situations, *Borom Sarret* is deliberately allegorical, structured to evoke national (and by implication continental) specificities, through the introduction of "fragmentary discourse" that reveals coded political messages. The contrast between the urban poor and the urban rich of Dakar served as the basic subject, but Sembene interweaves a series of vignettes to present African life in a neocolonial setting. But this neocolonial setting reflects, in the first place, the disappointment of being colonized. Here we see a poignant attack on the African elite who have replaced the white colonial administrator, on cultural alienation, and on social and economic exploitation, all pointing to the mantle of misery that was to prevail under neocolonial African governments – civilian or military.

[...]

Oral Tradition and the Aesthetics of Black African Cinema

Black African cinema and African artisan crafts, both influential vectors of oral tradition, share a sociocultural structure – a system of ideas and images – as collective synthesis of a society that never tires of defining itself to itself and to the rest of the world. Here lies the core of a tradition that gathers elements of reflection and introspection, provoking real-life discussion of the African condition. Using allegorical means, black African cinema achieves this, thus placing new emphasis on the well-known African tradition of making a point with stories – an important aspect of African life not widely disseminated to the outside world, except in literary circles.

The structure of African storytelling is composed of a variety of cultural and symbolic configurations. Much of this variety [...] is enunciated in the cohesive web surrounding the relationship among the text, the spectator (audience), and the performing artist (orator-narrator). This symbiotic relationship among the artist, text, and spectator, which African writers have so eloquently stressed[4] has also posed problems for African novelists and filmmakers, problems concerning language and the means of technical reproduction – the Africanization of the medium. For example, writing in Africa's languages is inhibiting since numerous languages abound. Chinua Achebe, Nigeria's veteran novelist, felt that the English language was capable of transporting his African views, noting that the language must "be a new English still in full communion with its ancestral home but altered to suit its new African surroundings."[5] This view is antithetical to Ngugi wa Thiong'o's radical advocacy of writing in African languages in order to restructure African literature.[6] Like other controversial passages in the article from which Achebe's statement was extracted, and seen in conjunction with early African writers who held similar views and who are often criticized by African writers,[7] Ngugi's dictum would also be limited and fails to provide an antidote to the problems of Ousmane Sembene, a novelist turned filmmaker. [...] With film, the visual images can spread the message more effectively. Even if the language used poses some problems, the message of the film image is still discernible to the viewer. Written literature and film depend on technology, but film transcends oral tradition and literature because it allows for wider coverage by producing audio and visual images simultaneously.[8]

The choice of film production means acceptance of European technology and codes of representation. But as to their application in the African context, it was only a short time before African filmmakers discovered the means of integrating traditional aesthetics into the stylistic repertory of world cinema. These modes of representation would resonate with indigenous codes and African sensibility. Like the African novels which developed precisely out of this instrument of cultural symbiosis, one of the expedient ways to inject African cinema with a dose of authenticity is to exploit the interlocking elements of the continent's cultural heritage. This tremendous fund of African imagery, ritual-spiritual language, music, dance, metaphor and proverbs, the mythic components and poetic resonances of the oral traditions, when adopted to filmic codes, would produce film aesthetics that are African.

Black African cinema, in this regard, has already dedicated itself to a genuine refurbishment of the continent's culture. The significance of its services to the African people is that it is persistent in highlighting images of historical experience, cultural identity, and national consciousness in past and present struggles. Whether some of the views expressed remain optimistic or pessimistic, whether they provide solutions to the impending crisis or not, the point is that these films are presenting debatable issues to the public by utilizing African cultural associations in a unique fashion no foreigner is capable of providing. How has African cinema imbued the dominant film structure with oral tradition to penetrate the African condition and bring to the surface African facts to inform the public? Is this tradition holding, and how has it been utilized in filmic narrative patterns?

Oral tradition and the aesthetics of African cinema are becoming the subject of exploration by African film historians and critics whose studies are pertinent to the understanding of African film practice, While Mbye Cham[9] links Sembene's storytelling capability to that of the *gewel* (griot or storyteller) and the *lekbat* (also storyteller), Françoise Pfaff[10] sees this trait encompassing Sembene's narrative techniques in such films as *Borom Sarret, Xala*, and *Ceddo*, where the griot's role is elaborated. In another perspective, while Manthia Diawara[11] analyzes the role of the griot in Sembene's films, this analysis is extended to the work of other directors – providing a detailed examination of oral tradition as an aesthetic device in cinematic narrative in the same way that Teshome Gabriel[12] explores oral narrative and film form in *Harvest: 3,000 Years*.

[...]

Ababacar Samb-Makharam's *Jom*, coproduced with Germany's Zweites Deutschen Fernsehen (ZDF television), is a good example of black African cinematic strategy completely reliant on oral tradition. In this film, a griot relates to his listeners the story of Dieri Dior (Oumar Seck), who murders a French colonial administrator. In the rage that follows the revenge, Dieri, rather than surrender, decides to die a dignified death by killing himself. The ramifications of this dignified act are recalled through the story of Khaly during a present-day labor strike. [...]

Narrated by a griot, the film reveals the multidisciplinary talent of the storyteller. Samb-Makharam acknowledges in his production notes that the griot "is also an endless source where painters, writers, historians, filmmakers, archivists, storytellers, and musicians can come to feed their imaginations."[13] In the oral tradition, the griot is endowed with multiple functions, as musician, dancer, and storyteller; he is the storehouse of oral tradition. The peripatetic nature of his performance enables him to recount to listeners the history of the entire community. His audience can in turn pass such knowledge on to others who are not present, in an endless transmission – passing from mother to sons and daughters, generation to generation. It is this type of knowledge that would precipitate, if need be, mass mobilization.

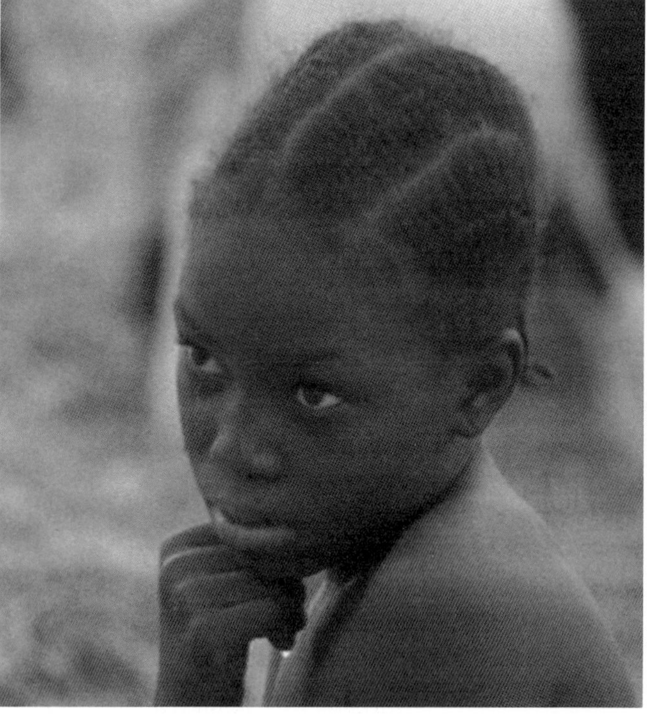

Figure 8.1 Gaston Kabore, *Wend Kuuni* (God's Gift), film, 1982, © Gaston Kabore.

[...]

If in *Jom* Samb-Makharam's structure illustrates the use of a historical narrative form of storytelling, Kaboré's *Wend Kuuni* is a prototype of creative candor for its definitive advancement in the effort to utilize specifically African cultural elements to create indigenous cinematic aesthetics. Basically,

Wend Kuuni is a revival of the family-oriented film fashioned after the African oral tale tradition; it depicts a young boy's traumatic experience of losing one family and finding another.

[...]

If one of the principal constituents of oral tradition is the organization, examination, and interpretation of society's past and present, *Wend Kuuni* shows that the fragmentation of linear images and their remolding in "new configurations and contexts," to use E. H. Gombrich's phrase,[14] can be achieved by blending oral art with cinematic art. In this film, the whole process of juxtaposition is conveyed by *découpage*,[15] specifically through parallel montage, extensive use of continuity editing, and with admirable characterization and performances by the nonprofessional cast. These elements, also comprising shifts and transgressions (of oral tradition and dominant cinematic conventions), assist in capturing the graphic images of the boy's transformation and the centralization of the film's rugged humanist qualities. As the narrative shows, Kaboré eschews chronological order by inverting the linearity of the tale as it would be told in oral narrative by employing the above filmic devices.

[...]

Visages de femmes by Désiré Ecaré, makes a different contribution to black African film aesthetics through oral tradition. Ecaré's innovative use of song and dance, here functioning as a vital narrative element, holds the film's structure together while other significant cultural oral traditions come into focus. [...]

Visages de femmes begins with ten minutes of song and dance. Beautifully composed and shot mostly in close-up with a few medium shots, it begins with two drummers dexterously providing the exhilarating music that draws a large village crowd in colorful traditional attire together, happily dancing the two-step. This wonderful scene, masterfully choreographed, catches the gay exuberance of the denizens of Loupou, in a sequence so compelling that J. Hoberman noted that "one would be proud to show [it to] a Martian as evidence of life on earth."[16] There is no dialogue omnisciently telling the viewer what is happening. The visuals are self-explanatory, providing an introduction to the African culture.

[...]

Like other filmmakers mentioned, who base their creative approach on oral tradition, Désiré Ecaré, actor, dramatist, and filmmaker who studied at the Institut des Hautes Etudes Cinématographiques (IDHEC) in Paris, also believes oral tradition to be a mainstay of African film language. In his work, oral tradition functions as a way of conceiving cinematic structure, a way of seeing, a view of the cosmic universe, and a way of articulating political and cultural possibilities. This means that, while the structural underpinnings in his films revolve around this cultural precept, his work is also based on an ideology that seeks to debunk rigid methodologies. Like Kaboré, Ecaré favors multiple narrative structure, as opposed to, for instance, Sembene's linear narrative style. But where Kaboré and Sembene clarify through simplicity and meticulous attention to detail, Ecaré uses an elliptical film style. [...]

[…] *Visages de femmes* is crafted around excellently choreographed dancing and singing. As in grammatical construction, where a punctuation mark breaks a sentence, the dancing and singing sequences play a similar role in the story line. Both are elements of form and content reinforcing the structure without breaking the flow of the diegesis; both also function as well-intended transition devices. In traditional African cultures the reason why oral tradition has had such an enormous impact on communication is its reliance on one of the most powerful elements of culture, the indigenous language, for its exposition. Since the employment of the oral tradition reflects patterns of everyday life, the narrative trajectory is easily understood. This sensitivity to a particular cultural heritage promotes a greater level of self-awareness and suggests avenues of social change. […]

From the marvelously well-orchestrated opening sequence of this film, one is immediately struck with the conviction that African music, as the adage goes, can emerge from African dance steps, lyrics can take their cue from oral poetry, and live performances can be a reassemblage of African rituals and folk opera. In the oral tradition, music and dance serve as bridges to the animating forces of nature, which is why in traditional cultures they are inextricably linked with aspects of everyday life. In this function, every rhythm generated is associated with particular activities, where rhythmic complexities serve to differentiate one particular African song and dance from another and one function from another. The rhythm of African music and dance is inspiring in its sophisticated and intended form. It evokes and manifests the cadences of creation, life and death struggles, and generally accompanies ordinary ceremonies usually requiring a group of musicians and dancers who perform communally with no strings attached. Contrary to the negative anthropological misinterpretations of African song and dance in Western films and television, which usually emphasize the exotic, for Africans, song and dance are not just accessories to life, they are transmitters of culture, indispensable to African existence.

[…]

Notes

1 A policy change was adopted in the late 1940s in recognition of Africa's role in defending France in World War II, when the Ministry of Colonies in the French cabinet was renamed the Ministry of Overseas France. Ironically, it was also during this same period (1944) that the French colonial authorities massacred the Senegalese infantrymen awaiting repatriation at Camp de Thiaroye (the title of Sembene's film) after they had fought for France during the bloody confrontations against the Axis.

2 Bernard Magubane, "A Critical Look at Indices Used in the Study of Social Change in Colonial Africa," *Current Anthropology* 12, no. 45 (October–December 1971): 419–43.

3 Although scripts were censored and politically explosive ones rejected, anticolonialist films such as *La noire de, Soleil O*, and others, whose productions could not be easily suppressed, could be manipulated through distribution. The Coopération could choose to control the impact of these films by buying the rights to distribute them only in French cultural centers in Africa (or not distribute them at all).

4 For instance, Ngugi wa Thiong'o, *Decolonizing the Mind: The Politics of Language in African*

Literature (London: James Currey; Nairobi: Heinemann, 1986); A. Hampaté Bâ, "The Living Tradition," and J. Vansina, "Oral Tradition and its Methodology," both in *General History of Africa: Methodology and African Prehistory*, ed. J. Ki-Zerbo (Berkeley: University of California Press, 1981), 166–203 and 142–65 respectively.

5 In his 1964 speech "The African Writer and the English Language," now in Achebe's collection of essays *Morning Yet on Creation Day* (London: Heinemann, 1975), 62.

6 In *Decolonizing the Mind*, Ngugi wa Thiong'o makes his position clear. See "A Statement," xiv, and especially chapter 1, "The Language of African Literature," 4–33.

7 See Ngugi, *Decolonizing the Mind*, 19.

8 For fuller discussion of technology and imagereproduction, see Jean-Louis Baudry's "Ideological Effects of the Basic Cinematographic Apparatus," *Film Quarterly* 28 (Winter 1974–5): 39–47.

9 Mbye Cham, "Ousmane Sembene and the Aesthetics of African Oral Traditions," *Africana Journal* 13 (1982): 24–40.

10 [Françoise] Pfaff, *The Cinema of Ousmane Sembene*. (Westport, CT: Greenwood Press, 1984).

11 Manthia Diawara, "Oral Literature and African Film: Narratology in *Wend Kuuni*," *Présence Africaine* no. 142 (2nd Quarter 1987): 36–49. Also "Popular Culture and Oral Traditions in African Film," *Film Quarterly* (Spring 1988): 6–14.

12 Gabriel, *Third Cinema in the Third World* (Ann Arbor: University of Michigan Press, 1982), 27.

13 From Production Press Kit, *Jom*.

14 E. H. Gombrich, *The Story of Art* (Oxford: Phaidon, 1978).

15 See Jean-Louis Baudry, "Ideological Effects of the Basic Cinematographic Apparatus," 40.

16 J. Hoberman, "It's a Mod, Mod World," *Village Voice*, 17 February 1987, 67.

9

On National Culture

Frantz Fanon*

Worldwide, a signature social role for the modern artist was to articulate and fabricate modern identities. For the black African artist, however, modern identity has had to be revealed and forged against an entrenched hegemonic Eurocentrism that set Western culture and the white race above all others.

Frantz Fanon (1925–61), the author of the following excerpt "On National Culture," from his path-breaking *The Wretched of the Earth* (1961), is referenced repeatedly in the debates concerning postcolonial identity, as is another anti-colonialist Martinique writer, Aimé Césaire (1913–2008), whose 1955 *Discourse on Colonialism* is introduced in the next chapter. These writers' exceedingly influential views are foundations of postcolonial studies and central to the arguments presented in this volume by Everlyn Nicodemus, Chika Okeke, Steven Sack, Michael Harris, Okwui Enwezor, and Octavio Zaya on modern art in Africa.

As you consider this brief commentary by Fanon and the following one by Aimé Césaire, ask what position each writer takes. How do their attitudes differ? Imagine a conversation between them about what an authentically "African" modern art would look like. Would their truly modern African artist restore and update precolonial African art traditions, or would he or she eschew the past and turn to the already synthesized forms and ideas of Western and colonial modernisms? Compare the views of Fanon and Césaire to those of Nigerian painter Uche Okeke, who specifically addresses the question of art in the selection included in the chapter "Natural Synthesis." Okeke's aesthetic manifesto, written in 1960, emerges from the same moment as Aimé Césaire's *Discourse on Colonialism* (1955) and Frantz Fanon's *Wretched of the Earth* (1961) from which our selections are drawn. All three

* Frantz Fanon (1963) "On National Culture." In *The Damned* (or *The Wretched of the Earth*) (trans. Constance Farrington, pp. 180–1). Paris, France: Présence Africaine.

Modern Art in Africa, Asia, and Latin America: An Introduction to Global Modernisms, First Edition.
Edited by Elaine O'Brien, Everlyn Nicodemus, Melissa Chiu, Benjamin Genocchio,
Mary K. Coffey, and Roberto Tejada.

commentaries were written in a time of radical transformation when Europe's African colonies were asserting nationhood. Africa, Europe, the United States, the entire world was awakening to "Black Power": a term coined by African American author Richard Wright in 1953, inspired by his visit to a Gold Coast on the verge of independence. To understand the global relevance of the commentaries by Fanon, Césaire, and Okeke for modern artists, useful comparisons can be made as well to other racialist texts excerpted in this volume: "Cannibalist Manifesto" by Brazilian Oswald de Andrade and Mexican José Vasconcelos's "Cosmic Race."

Further Readings

Gibson, Nigel C. (2003) *Fanon: The Postcolonial Imagination.* Cambridge, England: Polity Press.

Simeon-Jones, Kersuze (2010) *Literary and Sociopolitical Writings of the Black Diaspora in the Nineteenth and Twentieth Centuries.* Lanham, MD: Lexington Books.

[...]

In the sphere of plastic arts, for example, the native artist who wishes at whatever cost to create a national work of art shuts himself up in a stereotyped reproduction of details. These artists, who have nevertheless thoroughly studied modern techniques and who have taken part in the main trends of contemporary painting and architecture, turn their back on foreign culture, deny it and set out to look for a true national culture, setting great store on what they consider to be the constant principles of national art. But these people forget that the forms of thought and what it feeds on, together with modern techniques of information, language and dress have dialectically reorganised the people's intelligences and that the constant principles which acted as safeguards during the colonial period are now undergoing extremely radical changes.

The artist who has decided to illustrate the truths of the nation turns paradoxically towards the past and away from actual events. What he ultimately intends to embrace are in fact the cast-offs of thought, its shells and corpses, a knowledge which has been stabilised once and for all. But the native intellectual who wishes to create an authentic work of art must realise that the truths of a nation are in the first place its realities. He must go on until he has found the seething pot out of which the learning of the future will emerge.

[...]

10

Discourse on Colonialism

Aimé Césaire*

Like Frantz Fanon, anti-colonialist Martinique author and politician Aimé Césaire (1913–2008) is referenced repeatedly in the debates on postcolonial identity. For an expert sketch of Césaire's version of "Negritude" and conflicting African identity theories as they relate to visual culture, see the essay "Negritude, Pan-Africanism, and Postcolonial African Identity: African Portrait Photography" by Okwui Enwezor and Octavio Zaya in this volume.

Further Readings

Arnold, James (1998) *Modernism and Negritude: The Poetry and Poetics of Aimé Césaire.* Cambridge, MA: Harvard University Press.

Simeon-Jones, Kersuze (2010) *Literary and Sociopolitical Writings of the Black Diaspora in the Nineteenth and Twentieth Centuries.* Lanham, MD: Lexington Books.

[...]

A.C.: I would like to say that everyone has his own Negritude. There has been too much theorizing about Negritude. I have tried not to overdo it, out of a sense of modesty. But if someone asks me what my conception of Negritude is, I answer that above all it is a concrete rather than an abstract coming to consciousness. What I have been telling you about – the atmosphere in which we lived, an atmosphere of assimilation in which Negro people were ashamed of themselves – has great importance. We lived in an atmosphere of rejection, and we developed

* Aimé Césaire (1972 [1955]) *Discourse on Colonialism* (trans. Joan Pinkham, pp. 75–6). New York, NY: Monthly Review Press.

Modern Art in Africa, Asia, and Latin America: An Introduction to Global Modernisms, First Edition.
Edited by Elaine O'Brien, Everlyn Nicodemus, Melissa Chiu, Benjamin Genocchio,
Mary K. Coffey, and Roberto Tejada.

an inferiority complex. I have always thought that the black man was searching for his identity. And it has seemed to me that if what we want is to establish this identity, then we must have a concrete consciousness of what we are – that is, of the first fact of our lives: that we are black; that we were black and have a history, a history that contains certain cultural elements of great value; and that Negroes were not, as you put it, born yesterday, because there have been beautiful and important black civilizations. At the time we began to write people could write a history of world civilization without devoting a single chapter to Africa, as if Africa had made no contributions to the world. Therefore we affirmed that we were Negroes and that we were proud of it, and that we thought that Africa was not some sort of blank page in the history of humanity; in sum, we asserted that our Negro heritage was worthy of respect, and that this heritage was not relegated to the past, that its values were values that could still make an important contribution to the world.

[…]

11

Natural Synthesis

Uche Okeke*

The key work is synthesis, and I am often tempted to describe it as natural synthesis, for it should be unconscious not forced.

Uche Okeke, 1960

Uche Okeke (b. 1933) was the leading theoretician among the so-called Zaria Rebels, members of the Zaria Art Society founded in 1958 by art students at the Nigerian College of Arts, Science and Technology in Zaria who questioned the European curriculum there. Besides Uche Okeke, original members were Demas Nwoko, Yusuf Grillo, Bruce Onobrakpeya, Simon Okeke, William Olasebikan, E. O. Odita, Ogbonnaya Nwagbara, Oseloka Odadebe, Felix Nwoko Ekeada, and Jimoh Akolo. Although the group stayed together only three years, its legacy has had wide and lasting influence. Written in 1960, the same year in which Nigeria gained independence from Britain, we should perhaps read this manifesto, "Natural Synthesis," against the background of Nigeria as a nation in making, which would have to be forged together out of a great number of different ethnic and religious groups. While Okeke clearly states that an attempted revival of "traditional African art" would represent a lost opportunity in a world of change, the existing multitude of local strands of visual and oral traditions challenged the young artists in Zaria. The function of the "natural synthesis" that Okeke envisioned seems to have had to do both with this rich variety of popular cultures and with the poetic procedures of international modernism in honoring them. As a testimony from a group of young artists discussing at a crucial moment the role of the modern

* Uche Okeke (1995 [1960]) "Natural Synthesis." In Clementine Deliss (ed.) *Seven Stories about Modern Art in Africa* (pp. 208–9). Catalog of exhibition held at Whitechapel Art Gallery, London, England: Whitechapel.

Modern Art in Africa, Asia, and Latin America: An Introduction to Global Modernisms, First Edition.
Edited by Elaine O'Brien, Everlyn Nicodemus, Melissa Chiu, Benjamin Genocchio, Mary K. Coffey, and Roberto Tejada.

African artist, in what way do you think Uche Okeke's manifesto confirms the general account given in the preceding essay by Chika Okeke (no family relation), where the Zaria Art Society is put in context?

Further Reading

Okeke-Agulu, Chika (2006) "Nationalism and the Rhetoric of Modernism in Nigeria: The Art of Uche Okeke and Demas Nwoko, 1960–1968." *African Arts* 39(1) 26–37, 92–3.

Young artists in a new nation, that is what we are! We must grow with the new Nigeria and work to satisfy her traditional love for art or perish with our colonial past. Our new nation places huge responsibilities upon men and women in all walks of life and places, much heavier burden on the shoulders of contemporary artists. I have strong belief that with dedication of our very beings to the cause of art and with hard work, we shall finally triumph. But the time of triumph is not near, for it demands great change of mind and attitude toward cultural and social problems that beset out entire continent today. The very fabric of our social life is deeply affected by this inevitable change. Therefore the great work of building up new art culture for a new society in the second half of this century must be tackled by us in a very realistic manner.

This is our age of enquiries and reassessment of our cultural values. This is our renaissance era! In our quest for truth we must be firm, confident and joyful because of our newly won freedom. We must not allow others to think for us in our artistic life, because art is life itself and our physical and spiritual experiences of the world. It is our work as artists to select and render in pictorial or plastic media our reactions to objects and events. The art of creation is not merely physical, it is also a solemn act. In our old special order the artist had a very important function to perform. Religious and social problems were masterly resolved by him with equal religious ardour. The artist was a special member of his community and in places performed priestly functions because his noble act of creation was looked upon as inspired.

Nigeria needs a virile school of art with new philosophy of the new age – our renaissance period. Whether our African writers call the new realisation Negritude, or our politicians talk about the African Personality, they both stand for the awareness and yearning for freedom of black people all over the world. Contemporary Nigerian artists could and should champion the cause of this movement. With great humility I beg to quote part of my verse, *Okolobia*, which essayed to resolve our present social and cultural chaos. The key work is synthesis, and I am often tempted to describe it as *natural synthesis*, for it should be unconscious not forced.

Okolobia's sons shall learn to live
from father's failing;
blending diverse culture types,

the cream of native kind
adaptable alien type;
the dawn of an age –
the season of salvation.

The artist is essentially an individual working within a particular social background and guided by the philosophy of life of his society. I do not agree with those who advocate international art philosophy; I disagree with those who live in Africa and ape European artists. Future generations of Africans will scorn their efforts. Our new society calls for a synthesis of old and new, of functional art and art for its own sake. That the greatest works of art ever fashioned by men were for their religious beliefs [goes] a long way to prove that functionality could constitute the base line of most rewarding creative experience.

Western art today is generally in confusion. Most of the artists have failed to realise the artists' mission to mankind. Their art has ceased to be human. The machine, symbol of science, material wealth and of the space age has since been enthroned. What form of feelings, human feelings, can void space inspire in a machine artist? It is equally futile copying our old art heritages, for they stand for our old order. Culture lives by change. Today's social problems are different from yesterday's, and we shall be doing grave disservice to Africa and mankind by living in our fathers' achievements. For this is like living in an entirely alien cultural background.

12

A Historic Confrontation between Jean Rouch and Ousmane Sembène in 1965

"You Look at Us as if We Were Insects"

Jean Rouch and Ousmane Sembène*

This conversation is between two great cinematographers – one Senegalese, the other French – whose primary film subject was Africa. At the time of the interview, 1965, the Frenchman Jean Rouch (1917–2004) was at the forefront of European filmmaking. Acclaimed as an ethnographic director, Rouch was first to use the term *cinéma vérité*, applying it to *Chronicle of a Summer* (1960), his best-known film. Literally meaning "cinema truth," *cinéma vérité* is a genre that blurs fact and fiction and an influential film movement of the 1950s and 1960s. Rouch's lifelong attachment to African subjects began in 1941. His West African documentaries, such as *Les Hommes Qui Font La Pluie* [*Men Who Make the Rain*, 1951], *Les Maîtres Fous* [*Masters of Madness*, 1955], and *La Pyramide Humaine* [*The Human Pyramid*, 1961] show his fascination with magic and ritual. They also exemplify the ethnographic gaze associated with a primitivism couched in the rationale of the archive and Western science. "You look at us as if we were insects," Ousmane Sembène objects in this conversation.

Senegalese film director, producer, and writer of first importance, Ousmane Sembène (1923–2007) helped define modern Africa for the postcolonial era. The prize-winning success of his film *Borom Sarret* at the 1963 Tours International Festival in France, two years before this conversation took place, brought African film to the world stage. The previous commentary by Nwachukwu Frank Ukadike considered

* Jean Rouch and Ousmane Sembène (1965) "A Historic Confrontation between Jean Rouch and Ousmane Sembène in 1965: 'You Look at Us as if We Were Insects.'" In Okwui Enwezor (ed.) *The Short Century: Independence and Liberation Movements in African 1945–1994* (transcribed by Albert Cervoni and translated by Muna El Fituri, pp. 440–1). Munich, Germany: Prestel.

Modern Art in Africa, Asia, and Latin America: An Introduction to Global Modernisms, First Edition.
Edited by Elaine O'Brien, Everlyn Nicodemus, Melissa Chiu, Benjamin Genocchio,
Mary K. Coffey, and Roberto Tejada.

Sembène's films in the context of revisionist cinematography by black Africans and their aim to give an authentic voice to modern Africa. In this "historic confrontation" between Sembène and Rouch the question of authenticity – of who can represent Africa truly – is again emphatically underlined.

Questions for reading: What are Rouch's arguments in favor of the ethnographic viewpoint? How does Sembène counter? What is the dilemma for the artist and audience? How would you resolve it?

Further Readings

Gadjigo, Samba (2010) *Ousmane Sembène: The Making of a Militant Artist* (Moustapha Diop, trans.). Bloomington: Indiana University Press.

Stoller, Paul (2005) *The Cinematic Griot: The Ethnography of Jean Rouch*. Chicago, IL: University of Chicago Press.

[...]

OUSMANE SEMBÈNE: *Will European cinematographers, you for example, continue to make films about Africa once there are a lot of African cinematographers?*

JEAN ROUCH: This will depend on a lot of things but my point of view, for the moment, is that I have an advantage and disadvantage at the same time. I bring the eye of the stranger. The very notion of ethnology is based on the following idea: someone confronted with a culture that is foreign to him sees certain things that the people on the inside of this same culture do not see.

It is Not Enough to See

OUSMANE SEMBÈNE: *You say seeing. But in the domain of cinema, it is not enough to see, one must analyze. I am interested in what is before and after that which we see. What I do not like about ethnography, I'm sorry to say, is that it is not enough to say that a man we see is walking, we must know where he comes from, where he is going.*

JEAN ROUCH: You are right on this point because we have not arrived at the goal of our knowledge. I believe as well that in order to study French culture, ethnology having to do with France must be practiced by people on the outside. If one wants to study Auvergne or Lozere, one must be a Briton. My dream is that Africans will be producing films on French culture. As a matter of fact, you have already started. When Paulin Vieyra did *Afrique sur Seine (Africa on the Seine)* his purpose was indeed to show African students, but he was showing them in Paris and he was showing Paris. There could be a dialogue, and you could show us what we ourselves are incapable of seeing. I am certain that the Paris or Marseilles of Ousmane Sembène is not my Paris, my Marseilles, that they have nothing in common.

Moi, un Noir and Its Sequel

OUSMANE SEMBÈNE: *There's a film of yours that I love, that I've defended and will continue to defend. It's* Moi, un Noir. *In principle, an African could have done it, but none of us at the time had the necessary conditions to realize it. I believe that there needs to be a sequel to* Moi, un Noir, *to continue – think about it all the time – the story of this young man who, after Indochina, does not have a job and ends up in jail. After Independence, what becomes of him? Has something changed for him? I don't believe so. A detail: this young man had his diploma, now it so happens that most delinquent youth have their school diplomas. Their education doesn't help them, doesn't allow them to manage normally. And, finally, I feel that up to now two films of value have been made on Africa: your,* Moi, un Noir *and* Come Back Africa, *which you do not like. And then there's a third one, of a particular order, I'm talking about* Les Statues Meurent Aussi (Statues Die Too).

JEAN ROUCH: I would like you to tell me why you don't like my purely ethnographic films, those in which we show, for instance, traditional life?

The Trial of the Africanists

OUSMANE SEMBÈNE: *Because you show, you fix a reality without seeing the evolution. What I hold against you and the Africanists is that you look at us as if we were insects.*

JEAN ROUCH: As Fabre [Jean Henri Fabre (1823–1915), famous for his study of the behavior and anatomy of insects] would have done. I will defend the Africanists. They are men that can certainly be accused of looking at black men as if they were insects. But there might be Fabres out there who, when examining ants, discover a similar culture, one that is as meaningful as their own.

OUSMANE SEMBÈNE: *Ethnographic films have often done us a disservice.*

JEAN ROUCH: That is true, but it's the fault of the authors, because we often work poorly. It doesn't change the fact that in today's situation we can provide testimonies. You know that there's a ritual culture in Africa that is disappearing: griots die. One must gather the last living traces of this culture. I don't want to compare Africanists with saints, but they are the unfortunate monks undertaking the task of gathering fragments of a culture based on an oral tradition that is in the process of disappearing, a culture that strikes me as having a fundamental importance.

A Southerner and *Maîtres Fous*

OUSMANE SEMBÈNE: *But ethnographers don't collect fables and legends only of the griots. It is not solely about explaining African masks. Let's take, for example, the case of another one of your films,* Les Fils de I'Eau. *I believe that a lot of European viewers didn't understand it because, for them, these rites of initiation didn't have any meaning. They found the film beautiful, but didn't learn anything.*

JEAN ROUCH: While filming *Les Fils de I'Eau*, I thought that by seeing the film European viewers could do just that, go beyond the old stereotype of blacks being "savages." I simple showed that just because someone doesn't participate in a written culture doesn't mean they do not think. There's also the case of *Maîtres Fous*, one of my films that provoked heated debates among African colleagues. For me, it testifies to the spontaneous manner in which the Africans shown in the film, once out of their milieu, get rid of this industrial and metropolitan European ambiance by playing it, giving it as spectacle. I believe, however, that problems of reception do come up. One day, I showed the film in Philadelphia at an anthropological congress. A lady came to see me and asked: "can I have a copy?" I asked her why. She told me she was from the South and … she wanted to show … this film to prove that blacks were indeed savages! I refused. You see, I gave you an argument.

In agreement with the producers, the showing of *Maîtres Fous* has been reserved for art houses and cinema clubs. I believe that one should not bring such films to an audience that is too large, ill-informed, and without proper presentation and explanation. I also believe that the unique ceremonies of the people in *Maîtres Fous* make a primordial contribution to world culture.

Part II

Asian Modern Art

India, Japan, China

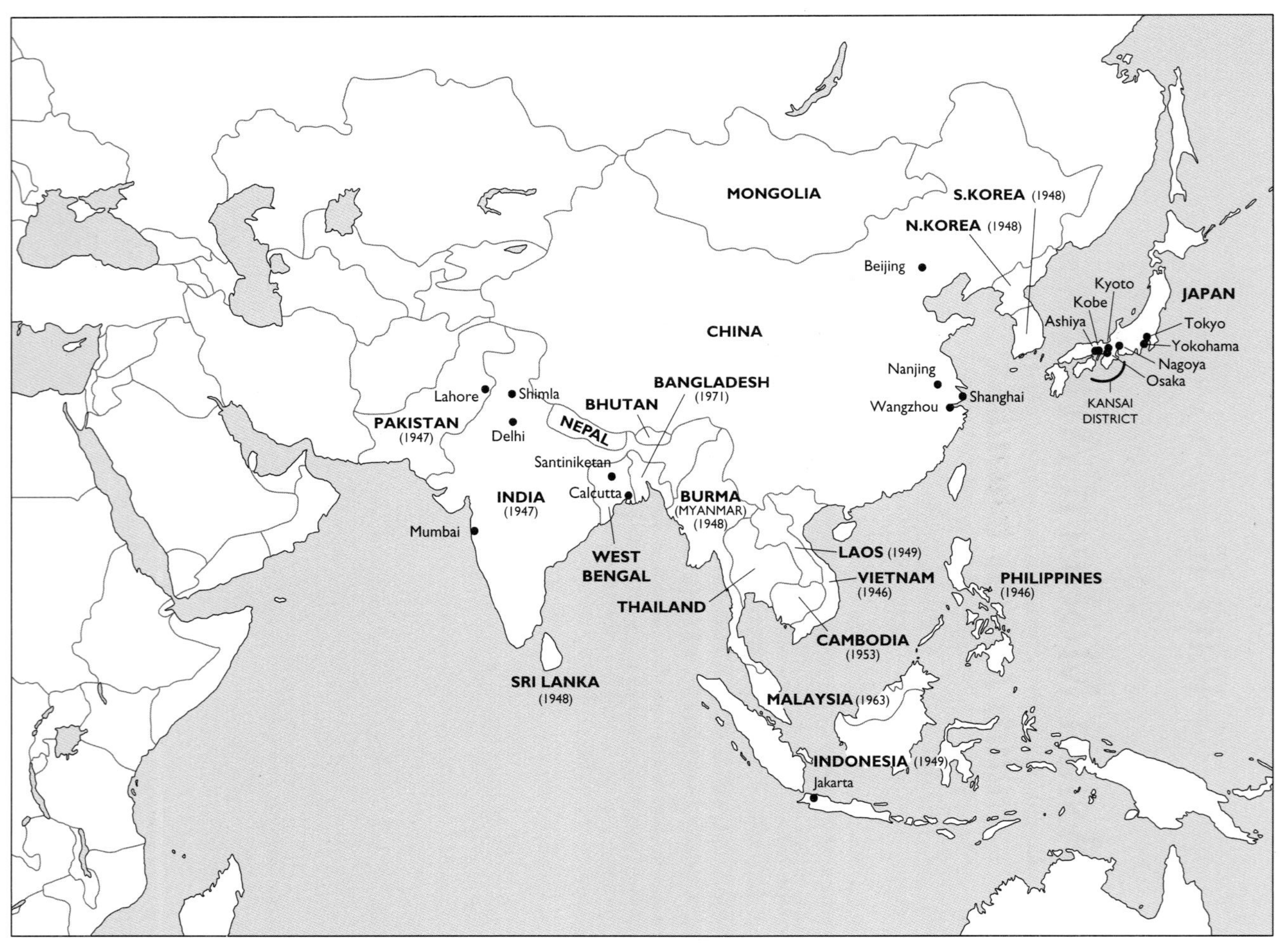

Map 2 Locations of Modern Art in Asia.

Introduction

Asian Modern Art: A Case of Alternative, Parallel, and Intersecting Modernisms

Melissa Chiu and Benjamin Genocchio

On May 2, 1930, an unusual exhibition of paintings by Rabindranath Tagore opened at the Galerie du Theatre Pigalle in Paris. Fascinated with Sigmund Freud's theories of the importance of dreams and the latent power of the unconscious, Tagore, the Indian poet and the first non-European to receive the Nobel Prize for literature, had lately begun to experiment with the possibilities of automatism in art, creating spontaneous, radically simplified yet lyrical and playful depictions of fantastic figures, faces, exotic animals, landscapes, and imaginary architecture (see Figure 17.1, this volume, p. 156). His semi-stream-of-consciousness painting style immediately appealed to the French avant-garde, who, as the Indian art historian Partha Mitter put it, "found a remarkable convergence of spirit between him and the European modernists" (Mitter 2007: 66; see also chapters in this volume by Mitter, Jamal, and Tagore).

Tagore's artwork seemed to share specific affinities in particular with Dada and Surrealist theory and practice. Published reviews of his show were enthusiastic, expressing delight at the raw beauty and imagination of the paintings. And subsequently the works were shown in various British cities. But Tagore is an exceptional figure in modern Asian art. He is exceptional insofar as his work was widely recognized and admired by the European avant-garde at a time when it was commonly believed in the West that there was no such thing as modern art in Asia. Meanwhile, in the Indian context his art stood out for being inwardly directed and mystical, and very much at odds with a more widespread local focus on "cultural authenticity" that was espoused by the Bengal School of Art, whose nationalistic assertions of the uniquely "Indian" were perceived as an appropriate, even necessary, expression of cultural resistance to British colonial rule as well as the more academic art styles promoted in local art schools. Tagore believed that by adopting more subjective approaches to art making along with the radical formalist

Modern Art in Africa, Asia, and Latin America: An Introduction to Global Modernisms, First Edition.
Edited by Elaine O'Brien, Everlyn Nicodemus, Melissa Chiu, Benjamin Genocchio,
Mary K. Coffey, and Roberto Tejada.

language of modernism in art, Indian artists could enliven their own culture and participate as equals in an increasingly cosmopolitan world. He espoused the idea of a "global modernity" decades before this concept became commonplace.

Modernity and modernism have a long, complex, and contradictory history in Asia that cannot be easily divorced from broader historical events during the nineteenth and first half of the twentieth centuries, especially colonialism. In the early decades of the twentieth century, much of Asia remained under European colonial rule, including all south Asia and large parts of southeast Asia. In east Asia things were more complicated. Japan had begun a process of national modernization and industrialization during the Meiji period (1868–1912) and by the early twentieth century was a colonial power, occupying Korea in 1905 (and effectively controlling the Korean peninsula until Japan's surrender to Allied forces on August 15, 1945) as well as parts of China, including Manchuria, between 1931 and 1945. China, for centuries the dominant cultural influence in east Asia, was in chaos following a series of local rebellions and wars with European colonizers, the collapse of the Qing dynasty in 1911 and failure of successive national unity governments leading to a takeover by the Communists in 1949. The takeover effectively ended nascent modern art movements in China, although modernism in art persisted or, better, reemerged later in a very different guise through the adoption of Soviet Socialist Realism as the nation's official painting style.

Colonialism had a powerful, transformative influence on the cultures in many Asian countries, as on life in general, providing a catalyst for both modernization and hybridization; Indonesia, for example, experienced the radical hybridization of its culture during 350 years of Dutch rule, while in India society was substantially transformed and reorganized under the influence of the British Raj (see Clark 1995, 1998, 2005). As old, traditional Asian societies were being remade anew, there was a widespread feeling of both liberation and tension. In general, there are similar experiences for progressive artists that can be described throughout much of the early twentieth century across Asia: first, an encounter with Western and other Asian modern art; second, a movement to modernize visual culture; third, attempts to adapt modernism to local aesthetic values and subject matter; finally, a self-conscious development of individual artistic voices coupled with the formation of modernist groups and in a number of cases an issuing of manifestos.

These impulses occurred at different times with different levels of intensity in each country in the region, reflecting, as the art historian John Clark has outlined in his wide-ranging and influential book *Modern Asian Art*, varying "modalities of transfer" of information from one place to another, including different infrastructure and exhibition models from country to country, the influence of colonialism and nationalism (nationalist movements as such were largely responses to colonial occupation), and, perhaps most importantly, the power and presence of a local avant-garde (Clark 1998: 49–69). Japan was the first nation in Asia to modernize, and its engagement with modernism was thus generally earlier and more widespread than for other nations. As early as 1910, Japan had widely embraced modern European art styles. In China, modern art was centered to a large extent (but not exclusively) in Shanghai, the center of trade with the West and site of extraterritorial "foreign concessions" on Chinese soil. Here, in the first decades of the twentieth century, there was a brief but intense flowering of Chinese modernist movements in photography, art, design, architecture, and film. After the Communist takeover in 1949, these movements were stymied and later discredited, providing an historical parallel with what happened to modern art under totalitarian regimes in Germany and Russia.

International travel played an important role in the entrenchment of modernism in Asian art. Several prominent artists spent a portion of their careers in Europe, returning with a new optimism and fresh ideas about how to reshape local artistic developments: from about 1910 Japanese artists were a continuous presence in Paris while the artists associated with the Shanghai School in China traveled en masse to Paris and Tokyo during the 1910s and 1920s and then returned to found the New Culture Movement. In other cases, modern art was mediated through other Asian artists and art centers; for example, prominent Japanese artists and art theorists visited India where they had a widespread influence. Japan also had an impact on Rabindranath Tagore, who made several extended trips there between 1916 and 1929. Modern art in Asia was thus frequently – and this is important to remember – a multilateral phenomenon, the product of more than just a bilateral relationship between Asia and the West.

Disparate modern artistic directions were thus manifested in Asian countries in accordance with a cocktail of local conditions, a phenomenon that in 1996, in a catalog essay for a pan-Asian contemporary art exhibition at the Asia Society Museum in New York, Indonesian curator and historian Jim Supangkat usefully characterized as "multimodernism" (Supangkat 1996). This essay is excerpted in a chapter in this volume. Supangkat makes an argument that in the best cases modernism was not imported wholesale or copied in Asia but adapted to different sets of cultural, political, and social circumstances; for example, in those countries under colonial rule, such as India, modernism often had a political dimension that went beyond aesthetic concerns, with modernist art movements initiated by nationalistic-minded artists as a challenge to the authority of their colonial rulers.

Moreover, this adaptation of modern art influences did not always correspond with the latest or even most fashionable art movement. Modernism in art is often characterized as an adoption of modes of expression which challenge the authority of local inherited traditions and that endeavor to reflect the spirit of their age. But as the Harvard-based Chinese art historian Eugene Y. Wang has pointed out in an influential essay, the relevant portion of which is included in this volume, traditions in Asia were very different from those in Europe, so Asian artists with modernist aspirations were frequently confronted with different challenges and, in turn, sought alternative, intersecting or parallel solutions (Wang 2001, see also chapter in this volume). For example Wang notes European academic realism with its use of fixed-point linear perspective, antithetical to the Western avant-garde, was taken up by Chinese modernists in the 1920s and 1930s as being, they believed, more "technologically advanced," and thus, paradoxically, "modern": it provided a possible alternative to what was perceived to be the stale, unscientific, and reactionary tradition of Chinese ink painting.

Let us end this introduction with a tentative definition of "modern" in relation to visual art in Asia, a definition which in turn informs our selection of essays for this volume. From our perspective, "modern" in Asian art is distinguished essentially by form or style, developed roughly between 1900 and 1950 interactively with Western visual modernism (for example, Impressionism, Fauvism, and Cubism) or other Asian modernisms in multiple cosmopolitan centers. Academic realism was also influential in this process, although more as a point of departure for experimentation for artists than as an end in itself.

What the following discussion and group of texts examine is how different kinds of modernism in three prominent Asian nations – India, China, and Japan – marked varying responses to new European modern art styles along with a changing social, political, and economic situation at the turn of the twentieth century. If, initially, modernism in Asian art meant simply advocating forms of Westernization, especially academic art, we can see a tendency over time to explore more nuanced ways of integrating European-inspired art and Asian art traditions. It is also important to recognize that this exchange marks far more than a unidirectional flow of ideas from West to East: just as Asian artists created their own distinctive modern art out of a process of cultural flow and exchange, Western artists also forged modernism out of an exchange of ideas with other cultures – witness, for instance, the influence of Japanese Ukiyo-e prints on the Impressionists, or the impact of Oceanic and African sculpture on the Cubists and Fauvists.

While the initial timeframe of modern art in Asia overlaps to some extent with that of modern art in Europe and in the United States, and in a few cases is all but concurrent, as in the work of Tagore or the Japanese Surrealism movement of the 1920s and 1930s, modern art in Asia often persists long after what many consider to be its accepted conclusion in the West at the end of World War II. Cubism, for instance, was especially popular among artists throughout Asia into the second half of the twentieth century, where it came to stand as a de facto symbol for the local avant-garde in opposition to older, traditional cultural forms and their practitioners. In Indonesia, for example, Cubism was adapted to local needs by the internationalist-oriented Bandung School during the 1950s. Then again, in the case of other art movements such as Gutai, originating in Japan in the mid-1950s, Asian artists were pioneering ideas that later influenced artists in the West. But however one looks at or theorizes what we would like to characterize as the "heterochronicity" of modern Asian art, what is indisputable is that modernism in Asia was something more than a locally flavored, belated manifestation of Euro-American art. We prefer to think of it more as a case of parallel yet at times also intersecting modernisms.

The following essays detail the complex interactions and transmissions between European and Asian artists in the early decades of the twentieth century. Engagements reveal that Asian artists were not docile receptacles of European ideas and forms, and most certainly not powerless colonized subjects aping colonial masters. Rather they were consciously picking and choosing ideas, styles, and forms that suited their own circumstances, reinvigorating their cultures through the kind of borrowings and exchanges of ideas that have been going on between artists everywhere for millennia. Let us look at some of these Asian modernisms more closely with respect to their social, political, and cultural meanings.

References

Clark, John (1995) *Asian Modernism: Diverse Development in Indonesia, the Philippines, and Thailand* (exhibition catalog). Tokyo: The Japan Foundation.

Clark, John (1998) *Modern Asian Art*. Honolulu: University of Hawai'i Press.

Clark, John (2005) *Cubism in Asia: Unbounded Dialogues* (exhibition catalog). Tokyo: The Japan Foundation.

Mitter, Partha (2007) *The Triumph of Modernism: Indian Artists and the Avant-Garde 1922–1947*. London, England: Reaktion Books.

Supangkat, Jim (1996) "Multiculturalism/Multimodernism." In *Contemporary Art in Asia: Traditions/Tensions* (exhibition catalog, pp. 70–81). New York, NY: Asia Society Galleries.

Wang, Eugene, Y. (2001) "Sketch Conceptualism as Modernist Contingency." In M. Hearn and J. G. Smith (eds) *Chinese Art: Modern Expressions* (pp. 102–61). New York, NY: The Metropolitan Museum of Art.

13

Multiculturalism / Multimodernism

Jim Supangkat*

In the past two decades, scholars in Asia as elsewhere have questioned the privileging common in standard art historical accounts that represent Europe and the United States as the originating center of modernism, and the rest of the world as the derivative, inauthentic periphery. With this questioning has come a realization of the need for new theoretical models that can accommodate other discourses that modernism elsewhere has engendered. In this essay Jim Supangkat, prominent Indonesian art critic and curator, asks us to consider the idea of modern art as inherently pluralistic and that in spite of surface similarities, specific local conditions in each country have caused modernism to take different forms. Supangkat characterizes this phenomenon in the Asian context as "multimodernism," providing a revisionist model with global relevance.

In the early to mid-1990s some US critics like Lucy Lippard and Suzi Gablik pointed out that modernism – the institutional version identified here by Supangkat as "codified in the 1950s" – had lost its relevance. To observers like Lippard and Gablik, multiculturalism had supplanted modernism as the actually existing mainstream of US art. They saw modernism and multiculturalism as opposites engaged in a culture war at the "end" of modernism and the "beginning" of multiculturalism. However compelling Supangkat found the US multicultural debates, he takes a different position. For him, a cosmopolitan Jakartan, modernism and multiculturalism had never been in opposition; modernism had not ended and multiculturalism had not just begun. Instead, what had occurred was a shift of cultural power and consciousness; the Eurocentric paradigm of world art was giving

* Jim Supangkat (1996) "Multiculturalism/Multimodernism." In *Contemporary Art in Asia: Traditions/Tensions* (exhibition catalog, pp. 76–8). New York, NY: Asia Society Galleries.

Modern Art in Africa, Asia, and Latin America: An Introduction to Global Modernisms, First Edition.
Edited by Elaine O'Brien, Everlyn Nicodemus, Melissa Chiu, Benjamin Genocchio, Mary K. Coffey, and Roberto Tejada.

way. Using Indonesian modernism as his example, Supangkat proposes that modern art was always already multiple, transcultural, and global.

Further Readings

Bahrani, Zainab and Shabout, Nada (2009) *Modernism in Iraq* (exhibition catalog). New York, NY: Miriam and Ira D. Wallach Art Gallery, Columbia University.

Furuichi, Yasuko and Nakamoto, Kazumi (1995) *Asian Modernism: Diverse Development in Indonesia, the Philippines and Thailand* (exhibition catalog). Tokyo: The Japan Foundation Asia Center.

"Contemporary Art in Asia: Traditions/Tensions" could be viewed solely as an exhibition of Asian art in America. The purpose of the show, as stated in the proposal, is "to introduce American audiences to the rich, flourishing art scene from among five Asian countries." Although this is the basic thinking behind the exhibition, I think the matter is not that simple. There was, for instance, an earlier exhibition at the Asia Society called "Asia/America: Identities in Contemporary Asian American Art," which presented work by Asian American artists. I think it is important to see the connection between these two exhibitions. The source of this link is easier to grasp in the case of the "Asia/America" exhibition. Since it addressed the issue of multiracial America, the "Asia/America" show seemed clearly related to the issue of multiculturalism, the subject of heated discussions in the United States over the past five or six years. And since these two exhibitions are connected, I get the strong impression that "Traditions/Tensions" is also in some way tied to the contestation over multiculturalism.

I first learned of the critical debates around multiculturalism in the United States through the writings of the American art critic Lucy R. Lippard. In her book *Mixed Blessings*, she outlines a pattern of cultural domination in the United States by a homogenized Euro-American society, and the consequent marginalizing of "mixed race" groups, who, although they can still be recognized as Africans, Native Americans, Asians, and Latin Americans, should not necessarily be viewed in relation to racial or ethnic differences in the general sense of those terms. As I understand it, "mixed race" is a social phenomenon reflected in the conflicts over race and gender differences and is not automatically linked to the idea of hybridity. Lippard describes the consequences, saying, "Participation in the cross-cultural process, from all sides, can be painful and exhilarating. I get impatient. A friend says: remember, change is a process, not an event."[1]

On the basis of such statements, I sense that within the development of contemporary art in America, multiculturalism exhibits a political dimension; in other words, art is not observed solely from the point of view of aesthetic values. Indeed, Lippard states,

> The contemporary art world, a somewhat rebellious satellite of the dominant culture, is better equipped to swallow cross-cultural influences than to savor them.... Ethnocentrism in the arts is balanced on a notion of Quality that "transcends boundaries" – and is identifiable by those in power. According to this lofty view, racism has nothing to do with art; Quality will prevail; so called minorities just

> haven't got it yet. The notion of Quality has been the most effective bludgeon on the side of homogeneity in the modernist and postmodernist periods, despite twenty-five years of attempted revisionism. The conventional notion of good taste with which many of us were raised and educated was based on an illusion of social order that is no longer possible (or desirable) to believe in. We now look at art within the context of disorder.[2]

Although Lippard is speaking about the situation in the United States, I have noticed that this cross-cultural exchange within multiculturalism has an international dimension. Lippard even includes within her study certain "Third World" artists from the developing countries of Africa, Asia, and Latin America. In order to justify this line of thinking, she quotes Vietnamese filmmaker and writer Trinh T. Minh-ha, who says, "There is a Third World in every First World and vice-versa."[3] Lippard also quotes artist Paul Kagawa's view that

> artists who create works which support the values of the ruling-class culture are ruling-class artists, no matter what their color. The "Third World artist" (hereafter T.W.A.) is one who produces in conscious opposition to the art of the ruling class, not just to cause trouble or to be "different," but because the artist is sympathetic with "Third World" people in other sectors of society and the world. Not all "Third World" people are aware of the oppression (or its cause), but all T.W.A.s must be because they are, by our definition, a voice of the oppressed.[4]

From these statements, I have formed a clear opinion of the relationship between "Tensions/Traditions" and multiculturalism in the United States. It seems that this is to be an exhibition of the works of what Kagawa calls "Third World Artists"; it is meant to follow the "Asia/America" exhibition, which displayed "Third World Artists within the First World." But, from what I can glean through reading about cultural developments in the United States, these exhibitions seem to be a major advance in the current debate over multiculturalism. Much has apparently changed since Lippard published *Mixed Blessings* six years ago.

For one thing, it seems the issue of multiculturalism is being ever more widely discussed in the United States. This is in part due to the controversies over the 1993 Whitney Biennial, which I gather was widely perceived as the "multicultural biennial." In a seminar in Jakarta in April 1995, American curator Mary Jane Jacob noted,

> The previous 1993 Whitney Biennial, which focused on the multicultural movement as an expression of artists, who were themselves outside the established mainstream, met with fierce objections because it threatened the existing power structure. . . . Here the American puritanical legacy, denouncing arts as unproductive and morally destructive for the society, came face-to-face with a multicultural agenda that promoted art as an expression of self identity, potentially restorative, and necessary to the creation of a new, more inclusive society.[5]

What interested me in this lecture was Jacob's constant reference to the "mainstream" as the dominant force opposed by the multicultural movement. I have found that this generalized notion of the mainstream comes up frequently in international art forums, and I can only infer that what is being referred to is the institutionalized version of cultural modernism that emerged in Europe and America around [the] mid-[twentieth-]century. This critical standard is based, as Lippard says, on "a notion of Quality that 'transcends boundaries' – and is identifiable only by those in power."

In her most recent book, *Conversations Before the End of Time*, American art critic Suzi Gablik also discusses this issue of the opposition between modernism and the multicultural movement. I get the impression from reading Gablik's book that this modernism-versus-multiculturalism controversy is a sign that change is coming in the United States. And I think Gablik sees this change occurring throughout the world, as well. This is particularly clear in her dialogue with the well-known art dealer Leo Castelli. In that conversation, auspiciously titled "A Farewell to Modernism," Castelli says,

> There was a certain sadness that I felt about it [multiculturalism], but, well, with the Whitney show, I realized that I had to change my attitude, and not be rejecting, as people generally are.... It was a sea change, not just any change: I would say that there is a clear and evident involvement with social problems of all kinds, and they are not filtered. They're there, brutally.[6]

At another point, Castelli remarks, "But there is also that sense that a new era had begun, and if we want to find a turning point – which is, of course, something that's a bit artificial – the Whitney show certainly was one."[7]

When Gablik prods Castelli further, urging him to comment on changes in the development of art worldwide, he says,

> There are lots of people who foresee total disasters, and probably we are heading toward immensely more important changes than have occurred, let's say, during the past century. Now we are beginning to realize, perhaps, that all these inventions, the wars, and the political and geographical changes are coming to a head. All this has been brewing for many, many decades, and it's becoming more evident that all these changes will have results that we can hardly foresee. For instance, America will be an entirely different country in 10, 20, 30 years from now with all these multicultures that we have.[8]

I do not think that the opinions expressed by Castelli are exaggerated. There is indeed a relationship between the social changes taking place in America and those occurring in the rest of the world. Outside of the United States, more and more signs of change are emerging. Critical discussions regarding domination by the mainstream are also expanding and developing. But if the domination of modernism is seen in America in the conventionalized practices of art institutions, outside of America it is seen more in the large international exhibitions, such as Documenta, the Carnegie International, and the Venice and Sydney biennials. These exhibitions constitute forums for the development of the international mainstream. And the impression has developed recently that these exhibitions do not show the works of artists who work outside the mainstream.

This critical attitude toward the domination of the mainstream has given birth to a number of international exhibitions that aim specifically to provide new forums. Among these new international exhibitions and forums are: the Havana Biennial in Cuba; the Asia-Pacific Triennial of Contemporary Art in Brisbane, Australia; the Johannesburg Biennial in South Africa; the Kwangju and Cheju biennials in South Korea; the Asian Art Show in Fukuoka, Japan; the Regional Artists Exchange (ARX) in Perth, Australia; and the "Contemporary Art of the Non-Aligned Countries 1995" exhibition in Jakarta.

In such forums, discussions of mainstream domination are clear and sharp. For instance, in her introduction to the catalogue of the "First Asia-Pacific Triennial of Contemporary Art" in Brisbane, Caroline Turner, curator of the Queensland Art Gallery, stated:

> While there is no theme for this exhibition, there is a thesis; that is that Euro-American perspectives are no longer valid as a formula for evaluating the art of the region. The confidence, relevance and vitality of the art will be a revelation to many curators in the West. The opportunities for intraregional interchange generated by forums such as the triennial will, it is to be hoped, provide new ways of looking at art on the basis of equality without a "center" or "centers" as well as an approach to cultural interchange open to the future in which we can recognize what we have in common and yet respect what is different.[9]

Turner even went so far as to identify the whole notion of the domination of the mainstream as a distinctly Euro-American construction. "What we have in Asia instead," she pointed out, "are strong intraregional cultural interchanges, which, like cross-cultural exchange in the multicultural movement in the United States, have caused discussions of contemporary art to take on a political dimension."

Having noticed a similarity between the movements opposing the domination of the mainstream/modernism around the world (in particular, in the writings of Lucy Lippard and in discussions at international art conferences), I fantasized about the possibility of a global multicultural movement. After all, isn't there already a general international struggle against the principles of modernism and the ruling-class values they reflect? And haven't many of the principles of multiculturalism already been reflected in changes in the international art discourse? Suddenly, I felt like predicting the worldwide emergence of cross-cultural exchanges among cross-cultural groups, all of them trying to achieve the sorts of breakthroughs that are now taking place in the United States.

But then I began to doubt that this could really happen. If multiculturalism were to become a global issue, would Asianness or Africanness not surface in contemporary art and head us directly back into the issues of ethnicity, indigenousness, and, finally, exclusivism? Besides that, what of the confrontation between "otherness" and the homogenized values of Euro-American society? Wouldn't the whole-thing simply return to an East-West dichotomy? Also, are Lippard's "cross-cultural exchanges" within the multicultural movement in the United States really the same thing as the "intraregional cultural interchanges" pointed out by Caroline Turner? And, finally, what makes us think that the changes in the art of the world as a whole will (or should) follow those occurring in the art of the United States?

These doubts became even stronger as I tried to delve into one small aspect of this situation: multiculturalism in Indonesia. But by analyzing the current conditions in a very familiar environment, I have arrived at an opinion and a conclusion that are far different from what I would have predicted.

A Multicultural Indonesia

The people of Indonesia, like the people of America, constitute a multicultural society. In Indonesia there are more than three hundred ethnic groups with vastly different traditions and over five hundred dialects. Although Indonesia experienced the hybridization of its culture during the 350 years it was ruled by the Dutch, it has not shown a similar hybridization process among its ethnic cultures during the past fifty years of independence. In fact, it was Indonesia's prolonged colonization that gave rise to the multicultural conditions that produced the new hybrid cultures. Many of the indigenous cultures were substantially transformed under the influence of the Western culture imposed by the Dutch colonial forces.

These new cultures were the product of the feudal elite, a small segment within each ethnic group who gained power by collaborating with the colonial forces. This phenomenon has caused many of the "traditional cultures" of Indonesia to become ambiguous. They are "original" and "hybrid" at the same time – having traditions that refect the influence of the West, while retaining the original ethnic traditions still embraced by the larger segment of society.

One example of this kind of hybrid culture is the High Javanese culture, which is now known as the traditional or classic culture of Java. (During the colonial period, Java Island was the base for all of the administrative and socioeconomic activities of the colonial administration.) Western influences entered High Javanese culture in a peaceful manner, without confrontation. And within the hybrid culture that developed, a tradition of "high art" emerged during the seventeenth and eighteenth centuries. This was particularly evident in the emergence of the art of painting in Indonesia. Previously, painting was unknown in any of the local ethnic cultures.[10]

This example raises the fundamental question of whether the occurrence of modernism in the development of Indonesian art is just a continuation of the Western-influenced hybrid culture and is, therefore, equivalent to the modernism that emerged in Europe and is associated with ruling-class values. Modernism is the key political force in the development of art in Indonesia. This can be seen in the fact that, since its emergence, modernism in Indonesia has had a political dimension that goes beyond artistic considerations. In the struggle for independence, for example, there was a social revolution in Indonesia. A majority of the population opposed not only the Dutch colonial government but also the feudal social structure that had been advocated by the Dutch. The modernist art movement in Indonesia in 1930s was sparked by nationalist artists who repudiated the colonial administration and feudalism, and modern art became the "expression of the people." For this reason, the emergent modernism was an important sign of a rejection of feudal elitist values in independent (modern) Indonesia.[11]

This modernism was not just a result of modernity or even part of the process of modernization. This modernism reflected idealism. There are similarities in the emergence of this modernism and the first stirrings of modernism in Europe. (Here, I am speaking of modernism as it evolved in the eighteenth century, not the late modernism that was codified in the 1950s.) As in the West, Indonesian modernists rejected conventional values and academic art, stood up for individual freedom, and focused on subjects that had their roots in social reality. But Indonesian modernism exhibited some differences as well. For one thing, it contained strong elements of idealism and socialism. The rejection of feudal and elitist conventional values in Indonesian modernism was coterminous with an opposition to the power and pressure exerted by the colonial administration. The themes of the people and of individual freedom (understood as the basic rights of freedom and independence) were colored by nationalistic sentiments that had been growing in Indonesian society since the beginning of the eighteenth century.[12]

But the rejection of colonialism was not the sole issue in the onset of Indonesia's struggle for independence in 1945. At that time, the fledgling state of Indonesia also faced the threat of disintegration due to the multicultural nature of its population: each of the archipelago's three hundred ethnic groups had its own traditions and its own brand of idealism. Since Indonesia had been a federation of states in which each ethnic group had autonomy and power over what went on in its individual region, there was considerable social tension during this revolutionary period. In addition to political turbulence, there was also bloodshed. All the signs seemed to indicate that the new nation would shatter apart. Thus, the multicultural situation that confronted modern Indonesia involved not only the problems arising from cultural diversity but also those stemming from a host of other, preexisting sociopolitical phenomena.

Edi Sedywati, an Indonesian anthropologist and archaeologist, once wrote of this type of multiculturalism:

> Within this state, every ethnic group has the same status as members of the unified nation. It seems that no notion of majority-minority dichotomy is put into any national discourse, regarding indigenous ethnic groups .... the idea of unification, regards towards one's primordial bounds is deemed necessary and positive, as it gives feeling of rootedness in one's culture, and at the same time that feeling will still be valid within the new nationality.[13]

Within this type of multicultural situation, modernist principles constitute political choices that can hinder disintegration. They can provide a neutral medium for the expression of unity. In Indonesia, they functioned to highlight the concept of an independent and unified nation, as opposed to a continuation of specific ethnic cultures. In particular, modernism and nationalism were attempts to avoid the privileging of Javanese culture ("Javanization" has long been an extremely sensitive issue in Indonesia), which, it was feared, would cause jealousy and suspicion among other ethnic groups.

The threats inherent in this kind of multicultural social condition have, in fact, made Indonesia modern. Whether or not this was agreeable to all, the political decision to state respect for and to acknowledge politically the traditions of the more than three hundred ethnic groups has meant that all are accepted as indigenous elements of a unified Indonesian culture. This point was specifically outlined in the constitution and is what made it possible for Indonesia to achieve independence.

Because of this necessity for forming a political consensus, Indonesia's modernist discourse did not include the rejection of tradition. This peculiarity meant that the avant-garde allegiance to progress and the new, which forms the basis for Western modernism, is no more than a thin layer of Indonesian modernism. In Indonesia, modernism developed without tension alongside many other kinds of art that remained within a traditional framework. In other words, modernism in Indonesia did not necessarily conform to the European modernist rejection of tradition, and the discourse of modernism/modernity in Indonesia cannot be fully interpreted as "modernization."

But neither can modernism in Indonesia be viewed as "Westernization." Even though the modernism of "the New" could be perceived as Western while the modernism that gathers together three hundred ethnic traditions is seen as Eastern, there is no necessary conflict between the two. However, echoes of the old West-East dichotomy are heard throughout Indonesia even today. There is no real basis for the development of that dichotomy. Rather, in investigating the propagation of the West-East debate between 1920 and 1940, I found that the artificial distinction was encouraged by the Japanese "Greater East Asia" campaign. In this prewar propaganda blitz, the Japanese attempted to use the notion of Easternness as a way of rejecting colonialism, which was identified with the West. Hidden behind this regional advocacy of Easternness – put forth by the Japanese in slogans reflecting their own fierce opposition to the West – was a fervent nationalism (national identity) which had been suppressed during the colonial period (the Dutch colonial administration was notorious for its policy of suppressing all forms of indigenousness). The view gained considerable influence in Indonesia during the Japanese occupation through the efforts of the main Japanese cultural institution, Keimin Bunka Shidoso.[14]

The Eastern pole of the East-West polemic in Indonesia also reflects the struggles of modern Indonesia to come to grips with its own multicultural nature. Since the national identity of modern Indonesia could not be derived entirely from any one of the three hundred ethnic traditions, an umbrella large enough to accommodate them all was required. The concept of Easternness turned out to be the most appropriate umbrella. Still, for the purposes of unifying those three hundred ethnic traditions, this overarching concept could just as easily have been "Westernness," except that Westernness was explicitly identified with the colonial administration.

In my opinion, both the Eastern and Western poles of this debate in Indonesia are options within a dialectical attempt to find the best way to move forward. In fact, the Eastern pole is often not fully concerned with Eastern values and ways of thinking, but is rather a stereotypical moral stance regarding spirituality, collectivity, and intuition. At the same time, the identification of the West is frequently colored with sentiments rooted in the colonial period, which gives even the valid aspects of Western views a negative connotation. But almost all West-East debates in Indonesia end up in a kind of syncretism that embraces neither the East nor the West. In fact, Western views are often seen as containing some "good" and are therefore capable of having a "good influence" which is needed and must be taken into consideration.[15]

Generally, though, the terms of this West-East dichotomy have been confined almost entirely to theoretical debate, and have not been reflected in the development of art as a practice or activity. There has been no movement to oppose Western aesthetics, for instance, and no revival of tradition; there has not even been an antitraditionalist movement. In Indonesia, the art academies teach only the modern art of the West, and never divide the program into modern Western styles and traditional Eastern styles, as is done in art schools in Japan, India, and Thailand, This indicates that art education in Indonesia – which is an important aspect of the development of modern Indonesian art – does not perpetuate the West-East split.

When the West-East issue does arise in discussions of art in Indonesia today it lacks the context of nationalism (since the once-pressing issue of national identity is no longer as relevant). But because no other context has emerged to replace nationalism, the West-East issue now seems hollow, it no longer has meaning. It lingers largely as a xenophobic, sloganistic expression of official rhetoric used to justify the government's political stances or its suspicion of developments it cannot comprehend.

In December 1993, when I organized the National Biennial in Jakarta, I was criticized by the mass media for advocating "the negative influences of the West," mainly in the form of postmodern installation art (this was the first time that installation art had appeared in a national biennial exhibition). A few months later, when an experimental art festival was held in Surakarta in Central Java, *Kompas*, Indonesia's largest and most influential independent newspaper, decided to "take action." They published an editorial deriding the Westernized art but assuring their readers that any negative influence would soon be "swallowed by time" They wrote:

> That this is a reaction to the sociopolitical and sociocultural situation can be understood, but the question arises as to whether our people are indeed so organized as to motivate this kind of "art." And if they destroy the arts and communication, which would mean anarchy, there is always the question as to whether that art is no

> longer art, but rather only a personal expression .... [Western] influence is always necessary because it is like a mirror in which we can look and see our own situation reflected. This kind of thing has become a kind of tradition in Indonesian society. The result is that many [negative] influences are simple swallowed up in time, while not a very few survive to become part of the cultural legacy of our people.[16]

Clearly, within the multicultural conditions of Indonesia, modernism carries no connotations of superiority. But then, the modernism that exists in Indonesia is a far cry from that of the far more homogenized Euro-American society, and does not reflect the values of the ruling class. In Indonesia, modern society has developed according to a different model than that followed in Europe and America. The ruling class and the elites in Indonesia have, for instance, remained closer to traditional values and in no way comprehend modernism. On the other hand, modernism in Indonesia does not contain the tensions of ethnicity, indigenousness, or difference of races. Neither is modernism mainstream nor are the nation's more than three hundred ethnic traditions marginalized. Rather, this modernism is limited to being a largely metropolitan phenomenon (since it occurs only in major cities). It does not force values, quality standards, or modernist thinking on traditional art, and there is no traditional art that "has the intention" of developing into modern art. In fact, Balinese art, like Aboriginal art in Australia, has maintained its traditional framework and yet has become more "contemporary" than most Indonesian modern art.

The fact that Indonesians have had to juxtapose three hundred ethnic traditions with an emergent modernism has fortified the pluralistic conviction that culture is always made up of a variety of substances and that it cannot be related to only one framework with one absolute truth. Indonesian modernism does not necessarily reflect hybridity or constitute a "melting pot" of the many ethnic traditions. This is in part because modernism is not based on those ethnic traditions and it is not the sole representation of modern/contemporary Indonesian culture. Although there has been some mixing of modernism and ethnic traditions, the mutual influence has failed to change the basic framework of either.

In this sort of multicultural context, it is hard to imagine cross-cultural exchanges like those cited by Lucy Lippard, which reflect "the deep social and historical awkwardness underlying that exchange." This is not to say that I do not agree with her view that the values of modernism as institutionalized in the United States are repressive and force homogenized Euro-American values on society. But Lippard implies that the debate over these values of modernism is black and white. In Indonesia, modernism is neither black nor white. It is gray. In fact, I would even say, it is a pale gray.

Multimodernism

Modernism in Indonesia is part of a global modernist movement but it has had only a selective interaction with more mainstream forms of modernism. Critics and art historians throughout the world can easily recognize modern Indonesian art; it reproduces the styles, idioms, and tendencies that are characteristic of the history of modernism. But Indonesian modernism, which is generally perceived as not showing a modernist development and assumed to constitute a part of Indonesia's local tradition, is a marginalized modernism.

Actually, it is not surprising that a concept of idealism, like modernism, should develop differently in a different context. Indonesian modernism has emerged from far different conditions than the dominant Euro-American modernism. Interestingly, though, there was once a close encounter between Indonesian modernism and American modernism. This occurred in 1990, when the "Festival of Indonesia in the United States" was being planned. This festival, which was intended to provide a total look at Indonesian culture, neglected modern Indonesian art almost entirely. All of the major galleries and museums in the United States refused to exhibit contemporary Indonesian art; they suggested that it be shown in anthropological museums instead.

That incident speaks for itself. The observations by Lippard and Jacob on art institutions in the United States make clear the situation which led up to that rejection. It is the same sort of refusal that had already been experienced by women artists and artists of color in the United States. However, there has been no need for a face-to-face confrontation. Unlike the Third World artists in the First World, who have to accept that situation whether they like it or not, Third World artists outside the First World, whose works have been rejected by the institutions of the United States, have other choices. Several international forums and exhibitions that have begun outside the mainstream have been particularly interested in exhibiting "marginalized" art. More and more, such opportunities have opened up over the past five years. This is a sign that there are changes in the development of art worldwide. And it is in these international contexts that Indonesian modernism has been presented.

This is also true of the various modernisms that have been developing in other Third World countries. In these new exhibition and discussion spaces – in Tokyo, Fukuoka, Brisbane, Havana, Johannesburg, Cheju, and Singapore (and the roundtable discussion at the Asia Society in New York in 1992, for that matter) – I have seen art historians, artists, and art critics from developing nations excitedly explain the development of modernism in their own individual countries, from the earliest to the most recent developments (including contemporary art). In my experience, these kinds of presentations have provided the main interest in these international forums outside the mainstream.

But the opposition to the domination of the mainstream that is demonstrated in these forums is not intended to force recognition or more opportunities to exhibit in the First World. Rather, what is suggested is that, despite surface similarities, local conditions and sociocultural backgrounds have caused modernism to take different forms in different places. Thus, mainstream modernism is simply that which has developed in Europe and America. It probably even encompasses differences within it. And the larger point is that none of the forms that modernism has taken should be rejected or discredited. Forms of modernism that exist outside the mainstream have been rejected by the mainstream not only because of the suspicion that their ties to tradition, ethnicity, and indigenousness are too strong but also because the very basis for their development is not understood. This lack of comprehension, I believe, is due to a very basic difference in perspective: mainstream modernism is convinced of the fixed, the absolute, and the universal, whereas modernism outside of the mainstream is based in pluralism.

To evaluate this situation properly, in my opinion, it is necessary to understand not only the differences that result from multiculturalism (i.e., ethnicity, indigenousness, differences among races) but also the differences within modernism itself. Those differences – particularly those that stem from various rates of development – depend not on discrepancies in cultural background but on substantial differences in both sociopolitical background and premodern exposure to Western culture.

When Caroline Turner set forth her views about intraregional cultural interchange at the Asia-Pacific Triennial of Contemporary Art in 1993, many suspected that she was raising the issue of cultural diplomacy in order to establish a program for friendship between nations that political diplomacy had failed to accomplish. But I think that Turner's statement must be seen as a step toward a serious consideration of the similarities and differences in the experience of modernism in the Asia-Pacific region. "We recognize what we have in common," Turner stated, "and yet respect what is different." This key concept is not limited to efforts to discuss the varieties of modernism from country to country; rather, it must be understood as an acknowledgment that modernism is a plural phenomena and that pluralism does not deny the universal aspects.

Unfortunately, it seems that it is impossible to link this concept of pluralism to the more specific discussions of multiculturalism, which are determined by the situation of each particular state. Pluralism is more directly related to the concept of "multimodernism," which constitutes an effort to evaluate and analyze a fundamental aspect of modernism that has been missing from most discussions; that is the recognition that there are many developments outside of the mainstream that are not often considered. The mainstream discourse of modernism, as can be seen in the views of Lippard and Jacob, has been shaped by a Western paradigm, one that presumes the domination of a homogenous, white, patriarchal Euro-American society.

Even so, multimodernism is related to the difficult and complex multicultural conditions that exist in America. Inherent in these conditions are many possibilities for misunderstanding, misinterpretation, and miscommunication. In fact, the situation reminds me of the story of the building of the Tower of Babel: there, the idealistic dream of constructing the monument failed because of confusions that arose from misunderstanding and miscommunication. Therefore, in order to give a clearer picture of the problem of art within the context of multimodernism, I would like to borrow the words of Lucy Lippard and describe it as "art within the context of disorder."

Multimodernism reflects a complex process of seeking. Art historian T.K. Sabapathy of the National University of Singapore best delineated the new premises and methodologies required to comprehend multimodernism when he wrote,

> Critics and historians of art will have to step outside their prescribed, privileged grounds, and become familiar with different or other models of articulating discussion or accounts of artistic practices and values. And among these are also to be included new or different usages of employing terminology which has art historical origins in the West.[17]

Thus, multimodernism not only analyzes the varying forms of modernism but also views them as material for rereading the analysis of the history of art. One of the very basic elements of multimodernism is the consideration of new, critical thinking toward the absolute, universal, totalizing character of modernism (and, for that matter, postmodernism, which may or may not be outside the mainstream).

As a methodology, then, multimodernism offers a quite different approach to modernism, one that makes clear that not all varieties of modernism develop under the paradigm of the West. It suggests, for example, that even theories of representation that are conceived in developing countries might be based on a wholly different point of view. As Palestinian-American literary theorist Edward Said has observed, most Western-based representation "has been repressive because it doesn't permit or make room for interventions on the part of those represented."[18] Multimodernism requires a multidisciplinary approach because within the confusion of existing theories (in which no confidence can be placed), only reality can function as the proper basis for the formation of new observations. Within this multidisciplinary approach, the sociopolitical, socioeconomic, and sociocultural aspects must be considered in order to properly analyze differences and similarities. Within this type of approach, the conditions of multiculturalism, those that are found in America as well as those found in Indonesia, must be important considerations.

So, this is not only a matter of taking into consideration the presence of hybridity, ethnicity, or indigenousness in modern or contemporary art. It is also a matter of considering the parallelism of modernism and traditional frameworks, each of which have their own idioms, convictions, and principles of aesthetics. We must accept that these are all radically different from one another and continue to develop, even now, as in the art of Bali or the Aboriginal art of Australia.

[...]

Notes

1 Lucy R. Lippard, *Mixed Blessings: New Art in a Multicultural America* (New York: Pantheon Books, 1990), p. 6.

2 Ibid., pp. 5, 7.

3 Ibid., p. 15.

4 Ibid.

5 Mary Jane Jacob, "The Audience, the Other" (paper presented at the seminar "Unity in Diversity

in International Art," Jakarta, April 1995), Department of Education and Culture, Republic of Indonesia, Jakarta, photocopied seminar proceedings, p. 17.

6 Suzi Gablik, *Conversation Before the End of Time* (London: Thames and Hudson, 1995), pp. 460–2.

7 Ibid., p. 472.

8 Ibid., pp. 468–9.

9 Caroline Turner, "Introduction," in *The First Asia-Pacific Triennial of Contemporary Art* (Queensland, Australia: Queensland Art Gallery, 1993), pp. 8–9.

10 Jim Supangkat, "Indonesian Contemporary Art: A Continuation" (paper presented at the seminar "Potential of Asian Thought," Tokyo, October 1994), Asia Center, Japan Foundation, Tokyo, photocopied seminar proceedings, pp. 53–68.

11 Jim Supangkat, "A Brief History of Indonesian Modern art," in *Tradition and Change: Contemporary Art of Asia and the Pacific*, edited by Caroline Turner (Queensland, Australia: University of Queensland Press, 1994), pp. 47–57.

12 Jim Supangkat, "The Emergence of Indonesian Modernism and Its Background," in *Asian Modernism* (Tokyo: Japan Foundation Forum, 1993), pp. 204–13.

13 Edy Sedywati, "Reflections on Multiculturalism" (keynote speech at the seminar "Unity in Diversity in International Art," Jakarta, April 1995), Department of Education and Culture, Republic of Indonesia, Jakarta, photocopied seminar proceedings, pp. 10–11.

14 Supangkat, "Emergence of Indonesian Modernism" p. 211.

15 See Achidat K, Mihardja, ed., *Polemik Kebudayaan* (Jakarta: Library of Education of the Department of Education and Culture, 1954). This book is a collection of articles regarding the East-West debate that occurred in Indonesia in the 1930s.

16 Unsigned editorial, *Kompas Daily* (Apr. 23, 1994).

17 T. K. Sabapathy, "International Contemporary Art: Artistic Movement within the Framework of International Contemporary Art, Some Implications" (paper presented at the seminar "Unity in Diversity in International Art," Jakarta, April 1995), Department of Education and Culture, Republic of Indonesia, Jakarta, photocopied seminar proceedings, p. 109.

18 Phil Mariani and Jonathan Crary, "In the Shadow of the West: An Interview with Edward Said," in *Discourses: Conversations in Postmodern Art and Culture*, edited by Russell Ferguson et al. (New York: New Museum of Contemporary Art, 1993), p. 95.

14

Negotiating Modernities
Encounters with Cubism in Asian Art

Ahmad Mashadi*

Ahmad Mashadi, a Singaporean art historian, moves us in this essay toward a comparative modern art. He wants us to eschew established (hermetic, formalist, progressivist) modern art historiography with its hierarchy of values based on concepts like authenticity and originality so that we can see Cubism at large as a heteronomy: a unity with parts that develop differently with different functions. Here he examines diverse engagements with the idiom of Cubism among Asian artists during the early and middle decades of the twentieth century. Mashadi argues that while a study of these various manifestations provides us with a basis for comparative study, each reflects different social, cultural, and political developments taking place in different parts of Asia, and that superficial similarities of style can mask the disparate uses to which Cubism was put. He also argues that artists "recoded" Cubism in the local context, detailing the ways in which Cubism in Asia was often narrative driven, making direct reference to Asian religion, myth, and folklore, as opposed to the more abstract and anti-representational strain dominating European Cubism in the early twentieth century. Furthermore, Mashadi reminds the reader that although European Cubism is distinct from Asian Cubism, it is also diverse and emerged from the same dialectical tensions of modernity – especially Self and Collective – that produced Asian Cubism. He turns to David Cottington's 2004 revisionist historiography of European Cubism, *Cubism and its Histories*, to help make his point that Cubism must be reseen as a world movement, each artwork manifesting a unique negotiation between the new syntax of Cubism and artists' individual political, social, and intellectual contexts.

* Ahmad Mashadi (2006) "Negotiating Modernities: Encounters with Cubism in Asian Art." In *Cubism in Asia: Unbounded Dialogues* (exhibition catalog, pp. 215–18). Singapore: Singapore Art Museum.

Modern Art in Africa, Asia, and Latin America: An Introduction to Global Modernisms, First Edition.
Edited by Elaine O'Brien, Everlyn Nicodemus, Melissa Chiu, Benjamin Genocchio, Mary K. Coffey, and Roberto Tejada.

Further Readings

Clark, John (1998) *Modern Asian Art. Sydney,* Australia: Fine Arts Press.
Sabapathy, T. K. (1995) *Modernity and Beyond: Themes in South East Asian Art.* Singapore: Singapore Art Museum.
Tadayasu, Sakai (1993) "Was Japanese Fauvism Fauvist?" In John Clark (ed.), *Modernity in Asian Art* (pp. 128–34). Sydney, Australia: Wild Peony.

> *Since the beginning of the 20th century, a new atmosphere has emerged in the European artistic community, comprised of the outcries of the Fauvists, the twists of the Cubists, the vehemence of the Dadaists and the cravings of the Surrealists ... It is time for a new atmosphere to emerge throughout the 20th century artistic community in China.*
>
> – *The Storm Club Manifesto* composed by Ni Yide[1]

[...]

Rather than a self-contained set of aesthetic principles sustained as a distinct conceptual category, Cubism appeared as part of a broad category of "Western art" or "Western painting", engaged, negotiated, adapted and advanced in relation to a broader societal need for cultural change – the need to move away from traditional systems of social organisation to ones that were considered more progressive. This was instigated by the colonial agency of change or the threat of being colonised, and/or a push towards an idea of a modern nation. The Chinese regard for Western art during the 1930s, as seen in *The Storm Club Manifesto* by Ni Yide above, is indicative of such shifts.

Modernity is not a singular phenomenon. Societies across Asia during the late 19th century and the early 20th century underwent dramatic processes of political, economic and cultural transformations. Common features of such transformations included the arrival of and negotiations with newer forms of knowledge and technology acquired from engagements with the West, often mediated through colonisation. Yet, differentiated histories and colonial legacies created modern experiences that were diverse, with multiple forms of reception, responses and outcomes.

By and large, Cubism is privileged as a Western art movement. Its use or adoption by modern Asian artists, whose practices were by and large lacking in their direct contributions to specific foundational discourses of modernism in Europe, is seen to be problematic. Seen in relation to limited concepts of originality and authenticity, questions into the merits and value of these Asian engagements were often raised. Yet, a critical consideration of history allows for the appreciation of discourses that bifurcate and evolve in conjunction to differing contexts and situations. In his 1964 reassessment of Cubism in Western art history – as an attempt to re-look at the critical emphasis for the "Analytical" over "Synthetic", and in doing so recover or recuperate Salon Cubism – Daniel Robbins questioned the privileging of Picasso's *Les Demoiselles d'Avignon* as the origin of Cubism, stating that such an assumption was unhistorical. Instead, he advocated a broader historical engagement by exploring and focusing on aesthetic developments that took place in the 19th century in art as well as critical writings on culture and society of the broad period. This involved the need to define the principal experience of the era connecting the many practitioners as well as the circulation of intellectual stimuli. For Robbins, "these involved the interaction of vast space with speed and action, with simultaneous work, commerce, sport and flight; with the modern city and the ancient country, with the river, the harbour and the bridge and, above all, with time, for the sense of time – involving memory, tradition, and accumulated cultural thought – created the reality of the world."[2] Writing in 2004, David Cottington recognises Robbins' assertion on the need to reassess the historical assumptions of Cubism. However, he remarked on Robbins' overemphasis on the analytical/synthetic binarism in Cubism and a tendency towards privileging formalisms found in Cubism, and as such his apologia for the academism of Salon Cubism. Cottington observed that Robbins' approach "failed to be radical enough", pointing towards the need to acknowledge the intensity and complexity of political and intellectual developments taking place in France and Europe at the time. These were contributive to the thinking amongst the avant-garde, a cause which Cottington took up and advanced in his book *Cubism and its Histories*. He advocates a notion of heteronomy in history given Cubism's development in relation to a number of discourses – independent in their origins and purpose but yet interconnected – that gave meaning to the experience of modernity in Paris and Europe [...]

This heteronomy may be extended to the survey of Cubism in other parts of the world including Asia. What follows is the consideration of geography and time, the processes of diffusion that involve encounters with localities and their histories, and given this process of diffusion, the "disjunctive" lag that suggests a dynamic purpose and intents over different times. Commonalty of experience occurred rarely and [was] mediated or made possible in most instances through political or communal relations between nations or groups. Comparable events or developments tended to occur at different times. Japan's engagement with European modernism took place early given the impetus of the Meiji Restoration of 1868. Developments in art quickly echoed those in Europe. Translations of writings by early European Cubists Albert Gleizes and Jean Metzinger appeared in Japan as early as in 1912, and works by Yorozu Tetsugoro during the 1910s indicated attempts to investigate the use of Cubistic elements. Korean and Chinese developments were also influenced by Japan given their proximity and relations with Japan during the early decades of the 20th century. But in other Asian countries, that adaptation or appropriation of Western modern styles, in particular Cubism, generally occurred later. Even then, the type of Cubism found in the internationalist Indonesian Bandung School showed greater interest in addressing the intense ideological struggle that pitted the "universalist-humanist" against the left-oriented art of the Yogyakarta School in a contest to shape Indonesian national identity during the immediate period of independence from Dutch colonial rule. As shown in Cubistic experimentations in Indonesia and elsewhere including India and Southeast Asia, artists were also susceptible to an engagement with European modernism as a broad series of stylistic propositions that were open to appropriations, to be recoded within specific localised discourses. Western styles were often engaged simultaneously given their historicity as well as the tendencies for artists to seek out individualised forms of expression concomitant to a wider notion of nationalism and internationalism that grew in force over the period of the 1950s, culminating in the dominance of Abstract Expressionism. Ahmad Sadali's *Central Park, New York* was painted in 1962, a work that demonstrated resistance against the heavy ideological onslaught of the cultural leftists of the Yogyakarta School supported by the Indonesian state and Sadali's insistence upon a universalist-humanist commitment to art development. Hence, although points of convergence between various national discourses across Asia may be identified and extrapolated, multiple modernity or modernities may be used to describe the varied cultural or artistic developments taking place in different parts of Asia. As described by John Clark,

> The various histories of art discourses within the field of modern Asian art take place within the wider histories of cultures and state units. These produce constraints, institutional structures, and the resource base for developments within art. They limit or facilitate its possibilities.[3]

For Jim Supangkat, such situation gave rise to particularised engagements that offers for each country,

> … its own modernism in reaction to specific artistic conditions, [these countries] adapted these aspects of European modernism that is most congenial to its soil, and finally pursued its own ways of appropriating and indigenising a European phenomenon. Modernism, then, was not a neutral process, welcomed with a fresh and unproblematic enthusiasm as a liberating impulse to an art floundering in academic formulas.[4]

Further, modern art influences such as Cubism made [their] way to Asia through varying channels, in both direct and indirect ways, arriving in various locales at various times often intermingled with other past or emerging modern idioms and forming a vast reservoir of aesthetic and stylistic ideas. Cubism's radical approach to image-making – spatial and temporal fragmentation, abstract qualities, rejection of past conventions, its appropriation of popular culture – was appealing for Asian artists in search of a vocabulary to express an age that was both hopeful and tumultuous, as well as to express emergent concepts of the Self. In Asia, the fascination with Cubism connects to the notion of the avant-garde. Rather than a tradition of avant-garde characterised by superseding of styles, developments in Asia have to be read in relation to function, rather than form, as noted by Clark, "… in terms of its anti-establishment stance considered against the modernism of the current … or in terms of its proclaiming an identity that would be followed by younger artists."[5] Hence he continues, "modernism can be seen as some set of procedures where the subject of art discourses is the way stylistic formalities operate on themselves in the material substratum of works, or serve as a means for the recoding of styles in the discourse of Interpretation. The group of artists who carry out these fraught and risky operations can be associated to the avant-garde."[6]

The avant-gardist "recoding" of modernism or Cubism can be contextualised by the concept of the Self and the Collective emerging during the early decades of the 20th century. In Western art, Cubism provided an unerring language for artists to describe and demonstrate the processes of change that took place during the early decades of the 20th century. It emerged during an era of widespread dissatisfaction with the positivism, materialism and determinism that accorded little to the concepts of "free will" and the place of individuals. Scientific models were increasingly seen to be insufficient to explain the complexity of the human condition. The writings and theories of philosophers like Henri Bergson and Friedrich Nietzsche challenged notions of absolutist truths and propounded the relativity of knowledge. The Cubist movement recognised through these writings the perceptual limitations of the human eye, and hence the illusionistic nature of empiricist approaches in image-making that were grounded in Euclidean geometry – which was the construction of space through perspective. New scientific and philosophical insights highlighted the inadequacies of material appearances in capturing realities hidden from vision, or perceptible through the contingency of the individual mind. Mental states, consciousness and duration provided a "simultaneity" that revealed a myriad variation of realities. For the Asian artists, the self-emancipating experience of modernity was made complex by the unique histories out of which they emerged and the unfolding realities concomitant to political and social changes, that resulted in tensions between the Self and the Collective. In Japan, an emergent ideology of individualism (*kojinshugi*) inspired by Western philosophical and political thought following the Meiji Restoration in 1868 was seen as a key defining factor in Japan's entry into the modern era. According to Gennifer Weisenfeld, "it broached serious questions concerning the locus of Japanese identity in the wake of the government's aggressive policy of westernisation, opened a discussion on the nature of the autonomous self, and prompted an unprecedented exploration of psychological interiority and subjectivity in the arts … it also addressed the issue of the social role of this newly autonomous individual."[7] This is echoed by Mark Sandler, whose study on Matsumoto Shunsuke's writings and the Japanese artistic discourse in the immediate period before World War II reveals "the contest between the claim of validity made for artistic self-expression and the assertion of cultural authority vested in the larger collectivity, as represented by the nation-state." In the case of Matsumoto, this discourse was characterised by a resistance against the hostile "state-defined concepts of [artistic and communal] value."[8] Early cubo-futurist [paintings from the 1920s] provide examples of artistic attitudes toward state and society, expressed through a sense of crisis, peril and pessimism.

In Republican China, such transformation of self was mediated through aesthetic education – giving rise to a new class of individuals and the avant-garde. As expressed by Ken Lum, writings by Lu Xun and the rise of modern Chinese literature were transformative in changing values away from feudalism, freeing artists from the dogmatic chain of Confucian morality. This is often described as the influence of Nietzsche's Existentialism on Lu Xun's thoughts, where a spirit of individualism situates the individual against the masses, and the individual against the collective. In contrast, Cai Yuanpei, China's Minister for Education during the Republican period was influenced by an organic Hegelian view of society in which an individual's measure was linked to his or her performance in and for society. Diverse intellectual approaches of Lu and Cai provided a unique complexion to the Chinese avant-garde that involved a dynamic confluence of the force of individualism and the moderating force of communitarian needs. While the May Fourth Movement of 1919 championed by Lu Xun attempted to implant into Chinese culture the concepts of "enlightenment (*qimeng*)", the 1920s and 1930s was a difficult period characterised by social and political challenges with "mounting social distress, negligent popular and economic support, and demands especially from the left, to surrender this brand of introspective, European rooted modernism to the project of nationalism, and political reform" in favour of "national salvation (*jiuwang*)."[9] Through the woodcut movement, points of confluence between competing notions of self were established. […] [D]evelopments along economic, industrial, military, social, cultural and intellectual fronts and such manifestations are symptoms of progressiveness, but they also exemplify the anxiety over changes in societal values and potential repercussions – foreshadowing the intensifying ideological struggles in China. In order to maintain art's communicative value for the masses, the centrality and the coherence of the figure is maintained. […] The Asian artist as an avant-garde oscillated between individualism and communitarian interests. As such, while Cubism deployed by avant-gardists offered an expression based on individual visions, it also advanced to address social and political concerns based on a broader communitarian vision.

That "recoding" of modernism can also be located within artistic attempts to seek access into international discourses. This can be highly problematic and even risky, as questions can be raised about the substantive value of Asian modern expressions in an international system dominated by the West, and artistic commitment to local political and cultural concerns. In describing the motivations of Indian modern artists from the 1950s, Dalmia locates this tendency towards internationalism as an irresistible outcome of cultural engagements which were multi-directional and promiscuous,

> Their exemplars were Paris, Munich, New York, and London. In situating themselves internationally, the artists were able, for a brief period, to be on an equal footing with the rest of the world. It has been contended that much of the work of the modernists was imitative of the West and hence "hybrid". Issues of cultural diffusion, however, can be informed by innate hierarchies. After all, direct influences were

> drawn from African and Oceanic art by Picasso, Persian art by Matisse, and Polynesian art by Gauguin. It is by now well established that art does not exist in isolation but always arises out of influences. Cultural diffusion is a universal phenomenon that cannot be privileged in any way as the exclusive domain of any country. It is far more fruitful to examine in what sense art is borrowed, and how it is invested in meaning.[10]

At the same time, these international engagements could not be undertaken with careless disregard for the need for discursive forms of continuities prefigured by critical artistic commitments made earlier,

> The artists had stepped into the difficult terrain of Indian art where variety of styles intermingled. They had to find a means of assimilating classical art, folk art, miniature painting and the different forms of western art that existed alongside and from this medley of schools they were to create their own mode of expression.[11]

Here, "to create their own mode of expression" is to project into modernity the imaginary of tradition and concepts of the past. Modern art was thus invested with forms that sought to clarify points of cultural anchoring or points of origination, or commitment to a national or communitarian ideal or type in the face of impending social and physical changes. Not surprisingly in Indian modern art, artists like George Keyt and N.S. Bendre made references to traditional and folk subjects or local iconographies. This susceptibility towards concepts of the tradition allowed Cubistic interests to develop in conjunction with decorative tendencies focusing on recuperation of motifs and design drawn from tradition.

The "belatedness" of Cubism in Asia has to be seen in relation to modalities of modernism and their capacity in appropriating newer aesthetic forms. Further, the seeming "disjuncture of time" between developments across Asia can also be seen in relation to the differing political resonances and their intensities. Formal and theoretical explorations in Japan and to some extent Korea and China occurred early. But continuities might have been subjected to broad political developments and state impositions on art. By 1949 with the formation of [the] People's Republic of China, leftist ideology became a dominant feature in cultural discipline. Subject to state scrutiny, avant-garde tendencies gave way to the more instructive interests of Social Realism. While the space for modernistic explorations in China became increasingly limited under Communist rule, elsewhere in Asia, post-War processes of de-colonisation and the rise of nationalism resulted in an intense search for notions of modernity grounded in the explorations of national and cultural identities. Given the extent to which such experiences were shared by many nations across Asia, the 1950s may be seen as one of the most significant periods in which positions constituting the modern were being explored and advanced by differing groups, at times in oppositional stance to each other. This may be expressed in relation to debates between "conservatives" and "modernists" and/or "nationalists" and "universalists/humanists". In most instances, those that constituted the "modernists" or the "universalists" would involve tendencies toward abstraction, characterised by the use of Cubistic techniques to advance new pictorial values. In Manila, the works of the Neo-Realists such as Vicente Manansala, Cesar Legaspi and Romeo Tabuena provided an expression of the modern, characterised by their use of fragmentation and transparency to evoke readings of the modern experience – with latent yet purposeful interests in social critique and popular struggles – through maintaining a clear line of interest in familiar subjects and themes drawning from folk and religious motifs. In British Malaya, artists of the Nanyang School, principal practitioners like Chen Wen Hsi and Cheong Soo Pieng – *émigré* artists from China – developed their Cubistic techniques through explorations into Southeast Asian imageries such as rural landscapes and their indigenous inhabitants. They engaged with issues of inter-ethnic engagements within a context of a nascent nationalism leading towards national independence of Singapore and Malaysia. Given their formative roots in Chinese academies, their artistic explorations in the *Nanyang* (Southseas) provided valuable insights into key directions in Chinese art taking place outside of China after the introduction of Communist rule. In China itself, it was only during the 1980s with the reopening of China that a belated return to formalistic explorations took place. In the context of communist China, Qu Leilei's work entitled *Youth* completed in 1980 carries a sense of the radical. It is a departure from the Realist conventions in favour of an abstracted space created by a play of lines and flat-coloured planes and the use of the female nude in place of conventional nationalistic themes.

From the above passages, several implications may be drawn. It is not possible to rigidly periodise Cubistic engagements in Asia in the same manner as historical readings in Western art. If the period between 1906 and 1914 is seen to be most congenial to an analysis of the development of Cubism in Europe, its presence in Asia was spread across different times at different geographical locations concomitant to the diffusion of ideas through varying points of access, education and evolving national histories. Asian engagements with Cubism [form] part of a larger artistic negotiation with shifting and evolving concepts and imaginaries of modernity. Heterogeneity of histories and cultures [informs] the nature and extent of such engagements. Predicated by specific discourses of Self, Society and Nation, and backgrounded by the seismic shifts in ideology and transformations of state structures, Cubism and Cubistic techniques offered currencies in which transactions with the modern experience might have taken place, and were advantageous for their foregrounding of modernistic sensations and sensibilities and that of the new. While developments in Japan, Korea and China occurred early through direct contacts with the West and influences from Tokyo to other emerging centres like Shanghai and Seoul, the 1950s offered greater depth in the articulation of Cubistic techniques in Asian art. In particular, the developments taking place in India and Southeast Asia were linked to varying intensities of post-colonial nationalism, and the ensuing political struggles that gave rise to varied cultural and artistic articulations. "Indigenisation" of Cubism occurred simultaneously in relation to emerging internationalist concerns which involved broad engagements with diverse Western art styles. These were largely approached in ways that were non-hierarchical, but yet leading towards abstraction as a dominant theme. Here we may witness the intermingling of Realist, Fauvist, Futurist, Impressionist, Surrealist and Expressionist elements which offered a syncretic synthesis for myriad expressions. These were often advanced as critiques against prevailing conventions in art making such as the lyrical academism found in genre paintings. These transactions involved necessary formal and conceptual negotiations, inflecting and transposing Cubism from its "originating" precepts found in European traditions and articulated in relation to functions it might have performed in preexistent fields of practice across Asia. Diffused over geography and time, engendered with differentiated or new formal and conceptual interests and disciplined by social and political circumstances, the hegemonic centrality of Cubism dissipates, and in its place a plurality of dynamic interlocking modernities and aesthetic visions have emerged.

Notes

1 Quoted by Zheng, Shengtal, "Waves lashed the Bund from the West: Shanghai Art scene in the 1930s", in Danzker, Jo-Anne Bimie et al. (ed.), *Shanghai Modern: 1919–1945*, Ostfildern-Ruit: Hatje Cantz, 2004, p. 193. [See "The Storm Society *Manifesto*" in this volume.]

2 Robbins, D., "Albert Gleizes: Reason and Faith in Modern Painting" in *Albert Gleizes 1881–1953*, exh. cat., New York: Solomon R. Guggenheim Museum, 1964, pp. 12–25; quoted by Cottington, David, *Cubism and its Histories*, Manchester University Press, 2004, p. 219.

3 Clark, John, *Modern Asian Art*, Sydney: Craftsman House, G + B Arts International, 1998, p. 19.

4 Supangkat, Jim, "The Emergence of Indonesian Modernism and its Background" in *Asian Modernism, Diverse Development in Indonesia, the Philippines, and Thailand*, exh. cat., Tokyo: Japan Foundation Asia Centre, 1995, p. 204.

5 Clark, 1998, p. 217.

6 Ibid, p. 220.

7 Weisenfeld, Gennifer, "Mavo's conscious constructivism: art, individualism, and daily life in interwar Japan – Japan 1868–1945: Art, Architecture, and National Identity", http://www.findarticles.com/p/articles/mi_m0425/is_n3_v55/ai_18798612/print, accessed June 2005.

8 Sandler, Mark H., "The living artist: Matsumoto Shunsuke's reply to the state – Japan 1868–1945: Art, Architecture, and National Identity", http://www.findarticles.com/p/articles/ml_m0425/is_n3_v55/ai_18798613/print, accessed June 2005.

9 Lum, Ken, "Aesthetic Education in Republican China: A Convergence of Ideals" in Danzker, op cit., p. 222.

10 Dalmia, Yashodhara, *The Making of Modern Indian Art: The Progressives*, New Delhi: Oxford University Press, 2001, pp. 47–8.

11 Ibid, p. 45.

Section 1

India

15

When Was Modernism in Indian Art?

Geeta Kapur*

This pioneering 1992 essay is an attempt by Geeta Kapur, a leading Indian art critic and curator, to locate Indian modernism both chronologically and ideologically. Her aim is to wrest Indian modernism from the Eurocentric paradigm of mainstream art history and theory that has discounted Indian modern art as belated and derivative. This densely written piece outlines an alternative critical structure for Indian modern art, one that comprehends the contexts and creative tensions of art making unique to India but relevant to other non-Western colonial/postcolonial nations.

India, the "jewel in the crown" of the British Empire, was colonized from 1858 to 1947, years coincident with modernism in Europe. While Kapur acknowledges India's early cosmopolitan moderns, such as Rabindranath Tagore and Amrita Sher-Gil, she sees continental Indian modernism as an "ongoing project" not truly launched until mid-century and bound up with the nationalist struggle for independence from British colonial rule. Kapur makes the case for the manifestation of modernity in Indian art as being different in almost every way from that in Europe and America. Because of the disjunctions, the author suggests a theoretical model for Indian modern art as simultaneously "modern" and "postmodern" according to hegemonic Euro-US definitions. Thus, for example, narrative abundance – magical and social realism – is

* Geeta Kapur (2000) "When Was Modernism in Indian Art?" In *When Was Modernism: Essays on Contemporary Cultural Practice in India* (pp. 297–324). New Delhi, India: Tulika Books.

Modern Art in Africa, Asia, and Latin America: An Introduction to Global Modernisms, First Edition. Edited by Elaine O'Brien, Everlyn Nicodemus, Melissa Chiu, Benjamin Genocchio, Mary K. Coffey, and Roberto Tejada.

characteristic of Indian modernism, yet in Europe and the United States narrative art is considered a postmodern "return of the real" signifying the "end" of modernism.

With the benefit of hindsight we can identify this essay as one of the earliest efforts by a regionally based scholar to take into account the specific cultural circumstances and references which shape and distinguish modern Asian art. Kapur's essay sets a powerful example for the development of new ideas of alternative, parallel, or intersecting modernities in Asian art, which have been developed and expanded by historians, critics, and curators, including many of those whose work is included in this volume.

Further Readings

Clark, John (1994) "Modern Indian Art: Some Literature and Problematics." Occasional Paper no. 21. Research Institute for Asia and the Pacific, University of Sydney, Australia.

Mitta, Partha (2007) *The Triumph of Modernism: Indian Artists and the Avant Garde 1922–1947*. London, England: Reaktion Books.

[...]

[...] it may be worth mentioning that modernism as it develops in postcolonial cultures has the oddest retroactive trajectories, and that these make up a parallel aesthetics. It is crucial that we do not see the modern as a form of determinism to be followed, in the manner of the stations of the cross, to a logical end. We should see our trajectories crisscrossing the western mainstream and, in their very disalignment from it, making up the ground that restructures the international. Similarly, before the west periodizes the postmodern entirely in its own terms and in that process also characterizes it, we have to introduce from the vantagepoint of the periphery the transgressions of uncategorized practice. We should reperiodize the modern in terms of our own historical experience of modernization and mark our modernisms so that we may enter the postmodern at least potentially on our own terms.

Modernization in India is a real if incomplete historical process. Dating from the British colonial enterprise, the process dovetails with the efforts of the post-independence Indian state to establish, through a large public sector and a planned economy, a balanced growth of industry. [...]

Modernity is a way of relating the material and cultural worlds in a period of unprecedented change that we call the process of modernization. It is also an ontological quest with its particular forms of reflexivity, its acts of struggle. Modernity takes a precipitate historical form in the postcolonial world, while its praxis produces a cultural dynamic whereby questions of autonomy, identity and authenticity come to the fore. These are desired individually but are sought to be gained in collectivity. Even the tasks of subjectivity, so long as they are unresolved, require acts of allegorical exegesis – often via the nation. There is a chronological fix between nationhood and modernity so that both may stand in for a quest for selfhood. Ever challenged in the postcolonial world, modernity continues to provide a cutting edge; it marks necessary historical disjunctures in the larger discourse on sovereignty.

[...]

Given [the] obstacle race of history it is possible to argue that Indian artists have only now become fully modern – in what is characterized as the postmodern age. I mean this in the sense of being able to confront the new without flying to the defence of tradition; of being able to cope with autonomy in the form of cultural atomization by invoking *and* inverting notions of romantic affiliation. That is to say, the mythology of an indigenous 'community' and the lost continent of an 'exile' – both alibis borrowed from the grander tradition of the romantic – are allowed to shade off into the current form of identity polemics. This already mature modernism means accepting the 'dehumanization' and decentering of the image. It means being self-conscious through an art-historical reflexivity; that is, through overcoming the anxiety of influence by overcoming the problem of originality itself. It is not surprising that in a country like India with its cultural simultaneities, its contradictory modes of production, modernism should have been realized through the promptings of postmodernism. For, in economic terms, modernization declares its full import when it comes to be propelled by global capitalism.

[...]

The Politics of Modernism

The 'when' in the title of this essay is of course polemically placed. It refers to a period of self-reckoning locked in with a commitment to collective social change. It refers to the project of figuring subjectivity as a locus of potential consciousness. The when is a site of vexed doubling within colonial/postcolonial identity and the permanent ambivalences that it launches.

The painful debate on identity, nowhere more viscerally handled than by Frantz Fanon,[1] is a debate within the modern consciousness at the last juncture of decolonization when the question of freedom is lifted out of an existential universalism and cathected upon the subordinated yet intrepid body-presence of the 'other'. A condensed unit of humanity drawn from an overwhelming demographical explosion caused by the emergence of the colonized people, this other displaces the safe space occupied by the pristine self in western ontological discourse. The entire western project for authentic being thus comes to be differently historicized in the moment of decolonization. Identity is seen not simply as a rational individuating project within the utopian plenitude of romantic community. It also involves reclaiming the ground lost (or never found) in history, the ground where the self may yet recognize itself in the form of a collective subject.

[...]

[…] it is worth recalling with Fredric Jameson that the modern itself had a politicality far greater than we are taught to recognize.[2] He notes the persistent use of the vocabulary of political revolution in the aesthetic avantgardes which complemented, perhaps even compensated for, the deep subjectivity to which modernist works were committed. That subjectivity itself prefigured a utopian sense of impending transformation where society was seen to be moving towards a greater democracy.

It is worth remembering this because there is a further case for reinforcing the fact in nonwestern societies where the modern, occurring in tandem with anti-colonial struggles, is deeply politicized and carries with it the potential for resistance. This is progressive as also polemical, so that there is a tendentious angle on modernity within our cultures whether they draw out theories of domination/subordination from the subaltern point of view (after Gramsci), or build an identity politics in a rhetorical mode (after Fanon). For Indians there is, besides, a profoundly paradoxical entry into the modern: the entire discourse against the modern (after Gandhi) gives us another utopian option to consider, one which is in its own way a negative commitment of tremendous force in the achievement of modern India.

The discrepancies in the stages of capitalist development in India remain so huge that the modern is charged with strong anomalies. Modernization, both desired and abhorred throughout the nationalist period, is continually contested even in the Nehruvian period. Indian modernity is often quite circumspect, mediated as it is to a point of handicap by negative evaluations of the very practice that it is evolving.

There is the further question as to what categories Indian modernism adopts. Is it the aristocratic/high art category or the more historicist one found in modernism's conjuncture with realism? Or does Indian modernism satisfy the condition of romantic radicalism in its bid to align with the 'liberating vanguard of popular consciousness'?[3]

The moderns anyway stage a mock confrontation between the mandarins and the luddites, a tantalizing play between the classical and the popular, which is worth our while to consider. More specifically, the modern period cherishes great artists who, as Fredric Jameson suggests, are seen to be holding over some archaic notions of aesthetic production, a handcraft aesthetic within a modernizing economy, and in the process valorizing perhaps for the last time a utopian vision of a more human mode of production.[4] This is especially true for third-world cultures. In India primitive techniques, artisanal skills, iconographic references are much valorized; and the modern, comprising the indigenous and the avantgarde, has a two-way relay and a paradoxical politics.

[…]

Indian Modernism: A Brief Account

If Indian artists have often appeared to be hamstrung over the progressivist as against 'correctly' modernist definition of modernism, if they have seemed to be stuck at the crossing-over, it is not so surprising. They are living out the actual material transition. Let me recall notationally the history of the modern in Indian art.

Indian artists have been tardy in making a direct avowal of modernism. They have moved on from the sceptical position held by Ananda Coomaraswamy and Abanindranath Tagore through the first three decades of the twentieth century to a more complex engagement that was developed in Santiniketan by Rabindranath Tagore, and taken over at different levels of complexity by Nandalal Bose, Ramkinkar Baij and Benodebehari Mukherjee from the 1930s. It is precisely at this juncture that a modernist vocabulary (as against initiatives which laid down, for half a century before, propitious ground for modernization) was introduced in several brave gestures. A rural boy in Tagore's Santiniketan, Ramkinkar Baij, ventured to introduce, in a somewhat hazardous manner, a postcubist expressionism and through that means to openly valorize primitive/peasant/proletarian bodies, to give them an axial dynamic. He thereby sought to bring through the ruse and reason of indigenous subject-matter a methodological shift in constructing the image.

This was differently taken up by Jamini Roy in Calcutta during the 1930s. Roy 'objectified' the tradition by bringing the question of folk iconicity and urban commodification face-to-face. Exactly at the same time there was an alternative in the form of the interwar realism initiated by the part-European, Paris-trained artist, Amrita Sher-Gil. With her intelligent masquerade as the oriental/modern/native woman, she gave to this emerging modernism a reflexive turn. She died a sudden death in Lahore in 1941, the year of death of the octogenarian savant Rabindranath Tagore. By then Indian art had begun to pose considerable formulations on modernism.

A reckless manner of cultural symbiosis was reenacted by the Bombay-based artists Francis Newton Souza and Maqbool Fida Husain in the late 1940s. They belonged to near working-class backgrounds and to minority communities (Christian and Muslim). Other important artists of this six-member group, significantly called the Progressive Artists' Group, were Sayed Haider Raza and the dalit artist K.H. Ara. Together these artists achieved, in the first decade of independence, a positively modernist stance. Several artists' groups claiming modernism came into existence during the 1940s and 50s in Calcutta, Bombay and Madras. Of these the Bombay Progressives were the most 'correctly' modernist: they worked with a mandatory set of transfer motifs of the dispossessed but they offered a formalist manifesto that was to help the first generation of artists in independent India to position themselves internationally.

The two enactments of modernism are seen developing together in India. In the romantic antecedents of that term the heralds and witnesses to social change ought to be carrying the flag of modernization (and thus also of modernism), which includes expressionist realisms of different shades. Thus in India M.F. Husain, K.C.S. Paniker, the Mexico-trained Satish Gujral and Ram Kumar, briefly inspired by the French left, held that position until the early 1960s. Just as artists with a commitment to social transformation set the terms revolt each in his/her context of community or nation, the outriders created the necessary disjuncture: the artists who established themselves in India became cultural emblems within a progressive national state, and those who left for Paris and London became equally emblematic outsiders of modern fiction. They embodied the modernist impulse of choosing metropolitan 'exile' – the first criterion of modernity, according to Raymond Williams.[5]

Like hundreds of garret artists in Paris and in London, these early 'settlers' – prominent among them Souza and Tyeb Mehta in London, Raza, Akbar Padamsee and Krishna Reddy in Paris – celebrated their solitude, their radical estrangement and the immanent 'truth' of art language, to become the first heralds of internationalism in India.

The premise of international art was not of course innocent of ideology. Even as it led the nonaligned movement, India stood closer to the second world than to the first and the west continued to be marked as imperialist, however alluring its cities, its citadels of modernism, may have been for Indian (and myriad other) artists. The older imperialist markings were transferred to postwar USA where, as we know, it had become ideology proper. The American cultural establishment elicited from the boldly original and freedom-loving artists grouped together as American abstract expressionists, the slogan of cultural 'freedom' vis-à-vis the socialist bloc. In the bargain, New York with its immense energy won the day even over the erstwhile Parisian fix. Those who had been part of the School of Paris, among them some of the best Indian artists of the 1950s, turned sympathetically to New York in the 1960s. They gained a fresh painterly ground and the poetics of an authorial gesture.

At the ideological level one may add that the US agenda to export cultural freedom came to India late. Fellowships for artists' residencies in New York were made available in the 1960s and 1970s to well-known Indian artists by the J.R.D. Rockefeller III Fund as a kind of postscript to its blatant strategies of intervention in Latin America; and the American side was highlighted by Clement Greenberg's visit to India in 1967 when he accompanied a large official exhibition of modern American painting sent by the Museum of Modern Art, New York. But the ideology as such did not make headway because of the nationalist self-regard persistent among even the most international of Indian artists.

Meanwhile there was a divergence in the Indian art scene itself. A generation of Indian modernists came to be attracted once again to a European, more precisely Italian and Spanish, rather than an American aesthetic. Artists like Jeram Patel, J. Swaminathan, Jyoti Bhatt, Himmat Shah and Ambadas responded to the informal aesthetic (of Antoni Tapies, Lucio Fontana, Alberro Burri, for example) and this showed up in the *Group 1890* exhibition of 1963. The exhibition manifesto was written by Swaminathan and the catalogue was introduced by the then Mexican ambassador to India, Octavio Paz. The attraction of the eleven-member Group 1890 to material/ritual/occult signs reissued the modernist enterprise in the coming years. It came to be situated with peculiar aptness in a visual culture of iconic forms still extant in India. This indigenism produced a playful modernist vocabulary replete with metaphorical allusions. Nagji Patel is an example. But the surrounding rhetoric of Indianness also grew apace in the 1970s and 80s. It acquired official support both in the National Gallery of Modern Art and the Lalit Kala Akademi with artists like G.R. Santosh gaining national status. This institutional aesthetic tended to shortcircuit some part of this enterprise, leaving a pastiche in the form of an overtly symbolic art proffered as neotantrism.

One is tempted to plot a tendentious narrative of oriental transmutation during the decades 1960–80: to show how the Parisian aesthetic was surmounted by the hegemonic American notions of freedom in the matter of world culture, how this was questioned by the liberationist rhetoric of the Latin world, and how all this contributed to form a distinct (rather than derivative) entity called modern Indian art. And how it acquired a national seal. For at the level of painterly practice many tendencies were recycled within the Indian sensibility. Exuberant forms of abstraction blazoned forth in Raza, Ram Kumar, Padamsee, V.S. Gaitonde. Abstract artists of the erstwhile Group 1890 and the so-called neotantrics held sway, especially the freer among them like Paniker and Biren De, who contributed a subliminal, even ironic symbolism. At the same time, the work of artists with an informal sensibility, like Mohan Samant and Bal Chhabda, surfaced. Finally, artists with an indelible ecriture shone out: I am referring to Somnath Hore's inscription in paper pulp of the social *wound* and Nasreen Mohamedi's capture of private grace in her ink and pencil grids.

These complex developments are only signposted here to fill out the contours of the larger narrative of the modern. By 1978, when the relatively old-style modernist Harold Rosenberg was invited by India to sit on the jury of the Fourth Triennale India, the more strictly modernist style in Indian art, especially abstraction, was on the wane. Rosenberg saw what he was to describe in his generously mocking manner as a 'much of a muchness' of representation by younger artists. He was referring to artists positioned against modernist formalism: late expressionists with a social message and artists trying to tackle the problem of reification in art language and the objects/icons of late modernism who had moved into popular modes and narratives, turning objects into fiction, icons into discourse.

Narrative Extensions

Noting that an interest in allegory had developed across the board but especially in the third world – from Gabriel Garcia Marquez to Salman Rushdie – Fredric Jameson provides an ideological twist to the impulse:

> Fabulation – or if you prefer, mythomania and outright tall takes – is no doubt a sign of social and historical impotence, of the blocking of possibilities that leaves little option but the imaginary. Yet its very invention and inventiveness endorses a creative freedom … agency here steps out of the historical record … and new multiple or

> alternate strings of events rattle the bars of the national tradition and the history manuals whose very constraints and necessities their parodic force indicts.[6]

During the 1970s not only third-world writers but also filmmakers and artists moved into magical realism, counting narrative abundance for deterministically motivating desire. In India this form of quasi-historical representational practice led equally deterministically to a variety of social realisms featuring artists as varied as Krishen Khanna, A. Ramachandran, Gieve Patel and Bikash Bhattacharjee. By the end of the 1970s an affiliation was formed with what was at the time the School of London after R.B. Kitaj – anathema indeed to Paris and New York but seen by several Indian artists of this generation as an antidote to the formalist impasse of late modernist art. This move also tried to take into account the lost phases of twentieth-century art: Mexican muralism, German new objectivity, American regionalism. That is to say, all those artists left in the wide margins of the twentieth century that a too-narrow definition of modernism ignores. This was the virtual manifesto of the 1981 exhibition *Place for People*, featuring Bhupen Khakhar, Gulammohammed Sheikh, Jogen Chowdhury, Vivan Sundaram, Nalini Malani and Sudhir Patwardhan.

The narrative move activated the strong traditions in Indian art itself, including its revived version in the nationalist period. At this juncture K.G. Subramanyan, the wise and witty father-figure linking Santiniketan with Baroda, took up genre painting (on glass) as a form of parody of the high modern. Parodying as well the ideologies of the popular, he slipped over the cusp – beyond modernism – and made a decisive new space for Indian art. This was extended by subversive tugs in social and sexual directions in the hands of an artist like Bhupen Khakhar. A regionalism developed in Baroda and it combined with the urban realism of Bombay. A representational schema for cross-referencing the social ground was realized. A reconfiguration also took place of the realist, the naive and the putatively postmodernist forms of figuration. Indian art, even as it ideologized itself along older progressivist terms, came in line with a self-consciously eclectic and annotated pictorial vocabulary.

If we argue that Indian efforts at finding an identity were reinforced by a kind of ethnographic overspill into fabulous narratives and new ideologies of narration, it can also help position the interest in pictorial narration in Indian contemporary art during the 1970s and 80s in a more provocative stance. To the traditions of K.G. Subramanyan and Bhupen Khakhar add Gulammohammed Sheikh, and we can see how these artists moved via pop art into a representational excess of signs to renegotiate several traditions at once. The intertextuality of their images, the art-historical references, the popular idiom serve as a more confident avowal of a regional and properly differentiated national aesthetic. Art language now affirms its multivalence, opening up the ideology of modernism to the possibility of alternative realities. By its transgressions what is retroactively called the post-modern impulse opens up the structure of the artwork, too-neatly placed within the high culture of modern India. The new narrators rattle the bars of national tradition and let out the parodic force suppressed within it.

During the 1980s a number of Indian artists assume the authorial confidence to handle multifarious references, to deliberately disrupt the convergent philosophy and language of Indian modernism. Prominent among them are women artists of a figurative ture. Arpita Singh, Nalini Malani, Madhvi Parekh and Nilima Sheikh are active in the 1980s. Anupam Sud, Arpana Caur and Rekha Rodwittiya reinforce the turn. These artists introject a subjectivity that is existentially pitched but does not devolve into the currently celebrated schizophrenic freedoms. Gender interventions come to mean that the narrated self is inscribed into the social body through allegorical means with a secret intent that exceeds its textual character. For there is always in our unresolved modernity and in our postmodern retroaction the haunting need to release a repressed consciousness, and in the case of the more politically inclined artists, to introduce a mode of intervention.

[...]

In India for the moment it looks as though there is a modernism that almost never was. The more political among Indian artists may be right after all in believing that the as yet unresolved national questions may account for an incomplete modernism that still possesses the radical power it has lost elsewhere. Positioned as an intrepid form of the human, signified in an order of verticality, thus John Berger introduced Picasso into the arena of the modern: as a vertical man.[7] Despite this male imagining of the modern it may be useful to place, like an archimedean point, a stake on an anthropomorphic truth of the modern revolution. For the Indian artist this stake is beyond irony, and beyond also the proclaimed death of the subject. Mapping the chronological scale of realism/modernism/postmodernism on to the lived history of our own deeply ambivalent passage through this [twentieth] century, it may be useful to situate modernity itself like an elegiac metaphor in the 'new world order'.

Notes

1 The following discussion takes off from Homi Bhabha, 'Remembering Fanon: Self, Psyche, and the Colonial Condition', in *Remaking History*, edited by Barbara Kruger and Phil Mariani, Bay Press, Seattle, 1989.

2 Fredric Jameson, *Postmodernism, Or, The Cultural Logic of Late Capitalism*, Verso, London, 1991, p. 311.

3 [Raymond] Williams, *The Politics of Modernism: Against the New Conformists*, Verso, London, 1989, p. 35.

4 Jameson, *Postmodernism*, p. 307.

5 Williams, *Politics of Modernism*, p. 34.

6 Jameson, *Postmodernism*, p. 369.

7 John Berger, *The Success and Failure of Picasso*, Penguin, Harmondsworth, 1965.

16

The Formalist Prelude

Partha Mitter*

UK-based Indian art historian Partha Mitter argues in this reading – the first chapter (or "formalist prelude") of his book on Indian Modernism – that the avant-garde was launched in India on December of 1922 with the opening of an exhibition in Calcutta of works by Paul Klee, Wassily Kandinsky, and other Bauhaus artists. The essay summarizes engagements with European modern painting in the early 1920s, chiefly Cubism and non-representational art, which superseded a late nineteenth century enthusiasm for European academic styles of realist naturalism adopted by Ravi Varma (1848–1906) and others. The focus is on the work of Gaganendranath Tagore (1867–1938), nephew of Nobel Prize winning poet and artist Rabindranath Tagore who figured so centrally in the development of international modernism in India.

Until the 1920s when Gaganendranath created the series of Cubist-inspired watercolors discussed here, he was an influential political cartoonist, his savage-fun lithographs appearing in Bengali satirical journals such as *Birup Bajra* (*Play of Opposites*) for the general Indian readership. Gaganendranath's cartoons specifically targeted Westernized Indians striving to be more English than their English colonizers. The unequivocal attitude toward authentic identity evidenced by the artist's cartoons supports Mitter's thesis that Gaganendranath's cubistic paintings were not merely weak, un-Indian copies of Western Cubism as English art historian W. G. Archer portrayed them in his 1959 *India and Modern Art*. Rather, in the text that follows, Mitter rereads Gaganendranath's modern paintings from outside the Eurocentric point of view of Archer and mainstream modern art historiography in general as unique transcultural syntheses, distinct not derivative. The claim here is that for Gaganendranath, as for

* Partha Mitter (2007) "The Formalist Prelude." In *The Triumph of Modernism: India's Artists and the Avant-Garde, 1922–1947* (pp. 15–27). London, England: Reaktion Books.

Modern Art in Africa, Asia, and Latin America: An Introduction to Global Modernisms, First Edition.
Edited by Elaine O'Brien, Everlyn Nicodemus, Melissa Chiu, Benjamin Genocchio,
Mary K. Coffey, and Roberto Tejada.

many cosmopolitan modern artists in Western Europe and around the world, Cubism provided a flexible transcultural language of art for individual expression only partly and ambiguously informed by national identity. Gaganendranath can be seen as the pioneering modern painter he was, who, largely eschewing the nationalist preoccupations of his Indian peers, sought to blend the formal qualities of Cubism with local allegorical themes. The results were fantasy-like paintings that depicted, as Mitter puts it, "a mysterious, twilight world of artificial lights and deep shadows that could not be easily deciphered."

Further Reading

Guha-Thakurta, Tapati (1992) *The Making of a New "Indian" Art: Artists, Aesthetics and Nationalism in Bengal, c.1850–1920* (South Asian series). Cambridge, England: Cambridge University Press.

To many of us Cubism's revolutionary mode of representation is synonymous with modernism. It was the first Western movement to attract Indian artists, although it failed to leave any lasting mark until its resurgence in the 1940s. We may take December 1922 as a convenient entry point for modernism in India. An exhibition of works of the Bauhaus artists in Calcutta in that year symbolized the graduation of Indian taste from Victorian naturalism to non-representational art. We first hear of the Western avant-garde in 1914 in the Bengali journal *Prabasi*, which described Brancusi's *Mlle Pogany* as unacceptably bizarre. Its author Sukumar Roy, a fervent believer in naturalism, had previously been a critic of orientalist distortions of reality. (I use orientalism, orientalist artists and oriental art in lower case to refer to the first nationalist art movement in India known as the Bengal School and use capitals for European Orientalists in the Saidian sense.) In his essay, 'Exaggerations [distortions] in Art', Roy acknowledged Cubism's revolutionary objective of challenging academic naturalism, but he rejected its extreme distortions of reality, while he condemned outright Futurist glorifications of war, the machine age and other odious trappings of progress.[1]

Others were more welcoming of modernism. In 1917, the widely read *Modern Review* carried an anonymous piece on 'automatic drawing', which dealt with Freud's impact on avant-garde art.[2] The poet Rabindranath Tagore, who had increasing misgivings about the nationalist Bengal School of art, was intent on broadening the artistic horizon of his university at Santiniketan. In 1919, during a visit to Oxford, he hired Stella Kramrisch (1898–1993) to teach art history at the fledgling art department (Kala Bhavan). Of Austrian-Jewish descent, Kramrisch had received a thorough grounding in art history at the University of Vienna, becoming a renowned authority on Indian art in later life. She became one of the foremost figures in the dissemination of Indian modernist art. At Santiniketan her personal knowledge of the avant-garde made it a living reality for the students.

In January 1922, the globe-trotting polymath and fervent nationalist Benoy Sarkar (1887–1949) decided on a 'much-needed infusion of modernism' into the art of Bengal. His controversial article 'Aesthetics of Young India', sent from Paris to the orientalist journal *Rupam* in 1922, prompted a heated debate.[3] Dismissing the Bengal School's much vaunted 'spirituality' of Indian art as a species of myth making, Sarkar made a passionate plea on behalf of the avant-garde 'aesthetics of autonomy', comparing it with the nationalist demand for self rule or autonomy from the Raj. Finally, he demanded the emancipation of Indian art from the tyranny of literary critics, historical analysts, nationalists and Bolsheviks. A 'dyed-in-the-wool' formalist, who extolled the objectivity of the 'artistic eye', Sarkar considered modernism to be a truly international style that overcame all cultural barriers.[4] Sarkar was in Berlin in the 1920s, where he came under the spell of modernism. His rousing manifesto welcoming formalism and the immediacy of art appreciation however recalls Clive Bell's notion of 'significant form' that distinguished art from 'descriptive painting'. In 1914, Bell asserted that in order to appreciate a work of art we need bring with us nothing 'but a sense of form and colour … Significant form stands charged with the power to provoke aesthetic emotion in anyone capable of feeling it.'[5]

The nationalists felt impelled to respond to Sarkar. Barindranath Ghosh, an intellectual and a former political prisoner, rejected Sarkar's ideas as inimical to Indian culture. Ordhendra Gangoly, editor of *Rupam* and the leading ideologue of the Bengal school, mocked Sarkar's presumption that Indians were unaware of recent developments in Western art: 'I have a secret sympathy for the latest Parisian craze over Negro sculpture. I can recall my own feeling of ecstasy at seeing Polynesian images when I first set foot in Java … I can therefore understand Picasso, Matisse and Derain's first thrills on viewing the Tami masks from New Guinea.'[6] Kramrisch exposed the flaws in Sarkar's formalist canon. A relativist, she rejected the primacy of Western art, arguing that 'significant form' in each individual artistic tradition was a product of a complex interaction of form, content and wider cultural values which suggests her familiarity with Alois Riegl. Referring to the Bengali painter Gaganendranath Tagore's recent experiments in Cubism, she contended that even if an Indian artist used a 'foreign' form such as Cubism, he would still remain Indian since he had internalized the peculiar cultural experience of India.[7]

This engaging dialogue in *Rupam* set the scene for the key date of December 1922, the year that introduced the works of Paul Klee, Wassily Kandinsky and other Bauhaus artists to Calcutta, an Asian city far removed from the metropolitan West. The German school of design (later architecture) in Weimar, the Bauhaus, had attracted radical artists, theoreticians and pedagogues to the institution. In 1921, the Indian Nobel Laureate, Rabindranath Tagore (best known in the West as Tagore), undertook one of his periodic trips to Europe. On 7 May he celebrated his sixtieth birthday in Weimar with readings from his poetry and a recital of his songs at the German National Theatre. Visiting the Bauhaus in Weimar, Tagore quickly sensed the affinities between its teaching methods, imparted by Walter Gropius, Johannes Itten and Georg Muche, and his own holistic experiments at Santiniketan (q.v.). As Oskar Schlemmer, also then at the Bauhaus, noted, there were two elements at the school, a penchant for mysticism and a commitment to the machine, the latter ultimately taking over. Muche and the mystically oriented Itten were deeply involved with Eastern philosophy. At Tagore's suggestion, Muche arranged for a selection of Bauhaus works to be shipped to Calcutta for an exhibition there.[8]

The 14th annual exhibition of the Indian Society of Oriental Art, which opened in Calcutta on 23 December, showcased the Bauhaus works. Among the 250 items shown at the exhibition, the most important were Kandinsky's two watercolours dated 1915 and 1921, and Paul Klee's nine watercolours.[9] There were also works by Lyonel Feininger, Johannes Itten, George Muche, Gerhardt Marcks, Lothar Schreyer, Margit Tery-Adler, Sophie Körner and 49 'practice work[s] in the course of instruction'. The show also included an original work by the English Vorticist Wyndham Lewis and reproductions of other European modern artists. The Bauhaus artists were interested in selling their works and priced them modestly but, with the exception of one of Sophie Körner's works, they remained unsold.[10]

The reverential press previews reaffirmed Kandinsky's international reputation, The *Statesman* of 15 December making it clear that he was the most important figure in the show. The *Englishman* congratulated the society for showing original works by the European avant-garde never before seen in India, paying homage to 'the great Russian', whose Art of the Spiritual had discovered 'emancipation in new forms of art undreamed of in its previous history'.[11] Kramrisch, who wrote the introduction to the catalogue, praised Kandinsky as the first artist to paint pictures without any subject matter and infusing his works with his inner experience. She exhorted the Indian public to study this exhibition, 'for then they may learn that European art does not mean naturalism and that the transformation of the forms of nature in the work of an artist is common to ancient and modern India'.[12] This was to remind not only the public but also critics such as Sukumar Roy that the Bengal School's anti-naturalist credo was akin to Kandinsky's rejection of a materialist conception of art. Her comment highlights the fact that while the artistic objectives of the Western abstract artists and the orientalists were different, they were making a common front against academic art.[13]

The exhibition offered a tantalizing glimpse of an art hitherto known mainly through publications to a milieu that had until now feasted on Alma-Tademas and Lord Leightons. The immediate impact of this show was not obvious but it sounded the death knell not only for academic art in India but also for orientalism, and its engagement with the past. Even Abanindranath, the archpriest of orientalism, quoted Kandinsky a few years later to repudiate his own historicism as an anachronism because, he confessed, it was impossible to live and feel like the ancients.[14] This was in the 1920s when the 'here and now' would seriously challenge historicism, which was administered the final coup de grâce by Abanindranath's own brother Gaganendranath. Once sympathetic to oriental art, Gaganendranath had gone down the path of modernism even before the Bauhaus show, and indeed made his 'Cubist' début at the very same show.[15]

Gaganendranath Tagore, a Poetic Cubist

Gaganendranath Tagore (1867–1938) was the only Indian painter before the 1940s who made use of the language and syntax of Cubism in his painting. Older than Abanindranath by a few years, Gaganendranath was an individualist, who impressed people with his intellect and personal charm. The English painter William Rothenstein met him in 1910 and was much taken with the breadth of his culture and reading. The former Governor of Bengal, the Marquess of Zetland, was a particular admirer of his, commenting on his dynamism tempered by an inner serenity and refinement.[16] Always keen to experiment, Gaganendranath began in the 1880s with 'phrenological' portraits inspired by his uncle's work, followed by delicate pen-and-brush paintings, learned from the visiting Japanese Nihon-ga painter, Taikan.[17] These black and white works, notably of rain-soaked crows, a familiar sight in Calcutta, prepared him for his later monochrome Cubist interiors. In 1908 he joined the oriental art movement, acquiring a major collection of Mughal and Rajput miniatures in the process.

Until the 1920s, Gaganendranath was best known for his brilliantly savage lithographs caricaturing the social mores of colonial Bengal.[18] In early 1922, he seized the 'modernist moment' to realize his artistic vision through Cubism. Evaluating Gaganendranath's Cubism in an essay published that year, Kramrisch asserted, somewhat provocatively, that even though Cubism was a European discovery, its formalist simplicity was neither unique nor significantly different

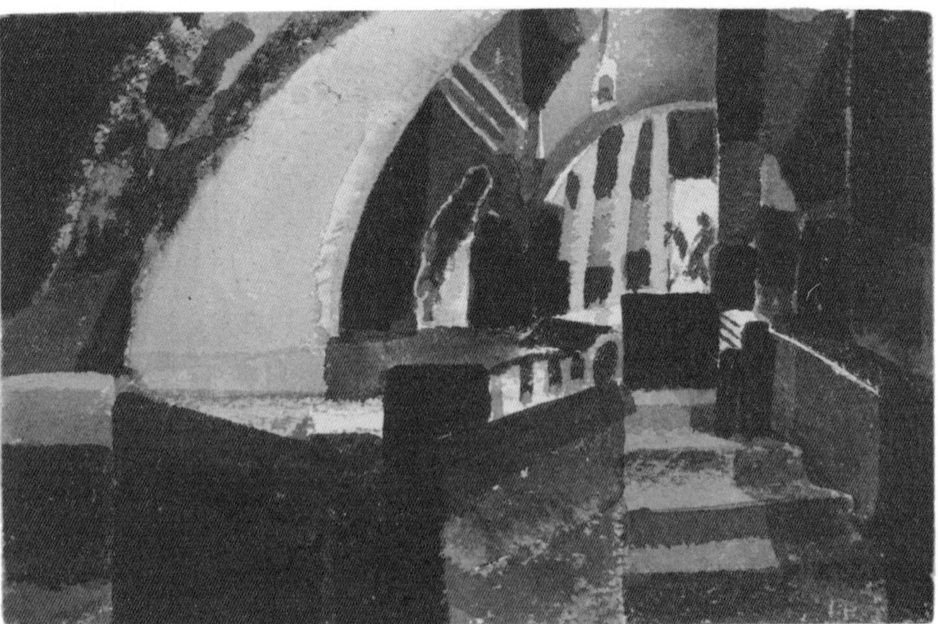

Figure 16.1 Gaganendranath Tagore, *Interior with Figures*, watercolor, India, c.1924. V & A Images/Victoria and Albert Museum.

from the objectives of other forms of non-illusionist art. The Indian artist's 'musical' paintings, she argued, avoided the danger of becoming a sterile form of abstraction by their blend of the allegorical and the formal. His cubes did not build up a systematic structure, but rather externalized the turbulent forces of inner experience, transforming the static geometry of Analytical Cubism into an expressive device. However, she cautioned that Gaganendranath's dynamic diagonal compositions tended to set up a contradiction between the flowing life of Indian art and the geometric rationality of Cubism.[19]

Gaganendranath's Cubist fantasies, including his well-known *House of Mystery*, had their first public exposure alongside the Bauhaus artists at the exhibition of 1922.[20] Two years later, he held an ambitious one-man show, mainly consisting of his Cubist works including *Aladdin and His Lamp, Duryadhana at Maidanab's Palace, The City of Dwarka, Symphony* and other well-known pieces. Kramrisch once again engaged in establishing his essential difference with the European Cubists. While not glossing over his failed experiments, she brought out his strength as a storyteller through his own brand of Cubism, as also his ability to soften Cubism's formal geometry with 'a seductive profile, shadow or outline of human form'.[21]

The paintings were well received in the daily papers, though the reviews dwelled more on his poetic qualities than on the new language of Cubism. The *Englishman*, which had been following his artistic career closely, described his Cubism as a new phase of oriental art, complimenting the artist on his beautiful colours.[22] While the *Statesman* admitted the difficulty of appreciating Cubism's revolutionary language, it praised the painting *Symphony* for successfully blending 'rigid telling cubist lines with mysterious lighting effects reminiscent of Rembrandt'.[23] *Forward* found him to be one of the finest painters of light, confessing that the appeal of his works lay in their beautiful colours, not to mention their intelligibility.[24] By 1925, the *Englishman* acknowledged the power of Gaganendranath's personal treatment of Cubism though it was less certain about Cubism as such.[25] Benoy Sarkar, the avowed modernist, gave Gaganendranath's exhibition at the Indian Society of Oriental Art his unqualified endorsement as 'object lessons in pure art'. 'In such compositions', he wrote, 'we begin to appreciate without the scaffolding of legends, stories, messages and moralizings, the foundations of a genuine artistic sense'.[26]

In 1928 Gaganendranath held his last major retrospective at the Indian Society of Oriental Art. The *Englishman*, once again reviewing the show, crowned him the 'master of modern art in Bengal'.[27] The *Welfare* gave an indication of its awareness of Roger Fry in describing the artist's synthesis of the Bengal School and Cubism as a quest for 'significant form'. Interestingly, the reviewer seemed uncertain about the worth of avant-garde formalism, suggesting that despite his eclectic sources, the Bengali artist had 'shown himself a great painter in the originality and the intenseness of his vision'.[28] In 1930, at 63, a cerebral stroke left the painter paralysed and speechless. He died eight years later.[29]

Around 1915, as Gaganendranath began quietly to withdraw from his brother's nationalist preoccupations, he moved into a poetic fairytale world drawing upon the Bengali stage and literature. While literature nourished his imagination, unlike the orientalists, he was not interested in painterly historicism. It was at this juncture that he discovered Cubism's possibilities. As he later confessed to the journalist Kanhaiyalal Vakil, 'the new technique is really wonderful as a stimulant'.[30] The multiple viewpoints and jagged edges of Cubism offered him the means to create compositions with many-faceted shapes evoking a remote mysterious world, for instance in his imaginary cities, such as the mythical Dwarka, the god Krishna's legendary abode, or Swarnapuri (The Golden City). Mountain ranges also gave him scope for the interplay of diamond-shaped planes and prismatic colours, resulting in fragmented luminosity. What held these zigzagging planes together was a tight formal structure. His other preoccupation was what he called the House of Mystery, inspired by his involvement with his uncle Tagore's plays staged in their home, for which he designed the sets. His growing preoccupation with imaginary interiors mysteriously illuminated by artificial lights hidden from view shows this involvement with the theatre. The painter conjures up a magic world of dazzling patterns, crisscrossing lights and shadows and light-refracting many-faceted forms. His paintings from the 1920s make constant references to stage props, partition screens, overlapping planes and artificial stage lighting. Their endless corridors, pillars, halls, half-open doors, screens, illuminated windows, staircases and vaults remind us a little of Piranesi's Carceri prints or Alain Resnais' film *L'année dernière à Marienbad*.

The obsession with 'prismatic luminosity' led Gaganendranath to look for mechanical devices for intensifying colour patterns. He is known to have often held up a crystal against the light to capture the rainbow colours on the paper placed below. He eventually possessed a kaleidoscope, a device that broke up objects into a fascinating variety of bright hues and geometric shapes. E. H. Gombrich suggests that the inventor of the kaleidoscope had vainly expected it to create 'a new art of colour music'. However, it is precisely this quality that enabled Gaganendranath to compose paintings described by critics as 'less pictures indeed, than visible music and pulsating light'.[31] As his pictorial language evolved, the Indian artist found the dynamic forms of the Futurists more suitable than the more static Analytical Cubism. Yet Gaganendranath's visual conventions remained within the bounds of oriental art. Despite the criticism of the nationalists, the artist insisted that Cubism had simply 'enabled me to [express] better with my new technique … than I used to do with my old methods'.[32] William Rothenstein was convinced that he remained an 'oriental miniaturist with his eye for exquisite lapidary details'.[33]

In the brief seven years (1922 to 1929) that Gaganendranath was engaged in his modernist excursions, he created a fairytale world with the 'language' of Cubism, but without ever spelling out the actual tales themselves. On the surface, his watercolours purported to tell stories, but the stories themselves were hidden behind a mysterious twilight world of artificial lights and deep shadows that could not be easily deciphered. The very ambiguities of his poetic imagery prevented the paintings from becoming illustrative, the whole effect heightened by his use of evocative titles, such as *The Poet on the Island of the Birds, The Seven Brothers Champa* or the *House of Mystery*. The *Englishman* aptly called these a 'new phase of oriental art' with their exquisite colours and miniature format. Gaganendranath's Cubism raises questions about the reception of modernism in India in the 1920s. Revelations of the Bauhaus show notwithstanding, his Cubist excursions threw into sharp relief the problem of reading the avant-garde visual language in a culture that had not yet fully confronted modernism. Today we perhaps take for granted modernism as the natural style of the twentieth century. However, in the 1920s, even in Britain modernism was still a minority affair, let alone in colonial India. At the same time, the initial unease about the new syntax began to give way to its gradual acceptance.[34]

Modernism and Colonial Art History

How are we to read these works – are they Cubist or are they oriental? It was this no-man's-land between Cubist formalism and a poetic narrative that infuriated the colonial art historian W. G. Archer, reared on Clive Bell and Roger Fry's separation of formalist purity from the 'sentimental clutter' and literary associations of narrative art. Fry's aesthetic polarity simply does not make allowances for works that do not fall into either of these categories. Let me take a striking passage in Archer: 'apart from their very evident lack of power – a power which in some mysterious way was present in the work of Braque and Picasso – Gogonendranath's [sic] pictures were actually no more than stylized illustrations … weak as art, but what was more important, they were un-Indian. Not only had Gogonendranath's style no vital affinities with other forms of Indian expression but its prevailing tone seemed frigidly indifferent to Indian feelings, interests or sensibility. As a result, his pictures, despite their modernistic manner, had an air of trivial irrelevance.'[35]

Archer's assessment of Gaganendranath's painting – illustrative quality, lack of power, un-Indian, modernistic 'manner' rather than substance – tells us a great deal about his art historical discourse. He accepted the Western modernist canon, as did his contemporaries, including Indians, as the standard against which all modernist art must be judged. The ideology of 'purity', with its moral connotation, was integral to modernism. Its critique of representational art was inspired by the Platonic distinction between truth and appearance. Its extreme form was the notion of the absolute values of abstract art.[36] His linked expressions, 'stylized illustration' and 'lack of power' were an essential foil to the 'pure' and robust formalism, the very antithesis of meretricious and fussy narrative art. The word 'power' also suggests obvious gender connotations, Archer's primitivist longing found the 'power', absent in Gaganendranath's painting, in abundance in India's tribal sculptures. In *The Vertical Man*, he expressed admiration for the 'masculine' vigour and abstract geometry of Indian tribal art, as he did for the 'peasant art' of medieval Britain. Primitivism had bestowed on modernist art criticism the notion of virility as standing for bold simplicity, as opposed to the weakness of complicated 'feminine' anecdotal painting.[37]

Archer's modernism found both the high sculptures of English cathedrals and Indian temples to be less 'authentic' than their respective examples of primitive art. Yet the English art historian's preference for Indian tribal art in comparison with Indian modernist art did not rest solely on his allegiance to the avant-garde. Notions of virility have been a compelling metaphor of power relations in colonial history, a metaphor derived from anthropology and its myth of the timeless 'primitive' tribes nestling in British protection.[38] Archer's idealization of tribal sculptures as the authentic art of India highlights his ambivalence about Indian nationalism, which he had to confront as a colonial civil servant. One of the persistent assertions of the Raj was that the nationalist movement was unrepresentative. Hostile to the Bengal School, Archer dismissed Gaganendranath's paintings as *déraciné* efforts that lacked the national mandate.[39] There are of course parallels between the new nationalist discourse of primitivism and Archer's idealization of tribal India. However, in contrast to the anti-colonial primitivism of Mahatma Gandhi, for instance, Archer's primitivism was grist to his colonialist mill. Archer's final objection to Gaganendranath's work was its failed modernism. Let us read on: 'His picture, Light and shadow … is made up of blacks, whites and greys and is a simple illustration of geometric architecture … There is no attempt to break the shapes into their fundamental structure or to link them into a single cohering rhythm … The artist merely selected a scene that looked Cubistic and set it down with academic care'.[40] I have already discussed Archer's conclusion that Gaganendranath's works were simply bad imitations of Picasso, and need not repeat the arguments here.

By what criteria can we judge Gaganendranath today? The artist named his paintings 'Cubist', even though he was perfectly aware that he was not seeking to reproduce Picasso. His Cubism makes sense in a global context and against the reception of Cubism in countries other than France. Analytical Cubism or the Braque/Picasso revolution of 1909–10, the great achievement of modernism, finally laid to rest the 500-year-old history of illusionism. Painters since Giotto had related different objects within a picture by means of consistent, directional lighting. Cubists set out to destroy illusionism by arranging objects within a picture formally, and by creating conflicting relationships of light and shadow. Thereby they restored the internal cohesion of a picture so that it was no longer a window to the external world. The implications of its revolutionary form did not affect other artists, Western and non-Western, so much as its flexible non-figurative syntax which could be put to different uses. The driving force behind the Expressionists, Franz Marc, Lyonel Feininger and Georg Grosz, behind the visual poetry of Marc Chagall and behind the orientalist Gaganendranath was the same: objects could be distorted and fragmented at will to create dazzling patterns. But their specific cultural contexts were as different as their artistic aims, not to mention their different artistic agendas. We now know that Eastern European artists created their own versions of Cubism that did not reproduce the Braque-Picasso experiment.[41]

The flexible language of Cubism, with its broken surfaces, released a new energy in Gaganendranath, enabling him to conjure up a painterly fairytale world.

The German avant-grade critic Max Osborn, reviewing the exhibition of modern Indian art in Berlin in 1923, singled out Gaganendranath's *Poet on the Island of the Birds* as having affinities with Feininger in its indifference to Analytical Cubism's formal implications.[42] The Indian artist represents the decontextualizing tendency of our age – a tendency shared as much by artists in the centre as in the peripheries, a tendency we come across again and again: styles past and present can be taken out of their original contexts for entirely new modernist projects.

In short, Cubism served as a point of departure for Gaganendranath, the particular Western 'device' yielding a rich new crop in the Indian context. Although its revolutionary language released a new energy in the Bengali artist, Cubism was merely a passing phase in India. It was primitivism that would dominate the decades of the 1920s and '30s. […]

Notes

1 S. Roy, 'Shilpe Atyukti', *Prabasi* (Asvin 1321 [1914], pp. 94–101. […]

2 'Gleanings: Automatic Drawing as a First Aid to the Artist', *Modern Review*, XXI/I (January 1917), pp. 63–5. […]

3 B. K. Sarkar, 'The Aesthetics of Young India', *Rupam*, IX (January 1922), pp. 8–24. Agastya (Canopus), 'Aesthetics of Young India: A Rejoinder', *Rupam*, IX (January 1922), pp. 24–7. In *The Futurism of Young Asia* (Berlin, 1923), Sarkar offered a blueprint for the modernization of India. […]

4 Sarkar, 'Aesthetics', pp. 16–18. See also his *Futurism of Young Asia*. […]

5 C. Bell, 'The Aesthetic Hypothesis', in *Art* (London, 1914), excerpted in C. Harrison and P. Wood, eds, *Art in Theory* (Oxford, 1992), p. 116. On Fry and Bell's influence in India, see Giles Tillotson, 'A Painter of Concern', *India International Centre Quarterly*, xxiv / 4 (Winter 1997), pp. 57–72.

6 Agastya, 'Aesthetics of Young India: A Rejoinder', p. 25. B. Ghosh, 'Panditer Lage Dhanda', *Bijoli* (15 Vaisakh 1329/28 April 1922). The sage Agastya was Gangoly's *nom de guerre*.

7 S. Kramrisch, 'The Aesthetics of Young India: A Rejoinder', *Rupam*, X (April 1922), pp. 65–6; 'An Indian Cubist', *Rupam*, XI (July 1922), pp. 107–9; In the early twentieth century, colonial representations of Indian art were challenged by critics led by E. B. Havell and A. Coomaraswamy (P. Mitter, *Much Maligned Monsters: History of Western Reactions to Indian Art* [Oxford 1977], chap. VI). Kramrisch in 'Indian Art and Europe', *Rupam*, XI (July 1922), pp. 81–6, rejected the colonial idea that the higher aspects of ancient Indian art were derived from Greece and Rome, an intervention that later flowered into her major studies of Indian art.

8 Johannes Itten's notes for 7 May 1921: 'Rabindranath Tagore tritt an seinem 60. Geburtstag mit einem Programm aus Rezitationen und liedern im Deutschen Nationaltheater auf'; and 1 October 1922–March 1923, 'Bauhaus-Ausstellung in der Society of Oriental Art in Kalkutta; Leitung: Dr Abanindranath Tagore (ein Neffe der Dichter's). Organisation in Weimer durch Georg Muche', in *Das frühe Bauhaus und Johannes Itten* (catalogue of exhibition celebrating 75 years of Bauhaus, Weimar), (Ost Fildern-Ruit, 1994), pp. 516, 518. R. K. Wick, *Teaching at the Bauhaus* (Stuttgart, 2000), p. 82. The works, expected to remain there from October 1922 until March 1923, never returned to Europe. The whole saga is recounted by R. Parimoo, *The Art of the Three Tagores* (Baroda, 1973), pp. 168–9.

9 'Internationale Kunstausstellung Das Bauhaus, Kalkutta, 1.12.1922–1.1.1923', in *Paul Klee: Catalogue Raisonné*, Paul Klee Foundation, Museum of Fine Arts, III (Berne and London, 1999).

10 *Catalogue of the 14th Annual Exhibition of the Indian Society of Oriental Art* (Calcutta, December 1922), International Section: Modern Phases of Western Art, Introduction by StK (Stella Kramrisch), pp. 21–3. [...]

11 *The Statesman* and *The Englishman* of 15 December 1922. Review in *Rupam*, XIII/XIV (January–June 1923), pp. 14–18.

12 *The Catalogue*, pp. 3–4.

13 S. Ringbom, 'Art in the Age of the Great Spiritual', *Journal of the Warburg and Courtauld Institutes* (1966), p. 389.

14 A. Tagore, *Bageswari Shilpa Prabandhabali* (Calcutta, 1962), p. 119. This lecture was given around 1922–3.

15 Kramrisch, 'An Indian Cubist', *Rupam*, XI (July 1922), pp. 107–9. See Mitter, *Art and Nationalism*, Epilogue, on the political reasons for the decline of orientalism. A review of Bauhaus works appeared in *Rupam*, XIII/XIV (January–June 1923), p. 18. The impact of Cubism in Bengal in this period is attested in a letter of Nandalal's, see note 21.

16 Obituary tributes to the Marquess of Zetland and William Rothenstein in *Visva Bharati Quarterly*, n.s., IV/I (May 1938), pp. 1–4.

17 The exhibition of Gaganendranath's works at the Academy of Fine Arts, Calcutta, on 26 May 1976, suggests early dates for his work such as 1888. See Mitter, *Art and Nationalism*, p. 275 on William Rothenstein's admiration for his uncle Jyotirindranath's phrenological portraits; Rothenstein had them published (*Twenty-five Collotypes from the Original Drawings by Jyotirindranath Tagore* [London, 1914]).

18 D. Chatterjee, *Gaganendranath Tagore* (New Delhi, 1964), p. 15; Purnima Devi, *Thakur Badir Gogonthakur* (Calcutta, 1381), p. 29, and Mitter, *Art and Nationalism*, on his cartoons, pp. 174–5 and colour pl. XI. Also S. Bandopadhaya, *Gogonendranath Thakur* (Calcutta, 1972).

19 *Rupam*, XI (July 1922), pp. 108–9. [...]

20 *The Englishman* (28 December 1922). Postcard from Gaganendranath to his ex-pupil Roop Krishna in Lahore. Postmark illegible but it belongs to a group written in the early 1920s. Obverse shows a 'Cubist' painting. Text on reverse: I am sending you a sample of my cubism. What do you think of it? (Sotheby Sale, 15 October 1984, lot 13). [...]

21 *Indian Daily News* (10 January 1924).

22 *The Englishman* (5 January 1924).

23 *The Statesman* (6 January 1924).

24 *Forward* (6 January 1924).

25 *Forward* (19 December 1925); *The Englishman* (29 January 1925, 19 December 1925).

26 B. K. Sarkar, 'Tendencies of Modern Indian Art', Review of the 17th Annual Exhibition of the Indian Society of Oriental Art, *Rupam*, XXVI (1926).

27 *The Englishman* (4 September 1928).

28 *Welfare* (24 September 1928).

29 Devi, *Thakur Badir Gogonthakur*, pp. 151–3; 'Indian Society of Oriental Art Exhibition', *The Englishman* (24 December 1929).

30 *Bombay Chronicle* (30 June 1926).

31 *Forward* (6 January 1924); E. H. Gombrich, *The Sense of Order: A Study in the Psychology of Decorative Art* (London, 1979), p. 149.

32 *Bombay Chronicle* (30 June 1926).

33 Obituary tributes to the Marquess of Zetland and William Rothenstein in *Visva Bharati Quarterly*, IV/I, pp. 1–4.

34 *Welfare* (24 September 1928). One of the more informed reviews of Gaganendranath's 1928 retrospective at the Indian Society of Oriental Art acknowledges Roger Fry's importance. See T. Steele, *Alfred Orage and the Leeds Arts Club* (Aldershot, 1990). [...]

35 W. G. Archer, *India and Modern Art* (London, 1959), p. 43.

36 See M. Cheetham, *The Rhetoric of Purity* (Cambridge, 1991).

37 *The Vertical Man: A Study in Primitive Indian Sculpture* (London, 1947). On his patronizing condescension towards Indian nationalism, see *India and Modern Art*, pp. 34–7. These primitivist sentiments, we know, were disseminated by Roger Fry, Clive Bell and later in Herbert Read, the conduits for modernism in the colonies.

38 On the essentializing myth of the 'good' docile primitive in Raj policy while suppressing actual tribal uprising, D. Rycroft, *Representing Rebellion: Visual Aspects of Counter-Insurgency in Colonial India* (New Delhi, 2006).

39 Similar sentiments were first expressed by Lord Curzon in 1905 (see Mitter, *Art and Nationalism*, pp. 235, 377 and passim), who dismissed the Bengali nationalists as being unrepresentative.

40 Archer, *India and Modern Art*, p. 43.

41 Golding, J. *Cubism: A History and an Analysis, 1907–1914* (London, 1968). Franz Marc and Lyonel Feininger created an imaginary world of animals and of architecture respectively while the left-wing revolutionary Georg Grosz put fragmentations and a distorted perspective at the disposal of a powerful political narrative, *Homage to Oskar Panizza*. [...]

42 Max Osborn's review, cited in *Rupam*, XV/XVI (July–December 1923), p. 74. [...]

17

E. B. Havell and Rabindranath Tagore

Nationalism, Modernity and Art

Osman Jamal*

In this essay UK-based Bangladeshi scholar, Osman Jamal, contrasts two conflicting approaches to modernity in colonial Indian art at the turn of the twentieth century. On the one hand, Rabindranath Tagore (1861–1941), the illustrious Bengali writer and artist, advocated for the inherent plurality of Indian art and a modernizing vision embracing Western influence. On the other hand, E. B. Havell (1861–1934), the influential English principal of the Calcutta School of Art and author of many books about Indian art and architecture, opposed European influence and called for a return to the "authentic" monoculture of the Indo-Aryan village. Havell's pro-imperialist Eurocentric posture paradoxically inspired an anti-European art movement beginning in Calcutta and then spreading across the subcontinent that took Indian artists back to their cultural roots. Where Havell insisted on fidelity to tradition, Tagore questioned the validity of tradition as a nationalist ideal. The author considers the aesthetic projects of both Tagore and Havell in the context of their respective, often contradictory, political positions on British colonial rule in India.

As a gesture towards the complexity of modern India's cultural identity, Jamal obliquely refers to several other influential figures in the debate. "Macaulayism," for example, refers to the ideology of an early colonial educational reformist, Lord Macaulay (1800–59) who made English the language of instruction in Indian schools. Macaulay's aim, expressed in his controversial 1835 "Minute" to Parliament, was to Westernize/modernize the colony and "to create a class of persons, Indian in blood and color, but English in taste, in opinions, in morals and in intellect." Other references in this essay are to prominent anti-modern moderns: the British art critic behind the

* Osman Jamal (2000–1) "E. B. Havell and Rabindranath Tagore: Nationalism, Modernity and Art." *Third Text* 53: 19–30.

Modern Art in Africa, Asia, and Latin America: An Introduction to Global Modernisms, First Edition.
Edited by Elaine O'Brien, Everlyn Nicodemus, Melissa Chiu, Benjamin Genocchio,
Mary K. Coffey, and Roberto Tejada.

neo-medievalist pre-Raphaelite movement, John Ruskin (1819–1900), and Mohandas Gandhi (1869–1948), leader of India's independence movement, both of whom advocated a rejection of industrial capitalist urban modernity and a return to the rural pre-modern past.

Questions for reading: What connections does Jamal make between colonialism, nationalism, and modern art in India? Why did Tagore reject Havell's form of Indian nationalism in his 1916 lecture in Japan? What was Tagore's opinion of nationalism, and what distinction did he make between the European *spirit* and European *nation*? Are paintings by Tagore, as presented in this essay, "authentically" modern Indian art?

Further Readings

Asher, Frederick M. (2007) "The Shape of Indian Art History." In Vishakha N. Desai, *Asian Art History in the Twenty-First Century* (pp. 3–14). Williamstown, MA: Sterling and Francine Clark Art Institute.

Jamal, Osman (1997) "E. B. Havell: The Art and Politics of Indianness." *Third Text 39* (Summer): 3–19.

E. B. Havell, as principal of Calcutta Art School (1896–1906), introduced certain curricular reforms, revising, to put it in his words, 'the whole course of instruction, making Indian art the basis of teaching'.[1] And for the rest of his life wrote a series of books on Indian art history from what he considered the Indian point of view, inspiring an art movement which took Indian artists back to their own old tradition. Though the art movement, which dominated Indian art for the first third of the twentieth century, enjoyed the generous patronage of the Empire, its progenitor, Havell, was lauded as 'the English prophet of Indian nationalism',[2] an apparent contradiction to which we shall return.

However, the movement did not go unchallenged. Controversies raged intermittently in Indian art circles on a range of issues.[3] Three decades after Havell introduced his reforms, when the movement was at the peak of its success, spreading out from Calcutta to other parts of India (with the exception of Bombay), Rabindranath Tagore, who had once supported Havell's reforms; addressed an audience at Dhaka University. His tone was urgent: 'I strongly urge our artists vehemently to deny their obligation to produce something that can be labelled as Indian art, according to some old world mannerism.'[4]

It was a powerful intervention seeking to liberate Indian artists from the claustral confines of a fossilised tradition, but it remained a one-off fusillade delivered from what was then a provincial town, and there is little evidence that it reached very far. Despite its importance in the trajectory of Tagore's own development as an artist, the Tagore 'industry' has shown little interest in this historically important address.

Though directed against the aesthetic practice of the Havell-inspired art movement, and not against Havell (Tagore does not mention him or anyone else involved in the movement), I present his 1926 lecture on 'Art and Tradition' in the context of the political positions of Havell and Tagore. The aesthetics are segments of total narratives; and I believe that the truth of an interpretation of any particular segment of a narrative – aesthetics, in this case – is verifiable in terms of its goal orientation with other segments. I have chosen to cradle their aesthetic projects in their respective political positions, in the light of which not only do the aesthetics reveal their true meanings but also appear less as history's passive reflections than as weapons in a struggle which constitutes that history.

Havell's art project was a response to a political crisis of the empire towards the end of the nineteenth century leading to popular discontent and a rising tide of nationalism. Havell as we shall see brought his Romantic anti-industrialism to read the Indian discontent as a protest against Westernisation and an urge to return to the Indo-Aryan village. From the perspective of a *culturist* Indian nationalism, he 'spoke' for the colonised, while reassuring the Empire of Indian loyalty.

While Havell read 'the Indian unrest' as a protest against Westernisation and called for a reversal of Macaulayist 'modernisation', Tagore accused imperialism for denying science to the colonised people. As opposed to Havell's reduction of Indian history exclusively to the moment of the Indo-Aryan, Tagore asserted the cultural plurality of India. And while the former fetishised everything Indo-Aryan (and whatever else he reduced to it), the latter spurned Indian nationalists for their indiscriminate idolatry of traditional institutions.

The Return to the Indo-Aryan Village

In his introduction to *The Ancient and Medieval Architecture of India*, Havell relates the civilisation introduced into India by the Aryan race to Empire building.[5] The Empire, he believes, should be *building* on the foundations laid by the Indo-Aryans and not erase them, as the British colonial administration had done, thus precipitating a political crisis. For 'the Indian unrest' towards the end of the nineteenth century, Havell blames the British bureaucracy's 'complete ignorance of [this] Indian history – the only history of India that matters'.[6] 'The history of India (he continues) is the history of Aryan institutions, traditions and culture' and this had 'dropped off the official file'.[7] Havell thus reconstructs the forgotten civilisation of India and deplores British tampering with 'the wonderful organisation of their village communities and the splendid culture which grew out of them'.[8] The cardinal sin the British had committed in India was to dig up the roots of Indo-Aryan civilisation and introduce Western forms of self-government for which Indians were unfit:

> The Anglo-Indian pedagogue has been sterilising Indian soil, so that he may plant in it seeds of Western culture which will not grow. The Anglo-Indian statesman digs up the roots of Indian civilisation and expects to maintain law and order upon principles totally foreign to the Indian mind and Indian masses are unfit for the Western forms of self-government and will remain so as long as the British Raj endures.[9]

Havell prescribes a radical *reversal* of the 'failed' Macaulayist project and concludes his glowing survey of ancient and medieval Indian society and architecture with an optimistic note: though 'the political institution of India has been broken up, the heart and soul of India are still in her villages, and if her voiceless millions are ever to become articulate, it must be by restoring the communal life of the Indian village'.[10]

This demand for the restoration of the Indo-Aryan village, shared later by a section of the Indian Congress, was a naive and potentially genocidal daydream but, in an unbearable situation where imperialism had irredeemably destroyed the economic and social base of India and then by its very nature failed to deliver what was promised in the name of modernity, this rhetorical statement of intent had a fatal attraction for the colonised. As far as the Empire was concerned, this would ensure her an indefinite lease of life: 'Only when [the restoration of Indo-Aryan village] is accomplished can it be said that the foundations of the British Raj are well and truly laid'.[11] Havell reassures the Raj that 'India is loyal to the core', and that 'the foul canker of anarchy bred in the foul slums of cities only penetrate to the village life because the law abiding instincts of the people there are denied the power of self-expression'.[12]

In the light of this political etiology and prescription, the meaning of Havell's art project becomes clear. The elements of the project – eg, his reforms at Calcutta Art School in 1896 and his dispersal of European paintings (except, significantly, medieval art) from the Calcutta Art Gallery so that his seminaries could now learn, undistracted, from their own tradition; the books he wrote in defence of Indian tradition, which held the Indian spellbound with their rhetoric; and, finally, the nationalist art movement he inspired – can be read as 'local' applications of his prescription for the ailing Empire to jettison the Macaulayist modernising project as well as the aspiration of the emerging Indian bourgeoisie (which had begun to demand a form of self-rule for India) and lead India back to her past.

Havell's ingenious concept of *Indianness* legitimises British rule in India. Related exclusively to the Indo-Aryan moment, the concept ties the coloniser and the colonised in a binary relationship where the dominance of the coloniser is established by a parallelism between two historical moments. In the first of these two moments the Indo-Aryans came to India and laid the foundation of Indian civilisation; in the second, the coming of the British, Havell implies, is a re-enactment of that hallowed moment. The British were to contemporary India what the Indo-Aryans were to ancient India. Havell admonishes the British 'successors' to take inspiration from 'the ancient Indo-Aryan empire builders', and build on the foundations they had laid. He recommends his *History of the Aryan Rule in India* (1920), to 'the present Aryan rulers': 'In honouring the Indo-Aryan forerunners of India, we shall honour ourselves and make the most direct and effective appeal to Indian loyalty.'[13]

Havell's construction of Indian nationalism is not a political weapon aimed against the Raj. There is no *raison d'être* for such a weapon where the Raj is the instrument for realising the nationalist aspiration for the restoration of the art, culture and society of the 'denationalised' Indian. This identity of interests empties the nationalist art of any anti-imperialist political content.

Tagore's Anti-Nationalism

[...]

In his *Nationalism* lectures, given in Japan and USA in 1916–17, Tagore rejects Indian nationalism. What he rejects is not the Havellian construct but the real thing he knew at close range. Which, nevertheless, is essentially similar to the Havellian object. [...] With the onset of the slaughter of World War 1, nationalism for Tagore, tore off its mask to reveal its ugly face of imperialism. Though his earlier objections to Indian nationalism are retained, the epicentre of the concept, moves from India to its origin in Europe, where nationalism emerged as a historically determined adjunct to modernity. The nationalism Tagore repudiates is virtually coterminous with imperialism: it is an European idea which a modern Nation deploys to mobilise its people for aggression against other Nations for the possession of *no-nations*, meaning 'premodern' colonised and colonisable people. Tagore does not use the term imperialism; he calls it by its chosen name, nationalism, but leaves no doubt about what he means by Nation[s] or the doctrine which animates them.

A Nation, he says, is 'a pack of predatory creatures that must have its victims' from among no-nations[14] and it was for the possession of no-nations that the Nations were at war,[15] threatening human civilisation. That these Nations might some day 'come into agreement for their mutual protection, based upon a conspiracy of fear' and create a stable world, held no consolation for no-nations. 'What remote chance of hope will remain (Tagore asks his American audience) for those others [i.e., no-nations] when instead of being numerous separate machines they [the Nations] become rivetted into one organised gregariousness of gluttony, commercial and political?'[16] A Nation, Tagore says, pointing to imperialism's denial of 'science' to its colonies, is exclusivist, 'unwilling to open the sources of power to those whom it has selected for the purpose of exploitation',[17] they 'act like dams to check the free flow of Western civilisation [meaning science, technology] into the country of the no-nations'.[18] He likens Nations trading 'on the feebleness of the rest of the world' to maggots 'bred in the paralysed flesh of victims kept just enough alive to make them toothsome and nutritious'.[19]

What worried Tagore was that Europe had set its own modernity's agenda for all other peoples. He rejoiced at Japan's achievement of modernity but feared that she would adopt the European paradigm and emulate their 'nationalism'. Nevertheless, as opposed to Havell, who wanted to turn the clock back, Tagore remained committed to modernity. [...] Tagore assumes a *contingent* link between modernity and nationalism (*his* variant of capitalism/imperialism pair), severable by a political choice. This position [...] allows Tagore to historicise nationalism as a European option determined by Europe's conflictual history and to admonish Japan to seek a substitute for nationalism in the ancient spiritual and human values of Asia.[20] The position also implies a Manichean view of Europe. The West is both *spirit* (good) and *Nation* (bad). By spirit Tagore means, roughly, modernity, the promise of Enlightenment. 'In India (he says) we are suffering from the conflict between the spirit of the West and the Nation of the West'; 'while the spirit of the West marches under its banner of freedom, the Nation of the West forges its iron chains'.[21] Though it is the Nation which rules India, Tagore hopes that by opposing the Nation with the spirit of Europe, 'we can claim herself as our ally in her resistance to her temptations ...'[22]

If nationalism is an ideology European Nations deploy to organise their peoples to wage colonial wars, it can hardly be a valid option for colonised no-nations like India. Tagore treats Indian nationalism as a proposition, rejecting it on at least two grounds, and in both his position is directly opposed to that of Havell. Havell reduces Indianness to the moment of the Indo-Aryan; Tagore considers an *ethnic* nationalism of the kind too exclusivist for a land so vast and varied. India, he argues, is 'many countries packed in one geographical receptacle', 'the opposite of what Europe truly is, namely, one country made into many'.[23] In India, where many races co-exist, 'the basis of [ethnic] nationalism is wanting'; 'India has never had a real sense of nationalism'.[24]

Secondly, if nationalism/imperialism is an option available only to a country which has acquired modernity, that option does not exist for premodern India. Nationalism in India, Tagore implies, would turn in on itself and, in its indiscriminate adoration of tradition, seek to perpetuate its anachronistic repressive social institutions. [...] Tagore warns: 'The same inertia which leads us to our idolatry of dead forms in social institutions will create in our politics prison houses with immovable walls.[25] The narrowness of sympathy,' he continues, pointing to the caste system, 'which makes it possible for us to impose upon a considerable portion of humanity the galling yoke of inferiority will assert itself in our politics in creating the tyranny of injustice.'[26] In short, what Havell believes would be a reign of freedom Meghasthenes talked about, Tagore foresees as a proto-fascist state running India on repressive principles.

Tagore and Modernism

For most of his life Tagore had considered painting subordinate to literature, illustrating it, carrying its meaning. Not long before Havell came to Calcutta to take up his post as principal of CAS, Tagore had advised his nephew, Abanindranath, who would soon lead the Havell-inspired art movement, to paint from the poetry of Chandidas. However, all that changed dramatically when he took to painting at the age of 67.

Tagore's 'invasion' of the art he had 'considered from a distance with unrequited love' was probably fortuitous. The story can bear repetition. On his way to Peru to attend the 1924 centenary celebration of that country's independence from Spain, Tagore fell ill in Brazil and stayed with Victoria Ocampo at her San Isidro residence. Ocampo found on the poet's bedside table a notebook of his manuscripts with decorative corrections. 'I make corrections dance', he later wrote, 'connect them in

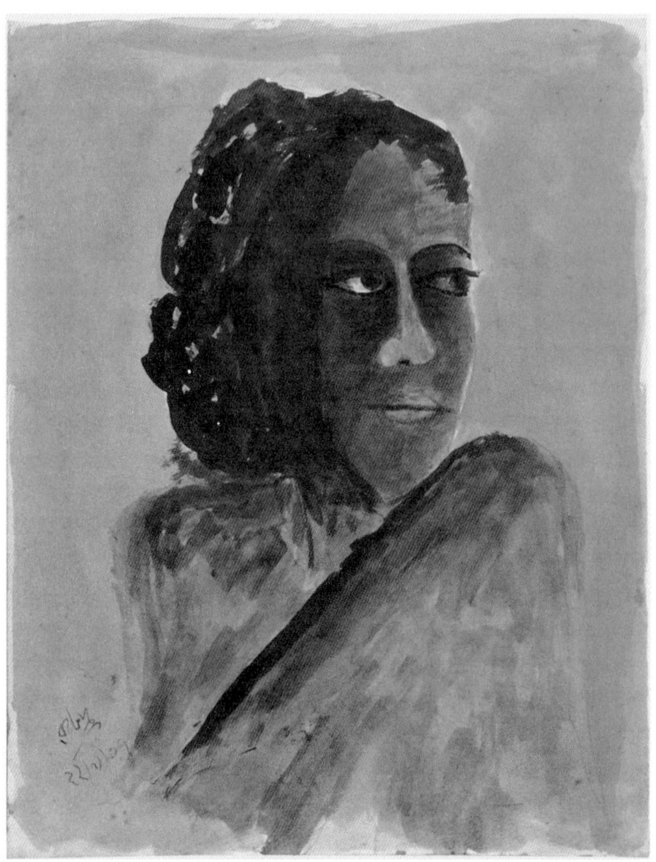

Figure 17.1 Rabindranath Tagore, *Untitled* (Woman's head against bright orange background), 1937. Colored ink on paper, 34 × 25 cm/ 13.4 × 9.8 inches, Rabindra Bhavana, 00-2514-16.

a rhythmic relationship and transform accumulation into adornment.'[27] The forms Ocampo saw on the corrected pages were works of art in their own right. She asked Tagore if she could photograph them. It would seem that by a sudden shift of perspective – from his own to that of Ocampo's, in whose eyes, perhaps the verses inscribed in a beautiful Bengali cursive of his own invention, unintelligible to her, were themselves part of a mosaic of artful corrections – Tagore became a painter of abstract forms. Soon so compelling would become his passion for painting, so beguiling its enchantment, that even writing, his life-long passion, would seem distasteful to him. He probably anticipated how his modern vision of art would estrange him from the art circle where the Havell-inspired art held sway.

In 1916, writing from Japan, Tagore had warned Abanindranath:

> Squatting all the time in the South Verandah [of Jorasanko house], you will never realise how important it is to have contact with the living art of Japan so that our own art may revive and flourish.[28]

A decade later Tagore addresses this insularity in his 1926 lecture at Dhaka University. He argues that there is no historical precedent for the kind of exclusive fidelity to tradition as practiced by Indian artists. He begins with a conception of art as 'response of man's creative soul to the call of the real', and attributes such differences as, say, between the Gandhara Buddha and the Buddha of the purely Indian mind to the fact that different people respond differently to the call of the real. These differences do not justify insularity. On the contrary, Persian influence in Indian art (the style of the Moghul miniature which Havell asked Abanindranath to emulate as an example of Indian tradition was itself a product of Persian influence) and the Chinese and Japanese acknowledgement of Indian influence in *their* arts, clearly indicate that there are 'no absolute caste restrictions' to cultural give-and-take.[29] For a more recent evidence of the benefits of cultural exchange, Tagore reminds his audience of Bengal's hospitable reception of European literature and thought in the nineteenth century which had brought about 'a great revolution in the realm of our literary expression'.[30] Supported by the examples of the past and of recent times, Tagore argues that now that the world had moved on since when people lived in 'relative segregation', 'a living soul' should embrace all that is worthy, though – here with a note of caution – 'not according to some blind injunction of custom or fashion, but follow his instinct for eternal value, the instinct which is a God-given gift to all real artists'.[31] With his vast personal experience in literature, Tagore reassures the Indian artist fearful of losing his identity, that Indian art would still havc 'a quality which is Indian', though it must be an inner quality, not 'an artificially fostered formalism', 'not too obtrusively obvious, nor abnormally self-conscious'.[32] There is an avuncular note to his rousing call:

> So let us take heart and make daring experiments, venture out into the open road in the face of all risks, go through experiences in the great world of human mind, defying unholy prohibitions preached by prudent little critics, laughing at them when in their tender solicitude for our safety they ask our artists to behave like good children and never to cross the threshold of their schoolroom.[33]

In his second argument Tagore seeks to free Indian artists from the institutional bondage thrust on them and to restore to them their individuality. At the cutting edge of European thought individualism is all but transcended; it is therefore all the more important to recall its revolutionary potential in a society where modernity is struggling to be born. Tagore deploys conceptions which have their roots in the Renaissance and the Enlightenment. While his idea of an 'instinct for eternal value, the instinct which is God-given gift to all real artists' echoes a Renaissance idea, his wish to see the artist outgrow his minority and be an adult reminds one of Kant's metaphorical equation of the Enlightenment with adulthood. For an artist, individualism has a particular importance. For unlike a child in whom 'individuality of physiognomy is blurred', his mind open to generalisation, an adult is an *individual*, 'difficult of classification', 'his manners and his responses to external stimuli unique',[34] where to be unique is a precondition of being an artist. Between the artist and his art, Tagore sweeps away the intermediaries. For like the artist endowed with his instinct for value, art too, with its own 'criteria of excellence', 'contemptuously refuses to be browbeaten into conformity with a rhetoric manufactured by those who are not in the secret of the subtle mysteries of creation'.[35] The artist alone has the key to the secret; he has no obligation to produce a so-called Indian art to order.

> I strongly urge our artists vehemently to deny their obligations to produce something that can be labelled as Indian Art, according to some old world mannerism. *Let them proudly refuse to be herded into pen like branded beasts that are treated as cattle and not as cows.* (Emphasis added) [36]

The distinction between cattle and cows is important: cows are individuals as opposed to cattle, a herd. This is a clear reposte to an art movement which had reduced Indian artists to a premodern status.

Finally, in a two-fold strategy, Tagore takes on tradition. As we have seen above, Tagore rejects Indian nationalism for its adoration of unjust and oppressive traditional institutions. His repudiation of an art committed to tradition is structurally homologous to his rejection of nationalism. What is common to the two levels is their ideological (nationalist) commitment to tradition. [...] Tradition-bound art, which aggressively cultivates 'a certain bigotry' of the past, 'smothers the soul', producing 'masks with exaggerated grimaces' that fail as art as they 'fail to respond to the ever changing play of life'.[37] Tagore criticises it for disengaging from life: when art takes root in 'a narrow soil of tradition' and, discouraged from 'allurements of all adventure, remains undisturbed by a mind that seeks the unattained, it is neither helped by the growing life of the people nor does it help to enrich that life'.[38] Tagore rejects this 'gorgeous sepulchre' in favour of a conception of art which 'belongs with the procession of life':

> Art is not a gorgeous sepulchre, immovable, brooding over a lonely eternity of vanished years. It belongs to the procession of life, making constant adjustment with *surprises*, exploring unknown shrines of reality along its path of pilgrimage to a future which is as different from the past as the tree from the seed. (Emphasis added) [39]

The word 'surprises' refers to the irreversible changes colonialism had wrought in India which Indian art brackets out, as if they could simply be wished away, in its ahistorical rehearsal of myth and tradition.

Secondly, Tagore de-reifies the tradition by locating its origin in *individual* action, in 'some gestures in the modes and mediums of expression that spontaneously came to a man of genius' and were then imitated by others.[40] [...] In other words, [imitative] rehearsal of tradition presupposes absence of creativity, death of art. For art – as 'the response of man's creative soul to the call of the real', where the real is assumed to be changing – demands a response commensurate with changing reality, which can only mean a continuous transcendence of tradition.

The Last Testament

With his ideological grounding in the Romantic anti-industrialism of Ruskin, Havell found in India a premodern society in a state of disintegration under a regime caught in the contradiction of its promise of unrealisable modernity, and called for a reversal of the 'modernising' project. He probably believed that by restoring to India its 'miniature republics' of the Indo-Aryan village, a pre-Raphaelite fantasy he expected the colonists and the anti-modernity Indian nationalists to buy, he would simultaneously offer imperialism a pristine field for colonial exploitation. In this sense, Havell could be said to have led the third phase of Orientalism in India. Despite substantial success in his art project, Havell felt let down by the British and died a bitter man.

Tagore never ceased changing, but he hung on to his faith in the spirit of Europe until the year before his death, when he grieved in what is taken to be his last testament:

> There was a time when I used to believe that the springs of civilisation would issue out of the heart of Europe. Today, as I am about to quit the world, that faith has gonc bankrupt.[41]

In 1947, six years after Tagore's death, the Indian subcontinent was partitioned, on the basis of two-nations theory, into India and Pakistan, which resulted in the massive intercommunal killings of about half-a-million Hindus, Sikhs and Muslims. In 1972, East Bengal (then East Pakistan) was separated – after a bloody struggle – from Pakistan and became the independent country of Bangladesh.

[...]

Notes

1 *The Studio*, vol. 44, 1908, p. 111.
2 Cited in Preface by Pramode Chandra to E. B. Havell, *The Art Heritage of India*, comprising *Indian Sculpture and Painting* and *Ideals of Indian Art*, revised edition [1927], Bombay, 1964, p. vi.
3 Tapati Guha-Thakurta, *The Making of a New Indian Art: Art Artists and Aesthetics in Bengal 1850–1920*, Cambridge, 1992, chap. 6.
4 Rabindranath Tagore, *On Art and Aesthetics*, Orient Longman, India, 1961.
5 E. B. Havell, *The Ancient and Medieval Architecture of India: A Study of Indo-Aryan Civilization*, London, 1915, p. xxii.
6 Ibid., p. xxiv.
7 Ibid., pp. xxvii–xxviii.
8 Ibid., p. xxv.
9 Ibid., p. xxxiv.
10 Ibid., p. 222.
11 Ibid.
12 Ibid.
13 E. B. Havell, *A History of Aryan Rule in India*, Harrap & Co., London, 1918, p. ix.
14 Rabindranath Tagore, *Nationalism*, Macmillan & Co., London, 1921, p. 21.
15 Ibid.
16 Ibid., p. 32.
17 Ibid., pp. 21–2.
18 Ibid., p. 21.
19 Ibid., p. 30.
20 *Nationalism*, p. 57.
21 Ibid., p. 24.
22 Ibid., p. 90.
23 Ibid., p. 114.
24 Ibid., p. 106.
25 Ibid., p. 123.
26 Ibid.
27 Rabindranath Tagore, 'My Pictures (ii)', *On Art and Aesthetics*, op. cit., p. 100.
28 Cited in Andrew Robinson, *The Art of Rabindranath Tagore*, London, 1989, p. 51.
29 Rabindranath Tagore, 'Art and Tradition', in *On Art and Aesthetics*, op. cit., p. 59.
30 Ibid., p. 60.
31 Ibid., p. 61.
32 Ibid.
33 Ibid., p. 60.
34 Ibid.
35 Ibid., p. 62.
36 Ibid.
37 Ibid.
38 Ibid.
39 Ibid.
40 Ibid., p. 63.
41 Rabindranath Tagore, 'Crisis in Civilization', *Towards Universal Man*, Asia Publishing house, London, 1961, pp. 358–9.

18

Art and Tradition

RABINDRANATH TAGORE*

In this essay the author, a world famous Indian poet, winner of the Nobel Prize for literature, and a widely admired expressionist painter, puts forward the thesis, radical for its time (1926), that there is no such thing as cultural purity, that all cultures borrow ideas and imagery from one another and that they have done so since the dawn of time. He therefore advocates that Indian artists reject nationalistic calls to produce "something that can be labeled as Indian art, according to some old world mannerism," thus freeing them from the limitations and confines of so-called tradition, and embrace the inherent cultural plurality of India out of which he believed artists could continue to make works of universal value. The text of the essay was first delivered as a public lecture at Dhaka University, Bangladesh.

Further Readings

Dutta, Krishna and Robinson, Andrew (eds) (1999) *Rabindranath Tagore: An Anthology*. New York, NY: St Martins Griffin.

O'Connell, Kathleen M. and O'Connell, Joseph T. (2009) *Rabindranath Tagore: Reclaiming a Cultural Icon*. Kolkata, India: Visva-Bharati.

There come in our history occasions when the consciousness of a large multitude becomes suddenly illumined with the recognition of something which rises far above the triviality of daily happenings. Such an occasion there was when the voice of Buddha reached distant shores across all physical and moral impediments.

* Rabindranath Tagore (1961 [1926]) "Art and Tradition." In *On Art and Aesthetics* (pp. 58–64). New Delhi, India: Orient Longman.

Modern Art in Africa, Asia, and Latin America: An Introduction to Global Modernisms, First Edition.
Edited by Elaine O'Brien, Everlyn Nicodemus, Melissa Chiu, Benjamin Genocchio,
Mary K. Coffey, and Roberto Tejada.

Then our life and our world found their profound meaning of reality in their relation to the central person who offered us emancipation of love. And men, in order to make this great human experience ever memorable, determined to do the impossible: they made rocks to speak, stones to sing, caves to remember; the cry of joy and hope took immortal forms, along hills and deserts, across barren solitudes and populous cities. A gigantic creative endeavour built up its triumph in stupendous carvings, defying obstacles that were overwhelming. Such heroic activity over the greater part of the Eastern continent clearly answers the question: *What is Art?* – Art is the response of man's creative soul to the call of the real.

But the individual mind according to its temperament and training has its own recognition of reality in some of its special aspect. We can see from the Gandhara figures of Buddha that the artistic influence of Greece put its emphasis on the scientific aspect, on anatomical accuracy, while the purely Indian mind dwelt on the symbolic aspect and tried to give expression to the soul of Buddha, never acknowledging the limitations of realism. To the adventurous spirit of the great European sculptor, Rodin, the most significant aspect of reality is the unceasing struggle of the incomplete for its freedom from the fetters of imperfection, whereas before the naturally introspective mind of the Eastern artist the real appears in its ideal form of fulfilment.

Therefore, when we talk of such a fact as Indian Art, it indicates some truth based upon the Indian tradition and temperament. At the same time we must know that there is no such thing as absolute caste restriction in human cultures; they ever have the power to combine and produce new variations, and such combinations have been going on for ages, proving the truth of the deep unity of human psychology. It is admitted that in Indian Art the Persian element found no obstacles, and there are signs of various other alien influences. China and Japan have no hesitation in acknowledging their debt to India in their artistic and spiritual growth of life. Fortunately for our civilisations, all such intermingling happened when professional art critics were not rampant and artists were not constantly nudged by the warning elbow of classifiers in their choice of inspiration. Our artists were never tiresomely reminded of the obvious fact that they were Indians: and in consequence they had the freedom to be naturally Indian in spite of all the borrowings that they indulged in.

A sign of greatness in great geniuses is their enormous capacity for borrowing, very often without their knowing it: they have unlimited credit in the world market of cultures. Only mediocrities are ashamed and afraid of borrowing, for they do not know how to pay back the debt in their own coin. Even the most foolish of critics does not dare blame Shakespeare for what he openly appropriated from outside his own national inheritance. The human soul is proud of its comprehensive sensitiveness: it claims its freedom of entry everywhere when it is fully alive and awake. We congratulate ourselves on the fact, and consider it a sign of our being live in soul, that European thoughts and literary forms found immediate hospitality in Bengali literature from the very beginning of their contact with our mind. It ushered in a great revolution in the realm of our literary expression.

Enormous changes have taken place, but our Indian soul has survived the shock and has vigorously thriven upon this cataclysm. It only shows that though human mentality, like the earth's atmosphere, has undoubtedly different temperatures in different geographical zones, yet it is not walled up into impassable compartments and the circulation of the common air over the entire globe continues to have its wholesome effect. So let us take heart and make daring experiments, venture out into the open road in the face of all risks, go through experiences in the great world of human mind, defying unholy prohibitions preached by prudent little critics, laughing at them when in their tender solicitude for our safety they ask our artists to behave like good children and never to cross the threshold of their school-room.

Fearfully trying always to conform to a conventional type is a sign of immaturity. Only in babies is individuality of physiognomy blurred, and therefore personal distinction not strongly marked. Childishness as a mentality can easily be generalised: children's babbling has the same sound-tottering everywhere, their toys are very nearly similar. But adult age is difficult of classification, it is composed of individuals who claim recognition of their personal individuality which is shown not only in its own uniqueness of manner but also in its own special response to all stimulations from outside. I strongly urge our artists vehemently to deny their obligation to produce something that can be labelled as Indian Art, according to some old world mannerism. Let them proudly refuse to be herded into a pen like branded beasts that are treated as cattle and not as cows. Science is impersonal: it has its one aspect which is merely universal and therefore abstract; but art is personal and, therefore, through it the universal manifests itself in the guise of the individual, physiology expresses itself in physiognomy, philology in literature. Science is a passenger in a railway train of generalisation; their reasoning minds from all directions come to make their journey together in a similar conveyance. Art is a solitary pedestrian, who walks alone among the multitude, continually assimilating various experiences, unclassifiable and uncatalogued.

There was time when human races lived in comparative segregation and therefore the art adventurers had their experience within a narrow range of limits, along the deeply cut grooves of certain common characteristics. But today that range has vastly widened, claiming from us a much greater power of receptivity than what we were compelled to cultivate in former ages. If today we have a living soul that is sensitive to ideas and to beauty of form, let it prove its capacity by accepting all that is worthy of acceptance, not according to some blind injunction of custom or fashion, but in following one's instinct for eternal value – the instinct which is a God-given gift to all real artists. Even then our art is sure to have a quality which is Indian, but it must be an inner quality and not an artificially fostered formalism; and therefore not too obtrusively obvious, nor abnormally self-conscious.

When in the name of Indian Art we cultivate with deliberate aggressiveness a certain bigotry born of the habit of a past generation, we smother our soul under idiosyncrasies unearthed from buried centuries. These are like masks with exaggerated grimaces that fail to respond to the ever changing play of life.

Art is not a gorgeous sepulchre, immovable brooding over a lonely eternity of vanished years. It belongs to the procession of life, making constant adjustment with surprises, exploring unknown shrines of reality along its path of pilgrimage to a future which is as different from the past as the tree from the seed. [...]

The art ideal of people may take fixed root in a narrow soil of tradition, developing a vegetable character, producing a monotonous type of leaves and flowers in a continuous round of repetitions. Because it is not disturbed by a mind which ever seeks the unattained and because it is held firm by a habit which piously discourages allurements of all adventure, it is neither helped by the growing life of the people nor does it help to enrich that life.

It remains confined to coteries of specialists who nourish it with delicate attention and feel proud of the ancient flavour of its aristocratic exclusiveness. It is not a stream that flows through and fertilises the soil, but a rare wine stored in a dark cellar underground, acquiring a special stimulation through its artificially nurtured, barren antiquity. [...]

The genesis of all art traditions must have been in some gestures in the modes and mediums of expression that spontaneously came to men of genius and were followed by others whose admiration naturally pursued the path of imitation. [...] All traditional structures of art must have sufficient degree of elasticity to allow it to respond to varied impulses of life, delicate or virile; to grow with its growth, to dance with its rhythm. There are traditions which, in alliance with rigid prescriptions of rhetoric, establish their slave dynasty, dethroning their master, the Life-urge, that revels in endless freedom of expression. This is a tragedy whose outrage we realise in the latter-day Sanskrit literature and in the conventional arts and crafts of India, where mind is helplessly driven by a blind ghost of the past.

And yet we may go too far if we altogether reject tradition in the cultivation of the arts, and it is an incomplete statement of truth to say that habits have the sole effect of deadening our mind. The tradition which is helpful is like a channel that helps the current to flow. It is open where the water runs onward, guarding it only where there is danger in deviation. The bee's life in its channel of habit has no opening: it revolves within a narrow circle of perfection. Man's life has time-honoured institutions which are its organised habits. When these act as enclosures, then the result may be perfect, like a bee-hive of wonderful precision of form, but unsuitable for the mind which has unlimited possibilities of progress.

Section 2

Japan

19

Western Style Painting in Japan
Mimesis, Individualism, and Japanese Nationhood

Gennifer Weisenfeld*

Gennifer Weisenfeld's essay is reproduced here from the first chapter of her book on Mavo, a radical avant-garde artist group that emerged in Japan in the 1920s. Artists associated with Mavo produced work ranging from performance art to painting, book illustration, and architecture, much of it collaborative and drawing inspiration from daily life. In part, the movement was a response to the rise of industrialism in Japan, which Mavo artists viewed critically as a source of uncertainty. Mavo artists also forged links with European modern avant-garde movements, including Futurism and Dada.

The selected text begins by outlining the social, cultural, and political context for the emergence of modern art in Japan in the late nineteenth century, specifically how the Japanese establishment (the artistic community and the government) perceived Western art and its influence. One official response was the establishment of the Institute for Western Learning, in 1855, which provided Japanese artists with first-hand information and training in Western art. Later, artists in

* Gennifer Weisenfeld (2002) "Western Style Painting in Japan: Mimesis, Individualism, and Japanese Nationhood." In *Mavo: Japanese Artists and the Avant-Garde, 1905–1931* (pp. 11–27). Berkeley, CA: University of California Press.

Modern Art in Africa, Asia, and Latin America: An Introduction to Global Modernisms, First Edition.
Edited by Elaine O'Brien, Everlyn Nicodemus, Melissa Chiu, Benjamin Genocchio,
Mary K. Coffey, and Roberto Tejada.

China, Korea, and Thailand were also given the opportunity to study Western styles and techniques in Japan. For modern art enthusiasts in Japan during the Meiji period of Westernization (1868–1912), Western art's preference for realism (mimesis) provided a more scientific approach to representation and was known as *yōga*. Not surprisingly, there was a countermovement that promoted a more "authentic" Japanese style in painting, *nihonga*. Conflicts between these two different modes of representation and their cultural underpinnings set the scene for the emergence of Mavo and other radical avant-garde groups of the early twentieth century, interrupted by World War II but begun again in the postwar period with Gutai and other groups.

Further Readings

Tōru, Haga (1971) "The Formation of Realism in Meiji Painting: The Career of Takahashi Yuichi." In Donald H. Shively (ed.), *Tradition and Modernization in Japanese Culture*, Princeton, NJ: Princeton University Press.

Takashina, Shūji (1987) "Eastern and Western Dynamics in the Development of Western-style oil painting during the Meiji Era." In Shūji Takashina, J. Thomas Rimer, Gerald D. Bolas (eds), *Paris in Japan: The Japanese Encounter with European Painting*. Tokyo: Japan Foundation.

Mavo's predecessors had been engaged in a discourse on Western-style painting *(yōga)* even before the inception of the Meiji state. Two core issues in this half-century-long debate were how to define the purpose of art and what role to assign the artist in modern Japanese society. These were not isolated issues: art and the artist were seen as deeply engaged in evolving conceptions of individualism, national identity, and culture, as well as the concerns more specific to Western-style painting, such as mimesis. Mavo joined into a complex and ongoing dialogue of artists, art theorists, and art bureaucrats, all trying to adapt to the rapidly changing sociopolitical context of Japanese culture.

By the early 1920s, when Mavo artists stepped into the fray, the Japanese state had attained sufficient stability and international economic parity to allow its intelligentsia to focus on more personal concerns. Mavo's project built on this emerging affirmation of the autonomous and unfettered individual, inherently a social being but nonetheless obliged to put the self first. By emphasizing self-awareness as an integral part of social awareness, Mavo inextricably linked individual and social concerns. Because "society" and the state were increasingly seen as distinct and sometimes even at odds, the artist was encouraged to maintain a critical stance toward both domains, thus allowing, it was thought, a more discriminating assessment of modernity in Japan.

Mavo group members, following the anti-academic trend of a preceding generation of artists, eschewed the mimetic representational function of Western-style art. They seized instead on expressionism, dadaism, and constructivism as tools to revolutionize Japanese artistic production and practice – their goal was to connect art more directly to everyday modern life.

Yōga in the Meiji Period

In the immediate post-Restoration period, with its "self-improvement movement" and credo of *risshin shusse* (success in life), the Meiji government sought to develop Japan technologically and economically by encouraging individual achievement in the service of the nation.[1] Many early Meiji artists and bureaucrats actively promoted art for its practical, educative, or commercial value; officials in Kyoto, for example, introduced the slogan "Enrich the country through the arts" *(bijutsu fukoku)*.[2] Already in the late Tokugawa period, *yōga* had been identified as a potentially useful tool for government purposes. Because it represented the natural world more "accurately" than traditional Japanese art forms, *yōga* appeared to be more scientific and utilitarian. To support the study of Western-style art along with other practical subjects, the Tokugawa government established the Institute for Western Learning (Yōgakusho) in 1855, renaming it the Institute for the Study of Barbarian Documents (Bansho Shirabesho) the following year.[3] Artists were able to examine reproductions of Western works of art in an institutional setting, albeit without guidance or instruction.

Preeminently concerned with transforming Japan into a modern nation, the Meiji oligarchy founded the Technological Art School (Kōbu Bijutsu Gakkō) in 1876 as the first official art school in Japan for the study of *yōga*. According to its constitution, the art school was founded "for the purpose of transplanting the techniques of modern Western art to original Japanese art as an aid to Japanese artists"; its mission was to teach "theoretical and technical aspects of modern Western art in order to supplement what is lacking in Japanese art and to build up the school to the same level as the best art academies in the West by studying the trends of realism."[4]

Three Italian artists were hired to teach at the new art school: Antonio Fontanesi (painting), Vincenzo Ragusa (sculpture), and Giovanni Cappelletti (drawing and the principles of geometry and perspective). Most *yōga* artists had their first experience with Western artistic pedagogy at the Technological Art School. The driving force behind the curriculum was Fontanesi, a well-known landscape painter in Italy and professor at the Royal Academy of Turin. He admired the Barbizon school, particularly Jean-Baptiste Corot, Charles François Daubigny, and August François Ravier. Even more than in the work of the Barbizon painters, Fontanesi's paintings relied heavily on somber pigments and indistinct delineation of forms; he transmitted these qualities to his students, who worked in resin-colored tones, often producing solemn and even lugubrious works.

Fontanesi defined the academic terms for "Western art," stipulating a uniform technique applied to predetermined pictorial and thematic paradigms, with little stress on innovation and originality. Fontanesi emphasized naturalism, like that in the works of Jean-François Millet and Jules Breton, along with conventional portraiture and landscape painting. Academic training at the

Technological Art School conditioned Japanese artists to seek similar teaching environments when they traveled abroad.

This unilateral introduction to academic Western-style painting reinforced the already strong Japanese valuation of *yōga* for its verisimilitude. One of the most influential proponents of *yōga* in the early Meiji period, Takahashi Yuichi, explained its appeal: "I happened to see a Western lithograph in the possession of one of my friends and found it so astonishingly lifelike and attractive that I made up my mind then and there to study the Western style of painting."[5] Takahashi believed that Western-style painting's *shashin* (representation of truth) allowed the painter to grasp and thereby comprehend the "substance" and "logic" of the material world, which in turn provided access to "the secrets of creation." But, as Takahashi stated in his memoirs, in order to paint *yōga*, he needed to "cleanse [his] dirty spirit" and, Haga Tōru surmises, "cut away within himself whatever had gone bad in traditional aesthetics. … [This was] a conscious, radical remaking of himself."[6] Thus Takahashi expressed the partial self-repudiation implicit in the Westernizing impetus propelling social and cultural development in the early Meiji period.

During the first decade following the Meiji Restoration, there was a torrent of enthusiasm for *yōga*, as for many new things from the West, such as pocket watches and bowler hats. But countermeasures to Western influence arose with the growing fear in the 1880s that indiscriminate importing of things Western would efface Japan's "national culture." The Dragon Pond Society (Ryūichikai), founded in 1879, promoted connoisseurship of traditional Japanese arts and inaugurated the system of designating national cultural treasures that is still in place today. The society's members included the president of the National Industrial Arts Exhibition, Kawase Hideharu, and the vice president, Sano Tsunetami, as well as the prominent bureaucrat Kuki Ryūichi, who later became head of exhibitions at the Imperial Museum (Teishitsu Hakubutsukan), which was established in 1889. The society was named the Japan Art Association (Nihon Bijutsu Kyōkai) in 1887 and continued to be a major force in the Japanese art world on and off well into the postwar period.

The hostility *yōga* engendered among nationalist-oriented intellectuals spilled over into the public debate about the value of a Westernized culture versus an "authentic" Japanese culture and eventually played a major role in the configuration of the art establishment. In the late 1870s, a group of artists and art connoisseurs, concerned by what they saw as a precipitous erosion of Japanese culture, sought to revitalize so-called traditional forms. One of their proposals was to adopt chiaroscuro shading and perspectival rendering in traditional styles of painting with ink and opaque pigments. Called *nihonga* (Japanese-style painting), the new movement vied with *yōga* for cultural preeminence, members of each group arguing that they alone worked for the good of the nation. Okakura Tenshin, a prominent ideological leader of *nihonga*, established the Japan Painting Association (Nihon Kaiga Kyōkai) in 1896; two years later, the membership of this artists' group became the core of the Japan Art Academy (Nihon Bijutsuin), opened under Okakura's direction as the central institution for instructing and promoting *nihonga*.

By the 1880s, the radical change in the political tide had also altered the balance of power between *yōga* and *nihonga*. *Yōga* became increasingly suspect and after 1882 was excluded from Japanese pavilions at international expositions. Moreover, the great popularity of "traditional" Japanese crafts *(kōgei)* that began with the 1873 Vienna exposition led bureaucrats to emphasize crafts and painting in ink and opaque pigments over *yōga*. While *yōga* was exhibited at domestic fairs sponsored by the Ministry of Industry and Agriculture, these national industrial arts expositions were designed to promote Japanese industry and treated painting and crafts like other industrial products, not like cultural artifacts.[7] In 1882 the government sponsored its first national painting exhibition, but *yōga* was intentionally omitted and *nihonga* promoted. Only in 1900 at the Paris exposition was *yōga* fully introduced into international exhibitions. In 1887, the newly founded Tokyo School of Fine Arts (where Okakura served as director) initially refused to include *yōga* in its curriculum. Although Western-style painting persisted in private studios, the official art establishment began to recognize the movement only when the *yōga* artist Kuroda Seiki returned from France in 1893. In 1894, the Tokyo School of Fine Arts began teaching *yōga;* two years later, a full section devoted to Western-style painting was added, with Kuroda in charge.

Before Kuroda's return, the majority of *yōga* painters justified their own work and Western-style art by defending its accurate portrayal of the external world. Kuroda was one of the first artists, and certainly one of the most influential, who tried systematically to communicate some of the philosophical underpinnings of Western painting to Japanese artists. Having studied with Raphäel Collin at the Académie Colarossi in Paris, Kuroda was exposed to a strong dose of French academicism. But unlike some of his academic colleagues who pursued allegorical historicism, Collin stressed painting *en plein air* (*gaikō* in Japanese) and integrated into academic representational modes an impressionist's response to the outdoors. At the same time, he explored a contemplative realm and a lyrical response to nature.

The powerful political position of Kuroda's family and the more receptive mood of the Japanese art establishment by the early 1890s enabled Kuroda to launch a full-scale *yōga* renaissance in Japan.[8] In addition to teaching at the Tokyo School of Fine Arts, Kuroda, with his distinguished social standing, helped legitimate painting as a vocation for the intelligentsia. As Kitazawa Noriaki has argued, Kuroda, inspired by the high social standing of artists in France, was instrumental in transforming the social identity of modern Japanese artists from artisans with technical skills *(gakō)* to fine artists *(geijutsuka/bijutsuka)*, full-fledged intellectuals who could express their individual impressions of the world. In the early Meiji period, being an artist was not considered a valid vocation for the intelligentsia. The Meiji elite, feeling that their sons should pursue a more dignified and serviceable profession, endorsed artistic activity and study abroad only insofar as they "civilized and enlightened" the nation, thereby facilitating Japan's campaign for national development. Art work produced during study abroad was categorized as belonging to practical studies *(jitsugaku)*, along with other technical skills, and was

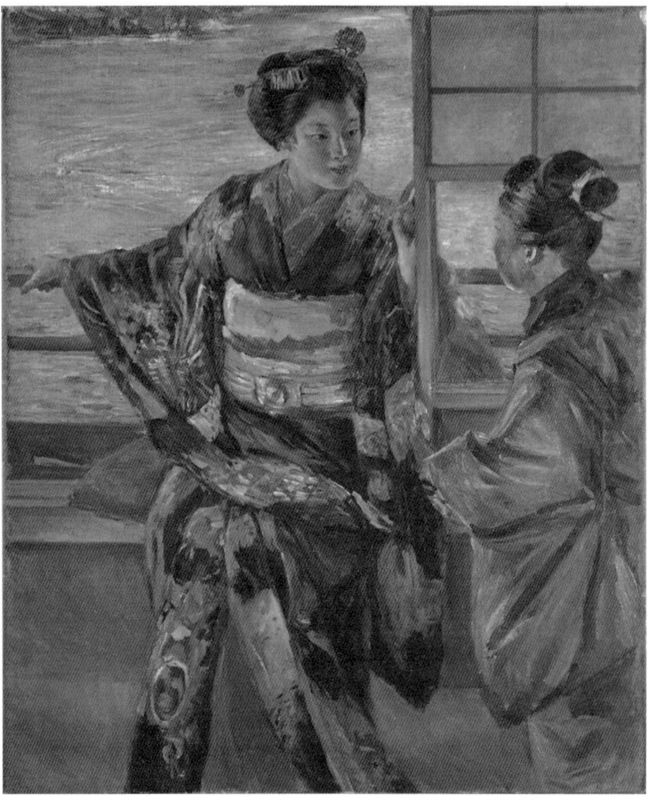

Figure 19.1 Kuroda Seiki, *Maike Dancing Girl* (Maike), 1893. Oil on canvas, 80.5 × 65.4 cm/32 × 26 inches. Tokyo National Museum/DNP Art Communications.

not appreciated for its inherent philosophical or aesthetic value.[9]

The work of Kuroda, because of his lyrical approach to painting, which matched traditional Japanese poetic sensibilities, was particularly well received at home. The lighter, purplish palette of the works of Kuroda and his followers, exhibited in the newly founded White Horse Society (Hakubakai), appealed more to Japanese viewers than the darker, resin-colored hues of the *yōga* artists who exhibited with the Meiji Art Society (Meiji Bijutsukai), who were predominantly heirs to Fontanesi's method.

True to his classical academic training, Kuroda depicted mythological or allegorical scenes that departed sharply from the images of modern life favored by the European impressionists. His pastoral genre scenes acknowledge a psychological interiority and a poetic yearning for Arcadia, and are differentiated from the classical Western academic landscape only because the figures are transmuted into Japanese women in kimonos. Kuroda's paintings have been credited with simulating a psychological introversion *(naikōka)* that came to be specifically associated with the Western-style artist *(yōgaka)*.[10] His "dreamscape" images bore no resemblance to the reality of his urban surroundings, nor did they address daily life in the rapidly changing Tokyo environment. Instead, Kuroda adopted themes from Japanese history and legends, set in familiar landscapes, in an attempt to naturalize his French academic style. He considered his main mission to civilize and enlighten Japan in the image of French high culture for the benefit of the Japanese nation-state *(kokka)*. Kuroda's attitude was reinforced by his experiences in France where, as Miriam Levin has pointed out, ideologues of the Third Republic viewed art and art pedagogy as means to foster national education and ensure industrial prosperity.[11]

In 1907, a group of concerned Japanese bureaucrats, led by the just-appointed Minister of Education Makino Nobuaki, convinced of the educational value of art and art exhibitions inspired by contact with European state cultural policies, established an officially sponsored national exhibition based on the French Salon. The Bunten, destined to be a strong force in the development of Japanese modern art, exhibited three categories of art: *yōga, nihonga*, and sculpture. (The term

"Bunten" is an acronym for the title of the Ministry of Education's art exhibition, Monbushō Bijutsu Tenrankai.) Through official use at the Bunten the term *bijutsu* (fine arts) came to designate painting and sculpture as the specific realm of the visual arts *(shikaku geijutsu)*. A neologism, *bijutsu* had come into common use only at the time of the 1873 exposition in Vienna; the term distinguished fine arts within the broader category of *geijutsu* (the arts), which included crafts and the decorative arts.[12] The inauguration of the Bunten marked the beginning of a national art collection. By supporting those artists recognized by the exhibition judges, the Bunten would serve as the central institution for evaluating and sanctioning art as well as educating the public. From the onset, the exhibition, held in Ueno Park, drew tremendous crowds. In 1912, attendance reached an unprecedented 161,805; most other public exhibitions of the time drew attendance only in the thousands.[13]

Kuroda Seiki's views were consonant with the bureaucratic, nationalist social agenda represented by the Bunten and other state initiatives, but this influence was not due solely to this similarity in ideology. Aesthetically, his dreamy and sentimental tableaux also struck a chord with the Japanese public. His work harmonized with and promoted the romanticism that emerged in Japanese art and literature in the late 1880s. It peaked with the nationalistic fervor roused by the Sino- and Russo-Japanese wars (between 1894–5 and 1904–5). Kuroda's students from his Tenshin Academy (Tenshin Dōjō) were inspired by romanticism; the paintings they exhibited with the White Horse Society were sentimental genre and historical scenes evoking strong emotions.[14] But then many *nihonga* painters associated with Okakura's Japan Art Academy (most notable was Hishida Shunsō) also injected a strong romantic emotionalism into their work, paralleling the developments in the White Horse Society even though the two societies were often at odds institutionally. Reproductions of works by Western artists involved in symbolism and art nouveau clearly encouraged this trend.

Among Kuroda's students, Aoki Shigeru (1882–1911) crystallized the romantic movement in the visual arts, according to Kawakita Michiaki.[15] Like Kuroda, Aoki employed a soft pastel palette, but rendered his forms indistinctly, like blurry, academic underpainting. Aoki took up history painting and, fueled by his intense interest in Japanese romantic literature, adopted Japanese myths and legends, such as those in the eighth-century *Kojiki* (Records of Ancient Matters), to express his emotional response to Japan as a nation and the abundance and beauty of nature itself. Aoki's depictions of heroic Japanese historical figures lauded the Japanese nation-state and the achievements of the Japanese people. But unlike Kuroda, whose main mission was to serve the nation and communicate an all-embracing philosophy, Aoki emphasized individual artistic expression and personal identity. His fascination with subjectivity and interiority, and decidedly secondary concern with realistic representation, are eloquently expressed in his many haunting expressionistic self-portraits. In this respect, his work, and that of the other romantic artists, served as a bridge to the postwar era of individualistic expression.

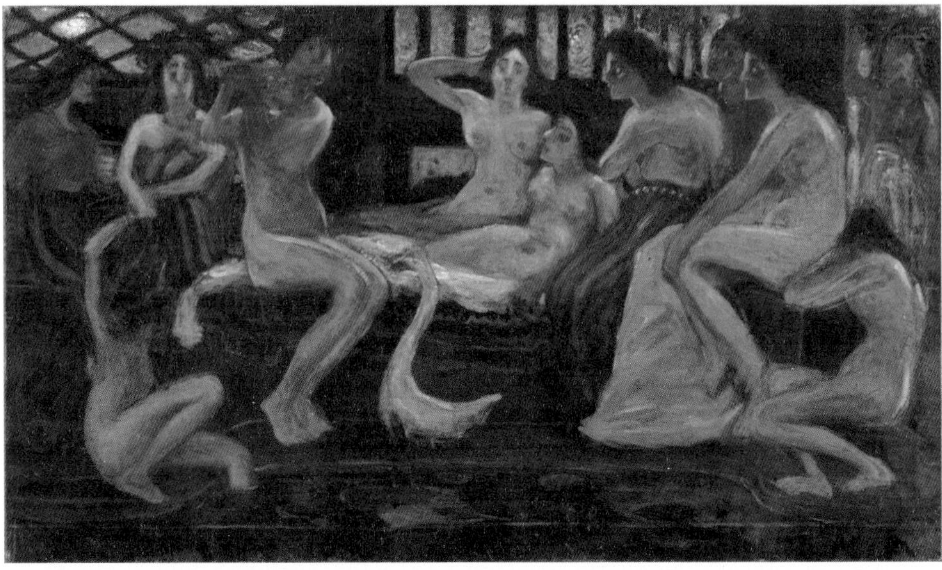

Figure 19.2 Aoki Shigeru, *The Tenpyo Era* (Tenpyo jidai), 1904. Oil on paper, 45.3 × 75.5 cm/ 18 × 30 inches. Bridgestone Museum of Art, Ishibashi Foundation, Tokyo.

Art, Individualism, and Self-Expression

In the late Meiji period following the Russo-Japanese war (1904–5), Japan experienced what Jay Rubin had identified as a "release from a total devotion to the national mission.[16] Economic hardship plus disappointment with the Treaty of Portsmouth, which stripped Japan of some of its war-won territory in northern China, inflamed a resentful and disillusioned populace that expressed its indignation at an antipeace demonstration in Hibiya Park. Despite this discontent, however, the general sentiment was that Japan had achieved its goal of national independence, and the sense of urgency over achieving parity with Western powers abated. This trend had profound implications for the intelligentsia's perception of what should be the individual's social role. Gradually there was a shift from the early Meiji conception of the link between individual success and familial and national prosperity to an emphasis on individual concerns with personal, social, and economic success, irrespective of family or state.[17] Moreover, the emphasis on inward directedness that developed sanctioned the cultivation of the "autonomous self." An individual's exploration of psychological interiority, subjectivity, and self-expression was now acceptable. In order to distinguish these new attitudes from nationalistic individualism, Henry Smith calls the postwar shift a movement of "self-concerned" individualism.

In the 1890s, a loose association of writers began to explore new discursive space, defined by the individual's putative daily experiences. These writers, referred to as the naturalists, championed an unmediated presentation of the experience of the individual – in an "authentic" voice. A strong sense of the oppressiveness and conformity of Meiji society also surfaced prompting a retreat to a more private arena of greater sexual and emotional autonomy.[18]

Although the novelist and renowned proponent of individualism Natsume Sōseki remained on the periphery of the naturalist movement, he addressed many of the questions raised by naturalism. Like the naturalists, he found the promotion of man's individualism deeply alienating. He saw this cultural shift as precipitating a collective nervous breakdown among the Japanese intelligentsia, rather than offering freedom from social constraints. Like other intellectuals of the late Meiji period, Sōseki recognized the problem of the individual's alienation in modern society but felt that the trend was irreversible and that there was no returning to a premodern consciousness. Sōseki came into public conflict with the government in 1911 because of his negative response to the Ministry of Education's establishing a Committee on Literature, which he criticized as the state's unprogressive attempt to counter naturalism so that it could promote its own view of a "wholesome" (*kenzen*) literature.

State authorities were troubled by the naturalists' assertion of individual autonomy, seeing the social consequences and political ramifications as potentially dangerous. Japanese nationhood was predicated on a tacit agreement by individuals, society, and the state to maintain consistent goals. The thought of each imperial subject establishing goals separate from those of the state seriously threatened national security. Bureaucrats, who had warily supported the liberation of the individual in the hope of harnessing the resulting energy for official objectives, could not sanction a divisive movement promoting absolute individual autonomy.[19] The total retreat from society proposed by the naturalists threatened the very fabric of Japanese nationhood. Eventually, Japanese authorities allowed naturalist writers to retreat into an apolitical realm, warning them to avoid in their works any criticism of daily life that might be construed as an indictment of the state. Censors remained alert to anything socially subversive or inconsistent with the moral imperatives of the state.

The issues that had prompted intense soul-searching by writers evoked a similar response among visual artists. Influenced by information about anti-academic trends in France brought back by traveling artists after the turn of the century, younger Japanese artists began to perceive academicism as passé. They searched for a new, more relevant mode of artistic expression and questioned the pedagogical and aesthetic foundations of academic training and the art establishment. An appreciation of post-impressionism and expressionism in Europe, combined with the pervasive influence of the naturalists, inspired a new individualism that asserted the primacy of self-expression (*jiko hyōgen*) and the centrality of the autonomous individual in art.

Some intellectuals, profoundly influenced by the naturalists' advocacy of individualism and individual experience, strongly criticized their relentless preoccupation with the dark side of human experience as well as their refusal to attempt to improve their lot. The artists and writers associated with the White Birch Society (Shirakaba-ha), which published the general arts periodical *Shirakaba*, epitomized this more positive attitude, and their opinions resonated widely.[20] While the naturalist writers were perceived as retreating from public life and social responsibility into a morass of negativity, Shirakaba-ha members were generally more optimistic about the individual's ability to improve society.

Undoubtedly, class differences affected the outlooks of these two groups. Unlike the naturalists, who for the most part were second sons of former samurai who themselves had been displaced socially and financially by changes during the Meiji Restoration, Shirakaba-ha members were all from privileged aristocratic families and had attended the elite Peer's School (Gakushūin). Buoyed by the advocacy of individual rights in the Western theories of democracy and liberalism, though equally disenchanted with political realities, Shirakaba-ha members, unlike the naturalists, espoused personal cultivation as a legitimate *social* goal. Believing that all could better themselves through education, Shirakaba-ha members viewed individual growth as a means to a more equitable society.

In the work of the Shirakaba-ha, the struggle for self-cultivation was transformed from a retreatist, world-denying attitude to a heroic gesture of the individual genius to improve society. Shirakaba-ha members emphasized the expression of emotion and intuition, particularly in response to nature. Their goal was to extract and express the aesthetic qualities of life. Both the neo-Kantian thought popular in Japan at the time and the Japanese Christian movement fueled their conceptions. Several members were initially involved with Christianity as followers of Uchimura Kanzō (1861–1930), one of the foremost Christian thinkers in Japan. Uchimura developed the concept of a "non-church" (*mukyōkai*) form of Christianity and combined neo-Confucianism and *bushidō* (the way of the warrior) morality with libertarian individualism to produce a deeply ambivalent philosophy that oscillated between nationalism and pacificism, fatalism and free will. Christians among the Shirakaba-ha claimed that through Christian dogma and its definition of the relationship between God and man they had discovered a new psychological and spiritual interiority.[21] Their particular Christianity included an element of utopian socialism, which was adopted into Shirakaba-ha thought as an egalitarian ideal, as well as an antagonism toward militarism and state imperialism abroad.

Not only was *Shirakaba* the organ for a wide-reaching and influential literary movement, but it also played a major role in introducing and disseminating information about European art. The magazine strongly encouraged the shift already under way from an interest in academicism to a new preoccupation with impressionism, post-impressionism, and expressionism. The Shirakaba-ha supported artists rejected from the Bunten by sponsoring its own *yōga "salon des refusés"* (*rakusenten*) in 1911. Many of the rejected artists had recently returned from study in Paris and were working in nonacademic styles. The following year, a number of these same artists were accepted into the Bunten, where the display of their work expanded that organization's aesthetic boundaries.[22]

C. Louis Hind's widely read book *The Post-Impressionists* (1911), with its explication of post-impressionism under the rubric of expressionism, shaped the way Japanese thinkers viewed Cézanne, Gauguin, Rodin, and Van Gogh, to name just a few of the most popular European artists.[23] No longer concerned with mimetic representation or historical and allegorical themes, the post-impressionists were viewed as the consummate icons of the cult of the self. The subjective vision in their work appealed to Japanese artists also struggling toward self-expression. These European artists became heroes to the Japanese, for they exemplified a heroic struggle similar to that expressed by the Shirakaba-ha theorist Mushanokōji Saneatsu: "I only understand myself; I only do my work; I only love myself. Everyone else, even my parents, my brother, my master, my friends, my beloved, are enemies to my growing self. Hated though I am, despised though I am, I go my own way.[24]

The Shirakaba-ha had several counterparts in the visual arts. A short-lived gathering of artists under the title of the Fusain, or Sketch Society (Fyūzan-kai), was among the first publicly to assert the philosophical and stylistic imperatives of individualism, generally opposing Bunten institutionalism. Resenting the authoritarianism of official public exhibitions, Fusain artists demanded greater stylistic and thematic autonomy and the ability to judge their own works. Similarly, in 1914, a group of *yōga* artists formally withdrew from participation in the Bunten after unsuccessfully petitioning to divide the *yōga* section into two categories, called *ikka* and *nika* (for older and newer artistic idioms); they wanted what they perceived as different stylistic trends to be judged separately. Called Nika-kai (the Association of the Second Section), the secessionist group went on to become the largest and most influential independent exhibiting society of so-called progressive artists. A number of other similarly minded coteries also formed around this time, and artists often exhibited in several different groups at once.

A strong autobiographical quality characterized the work of many Nika artists. Art and art making had become a mirror of the individual's spirit and personality, and a means by which artists could analyze themselves as the subject. The striking preponderance of self-portraits produced by such artists as Kishida Ryūsei, Arishima Ikuma, Umehara Ryūzaburō, Yamashita Shintarō, and Yasui Sōtarō, among others, attests to their great "self-concern." Many Nika artists believed the viewer could judge the artist's personal authenticity based on the art works' expression of sentiment and experience.[25] Like the naturalist writers, Nika artists believed in the need to reveal the truth of one's experiences – no matter how painful the result – a belief that left the artist to contend with the dual "burden of authenticity and individuality."[26]

Nika artists, like members of the Shirakaba-ha, implicitly grappled with the problem of uncoupling the individual from the state, seeking to establish the primacy of subjectivity and self-expression in the arts as well as promoting their social value. Responding to the still dominant discourse of academicism and representational art in *yōga* circles, Shirakaba-ha member Takamura Kōtarō, a well-known artist, poet, and critic, articulated a credo that echoed the sentiments of his contemporaries. In line with Sōseki's statement that "art begins with the expression of the self and ends with the expression of the self.[27] Takamura penned the now famous essay "Green Sun" (Midori iro no taiyō), published in *Subaru* in 1910.[28] Takamura took Kuroda's lyrical response to nature one step further by arguing for an entirely expressionistic response that need not relate to the appearance of the natural world:

> I am seeking absolute freedom in art. I recognize the infinite authority of the artist's personality. In every sense I want to think of art from the viewpoint of one single human being, and I want to evaluate a work by starting from consideration of the personality as it is and not to admit a great number of doubts. If I think of something as blue and someone else sees it as red, criticism should start from the point of view that this person sees the object as red and then confine itself to the question of how the red is treated. I see no reason to go on complaining because the artist sees the object differently from the way I do. Instead, I consider it a pleasant surprise to find a different view of nature from my own. I prefer to consider how this artist has arrived at the nucleus of nature and how he has fulfilled his personal feelings. It does not matter to me if two or three people paint something called a "green sun," because I might from time to time see the same thing myself.[29]

Takamura's criticism of art's slavish attachment to mimetic representation and his championing of unfettered self-expression was a rallying call for many artists ultimately categorized as "post-impressionists" *(kōki inshō-ha)* and "expressionists" *(hyōgenshugisha)*. These terms, used broadly and sometimes indiscriminately, came to encompass all art work centered on self-expression, regardless of social, political, or artistic attitude. Hence, the Japanese futurists and Mavo were both termed expressionists.

Mavo and Late Taishō Japan

By the end of World War I, in the middle of the Taishō era, artists had entered a new ideological landscape, and the discussion of individualism took on stronger sociopolitical overtones. Nationally, there was guarded optimism and confidence about Japan's situation vis-à-vis the European powers. Japan had experienced rapid industrial expansion as a wartime supplier to the allies, and the re-opening of China after the war bolstered the Japanese imperialist project. The postwar reordering of social and economic structures resulted in a steady migration of worker to urban areas and the emergence of both a sizable industrial working class and a new middle class of civil servants, white-collar workers, and professionals. Little of the national prosperity, however, trickled down to the working classes. In fact, wartime inflation had reduced the value of wages, which, combined with crowded urban living conditions, exacerbated feelings of discontent. Moreover, although Japan had suffered no physical destruction during the war, afterward, as a participant in the world economy, it experienced a severe postwar depression. This abrupt economic downturn caused high unemployment, which increased the social unrest.

Historians have written of a crisis in political and social consciousness among the intelligentsia in the period. The same forces that were acting to "democratize" and "liberalize" Japan's historically rigid social system were also generating incendiary political conflict and social upheaval. Peter Duus has noted that by the mid-Taishō period many liberal intellectuals had turned from a "consensus model" of Japanese society to a "conflict model" – that is, from a belief in the shared values of state and society with the ultimate goal of equal opportunity achieved through constitutional government, to a conviction that social conflict was linked to poverty, itself rooted in class inequity.[30] This shift was a response to increasing signs of social strife, starting with the anti-Portsmouth treaty demonstrations, escalating with the 1912 rallies against the Diet in Hibiya that resulted in the mass resignation of the cabinet, and culminating in large-scale urban and rural strikes after 1918. In response, many intellectuals, including artists and writers, began to look to leftist political thought, seeing "struggle between interest groups or classes as the central motif to human history, and … ascrib[ing] the existence of social conflict in Japan not to transient maladjustments in the social mechanism but to deep-seated imperatives of social life."[31] Fueled by this new social awareness, intellectuals turned their search outward to locate a means by which the individual could be more actively engaged with society.

Many liberal and leftist-oriented intellectuals condemned the Shirakaba-ha's elitism and focus on inner cultivation. After World War I, the intelligentsia came to share the long-standing concerns of the novelist and Shirakaba-ha member Arishima Takeo about the social impotence of the intellectual and his call for a stronger link between thought and action. Like the naturalists, Arishima was intensely distressed and anxious about the modern condition. A strong believer in individualism, Arishima was also concerned about the working classes and the need for action on their behalf. In the end, he gave up his property to a collective of tenant farmers, a gesture mirrored in Mushanokōji's ultimately unsuccessful attempt to set up an experimental utopian community in Hokkaidö called "New Village" (Atarashiki Mura). Morbidly disillusioned, Arishima made a socially symbolic act of his despondency: he committed suicide in June 1923.

A month later Mavo publicly announced its formation. The artists of Mavo's generation, most of whom came of age in the late Taishō period, were confronted by the same tumult that so troubled Arishima Takeo. They felt it imperative to respond with social action. To cultivate subjective interiority now seemed inadequate. Yet, although the works of Mavo artists attest to the group's strong commitment to social revolution, Mavo members always considered themselves artists first. They consistently concerned themselves with the formal qualities of their work, attempting to innovate within the field of art. Seeking a new definition of the artist and a new role for art, they questioned the validity of existing artistic methods and the exclusivity of the *gadan*. Reforming art had to begin with restructuring its institutions. By the 1920s, the *gadan* consisted of a number of exhibiting societies and art schools (in effect, institutional cartels) that greatly influenced the development of the art world aesthetically and professionally. *Yōga* artists considered the Tokyo School of Fine Arts the best training ground for professional success. Following close behind were the private ateliers affiliated with teachers at the school, particularly those associated with Kuroda's White Horse Society, which helped successive generations of artists pursue studies abroad and reestablish themselves upon their return to Japan.

Despite criticism, the Bunten, under the watchful eye of its sponsoring agency, the Ministry of Education, remained the most prominent and prestigious state-sponsored public art exhibition venue. Just before World War I, the return from their studies abroad of a host of younger well-connected White Horse Society-trained painters, such as Fujishima Takeji, Yamashita Shintarō, Shirataki Ikunosuke, Yuasa Ichirō, Tsuda Seifū, and Arishima Ikuma, exerted pressure to change the stylistic boundaries of the official exhibition. These painters had studied together in Europe, often becoming friends, and they shared an interest in the new modernist styles of post-impressionism. While some continued to support the Bunten, others remained dissatisfied with the organization's lack of stylistic diversity and exclusivity, prompting them to form the purportedly more progressive Nika art association. Within several years of its founding, however, the Nika exhibition and its various smaller spinoffs, the Sōdosha and the Shun'yōkai, had themselves become exclusive organizations, though still open to a much greater diversity of formal styles than the official salon. In fact, by complementing the Bunten, these groups reinforced the existing structures of the art establishment.

In 1918, the Bunten was renamed the "Exhibition of the Imperial Academy of Fine Arts," or Teiten (Teikoku Bijutsuin Tenrankai), and came under the purview of a newly appointed governing body of established artists, the Imperial Art Academy (Teikoku Bijutsuin), which, while opening its ranks to modernist painters, notoriously engaged in cronyism by promoting its own academy members and their students. Unaffiliated artists or those who sought to circumvent the seniority system had little hope of recognition from the Teiten. Moreover, the vast majority of *gadan* artists were dedicated to the production of autonomous fine art, and unconcerned with the issues of praxis emerging in artistic discourse in the Soviet Union and Weimar Germany.

Mavo artists, attuned to these Western debates, believed that by revolutionizing artistic practice they would also revolutionize Japanese society. Unable to break into the exclusive sphere of the *gadan*, they instead opposed it, as disaffected youths contemptuous of the nation's moral and sociopolitical agenda. Feeling deeply alienated, they chose to be intellectual dissidents or social bohemians, gravitating to various strains of socialist thought, most prominently anarchism, as an alternative to state-promoted capitalism. In the process, they appointed themselves spokesmen for the disenfranchised, speaking out against social inequity. Originally emerging out of the rebellious and anarchist-inclined Futurist Art Association (Miraiha Bijutsu Kyōkai), Mavo artists emphasized the anarchist tenor of their work. However, like the multifaceted anarchist movement, the group expressed many ambivalent attitudes – social and antisocial, political and antipolitical, egoistic and collectivist – so that they left a dialectical rather than a programmatic legacy.

Notes

1 Earl Kinmouth, *The Self-Made Man in Meiji Japanese Thought: From Samurai to Salaryman* (Berkeley: University of California Press, 1981).

2 The expression was coined by Makimura Masanao, vice-governor of Kyoto. Ellen Conant, "The French Connection: Emile Guimet's Mission to Japan, A Cultural Context for *Japonisme*," in *Japan in Transition: Thought and Action in the Meiji Era, 1868–1912*, ed. Hilary Conroy, Sandra Davis, and Wayne Patterson (Rutherford, NJ: Farleigh Dickinson University Press, 1984), 128–30.

3 Languages taught at the institute and translated there included Dutch, English, French, and German. The curriculum was largely dedicated to subjects related to the military, including metallurgy, surveying, navigation, mathematics, physics, chemistry, and mechanical engineering. [...]

4 Michiaki Kawakita, "Western Influence on Japanese Painting and Sculpture," in *Dialogue in Art: Japan and the West*, ed. Chisaburoh Yamada (Tokyo: Kōdansha International, 1976), 83.

5 Kawakita, "Western Influence," 82.

6 Haga Tōru, "The Formation of Realism in Meiji Painting: The Artistic Career of Takahashi Yuichi," in *Tradition and Modernization in Japanese Culture*, ed. Donald H. Shively (Princeton: Princeton University Press, 1971), 228, 253.

7 The National Industrial Arts Exhibitions (Naikoku Kangyō Hakurankai) began in 1877 and were mounted again in 1881, 1890, 1895, and 1903.

8 Kuroda Seiki's adoptive father, Kuroda Kiyotsuna, was from the powerful Satsuma clan and an important figure in the Meiji Restoration who served as an oligarch *(genrōin)* in the early Meiji government.

9 Kitazawa Notiaki, *Kishida Ryūsei to Taishō avangyarudo* (Kishida Ryūsei and the Taishō avant-garde) (Tokyo: Iwanami Shoten, 1993), 32–6.

10 Kitazawa, *Kishida Ryūsei*, 38.

11 Miriam Levin, *Republican Art and Ideology in Late Nineteenth-Century France* (Ann Arbor, MI: UMI Research Press, 1986).

12 Kitazawa Noriaki, *Me no shinden (Palace of the eye)* (Tokyo: Bijutsu Shuppansha, 1989), 164–82; Kitazawa, *Kishida Ryūsei*, 30–31.

13 Takashina Shūji, "Natsume Sōseki and the Development of Modern Japanese Art," in *Culture and Identity: Japanese Intellectuals During the Interwar Years*, ed. J. Thomas Rimer (Princeton: Princeton University Press, 1990), 273–4.

14 Kawakita Michiaki, ed., *Aoki Shigeru to rōmanshugi* (Aoki Shigeru and romanticism), Kindai no bijutsu, no. 1 (Tokyo: Ibundō, 1970), 33–4.

15 Kawakita, *Aoki Shigeru to rōmanshugi*, 18.

16 Jay Rubin, *Injurious to Public Morals: Writers and the Meiji State* (Seattle: University of Washington Press, 1984), 60.

17 Yoshitake Oka, "Generational Conflict After the Russo-Japanese War," in *Conflict in Modern Japanese History*, 197–9, 206.

18 Sharon Nolte, *Liberalism in Modern Japan; Ishibashi Tanzan and His Teachers, 1905–1960* (Berkeley: University of California Press, 1987), 16.

19 Individualism was seen as incompatible with the maintenance of the Japanese national polity *(kokutai)* and the emperor system *(tennōsei)*, "which demanded absolute loyalty and obedience"; reconciliation could only come from imperial benevolence. Japanese nationalists believed that "the corporate imperial state transcended not only individual interests but the whole people." Nolte, *Liberalism*, 55–6.

20 [...] *Shirakaba* achieved an unprecedented circulation for a "coterie magazine" *(dōjin zasshi)*. At the highest point of circulation, a single issue sold 10,000 copies, a statistic that does not take into consideration the widespread sharing of published material in the period. [...] Edward Fowler, *The Rhetoric of Confession* (Berkeley: University of California Press, 1988), 132.

21 Kitazawa, *Kishida Ryūsei*, 27.

22 *Nika nanajū nenshi* (Seventy-year history of Nika) (Tokyo: Zaidan Hōjin Nikakai, 1985), 8–9.

23 Takashina Shūji, "*Shirakaba* to kindai bijutsu," in *Nihon kindai no biishiki* (Tokyo: Seidosha, 1993), 327.

24 Mushanokōji's comment on the wrenching struggle involved in individual liberation was originally published in *Shirakaba* (August 1911). [...]

25 Rimer, "Tokyo in Paris," 60–1.

26 Ibid., 66. Yamashita Shintarō, 1881–1966; Yasui Sōtarō, 1888–1955.

27 Takashina, "Natsume Sōseki," 277.

28 Takamura Kōtarō, "Midori iro no taiyō" (A green sun), in *A Brief History of Imbecility*, trans. Satō Hiroaki (Honolulu: University of Hawaii Press, 1992), 180–6.

29 Translated in Kawakita Michiaki, *Modern Currents in Japanese Art, The Heibonsha Survey of Japanese Art*, no. 24, trans. Charles Terry (New York and Tokyo: Weatherhill/Heibonsha, 1974), 96.

30 Peter Duus, "Liberal Intellectuals and Social Conflict in Taishō Japan," in *Conflict in Modern Japanese History*, ed. Tetsuo Najita and J. Victor Koschmann (Princeton: Princeton University Press, 1982), 412–15.

31 Duus, "Liberal Intellectuals," 426. […]

20

Artistic Subjectivity in the Taishō and Early Shōwa Avant-Garde

JOHN CLARK*

For an artist, being modern in Japan in the early years of the twentieth century was not just about making art that conformed to European art styles. Australian art historian John Clark displays the diverse range of assimilations and transformations of European modern art styles in Japan during the first half of the twentieth century, from the experimental 1920s through the 1930s and the increasing censorship of the avant-garde, effectively silenced by the time of Japan's involvement in World War II.

Clark's survey begins at the end of the Meiji era of intensive Westernization (1868–1912) and the shift away from the mimetic style of academic realism associated in Japan with objectivity and modernization to the radically "subjective" anti-academic modern movements from Expressionism to Dada and Surrealism. In addition to canvassing the main artists and movements, the author argues that bound up with this process of assimilation was the emergence of new ideas about the place and purpose of the artist in Japanese society, showing how artists began to focus energy on their own subjective interests and preoccupations, rather than seeing their art as the expression of a wider national consciousness.

The Taishō (1912–26) and Shōwa (1926–89) of Clark's title are, like Meiji, names for eras corresponding with the reigns of Japanese emperors. The term "artistic subjectivity" identifies a universal hallmark of modernism. Although as Clark notes, subjective individualism took a very different shape in Japan than in the West, all modern art is subjective in that it is freely created by an individual to convey his or her unique feelings, beliefs, and ideas. The hermeneutic opposite would be "objective" art, that is, art that serves a purpose – political, religious, economic – other than self-expression. No artwork,

* John Clark (1994) "Artistic Subjectivity in the Taishō and Early Shōwa Avant-Garde." In Alexandra Munroe (ed.) *Japanese Art after 1945: Scream against the Sky* (pp. 41–53). New York, NY: Harry N. Abrams.

Modern Art in Africa, Asia, and Latin America: An Introduction to Global Modernisms, First Edition.
Edited by Elaine O'Brien, Everlyn Nicodemus, Melissa Chiu, Benjamin Genocchio, Mary K. Coffey, and Roberto Tejada.

however, is entirely subjective or objective. To Clark, even Japanese Proletarian art, modeled on Soviet socialist realism and meant to promote international communist objectives, had subjective qualities.

For more on how these and other rhizomatic concepts of global modernism assumed hybrid forms in Japan, see the essay in this volume by Gennifer Weisenfeld, "Western Style Painting in Japan: Mimesis, Individualism and Japanese Nationhood."

Further Readings

Clark, John (1986) "Modernity in Japanese Painting." *Art History* 9(2): 213–31.

Menzies, Jackie (ed.) (1998) *Modern Boy, Modern Girl: Modernity in Japanese Art* (exhibition catalog). Sydney, Australia: Art Gallery of New South Wales.

Rimer, Thomas J. (1990) *Culture and Identity: Japanese Intellectuals during the Interwar Years*. Princeton, NJ: Princeton University Press.

Shūji, Takashina and Rimer, J. Thomas (with Gerald Bolas) (1987) *Paris in Japan: The Japanese Encounter with European Painting (exhibition catalog)*. St Louis, MO: Washington University.

Tsutomu, Mizusawa (2000) "The Artists Start to Dance: The Changing Image of the Body in Art of the Taisho Period." In Elise K. Tipton and John Clark (eds), *Being Modern in Japan: Culture and Society from the 1910s to the 1930s* (pp. 15–24). Sydney, Australia: Fine Arts Press.

A new kind of artistic subjectivity developed in Japan during the Taisho era (1912–26) and more obviously during the early Showa era (1926–late 1930s). The change was due to various developments in art practice, but was also a reaction to the state nationalism of the preceding Meiji era (1868–1912). Among the small number of Japanese Futurists, Dadaists, and, by around 1935, far larger number of Surrealists, there began a private discourse about the situation of the creative artist in the world. This discourse cut across a quite diverse range of stylistic assimilations from, and transformations of, European modern painting. While Japanese painters of Taisho and early Showa followed their Meiji forbears in their conscious redeployment of "Western" styles, they placed their own self-consciousness at the center of their creative practice. Artists and their works no longer represented a site for the discourses of national consciousness; the national was only one of many sites for the discourse of the artist's identity. Artists focused the discourse on themselves and their own sympathies and identification, not on a social or international other given to them by the state or, more broadly and abstractly, by Japan's historical situation. One can even see the short-lived Proletarian Art movement (1926–34), despite its focus on others in society, as an example of the development of such subjectivism, on a par with the more directly subjectivist Surrealism that was practiced in the Japan of the 1930s and 1940s.

As in Europe, the avant-garde in prewar Japan arose not only as the bearer of formal innovation and creator of new types of art institutions, but its stylistic discourses came at the historical conjunction of a repositioning of the artist in relation to the work itself, which was no longer an extension of received or necessary national taste. At the same time, the work could be far more inner-directed even as it was intended for public exhibition.

By the 1920s, the Japanese government had established a secure, conservative salon system. It was the official salon, *Bunten* (Ministry of Education Fine Arts Exhibition, inaugurated in 1907),[1] and its successors that favored a mixture of French *pleinairiste* and British Victorian and Edwardian styles, that presented an authority that an avant-garde could contest. This avant-garde did so from the same position of informed "knower" of the "West" that had once empowered the intellectuals and artists of the Meiji era. There is no room here to examine all the implications of this problematic for the art world: what this essay examines is the way different kinds of artistic subjectivity marked various responses to new styles and to new social and political situations during the 1920s and thirties.

Artistic Subjectivity and the Avant-Garde

The questioning of artistic subjectivity presented by the Japanese avant-garde had three moments before 1945: the inception of avant-garde groups from around 1910 to 1914; the social positioning of artists and art objects of the Dada and Proletarian Art movements from 1920 to 1934; and the rise of Surrealism and abstract art as a permitted, tacitly anti-establishment practice from 1929 to 1941.

How to be modernist, avant-garde, and Japanese had been a continual dilemma for artists since the turn of the century. It was partially resolved by the sculptor, painter, and poet, Takamura Kōtarō (1883–1956), who stated in his manifesto, "The Green Sun" (*Midori-iro no taiyō*), published in the April 1910 *Subaru*:

> I hope Japanese artists will try to use all *möglich* techniques without being put out by interpretation. I pray that when they do so, consequent on their interior psychological demands, they are not afraid of what is un-Japanese. However un-Japanese this might be, if a Japanese person creates it, it must be Japanese.[2]

[...]

Contemporary with Takamura's manifesto was the appearance of the journal *White Birch* (*Shirakaba*), which idealized the artist's life itself and maintained that it was not the production of, nor created in reaction to, a given artistic discourse. According to the art historian Takashina Shūji, the White Birch Society's emphasis on the self was a sort of romanticism, but one different from that of Western romantic artists who, when they absolutized the "self," had the implicit model of man's relation to God available to deny. For a Westerner to absolutize the self was to deny God. In Japan, what corresponded to God was an amorphous social "other" that existed in an ideological space. Since Meiji, this space had been occupied by the state and its mores. "Self-assertion" could only mean expanding the self by gaining "colonies," and doing one's best to hold on to one's domain while surrounded by others. Self-assertion meant either denying the other or turning one's back on the other. This meant that in understanding one's "self," there was only oneself to rely upon.[3]

In the 1910s, the White Birch artists took a humanist position in their absolutization – and ahistoricality – of the artistic subject. There are curious analogies in this humanist absolutization to the nihilistic position of the Futuro-Dadaists of the twenties that negated both the art work and artist. Their position is most clear in the 1920 manifesto of one of the more important early Futurists, Kanbara Tai (b. 1898):[4]

> Painters be gone! Art critics be gone! Art is absolutely free. There is no poetry, no painting, no music. What exists is creation only. Art is absolutely free. The freedom of its form is also absolute. Say, nerve, reason, sense, sound, smell, color, light, desire, movement, pressure – and furthermore, true life itself which stands at the end of all – there is nothing that does not fit the content of art; any material and any form cannot be useless in the course of creation.[5]

Such absolute non-dependency echoes Buddhist ideas about an unconditioned realm beyond karmically conditioned perception. The manifesto's ahistoricality is problematic because it recognizes neither the long development of European modernism, nor the way in which the history of Japan's introduction to European art was premised on different kinds of artistic subjectivities. [...]

There are two ways out of this ahistoricality: to refuse to accept inauthentic imitation; or to ground the practice of art in a social rather than an autonomously artistic discourse. Both ways were adopted, in succession, by the Dadaist and Constructivist Murayama Tomoyoshi (1901–77) who, after returning from Berlin, castigated the artists who participated in the second exhibition of the avant-garde group Action (*Akushon*)[6] in 1924 :

> Throw away your albums. Stand up by yourselves. I beg you to stop acting like monkeys. Respect yourselves more.... The worst things in this exhibition are Nakahara Minoru's copy of Grosz, Asano Takeshirō's reproduction of Archipenko, ... Yokoyama Junnosuke's reprinting of Rousseau and the copies of the constructionism of the Italian Futurists. There's even someone whose name I've forgotten who has borrowed [de] Chirico and Ernst's mechanical doll. Most of it is an imitation of spineless French imperial salon style boiled down from Picasso and Braque. There's nothing more shameless than this for the Japanese painting world. It makes you want to puke. Oh mates, how far will you be slaves? It's as if you had been born slaves for generations.[7]

[...] This important critique was delivered by an artist who was remarkably familiar with European modernism: Murayama had, while in Berlin, painted Dada-Constructivist schemes in the manner of Hannah Höch's collages, and, upon his return to Japan, assembled Dadaist *objets*. Murayama's critique marks the beginning of an attack on Japanese modernism for being merely the local imitation of a tendency elsewhere, an attack which was to reappear in various guises during the 1950s and sixties.

Murayama initially pursued something he called "Conscious Constructivism" which, in practice, was an idiosyncratic synthesis of radical theater, installation-performance, and a consciousness of the social implications of avant-garde practice.

His contribution to the May 1925 "Theater of the Third Section" (*Gekijō no Sanka*), a temporary alliance of different members of the avant-garde that presented Dadaist and Expressionist theatrical sketches, has been described as follows: After an opening accompaniment similar to the well-known folk tune *Yagi-bushi*, the curtain rose and a child selling newspapers came out on stage. Then a prostitute with a distended belly appeared, wearing a pink, Western-style dress. This woman gave birth to children squatting directly on the ground, and the babies then rose up into heaven. Another report of the performance speaks of five or six rubber dolls hung from a bamboo pole that amused the audience when they were lifted to the ceiling.[8] Murayama's performance at the "Theater of the Third Section" may have been artistically radical, but there was some pessimism about the group's revolutionary potential, reflecting a new interest in socialist issues. Okada Tatsuo, a friend of the group and former member of Futurist Art Association (*Mirai-ha Bijutsu Kyōkai*),[9] wrote in the July 1925 issue of the journal *Mizue*: "the egg which *Sanka* has delivered does not appear to be strong enough to permeate into the kernel of the times and rupture; it cannot become the fuse for a social revolution, an individual revolution, nor a revolution in the life of the masses."[10]

The "Theater of the Third Section" soon broke apart and Murayama allied himself with the new current of Soviet art introduced into Japan around 1927. Murayama became a proletarian artist and was subsequently imprisoned during the militarists' anti-Communist purges in the 1930s. He later claimed that "*Sanka* was destroyed by anarchism and nihilism"[11] and that "from this time the distinction became clear between those who were moving vaguely towards a socialist art without understanding the distinction between Communism and anarchism, and those who were for artistic suprematism."[12]

Although this statement belies Murayama's partisan position and a certain amount of revisionism, it was certainly true that from around 1925, the Japanese avant-garde appeared to be going in two directions; it is not surprising that it eventually split.

Some artists began to explore a kind of formalism. Recently-imported European styles such as Cubism, and new subject matter for painters, such as scientific fantasy, led artists increasingly to regard avant-garde practice as outside of, or at least parallel, to society. In the 1930s, artists were exposed to late École de Paris work and illustrations of Jean Arp, Joan Miró, and the Bauhaus; formalism developed into a kind of organic abstraction, which, in the late 1930s, became what some have called Constructivist abstract expression.

The other trend was socially concerned art. Some artists, like Yabe Tomoe, who had earlier made Decorative Cubist works, were, by the late 1920s, to become wholly committed Socialist Realist painters, making art they thought was understood by ordinary workers. Proletarian Art arose from a late-1920s reinterpretation of the critical possibilities of salon realism via the Soviet example. In Japan, it also developed out of a long tendency to satirize the political via grotesque imagery, which, since late Meiji, the state had never quite succeeded in repressing. Many artists were influenced by George Grosz's illustrations in the German periodical *Simplicissimus*, and by Expressionist-humanist prints such as those of Käthe Kollwitz. Perhaps the most lasting expressions of the Proletarian Art movement were the newspaper collages of Yanase Masamu (1900–45), a leading member of the group who was arrested in 1932 for his practices. [...]

Murayama's statement about the break between political progressives and formalists seems, in retrospect, to have had some validity. With the importation of a new international Surrealist style concurrent with a redefinition of artistic subjectivity, the socially-conscious style of the late 1920s would simply be a convenient gloss on a revised national(ist) ego. The art historian, Tanaka Yoshio notes, "what was dangerous was that 'internationalization' and 'informationalization' would give birth to superficial misinterpretation. It was clearly visible that 'one's own art' changed its clothes into 'the art of Japan.' In our country, where the individual was not established, 'the art of Japan' easily slipped into becoming 'the art of Fascism.'"[13]

Surrealism and the Artistic Subjectivity of the Avant-Garde

A negative example of the possibilities for artistic subjectivity is reflected by opposition within the avant-garde to Surrealism. The anarcho-Futurist tone of Kanbara Tai's reply to a 1937 questionnaire exemplifies this opposition:

> [Surrealism is] just the twisted outlet for doubt, criticism, derision, discontent, and disaffection on the part of an isolated stratum of the liberalists, who cannot even follow blindly and are incapable of struggling against the domination of current state integration. As the social crisis intensifies further, the chimeral social attitude of the Surrealists will no longer be permissible, and their paintings will probably secrete themselves from the streets into the bedroom. That some of these paintings have recently become "pornographic" gives us that information.[14]

Kanbara saw Surrealism as a bourgeois strategy for avoiding reality, first by making various disaffected public stances, then by an inner emigration, and finally by pursuing nihilist eroticism.

In 1937, the artist Fukuzawa Ichirō (1898–1992)[15] questioned whether Surrealism in Japan at that time was an exotic flower transplanted from a distant land and cultivated in an enclosed garden by several artists besotted (*épris*) by European culture. He likened these artists to the Meiji aristocrats of the 1890s who had dressed up in Western garb to dance with foreigners at Tokyo's exclusive dance hall, the Rokumeikan (Deer-Cry Pavilion).

Although his work resembles Surrealism in its metaphorical use of collage techniques that he derived from Max Ernst, Fukuzawa should be seen as a kind of realist who used Surrealist techniques and concepts to give his work more of a critical edge. His odd juxtapositions, twisted compositions, and strange magical lighting that infused his figurative elements [reflect] his resistance to naturalization, despite the fact that he used recognizable image forms. He made socially absurdist schemas that used visual material and compositions drawn from such sources as contemporary illustrations and popular scientific magazines. Fukuzawa even did savage parodies, like his *Oxen* of 1936, completed after a visit to Manchuria. He used the bull motif to rail against militarist barbarism, and anticipated Picasso's *Guernica* of the following year.

Fukuzawa was indebted to Giorgio de Chirico and Max Ernst, but he used few of the other typical Surrealist techniques, such as automatic writing and *decalcomanie*,[16] the latter first experimented with in Japan in 1937 by the Surrealist painter Kitawaki Noboru (1901–51). Indeed, Fukuzawa sought symbols found in "profound reflection born of conscious experience" rather than ones that were products of the psychological experience of the unconscious.

In an article in the journal *Atorie* (June 1937), Fukuzawa speaks of the political significance of an integration of self and world, which he saw his critical use of symbols as leading to. Surrealism too, "in order to respond to the need for an overall revival of the value of the real, demands contact and unification between our inner and outer mental worlds," and "it was [André] Breton who did not hold back from the interpretation that strange and wondrous inner forms could be planted in the outer soil of Communism."[17]

[...]

[...] the painter Migishi Kōtarō (1903–34) represents a more typical late 1920s artist, a Fauvist who became avant-garde after seeing Surrealist works at the "Tokyo-Paris Exhibition of Rising Art" in December 1932. He was among the first Japanese artists to work with automatist techniques with his *Orchestra* (1933), and, along with a number of early Surrealists like Yoshihara Jirō (1905–72), also began to make more purely abstract compositions. These he created, however, not with lines as an expression of the unconscious, but through his sympathetic intoxication with musical rhythms. Migishi's practice was eclectic: he also explored notions of mechanical beauty that were influenced by the work of Le Corbusier. And by early 1934, he tried to stop time by depicting a quiet, motionless world of sea, butterflies, and shells. His works manifest a dry eroticism with desiccated motifs laid out before a nominal and naturalistic landscape in the manner of Salvador Dalí, whose works he must have seen in reproduction a few years earlier. Migishi saw his last works as having fused "the still, bright, centripetal beauty in the oriental spirit and the simple, clear, centrifugal beauty of Western Europe."

[...]

Surrealism as Art Discourse in Japan

In 1928, Surrealism was the latest wave of the European avant-garde to arrive in Japan, and its more superficial exponents were roundly criticized by those who disliked shallow imitation of European trends, or by those like Murayama and Fukuzawa, who had been to Europe, had direct experience, and thought they knew better. Surrealism was introduced in a context where three currents of figurative art were dominant. [...]

The trends of figuration consisted firstly of the old survivors of a wide variety of style, from late-Victorian academic realism through to the Japanified Post-Impressionist painting that dominated the government salon *Teiten* (Imperial Fine Arts Exhibition, 1919–34) and the anti-mainstream establishment-in-waiting, *Nika-kai*. These old survivors were surrounded by a second stream who would become prominent in the early 1930s, and after 1936 would be the main jurors of the reformulated government salon, *Shin-Bunten* (New Ministry of Education Fine Arts Exhibition). There was also a new group of figurative artists who practiced a mixture of late-1920s École de Paris mannerisms and some of the *Neue Sachlichkeit* styles that could be found in Paris and Berlin in the early 1930s. [...]

Surrealism also arrived just as two pressures were disrupting Proletarian Art. One was the effect of the special police investigations of all kinds of left-wing activity, including broadly cultural ones. The other was its own artistic bankruptcy: despite several notable exceptions, Proletarian Art seems largely to have been composed of propagandistic works in approved figurative manners.

[...]

One suspects that the appeal of Surrealism for many Japanese avant-garde artists was that it could render tangible things unseen, and that it was avoided by the establishment figurative artists at *Shin-Bunten* and elsewhere. Asano describes the quest for the unknown among the Surrealists, figuratives, and some abstractionists:

> Surrealist painting opens up several methods in the process of that search. Those methods suggest an extremely large world of expression. Although separated perhaps from the original modalities of Surrealism, it was possible by using those methods as a kind of metaphor to criticize reality and society, together with constructing a world of poetic fantasy, to escape from it. The possibility which such Surrealism hinted at seemed to have taken over the hearts of young artists who were sensitive to the atmosphere of this era, an era that gradually increased its oppressiveness. In exact contrast to the atrophy of the Japanese Proletarian Art movement which had prioritized the propaganda and enlightenment of political ideology, it is a phenomenon worthy of attention that fantasy painting under the influence of Surrealism came to have such strength.[18]

The great appeal of Surrealism as a public discourse in art was that by its handling of the unconscious it could criticize the world which denied it, and yet it was precisely this that laid Surrealism open to criticism. The critic Ogawa Takei wrote a series of articles in 1937 in *Atorie*, saying that he "saw Surrealism as 'a kind of hysterical phenomenon' that had appeared in the field of art as the outcome of the pain and anguish of a transitory period of crisis .... This ideology, born as a hysterical paroxysm in a repressed era, had left its original purpose of a passive means to the realization of desires and had gradually approached an authentic disorder."[19] 1937 was also the year when increasing information about Dalí was available in Japan through various art journals, and when Kitawaki worked in a Dalí-esque manner. Kitawaki's works were probably the first to make a high level critique of Surrealism, even though they investigated neither its historical development in France nor its peculiarities in Japan.

The argument from a realist position against Surrealism was made by the scholar of aesthetics, Sagara Tokuzō, in the March 1938 issue of *Atorie*. He wrote that the "revolution of Surrealism was not realistic, and therefore was anti-revolutionary, and also the 'imagination' of Surrealism was not realist and was therefore anti-social."[20] He was counter attacked by the poet and critic Takiguchi Shūzō in the April issue of *Mizue* of the same year. Takiguchi used the metaphor, "if the war gets more serious, art will probably go into mourning."[21] [...] Takiguchi believed that modern Surrealist painters were already qualified to be included in the chapter about fantastic painting in future art history.[22]

[...]

Avant-Garde Art and the State in the 1930s

There was a proliferation of small artists' groups throughout the 1930s, particularly short-lived ones associated with graduates from the main art schools. Many of the artists worked in Surrealist or abstractionist manners from around 1937. It is difficult now, even with considerable hindsight, to reconstruct how these groups were viewed by the authorities, but there can be little doubt that the political police linked Surrealism to Communism, and that the clubs and critics associated with them were under surveillance from at least 1936.[23] The Surrealist artists who were politically conscious were, in most cases, aware of the deliberately radical content of their work, and were careful about their public pronouncements. For example, at the first exhibition of the Art Culture Association (*Bijutsu Bunka Kyōkai*) in 1939, Fukuzawa stated, "in view of the times, I would like everyone to be careful not to mention those matters which are taboo to the authorities from the point of popular mores and ideas."[24] Art critics discussed young artists' Surrealist work as "unhealthy" because by implication it was too tied up in the formal grammar of its style, but said Fukuzawa's work was "healthy" because he appeared to be trying to abandon it. Such formalist criticism seems to be only a step away from the position soon to be adopted by the state for its political ends.

The real concern of the authorities fighting vestiges of Communist thought in the art world became clear only after the arrest and subsequent investigation of Fukuzawa and Takiguchi on February 19, 1941. They were released in November 1941, one month before the outbreak of the Pacific War. Takiguchi recorded the course of their investigation in his "Chronology in My Own Hand" (*Jihitsu nenpu*):

> I was investigated about once a week. The center of the investigation lay on the single point of whether or not the Surrealist movement had any connection with international Communism (of course, without basis). Among my handwritten texts a correspondence with Breton was found and I was intensely pursued on this. In the summer [of 1941] I was put under prosecutorial detention and reinvestigated, but the argumentation got a bit more on track, and I could see a perplexed look on the young prosecutor as the give and take got confused when we mentioned the relation between real politics and the essential theory of Surrealism.[25]

Clearly the police saw all avant-garde art activity as potentially subversive, but this may have been because of their need to find further enemies after crushing the Communist Left and its allied Proletarian Art movements by 1934. The 1939 Interior Ministry Police Protection Bureau report, *Current State of Cultural Movements* listed forty so-called avant-garde artists as participating in the major cultural groups. In 1940, a similar document mentioned the Art Culture Association, exposing the names of its forty-four members, including Fukuzawa's. It described the group as "having a tendency to Surrealism as before, despite having held an exhibition to commemorate the 2,600-year Imperial rule."[26] A 1941 report includes a 600-character definition of Surrealism as a movement having the mission of spiritual revolution, but thereafter as having served as the cultural mission of Communist revolution since the publication of Breton's *Second Surrealist Manifesto* of February 28, 1930. Clearly the police confused Japanese artists, who were part of a liberal and latently subversive intelligentsia, with the membership of the much more directly destabilizing Communist movement.

[...]

Consequences for the Postwar Avant-Garde

It was the onset of the Korean War that marked the boundary between the pre-and postwar art worlds. After 1945, the art world war filled with recriminations against the war artists, chiefly Fujita Tsuguharu and those he had supported in the New Production School Association. The natural resurgence of the Left in the art world in 1945 and 1946 (after such suppression in the 1930s, and the resigned inner emigration of many Surrealists) meant that the extraordinary war paintings of Fujita and some others have never been viewed as the culmination of certain artistic tendencies that began in the Meiji era, rather than their negation. The postwar antipathy on the part of the avant-garde for all types of academic realism resulted in a kind of nihilist cynicism towards humanist painting coupled with a dislike for the disingenuousness of the decorative "Japanese-style" Expressionism and Fauvism.

[...]

The full prescience, if also the isolated preconciousness, of the prewar avant-garde may be finally exemplified by Sawa Hajime's introductory statement in the exhibition catalogue of the Association of the Absolute Image School (*Zettaizō-ha Kyōkai*) at Tokyo's Nichidō Gallery in May 1939 (the words distinguished below indicate foreign loan-words in the original):

> In the so-called *abstract* art of this country, a *human element* intensely hinged to reality is certainly missing. But when that is provided for the first time the character of our art will begin to be different from that of the continent, and will even be a way to the expression of an artistic feeling which is more acute and fresh than *decorative*.

The distinguishing feature of modern painting lies in the discovery of a radical form of expression which reflects the age. At the same time, human intellect and feeling must transcend the yoke of the machine, and shine beautifully and resolutely.

The members of the Absolute Image Group, which is based on the pursuit of plastic form, are concerned with the sublation of existing concepts and the dynamic display of the human consciousness that accompanies the construction of a new beauty.[27]

Notes

1 *Bunten* was the first government-supported painting salon organized largely at the instigation of Kuroda Seiki on the lines of a French Salon, as the Ministry of Education Fine Arts Exhibition (*Monbushō Bijiutsu Tenrankai*) in 1907. It was held annually until 1918.

2 For other English translations of parts of this important manifesto, see John Clark, "Modernity in Japanese Painting," *Art History* 9, no. 2 (June 1986), pp. 213–31 and Takashina Shūji and J. Thomas Rimer with Gerald Bolas, *Paris in Japan: The Japanese Encounter with European Painting*, exh. cat. (St Louis: Washington University and Tokyo: The Japan Foundation, 1987).

3 Takashina Shūji, *Nihon kindai no bi-ishiki* (Aesthetics in Modern Japan), (Tokyo: Aoni-sha,1986), p. 356.

4 Kanbara Tai began to write avant-garde poetry around 1916, having learned French, Latin, and Italian after graduating from Chūō University. He first exhibited at *Nika-kai* in 1917, and was a member of a number of avant-garde groups, including Action (*Akushon*), from September 1922 until 1927, when he stopped painting to write poetry and art criticism.

5 Won Ko, *Buddhist Elements in Dada: A Comparison of Tristan Tzara, Takahashi Shinkichi and Their Fellow Poets* (New York: New York University Press, 1977), pp. 17–18.

6 Action (*Akushon*), a group whose name was chosen by Kanbara Tai presumably because of its Futurist connotations, exhibited from September 1922 until October 1924. It was made up of thirteen artists practicing Dadaist and Cubist styles who were trying to create art on the basis of freedom and individuality. [...]

7 See Tanaka Yoshio in *Shōwa no bijutsu 1926–1935* (Art of Showa, 1926–1935), vol. 1 (Tokyo: The Mainichi Shimbun, 1990), p. 173.

8 Omuka Toshiharu, "Taishō-ki no shinkō bijutsu undō to 'Gekijö no Sanka'" (The Progressive Art Movement in the Taisho Period and the "Theater of the Third Section"), *Art Vivant*, no. 33 (July 1989), p. 89.

9 Futurist Art Association (*Mirai-ha Bijutsu Kyōkai*) was active between 1920 and 1922. [...] Although Futurism had long been gathering its own momenturn as one frame in which Japanese avant-garde art would appear in the early 1920s, the movement was considerably helped by the presence in Japan of the Russian Futurist David Burliuk from October 1920 to August 1922, who brought works from Russia and showed his own.

10 Nakamura Giichi, "'Chōgenjitsu-shugi no botsur-aku' ronsō" (Debate on the Fall of Surrealism) in *Zoku Nihon kindai bijutsu ronsō-shi* (History of Modern Japanese Art Debates, Continuation), (Tokyo: Kinryūdō, 1982), p. 188. Hereafter referred to as *Ronsō-shi*.

11 Ozaki Makoto, "'Kôsei' to iu na no jumon to jubaku – Murayama Tamoyoshi no 'Mavo' tai-ken" (The curse and the spell with the name of "Construction" – Murayama Tomoyoshi's experi-ence of "Mavo"), in the special issue "Mavo no Jidai" (The Age of Mavo), *Art Vivant*, no. 33 (July 1989), p. 42.

12 Omuka, *Art Vivant*, p. 93.

13 Tanaka Yoshio in *Shōwa no bijutsu*, p. 174.

14 Nakamura, *Ronsō-shi*, p. 215.

15 Fukuzawa [...] went to France in 1924, and was first attracted to Chagall, but from about 1929 became interested in de Chirico and Ernst. He

experimented with Surrealist collage techniques and sent works from Paris to the fifth and last exhibition of the 1930 Association (*1930-nen Kyōkai*, 1926–30). In 1931, he sent thirty-six other works for the special exhibition at the first exhibition of the Fauvist/Surrealist Independent Fine Arts Association (*Dokuritsu Bijutsu Kyōkai*, 1930–present). He returned to Japan soon after this. [...]

16 *Décalcomanie* is a method of making a spontaneous monotype [...]

17 Nakamura, *Ronsō-shi*, pp. 211–12.

18 Asano Tōru, *Zen'ei kaiga* (Avant-Garde Painting), Genshoku gendai Nihon no bijutsu (Modern Japanese Art in Full (Color), vol. 8 (Tokyo: Shōgakkan, 1978), p. 164.

19 Nakamura, *Ronsō-shi*, pp. 216, 217.

20 Ibid., p. 220.

21 Ibid., p. 220.

22 Ibid., p. 222.

23 By 1936, the Avant-Garde Artists Association (*Zen'ei Bijutsuka Kyōkai*) was under surveillance by the Special Higher Police; see Nakamura, *Ronsō-shi*, p. 223.

24 Nakamura, *Ronsō-shi*, p. 223.

25 Ibid., pp. 223–4.

26 Ibid., p. 225.

27 Quoted by Ozaki Mazato in Okuma, *Nihon nochūshō kaiga*, p. 128.

21

The Age of Modernism
From Visualization to Socialization

Joe Takeba*

Photography was invented in France and England in 1839 and by mid-nineteenth century had transformed visual culture worldwide. This new, most modern of mediums, child of Western science and aesthetics, recorded modernity everywhere and shaped the way it was seen. When reproduction became possible in the late nineteenth century, photographs became a global industry, making distant visual cultures available to each other as never before.

In Japan, the history of photography began with and reflected the modernization of the country. The first photographs of Japan were taken by the US painter and daguerreotypist, Eliphalet Brown (1816–86), a member of Commodore Perry's 1854 expedition to negotiate the opening of Japan to trade after two centuries of isolation. By 1859 foreigners had set up photography shops and trained Japanese photographers, and by the end of the century little to no time lag remained between developments in Euro-American and Japanese photography. They can be seen as parallel modernisms.

Takeba Joe, curator at the Nagoya City Art Museum and specialist in Japanese photography, begins this essay on the development of modern photography in Japan with a usefully succinct summary, from the pictorialist tendencies of 1900 through 1920 and modernist sensibilities that began in 1924 and continued through World War II. For Takeba, photographic expression in Japan during the 1920s and 1930s comprised an "oscillation between objective depiction and subjective representation." This played out across a multitude of forms that saw the emergence of photographic clubs and a range of journals and magazines such as *Photo Times, Asahi Camera, Monthly Photo Journal* (*Shashin geppō*) and *Photo* (*Kōga*). Takeba's essay chronicles their activities, with

* Joe Takeba (2003) "The Age of Modernism: From Visualization to Socialization." In *The History of Japanese Photography* (exhibition catalog, pp. 142–57). Houston, TX: The Museum of Fine Arts.

Modern Art in Africa, Asia, and Latin America: An Introduction to Global Modernisms, First Edition.
Edited by Elaine O'Brien, Everlyn Nicodemus, Melissa Chiu, Benjamin Genocchio, Mary K. Coffey, and Roberto Tejada.

special attention to some of the differences between those in western Japan and Tokyo. In the western region of Kansai for example, the Naniwa Photography Club and its offshoot Ashiya Camera Club generated considerable national attention, especially with the latter's first Tokyo exhibition in 1931. The author identifies certain key influences such as Hungarian international constructivist László Moholy-Nagy and the US Surrealist Man Ray. Japanese modernists like Horino Masao (1907–2000) and Koishi Kiyoshi (1908–57) were in dialogue with the international avant-garde of New Objectivity, Bauhaus, Surrealism, and Soviet photography. Takeba also offers some of the sociohistorical contexts that affected photographers during the period. One of the most important was the militarization period of the 1930s that erupted with the Sino-Japanese war in 1937. A significant effect was governmental censorship of the term "avant-garde" because it had been translated into Japanese with the same Japanese words for "communist vanguard." As a consequence, "avant-garde" disappeared from Japanese artistic group names, although according to Takeba there is little evidence of an official crackdown on artists. At the dawn of the 1940s photojournalism was on the rise and photographers were caught up in their increasingly totalitarian country's nationalist mythology and patriotism, marking the end of avant-garde photography in Japan.

Further Readings

Dower, John (1980) *A Century of Japanese Photography*. New York, NY: Pantheon Books.

Ozawa, Takeshi (1981) "The History of Early Photography in Japan." *History of Photography* 5(4): 285–303.

The modern era of Japanese history is generally defined as the period from the Meiji Restoration in 1868 until the end of World War II in 1945. (The period after the war is called the contemporary era.) Within this span, photographic expression is usually divided into three further periods: the early, in the nineteenth century; the pictorialist, from the early 1900s into the 1920s; and the modernist, from 1924 to the end of World War II.

Nineteenth-century photography was characterized by a focus on the external world, with straightforward photographic techniques used to document an ever-increasing range of subjects in an evolving nation. During the pictorialist years, a broader palette of techniques was employed in the pursuit of higher aesthetic expressions, characterized by expansive landscapes and romantic, pastoral scenes that evoked a lyrical appreciation of the natural world. Modernism represented a decisive break with the pictorialist aesthetic – in some cases, its explicit rejection – and a return to a more fundamentally photographic expression that focused on the representation of reality.

Driven by advances in the versatility and precision of the medium, the modernist movement encompassed a wide range of experimentation aimed at discovering new realities and new ways of seeing. During the early years of the modernist decades, these experiments came under the rubric of New Photography (*shinkō shashin*), which was strongly influenced by the German New Objectivity

(*Neue Sachlichkeit*) and the Bauhaus design movements. Later, in the 1930s, surrealism enjoyed widespread popularity and formed the core of what was known as "avant-garde photography" (*zen'ei shashin*). These tendencies responded in various ways to an increased consciousness of the social role of photography, which came to the fore at the end of the period with the ascendance of photojournalism.

This chapter will track these developments in photographic expression in the age of modernism and also trace the continuing oscillation between objective depiction and subjective representation that characterized this era. Just as the period between the world wars has proved useful for discussing developments in modern European history and culture, in Japan, especially with regard to photographic expression, the urban culture that developed and exhausted itself in the two decades between the catastrophes of the Tokyo Earthquake of 1923 and the end of World War II is taken as the locus of modernism.

In social terms, the capital city of Tokyo emerged from reconstruction after the earthquake as a substantially modernized city, and great changes took place in social structure, ways of life, and popular culture. The urban environment was transformed, with the emergence of a full-fledged mass culture, the development of the mass media, and the introduction of socialist thought. This increasingly cosmopolitan milieu, invigorated by a spirit that embraced new ideas and perspectives, provided the context for the spread of modernism.

At the same time, Japan was preparing to embark on a campaign of territorial expansion on the Asian continent, first in Manchuria in 1931 and then in China in 1937, which quickly led to war throughout Asia and the Pacific. This Fifteen-Year War, as the Japanese later termed it, was accompanied by escalating campaigns of social mobilization and ideological control that by about 1940 had severely constrained modernist explorations and forced photographers to choose between serving the militarist agenda or retreating, as some did, into more benign forms of cultural documentation.

Although tying the starting points in the development of Japanese photographic expression to social phenomena and historical events risks distorting historical fact, individual aesthetics, and the actual conditions of the times, it is nonetheless true that never before had a period exerted so strong an influence on individual self-consciousness. Photography had followed the course of the development of the modern Japanese nation, reflecting its changing conditions and shaping the modern visual sensibility of its people. As the medium entered the uncertain era of the 1930s, in which photographers as individuals could not separate themselves from an increasingly totalitarian society, photography moved from individual, aesthetic expression toward a societal function, or social character.

Objectivity and the New Photography, 1924 to the Early 1930s

The Tokyo Earthquake (called by the Japanese the Great Kantō Earthquake), which devastated the Tokyo-Yokohama region on September 1, 1923, represented a major turning point in the modernization of Japan. The flowering of urban modernism in the effort to rebuild from the ashes of the earthquake symbolized this change. Where Japanese modernist expression had been conventional and imitative before the earthquake, in its aftermath artists began to explore a new range of avenues for the active engagement of art and society. Of course, even before the earthquake, contemporary currents of thought had been entering Japan from overseas. The Shirakaba school was particularly instrumental in stimulating individuality in literature and art, and the exuberant embrace of new forms was common.[1] But as artists began modernist cultural activities again from scratch after the earthquake, they exhibited a stronger social orientation and a greater willingness to view the world from entirely new perspectives.

These developments were epitomized by the 1924 founding in Tokyo of the Tsukiji Little Theater (Tsukiji Shōgekijō), an influential company in the *shingeki* (new theater) movement.[2] Inspired by the contemporary theater scene in Moscow and Berlin, the Tsukiji company took on the character of an experimental laboratory, stretching the boundaries of theater not only through its plays but also in stage design and theatrical photography. Horino Masao, a student at the Tokyo Higher Technical School, frequented this theater to pursue research and experiments in theatrical photography. As we shall see, his efforts to express motion in posed photographs would bear fruit when applied to different subject matter in the 1930s.

New ventures in publishing quickly established the context in which the coming generation of photographers would work. Both *Photo Times*, a magazine for commercial photographers launched in March 1924, and the broader-based *Asahi Camera*, begun in April 1926, had clearly cosmopolitan content that stood in contrast to established photography magazines like *Shashin geppō* (Monthly Photo Journal). The new magazines challenged the dominant authority of pictorialism and carried essays calling for a new direction based on the fundamental functions of photography.

The post-earthquake cultural environment spawned a new population of photography fans, and the newly launched magazines responded by introducing contemporary international trends in photography. Beginning around 1926, they regularly featured László Moholy-Nagy and Man Ray as exemplars of the new wave. The Hungarian Moholy-Nagy, working at the Bauhaus in Weimar, became known as a photographer with a strong consciousness of the "camera eye": the unique perspectives that are captured by the mechanical lens of the camera, often in ways that are not perceptible to the human eye. His 1925 Bauhaus book, *Malerei, Fotographie, Film* (Painting, Photography, Film), became the benchmark for the New Photography, especially after it was published in Japanese journals beginning in 1930. Man Ray, an American surrealist artist living and working in Paris, was first introduced as an early practitioner of the photogram: an image formed by placing material directly onto a sheet of sensitized film or printing paper and then exposing the sheet to light. These two artists, whose work continued to be closely followed into the 1930s, exerted a profound influence on Japanese modernist photography.

The new tendencies developing in photographic expression became manifest in 1929. In February, Horino Masao joined a group of avantgarde artists and sculptors he had met through his association with the Tsukiji Little Theater to establish the International Photography Association (Kokusai Kōga Kyōkai). During the previous year, the shingeki movement had started to shift toward proletarian theater, with a social consciousness that was influenced by postrevolutionary Soviet thought. In a similar spirit, the International Photography Association sought to develop the social and documentary functions of photography. The association later hosted the international traveling exhibition of the seminal *Film und Foto* show, originally staged in Stuttgart in 1929.

Meanwhile, in June, *Photo Times* inaugurated a monthly "Modern Photo Section" that followed trends in European photography and introduced experimental efforts and theory. The art of the photogram received particular attention, along with other techniques of New Photography, such as the typophoto (the incorporation of typography in the layout of published photographs) and photomontage. In May 1930 photographers involved with *Photo Times* formed the New Photography Research Society (Shinkō Shashin Kenkyūkai), which held its first exhibition and began publishing a journal, *Shinkō shashin kenkyū* (New Photography Studies), later that year. The journal, edited by *Photo Times* editor Kimura Sen'ichi, published only three issues, featuring work from the society's exhibitions, before the group was disbanded (its final exhibition was in 1932), but it helped establish New Photography as a movement.

One of the influential figures of New Photography was the art theorist Itagaki Takao, who had studied in Europe and been exposed to German visual sensibility, particularly the New Objectivity movement led by Franz Roh. After returning to Japan, Itagaki began publishing essays promoting an art of mechanical civilization in all genres of expression. In magazine essays that introduced and elucidated German expression and books like *Kikai to geijutsu to no kōryū* (The Interrelation Between Machine and Art, 1929), Itagaki emphasized the documentary function of photography and advocated a "mechanical aesthetics." His main adherent in this approach was Horino Masao.

In June 1930 Horino published a collection of essays, *Gendai shashin geijutsu ron* (Contemporary Photographic Art Theory), and in November he began another series in *Photo Times*, entitled "The Path to a New Photography." Since the spring, Horino had been photographing luxury liners as an experiment in depicting the properties of mechanical structures. This effort taught Horino the "vital importance of the camera angle," and the results were published at the end of 1930 in a book, *Yūshūsen no geijutsu shakaigaku-teki bunseki* (A Sociological Analysis of the Art of Superior Ships), for which Itagaki provided the text.[3] Horino's exploration of mechanical structures was further developed in a collection entitled *Kamera. Me x tetsu. Kōsei* (Camera: Eye x Steel: Composition), which appeared in 1932, but by the time the book was published he had already turned toward a more explicitly social reportage. The first product of this new approach, again done in collaboration with Itagaki, was an extended photomontage combined with typography that aimed to "depict the character of Tokyo," published in a popular magazine in October 1931. Horino continued his ambitious experiments with photomontage (which will be discussed below) throughout the following year.

In April 1931 the *German International Traveling Photography Exhibition*, based on the *Film und Foto* exhibition staged in Stuttgart in 1929, opened at a hall in the Tokyo Asahi Shimbunsha (a major newspaper company), hosted by the International Photography Association. Under the banner of "new realism," the show exhibited some 1,180 photographs, including work by such photographers as Moholy-Nagy and Albert Renger-Patzsch that had previously been introduced in photography magazines and examples of new techniques like microscopic and X-ray photography. The exhibition (which later traveled to Osaka) was an exhaustive presentation of the functional range of photography as well as of emerging trends in the medium, and it is generally considered a seminal event in spreading the influence of New Photography throughout Japan. Its impact was diminished by its huge scope and by the cultural distance between Japan and Europe, but the opportunity to examine samples of work they had only seen as published illustrations left a lasting impression on many photographers.

For the New Photography movement, the founding of the small-press magazine *Kōga* (Photography) in 1932 represented a fulfillment of sorts. The inaugural issue of the magazine carried the first concise declaration of a parting of the ways with pictorialism, in an essay entitled "Return to Photography" by the critic Ina Nobuo. Coming after several years of experimentation and theorizing about New Photography, this somewhat belated manifesto called for "a break with art photography" and repeatedly emphasized the medium's mechanistic nature. The photographer's role, Ina argued, was to express aspects of social life through the camera's eye. The essay introduced the concept of the Real Photo to describe the new tendency and form, which incorporated three elements: expression of the beauty of the object, documentation of the era and reports on people's lives, and photographs produced through the sculptural properties of light and shadow.

The work of the three founders of *Kōga*, Nojima Yasuzō, Kimura Ihee, and Nakayama Iwata, essentially embodied these three elements of the Real Photo. Nojima, the patron of the magazine and oldest of the three, had been producing conventional, if distinctive, pictorialist work for more than twenty years when around 1930 he shifted to a more experimental, spontaneous style under the influence of European photography. He began to specialize in nudes and portraits, employing compositions that broke all the rules of the genre. Kimura was a pioneer in the use of the versatile Leica 35 mm camera, which he used to produce candid snapshots of daily life in working-class Tokyo; he later became one of Japan's leading photojournalists. Nakayama had operated a portrait studio in New York and spent time in Paris in the 1920s, where he had committed himself to "pure art photography" and begun experiments with photograms and photomontage, which he continued after settling in Ashiya, near Kōbe in western Japan, in 1929.

During the short, eighteen-issue duration of *Kōga*, the magazine published these photographers' work, along with essays and photographs by other leading figures in New Photography, including Horino Masao and Hanaya Kambei, an Ashiya colleague of Nakayama's. It ceased publication at the end of 1933, in part due to financial pressures but also because Kimura and Ina Nobuo, who had joined the coterie, had moved on to more direct involvement with photojournalism. This short lifespan was typical of the associations involved with New Photography in the Tokyo area, where photographers tended to focus on the commercial applications of the new techniques. This was much less true of New Photography in western Japan, and it was there that the movement experienced its most sustained development.

The first Tokyo exhibition of the Kōbe-based Ashiya Camera Club (formed in 1930), which was led by Nakayama Iwata, took place by chance in the same exhibition hall as the *Film und Foto* exhibition, opening just a few days after the German show, in April 1931. The Ashiya show won higher critical praise as a demonstration of Japanese interpretation of New Photography and, in one stroke, brought national attention to the developments in this tendency taking place in the photography circles of Kansai (western Japan). This work was featured in *Kōga* when it was launched the following year.

The insurgent New Photography movement of the 1930s had made its appearance on the scene in Kansai in a truly dramatic fashion. The leading photography association there, the Naniwa Photography Club (Naniwa Shashin Club, of which the Ashiya club was an offshoot), had been a bastion of pictorialism for more than twenty years, but within a relatively short period of time around 1930, the club shifted its focus and embraced New Photography.

In August 1930, at the annual *Namiten* exhibition of the Naniwa club, a young photographer named Koishi Kiyoshi exhibited a work called *March On!* that employed intentional camera movement. This now-legendary photograph heralded the arrival of a new generation of expression, and the club soon began to favor the snapshot over the deliberate pigment-printing techniques of pictorial photography. Two years later, in October 1932, the Naniwa Photography Club held its first Tokyo exhibition since the 1923 earthquake. In the exhibition, Koishi presented a series of ten photographs called *Early Summer Nerves*, photomontages that represented his individual vision of a "poetic reality." Though presented as an experiment in New Photography, Koishi's photographs incorporated a passionate, lyrical quality that had never been seen before in works of the movement, and this generated an intense critical response from New Photography's proponents in Tokyo.

At a research meeting of the *Kōga* magazine coterie, Itagaki Takao criticized the connection between the photographs and the three lines of poetry ("In my youth/ In my flesh/My sun dwells") that introduced the series. Yamawaki Iwao, who had studied at the Bauhaus and believed that the use of photomontage should be limited to media publications, argued that the work of Koishi and the Ashiya group "ran the risk of indulging in eroticism and the grotesque." Koishi responded to this criticism by deriding the Tokyo school of New Photography for engaging in dogmatic, "fragmented mechanical analysis" and declared that photographers should pursue the expression of a new sensibility that lies "on the far shores of realism."[4] This new sensibility would, in time, be equated with surrealism, which was just beginning to make its presence felt in Japan. Koishi continued to experiment with such techniques as multiple exposure, infrared photography, solarization, and photomontage, and in 1936 he collected his experiments in a book, *Satsuei/sakuga no shingihō* (New Techniques for Shooting and Producing Photographs), that offered technical guidance to amateur photographers and further articulated the artistic orientation of Koishi and his colleagues.

[…]

The "new sensibility" that the experimental Koishi and others were pursuing "on the far shores of realism" represented a revival of narrative content in photography. The objectivist, functionalist school of New Photography had rejected such content, along with the lyricism of pictorialism, as an unwelcome intrusion of subjectivity. […]

The lyricism of pictorialist expression continued to exert its pull on some younger photographers into the 1930s. For example, Tamura Sakae and Takao Girō, two photographers of the younger generation who were driving forces behind New Photography in the pages of *Photo Times*, were at the same time producing pictorialist photographs as leading members of the Kyoto-based Japan Photography Association (Nihon Kōga Kyōkai), led by Yamamoto Makihiko. Their pictorialist photographs, modeled after impressionist painting, were considered works of nonrepresentational subjectivity, as were works of the newly introduced surrealism. It was one of the characteristics of this period of transition that objective realism and subjective presentation often coexisted within the work of one artist. This push and pull between the two continued as surrealism and avant-garde photography came into prominence in the late 1930s.

Subjective Presentation and the Search for Avant-Garde Photography, Late 1930s

The seeds of Koishi's new sensibility began to germinate in the Kansai area in the late 1930s. In 1937 Naniwa Photography Club spokesman Hanawa Gingo established the Avant-Garde Image Group (Avant-Garde Zōei Shūdan) to pursue radical forms of expression, with Tampei group members Hirai Terushichi and Honjō Kōrō among the founding photographers. Hanawa exhibited his *Complex Imagination* at the twenty-seventh *Namiten* exhibition in 1938. Although Itagaki Takao, the art critic who had been a strong promoter of New Photography, denounced the photograph as trapped in the dadaist tendency of the late 1920s, his influence had already begun to wane.

At the same *Namiten*, Hanawa also exhibited *The Creator's Mechanicity*, which is not extant, as a companion to *Complex Imagination*. The titles of these two works, both assemblages, suggest the sensibility of the Machine Age, as well as Hanawa's sense of humor (there is a punning rhyme in the Japanese words for "imagination" and "creator"). They also convey the position of a photographer at the moment of transition between objectivity and subjectivity, and the groping exploration this entailed.

As can be seen in Hanawa's work, the effort to move away from objectivity to pursue subjective expression had led the photographer to embrace surrealism, and he began producing works that employed painterly compositions and montage techniques in order to explore dreams and illusions. Also typical of this effort is the work of Hirai Terushichi, a fellow member of the Avant-Garde Image Group. The work of these Kansai photographers, along with their use of the designation *avant-garde* in place of *new*, influenced amateur photographers throughout Japan, but they also met with counterattacks in the critiques and photographs of artists who argued for the restoration of photography's original functionality. These differences regarding the value of surrealism and its presentation in photography once again highlighted the divergence between the Tokyo and Kansai schools of expression.

The efforts in Kansai to explore the new sensibility would probably have ended as a strictly local phenomenon if the monthly *Photo Times* had not taken notice and identified the Kansai-based avant-garde as the next generation in photography, promoted its work, and helped spread its influence throughout Japan. However, *Photo Times* had entrusted its writing on new photography to the art critic Takiguchi Shūzō, and from his perspective Kansai avant-garde photography was too pictorial in its evocation of a "surreal world."[5] He argued for a return to objectivity, which he considered fundamental to photography, and advocated a surrealism that was based on the camera eye, which had been stressed during the era of New Photography but was now being abandoned.

Takiguchi, who was also a symbolist poet, had translated André Breton's *Le Surréalisme et la peinture* (Surrealism and Painting, 1928) and wrote extensively on surrealism for Japanese art magazines. In 1938 he published two essays in *Photo Times* that discussed the development of surrealism in photography: "Photography and Surrealism" in February and "The Interchange Between Painting and Photography" in May. In the latter essay, Takiguchi credited cubism with having brought about a visual revolution by "providing a new subjectivity, or a new dynamism, to the space of a painting." In a similar manner, he claimed, we could expect a new subjectivity to be derived from the objective function – the documentary character – of photography. He suggested that the dialectic of surrealism be pursued through the objectivity of photography, rather than by modeling photographs after surrealist painting.[6]

In June, Takiguchi became the theoretical guide for a group of young artists who formed the Avant-Garde Photography Association (Zen'ei Shashin Kyōkai) to pursue surrealist expression through photography. In contrast to the movement in Kansai, which was led solely by photographers, most of these artists had no connection to the photography clubs that had produced pictorialism, and they were able to explore radical and experimental modes of expression on a purely individual level. On the occasion of the Naniwa Photography Club's Tokyo exhibition, also in June 1938, the group held an "Avant-Garde Photography Symposium," sponsored by *Photo Times*, which represented the first exchange among the various proponents of surrealism in Tokyo and Kansai.[7]

The symposium began with a discussion of the meaning of *avant-garde*, in which the Tokyo group criticized the Naniwa exhibition and the Kansai group defended it. Takiguchi and his cohorts roundly attacked the Naniwa group for taking a "diagnostic," contrived approach to surrealism, whereas they looked to the dialectic of surrealism as a means to transcend photography and painting. The debate featured differing perspectives on subjectivity and objectivity, on the nature of presentation and reproduction in photography, and on the function and expression of surrealism in photography, but the meeting also provided the first (and, as it turned out, the last) opportunity for the two groups to examine surrealist photography together.

Writing in *Photo Times*, Takiguchi had noted that "it can be said that photography truly influenced painting when photography discovered the poetry of objects," and soon afterward he addressed the subject of *objet* that had begun to appear in avant-garde photography.[8] In an August 1938 essay in *Photo Times*, Takiguchi defined *objet* and introduced examples of its use, advocating the use of objects as a means of awakening the viewer to the extraordinary that lies within the everyday, in contrast to surrealist photography, which produced images of dreams and illusions in a picturesque manner. "The function of photography is to discover objet and provide us with revelation," he argued. Takiguchi's definition and classification of objet was, in a sense, an attempt to fix an objective gaze on things and to provide an opportunity to reflect on Japanese works of still life.[9]

Japanese photographers took up the exploration of objet with relish, but the results rarely went beyond a kind of metaphoric humor produced by abstracting objet from natural forms, rather than offering the deeper reflection that Takiguchi was promoting. This failure to fully digest an imported artistic tendency was typical of prewar Japan, where the rapid pace of Westernization meant that many forms of expression were introduced without being fully understood. There was a strong tendency to find Japanese equivalents that would make Western expression easier to assimilate. For example, the wordplay called "exquisite corpse" (*Le Cadavre exquis*) that surrealists engaged in Paris was quickly deemed the equivalent of Japanese haiku and *renga* (linked verse), which often had a humorous twist. Japanese photographers were already producing photographs inspired by the humor or irony of poets like Bashō, and for these artists the discovery of objet was certainly opportune. They began looking for humorous and metaphoric images suggested by the objet, rather than exploring the objet itself.

The photographer who came closest to meeting Takiguchi's standards was the painter Abe Yoshifumi (Nobuya). A member of the anti-mainstream Independent Art Association (Dokuritsu Bijutsu Kyōkai), Abe had pursued a different approach to surrealism from that of other photographers and published his work in *Photo Times*. Working along the same lines as Takiguchi, Abe eschewed objet photography and the tendency to imbue subjects with humor, and turned his camera instead to unusual vistas encountered in everyday life, eventually discovering a way to express what he called the "objective accident."

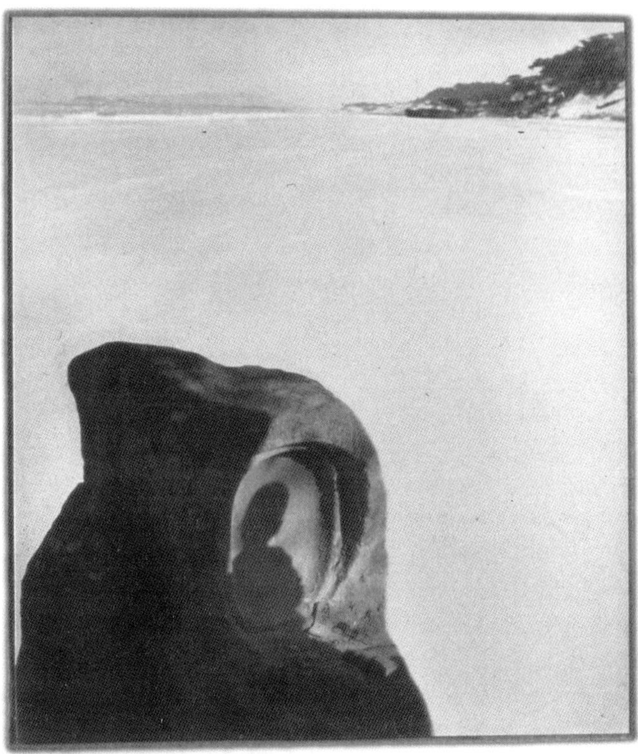

Figure 21.1 Takahashi Wataru, *Untitled*, 1939, Gelatin-Silver photograph, Takahashi Family Collection, Fukuoka City, Joe Takeba.

Avant-garde photography spread quickly throughout Japan, invigorated by the revival of thematic content and employing the newly acquired tool of the objet. In February 1939 the Nagoya Photo Avant-Garde was established by Sakata Minoru, who is best known for his close-up studies of natural objects; the poet Yamamoto Kansuke, discussed above; the painter Shimozato Yoshio; and others. The following October, Takahashi Wataru, Hisano Hisashi, and others formed Société Irf in Fukuoka, Kyūshū;[10] this group became known for combining a distinctive regional flavor with the international influence of surrealism. Even in the Japanese-occupied Manchurian cities of Dalian and Harbin, groups championing avant-garde photography were established.

There were differences in intensity between the various cities in the "homeland" and on the continent, but these new groups broke down the bipolar Tokyo-Kansai structure of the avant-garde and created more diverse opportunities for interaction. Sakata, for example, maintained an active correspondence with both the Avant-Garde Photography Association in Tokyo and Société Irf in Kyūshū; he also delivered regular lectures to Société Irf from 1939 to 1941. Beginning with the use of close-up techniques, in time a style developed where the objet lost its context and filled the entire frame with geometric patterns, especially in the work of Sakata and Tajima Tsugio in Nagoya, and Takahashi and Hisano in Fukuoka. These later avant-garde photographers modified surrealism as they went along, until the image became an entirely abstract composition.

By the late 1930s, the Japanese avant-garde had gained an increasingly sophisticated understanding of international art movements. For example, the "Abstract Art Movement" chart that appeared on the cover of the catalogue for the 1936 New York Museum of Modern Art exhibition *Cubism and Abstract Art* was translated and introduced in the June 1937 issue of the art magazine *Atelier*. This allowed Japanese artists aspiring to the avant-garde to judge their own direction with an overall perspective on trends in Western expression, which had entered Japan in a fragmentary manner. Sakata Minoru published an analysis of the chart in the May 1939 edition of *Shashin Salon* (Photography Salon).[11]

At the same time, the rise of Japanese militarism, especially after the outbreak of war in China in 1937, was bringing intensified ideological pressure on artistic expression. In particular, the term *avant-garde* was coming under attack since it carried the threatening political associations with the Communist *vanguard* (the Japanese used the same word to translate both terms). The avant-garde photographers were subjected to criticism by those who did not share their aesthetics, and, in what might be called an act of self-defense, *avant-garde* began to disappear from the names of photography associations. The Avant-Garde Photography Association renamed itself the Experimental Photo Group (Shashin Zōkei Kenkyūkai), and the Nagoya Photo Avant-Garde changed its name to the Nagoya Photography Culture Association (Nagoya Shashin Bunka Kyōkai). The name of the tendency itself was changed from *zen'ei* (avant-garde) to *zōkei* (creating form). *Zōkei*, a neologism that was apparently inspired by *photo-plastic* – Moholy-Nagy's term for his photograms – was a versatile, if benign, term that came to be applied to all manner of image creation. Perhaps tellingly, there is no good English equivalent, and it was free of the dangerous, foreign connotations of both *avant-garde* and *surrealism*.

Photographers inclined toward abstract art took this new appellation of "zōkei photography" and changed it to "abstract zōkei," moving another step in the direction of an even more radical subjectivity. These repositionings reflected the desire to pursue a pure photographic art to the end – but this too was soon constrained by the ideological thrust of the times. There is little evidence of a direct crackdown by the Japanese special police on the radical expression of these groups, but by changing their names the groups had created the climate in which internal splits were inevitable as they moved steadily toward conformity to the slogans of the day. For example, when the Nagoya group changed its name in November 1939, Sakata Minoru proclaimed the new direction the "union, through photography, of reform and nationalism," to which Yamamoto Kansuke took exception, and he left the group.[12] Sakata took over the leadership, but he eventually took the path of cultural cooperation and "national service" in the war effort, and the group is thought to have ceased activities some time in 1941.

From the time of its founding, the Avant-Garde Photography Association in Tokyo had encompassed both the avant-garde as artistic expression and photojournalism as social expression. One reason for this was Takiguchi Shūzō's repeated emphasis on the documentary character of photography; but it also reflects the situation in which photography found itself as the standard-bearer of the avant-garde of two distinct spheres: presentation and documentation, art and society. What truly awakened photographers to the documentary character of photography, however, was the outbreak of hostilities in China on July 7, 1937, at a bridge near Beijing called Lugouqiao (known in the West as the Marco Polo Bridge). This soon expanded into what was called the China Incident and then into full-scale war between Japan and China. Photographs in the daily newspapers and in magazines like *Asahi Graph* that depicted conditions at the front suddenly drew the attention of amateur photographers to the possibilities of news photography. In contrast, the self-restricted photography that was now offered by the renamed avant-garde was unable to excite the enthusiasm that surrealism had enjoyed.

Instead of being seen as a means for individual contemplation and expression, photography was now being asked what it could do, as a medium, to cooperate with the national culture – in other words, how it could contribute to national service. These changed conditions were clearly reflected in the conversion of *Photo Times*, the journal that had followed and promoted the transition from New Photography to the avant-garde. On the last page of its report on the June 1938 "Avant-Garde Photography Symposium," in which photographers from the western and eastern parts of the country had exchanged opinions on the meaning and direction of the avant-garde, the magazine tellingly published the bylaws for the Young People's Photojournalism Research Association (Seinen Hōdō Shashin Kenkyūkai), a spin-off of the Avant-Garde Photography Association. Later, while covering the transition from avant-garde to zōkei photography in 1939, the magazine shrewdly also followed developments in photojournalism. Although the editors were simply responding to trends in photographic expression and meeting the demands of the era, it was clearly evident that the journal was also constrained by the times.

In the January 1940 issue, *Photo Times* carried a special feature with a questionnaire entitled "Toward Photography in the 2,600th Year of the Imperial Reign," and in October it declared itself a "news photography magazine." *Photo Times* ceased publication with its December 1940 issue, effectively bringing down the curtain on the era of avant-garde photography.

Engagement and Conversion: Perspectives on Society and the Other, 1940–5

In addition to the artistic experimentation we have just examined, the other major strand of photography in the 1930s was social realism, which brought previously neglected aspects of society into view. Since the Meiji period, there had been a market for documentary photographs of "the Other" as represented by the minority peoples on the periphery of the expanding territory of the Japanese Empire. As capitalism extended its reach, and cities expanded owing to migration from the countryside, pockets of extreme poverty began to emerge, especially after 1930, when the Japanese economy began to suffer the effects of the Great Depression in the West. It was natural that photography should now turn toward what might be called the "internal Other": subjects in everyday life that lay closer to home. In fact, works of German New Objectivity exhibited in Japan had included images of poverty as examples of social realism. As Japanese New Photography was establishing its organizational base in the early 1930s, efforts were made to document the face of the poverty lurking in the shadows of the cities, in what was dubbed "beggar photography."

These efforts were also stimulated by the introduction of Soviet photography and socialist thought in the wake of the Russian Revolution. A trend toward the realistic depiction of the dark side of modern urban life appeared in both Japanese-

and Western-style painting of this period. In the photography that aimed at objective realism, the "internal Other" was consciously expressed as an ordinary presence.[13] For the most part, however, the lower classes were simply treated as subjects, and there was little connection between the photographs of them and movements for social reform. That photography was unable to perform a critical social function in Japan during this period reflects the political constraints imposed by the rise of militarism; it was also the result of the somewhat formulaic response of Japanese photographers to New Photography. In other words, photographers may have pointed their cameras at the underside of capitalist society, but they appeared to be blind to the reality of what they were seeing.

In this context, there was one effort that stood out as a document of high quality: the experiments in photomontage conducted by Horino Masao in the early 1930s. In the October 1931 issue of *Chūō kōron* (Central Review) magazine, Horino published *The Character of Greater Tokyo*, a montage constructed of photographs and typography that repeated the words *tempo* and *jazz*. An experiment in New Photography, *The Character of Greater Tokyo* evoked a sense of speed and offered a hymn to the bright side of urban modernism.

[...]

As awareness of the photo story documentary took hold in the late 1930s, a number of notable portrayals of the Other were produced. In May 1941 six members of the Tampei Photography Club, including Yasui Nakaji and Shiihara Osamu, exhibited *Wandering Jew*, a collaborative series of photographs of eastern European Jewish refugees who were temporarily residing in Kōbe. This was an exceptional document, photographed with a sympathetic eye that set it apart from other contemporary photojournalism. A similar vision was reflected in a series of photographs of White Russian immigrants in a northern Manchurian village, produced in 1939 by members of the Manchuria Photographic Artists Association. Although in both cases the Western subjects were considered particularly photogenic to Japanese eyes, the emotional depiction of these sorrowful figures is worthy of attention as a modernist expression. The issue of the photographer's distance from the subject had been raised in the debates over subjectivity and objectivity within modernism; these series, while retaining a certain lyrical distance, can be considered the first fruit of photographers' efforts to identify with their subjects.

Meanwhile, a number of individual photographers produced work that fell outside the framework of the avant-garde and photojournalism. Kimura Ihee's scenes of Tokyo and the snapshots that Kuwabara Kineo was taking in the older sections of the city reflected the vision of urban observers who had attained a modern individuality. Likewise, the uncommon modernist Ueda Shōji had begun producing staged portraits of his family and himself on the sand dunes near his birthplace on the northern coast of Japan, a project he continued throughout his life. All these photographs were animated with a human vitality that reflected the fundamental function of photography, independent of any "-ism," and in hindsight it is clear that these exceptional individual expressions were also the fruit of the gropings for visualization cultivated during the era of modernism.[14] However, as the war in China escalated, this kind of individual expression became increasingly constrained, and photographers who chose not to engage in propaganda were forced to find other avenues.

As we have seen, by the end of the 1930s photojournalism was clearly in the ascendant, and government policy redirected the purpose of photography from individual expression to the glorification of the nation. The zōkei photography that carried forward the abstract expression of the surrealist avant-garde responded to the times by turning to "cultural cooperation" and "patriotic" efforts. Photographers turned their focus to Japanese architecture and folk crafts and attempted to locate in their details a traditional beauty that could supplant modernist expression, giving rise to the paradox of radical modernism looking in retrospect on traditional forms.

Beginning in 1940 increasing numbers of photographers turned their attention to folklife and folklore. In a parallel development, many of the young political idealists who had been drawn to radical socialism in the early 1930s, and who now found themselves in danger of arrest and other forms of political repression, became followers of Yanagita Kunio, the father of Japanese folklore studies. In the late 1930s Yanagita's efforts to trace the roots of the Japanese national character served as a vehicle to mobilize the popular consciousness of the Japanese as a "people," by turning attention to traditional ways of life and evoking a lyrical appreciation of the simple life and its manners. Photographers of this time – including Sakata Minoru, one of the driving forces behind zōkei photography, and Hamaya Hiroshi, who left the Tōhōsha agency (which was publishing *Front* and other propaganda magazines) to take up residence in remote Niigata Prefecture – can be said to have turned to folklore subjects in self-defense against the pressure of the times. However, their work, although produced with the fundamental analytical and investigative techniques of photography, expressed not the hardship of rural life but a yearning for the olden days.

This was precisely the role the state expected photography to play, and for these erstwhile avant-garde photographers engagement with folklore (as opposed to ethnography) meant participating in the construction of a nationalist mythology. In the process, avant-garde photography and photojournalism, which had previously been at odds over the social role of photography, now found themselves, ironically, channeled into a shared exploration of folklore.

Japanese photographers who moved from the city to the country as the war in Asia intensified also documented the lives of the ordinary people, and this work carried over into postwar realism. On August 15, 1945, in the town of Takada in Niigata Prefecture, where he had taken refuge during the war, Hamaya Hiroshi heard the emperor's radio broadcast accepting defeat and immediately went outside to take a photograph, an extremely symbolic gesture. This photograph, *The Sun on the Day of Defeat*, resulted, both literally and figuratively, in a negative of the Rising Sun, the symbol of Japan. The symbolic realism that accompanied this act became a benchmark of postwar Japanese photographic expression.

Postwar photography would develop with documentary realism at its core, but this would not represent a continuation of the prewar explorations. Rather, in an effort to break the spell of lyrical presentation and modernist metaphor, Japanese photographers began taking a decidedly ideological approach to the problems of subjectivity and objectivity in the representation of the lives of "the ordinary Japanese."

Notes

1 The Shirakaba school was a group of writers who took their name from *Shirakaba* (White Birch), a monthly journal of literature and art criticism, published between 1910 and 1923. The magazine introduced the works of European impressionist and postimpressionist painters, as well as contemporary Japanese and European writers. The humanist aestheticism of the magazine is considered one of the more powerful cultural currents of the Taishō period.

2 *Shingeki* ("new theater," in contrast to traditional Kabuki and No) is comparable to modern Western theater, employing conversational dialogue and psychological realism. It began in the early twentieth century and continues as the mainstream Japanese theater today.

3 Horino and Itagaki discussed this project, including Horino's observations on camera angles and the versatility of the hand-held camera, in *Photo Times*, September 1930, 98–104.

4 Reported by Ina Nobuo, "Kōgakai kiji" (Kōgakai Report), *Kōga*, June 1933, 156–7. Yamawaki Iwao, "Nihon no fotomontāju o miru" (Viewing Japanese Photomontage), *Photo Times*, April 1934, 509–16. Koishi Kiyoshi, "Seimei no gangu" (Life's Toys), *Shashin shimpō*, September 1934, 18–24.

5 Takiguchi's contributions to *Photo Times* began with an August 1931 essay on Man Ray. In a 1934 discussion of the French photographer Eugène Atget, he stressed the objective function of photography for the first time.

6 Takiguchi Shūzō, "Shashin to kaiga no kōryū" (The Interchange Between Painting and Photography), *Photo Times*, May 1938.

7 A report on this symposium appeared in the September 1938 issue of *Photo Times* (6–25). [...]

8 Takiguchi, "Shashin to kaiga no kōryū." *Objet*, the French word for "object," referred to often everyday objects that were modified or photographed to reveal a deeper meaning. Awareness of the objet in surrealism resulted from the May 1936 issue of the French art magazine *Cahiers d'art* and a major exhibition on this theme at the Charles Ratton Gallery in Paris, also in May 1936.

9 Takiguchi Shūzō, "Buttai to shashin: Toku ni shururearisumu no obuje ni tsuite" (Objects and Photography, Especially Concerning Surrealist Objet), *Photo Times*, August 1938. [...]

10 "Irf," read in Japanese as "irufu," is the reverse of *furui* (old). The name thus implied that the reverse of the old is new.

11 Sakata Minoru, "Chōgenjitsu-shugi shashin to chūshō zōei no gutaiteki na kaisetsu" (A Concrete Interpretation of Photo-Surrealism and Photo-Abstraction), *Shashin Salon*, May 1939.

12 Quoted by Yamamoto Kansuke, "Iyū: Sakata Minoru no koto" (My Esteemed Friend: On Sakata Minoru), in *Zōkei shashin 1934–1941: Sakata Minoru shashinshū* (Structure in Photography: Sakata Minoru Anthology) (Nagoya: Arumu, 1988) [...]

13 The third and final issue of *Shinkō shashin kenkyū*, published in July 1931 by the New Photography Research Society (established the previous year), carried an article entitled "Kojiki no seikatsu kiroku yori 'Jyānarizumu/kansatsu'" ("Journalism/Observation" in Documenting the Lives of Beggars).

14 Ueda Shōji, who developed his own expression independent of the avant-garde movements of Tokyo and Kansai, noted that he had "learned composition of the frame and sensibility" by studying avant-garde photographs ("Kansō" [Impressions], *Camera Art*, October 1939).

22

The Architectural Profession in Japan, 1850–1930

Jonathan M. Reynolds*

The professionalization of architectural education and practice is modern, beginning in Europe in the early to mid-nineteenth century with industrial modernization and new building materials and methods. Modernist architecture called for engineering and design skills that, with important exceptions, were learned in institutions created specifically to teach them. By the 1880s, architectural associations and credentialed architects were on the rise in industrialized nations and their colonial branches. In this essay, the first chapter of a book-length study of leading modern architect Kunio Maekawa (1905–86), Jonathan Reynolds, historian of Japanese architecture, gives a brief account of the making of the architectural profession from which Maekawa would emerge.

In Japan, the architectural profession was first formed to create European-style buildings. The Westernizing Meiji government established the Imperial College of Engineering (later the Faculty of Engineering of the Imperial University) in Tokyo in 1873 and brought in European architects such as Josiah Conder (England, 1852; Japan, 1920) as instructors. After decades of dominant academic historicism, in 1920 six graduates from the architectural department at the Tokyo Imperial University – Horiguchi Sutemi, Yamada Mamoru, Ishimoto Kikuji, Takizawa Mayumi, Morita Keiichi, and Yada Shigeru – created the influential Bunriha Kenchikukai (Secessionist Architectural Group) to promote modern style architecture. Other avant-garde groups such as Sōusha (Creation of the Universe Society) promptly followed. Their manifestos, quoted in this essay, stridently assert universal avant-garde values.

* Jonathan M. Reynolds (2001) "The Architectural Profession in Japan, 1850–1930." In *Maekawa Kunio and the Emergence of Japanese Modernist Architecture* (pp. 9–37). Berkeley and Los Angeles, CA: University of California Press.

Modern Art in Africa, Asia, and Latin America: An Introduction to Global Modernisms, First Edition.
Edited by Elaine O'Brien, Everlyn Nicodemus, Melissa Chiu, Benjamin Genocchio,
Mary K. Coffey, and Roberto Tejada.

Reynolds tells the story of how, from 1850 until 1930, when militarist censorship silenced the avant-garde, professional architects negotiated the tensions between Japan's architectural heritage and Western modern practices, especially the use of new technology and building materials, eventually leading to a new architectural style that synthesized Japanese and Western elements and transcended national boundaries. As did principal European modernists like Walter Gropius and Le Corbusier, Japanese modernists wanted to create an "international architecture," one that shared and promoted a common cause among architects around the world.

Further Readings

Jinnai, Hidenobu (1995) *Tokyo: A Spatial Anthropology.* Berkeley: University of California Press.
Stewart, D. B. (1987) *The Making of Modern Japanese Architecture.* Tokyo, Japan: Kodansha.

[...]

The Introduction of Western Architecture

The beginnings of a modern architectural profession in Japan can be traced to the middle of the nineteenth century. Even before Commodore Perry presented an ultimatum to the shogun's officials in 1853, demanding that Japan open its borders to the West, the leaders of some of the great feudal domains had sought out Western technology to build the foundries and factories they needed to compete with domestic rivals and to protect themselves against foreign encroachment. As a part of this effort, the Saga clan employed Western building methods to construct a reverberatory furnace in Nagasaki in 1850 to produce steel for weapons. This was perhaps the first structure in Japan built of fired brick. The Shogunate and other domains soon followed suit, constructing foundries, weaving mills, and shipyards.[1]

A succession of treaties signed with the Western powers from 1858 onward opened certain Japanese ports to trade and led to the establishment of foreign settlements. This led to a dramatic increase in Western-style building in Japan, as Japanese workmen constructed houses, churches, and warehouses for members of these communities. Many of these structures, particularly in the early years, blended Western and Japanese forms and building techniques.

[...]

When the Meiji government came to power in 1868, it was deeply committed to transforming Japan into a modern nation capable of interacting with the Western powers on equal terms. The government actively sponsored modern industry, which accelerated the absorption of Western industrial building practices. The government itself needed modern office buildings for its burgeoning bureaucracy and looked to the West for practical solutions. Yet style was just as important as technique. For the nation's leaders, the novel Western architectural styles projected a dignified and up-to-date image that served as a tangible expression of their aspirations.

[...]

During the first decade of Meiji, Japan continued to rely heavily on Western advisors in technical fields, including civil engineering and architecture. To reduce this dependence, the government established the Imperial College of Engineering in 1873; in 1886 the college was incorporated into the Imperial University as the Engineering Department. At first the students were taught by foreign instructors, such as the English architect Josiah Conder (1852–1920), who was invited to Japan in 1877.[2] He shepherded the first class of academically trained Japanese architects through their graduation in 1879. Conder remained a full professor at the college until 1884 and continued to lecture until 1888. Conder also served the Japanese government as an architectural advisor to the Home Ministry and the Imperial Household; he produced designs for the homes of Japan's government and business elite, practicing in Japan until his death in 1920. After Conder stepped down as full professor, one of his first students, Tatsuno Kingo (1854–1919), took his place, and gradually the responsibility for education in Western-style architecture in Japan passed into Japanese hands.

Some Japanese ventured abroad to expand their knowledge of Western architecture. Tatsuno traveled to England to work with Conder's mentor, William Burges, from 1880 to 1883 and to study at the University of London. Yamaguchi Hanroku (1858–1900) studied in Paris for several years before returning to Japan in 1879. Tsumaki Yorinaka (1859–1916) attended Cornell University (1884–5) and worked in Germany for two years, beginning in 1886. Sone Tatsuzō (1852–1937) went to the United States in 1893 to learn more about iron construction. Although overseas study was generally limited to the elite architects and engineers, the government even sent a group of building craftsmen as well as architects for training between 1886 and 1889.

This educational program soon bore impressive fruit, as one can see from Tatsuno Kingo's design for the Bank of Japan, a building completed in 1896. This gray edifice presiding over Tokyo's business district was constructed with iron-reinforced brick faced with stone. Tatsuno took an exhaustive study tour of Europe to ensure that the building would meet the standards of the day, and the Banque National de Belgique (1874) is thought to have been the primary model for his complex neobaroque design.[3] The imposing Bank of Japan building eloquently communicates the expanding ambitions of the Japanese government in the later Meiji period and vividly demonstrates the speed with which the radically different Western-derived approach to design and construction had matured in Japan.

The first professional organization, the forerunner of today's Nihon Kenchiku Gakkai (Architectural Institute of Japan), was formed in 1886. The Zōka Gakkai (Building Institute) was modeled to a great extent on the Royal Institute of British Architects (RIBA), which had been very successful at advancing architectural standards and improving the status of its members since its founding in 1834. The founders of the Zōka Gakkai hoped that they too would be able to improve the position of members and the profession as a whole. As the group's initial statement of principles declares, the "organization's aim [wa]s to measure the improvement

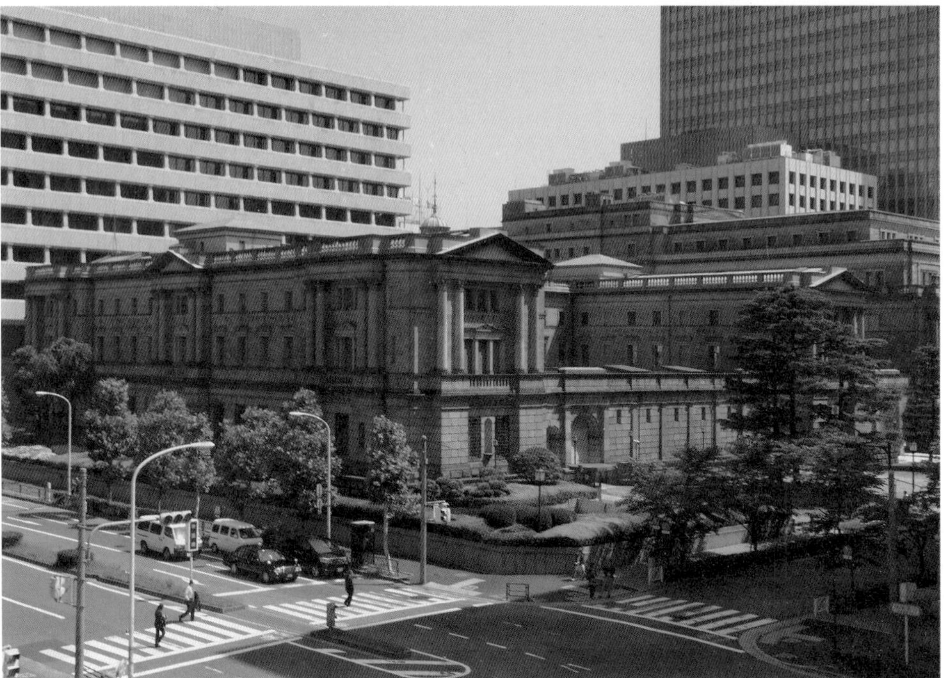

Figure 22.1 Bank of Japan, 1896. Designed by Tatsuno Kingo. Wikimedia Commons, wiii, 2010.jpg.

and progress of the building industry through the exchange of knowledge."[4] To that end the Zōka Gakkai met regularly, sponsored lectures, and produced Japan's first major architectural journal, *Kenchiku zasshi* (*Architectural Journal*). The publication both disseminated technical articles and provided a forum for examining broader issues of interest to the nascent profession. The emphasis on "the exchange of knowledge" reflects the founders' positivistic belief that "progress" in architecture depended on the production of a specialized field of knowledge.

Within a few decades, architects had established a Western-style profession in Japan. By the turn of the century, a solid program for the education of architects and civil engineers was in place at the Imperial University and was being run without foreign assistance. Through study both at home and abroad, Japanese architects had mastered contemporary Western building technology and architectural styles, and a pool of contractors and craftsmen skilled with the new materials and techniques was available to execute their designs.

Tradition and Modern Architectural Practice in Japan

The architectural profession in Japan was formed to design and construct buildings using modern technology and Western styles. In its early years, many of its members were unfamiliar with Japan's own architectural legacy. Indeed, although Conder and others did mention premodern Japanese architecture in their general surveys of architectural history, the Architecture Department of the Imperial University did not offer a course focusing on Japanese architectural practices until 1889, thirteen years after instruction began there.[5] Furthermore, there was little interest in incorporating Japan's premodern architectural practices into new designs.

Ironically, foreign advisors often showed more enthusiasm about employing "traditional" Japanese forms in their designs than did their Japanese colleagues or patrons. When Conder, who had a deep respect for Japan's art and architecture, attempted to draw from premodern Japanese architecture in his designs for public buildings, he was sometimes rebuffed by the Japanese government, which desired architecture like that in the European capitals.[6]

[...]

During the early years of Meiji, rapid change seemed unavoidable in the drive to achieve national security and independence. By the mid-1890s Japan had laid the foundations for a modern industrial economy, instituted nationwide compulsory education, and promulgated a constitution. With its victory over China in the Sino-Japanese War of 1894–5, Japan had also demonstrated its growing military potential. Yet despite these achievements, the Western powers were still unwilling to treat Japan as an equal. Although after prolonged negotiations Britain signed an agreement with Japan in 1894 establishing a timetable for eliminating extraterritoriality, many Western governments continued to insist on maintaining this legal privilege. Japan was also pressured into surrendering the Liaotung Peninsula, which it had obtained in the Sino-Japanese War. These developments, combined with anti-Asian immigration laws in the West, disillusioned many Japanese who had been aggressively pro-Western.[7]

The ranks of the disillusioned included architects. Just as Japanese architects began to replace their Western teachers and consolidate their leadership over the architectural profession, they also began to question the wholesale adaptation of Western practices, which had continued unabated for a generation. Academically trained practitioners and historians expressed new interest in Japan's architectural heritage.

Itō Chūta (1867–1954) is representative of this new development within the architectural community. Itō had mainly studied Western architecture at the Imperial University; indeed, his graduation project of 1892 was a Gothic cathedral. During his long career, Itō completed designs in a number of Western historical styles, including a neoclassical artist's studio in the Tokyo suburb of Den'en Chōfu (1927) and the Italian Romanesque-style Kanematsu lecture hall at Tokyo Higher Commercial School (now Hitotsubashi University; 1927).

But despite his immersion in Western architecture, Itō developed a deep appreciation for Japan's architectural history as well. At the Imperial University he worked closely with the master carpenter Kigo Kiyoyoshi (d. 1915), under whose guidance he participated in field surveys of premodern Japanese architecture. He thereby gained much greater exposure to historically significant buildings than most of his senior academically trained colleagues had experienced.[8] Itō's engagement with premodern Japanese culture was also stimulated by the work of Okakura Kakuzō (1862–1913), who, together with the American Ernest Fenollosa (1853–1908), campaigned for a renewed appreciation of Japanese arts. In 1889 Okakura succeeded in convincing the government to reopen the Japan Art Academy, which offered instruction in traditional methods (the predecessor to today's Tōkyō Geijutsu Daigaku, or Tokyo Institute of the Arts).[9] Itō similarly found himself fighting the neglect of Japan's own architectural roots within the Japanese architectural community.[10]

Itō's numerous contributions to the history of Japan's premodern architecture began with a groundbreaking work, published in 1893; on the seventh-century Buddhist temple complex at Hōryūji.[11] He helped restore and reconstruct many historic buildings and collaborated with his former teacher Kigo Kiyoyoshi in constructing the Heian Shrine, a replica of a portion of the late-eighth-century Imperial Palace produced in 1895 to commemorate the city of Kyoto's 1,100th anniversary.[12] In his role as a professor at Tokyo Imperial University, Itō was also instrumental in expanding other architects' awareness of Japanese architectural history.[13]

Though Itō designed a number of buildings based on premodern architectural forms, he never abandoned modern materials. His memorial to the victims of the Great Kantō Earthquake of 1923, which was completed in Tokyo in 1930, was constructed in steel and reinforced concrete – materials that were particularly fitting, since they were relatively resistant to earthquake and fire damage. The design is a fusion of Japanese and Western architectural sources. The plan of the entire hall vaguely resembles the cross-shaped plan of a Christian church. A pagoda 41 meters high rises at the back (west end) of the hall. At the base of the tower is an ossuary for the ashes of thousands of earthquake victims. The pagoda form is appropriate here, for pagodas were one type of memorial structure, serving as reliquaries in Buddhist temples. In temple complexes, however, pagodas were usually freestanding buildings; Itō instead incorporated the pagoda as an integral element in the main memorial building. It is the primary visual focus for the entire design, functioning in much the same way as would a tower or dome over the crossing of a Christian church (the cathedral Itō designed as a graduation project had a prominent crossing tower). The memorial hall was an outgrowth both of Itō's Western academic training and of his research into early Buddhist precedents.

There were unmistakable nationalistic overtones to Itō's work, which recalls in this regard the nationalistically driven historicism that was widespread among northern European architects in the second half of the nineteenth century.[14] Itō did not, however, advocate purging architectural practice in Japan of Western influence and returning to an idealized premodern and pre-Westernized past. To the contrary, he shared with many Meiji intellectuals a faith in the idea of technological progress and continued to employ Western-derived architectural practices throughout his career.[15] But Itō's study of premodern Japanese architectural history had convinced him that it would not be possible to adopt Western architecture unmodified. Japan could not move forward until it got back in touch with its own artistic and spiritual roots. Just as Western historical styles were an appropriate expression in the modern world of those countries' cultural heritage, Itō believed that premodern Japanese architectural styles were relevant for contemporary Japanese architectural practice as a reflection of Japan's unique culture. Therefore he argued for the development of a new architectural style partaking of both Japanese and Western elements.[16] To that end, Itō not only produced hybrid designs, such as the Kantō Earthquake Memorial Hall, but also became a prominent supporter of the style known as *Nihon shumi* (Japanese taste), associated with public buildings of the late 1920s and 1930s.[17]

[...]

The Bunriha

In 1920 six graduating students from the architecture department at Tokyo Imperial University – Horiguchi Sutemi, Yamada Mamoru, Ishimoto Kikuji, Takizawa Mayumi, Morita Keiichi, and Yada Shigeru – formed what might be considered Japan's first organization of modernist architects, the Bunriha Kenchikukai (Bunriha Architectural Society). The Bunriha first displayed its designs in a waiting room at the Imperial University in February 1920. That summer the group organized an exhibition at the Shirokiya Department Store in Nihonbashi in Tokyo and produced a catalogue containing designs and essays by the members.

Although the Vienna Secession may have inspired the choice of the name "Bunriha" (literally, "Secessionist Group"), the group did not perceive itself as a mere offshoot of the Viennese movement. One of the Bunriha members, Yamada Mamoru (1894–1966), concerned that their name might be misunderstood, emphasized that it should be interpreted broadly, as expressing the group's intention to secede from certain practices current in the architectural profession at that time.[18] The group's objectives might coincide to some degree with those of their European colleagues, but the Bunriha had its own distinct agenda and aspirations. Yamada's worries about the translation of the group's name suggest that he anticipated a potential international audience for the Bunriha's work – a hint at great ambitions on the part of this fledgling architect and his colleagues.

Following in the footsteps of European groups such as the futurists and De Stijl, the Bunriha issued a dramatic manifesto. The young architects declared:

> We arise!
> We break away (*bunri shite*) from the realm of past architecture so that we might create a new architectural realm where all of the architecture that we produce is given genuine significance.
> We arise!
> In order to awaken all that is sleeping in the realm of past architecture,
> In order to rescue all that is in the process of drowning.
> In a state of joy, we dedicate everything that we have to the attainment of this ideal and we will wait expectantly for it until we collapse and die.
> In unison, we declare this to the world![19]

The emotionally charged declaration was a call to action – a pledge to win freedom from the fetters of a complacent architectural establishment. Yet the manifesto addressed the profession's weaknesses only in the most general terms and was not burdened with specific proposals for reform. The core of the message was its sincere and idealistic spirit; this manifesto's heroic tone would come to characterize modernist pronouncements in the future.

The Bunriha members wished to break with the academic historicism that dominated architectural practice in Japan. They believed that architectural design had been reduced to a process of choosing from a fixed repertoire of styles and superficially manipulating ornament. One of their leaders, Horiguchi Sutemi (1895–1984), examined the uses of ornament in contemporary architecture in a 1921 essay titled "Thoughts on Art and Architecture," published in the catalogue of the group's second exhibition. He likened traditional forms pasted onto contemporary architecture to moss and duckweed floating on stagnant water.[20] In this attack, Horiguchi was echoing a criticism being voiced with increasing frequency by European architects, who were challenging traditional academic formulas for the use of ornament. Yet while many modernists assailed "superfluous ornament" in design, even the extremist Adolf Loos did not insist on eliminating it altogether.[21] Similarly, Horiguchi had no intention of purging ornament, but he believed that its employment must be appropriate to and properly integrated with the project at hand.

Although the Bunriha architects condemned the misuse of past architectural forms, they did not turn their backs on the various architectural practices – Japanese and non-Japanese – that they had inherited. To do so would have been both impossible and undesirable. Horiguchi wrote, "There is no doubt that modern architecture could not have come into being detached from architecture of the past. In this sense, we have absorbed tradition deeply into our blood and muscle and it has matured in every cell in our bodies – we could never just decide to separate ourselves from it."[22] To the Bunriha members, particularly Horiguchi, Japan's architectural heritage was as relevant as it had been to Itō Chūta and other architects of the previous generation. At this time, Horiguchi was beginning a lifelong study of premodern Japanese architecture that would significantly affect many of his designs.[23] Gradually he and other modernists would construct a vision of Japan's architectural traditions on which they could draw in a way consonant with their modernist principles and without trivializing the past.

[...]

The sense of national crisis that was still so acute in the 1890s was less pressing in the early 1920s. At a time when Japan's economy was stronger and its position in the world seemed somewhat more secure, Horiguchi and his fellow Bunriha members did not feel compelled to relate their work to national development. Instead, they directed their attention inward and strongly emphasized the individual; in the personal, inner world they sought a new source for artistic inspiration. According to Horiguchi, "The freedom of our inner lives can be obtained only when we stand independent of others and form a style that is most appropriate to ourselves as individuals; only then will a world of individuality be born. The style of this world will come to be expressed through our creations."[24] In order for the architects' art to remain vital, they must strive for personal expression.

The group's designs reflected a wide variety of stylistic sources, including the Vienna Secession, expressionism, the Amsterdam School, and the Bauhaus. When the Bunriha was established in 1920, members relied primarily on architectural magazines for information about European modernism; but soon several members traveled to Europe to meet leading modernist architects and see their work. Horiguchi Sutemi visited Vienna, Paris, Brussels, Amsterdam, and the Bauhaus in Weimar from 1923 to 1924. He was so impressed with the Amsterdam School that on his return to Japan, he published a study of contemporary Dutch architecture.[25] Ishimoto Kikuji traveled to Germany to work with Gropius in 1922. Yamada Mamoru also made a pilgrimage to Europe, but not until 1929, after the group had disbanded.

[...]

Horiguchi incorporated ideas from both Japanese and contemporary Dutch architecture in his Shiensō, a private residence he completed in 1926. One remarkable feature of the Shiensō was a steeply pitched pyramidal roof. Horiguchi juxtaposed the thick roof thatching with comparatively thin horizontal roof slabs placed over one corner of the first floor, over the entryway, and over a second-floor gable. A number of Dutch architects employed very similar roofs (several such examples were included in Horiguchi's study of Dutch architecture), and he was clearly drawing on these designs.[26] At the same time, the thatched roof also alludes to Japan's own rustic teahouse (*sōan*) tradition. The first-floor interior has Western-style furniture and hardwood floors (rather than tatami mats). Horiguchi provided tatami mats in Japanese style for the second-story room. [...]

This combination of Western and premodern Japanese sources might at first seem inconsistent with Horiguchi's own criticism of historicism. But the sources in the Shiensō are both more historically ambiguous and more thoroughly integrated into the design as a whole than were those drawn on by the academic eclectics whom Horiguchi condemned. Is the roof based on Dutch or Japanese vernacular? Are the windows traditionalist or modern? The complex layering of Japanese and European modernist sources suggests the complexity of the historical situation in which Horiguchi and his Bunriha colleagues found themselves. If we accept Horiguchi's word that they had "absorbed tradition deeply into [their] blood and muscle," then his conception of "tradition" clearly included the architectural legacy of both Japan and Europe. In Horiguchi's Shiensō those sources were brought together in a fundamentally new way.

The establishment of the Bunriha greatly influenced the development of modernism in Japan. During the eight years that the group was active, it organized a total of seven exhibitions (the last in 1928), providing these young architects forums in which to present their ideas to the public. The Bunriha explored new developments in European architecture and promoted these ideas within Japan's architectural community. When its members declared forcefully that they were breaking away from the establishment that had trained them to pursue a new architecture, they helped catalyze a modernist identity separate from the architectural mainstream. The act of forming an association to achieve their goals was itself important, because the Bunriha became a valuable model for the kind of social institution that was essential for modernism's emergence as a viable architectural movement.

The Sōusha

The Sōusha (Creation of the Universe Society) was established in the fall of 1923, soon after the Great Kantō Earthquake. Most of the organizers – who included Yamaguchi Bunzō, Ogawa Mitsuzō, Umeda Yuzuru, Hiroki Kamekichi, and Sento Eiki – were working at the time as draftsmen or as junior engineers in the Ministry of Communications. The ministry carried out an extensive building program with its own talented group of architects and engineers, producing bridges, post offices, telegraph offices, meteorology stations, and other structures. A core mission was to promote and disseminate new technology, and under the leadership of architects such as Yoshida Tetsurō (1894–1956) and Yamada Mamoru, the ministry relied increasingly on modernist architectural forms to project a fittingly progressive image.[27] The Ministry of Communications became the most important governmental patron of modernist architecture and completed some of the best pre-World War II modernist designs in Japan. It is particularly striking, given the antiestablishment rhetoric that predominated in modernist circles before the war, that the Sōusha was founded by employees of a government ministry and that that ministry was so supportive of modernist design.

In the beginning the Sōusha was strongly affected by the Bunriha. One of the Sōusha's leaders, Yamaguchi Bunzō (1902–78),[28] had been a member of the Bunriha since 1921, and Sōusha members were acutely aware of Bunriha activities. Like the Bunriha, the Sōusha proclaimed its objectives in an idealistic manifesto:

> Attaining a purity of heart like that of the ancients
> We are devoted to the spirit of creativity, and we attempt to remain
> Untainted by impure fads and fashion of imitation
> We carry with us a yearning for the Eternal Mother
> We wait expectantly for the awakening of a modern architecture which is [at present] infected by the degenerate and the trite
> The symphony of our lives – We exert ourselves single-mindedly so that the beautiful, sacred mass of our souls might resound in the universe.[29]

The rhetorical intensity of the Sōusha manifesto closely resembled that of the Bunriha. The Sōusha viewed the practice of architecture in highly moralistic terms, pitting their "purity of heart" against the "degenerate and trite." There was no room for incremental reform or compromise in their program! Like the Bunriha, at this stage the Sōusha conceived of the creative process in very personal terms. Their mission depended on the integrity and unswerving commitment of each member of the group.

The Sōusha's manifesto was infected with the same visionary spirit that inspired the writings of the Bunriha and certain European contemporaries. For example, consider the following passage from a 1919 essay by Bruno Taut: "Art seeks to be an image of death … to furnish the threshold at which mean preoccupation with earthly things dissolves in contemplation of that which opens up beyond death. … [The artist] assigns everything to its place. … Light casts its radiance over all. … The earth itself sparkles with the New; as the impossible becomes possible, 'hard' reality yields up miracles."[30] Like Taut, these architects saw architectural production as a pseudo-religious act that transcended normal daily experience and had significance beyond all boundaries of time and space. Taut offered the promise of miracles, and the Sōusha wrote of "the beautiful, sacred mass of our souls." But there were clear differences as well: while Taut envisioned art as a process through which one comes to terms with death, the Sōusha appealed to both an atavistic fantasy of lost ancient culture and a desire to return to the womb.

At the end of the 1920s, there was a major shift in Sōusha writings; while no less idealist and moralistic than the manifesto had been, they became less mystical in tone. The "yearning for the Eternal Mother" had somehow subsided, replaced by the dream of constructing a just society. Instead of striving to "reveal their souls to the universe," members directed their attention toward more pragmatic concerns such as finding ways to utilize new construction materials that might reduce building costs and to explore designs that exploited natural light for maximum benefit. "Rationalism" was the key. In the later essays by Sōusha members, the word "rationalism" (*gorishugi*) took on a special, almost magical, power. A rationalist approach to design would lead to positive social change by creating efficient and comfortable living and working environments.

This shift can be explained, in part, by the education of the Sōusha architects – they were trained primarily in technical schools and within the engineering department of the Ministry of Communications. In contrast, most of their colleagues in the Bunriha were products of the elite Tokyo Imperial University. At the ministry they worked daily as draftsmen and engineers on very down-to-earth projects, building bridges, dams, and post offices. It is not surprising that over time their idealism would be directed toward more pragmatic goals. Their emphasis on rationalism was also connected with a growing commitment to Marxism. Although the Sōusha never became as explicitly political as did some contemporary proletarian arts groups, Marxism had a powerful impact on the architects' writings and designs.[31]

[…]

Not all modernist architects active in the 1920s sympathized with leftist politics, but Sōusha members did become increasingly radical. As they studied Marxism, they began to reconsider the role of architecture in society and became convinced that a rational, scientific approach to building would meet the pressing needs of the proletariat most effectively.[32]

[…]

The changes in the Sōusha are visible in the group's exhibitions as well as its writings. The final two exhibitions concentrated on themes that reflected members' political commitments.[33] One social problem of special concern […] was the shortage of decent housing for workers. The Sōusha architects were inspired by the many housing projects constructed in Weimar Germany by architects with similar social concerns, such as Ernst May, Walter Gropius, and Bruno Taut. Just as the *Siedlung* was the characteristic building type of the modernists working in Berlin and Frankfurt in the 1920s, so workers' housing became the most common building type in the Sōusha's later exhibitions.

A project for housing female textile workers that Yamaguchi [Bunzō] contributed to the last Sōusha exhibition, in October 1930, is thus representative of later Sōusha designs. The theme is itself significant: textile workers, the most numerous factory workers in Japan, were especially hard hit by the economic downturn in the late 1920s. The design has formal similarities with German housing projects such as Gropius's Siedlung Törten in Dessau (1927).[34] Yamaguchi alternated blocks glazed with bands of horizontal windows and blocks glazed with vertical windows, just as Gropius had done in the low-rise portion of his design. The expanses of white walls and glass uncluttered by surface decoration created a bold, clean, efficient look.

[…] In 1929 Yamaguchi was both more politicized and further to the left than most of his fellow modernists, but many would generally have sympathized with [his] social critique […]. In the late 1920s, articles frequently expressed concern over social problems generated by industrial capitalism, including the shortage of high-quality housing for workers. But at the same time, the government was growing more intolerant of social criticism, especially from the Left. In the fall of 1930, the authorities pressured a newly formed group of architects to disband, seemingly with less provocation than Yamaguchi had offered […]. Changes in the political environment would effectively silence this important strain within modernist discourse, just as it was beginning to develop. In December 1930 Yamaguchi departed for Europe, where he worked under Gropius in the Bauhaus. He established ties with various leading modernist architects and progressive arts groups before returning to Japan in 1932.[35] Yamaguchi had played a central role in the Sōusha, and with his departure for Europe the group's activities ended.

Despite the intolerant political climate, former Sōusha members continued to pursue their political ideals. Umeda Yuzuru (1904–83) joined the Communist Party some time after the breakup of the Sōusha in 1930. By that time, the party was outlawed: Umeda was arrested and given a suspended sentence. Imaizumi Zen'ichi (1911–85), who contributed designs to the group's final two exhibitions, also joined the Communist Party. He participated in the famous Ōmori bank robbery – a desperate attempt to seize funds for the party in October 1932 – was arrested, and served more than eleven years in prison. Those who sustained their political beliefs even in the face of intense government repression in the 1930s established a precedent for political commitment that would strongly influence modernist architects after World War II.[36]

An International Architecture

Many European modernists of the 1920s cherished dreams of building a truly international architectural movement. Leaders of the movement, such as Walter Gropius, conceived of international architecture not as an eclectic portfolio of styles from many nations but as an approach to design founded on principles of science and technology that would transcend national boundaries.[37] The theme of internationalism appealed strongly to Japanese modernists as well. Believing that the principles of science were universal and that scientific and technological progress was unstoppable, they saw the success of an architectural style firmly grounded in technology as assured. Furthermore, internationally oriented Japanese hoped that by reaching out to like-minded colleagues around the world, they might be able to break out of the confines of their small and isolated community.

Publications from the period attest to the strong identification of internationalism with modernism. By the late 1920s, the expression "international architecture" (*kokusai kenchiku*) appeared in modernist writings almost as often as "modern architecture" (*gendai kenchiku*). One of the most influential modernist magazines of the period bore the title *Kokusai kenchiku* (*International Architecture*).[38] Articles and designs by foreign and Japanese architects were interspersed in each issue. The magazine emphasized shared values and promoted the spirit of a common cause among modernists around the world. Indeed, the magazine frequently provided captions and indexes in English, German, and even Esperanto, as well as in Japanese. In 1934 the magazine published an entire article in Esperanto, titled "The Functional Basis of Japan's Past Architecture and Modern Thought."[39] This manifestation of internationalism appeared in a special issue devoted to premodern Japanese architecture; clearly, neither the editors nor the readers of *Kokusai kenchiku* believed that interest in Japan's architectural legacy was at odds with their internationalist objectives.

In July 1927, six architects from the Kyoto-Osaka region met in Kyoto to form an architecture organization that they named the Nihon Intānashonaru Kenchikukai (International Architecture Association of Japan). One of the six was Motono Seigo, the author of the article in Esperanto. The other founding members were Ishimoto Kikuji (also a founder of the Bunriha), Itō Seibun, Ueno Isaburō, Shinmyō Kazuo, and Nakao Tamotsu. Takeuchi Yoshitarō also became involved in the organization at an early stage. Ueno had become friends with Gropius and other modernists while he was in Europe. When he indicated that he wanted to establish an international architectural group in Japan, the Europeans promised to lend their support, and Gropius and nine other European architects were invited to become members of the new organization.[40]

In Europe many found the concept of internationalism threatening, and it produced a significant rift within the architectural community. As the architectural historians Richard Pommer and Christian F. Otto have observed, "The establishment of the International Style had a far greater political consequence: it consolidated the opponents to the Modern Movement and drove them closer to the Right. Their reaction found justification in the double connotations of the term 'international' in Germany, where it implied not only the links between nations, but an absence of patriotic feeling – for the Left a virtue, for the Right a reproach."[41] Even the word "international" was problematic in the years immediately following World War I, because for many it carried leftist political connotations.[42] In Japan, too, the concept of internationalism became suspect as the political climate in the late 1920s once again grew nationalistic. Politicians and prominent architectural leaders insisted that public projects be demonstrably "Japanese". The organizers of the Nihon Intānashonaru Kenchikukai were concerned that if they appeared to advocate internationalism too aggressively, they might be subject to political attack from the Right. Members even debated the merits of changing their name by substituting the Japanese word *kokusai* (international) for the Western loanword *intānashonaru*, which was problematic for two reasons: it was foreign in origin, and, as in Europe, it was associated by some with the Left. Members did not want to be branded as either "un-Japanese" or "red."[43] *Kokusai* would have been a more neutral term. In the end, however, the members agreed to keep their original name and risk attack.[44] The serious political significance ascribed to such apparently subtle distinctions indicates how politicized and polarized the Japanese cultural community was becoming. Architects were entering into an era in which greater political caution was necessary for survival.

The Nihon Intānashonaru Kenchikukai issued a manifesto and a statement of principles expressing its objectives:

Manifesto

1. We will think of human survival whenever we try to solve basic problems arising in the future course of our architecture.
2. We will design a style appropriate to the new life that emerges with the progress of mankind.
3. With resolution of Japan's problems as an objective, we will cooperate with comrades (*dōshi*) in various countries of the world and continue [to work] toward shared goals.

General Principles

1. As for architectural style, we reject dependence on traditional forms; and yet, without adhering to [ideas of] national character (*kokuminsei*) in a narrow sense, we place our roots in an authentic localism (*shinsei naru "rōkaritei"*).
2. As for the limits of our research and creative work, with architecture at the center we include everything related to human life.
3. In order to realize the principles and goals in this manifesto, we will hold exhibitions and symposiums whenever required, and we will set up mechanisms for ongoing research and education.[45]

This manifesto is idealistic, but its language is far less hyperbolic than that of the Bunriha or the Sōusha. The search for an architecture rooted in modern life lay at the heart of the Nihon Intānashonaru Kenchikukai program ("a style ... in step with the progress of mankind"), as well as the programs of their modernist colleagues in both Japan and Europe. The authors appeared less insistent about asserting independence from established architectural practices than their manifesto-writing predecessors had been, perhaps because in the few years between 1920 and 1927, the sense of distinct identity within the modernist architectural circles had already grown stronger.

One especially important feature of this manifesto was its emphasis on "an authentic localism." Although the architects of the Nihon Intānashonaru Kenchikukai were committed to international architecture, they shared with other Japanese modernists the desire to ground their work in its Japanese context. Therefore, the manifesto was inclusive; the architects made a special point of rooting themselves in the best aspects of their local practices, while at the same time reaching out to embrace the goals of the international movement.

The group was strongly indebted to Gropius's introduction to *Internationale Architektur*, which championed the modernization process that he hoped would unite architectural practices across old political or cultural boundaries. There Gropius wrote:

> Impelled by worldwide trade and technology, a unification of modern architectural characteristics is progressing in all civilized lands, across the natural borders to which peoples and individuals remain bound.
>
> Architecture is always national, always individual, too; but of the three concentric circles – individuality, nationality, humanity – the last category includes both of the others. Therefore the title:
>
> "INTERNATIONAL ARCHITECTURE."[46]

Gropius considered the new transnational links of international architecture to be most important. Nonetheless, by also acknowledging here and elsewhere that architecture would inevitably reflect the character of individual architects and of the local conditions in which it was created, he provided justification for the Nihon Intānashonaru Kenchikukai to feature "authentic localism" even more prominently in its own statement.[47] Earlier modernist writings had certainly embraced Japanese "tradition," but the theme's prominence in the group's manifesto suggests a growing defensiveness – clearly members were anxious about the threat of attack from nationalists.

In 1929 the Nihon Intānashonaru Kenchikukai established a magazine, *Nihon intānashonaru kenchiku* (*Japanese International Architecture*), which it published for three years. It also sponsored exhibitions and other activities before disbanding in 1933. Undoubtedly, the Nihon Intānashonaru Kenchikukai had less impact on the modernist movement than did the Bunriha or the Sōusha.[48] Still, the members as individuals were active participants in the modernist architectural community, contributing articles in various publications and even (in the case of Ueno Isaburō) helping to bring Bruno Taut to Japan in 1933. Moreover, the organization's strenuous efforts to temper its commitment to internationalism with "authentic localism" in response to the threat posed by increased nationalism significantly affected the subsequent history of the modernist movement in Japan.

Modernist Expression in Japan in the 1920s

Any account of the early stages of the modernist movement in Japan must begin by recognizing the importance of the architects and professional institutions that proceeded it. Although the Bunriha architects declared that they were seceding from the architecture of the past, they were the children of that past. They and others built new institutions but also continued to participate in some of the well-established institutions of the old order. It is also clear that in their positions on many of the problems of concern to the profession, the modernists showed some continuity with the approaches of their teachers' generation.

The variety of architectural forms generated by architects associated with modernism during this period is striking, ranging from contorted "romantic" designs inspired by European expressionism to coolly regular glass and concrete boxes suggestive of the "new objectivity" associated with the Bauhaus. The diversity offered in the architectural writings during this period is just as remarkable. While Horiguchi Sutemi of the Bunriha described architecture as a medium of personal expression, Yamaguchi Bunzō of the Sōusha concentrated on the importance of architecture as a tool for social change. But despite their differences, these architects shared a keen sense of group identity – they were comrades engaged in a struggle to forge new architectural solutions appropriate to the modern world. These modernists deployed a highly charged, combative rhetoric filled with heroic idealism, and this distinctive language reinforced their faith in a common mission.

[…]

Notes

1 Inagaki Eizō, *Nihon no kindai kenchiku: Sono seiritsukatei*, vol. 1 (Tokyo: Kajima Shuppankai, 1979), pp. 28–9. […]

2 […] Onogi Shigekatsu, *Yōshiki no ishizue*, vol. 2 of *Nihon no kenchiku: Meiji, Taishō, Shōwa*, ed. Muramatsu Teijirō (Tokyo: Sanseidō, 1979), pp. 99–101; Stewart, *Modern Japanese Architecture*, pp. 33, 35–7.

3 Suzuki Hiroyuki and Yamaguchi Hiroshi, eds., *Kindai gendai kenchikushi*, vol. 5 of *Shin kenchikugaku taikei*, ed. Uchida Yoshichika et al. (Tokyo: Shōkokusha, 1993) p. 257.

4 Ibid., p. 263.

5 Suzuki Hiroyuki mentions Conder's coverage of Japanese architecture in his survey course in Suzuki, *Vuikutorian goshikku no hōkai* (Tokyo: Chūō Kōron, 1996), p. 109. For a discussion of the introduction of Japanese architectural practices into the curriculum at the Imperial University, see Cherie Wendelken, "The Tectonics of Japanese Style: Architect and Carpenter in the Late Meiji Period," *Art Journal* 55, no. 3 (fall 1996): 28–37.

6 Suzuki Hiroyuki, "Meiji Architecture as an Expression of the Meiji Mind" (paper delivered at Princeton University, April 1987), p. 4.

7 See, for example, Kenneth B. Pyle's discussion of the effects of the war and the retrocession of the Liaotung Peninsula on the once pro-Western writer and social critic Tokutomi Sohō; Pyle, *The New Generation in Meiji Japan: Problems of Cultural Identity, 1885–1895* (Stanford: Stanford University Press, 1969), pp. 163–87.

8 For a discussion of Itō's work with Kigo, see Wendelken, "The Tectonics of Japanese Style," pp. 32–3.

9 Ota Hirotarō, *Kenchikushi no sendatsutachi* (Tokyo: Shōkokusha, 1983), pp. 24–5. For a discussion of the efforts of Okakura and Fenollosa, see John M. Rosenfield, "Western Style Painting in the Early Meiji Period and Its Critics," in *Tradition and Modernization in Japanese Culture*, ed. Donald H. Shively (Princeton: Princeton University Press, 1971), pp. 181–219.

10 Itō told a story that reflects his frustration at the dominant attitudes: When his teacher Tatsuno Kingo was working in Burges's firm, Burges said to Tatsuno, "Japan has a long history and must have unique characteristics from its distant past. What are some of the features of Japan's old architecture?" When Tatsuno replied that he didn't know anything about it, Burges continued, "A number of ancient buildings must still survive. What are they like?" Tatsuno answered that he knew nothing about that either, and Burges responded, "Before you begin studying European architecture, you should know something about the architecture of your own country." Whether or not this conversation actually occurred, it suggests how Itō's concern about the neglect of Japan's traditional architecture helped motivate his research. See Itō Chūta, "Hōryūji kenkyū no dōki," *Kenchiku shi kenkyū* (1940); quoted in Itō Michiō and Maeno Masaru, *Yōshikibi no banka*, vol. 8 of *Nihon no kenchiku: Meiji Taishō Shōwa*, ed. Muramatsu Teijirō (Tokyo: Sanseidō, 1982), p. 97.

11 Itō Chūta, "Hōryūji kenchiku ron," *Kenchiku zasshi*, no. 83 (November 1893): 317–46.

12 Kigo was the instructor in the Imperial University's first course (in 1889) focusing on premodern Japanese architectural practices; see Wendelken, "The Tectonics of Japanese Style," p. 31.

13 Itō began to lecture at Tokyo Imperial University in 1897 and became a full professor in 1905.

14 Peter Collins, *Changing Ideals in Modern Architecture, 1750–1950* (Montreal: McGill-Queen's University Press, 1965), pp. 100–5.

15 Itō's commitment to modern building materials such as concrete was strengthened after the Great Kantō Earthquake of 1923 – he saw that wooden construction was too vulnerable to fire, especially in crowded cities. See Itō Chūta, "Shin Nihon kenchiku no sōzō," *Nippon*, January 1927; reprinted in Itō Chūta, *Ronsō, zuihitsu, mampitsu* (Tokyo: Hara Shobō, 1982), pp. 294–300.

16 Itō Chūta, "Kenchiku shinka no gensoku yori mitaru wagakuni kenchiku no zento," *Kenchiku zasshi* 23, no. 265 (January 1909): 31–2; reprinted in Itō, *Ronsō, zuihitsu, mampitsu*, pp. 54–5.

17 *Nihon shumi* [...] was characterized by modern building materials and the selective incorporation of premodern Japanese architectural details, especially tiled, upswept roofs.

18 Yamada also stated that to avoid confusion, the group's name should be transliterated "Bunriha" and not translated in foreign languages; I have followed Yamada's wishes here. See Yamada Mamoru, "Dai ni kai Bunriha tenrankai ni okeru watakushi no kenchikukan," in *Bunriha Kenchikukai sakuhinshū*, vol. 2 (Tokyo: Iwanami Shoten, 1921), pp. 25–6.

19 The manifesto was printed in the Bunriha's first catalogue, "Bunriha Kenchikukai sengen," in *Bunriha kenchikukai sakuhinshū*, vol. 1 (Tokyo: Iwanami Shoten, 1920), n.p., and was included in the group's later catalogues as well. The manifesto is reprinted in Fujii Shōichirō and Yamaguchi Hiroshi, eds., *Nihon kenchiku sengen bunshū* (Tokyo: Shōkokusha, 1973), p. 126.

20 Horiguchi Sutemi, "Geijutsu to kenchiku to no kansō," in *Bunriha Kenchikukai sakuhinshū*, vol. 2, p. 8; also in Fujii and Yamaguchi, *Nihon kenchiku sengen*, p. 154.

21 Reyner Banham points out that although Loos went so far as to equate ornament in modern design with crime (in his polemical essay "Ornament and Crime"), he himself made use of classical details in his design for the American Bar in Vienna; see Banham, *Theory and Design in the*

First Machine Age (Cambridge, MA: MIT Press, 1960), pp. 88–97.

22 Horiguchi, "Geijutsu to kenchiku to no kansō," p. 8; also in Fujii and Yamaguchi, *Nihon kenchiku sengen*, p. 154.

23 Horiguchi conducted extensive research into *sukiya* style (characteristic of the Edo period) and into the teahouses associated with Sen no Rikyū. He incorporated aspects of *sukiya* style into many of his works, including the Shiensō, which is discussed later in this chapter.

24 Horiguchi, "Geijutsu to kenchiku to no kansō," p. 7; not included in Fujii and Yamaguchi's abridged edition.

25 Horiguchi Sutemi, *Gendai Oranda kenchiku* (Tokyo: Iwanami Shoten, 1924); reprinted in Horiguchi Sutemi, *Kenchiku ronsō* (Tokyo: Kajima Shuppankai, 1978), pp. 29–165.

26 In his discussion of thatched houses designed by Dutch architects associated with the magazine *Wendingen*, Horiguchi refers to the buildings as examples of "the bravest and freest expression"; see *Kenchiku ronsō*, p. 141. He also discusses examples of "high art" thatched architecture, including the cottage built for Marie Antoinette at Versailles and Japanese teahouses (ibid., p. 145).

27 Yoshida was the chief designer of the Tokyo Central Post Office of 1931 and Yamada, as discussed above, designed the Tokyo Central Telegraph Office. Both architects were older than the Sōusha members; while not directly involved with the group, they affected the careers of the younger architects. For example, Yamada was instrumental in bringing Yamaguchi Bunzō into the Bunriha before the Sōusha was formed. Yamada was also Yamaguchi's supervisor when he was assigned to work on bridge designs for the ministry in the mid-1920s.

28 Yamaguchi Bunzō was born Yamaguchi Takizō. During the Sōusha years he called himself Okamura Bunzō. To avoid confusion, I refer to him throughout as Yamaguchi Bunzō, the name by which he is best known and which he took in 1942.

29 The Sōusha manifesto is reprinted in Fujii and Yamaguchi, *Nihon kenchiku sengen*, p. 164.

30 Taut's essay is quoted in Wolfgang Pehnt, *Expressionist Architecture* (New York: Praeger, 1973), p. 55.

31 Two of the most prominent proletarian arts groups were the Japan Proletarian Literary Arts League (Nihon Puroretaria Bungei Renmei), which was formally established in 1925, and the All-Japan Federation of Proletarian Arts (Zen Nihon Musansha Geijutsu Renmei, known as NAPF, the acronym formed from its name in Esperanto), established in 1927; for a brief discussion of these groups in their political context, see George M. Beckmann and Okubo Genji, *The Japanese Communist Party: 1922–1945* (Stanford: Stanford University Press, 1969), pp. 213–14.

32 Inagaki discusses this link between rationalism and Marxism in the thought of the Sōusha members; see *Nihon no kindai kenchiku*, vol. 2, pp. 310–14.

33 The last Sōusha exhibition, in 1930, included ten multiunit housing projects, three medical facilities, three schools, three public administration buildings (all designed by Maekawa), and two retail stores (one by Maekawa). When selected designs from the exhibition were published together with essays by the members, the distribution of building types was calculated and the preponderance of housing in the exhibition was highlighted; see Ishihara Kenji, "Atarashiki shakai gijutsu e," *Kokusai kenchiku* 6, no. 11 (November 1930): 1–2. Although Maekawa was not a member of the Sōusha, he and several other nonmembers exhibited designs with the group; see chapter 3.

34 Siedlung Törten and other Gropius designs were published in the magazine *Kokusai kenchiku* four months before the exhibition (*Kokusai kenchiku* 6, no. 6 [June 1930]: pls. 16–20). A special article on Gropius had appeared in *Shinkenchiku* in August 1927 (Okada Takao, "Warutā Guropiusu shi oyobi Bauhausu no kinkyō," *Shinkenchiku* 3, no. 8), and Gropius's work would have been readily available via Western publications as well.

35 RIA Kenchiku Sōgō Kenkyūjo, ed., *Kenchikuka Yamaguchi Bunzō* (Tokyo: Sagami Shobō, 1982), pp. 73–5.

36 See Imaizumi, "Ōmori jiken," pp. 30–3. [...]

37 See Gropius, *Internationale Architektur*.

38 The journal first began to publish in 1925 under the name *Kokusai kenchiku jiron* (Contemporary Opinion on International Architecture) and became *Kokusai kenchiku* in 1927.

39 Motono Seigo, "Funkciecaj elemento de malnova Japana arkitekturo kaj nova sento," *Kokusai kenchiku* 10, no. 1 (January 1934): 54–9. It is unclear how many of the magazine's readers could actually read Esperanto.

40 The other European architects were Bruno Taut, Erich Mendelsohn, Gerrit Rietveld, Josef Hoffmann, Jan Wils, J. J. P. Oud, Peter Behrens, André Lurçat, and Richard Neutra. This list illustrates the interests among Japanese modernists at this time: strong representation from northern Europe, only one French architect, and no Italians. Le Corbusier was not included – he was still not very well known in Japanese modernist circles in 1927. See Takeuchi Yoshitarō, *Nenrin no ki: Aru kenchikuka no jigazō* (Tokyo: Sagami Shobō, 1978), pp. 502–3.

41 Richard Pommer and Christian F. Otto, *Weissenhof 1927 and the Modern Movement in Architecture* (Chicago: University of Chicago Press, 1991), p. 164.

42 Ibid., p. 161. Pommer and Otto indicate that by the middle of the 1920s these associations began to fade, at least in Germany.

43 Probably few if any members of the Nihon Intānashonaru Kenchikukai were communists, but, as Inagaki points out, their writings reflected leftist political sympathies; see Inagaki, *Nihon no kindai kenchiku*, vol. 2, p. 316.

44 According to Takeuchi Yoshitarō, the issue of the organization's name was discussed at his house when Ueno came to Tokyo in 1927 to organize support there. See Takeuchi, *Nenrin no ki*, pp. 503–7.

45 Reprinted in Fujii and Yamaguchi, *Nihon kenchiku sengen*, pp. 168–9.

46 The emphasis is Gropius's; quoted in English in Pommer and Otto, *Weissenhof 1927*, p. 161.

47 Inagaki cites this passage from Gropius's essay and discusses the discrepancy between Gropius's position and that of the Nihon Intānashonaru Kenchikukai in *Nihon no kindai kenchiku*, vol. 2, p. 316.

48 Inagaki Eizō describes the output of the group as "meager" in terms of new ideas and technology; see ibid., p. 317.

23

Dangen wa Dadaisuto

TAKAHASHI SHINKICHI*

Zen poet Takahashi Shinkichi was the pioneer of Japanese Dada, a small-scale, short-lived and even less coherent movement than it was in Europe. This manifesto was authored by Takahashi and served to attract other poets. The impact of Dada was most clearly felt by poets while for visual artists Surrealism was more influential. Yet, this manifesto is significant because its inflection of Buddhist references provides a compelling example of the multiplicity of modernism in an Asian context. Takahashi was one of the key figures in Japanese modern literary circles having published 17 books of poetry, 10 volumes of essays on art, and 3 collections of literary essays.

Further Readings

Sas, Miryam (1999) *Fault Lines: Cultural Memory and Japanese Surrealism.* Stanford, CA: Stanford University Press.

Stryk, Lucien and Ikemoto, Takashi (translators) (1970) *Afterimages: Zen Poems of Shinkichi Takahashi.* Chicago, IL: Swallow Press.

The Dada "Assertion" Manifesto

Of Takahashi's early poems published in 1922, "Dangen wa dadaisuto" (literally, "Assertion is Dadaist"), which opens his 1923 volume, *Poems of Dadaist Shinkichi*, is

* Takahashi Shinkichi (1977 [1923]) *Dangen wa Dadaisuto* (Assertion Is Dadaist). In Ko Won, *Buddhist Elements in Dada: A Comparison of Tristan Tzara, Takahashi Shinkichi, and Their Fellow Poets* (excerpt from chap. 2, "Poems of Dadaist Shinkichi: Comparisons," pp. 31–4). New York, NY: New York University Press.

Modern Art in Africa, Asia, and Latin America: An Introduction to Global Modernisms, First Edition.
Edited by Elaine O'Brien, Everlyn Nicodemus, Melissa Chiu, Benjamin Genocchio,
Mary K. Coffey, and Roberto Tejada.

most important in that it exemplifies the basic ideas and the manner of expression of Takahashi as a Dada poet. In fact, this is the first and only Dada manifesto per se ever proclaimed in Japan. The poet himself speaks of this sixty-line prose poem as "a manifestation of the Dadaism I seized and conceived." Because of its significance, it is translated here in its entirety.

DADA asserts and negates all.
Infinity, naught – only reecho the sound "cigarette," or "waistband," or "word."
What gushes in imagination is reality.
The whole past is contained in the soybean's future.
Each man and his brother imagine that fantasies beyond reach of man can be thought of by a stone or a sardine's head.
DADA finds the self in all.
In the air's vibration, in the hatred of a gem, and in the stink of the word "self," there too it finds the self.
All is not two. A saying from the Buddha's clear vision emerges: all is all.
All is seen in all.
Assertion is all.

The universe is a cake of soap; soap is a pair of trousers.
All is possibility.
To Christ stuck on a fan, jelly wrote a love letter.
Everything is true.
Is it possible for the nonsmoker *Mr God* to imagine anything which cannot be asserted?

Christ said that God is almighty.
DADA asserts that everything is almighty.
Therefore, DADA asserts that the Almighty is something like a light bulb which, even when tossed into the Okhotsk Sea, lights up from time to time at the bottom.
DADA negates everything.
It pierces and rips up the no-self.
In explosion, it pisses inexplicably into the place of Nothing, from where the Buddha can exit less easily than an ant.
DADA knows no place to stay.
DADA embraces all.
DADA rises high. Nobody can love DADA.
DADA cares about everything, for it avoids nothing.

A melon which grew insensitive to the contradiction and harmony of things did not fail to become a Dadaist. No, that is not so. Contradiction and harmony are also Dadaists.
Existence is Dadaistic.
Everything can be skewered and turned over.
Change equals value, and value is a Dadaist.

Who can say a Dadaist is not edible? Is he then a thing that cannot be licked?
All is food, and food is an anarchist.

A certain Dadaist died. It happened a century before he was miscarried, while he was an embryo.

There is a Dadaist who foresaw that the earth would shrink to the size of a tadpole or a man's eye socket on October 9, 1922, at 12:34 AM. It's clear. He is invulnerable life. Each of predictions is accurate.
Another Dadaist has invented a medicine which, when taken, gives him power to work with ease – without food for a half a millennium. He is now ready to distribute it to each proletarian when the class war reaches its peak.
A young woman visited me from the North Pole on a single-wheeled vehicle, taking only 1.22 seconds.
She said she hated the bourgeoisie.
The mere word capital made her tremble.
She said she had brought a magnet which converts gold, silver, nickel, and platinum to saliva in seconds. And she taught me an incantation and how to chant it.
Any time you think you need it – she said.
A Dadaist said she was a phosphoric pronunciation.

He was strolling about the streetcar tracks in the heat, with an empty matchbox and some secrets placed in the right pocket.
The Dadaist was the subject of gossip for his friends for he had recently ceased frequenting the red light district in the outskirts all night, no longer buying whores, and had become a puritan.
He threw out his wooden sandals and stripped stark naked. Then he bound up his clothes in a lump to strike at the trolley tracks.
His pockets were smoking – that's why.
A police station was nearby, but the cops were too timid to take action.
He mentioned the other day that he could boil up the Pacific with a lit match with great ease.

A man practices pistol daily from dawn to dark, even in bed.
This Dadaist says he won't loosen his grip on the pistol until he has killed seventy million people in a street fight.

A Dadaist wrote his will that no matter how trivial and hard life might be, he hated to die, wanted to live even a second longer.
He hanged himself with a lamp string in a library on the third floor of an association office.
In his lifetime he was very gentle, always faithful to the organization's rules, totally trusted by everybody.
Another Dadaist received a PhD for his chemical analysis of a variety of tears.
DADA gives birth to all, splits and synthesizes all.
All is encamped behind DADA.
Nobody can be on DADA's side.
DADA is female, but has no sexual cravings.
That is why DADA is equipped with sex organs and all kinds of weapons.
DADA is the most cowardly creature. Since it keeps a furious fighting spirit at its waist, it is in constant explosion, smashing and destroying.
All is enemy to DADA.
DADA curses everything to death, swallows everything up, and yet its tongue, still dissatisfied, flicks in and out like an eternal have-not.

Section 3

China

24

Sketch Conceptualism as Modernist Contingency

Eugene Y. Wang*

In this essay, Eugene Y. Wang, noted US-based historian of Chinese art and Buddhist visual culture, explores the complexity of modern art in China, especially in relation to the literati tradition of ink painting, *xieyi*. Translated here as "sketch conceptualism," *xieyi* had prevailed in China as an individualist art practice since the thirteenth century. By comparing the art, philosophy, and life choices of two modern painters, Xu Beihong (1895–1953) and Chang Yu (1901–66), this reading displays the paradoxical (or, as in the title, "contingent") correlation between the abstract, gestural style and subjective content of *xieyi* and the Western modern paintings of artists such as Henri Matisse with its hallmark "sketch conceptualist" simplification, flatness, and eschewal of realism. Sketch conceptualism can thus be understood as both traditionally Chinese and universally "modern."

Although the impetus to revitalize Chinese art and culture saw a wave of artists study in Paris in the 1910s and 1920s, Wang carefully dissects the differences among their artistic approaches using Xu Beihong and Chang Yu as archetypes. Far from a wholesale appropriation of European modernist styles, Chinese artists responded to European art with an eye on how it might be used to modernize Chinese

* Eugene Y. Wang (2001) "Sketch Conceptualism as Modernist Contingency." In Maxwell K. Hearn and Judith G. Smith (eds) *Chinese Art: Modern Expressions* (pp. 102–61). New York, NY: The Metropolitan Museum of Art.

Modern Art in Africa, Asia, and Latin America: An Introduction to Global Modernisms, First Edition.
Edited by Elaine O'Brien, Everlyn Nicodemus, Melissa Chiu, Benjamin Genocchio, Mary K. Coffey, and Roberto Tejada.

art. On one side of the spectrum was Xu Beihong, who studied academic painting in Paris for eight years and stridently opposed avant-garde modernism in favor of academic realism – in his view more scientific and therefore more advanced. In contrast, the subjective, sketch conceptualist paintings of expatriate Chang Yu identify with avant-garde modernism and can be seen as a strategic re-appropriation of European modernism's massive appropriation of Chinese painting in the early twentieth century. Both Xu and Chang were arguing for modernism, but they employed vastly different methods.

Wang's essay shows that the dynamic engagement between Western modernism and Chinese modernism was a process fraught with tensions and philosophical differences. One of the main questions the essay raises is what impact traditional Chinese literati paintings had on the formation of China's modernism since modernism was everywhere – local and universal – and based not only on a particular social and historical set of circumstances but also on artistic traditions. Wang succinctly expresses this as: "One's traditionalism is another's modernism."

Further Readings

Andrews, Julia (2003) "The Traitor of Art and Chinese Modernity: Liu Haisu and the Nude Controversy." In Richard Vinograd (ed.), *Images in Exchange*. Berkeley: University of California Press.

Croizier, Ralph (1989) "Reverse Current Early Twentieth Century Influence on Chinese Painting." In Yue-him Tam (ed.), *Sino-Japanese Cultural Interchange: Aspects of Archaeology and Art History*. Hong Kong: Chinese University.

Yiu, Josh (ed.) (2009) *Writing Modern Chinese Art: Historiographic Explorations*. Seattle, WA: Seattle Art Museum.

It is ever vexing to invoke modernity in Chinese art, as we are never entirely sure what it is. The confusion arises not so much from the legion of rival definitions – though certainly they have clouded the matter – as from a historical complexity underlying modernist aspirations in Chinese art. Shifting contexts and frames of reference further complicate the matter. If we follow the general understanding of modernism as a radical mutiny around the beginning of the twentieth century against the authority of tradition, we find that Western modernists and their Chinese counterparts were confronted by different traditions, and hence also different tasks. European modernism broke away from mimetic illusionism by constructing a utopian purism of subjectivity and sensation.[1] Reformers of Chinese art, however, faced a different burden of tradition. The primacy of spiritual vision and anti-illusionism that European modernism was working hard to create was precisely the burden of the literati tradition that modern-minded Chinese radicals were trying to unload. In fact, the Academic Realism that was an anathema to European modernism was at one point envisioned by some leading radical reformers as the needed corrective to what was perceived as the moribund tradition of Chinese painting. One's traditionalism is another's modernism. This led to a curious historical paradox: apologies for traditional

Chinese literati painting often justified its relevance to modern times on the ground of its spiritual affinity – its intensely subjective orientation and determined renunciation of verisimilitude – with European post-Impressionism, Cubism, Futurism, and Expressionism.[2]

This neatly polarized situation did not last long. The initial modernizing clamor of the 1910s evolved in the late 1920s and the early 1930s into situations far too complex to be described purely in clear-cut polarities. It is beyond the scope of this essay to offer a definition of Chinese modernism in art (leaving aside the question whether that is even feasible). Instead, it focuses on one area where the terms "traditionalism" and "modernism," "East" and "West," "radicalism" and "conservatism" tend to converge or collide, an area that well demonstrates the historical complexity underlying Chinese modernist aspirations. If this narrative does not result in a neat ordering of the entangled problems, it may at least lead to, following T. J. Clark, either "a thickening or thinning" of some kind of pattern that underlies the modernist situation in Chinese art.[3]

That area of focus is "sketch conceptualism" (*xieyi*), a pictorial genre and mode of execution that can be traced back to the thirteenth century or earlier, depending on how we frame our narrative. In its traditional usage, this term implies an underlying assumption that such painting serves only as a means – by way of highly abbreviated, sketchy forms – to evoke conceptual overtones and spiritual resonance beyond tangible formal properties. To this end, a cultivated amateurism, suggestive of a scholarly or "writerly" (i.e. literati) taste, is favored over professional craftsmanship with its painterly interest in verisimilitude. Economy of execution is favored over detailed and textured refinement. The articulation of this ideal or aspiration enabled scholar-amateurs over time to appropriate painting as a scholarly pursuit. It also justified lesser efforts – the irresponsible splashy throwaways – to masquerade as respectable works of the "spirit." In the early twentieth century, sketch conceptualism became the flash point in the debate between reformists and traditionalists. Radical reformers held that the codification of brushwork at the expense of modeling led to a diminution of creativity and the consequent degeneration of Chinese painting in late imperial times. Enlightened "traditionalists," on the other hand, saw sketch conceptualism as a point of contact between time-honored Chinese literati painting and Western modernism, and hence argued against its rejection or the radical "modernization" of Chinese painting. For many young Chinese artists, sketch conceptualism was the aspect of Chinese tradition that they were most able to capitalize on and explore in their attempts to appropriate or internalize European modernist models. It was also where demarcations between "traditionalism" and "modernism" were most likely to founder and unravel.

Xu and Chang: Two Sides of the Same Sheet

This dichotomy was literally illustrated by two artists in a rare historical document of the early 1920s. On the front of this single sheet is a flower painting, dated 1921, an example of traditional Chinese ink-and-color sketch conceptualism by Chang Yu (1901–66), an artist from Sichuan who went to Paris around 1920 to study art. On the back is a drawing of lions by Xu Beihong (1895–1953), an artist who would become one of the key forces in shaping the contour of twentieth-century Chinese art. Xu arrived in Paris in 1919 with his wife, Jiang Biwei, on a government scholarship. In 1921, when the scholarship was temporarily discontinued, Xu took up residence for half a year in Berlin, where the cost of living was then significantly lower. Ever hard-working, Xu spent time at the Berlin zoo, honing his skills by sketching and drawing lions. The drawing in question is among his copious exercises.

Strikingly, the two sides of this sheet correspond to the two contending viewpoints on Chinese painting, and epitomize the tension within Chinese art circles concerning what was to be done with traditional sketch conceptualism. Apparently, Chang had meant his painting as a gift and a token of friendship. Xu's decision to recycle a fellow artist's painting may point to the depth of his financial embarrassment; no sheet of paper was to be wasted. However, the decision also registers his attitude: the painting was no more than scrap paper to be recycled. In other words, Xu did not think much of Chang's effort and could just as well have disposed of it.

Xu Beihong's act should be viewed against the larger historical backdrop. The artist's formative years coincided with one of the most volatile periods in modern Chinese history. He was right in its vortex. In 1915 Xu, a provincial from Yixing, Jiangsu Province, had arrived in Shanghai to pursue a career as a painter.[4] After a period of poverty, frustration, and despair that nearly drove him to suicide, a turning point came in 1916. Xu answered an advertisement from the Hartung Garden, a wealthy Jewish estate in Shanghai, calling for a picture of Cangjie, the primordial deity who in Chinese myth had invented writing. Xu's painting, a giant with "four eyes radiating divine light," was chosen. He was subsequently invited to be the resident tutor and professor of fine arts at an institute attached to the Hartung Garden, the University of the Sage Cangjie and Enlightenment (Cangsheng Mingzhi Daxue), where members of the cultural elite such as Kang Youwei (1858–1927) and Wang Guowei (1877–1927) were frequently invited to lecture. Xu came under Kang's tutelage. In the course of viewing art and practicing calligraphy under his guidance, Xu was to acquire his mentor's radical art-historical stance. In 1918 Xu went to Beijing, where he met Cai Yuanpei (1868–1940), president of Beijing University, who appointed him a tutor in the university's Society of Research on Pictorial Method.

Thus, in a few short years, Xu's career path intersected the lives of two of the leading radical thinkers in modern Chinese history. Kang Youwei, a noted political reformer, held that Chinese literati painting, with its preference for sketch conceptualism over professional craftsmanship, was responsible for the decline of Chinese pictorial art, which Kang thought paled in comparison with Western art. His solution was to return to the realistic style of the art of the Tang dynasty (618–907).[5] Cai Yuanpei reached the same conclusion from another route. Compared with Western art, Cai argued, Chinese art emphasized conception and copying rather than the depiction of actual external appearance. He considered Western painting more advanced by virtue of its affinity with science. To modernize Chinese art required, according to Cai, the infusion of a "scientific" spirit by way of verisimilitude.[6]

Underlying both of these men's radical views was the conviction that historical progress was propelled by advances in science and technology. Western realism, with its linear perspective and illusionist devices, was seen as technologically more advanced. For Kang and Cai, the traditional ideals of quietude, eremitism, and self-cultivation evoked by sketch-conceptualist painting appeared increasingly out of sync with the emotional needs of modern Chinese intellectuals. The pictorial mood of understatement, restraint, and effeminate fragility conveyed through such paintings seemed incongruous at a time when China was reeling from repeated humiliating defeats dealt by foreign powers and when the rallying call was for national self-strengthening.

These radical voices combined to inform Xu Beihong's views on Chinese art. But none of these thinkers ever took up brush to paint. Despite their prominence in intellectual circles, it is not clear to what extent their radical views influenced the painters of their day. Xu Beihong, however, was a painter, and a serious one. His own upbringing, while by no means revolutionary, prepared him well for such a radical challenge to traditional literati painting.

Xu Beihong was steeped in a family artistic tradition with a penchant for verisimilitude. His father, Xu Dazhang (1867–1914), specialized in portraits. A painting by Xu Dazhang portraying himself and his son, with its realistic treatment of the sitters' faces, continues the late-Ming tradition of European-influenced portraiture practiced by Zheng Jin (1568–1650) and others. Until Xu Beihong's time, such portraits were held in low esteem, regarded as mere craftsmanship when compared with the literati tradition of sketch conceptualism. Xu learned this art from his father, beginning at age ten. He copied daily the printed images of the popular Shanghai illustrator, Wu Youru (d. 1893).[7] Xu's training in this realistic mode of painting enabled him to embrace the reformist challenge to traditional literati painting. Unlike Kang Youwei and Cai Yuanpei, he was able to embody the radical viewpoint in pictorial practice. We can imagine the excitement of this twenty-three-year-old as he joined the exalted ranks of Beijing University's Painting Society, among them the much-revered Chen Hengke (Chen Shizeng, 1876–1923). Moreover, he had the audacity to address, if not dress down, his gray-haired fellow tutors in his lecture "On Ways of Reforming Chinese Art." He blasted the current state of Chinese painting as a "ruin" and a "disgrace and shame." He deplored the smug self-complacency of Chinese painters and their blindness to Western painting, and called for "uttermost verisimilitude" as the solution to Chinese painting's present dismal situation.[8] When he was given the opportunity to go to Paris to study European art on a government scholarship, he went with a strong sense of mission.

By the time Xu Beihong arrived in Paris in May 1919, the art world there had undergone a fundamental change. The French academic standard that had dictated artistic practice and regulated pictorial taste had been all but completely eroded, replaced by "a welter of conflicting artistic styles and philosophical obligations."[9] Intent on resuscitating what he and his radical contemporaries saw as the degenerated and moribund state of Chinese painting, Xu seems to have been unfazed by the modernist buzz in the Parisian air. A year after arriving in Paris, he passed the rigorous entrance examination to the École des Beaux-Arts, a stronghold of academic tradition.[10] He also apprenticed himself to Pascal Dagnan-Bouveret (1852–1929), student of Corot, whose kind of art was largely passé.

Like Xu, Chang Yu also received his early painting lessons from his father, starting at the age of twelve. Again like Xu, he had traveled to Japan before going to Paris. Chang, however, had grown up in a well-to-do family, and had not suffered the kind of maddening poverty that had afflicted Xu in his youth. This no doubt contributed to the fundamental difference between the two. While Xu's involvement with art always had a sense of urgency to it – either as a means of survival or as the fulfillment of a historical mission – for Chang, art was simply a way of life.

Chang Yu arrived in Paris a year after Xu Beihong, and the city meant different things to him. To Xu, Paris embodied a massive and solid artistic legacy that he intended to appropriate as a force for changing the direction of Chinese art. To Chang, the city offered a liberating, bohemian lifestyle and a place for self-discovery and fulfillment. His temperament made it easy for him to quickly imbibe the modernist ethos of the avant-garde art world, just as he was repelled by the idea of studying at the École des Beaux-Arts. When Pang Xunqin, a fellow Chinese expatriate, who was considering studying at the École, sought Chang Yu's advice, he was taken aback by Chang's vehement dismissal of the institution. Chang's allegiance was to a private art studio known as the Académie de la Grande Chaumiere, located in the heart of Montparnasse.[11] Founded in 1902 and directed by artists such as Bourdelle, Zadkine, and Othon Friez,[12] the studio maintained a relaxed, freewheeling atmosphere. The atelier held more than a hundred people seated in four rows, and anyone paying the negligible entrance fee was allowed to sketch the mode.[13] While others used charcoal to sketch, Chang would at times use Chinese brush and ink, drawing admiring crowds. Instead of sketching the model on stage, he often drew his fellow painters. Verisimilitude was never his concern. Regardless of the gender and age of his "sitters," he invariably gave them a corpulent female body. No one found this offensive; such whims were to be indulged in the Grande Chaumière. Chang also found the open environment of the Montpartnasse cafés accommodating for his capricious art practice.

We do not know why Chang Yu painted in Paris a peony in the traditional Chinese ink-and-color sketch-conceptual method and gave it to Xu Beihong as a gift. Was it a showy testimony to his early training in Chinese art? A pledge of the bond between two Chinese compatriots? Or a veiled signal of flirtation with Jiang Biwei, Xu's coquettish and often neglected wife? The immediate circumstances and motivation elude us. But the work conveys Chang's conviction – one that Xu Beihong certainly did not share – that a flower painting in the Chinese ink-and-color mode of sketch conceptualism was not out of place in 1920s Paris.[14] This is all the more remarkable considering Chang's embrace of Matisse and other modernist trends in Paris. Could it be that Chang Yu sensed some kind of an affinity, or some relevance in mood or spirit, between certain strains in contemporary European modernism and traditional Chinese sketch conceptualism?

Why would Chang Yu, knowing Xu's realist preferences, give him such a painting, unless he meant it as a gesture of persuasion? The two artists must have exchanged their views on art: Xu would most likely have attributed the perceived degeneration of Chinese art to the tradition of sketch conceptualism, and rave about Delacroix and others as the modernizing remedy, while Chang would have insisted on the affinity of Chinese sketch conceptualism with the vision of a Matisse.

The difference between Chang Yu's ink-and-color sketch of a peony and Xu Beihong's academic drawing of lions is not a matter of technical skill or talent. Xu could just as well have done an ink-and-color work in the sketch-conceptual mode. The fact that he did not do so shows that it was his intention to throw out that baggage. Chang Yu apparently thought otherwise. In any case, the two different drawing modes encapsulate the two divergent convictions among Chinese art students in Paris at the time. According to one French critic's assessment, in reviewing a Chinese art exhibition in Strasbourg in 1924, Chinese artists in France were divided into two groups: the Association des Artistes chinois en France and the Société chinoise des Arts décoratifs a Paris.[15] The former pledged allegiance to "chefs-d'œuvre européens," while the latter was committed to the Chinese pictorial tradition. This juxtaposition of the two groups, as Craig Clunas has demonstrated in a recent study, is somewhat misleading. The followers of the European tradition exhibited works on silk with titles like "Printemps pluviex" and "Idée antique," while the supposedly Chinese "traditionalists" exhibited an embroidery entitled Portrait de M. Clemenceau."[16] Except for Xu Beihong (during his Paris years at least) and a few others whose break from Chinese tradition appears resolute and uncompromising, there was a general tendency among Chinese art students in France to explore ways of integrating European modernism and Chinese tradition.

The general atmosphere in the Parisian art world encouraged such efforts. Chinese art students, like those from other countries, found themselves thrown into excitement and confusion. They had come with the preconceived notion of European art as a codified set of skills. Instead, they found themselves in a bewildering arena where rules were challenged and broken in an atmosphere that encouraged freedom and the exploration of new possibilities. Their modernist mentors urged them to disengage themselves from all entrenched models and find a unique "self." But the pictorial construction of a stylistic "self" has to rely on some sort of a schema, no matter how strong the desire for originality. Matisse, for example, had sought inspiration in Oriental carpets and other exotic sources, in so far as they posed a viable alternative to the European tradition. This new interest in Eastern traditions may explain the massive upsurge of interest among European scholars in ancient Chinese art in the early twentieth century.[17] Some Chinese art students were told by their French mentors to value their own artistic tradition.[18] Such exhortations prompted Lin Fengmian (1900–91) to frequent the Oriental

Museum and Oriental Ceramic Museum in Paris. In any case, the quest for novelty in the European modernist movement meant that Chinese art students in Europe could draw upon traditional Chinese art to achieve that effect.

There are close parallels between the works of some Western modernists, such as Matisse, and traditional Chinese sketch conceptualism. Both tend toward simplification and abstraction, both accentuate curvilinear flatness, and both renounce any interest in verisimilitude. Furthermore, the languid, loose, and seemingly effortless quality of Chinese sketch conceptualism harmonizes with the free-spirited European modernist temperament. None of this seems to have been lost on Chang Yu. He insisted on using Chinese ink and brush to do his sketches in the Grande Chaumière. His paintings show a growing tendency toward simplification that borders on minimalism. "To simplify, and again simplify," is one of the few artistic dictates he left us.[19] For Chang Yu, unlike Xu Beihong, verisimilitude was never a preoccupation. His sketches in the atelier setting were deliberately "deconstructive," as pointed out above.

The Two Xus Debate and Two Views of Modernity

Xu Beihong first returned to China in 1926, landing in Shanghai, and was an instant celebrity. Newspaper reporters dogged him, and interviews with him and lectures by him were aired on the radio or instantly printed in the newspapers. Xu seems to have thrived on this notoriety. If he had been bold in his attacks on the Chinese literati tradition before his departure for Paris, he now became even more confident in pronouncing his judgments on art. Eight years of immersion in the European art world had provided him with a solid basis for making well-informed comparisons.

Though he deplored the ineffectiveness of the Chinese language in describing and communicating various subtleties of aesthetic quality, he nevertheless continued to use some traditional Chinese art-historical terms in his discussions of contemporary art, probably to make his views more accessible to his Chinese audience. The terms he used most frequently were the antonyms *xieshi* (realistic depiction) and *xieyi* (conceptual depiction, or sketch conceptualism). The art of the world, said Xu, may be diverse, including Classicism, Romanticism, Impressionism, post-Impressionism, Cubism, Futurism, and so on, but these movements fall largely into two categories, *xieshi* and *xieyi*,[20] "realism" and "conceptualism." Realism emphasizes images and objects, while conceptualism concerns itself with mental states and emotions. Realism stems from close observation; conceptualism thrives on sensation. Xu cited Rodin as the epitome of realism and Chavanne[s] as the paragon of conceptualism. Wary that such a rigid dichotomy might be too limiting, he acknowledged that the greatest artists often transcended this division. He cited Dagnan-Bouveret, his French mentor, as the model of reaching the state of conceptualism by way of initial mastery of realism. Xu further pointed out the dialectical relationship between these opposed categories: realism is never devoid of a conceptual framework; and conceptualism cannot be sustained without some kind of representational quality.[21] While theoretically granting equal validity to the two categories, Xu warned against pretensions to and the potential abuse of conceptualism.[22] His examples of the latter include European modernism as exemplified by Cézanne, Matisse, and others.

Xu Beihong's assessment of European art in terms of realism versus conceptualism is only a prelude to his radical revision of Chinese art-historical orthodoxy. He maintained that a similar dichotomy existed in traditional Chinese art: *gongbi* (crafted depiction) versus *xieyi* (conceptual depiction), terms that largely correspond to his realism/conceptualism scheme. While, in Chinese art discourse, "crafted depiction" and "conceptual depiction" generally pertain to two distinct modes of execution, they are often correlated with two distinct pictorial traditions, namely the courtly and the literati. It was Dong Qichang (1555–1636), the seventeenth-century arbiter of taste, who codified this bifurcation of Chinese painting. Following the formulations of Chan Buddhism, Dong divided the traditional corpus of Chinese painting into Northern and Southern schools, the former characterized by professional craftsmanship and realist virtuosity, and the latter by a conceptual approach that valued self-cultivation and disdained technical virtuosity and interest in verisimilitude. This value-laden bifurcation had a profound impact on taste, so that by Dong's time even professional painters had to affect an amateurish style in order to measure up to the perceived high standards.

Xu Beihong wanted to reverse this entrenched hierarchy. The Northern school, he pontificated, with its "endless resourcefulness" and "overwhelming magnitude and strength" manifested in its "crafted depiction," far excelled and overshadowed the Southern school, whose "elegant small pieces are sufficient to please but are not able to inspire awe.[23] Furthermore, Xu's aversion to ink-splashing masquerading as conceptualism is apparent: "What is so special about [works by] those who only know how to flip their brushes and dash their ink, daubing in random abandon without a governing principle?"[24]

Notwithstanding his pronouncements on the value of craftsmanly painting, Xu initially assumed a "modernist" stance in the Chinese context. Soon after he returned to China permanently, in September 1927, Xu established a close association with Tian Han (1898–1968), a dramatist of modernist proclivity who was an admirer of Baudelaire[25] and an explorer of "sub-consciousness." Tian was the editor of a supplement of the *Central Daily* newspaper, titled *Modeng*, a Chinese transliteration of the English "Modern," and Xu designed the letterhead for it.[26] Xu also published his writings in the supplement, including a rather dashing "Four Chapters of Revolutionary Lyrics" in the inaugural issue.[27] In early 1928, at the invitation of Tian Han, Xu was involved in the establishment of an art school, the South China Art Academy (*Nanguo yishushe*). Intended as a modern establishment, the school offered courses in literature, drama, and painting, with Xu in charge of the last. An advertisement declared the school's intention to be "the pioneer of the new age." It also claimed that the founders of the school were "all of the Bohemian class," with the word "Bohemian" printed in French: "Bohémienne."[28] The founders listed included Xu Zhimo (1896–1931), Yu Dafu (1896–1945), Ouyang Yuqian (1889–1962), and other young cultural elite of Shanghai who certainly qualified for the epithet "modernists."

At the time, Xu embodied modernity, which in Shanghai consisted primarily of advocating Westernization. As someone who had lived in Europe for eight years, Xu had firsthand experience of what was "modern." [...] His works appeared in journals and magazines, such as *Young Companions*, which projected the kind of chic urban glamour that contributed to the cultural imaginary of modernity in Shanghai around 1930.[29]

However, Xu's modernist role did not extend to his fundamental vocation – painting. In the late 1910s, even before his departure for Paris, he had spoken out against the moribund state of the Chinese pictorial tradition and called for the introduction of European realism as a path to reform and modernization. Returning to China in the late 1920s, he faced an audience that had already been exposed to European culture, including the latest trends in the art world. The choice was no longer between a Chinese art that was stagnant and backward and a "scientifically advanced" Western art. It was between pre-twentieth-century European art and everything that came after post-Impressionism.

With his deep attachment to pre-twentieth-century European art, and realism in particular, Xu now found himself in the "Paris of the Orient," where the creative buzz was hardly a beat behind that of its namesake. Few of his fellow artists – many of whom had just returned from Paris or other parts of Europe and Japan – shared his pictorial taste. If he had been able to avoid modernism in Paris, he was no longer able to do so in Shanghai, a city taken with anything "new," and where he was supposed to represent the latest Parisian trends. His recently acquired European art skills indeed put him in a position to inject new spirit into the Chinese art world. Yet, he soon found himself playing a role opposite to that which might be expected of a reformer.

In January 1929, Xu Beihong was nominated a member of the standing committee of the first National Exhibition of Chinese Art, sponsored by the Nationalist government.[30] Xu Zhimo, his former colleague at South China Art Academy and a romantic poet who had studied in the United States and at Cambridge, was the editor of the journal, *Meizhan* (*Art Exhibition*), that accompanied the exhibition. The two Xus (who were not related) were soon to engage in a public debate about the relevance of European post-Impressionism to China. The exhibition opened on April 10 in the Xinpuyu Auditorium in Shanghai, and from the outset was ominously tension-ridden. Protesting that the exhibition was being hijacked by "formalists," Xu Beihong withdrew his paintings.[31] Xu Zhimo tried, unsuccessfully, to coax him into cooperating. A debate between the two erupted when Xu Beihong made public his aversion to European modernist strains represented by Cézanne, Matisse, and Bonnard. In his view, the European "psyche" had been warped since World War I, and the "dignity" of European art epitomized by Leonardo da Vinci had been "eroded," having fallen prey to faddishness and market manipulation by dealers. Xu believed that the current hankering after novelty was simply the result of having ingested so many delicacies that the appetite craved a momentary change. He thereby proclaimed Manet "mediocre," Renoir "vulgar," Cézanne "flippant," and Matisse "low." Denying his anti-modernist stance, he acknowledged Rodin, Carrierre, Monet, and Besnard as "giants among the new school," but dismissed those artists who could easily churn out two works a day. To Xu Beihong, artistic greatness meant something beyond *his* own capabilities.[32] In other words, technical virtuosity remained his ultimate criterion of quality.

Xu Zhimo's defense focused on Cézanne. In spite – or maybe because – of his immersion in Western romanticism, Xu Zhimo's language is squarely couched in idioms from traditional Chinese literati discourse:

> In the history of modern painting, there are those [painters] who have the character of aloofness, willing to remain indifferent to worldly success, completely independent of the madding crowd, whose lifelong commitment is to realize their distinct personal "transcendent realm" (*jingjie*). Cézanne is one of them … He wants to convey his personal feeling, to arrange "the architecture of color," and fulfill his irrepressible desire to represent "the experience of personal sensibility" (xingling, or lingxing). Can we think of an artist more devoted to a pure art?[33]

In this debate, it was Xu Beihong, the radical and harsh critic of the Chinese literati tradition, who adopted a hardened "traditionalist" view of Western art, while Xu Zhimo, the defender of European modernism, adopted the language of a traditional Chinese literati. Xu Zhimo's characterization of Cézanne could just as well have been applied to Dong Qichang.

Chang Yu as the Projected Participant in the Two Xus Debate

The issues in the debate between Xu Beihong and Xu Zhimo parallel the issues that divided Xu Beihong and Chang Yu. Xu Zhimo visited Paris in the early 1920s and revisited Europe in 1925 and 1928, where he and Chang Yu became good friends. Writing to Liu Haisu (1896–1994), who was in Paris at the time of the two Xus debate, Xu Zhimo continued to make inquiries after Chang Yu. He enclosed a copy of the open letters he had exchanged with Xu Beihong for Liu to circulate among Chinese art students in Paris, in hopes of enlisting their support since their intimate knowledge of the European art world would add credence to his defense of modernism.[34] Chang Yu was most likely to be among his allies. Although rarely given to pronouncements on art, Chang supplied Xu Zhimo with ammunition. He sent him a painting of a female nude, causing Xu to marvel at her "cosmic legs."[35]

Chang Yu's artistic career in Paris had taken off by this time. His works were exhibited at the Salon d'Automne in 1925, and in 1929 the art collector Henri-Pierre Roché who brought Picasso and the Steins together,[36] recognized Chang Yu's talent and purchased his works. Between 1931 and 1932, his works were exhibited at various Parisian galleries, including Éditions Bonaparte, Galérie van

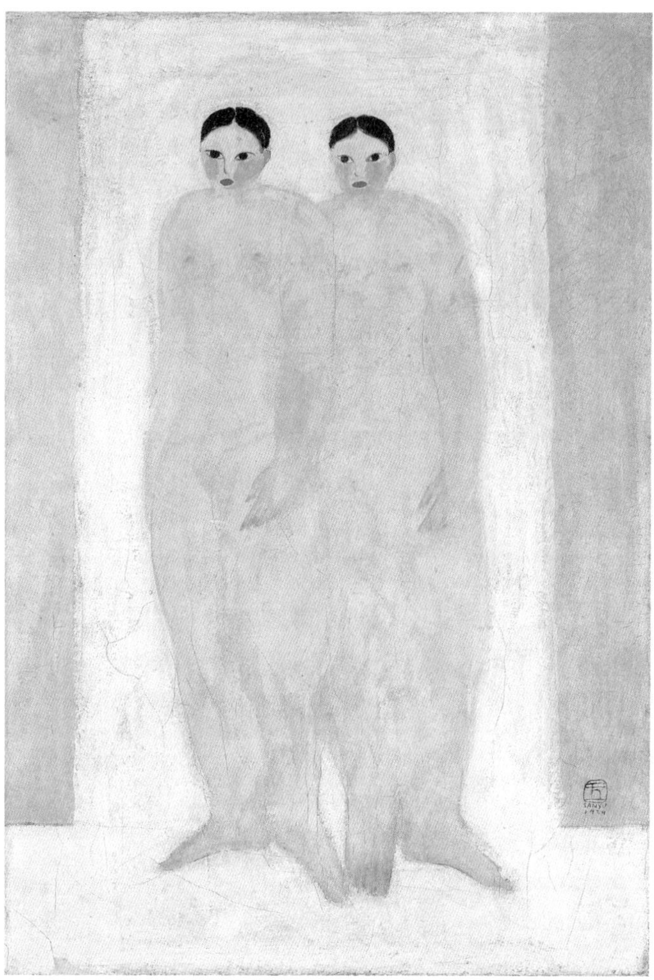

Figure 24.1 Sanyu (Chang Yu), *Two Pink Nudes*, 1929, oil on canvas. Private Collection / Photo, © Christie's Images / The Bridgeman Art Library.

Ojien, Salon des Indépendants, and Salon des Tuileries. Between 1932 and 1934, several galleries in Holland, among them J.H. de Bois, in Haarlem, and Galérie van Lier, in Amsterdam, showed his art. He was listed in the *Dictionnaire biographique des artistes contemporaine 1910–1930*, published in 1932.

During this period, Chang Yu's pictorial subjects consisted primarily of female nudes and still lifes of flowers. The minimalist tendency in his work was already evident. Linear economy and minimal detail seem to have been his overriding pictorial concerns. To this end, he used Chinese ink and brush to outline the contours of his figures. He then applied touches of charcoal and watercolor to give a suggestion of shading and volume. While these sketches might suffice in their own right as Chinese-style conceptual depictions, Chang Yu would sometimes translate them into oil paintings. As this medium is not the optimum vehicle for such linear drawings, his sketches were probably intended merely as preparatory exercises for larger works to be executed in oil on canvas. Clearly, the formal concerns apparent in these sketches are carried over to the oil paintings. [*Two*] *Pink Nude*[*s*] painted in 1929, for example, may be based on [such sketches].

[…]

It is not necessary to engage in an iconographic analysis of Chang Yu's works here. Formal concerns are most likely his primary preoccupation. Paintings such as *Nude in Geometric Shape* may be seen as evidence of Chang taking cues from Matisse and others. He may indeed have shared the same pictorial interests underlying some of Matisse's works, such as *Lorette Reclining*, namely, the interplay between volume and flat decorative patterns and its resulting visual effect. But Chang is more of a minimalist, and appears more interested in the effect of blankness. "European painting is like a lavish feast where there are roasts and fried foods and all kinds of meat," Chang Yu once said in one of his rare statements on art. "As for my works, they are like vegetables, fruits, and salads. They can help you put aside your usual tastes in painting."[37] He brings to his canvases a sensibility distinct from that of his European contemporaries. While sharing the Parisian interest in voluptuous sensuality, his paintings have a quieter and more meditative quality, evoking a remote otherness, particularly as evidenced by *Nude in Geometric Shape*.

It is difficult to formulate the elusive qualities of a sensibility. Keeping in mind the cultural baggage he carried, we can place many of Chang's works in the context of Chinese sketch conceptualism or conceptual depiction. There are the unmistakable signs of striving after what minimalism may evoke rather than represent, the yearning for what is beyond the images. What the Parisian modernist experience does to Chang's Chinese sensibility is to infuse it with a liberating spirit, provoking an unabashed indulgence in fantasies about the sensuality of the body as a landscape that sublimates and crystallizes the Parisian bohemian lifestyle. What Chang's Chinese sensibility does to his newly acquired Parisian taste is to make it more ethereal and "spiritual." These two traditions and contexts converge in Chang to produce a distinct kind of conceptual depiction. By bringing Chinese sketch conceptualism to Paris, where it was geographically and culturally displaced but spiritually at home, Chang Yu tested its potential, pushed its limits, and put it in touch with alternative traditions of conceptual depiction from other cultures. This new chapter in the history of Chinese sketch conceptualism is yet to be acknowledged by scholars in the field of Chinese art history. In Paris, however, it did not go unnoticed. European art critics took note of "these subtle paintings of pink women and animals alone in a vast dizzying space." Pierre [Joffroy], who reviewed Chang Yu in 1946, described him as an "inventeur de l'essentialism":

> The curious could ask if Sanyu [Chang Yu] is a Chinese who is an artist or an artist who is Chinese. There is no answer to this question. The particular gift of this artist is to unite East and West in his paintings, not in a confused, sacrilegious way, but with an elevated awareness where one loses usual points of reference. Sanyu has found one word to describe his minimalist art using basically three tones of color: simplicism. Some people have substituted this, perhaps somewhat inappropriately, with the word "essentialism," which may not be better, but could allow critics to differentiate it from other groups of cliques of 'isms.[38]

Chang Yu was one of the few Chinese artists who chose to stay in Paris to pursue their artistic careers. This dislocation meant that he could explore possibilities in art unhampered by the circumstantial pressures faced by his contemporaries in China, a fact that is in itself interesting. At the same time, he was not entirely irrelevant to the cultural landscape of China around 1930. The painting of the "cosmic legs" that he sent to Xu Zhimo aligned him firmly with the latter in the debate between the two Xus. In other words, Chang Yu remained Xu Beihong's opponent, albeit unwittingly. Xu Beihong apparently grudgingly acknowledged Chang's talent, although he was quick to find faults with Chang's art. Reviewing Chang's works in an exhibition held in Shanghai in 1927, Xu commented: "There is a special flavor (*qiqu*) in the drawings by my friend Chang Yu. Regrettably, he pays no attention to construction. His works are therefore always slightly flawed."[39]

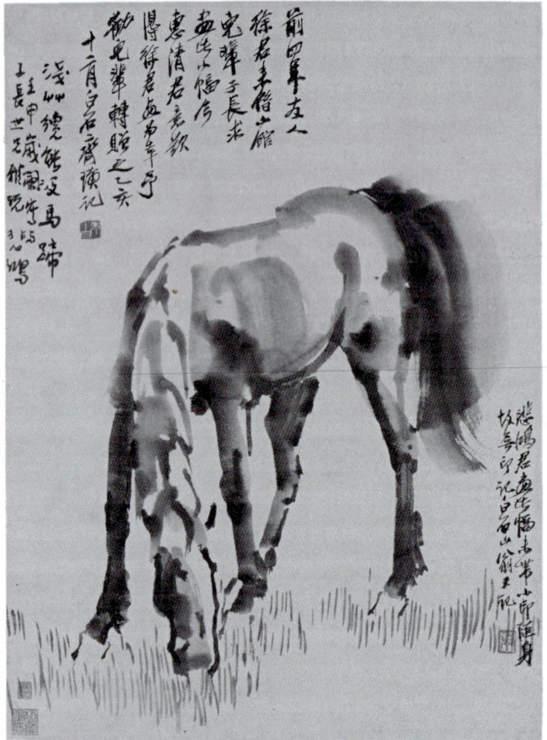

Figure 24.2 Xu Beihong, *Grazing Horse*, 1932, ink/hanging scroll from the collection of the Metropolitan Museum of Art, New York City. Scala.

[...]

Ironic Reversal: Xu Beihong's Turn Toward Sketch Conceptualism

A major paradox underlies Xu Beihong's career as a painter. He burst upon the cultural stage in the late 1910s blasting the literati tradition of sketch conceptualism and hailing Western realism as the needed catalyst for reinvigorating Chinese painting. His rigorous training at the École des Beaux-Arts in Paris in the 1920s equipped him with the technical facility for realizing his avowed goal of pictorial realism. After his return to China, however, he worked in the traditional Chinese medium of brush and ink more often than in oil on canvas. While this may be understood as an effort to make good on his early promise to reform Chinese painting, it is curious that the bulk of his output after his return from Paris increasingly tended toward sketch conceptualism, the antithesis of his realist ideals. In public pronouncements, Xu never quite recanted his earlier positions, and he continued to churn out the occasional essay reiterating his early radical stance and attacking traditional literati sketch conceptualism. His practice, however, points to an impulse that was, at times, counter to his manifestos. True, we discern in his ink paintings traces of his training in realist oil painting: the anatomical precision, the attention to shading, modeling, and spatial relationships. In other cases, however, his ink paintings do not seem to stray far afield from the traditional sketch conceptualism. In these instances, we detect very little of the impact of his Paris training. Rather, it seems as if Xu had taken his cue from such masters of sketch conceptualism as Qi Baishi (1864–1957), whom Xu respected and promoted vigorously. The ultimate irony is that Xu's reputation increasingly rested not on his realistic works but on a corpus of horse paintings that are largely in the mode of sketch conceptualism, and that he could have done just as well without his Paris training. Critics were quick to take note: "Western painting has been advocated in China for more than two decades. What is the result? Lately those practitioners *cum* admirers of Western-style painting have all scrambled to take up Chinese painting instead."[40]

The variety of circumstances that may have caused Xu to turn toward sketch conceptualism is complex and largely unacknowledged among critics and scholars. While we have no reason to discount his commitment to reform Chinese painting, it does not fully explain his choice of sketch conceptualism as his increasingly favored mode of execution. A more significant factor may have been the surge of nationalism in China after 1926. The Chinese – in particular intellectuals – were caught in a double bind. They were attracted to many aspects of the modern West, yet they resented the West's imperialist encroachment. Nowhere was this ambivalence felt more intensely than in Shanghai around 1930, where the texture of life was suffused with Western ideas and things, and yet the arrogance of the foreign powers and their infringement on China – embodied in their territorial rule in the Concessions – was ubiquitous, a constant reminder of national humiliation. The increasingly menacing behavior of Japan further excited feelings of nationalism. One effect of this nationalism in the art world was the call for "preservation of national essence." Journals increasingly turned to comparisons between Chinese and Western art, emphasizing their differences and relative merits. This was a marked departure from the tone of discourse in the 1910s, which was focused on how Western art could resuscitate Chinese art. It was partly in this context that the term "national painting" (*guohua*), meaning painting in the traditional Chinese manner, gained a wide currency.[41]

Xu Beihong, ever a passionate patriot, was moved by the urgency of this national ethos. As early as 1928, he was publishing poems that exhibited an intense nationalist fervor.[42] In February 1932, Japanese gun ships began to bombard Nanjing, where Xu was teaching at the National Central University. He encouraged some of his students to join the Nineteenth Route Army to participate in the resistance. On February 12, Xu went to Beijing, where he stayed with Hu Shi (1891–1962), a Western-educated intellectual and one of the leaders of the May Fourth Movement (1919). In the same month, he produced three notable Chinese ink paintings: *Ancient Cypress, Rumination*, and *Running Horse*. Of the three, *Rumination* is particularly revealing, as it contrasts sharply in style with *Ancient Pines and Cypresses at West Hill*, which Xu painted in 1918, prior to his study in Paris. That earlier painting, with its refined craftsmanship and spatial illusionism, displays Xu's penchant for realistic depiction and corroborates his conviction about the future direction of Chinese painting. *Rumination*, a post-Paris work, however, bears little imprint of Xu's Paris training. It is in many ways at odds with his programmatic call for realism. The composition is taken up by large, hastily brushed ink daubs. The sole human figure – very likely Xu himself – is reduced in scale, a detail added to make the theme explicit. The painting is apparently Xu's pictorial response to the political situation of 1932. In coping with his need to express his emotions through his art, Xu may have found his Parisian training in realism a limitation. Ironically, it was only through ink sketch conceptualism that he could respond to his expressive urge.

[...]

Xu's newly tempered skills in realistic depiction could readily have been applied to the human figure in *Rumination*. Instead, the figure is reduced to a miniscule scale, a symbolic act that inadvertently signals Xu's conversion to ink sketch conceptualism, though he would not have openly admitted to such a development.

Xu also painted *Landscape Light* under the same circumstances and in the same year.[43] His inscription explicitly describes the time as a "moment of crisis." The painting, appropriately in the mode of ink sketch conceptualism, was intended as a gift for a friend. Xu would not have considered it appropriate to employ a realistic mode of painting to share his private sense of anxiety. The personal touch and emotional immediacy of sketch conceptualism, qualities that made it the traditionally preferred way for Chinese painters to interact with patrons and with one another, are among the forces that prompted Xu's return to that mode of painting. Celebrated artists faced constant requests for paintings from all sorts of people,[44] and also took delight in exchanging works with fellow artists or scholars. Their social gatherings often resulted in works done on the spur of the moment, at times involving several artists and scholars collaborating on the same scroll. A typical pictorial subject for such an occasion would be the "Three Friends" – bamboo, plum, and pine – plants hardy enough to brave winter's adverse conditions. Xu had done such paintings in his pre-Paris years, and continued to rise to such occasions in his post-Paris phase.[45] A painstakingly executed Western realist-style painting would be too cumbersome and time-consuming to satisfy such demands, particularly at social occasions where swift improvisation and dashing performance were called for. A conceptual sketch was the easy solution. In a 1934 article, Yu Jianhua (1895–1979), an ardent apologist for Chinese painting, trenchantly summarized the situation:

> There are many advantages to Chinese painting in [fulfilling] social obligations. In Chinese society, painting has long been a form of social courtesy. An album leaf, a pair of hanging scrolls, or a fan can all constitute either a conduit of emotional bonding or a chance to demonstrate one's talent. In many ways, they come in handy in fulfilling social obligations. If you become proficient [in Chinese painting], you may in future become a specialist, able to earn a living through brush-moistening (*runbi*, or fees). As for Western painting, the public understands little about it and demands little of it. Even if you become a specialist, and set your price high, you can only indulge in solipsism, for others care little for it. Among friends, there are those who know you are a painter; but little do they know that you are only a Western-style painter. Now and then they press you for a pair of hanging scrolls or a fan painting. You are unable to comply [but] decline, and you show no respect for your friends. It takes endless explaining and, even then you can hardly absolve yourself. This embarrassment commonly befalls [Chinese] specialists of Western-style painting.[46]

Xu Beihong was hardly immune to this predicament; to maintain his celebrity as a painter, he had to take up Chinese ink and brush.

[…]

[…] Although his sketch conceptualism did not pass muster with those hardened traditionalists whose eyes were accustomed to idiomatic uses of *bi* (brushwork) and *mo* (ink gradation), his apologists dismissed such criticism as irrelevant.[47] Indeed, public reactions to Xu's ink painting were largely positive. In 1930 a caption accompanying the reproduction of his ink paintings in *Shidai huabao* (*Times Pictorial*) called attention to this new move: "Mr. Xu, a specialist in Western painting … has lately begun to pursue Chinese painting (*guohua*)."[48] In 1931 the editor of

Beicheng huakan (*Northern Morning Pictorial*) went further: "Xu is not only known for his Western painting, he also has an elegant mastery of Chinese painting … Even if Dongxin [Jin Nong, 1687–1764] were alive, he would defer to Xu."[49] In 1932 Zong Baihua (1867–1986), a prominent scholar of aesthetics, characterized Xu in the context of Chinese painting. Having captured "the innermost secret of Western-style realism," Zong wrote, Xu was now able to "daub with ease his meaningful brush in Chinese painting … whereby the authentic flavor of his individual nature is manifested."[50] By 1935 Xu's ink painting had won unadulterated acclaim. "[Xu's paintings] are robust, refined, and solid," enthused the editor of *Dazhong huabao*. "He is a leader in the world of Chinese painting."[51]

Xu's turn to sketch conceptualism was a tactical response to modernism. In the late 1910s, he had been at the forefront in challenging the overbearing tradition of literati conceptualism. A decade or so later, having returned to China from Paris, he found himself no longer on the cutting edge. His contemporaries had forged ahead, experimenting with new possibilities raised by European modernism. While he held on to an increasingly outmoded realist ideal, Xu appears to have been aware of his tenuous position, and resented being called a practitioner of French Academicism. Riding the crest of nationalism in China amid the call for "cultural construction of the Chinese base,"[52] Xu found sketch conceptualism (the more dashing variety) an effective response to the challenge of other Chinese artists' appropriation of European modernism. What is less apparent is that he was acting on some of the same principles held by his contemporary avant-garde artists: if modernism has an "orientalizing" streak, then why not go directly to its source, namely, China's own traditions? There are, of course, differences. Artists such as Lin Fengmian and Pang Xunqin were looking for ways to meld Chinese sketch conceptualism with European modernism. Xu, on the other hand, was resurrecting sketch conceptualism *in lieu of* modernism, while acknowledging the underlying spiritual affinity between the two.[53] Xu was exploring the possibility of "modernizing" Chinese painting by honoring one fundamental modernist principle – formal abstraction. He did so by tapping into one strain of traditional sketch conceptualism, the more bravura mode practiced by Xu Wei (1521–93) and his followers, a manner largely rejected by the more orthodox tradition.

[…]

Reversal of Fortune: Chang Yu in the Western Context

[…] In spite of Chang's determination to be part of the Parisian art world, and the Western and modern appearance of his painting to Chinese viewers, he remained essentially an Eastern artist in the eyes of most European critics of his time. Johan Franco notes an "ethnic distinction" in his paintings, which bear only "a little European influence" but overall are "close to complete sinicization."[54] A Dutch critic, reviewing Chang Yu's exhibition at the Galérie van Lier in Amsterdam in 1933, observed:

> Sanyu ... attempts to create a certain effect in the oil medium ... which would probably have been achieved more immediately with pencil or brush and ink. With the quick and sensitive hand of a Chinese calligrapher, he etches lines of flower baskets and horses out of the thick layer of oil ... It is hard to figure out though why he needs to resort to oil to accomplish his creative purpose.[55]

It is apparent from these reviews and his surviving works from around 1930, a period in which he enjoyed some fame, that Chang Yu was practicing a minimalist curvilinearism, described by the French critic Joffroy in the makeshift and deceptive terms "simplicism" or "essentialism." Johan Franco formulates his impression of Chang's paintings in this way:

> At first, his works give most viewers a feeling of artlessness; only after long and repeated viewings do they make a deep impression. He knows how to depict the essence and often the humor of things with astonishing economy.[56]

In Chinese terms, this is sketch conceptualism, pure and simple.

Chang's minimalist pictorial vision began to crystallize around 1930. A typical example is *Horses in Landscape*. The canvas is neatly divided into three horizontal bands of color. From the pink band, in the middle, emerges a black horse with an evenly daubed coat of dark pigment (the white horse was not added until 1945). A photograph of the exhibition of Chang Yu's works held in Amsterdam in 1933 shows a similar painting with a single piebald horse. The photo also reveals a peculiar practice of the painter. On the table in the foreground is a ceramic horse by Chang, which appears to be the model for the painted horse. By juxtaposing ceramic and painted images, the artist seems to suggest that his model for the painting was not reality but art. The painting is a formal construct that deals primarily with pictorial concerns. Chang apparently delighted in transferring visual effects from other media to his works in oil on canvas. For example, he incorporated in his oil painting the crispness of etchings and prints, and also relished the feel of saturated dark ink, a medium with which he was intimately conversant. Translating a three-dimensional sculptural model into a two-dimensional painting shows a similar predilection. Such transferals resulted in a refreshing effect of cultivated awkwardness and childlike innocence. Chang's cultural background would have provided him with a set of prompts derived from the literati vocabulary: *zhuo* (clumsy; awkward) and *zhi* (childlike; innocent), value-laden stylistic qualities often touted in the literati's evaluations of painting. On the personal level, such paintings fulfilled the expressive and emotional urges of a man in love, in the same way that ink sketch conceptualism excited Xu Beihong in the early 1930s.

Sketch conceptualism carries with it the cultural baggage of traditional Chinese literati. It implies a disposition and an attitude – and sometimes a pretension – that painting is a leisurely pastime, something that ought to come naturally instead of being a toilsome effort. On the moral level, it often carries transcendental and eremitic associations, though not always fulfilled, and a deeply ingrained disdain for material success.[57] Chang Yu not only practiced his own form of sketch conceptualism; to some extent he enacted the values embedded in it, rather like a traditional literatus. Perhaps his upbringing and temperament were such that sketch conceptualism suited him best. Until the early 1930s, he was well provided for financially. Paris offered him a carefree, bohemian lifestyle.[58] Painting was a matter of dilettantish dabbling. This was to be Chang's undoing. His carefree attitude, his lack of ambition and motivation, his disinterest in advancing his career, his distrust of dealers, and his longing for money yet guarded sense of dignity and self-esteem made it difficult for influential dealers, such as Roché, to promote him.[59]

[...]

[...] During the last decade of his life, he resumed painting with renewed intensity and a matured vision.[60] Ironically, it was during this final phase of his career, when he could no longer afford to paint as a carefree activity, that his art acquired a new power. He painted human figures, still lifes, and landscapes with small, isolated figures.

No matter how intriguing Chang's newly tempered sketch conceptualism was in its own right, it did not sit well in the context of post-World War II Western modernism. Abstract expressionism was the rage, and Zhao Wuji (Zao Wouki, b. 1921), who arrived in Paris from China in 1948, quickly warmed to the new trend by capitalizing on his training in Chinese ink painting. Zhao captured the Parisian imagination with his orientalizing abstract expressionism. Perceived as a fitting cultural spokesman from the East, Zhao enjoyed considerable success and fame. Chang Yu's painting, a rehashing of his work of the early 1930s, appeared somewhat quaint and out of touch with the latest trend in the Western art world. Abstract expressionism was primarily non-figurative; Chang's art was based on figural representation. Abstract expressionism thrived on broad swaths or explosive splashes of paint; Chang's strength was rooted in a sparing, disciplined, crisp curvilinearity.

Viewed within the context of his own œuvre, however, the paintings produced by Chang in the last decade of his life achieved a new profundity, bringing his brand of sketch conceptualism to a new height. He reworked the figural sketches of decades earlier, accentuating the figures' contours with dark lines, while creating a variety of intriguing abstract forms.

[...]

More illustrative of his new sketch conceptualism are Chang Yu's minimalist compositions of lonely figures in vast, abstract landscapes. Such schemes are already heralded by his works of the 1930s, except that in those earlier paintings the frolicking animals form a larger presence against a backdrop of colored bands. His later compositions follow the same formula but drastically reduce the size of the figures. Female nudes, cats, horses, and leopards appear in a miniscule size that seems deliberately disproportional to the vast expanse of the abstract landscape. Existentially, the paintings convey the profound sense of loneliness, alienation, and desolation that gripped Chang Yu in his later years. Art historically, they appear to speak to the painful process of coming to grips with abstract expressionism, and an awareness of the increasing irrelevance in a changed art world of the figural art that defined his life's work. This realization may have added to his feelings of inadequacy and his increasing estrangement.

[...]

The impact of such paintings stems in part from Chang's relentless urge to minimize. Such a minimalist sensibility was rooted in his penchant for sketch conceptualism and reinforced through his early exposure to 1920s modernism. It is already evident in his works of the 1930s, though it served a different artistic purpose. The deepening hardship of his personal circumstances and increased estrangement from the world imbue this formal impulse toward minimalism with existential overtones. [...]

Some of his surviving works testify to this inexorable urge. In one painting of around 1955, a leopard gingerly gropes its way along a branch of a bleached, bare tree set against a dark green background. In another painting of leopards, large expanses of black above and yellow below divide the canvas into two sharply contrasting areas, suggesting heaven and earth. The two colors appear to be painted over a bare tree [...] which is still discernible beneath the over-painting. By obliterating the tree, Chang leaves the two leopards homeless in the desolate vastness of the yellow land [...] both paintings are an outcome of a reductionist impulse. As Chang confided to a close friend in the last year of his life. "I first paint, then simplify it,...[and] further simplify it."[61] His final work shows a tiny elephant running across a vast empty space. He pointed to the elephant and remarked to his friend with an inscrutable smile: "This is me."

In 1966, Chang Yu died in obscurity and loneliness in his Paris home. Xu Beihong, his one-time friend and stylistic opponent, had passed away thirteen years earlier, in 1953, while serving as director of the Central Academy of Fine Arts, in Beijing.

[...]

Abbreviations of sources cited in the notes

XBNP	Xu Boyang and Jin Shan, *Xu Beihong nianpu* (A Chronology of Xu Beihong) (Taipei: Yishujia chubanshe, 1991).
XBPJ	Wang Zhen ed., *Xu Beihong pingji* (Collection of Critical Essays on Xu Beihong) (Guilin: Lijiang chubanshe, 1986).
XBYS	Wang Zhen, ed., *Xu Beihong yishu suibi* (Xu Beihong: Essays on Art) (Shanghai: Shanghai wenyi chubanshe, 1999).
XBYW (1987)	Xu Boyang and Jin Shan, eds., *Xu Beihong yishu wenji* (A Collection of Essays on Art by Xu Beihong) (Taipei: Yishujia chubanshe, 1987).
XBYW (1994)	Wang Zhen and Xu Boyang, eds., *Xu Beihong yishu wenji* (A Collection of Essays on Art by Xu Beihong) (Yinchuan: Ningxia renmin chubanshe, 1994).

Notes

1 T. J. Clark, *Farewell to an Idea: Episodes from a History of Modernism* (New Haven and London: Yale University Press, 1999), p. 9.

2 Chen Hengke, "Wenrenhua zhi jiazhi" (Values of Literati Painting), in *Meishu lunji* (Essays in Fine Arts), edited by Shen Peng and Chen Lüsheng (Beijing: Renmin meishu, 1986), vol. 4, p. 16.

3 My strategy here is indebted to T. J. Clark, *Farewell to an Idea*, p. 7.

4 He first went to Shanghai in 1912 at the age of 17. See XBNP, p. 6.

5 Kang Youwei, "Preface," *Wanmu caotang canghua lu* (Catalogue of Paintings at the Thousand-Tree Thatched Hall) (1917), in *Meishu lunji*, vol. 4, pp. 1–3. [...]

6 Cai Yuanpei, "Zai Beida Huafa yanjiuhui zhi yanshuoci" (Speech at the Society of Research on Pictorial Method, Beijing University), in *Cai Yuanpei meixue wenxuan* (Selected Works on Aesthetics by Cai Yuanpei) (Beijing: Beijing University Press, 1983), pp. 80–1. [...]

7 Xu Beihong, "Beihong zishu" (Autobiography), in XBYS, p. 159.

8 Xu Beihong, "Zhongguohua gailiang zhi fangfa" (On Ways of Reforming Chinese Art), in XBYW (1987), vol. 1, pp. 39–45.

9 J. Thomas Rimer, "Tokyo in Paris/Paris in Tokyo," in *Paris in Japan: The Japanese Encounter with European Painting*, edited by Shūji Takashina et al. (Tokyo: The Japan Foundation; Gallery of Art of Washington University at St. Louis, 1987), pp. 65–6. [...]

10 The École was still a prestigious institution, whose rigorous entrance exams included not only demonstration of technical skills but also comprehensive knowledge of European art history. The situation made it virtually impossible for foreign students fresh on French soil to pass the exams. Xu was one of the few Chinese students to have been admitted to the school. [...] See XBNP, pp. 24–5. [...]

11 See Leslie Jones, "Sanyu: Chinese Painter of Montparnasse," *Res: Anthropology and Aesthetics* 35 (Spring 1999), pp. 225–39.

12 See *The Johan Franco Collection of Works by Sanyu*, Sotheby's catalogue, Taipei, October 15, 1995.

13 Pang Xunqing, *Jiushi zheyang*, pp. 99–100.

14 Chang's inscription on the painting reads: "1921. Chang Yu, at the time residing in Paris." The emphasis on the location is significant.

15 Craig Clunas, "Chinese Art and Chinese Artists in France 1924–1925," *Arts Asiatiques* 44 (1989), p. 102.

16 Ibid.

17 This interest is evidenced in the work of Chavannes, Pelliot, Roche, Sirén, Hobson, Kop, Waley, and Bushell. See ibid., p. 105.

18 Chen Yanfeng, *Chang Yu*; *Sanyu* (Taipei: Yishujia chubanshe, 1995), p. 19.

19 Cited from ibid., p. 41.

20 Wan Ye, "Liu Fa yishu zhuanjia Xu Beihong jun fangwen ji" (Interview with the Art Specialist, Xu Beihong, a Returned Student from France), *Shibao* (March 5, 1926); reprint XBYW (1994), p. 43.

21 Xu Beihong, "Mei de jiepo" (Anatomy of Beauty), *Shibao* (March 19, 1926); reprint XBYS, pp. 3–4; Wan Ye, "Meishujia Xu Beihong zhi tanhua" (Interview with the Artist Xu Beihong), *Shibao* (March 5, 1926); reprint XBYS, pp. 12–17; Xu Beihong, "Faguo yishu jingkuang" (The Recent Situation of French Art), *Shibao* (March 5, 1926); reprint XBYW (1994), pp. 41–3.

22 Xu Beihong, "Mei de jiepo," in XBYS, p. 10.

23 Wan Ye, "Interview," in XBYW (1994), p. 43.

24 Wan Ye, "Interview," in XBYS, p. 15.

25 Tian Han praises Baudelaire's *Les Fleurs du mal* as "great poem[s] for 'rebels.'" Tian acknowledges that his play *Death of a Famous Actor* was inspired by Baudelaire's *Brave Death*. See "Preface to vol. 4," in *Tian Han xiju ji* (Collection of Plays by Tian Han); cited from *Zhouxiang shijie wenxue* (Toward World Literature), edited by Zeng Yi (Changsha: Huna wenji chubanshe, 1986), p. 598.

26 XBNP, p. 47.

27 Ibid., pp. 47–8.

28 See "Nanguo yishu xuexiao chuang xiao zhaoshen" (South China Art Academy Founded; Now Taking Applications for Admission), *Xinwenbao* (January 26, 1928); Wang Zhen, *Xu Beihong yanjiu* (Study of Xu Beihong), pp. 16–17.

29 Leo Lee, *Shanghai Modern: The Flowering of a New Urban Culture in China, 1930–1945* (Cambridge, MA: Harvard University Press, 1999), p. 67.

30 Among the other committee members were Wang Yiting, Li Yishi, Lin Fengmian, Liu Haisu, Jiang Xiaojian, and Xu Zhimo. See XBNP, p. 57.

31 Xu's complaint about the "formalist" (i.e., modernist) dominance of the exhibition shows how much at odds he was with the mainstream Shanghai art world. [...] See Li Chao, *Shanghai youhua shi* (History of Oil Painting in Shanghai) (Shanghai: Shanghai renmin meishu chubanshe, 1995), p. 57.

32 Xu Beihong, "Huo" (Perplexity), in XBYW (1987), vol. 1, pp. 131–4. Xu Beihong, "Huo zhi bujie (1)" (Perplexity Unsolved, part 1), ibid., pp. 135–41. Xu Beihong, "Huo zhi bujie (2)" (Perplexity Unsolved, part 2), ibid., pp. 143–5.

33 Xu Zhimo, "Wo ye 'huo'" (I Too Am 'Perplexed') in *Xu Zhimo quanji* (Complete Works of Xu Zhimo), (Hongkong Shangwu, 1983), vol. 4, pp. 100–1.

34 Xu Zhimo, "Letter to Liu Haisu" (April 25, 1930), in Xu Zhimo quanji, vol. 5, p. 139.

35 Xu Zhimo, "Letter to Liu Haisu," (February 9, 1931), ibid., p. 145.

36 See Carlton Lake and Linda Ashton, *Henri-Pierre Roché: An Introduction* (Austin: The University of Texas at Austin, Harry Ransom Humanities Research Center, 1991), p. 10. Roché was active in the circle that included Picasso, Braque, Marie Laurencin, Erik Satie, and Brancusi.

37 Pierre Joffroy, "Inventeur de 'l'essentialism': San-Yu, peintre chinois de Montaparnassee," *Le Parisien Libre* (December 25, 1946). Translation from *Robert Frank's Sanyu*, Sotheby's catalogue, Taipei, October 19, 1997, p. 34.

38 Pierre Joffroy, "Inventeur de 'l'essentialism'," in *Robert Frank's Sanyu*, p. 34.

39 Xu Beihong, "Meishu lianhe zhanlianghui jinue" (Brief Notes on the Coordinated Art Exhibition), in XBYS, p. 45.

40 Yu Jianhua, "Zhongxiaoxue yi shou guohua yi" (On the Necessity of Teaching National Painting in Elementary Schools and High Schools), *Guohua yuekan*, no. 6 (1935); cited from Shui Tianzhong, "Zhongguohua lunzheng 50 nian" (Fifty Years of Debate Concerning Chinese Painting), in *20 shiji Zhongguohua: chuantong de yanxu yu yanjin*, p. 53.

41 Tong Guang, "Guohua mantan" (Random Notes on National Painting) (1926), in *Zhongguohua taolun ji* (Discussion of Chinese Painting), edited by Yao Yuxiang (Beijing: Lida shuju, 1932), p. 137.

42 See, for example, Xu Beihong, "Geming geci sizhang" (Revolutionary Lyrics: Four Cantos), *Zongyang ribao* (Central Daily) (February 2, 1928), supplement "Moden" (Modern), no. 1.

43 Xu Beihong Memorial Museum, ed., *Xu Beihong huaji* (Paintings by Xu Beihong) (Beijing: Beijing chubanshe, 1981), vol. 1, p. 44.

44 See James Cahill, *The Painter's Practice: How Artists Lived and Worked in Traditional China* (New York: Columbia University Press, 1994), pp. 32–50.

45 One night in the winter of 1930, for instance, Xu had a gathering with two other like-minded artists. The party culminated in a painting of "Three Friends in Winter," with Xu painting pines, and the other two painting plum and bamboo, respectively. See XBNP, p. 71.

46 Yu Jianhua, "Zhongxiaoxue huake yi shou guohua yi" (On the Necessity of Teaching National Painting in Elementary Schools and High Schools) (1934), in *Yu Jianhua meishu lunwen xuan* (Essays on Art by Yu Jianhua), edited by Zhou Jiyin (Ji'nan: Shandong meishu chubanshe, 1986), p. 403.

47 XBPJ, p. 184.

48 XBNP, p. 68.

49 Ibid., p. 77.

50 Zong Baihua, "Xu Beihong yu Zhongguo huihua" (Xu Beihong and Chinese Painting), in *Bainian Zhongguo meishu jingdian* (Classics in Chinese Art), edited by Gu Sen and Li Shusheng (Shenzhen: Haitian chubanshe, 1998), vol. 1, p. 79.

51 XBNP, p. 108.

52 Wang Xinming et al., "Zhongguo benwei de wenhua jianshe xuanyan" (Manifesto on Cultural Construction of the Chinese Base), *Duli pinglun*, no. 145 (April 1935), reprinted in *Hushi yu Zhongxi wenhua* (Hu Shi and the Chinese and Western Cultures) (Taipei: Buffalo Book, 1967), pp. 127–31.

53 [...] See Xu Beihong, "Notes from Lectures on Art at the Central University," in XBYW (1994), p. 204.

54 See the Chronology compiled by Rita Wong, entry 1932, in *The Johan Franco Collection*, n.p.

55 Ibid., entry 1933.

56 Johan Franco, "Preface" for Sanyu's Holland exhibition brochure, September 15, 1932. Cited from *The Johan Franco Collection*, n.p.

57 This is not to say that anyone practicing this style necessarily subscribes to this set of values. Recent scholarship has done much to dispel the idealistic cloud shrouding literati art and practice. See James Cahill, *The Painter's Practice*, pp. 1–2.

58 In his later years, Chang confided to a friend that "previously, I was by myself and really enjoyed myself. … If I wanted to paint, then I painted. If I wanted just to fool around, then I fooled around. I felt really free." Cited from Chen Yanfeng, *Chang Yu*, p. 47.

59 Chen Yanfeng points out that the lack of regular exhibition venues was also one of the factors that impeded Chang Yu's career. See Chen Yanfeng, *Chang Yu*, p. 30.

60 See Rita Wong, in *Robert Frank's Sanyu*, p. 16.

61 Dahan's memoir, cited from Chen Yanfeng, *Chang Yu*, p. 41.

25

Post-Impressionists in Pre-War Shanghai

The Juelanshe (Storm Society) and the Fate of Modernism in Republican China

Ralph Croizier*

The Republic of China (1911–49), established with the overthrow of the Imperial Qing dynasty, led a fragmented, politically and economically struggling nation overwhelmed by Western, Japanese, and Russian imperialism. In order to survive, republican China had to become a modern state equal to Japan and the West. The New Culture Movement of the mid-1910s and 1920s called for the renovation of Chinese culture based on Western standards, especially democratic revolution, progressivism, and science. In the visual arts, these values were associated with European academic realism, not modernism.

Canadian historian of modern China, Ralph Croizier, chronicles in this piece key intellectual debates of the 1930s that saw efforts to establish Chinese modern art against the grain of an academic realism backed by both nationalists and communists who grew increasingly hostile to the subjective individualism of the avant-garde. According to Croizier, the famous realism versus modernism dispute between Xu Beihong (1895–1953), the so-called father of Chinese socialist realism, and the literary modernist, Xu Zhimo (1895–1931) – inspired by the 1929 *National Exhibition of Chinese Art* in Nanjing – marks the beginning of modern art in China.

Two years after the watershed Nanjing exhibition, the Storm Society (1931–5), comprised initially of five painters just returned from Paris and Tokyo led by Pang Xunqin (1906–85) and Ni Yide (1901–70), converged, as Croizier puts it, "in the center of everything modern in China, Shanghai." Espousing post-Impressionism

* Ralph Croizier (1993) "Post-Impressionists in Pre-War Shanghai: The Juelanshe (Storm Society) and the Fate of Modernism in Republican China." In John Clark (ed.) *Modernity in Asian Art* (pp. 135–54). Sydney, Australia: Wild Peony.

Modern Art in Africa, Asia, and Latin America: An Introduction to Global Modernisms, First Edition.
Edited by Elaine O'Brien, Everlyn Nicodemus, Melissa Chiu, Benjamin Genocchio, Mary K. Coffey, and Roberto Tejada.

and Expressionism, the Storm Society held monthly meetings, annual exhibitions, and reproduced their works in magazines and journals. Croizier identifies an initial receptivity to their brand of anti-establishment avant-garde thinking after the Nationalist Government came to power in 1927 and a prevailing dissatisfaction with the status quo for which the Storm Society's mantra of change had much appeal. (See the Storm Society manifesto reprinted in this volume.) Yet later, when war with Japan became imminent, expectations of artists began to revolve much more around issues of nationalism. Some artists adapted, but nationalism was fundamentally antithetical to the individually driven content and stylistic innovations at the core of modernism. The brief modernist movement did not survive when the Communists triumphed in 1949. A renewed engagement with Western art and modernism would emerge again in the 1980s with a new generation of artists seeking a fresh visual vocabulary.

As you read, consider the political situation for modern artists in Shanghai in the 1920s and 1930s. How did it compare to what modern artists faced in Tokyo and Calcutta, Mexico City and São Paulo at that time? How could art exhibitions – like the 1929 first *National Exhibition of Chinese Art* in Nanjing, and the 1922 Calcutta Bauhaus exhibition – be so influential that they are said to mark the beginning of modern art in their countries?

Further Readings

Andrews, Julia and Shen, Kuiyi (1998) *A Century in Crisis: Modernity and Tradition in the Art of Twentieth Century China*. New York, NY: Guggenheim Museum.

Kuo, Jason C. (ed.) (2007) *Visual Culture in Shanghai 1850s–1930s*. Washington, DC: New Academia.

Sullivan, Michael (1996) *Art and Artists of Twentieth Century China*. Berkeley: California University Press.

"Modernism", as a term and an approach to art, came to China relatively late and disappeared rather quickly. Why then is it worth resurrecting a small group of avant-garde painters from the 1930s? The answer comes in part from the revival of interest in modern art with China's second opening to the West in the 1980s, but also from what the short history of China's first "modernist movement" tells us about the attractions and problems of artistic modernism in twentieth-century Asia.

Before 1929 few, even among China's Westernized intellectual élite, had heard of modernism. It first leapt into prominence with the initial National Exhibition of Chinese Art held that year in the Nationalist Government's new capital of Nanking. Although the "Western Art" section of the exhibition had few pieces that would have been considered "modernist" by contemporary Parisian standards, these were enough to provoke the ire of Xu Beihong (1895–1953) recently returned from studies at the L'École des Beaux Arts and leader of Western-trained academic realists in the Chinese art world.

In a short, vitriolic article entitled "Doubts", he denounced Cézanne, Matisse and their ilk as deviants from the great tradition in Western art and ridiculed their Chinese followers in abusive terms that equally mixed scorn and outrage. Xu Zhimo (1895–1931), editor of the Exhibition's supplementary journal, *Meizhan huikan* (Art Exhibition Report) took exception to the condemnation of twentieth-century art and replied in a longer essay, "I Also Have Doubts". The second Xu (no relation), was not an artist but, through his Oxford education and national reputation as a romantic poet and modern thinker, he was admirably equipped to argue the modernist case. With a defter literary touch he used biting satire to cast the academic artist in a light of unreasonable conservatism at a time when reason and progress were regarded as beacons for the new China. Obviously stung, Xu Beihong replied with a long two-piece essay, "Doubts Unresolved", defending in more detail the need to maintain standards and particularly the importance of a truthful and scientific depiction of form. Li Shiyi (1886–1942), another Western-trained academic realist, Glasgow School of Fine Arts 1916, joined in with a piece, "I Have No Doubts", generally supporting Xu Beihong's insistence on realism in form, especially for a China just beginning to assimilate Western culture and science.

So the Chinese debate on modernism focused on questions of style rather than substance or subject matter, but behind that question loomed larger issues about the nature of art, the role of artists, and the meaning of modernity. This well-publicized exchange of "Doubts" made at least the Westernized urban élite aware that the West itself was divided over new directions in art and culture. Still trying to come to terms with the Western cultural assault on Chinese tradition, Chinese intellectuals were now clearly shown the modernist challenge to all accepted standards. The perplexities and possibilities for cultural change suddenly expanded.[1]

Within the small circle of Chinese artists familiar with Western art, the modernist-realist tension had been growing for some time. The National Exhibition and its controversy only publicized and hardened the split within the ranks of Westernizers. Early in the twentieth century, Western art had appealed to educational modernizers because of its realism and supposed association with science and progress. The first government schools to teach Western art had emphasized draftsmanship – perspective, light and shade for volume, accuracy of depiction – as part of the new art education. And, among Chinese brush painters, a small group of young Cantonese, the Lingnan School, went to Japan to learn how to incorporate realistic elements of Western art into a rejuvenated Chinese painting capable of depicting and inspiring a revolutionary new China.[2]

But it was not until well after 1911 that leaders of the general intellectual revolution seriously took notice of art. When they did it was the realism and progressiveness of Western art that struck them as a useful solvent for the stagnation and obscurantism of the old culture. In August 1917, Cai Yuanpei (1868–1940), president of Peking University and probably the most influential educator in China, first proposed his famous slogan "aesthetic education as a substitute for religion."[3] He did not totally opt for Western art, and he did not even recognize the modernist-traditionalist controversy, but it was the supposedly rational spirit behind Western art that inspired his vision of a higher and more humane culture.

In 1918, Chen Duxiu (1879–1942), then editor of the leading new intellectual journal, *Xin qingnian* (New youth), was more explicit in his call for a "revolution in art."[4] He saw the "realistic spirit" of Western art as a cure for the repetition and irrelevancy that characterized Chinese painting. But his insistence on realism was accompanied by a call for creativity and innovation – no more copying of old masters – and this, of course, could open the door for modernism.

Some of the first generation of Chinese artists to study Western art, either abroad or in China, had already peeked in that door. Li Shutong (1880–1942), the first oil painter and art educator to return from Japan, evidently leaned more towards Kuroda Seiki's impressionist style than the more conservative Meiji Society of Fine Arts. Liu Haisu (b. 1896), precocious founder of the Shanghai Art School in 1912, was fascinated by the bold colours and free brushwork of the Post-Impressionists and Fauves while he struggled to master and transmit the basics of oil painting technique. By the early 1920s, trips to Japan had confirmed him in his generally modernist orientation.

But it was the return to China of a new generation of "returned student" painters in the mid-1920s that really set the stage for a modernist movement and its clash with the academic realists. From Tokyo, where Fauvist currents ran strongly in post-war Japan, came Ding Yanyong (1902–78), Guan Liang (1900–85) and, most important for our purposes, Ni Yide (1901–70). More artists also started to return from the font of Western modernism, Paris. By far the most important was Lin Fengmian (b. 1900) who, immediately after his return in 1925 provided a series of distorted, even tortured works (now preserved only in smudgy magazine photos) that smacked more of German Expressionism than the school of Paris and that differed markedly from the lyrical, syncretic style he adopted in the 1930s.[5] Most important at the time, however, he established a position opposite to the academic realism championed by Xu Beihong and as head of first the Peking Art School and then the Hangzhou Academy of Fine Arts, Lin was able to influence the direction of the new Chinese art world through his writings and other activities. His call for unrestricted individual creativity paved the way for the two Xu's exchange of doubts in 1929 and the emergence of an unabashedly militant modernist group soon afterwards. That group was the Juelanshe (Storm Society).

The genesis of that society occurred when Pang Xunqin (1906–85), freshly returned from Paris, met Ni Yide, well-connected modern man-of-letters and artist who had studied in Tokyo in the 1920s. Thus the two main sources of influence on modern Chinese art, Paris and Tokyo, converged in the centre of everything modern in China, Shanghai.[6]

Pang had gone to Paris at nineteen, studied at the modernist-inclined Académie Julien, and familiarized himself with a wide-range of contemporary styles.[7] He did not identify with any particular school or "ism", but his generally modernist inclination was clear as was a Paris-stimulated interest in combining the decorative arts

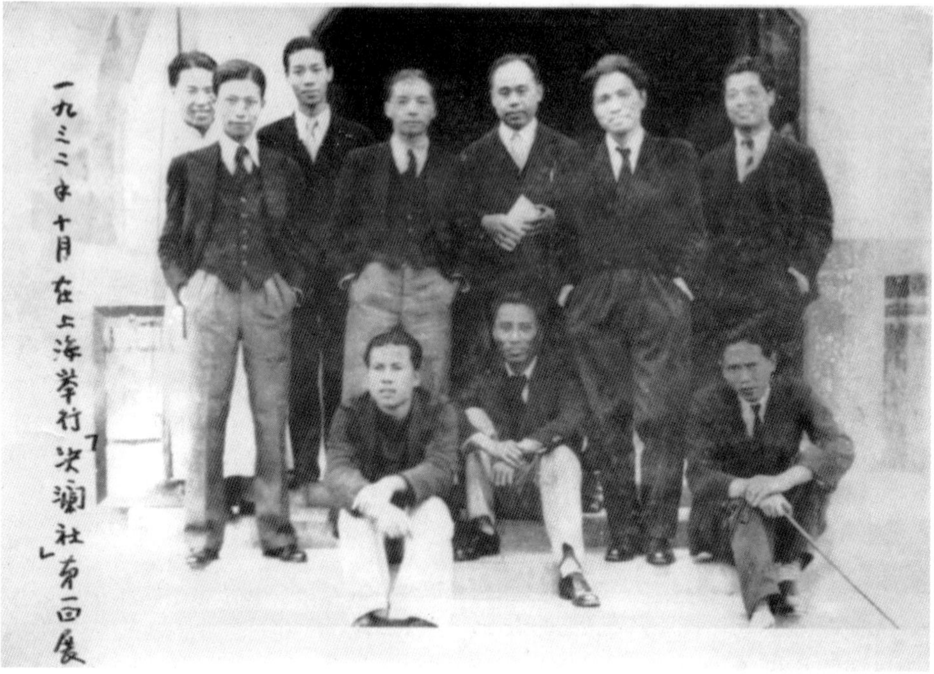

Figure 25.1 Group photograph, first exhibition of the Storm Society, October 9, 1934, Chinese Scholarship Society, Shanghai. Collection of Liang Xihong. Courtesy of Liang Ya.

with formal easel painting. Upon returning to Shanghai in 1929, he shared a studio in the French Concession with the older Western-style painter, Wang Jiyuan (1893–1975), hoping to transplant a modernist Parisian art salon in Shanghai. His contemporary French art and acquired Parisian mannerisms seem to have created a small stir among Shanghai's cultural cosmopolites but this salon was less than a resounding success, certainly not financially.[8] Its most significant outcome was that curiosity about the salon brought Pang and Ni Yide together.

Ni was a few years older, graduating in 1922 from the earliest training ground for modern Western art in China, the Shanghai Art School. By 1930 he had made a name for himself as an art critic, theorist, and creative writer, as well as an oil painter. Most significantly he had been to Japan to study Western art and art history. This meant that Ni knew Tokyo's modern art scene at a time when far more Chinese art students could afford to go there than to Paris. And he knew the Shanghai scene far better than Pang. It was a fortunate meeting for modernism in China, bringing together foreign experience and local connections, youthful enthusiasm and theoretical knowledge.

Still, it took almost two years for them to organize the first consciously modernist art society in China. Ni left Shanghai for a temporary position at the Wuchang Art School. When he returned in the spring of 1931, Pang had been forced to close his salon and was eking out a living on part-time teaching and very occasional commissions. The two agreed that a modern art movement in China needed its own art journal and a dedicated group of modern-minded artists to support such a publishing venture. The idea was not entirely novel, for modern-minded writers and artists had shown a proclivity for groups, societies, and associations since the early 1920s. The most significant of these for modern art had been the Tian Ma Hui (Heavenly Horse Society) organized around Liu Haisu's Shanghai Art School. But Ni, already experienced in organizing a Chinese art students society in Japan, had in mind something smaller and more radical, the focus for a Shanghai-based avant-garde.

The inaugural meeting was delayed another half year because of the Japanese invasion of Manchuria and the concomitant fighting in Shanghai. National crisis delayed the art revolution – an ominous portent for the fate of modernism in Republican China. Finally, in the winter of 1931, Ni succeeded in bringing Pang together with five keen young modernist painters and the Storm Society was born.

Their purpose was to promote the new art and incidentally their own careers in an indifferent, if not hostile, environment. Ironically, the art magazine itself proved beyond their limited means, but Ni Yide, through his contacts with Liu Haisu and the Shanghai Art School, was able to mobilize a larger number of artists in a broader-based, less radical association called the Mo She (Muse Society). It had the resources to publish a thrice-monthly journal, *Yishu xunkan* (*L'Art*) which supported and publicized the Storm Society's avant-garde position.[9] Thus, the Storm Society provided the shock troops for the modernist assault on conservatism – both traditional Chinese and imported Western academicism.

As the spearhead of China's modernist movement, the Storm Society was expected to be radical or tempestuous. The name they chose literally meant a great wave; "Storm Society" was their choice for an English name. Wang Jiyuan explained its significance, "… we want to hit the rotten art of contemporary China with a powerful wave."[10] Their "Manifesto" proclaimed, in the best tradition of modernists everywhere, that they were suffocated by the stagnant old society and had to break free.[11] As for painting, "… it is definitely not a copy of nature … the reproduction of dead forms." Here their attack turned more on Western-trained rivals who made realism the standard for a new art rather than on old-style Chinese painting, for in the wake of the two Xu's debate, it was now a contest between westernizers over who possessed the real essence of Western art and supposedly the future of China. The manifesto clearly showed where their inspiration would come from:

> … The war cry of the Fauves, the transformed shapes of Cubism, the fierceness of Dadaism [printed in English], the violent awakening of Surrealism. … The Chinese art world should also create a new climate.

There were just enough favourable circumstances in the China of the early 1930s to make their naive optimism not entirely without basis as a number of factors came together to give modern art and modernist ideology a brief moment of opportunity in a generally hostile environment. To begin with, knowledge of recent developments in European art and culture had reached China, most directly through returned artists, such as Pang or Lin Fengmian, but also through reproduction volumes, art journals, and the writings of critics and publicists such as Ni Yide.[12] This swelling literature, almost all of it published in Shanghai, reached others than just artists. Several of the leading newspapers carried weekly art supplements and broad interest pictorial magazines regularly covered modern art events. The longest running and most important of these, *Liang you* (The good companion), for instance, had photographic spreads on all four of the Storm Society's exhibitions. This meant that the urban reading public at least knew of the existence of modern art, while art students had direct contact with returned teachers as well as access to recent Japanese publications.

In one of his magazine articles on the contemporary Shanghai art scene, Ni Yide explained how two of the young talents in the Storm Society, Yang Qiuren and Yang Taiyang, had become familiar with the latest art movements in the West. Mainly, he claimed, through Japanese publications on famous modern Western artists.[13] Years later Yang Taiyang confirmed the importance of the Japanese connection for artists staying in China by recalling how, in addition to selling the reproduction volumes, he had met modernist Japanese oil painters at the studios of Chinese painters who had studied in Tokyo.[14]

Sources for the transmission of styles and ideas from the West were a necessary, but not sufficient, condition for the growth of a modernist art movement in China. Intellectuals, including artists, also had to be dissatisfied and receptive to outside influence. Since the outburst of cultural iconoclasm in the May Fourth era, roughly 1915 to 1922, this was generally the case. More particularly, many intellectuals were disappointed and chagrined by political events after the Nationalist Government came into power in 1927. There was a definite let-down after the extravagant hopes of the 1920s, but the rightward turn of the revolution had provided the modicum of social and political stability that made an expanding cultural life possible.

So, in some ways, the situation was amenable for the emergence of an anti-establishment avant-garde. There was a conservative political authority which they could legitimately regard as repressive, but it was neither repressive nor powerful enough to squash dissent or innovation. There was a bourgeois society, especially in Shanghai, whose materialism and philistine values they could despise while, as with the sons and daughters it sent to their modern art schools, that bourgeoisie provided some support for their economic existence. Moreover, in art, there were two establishments to attack, both of which were unsure of their positions. Traditional Chinese painters still predominated in numbers and sale of paintings but, with so much else in the ferment of change, they could not be sure of their future. Western-trained academic realists who, in terms of government patronage and position in the Academies constituted the mainstream of Western art, felt threatened by the modernists' claim to be more up to date, as Xu Beihong's vehement attack on all modern schools had indicated. Here, too, the forces of the establishment looked strong but vulnerable. The modernists, claiming modernity as their own and trumpeting individual emancipation, were able to take up the mantle of challengers to the *status quo* in a society where change was recognized as a paramount necessity. On balance, however, the negative factors were more formidable. The economic basis for a modernist movement, or any foreign-style art development, was still weak. There was no gallery system and, though modern-minded intellectuals might be interested and some of the Westernized Shanghai bourgeoisie mildly curious, the former could not buy paintings and the latter would not.[15] Government commissions were rare and certainly did not go to modernists. Some could earn money by doing magazine illustrations or even advertisements, but mainly they had to depend on teaching for a livelihood. As Ni Yide had complained several years earlier, to teach sounded appropriate but elementary classes for untalented and marginally motivated students provided a poor creative environment for independent-minded artists.[16] It also did not pay much.

Still, so long as business continued in the treaty ports and foreign concessions, and they remained open to the outside world, the Western-style modernists could eke out a living. More difficult problems arose on another front. The old charge of foreignness and incompatibility with a Chinese essence had lost some of its sting after three decades of revolution, although it continued to be echoed by cultural conservatives. Much more serious for an obviously Western-inspired and avowedly individualistic modern art movement was the accusation that they were both foreign and irrelevant to China's present needs.

By 1932, the year of the Storm Society's first exhibition, the left-wing art movement was well underway. Lu Xun, the most famous writer and leftist intellectual in China, had sponsored the new woodcut movement that linked the visual arts directly with social and political concerns.[17] An umbrella organization of those who saw art as a weapon for social struggle had been formed in 1931, The League of Left-Wing Artists.[18] As one of its leading lights, Xu Xinzhi, explained in a proclamation on "The Outlook for China's Art Movement",[19] the days of the old bourgeois art from Europe were over since, along with the Chinese bourgeoisie, it had turned reactionary after 1927. Now all progressive artists, and as a Tokyo-trained oil painter he had in mind mainly Western-style artists, should unite and follow the proletarian revolutionary struggle. He did not explicitly repudiate modern styles. Indeed, his own work came out of Japanese "proletarian art" that had been strongly influenced by French Post-Impressionists whereas much of the left-wing woodcut movement drew on later German Expressionism. But his denunciation of factional schools (*liu pai*), of "painting for painting's sake", and of prominent modernist figures such as Liu Haisu and Lin Fengmian, left no doubt that he had in mind a different kind of art – one that could reach the workers and serve the revolutionary cause. For the left, the modernist exploration of style as a new language for communication of personal feelings was useless for China's real needs.

This was somewhat similar to the accusations levelled by Xu Beihong and other academic realists, but the angle of attack had shifted. The academicist-modernist debate had been over style; the leftist critics attacked the modernists over content and purpose.

So long as the attack came only from the politically committed left, Communists and their sympathizers, the modernists could hope to fill the centre of a political-cultural spectrum between political radicals and new or old style cultural conservatives. Over two decades, Ni Yide used his considerable literary skills to defend stylistic innovation and personal creativity as the essentials for a modern art in modern China.[20] But as renewed threats of foreign invasion reinforced internal demands for "national salvation", it became harder and harder to argue the modernists' case. What T. C. Hsia has called the "burden of China" in twentieth-century literature – the need to address social and political problems before individual needs – came to weigh heavier and heavier on artists as well as writers.

Modernism was ill-prepared to shoulder such a burden: first because of its stylistic and individualistic thrust, second, and most relevant to the Chinese situation, because of its obviously foreign character. In a time of mounting national crisis it was a fatal liability. The modernists themselves might protest that they were as patriotic and progressive as any Chinese, but as the storm clouds gathered in the 1930s they were in danger of being brushed aside by the onrush of larger events. The first exhibition of the Storm Society was delayed almost a year by the Manchurian Incident of 1931. The exhibition finally took place in October of 1932. As a sympathetic reviewer wrote, it was intended to be "a great flood … a hurricane angrily roaring through the dead still night."[21] Actually, the roar was rather muted. Because of limited finances, they could only afford the reception hall of the Chinese Art Students Society which was rather poorly located for drawing the attention of the general public and had inadequate light for showing the paintings.[22]

The selection committee consisted of Pang, Ni, and the well-established, somewhat older oil painter, Wang Jiyuan, but most of the exhibitors were younger members still in their early twenties.[23] The most notable addition was the figure painter, Zhang Xuan (d. 1936), who had returned from a second trip to Europe generally impressed by the sketching techniques of Degas, Matisse, and Derain, but particularly influenced by Picasso's figures in his brief neo-classical phase. The others, according to Ni Yide's commentary, were variously influenced by Modigliani, Picasso and Derain, but had not yet settled on a stable style.[24] After all, creativity, innovation and change were supposedly to be the hallmarks of the Society. Ni contributed pieces which were modernist but still recognizably representational. Pang may have had more works shown than any other individual for he included sketches, pastels, and watercolours as well as oils – some from his Paris period and some done since returning home.

Did this "powerful wave" shake the Shanghai art establishment and rouse the general public? As suggested above, the location of the exhibition and the restricted publicity limited its impact. It received a rousing welcome from modern-minded critics like Li Baoquan and Fou Lei in their house journal, *L'Art*.[25] Fou Lei was a contemporary of Pang's in Paris who through his translations of French literature, notably Romain Rolland, became one of the better known new-style "men of letters" in cosmopolitan Shanghai. He was an articulate spokesman for the modernist position and Pang Xunqin's "reality transcending dream" in particular.[26] But here he was mainly preaching to the converted. There was not very much critical reaction in larger circulation journals perhaps because, as Ni Yide had noted earlier, the Chinese art world still lacked a tradition of stimulating criticism.[27] The leading Shanghai newspaper, *Shen bao*, ran a brief notice and some photographs appeared in the monthly pictorial magazines, but for such an ambitious wave it had made a fairly small splash. It was not that there had been much hostile reaction, not indeed much reaction at all.

The Storm Society pressed on with its mission – holding monthly meetings, attracting new members, and sponsoring group exhibitions each October. The 1933 exhibition had a change of venue when for economic reasons they moved to what Pang considered an even less desirable location. Attendance was down, "mainly Shanghai Art School and New China Art School students plus friends in cultural circles"[28] but magazine coverage increased and there were more exhibitors with an even wider range of styles and subjects,[29] inspired by European movements as far back as the post-impressionists, as with Wang Jiyuan's landscapes, or as contemporary as the surrealistic "Still Life of Yang Taiyang". This stylistic diversity was a hallmark of the Society. The younger members, scarcely out of art school, were obviously experimenting in an effort to reach their own individual style, one could almost say ransacking the field of European modernism. The more established artists of the group were not necessarily more stable. Zhang Xuan evolved rapidly from his infatuation with Picasso's neo-classical mode towards experiments with Chinese techniques in figure painting. Wang Jiyuan left after the second exhibition. Perhaps he felt his relatively stable style was incompatible with the group's state of flux; perhaps the reasons were personal. Ni Yide's paintings, which he characterized as "neo-realist," were just as "conservative" as Wang's, if that is the right word in this Chinese context. From the few colour reproductions available of his early work, Ni seems to have followed a later- or post-Fauvist style, Derain and Vlaminck without the bright colours of their early Fauvist period. This may have come from Ni's brief training under the Japanese post-impressionist master Fujishimu Takeji.

Pang Xunqin, however, was quite different, more like the younger artists in his sudden leaps from style to style. He was, himself, still in his twenties despite his four years in France. During this Shanghai period he did a wide variety of subjects in styles ranging from fairly representational to almost abstract, from free and lyrical line drawing to geometric or montage-like compositions. There are traces of the Cubists, the Fauves, Matisse, Léger and others. Much later, Pang would remark to the author that he never did more than three paintings in the same style. For these years, that seems to have been true.

But it was not Pang's "Design" of vaguely Léger-like automatons or the surrealistic still lifes of Zhou Duo and Yang Taiyang that attracted the most attention at the second exhibition. The biggest controversy arose over a prize-winning entry by the only woman member, Qiu Ti (Mrs Pang Xunqin). Reproduced in several magazines (unfortunately not in colour) what disturbed critics and casual onlookers

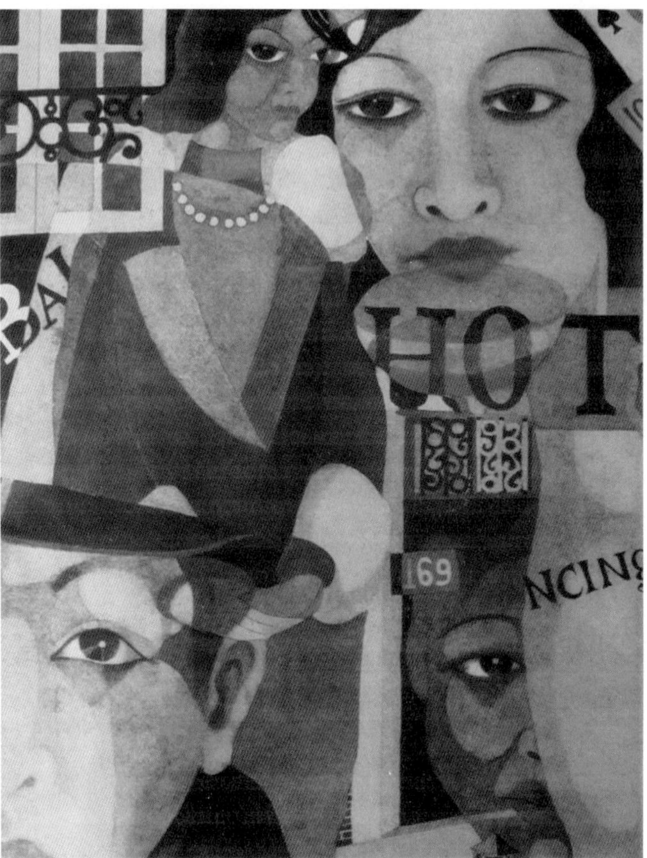

Figure 25.2 Pang Xunqin, *Such Is Paris*, 1931, oil on canvas, courtesy of James D. Chang, http://en.wordpress.com/tag/old-shanghai.

was the fact that in a decorative picture of a potted plant she had painted the leaves red and the flowers green.

Writing about this public flap over unnatural colours, Ni Yide cited it as proof of China's backwardness where most people still did not understand artistic expression, "that painting is sometimes done for decorative effects and there is nothing wrong with changing natural colours."[30] And nothing wrong with changing anything about nature – the mere outward manifestation of reality – in order to express the artist's own feelings or inner vision. The Storm Society's Manifesto had said it clearly, "… painting is not a copy of nature … the reproduction of dead forms".

We are back again to the heart of the realist-modernist controversy and perhaps to the essence of what modernism meant in China: it was subjective, individualistic, innovative, and, by implication if not intent, élitist. The emphasis on the individual's inner vision and constantly changing creativity meant that it could brook no rules or regulations, no source of external authority.

Pang Xunqin's contributions to the journal *L'Art*, published in each issue as "Random Remarks", repeatedly emphasized the paramountcy of "the self" (*ziwo*).[31] However, for a foreign-trained modernist, there was one curious aspect to Pang's defence of the self in art, for he started with a reference to the *locus classicus* of traditional Chinese literati painting theory – Xie He's principle of *qiyun* (usually translated as "spirit resonance"). Here was an unlikely affinity between Western-inspired modernists and the Chinese painting tradition. Both despised a literal depiction of reality, the realism championed by some of China's modernizers, and valued the artist's subjective interpretation. Beyond that, the old-style Chinese painters and the modernists parted company, occupied different worlds, but the affinity over the subjective element in art offered a potential point of reconciliation with their own national tradition for these foreign-inspired modernists, one which events of the 1930s foreclosed.

The Storm Society lasted only two more years. Its third annual exhibition, in October of 1934, drew the largest attendance as it continued to offer a wide range of styles with some non-members exhibiting. This was an indication that the

Society was acting as something of a magnet for modernist-inclined painters in Shanghai, or perhaps just provided one of a limited number of opportunities to show their work. Among "the older generation" of outside exhibitors, the most prominent was Guan Liang, who showed strong traces of 1920s Japanese Fauvism. But younger artists like Li Zhongsheng and Liang Xihong were more inspired by the Tokyo surrealists and brought an even more contemporary flavour to the exhibition.[32] So the Storm Society kept its styles up-to-date, but it was a question of subject matter, not style, that caused the most trouble.

Pang showed a work inspired by observation of drought victims in the countryside near Shanghai. Fortunately the picture survives in the form of a pastel draft for the final oil version. It is a surprisingly Western-looking modern Pietà complete with a cross in the background. The elongated sorrowing figures of the mother and father holding a dead son are not "realistic" by academic standards but they are not much distorted. There is a gentle sadness, and a touch of Pang's softly lyrical or decorative temperament, to the picture. It does not look very angry, shocking, or controversial, but it provoked more than just art criticism. Certain unnamed persons thought it looked too much like left-wing social art and Pang received threats on his person as well as criticism of the painting.[33] This must have been disappointing, as well as frightening, since the modernists were trying to convince the public that it was how a painting was done, not what was shown, that mattered. However, in China, subject matter still attracted the most interest.

The episode also raises the question of these artistic radicals' political attitudes. As mentioned before, they rejected the idea that painting should serve politics by doing pictures that the broad masses could easily recognize. But that did not mean that the artists were at all satisfied with the *status quo*. Yang Qiuren and Yang Taiyang had both been active in the Communist Youth League during the revolution of the 1920s. Pang was out of the country then, but on his return he got in trouble with the French Concession police for associating with communist sympathizers who had studied art in Japan.[34] His memoirs, written in the 1980s, may exaggerate his political consciousness at the time, but there is no reason to suppose that he did not share the widespread distaste for the Nationalist regime among intellectuals or their anxiety about the future of the country in the face of mounting Japanese aggression. By the late 1930s some of his works were unquestionably motivated by socio-political concerns, but when the Storm Society was in existence, Pang and the others seem to have been more concerned with cultural politics than political action. As Yang Qiuren pointed out in retrospect, with the exception of Pang's "Son of the Earth", all the other works exhibited were portraits, scenery, still life and nudes.[35] They were promoting a revolution in art, one that would promote a revolution in consciousness, but most of them were not active in political causes during these years. Pang, himself, although not accepting the controversial slogan "art for art's sake" propounded by one of the Society's admirers, Li Baoquan, also would not endorse the left-wing art movement's line, "art for life's sake" (i.e. for social purposes).

But, in the China of the mid-1930s, it was not so easy for artists to stick to art, the propagation of new styles and expression of inner feelings. At the Storm Society's final exhibition in 1935, there were, amid the "portraits, scenery, still life, and nudes", two works which shifted into the area of social or political commentary. One was a soberly realistic painting of an overalled worker repairing a large piece of machinery. The style has more in common with contemporary American social realism than anything from the School of Paris, but the provenance is probably "proletarian art" in Japan. The painter, Zhou Zhentai, had studied there, and had at one time been arrested for leftist activities. It was not the type of explicitly political art being practised by the left-wing woodcut movement, but it was not devoid of political meaning either.

The other controversial work was by Pang Xunqin. The style was more modern as Pang continued his protean shifts between different modes of modernist expression by doing something that could be called mechanical surrealism. It shows a mechanical man or robot turning the screws on a giant press while a doleful woman watches. Much later, in the People's Republic, he explained the picture as

> symbolizing developed industry of capitalist countries and backward Chinese agriculture "with" ... the three [actually there are four] giant fingers turning the press to symbolize the power of imperialism, reactionary rulers and feudalism. These were the three forces that squeezed our country's people, also the three forces that forced me into this blind alley.[36]

Seldom do we have such an explicit explanation of a modernist work but in this case we should be careful about taking it at face value. Apart from miscounting the fingers, and thus spoiling the neat three oppressive forces symbolism, Pang neglects to explain why the woman symbolizing Chinese agriculture stands alongside the robot and why in the distance there is a Matisse-like circle of women dancers about to be joined by another parachuting from the sky. Perhaps Pang was hiding his seditious intent from reactionary enemies, but the picture must have been more mystifying than inspiring to its contemporary viewers. The other published works from the exhibition look generally innocuous.

In any event, it was the group's last exhibition. Pang Xunqin left Shanghai for a teaching position at the Peking Art School. Ni Yide continued to be very active as critic and author, but not as an organizer. Yang Taiyang went to Japan; others who remained in Shanghai went their separate ways artistically. Four years was not a bad run for an avant-grade group, but Chinese modernism needed a successor to sustain the enthusiasm of the early thirties.

There was only one group that could possibly be seen in that light and it did not arise in Shanghai. Zhonghua Duli Meishu Xiehui (The Chinese Independent Artists Association) was originally formed in 1933 by a group of Cantonese students in Tokyo who transferred it to Canton after returning home.[37] Like the founders of the Storm Society several years before, they were impatient with the alleged stagnation of China's art world and were determined to shock it into life, in their case with surrealism which they featured in a well-publicized exhibition in Shanghai in the Fall of 1935. This was not quite the first introduction of surrealism to China. Ni Yide had written about it in *L'Art* in 1933 and some of the works at Storm Society exhibitions had shown surrealist influences.[38] At the new exhibition, works like Bai Sha's Daliesque painting "Desire" (*Yuwang*) and Zhao Shou's more original, "Jump!" (*Tiaoyue ba*) must have given viewers a start.[39] That same year several of the Association's members, Li Dongping, Liang Xihong and Zeng Ming, contributed essays to a special issue on surrealism in the important art journal, *Yifeng* (Art wind).[40]

They had done a fairly good job of introducing the most up-to-date art movement from Europe, even if their understanding of it had been filtered through Japan. But it did not catch on in Shanghai, centre of the Chinese art world. They retreated to Canton where they edited a journal, *Xiandai meishu* (Modern art) and showed their works. When Xu Beihong held an individual exhibition in Canton in early 1937, one of the Association's spokesmen caused a minor furor by attacking that famous national figure.[41] But it did not rekindle any realist-modernist debate similar to that in which Xu had engaged eight years earlier. Time was running out on that issue and the Cantonese surrealists could not succeed where the Storm Society pioneers had failed. Leading lights of the Storm Society continued their efforts after 1935. Ni Yide fired a true modernist shot at the Second National Art Exhibition when, criticizing the judges for their conservative bias, he dismissed "official art" with the argument that in France real progress always came outside of the government salon.[42] Meanwhile, Pang stirred up more controversy with his entry to the Third National Exhibition, another modern-styled allegory on the nation's suffering.

It was, however, too late or simply impossible for modernists to turn the central canons of their movement in the direction of serving national interest. As the crisis that would lead to war in the summer of 1937 deepened, the modernists' individualistic and foreign-based position became less and less tenable. This was apparent in the rising demands from critics and interested intellectuals that China's new art do two things: one, manifest a strong national character; two, be useful to the nation in its hour of peril. Nowhere have nationalism and utilitarianism been the strong points of modernist movements. The former flies in the face of modernism's disdain for tradition and its symbols; the latter negates the individualistic ethos of modernism.

Thus, as realist adversaries charged modernists with being unintelligible to the great majority of Chinese, "... not expressing real life or caring for the nation's soul",[43] the modernists' insistence on modern style and spirit as the key to national rejuvenation grew more and more strained. And as nationalistic critics demanded "Chineseness" in their works and an end to copying European styles,[44] they could only, in the face of direct visual evidence to the contrary, assert that they were not following Europe's lead.

A kind of verbal *coup de grâce* to modernism in China came from an unexpected quarter at the beginning of 1937. The generally liberal and cosmopolitan

English-language intellectual journal, *Tien Hsia Monthly*, which had been sympathetic to modern trends in Chinese art, started to demand national character and useful realism. The "Editorial Commentary" declared:

> ... oil painting by Chinese can never be much until it ceases to ape the West. ... Art has to have its roots in the soil ... it has to be intensely national.[45]

And Chen Yifan elaborated on the issue:

> Only that art can be considered modern that is inspired by revolutionary democratic nationalism. The test of a modern art is its value to the progress of China. ... It is the prime need of China and her millions to be able to see and feel and visualize things realistically. ... In the creation of a realistic art the artist completely fulfils his social and political duties.[46]

"Social and political duties" had never been the long suit of the Chinese modernist. When the war broke out they tried to bend their art to these purposes. Ni Yide assumed a fairly important position with the Government's "United Front" propaganda organizations as he and other modernists worked on the kind of popular, realistic art their leftist critics had demanded all along.[47] Some made sporadic attempts to use surrealist elements in their wartime propaganda efforts but the results were curious if not ludicrous. As the war dragged on, occasionally neo-realistic styles, echoes of Germany's *Neue Sachlichkeit*, could convey the grimness of life and alienation of artists trapped in China's backward interior.[48] But, on the whole, the purveyors of Western modernism were very much out of their element. Cut off from the West and pressured by demands for national content and social usefulness, some adapted in order to survive, others dropped from sight. The Communist rise to power in 1949 wrote a definitive end to a period in modern China's art history and cultural interaction with the West that was already over.

Not until the 1980s would the names and styles of European modernism – Matisse, Picasso, Fauvism, Cubism, and all the rest – re-enter the Chinese art world. Then it was in a different context with a different meaning as, after a hiatus of almost fifty years, China had to cope with all the complexities of later and post-modern discourse as well as classic, turn-of-the-century modernism.

The earlier pioneers of modernist art in China, Storm Society members and others, did not really act as a bridge between the two periods, although some survived into the 1980s. But they did serve as an example for the new generation of modern artists and critics.[49] Even more important, as these efforts are resurrected from decades of neglect, they serve as a reminder that it was historical circumstances, not any eternal incompatibility between East and West, Chinese and Western culture, that defeated the Shanghai modernists. The fate of modernism in the 1930s need not prove a model for Chinese, or world, cultural history in the late twentieth or twenty-first century.

Notes

1 The essays in this debate all appeared in the magazine *Meizhan huikan* (Art Exhibition Report), the National Exhibition's supplementary journal under the editorship of Xu Zhimo. They appeared as follows: Xu Beihong, "Huo" (Doubts), No. 5 (22 April 1929), pp. 1–2; Xu Zhimo, "Wo ye 'huo'" (I also have "doubts"), No. 6 (25 April 1929), pp. 1–4; Li Yishi, "Wo bu 'huo'" (I have no "doubts"), No. 8 (1 May 1929), pp. 1–2; Xu Beihong, "Huo zhi bu jie", (Doubts unresolved), No. 9 (4 May 1929), pp. 1–4 continued in *Meizhan huikan zengkan* (supplement to the Art Exhibition Report), no date given.

2 Ralph Croizier, *Art and Revolution in Modern China: The Lingnan (Cantonese) School, 1906–1951* (University of California Press, 1988).

3 Cai Yuanpei, "Yi meiyu dai zongjiao shu" (On aesthetic education as a substitute for religion), *Xin qingnian* (New youth), Vol. 3, No. 6 (August 1917).

4 Chen Duxiu, "Meishu geming" (Revolution in art), *Xin qingnian*, Vol. 6, No. 1 (January 1918), pp. 85–6.

5 Only poor quality black and white photographs remain of his works from the 1920s. They can be found in the recently reprinted pictorial magazine *Liang you*, No. 17 (1927), p. 38.

6 We are quite well served for accounts of the origins of the Storm Society as its two principal organizers Pang Xunqin and Ni Yide both left accounts. Pang Xunqin, "Juelanshe xiao shi" (A small history of the Storm Society), *Yishu xunkan* (*L'Art*), Vol. 1, No. 5 (1932), p. 9 and *Jiu shi zheyang zuoguolai de* (It went exactly that way; Xinhua shudian, Peking, 1988), especially chapters 62 and 63. Ni Yide, "Yiyuan xiaoyou ji" (Record of travels through the art world), *Qingnian jie*, Vol. 8, No. 3 (October 1934), pp. 65–70 and "Juelanshe de yi qun" (The Storm Society Group), *Yiyuan xiaoyou ji* (Liangyou Book Company, Shanghai, 1936), pp. 1–12. The author was also able to interview Pang Xunqin in Peking in 1983 and another of the original Storm Society members, Yang Taiyang, in Guilin in 1988.

7 In much later recollection he referred specifically to Fauvism, cubism, and abstraction. Interview with Pang Xunqin, Peking, 1 July 1983. But his early works show that he was also exposed to Léger, the Surrealists, and other fashionable movements of the 1920s.

8 Five years later, Ni Yide recalled both the impact of "the rich artistic feeling" in Pang's studio and his "... mannerisms of a Paris artist, black frock coat, beret on the side of his head, both hands stuck in his pockets, long and dishevelled hair, cigarette butt always hanging from his mouth." Ni Yide, "Juelanshe de yi qun", pp. 3–4. The essay is dated 1 October 1935.

9 The general situation, though not this interpretation of the relationship between the two societies, is told in Zhu Boxiong and Chen Ruilin, *Zhongguo xihua wushinian, 1898–1949* (Fifty years of Western painting in China; People's Art Publishing House, Peking, 1989), pp. 301–2. Pang Xunqin personally confirmed to the author that the Storm Society members had been too poor to support a journal. Interview, Peking, 1 July 1983.

10 Quoted in Zhu and Chen, *op. cit.*, p. 302.

11 The Manifesto was first published in *Yishu xunkan*, Vol. 1, No. 5 (October 1932), p. 8. It has been reprinted several times, most recently and perhaps most conveniently in Zhu and Chen, *op. cit.*, p. 592.

12 A collection of his essays, most of which had originally appeared in art and general interest periodicals, had already appeared. Ni Yide, *Yishu mantan* (Random talks on art; Guanghua Press, Shanghai, 1928). During the 1930s he produced no less than nine books and numerous articles on Western art theory, techniques and history.

13 Ni Yide, "Yiyuan xiaoyou ji", p. 69.

14 Interview with Yang Taiyang, Guilin, 7 June 1988. This is obviously an area requiring much more research. Which Japanese oil painters taught or influenced the Chinese artists who went to Japan in the twenties and thirties? Equally important, what European modernist works were available in Japanese reproduction volumes? Which of these were available in China?

15 Pang Xunqin's memoirs recount the difficulties of supporting himself as an avant-garde painter in early thirties Shanghai. See Pang's *Jiu shi zheyang zuoguolai de*, pp. 164–90 *passim*. In interviews several modernist oil painters from the 1930s all stressed the impossibility of supporting themselves by selling paintings. Interviews, Zhu

Qizhang, 14 June 1983; Yang Taiyang, 7 June 1988; Pang Xunqin, 1 July 1983; Guan Liang, 10 February 1983.

16 Ni Yide, "Yishujia de shenghuo wenti" (The livelihood question for artists), *Yishu mantan*, p. 117.

17 Well covered in both English and Chinese. Shirley Sun, "Lu Hsün and the Chinese Woodcut Movement, 1929–1935" (PhD dissertation, Stanford University, 1974). Li Hua, Li Shusheng and Ma Ke, *Zhongguo xinxing banhua yundong wushinian, 1931–1981* (Fifty years of China's new woodcut movement, 1931–1981; Liaoning Art Publishing House, Shenyang, 1981).

18 The left-wing art movement is the most thoroughly, if least critically, covered area of twentieth-century art history in the People's Republic. For general accounts: Zhu and Chen, *op. cit.*, pp. 283–94; Li Shusheng (ed.), *Zhongguo meishu tongshi*, Vol. 7, pp. 27–37 and pp. 227–76. There are also more specialized studies such as Wu Bunai (ed.), *Yiba She* (The eighteen society; People's Art Publishing House, Peking, 1981).

19 Xu Xinzhi, "Zhongguo meishu yundong de zhanwang" (The outlook for China's art movement), *Shalun* (Salon; 16 June 1930), pp. 21–33.

20 An early example was in 1923 when he compared painting to music, using formal elements rather than explicit content, to convey an emotional meaning. Essay reprinted in Ni Yide, "Chenguang Meishuhui disan jie zhanlanhui" (The third exhibition of the Daybreak Art Society), *Yishu mantan*, pp. 63–4. As late as June of 1937 he was arguing the importance of style over content. Ni Yide, "Zuofeng de wenti" (The question of style), *Meishu zazhi* (Art magazine), Vol. 1, No. 4 (June 1937), pp. 79–80.

21 Li Baochuan, "Hongshui fan le" (A great flood rises), Yishu xunkan, Vol. 1, No. 5 (September 1932), p. 9.

22 These are Pang Xunqin's much later recollections of the first exhibition. Pang, *Jiu shi zheyang zuoguolai de*, p. 171.

23 There is some uncertainty about who participated in the first exhibition and who joined only in the second exhibition the following year. Although Pang Xunqin recalls there was a catalogue printed, apparently it has not survived. Pang Xunqin, *Jiu shi zheyang zuoguolai de*, p. 172. The participants seem to have been Pang, Ni, Yang Qiuren, Yang Taiyang, Zhou Duo, Duan Pingyu, and Zeng Zhiliang, all original members, plus Zhang Xuan and possibly Ding Yanyong. According to Pang, Wang Jiyuan only entered works in the second exhibition.

24 Ni Yide, "Yiyuan xiaoyou ji", pp. 69–70.

25 *Yishu xunkan*, Vol. 1, No. 5 and subsequent issues.

26 Fou Lei, "Xunqin de meng" (Xunqin's dream), *Yishu xunkan*, Vol. 1, No. 13 (1932), pp. 19–20.

27 Ni Yide, "Piping yu chuangzuo" (Criticism and creation), *Yishu mantan*, pp. 100–2.

28 Pang, *Jiu shi zheyang zuoguolai de*, p. 178.

29 Full page photo coverage in *Liang you*, No. 82 (November 1933), p. 30 and *Shidai huabao*, Vol. 5, No. 1 (November 1933).

30 The prize announcement and a smudgy black and white photograph can be found in *Shidai huabao*, Vol. 5, No. 4 (December 1933), p. 13. Ni's remarks are in *Qingnian jie*, Vol. 8, No. 3 (October 1934), p. 70.

31 See particularly Vol. 1, No. 1 (September 1932), and No. 4 (October 1932).

32 Information on the outside exhibitors in the last two Storm Society exhibitions comes from Yang Qiuren, "Huiyi Ni Yide he Juelanshe" (Recalling Ni Yide and the Storm Society), *Meishujia* (The Artist), No. 31 (April 1983), p. 20.

33 The episode is described by Ye Yonglie, "Pang Xunqin de huabi" (The painter's brush of Pang Xunqin), *Renwu* (March 1987), p. 170. See also Pang, *Jiu shi zheyang zuoguolai de*, pp. 181–2.

34 *Ibid.*, pp. 154–5.

35 Yang Qiuren, "Huiyi Ni Yide he Juelanshe", p. 20.

36 Pang, *Jiu shi zheyang zuoguolai de*, p. 184.

37 The group's history is briefly told in Zhu and Chen, *op. cit.*, pp. 380–2 and even more briefly by one of its founders Liang Xihong, "Zhongguo yanghua yundong" (China's foreign painting movement), *Dagongbao* (Canton, ed.), 26 June 1948, p. 4.

38 Ni Yide, "Chaoxianshizhuyi de huihua" (Surrealist painting), *Yishu* (January 1933), pp. 1–5. The essay, which quoted André Breton, listed four schools of surrealism, according to Ni: Picasso-Braque [!], de Chirico, Miró, and Ernst. A bit dated and somewhat peculiar, but surrealism was

introduced to Chinese readers. The essay was reprinted in Ni Yide, *Xihua lun ye* (Discussions of Western painting; Shanghai, 1936), ch. 15.

39 Published in *Liang you*, No. 111 (November 1935).

40 *Yifeng* (Art wind), Vol. 3, No. 10 (1935).

41 One of his barbs was published as "Ping Xu Beihong ge zhan" (Criticizing Xu Beihong's individual exhibition), *Meishu zazhi* (Art magazine), February 1937, pp. 96–7.

42 Ni Yide, "Quan guo meizhan gei wode xin zhanwang" (The new outlook which the National Exhibition gives me), *Meishu zazhi* (February 1937), pp. 12–13.

43 Wu Zuoren, "Yishu yu Zhongguo shehui" (Art and Chinese society), *Yifeng*, Vol. 3, No. 4 (April 1935), p. 81.

44 Lu Jie, "Ping Guangdong Meizhan" (Criticizing the Guangdong Art Exhibition), *Meishu zazhi*, Vol. 1, No. 4 (June 1937), p. 22.

45 "Editorial Commentary", *Tien Hsia Monthly* (April 1937), p. 376.

46 Chen Yifan, "The Modern Trend in Contemporary Chinese Art", *Tien Hsia Monthly* (January 1937), pp. 47–8.

47 Information on Ni Yide's life came from an interview (24 May 1988, Hangzhou) with his widow, Liu Wei. His later paintings are well represented in *Ni Yide hua ji* (Collected paintings of Ni Yide; People's Art Publishing House, Shanghai, 1981). Ni's conversion to a realistic art which "the masses understand" was expressed in his wartime article "Cong zhanshi huihua shuo dao xieshizhuyi" (From wartime art to realism), *Meishu jie*, Vol. 1, No. 1 (December 1939), pp. 2–3.

48 Some of these are reproduced and discussed in Michael Sullivan, *Twentieth Century Chinese Art* (University of California Press, 1959).

49 The most notable example of revisionist art history is Zhang Shaoxia and Li Xiaoshan, *Zhongguo xiandai huihua shi* (A history of China's modern painting; Jiangsu Art Publishing House, Nanjing, 1986), pp. 51–2. For a review article covering this and some of the other recent books on modern Chinese art history published in China, the United States, and Hong Kong, see Ralph Croizier, "Art and Society in Modern China: A Review Article", *Journal of Asian Studies*, Vol. 49, No. 3 (August 1990), pp. 587–602.

26

Films and Shanghai

ZHENG DONGTIAN*

Award-winning filmmaker and academic Zheng Dongtian published this essay in a catalog for *Shanghai Modern 1919–1945*, one of the first exhibitions to focus exclusively on Shanghai's modern period, held at the Villa Stuck in Munich in 2004–5. Zheng offers an account of how the film industry evolved in China and came to be centered in Shanghai – from the first public screening in 1896 to its heyday during the decades of the 1920s through to the 1940s when nearly half of Chinese films were produced exclusively in this city. The essay identifies some of the key films and how they had begun in the 1930s to receive international recognition, reinforcing the idea that cosmopolitan urban life and visual culture, in this case the film industry, were significant factors in Chinese modernism, as they were in all global modernisms.

Further Readings

Fu, Poshek (2003) *Shanghai and Hong Kong: The Politics of Chinese Cinemas*. Stanford, CA: Stanford University Press.

Zhang, Yingjin (ed.) (1990) *Cinema and Urban Culture in Shanghai 1922–1943*, Stanford, CA: Stanford University Press.

"Shanghai has only businessmen, but no noblemen," wrote the Shanghai-born woman writer Wang Anyi and, although her words did not refer to films, they reveal some of the mystery that has made Shanghai the cradle of China's film

* Zheng Dongtian (2004) "Films and Shanghai." In Jo-Anne Birnie Danzker, Ken Lum, and Zheng Shengtian (eds) *Shanghai Modern, 1919–1945* (exhibition catalog, pp. 298–306). Ostfildern-Ruit, Germany: Hatje Cantz.

Modern Art in Africa, Asia, and Latin America: An Introduction to Global Modernisms, First Edition.
Edited by Elaine O'Brien, Everlyn Nicodemus, Melissa Chiu, Benjamin Genocchio,
Mary K. Coffey, and Roberto Tejada.

industry. China's first film was, however, not filmed in Shanghai. When films were first mentioned in the Chinese press, they were called "electric light shadow plays", meaning plays or dramas recorded with light. It was in the autumn of 1905, at a photo studio about one kilometre from the Forbidden City in Beijing, that Peking Opera performer Tan Xinpei performed a few episodes from the opera *Conquering Jun Mountain* in front of a hand-cranked film camera. Everybody from the noblemen in the Imperial Court to the ordinary person in the street knew this 60-year-old performer. However, he himself was probably not aware that the "electric light shadow play" that he spent 30 minutes performing in front of a camera made him the first film star in Chinese history.

Theories abound as to why the film business did not have the opportunity to grow in Beijing, one of them being quite intriguing. At Empress Cixi's 70th birthday celebration, held in the Imperial Court, the British Minister brought a film projector as a gift. To everybody's surprise, just as the film was beginning, the electricity generator suddenly exploded into flames. Taking this as an ominous sign, her Majesty burst out in anger, and forbade any films in the Imperial Court after the accident.

Without an Imperial Court, Shanghai became a perfect paradise for adventurers. With China's most fertile "land of rice and fish" backing on to the nation's largest ocean port, Shanghai offered its residents a relatively abundant life, and broad, flexible perspectives preparing them for an earlier awareness and acceptance of new things and ideas. This openness provided more opportunities for companies from abroad. In the history of 'importation' of modern civilisation, Shanghai and its neighbouring cities have functioned as a testing ground for almost all modern concepts and goods shipped into China from overseas.

According to historical records, the first film-showing in Shanghai took place in August 1896 in a private garden on Tiantong Road, less than a year after the Lumière brothers' film was first shown in Paris. Shortly afterwards, representatives from the American, Spanish, Italian and Portuguese film industries visited Shanghai, one after another. In 1898, the Thomas Edison Company in the United States sent a cameraman to Shanghai to shoot a documentary entitled *Shanghai Police*, which marked the beginning of film-shooting in China. In 1908, Romas, a Spanish businessman, built the first cinema in China on a roller-skating rink located at the busy Haining Road and Zhapu Road crossroads in Shanghai's Hongkou district. This 250-seat facility was named the Hongkou Movable Cinema House. One year later, American businessman Benjamin Brasky established Asia Films in Shanghai; this was the first film production studio ever set up in China. The metropolitan atmosphere of Shanghai not only drew adventurers from overseas and made the city their first choice for marketing films, it also attracted a large number of Chinese businessmen, artists and technicians who moved to the city to start China's own film industry. Four years later, in 1912, Zheng Zhengqiu, Zhang Shichuan and other young people formed a company, Xinmin (New People), to produce for Asia Films. Their first film, *The Difficult Couple* (also named *The Wedding Night*), an hour-long drama, is now recognised as China's first feature film.

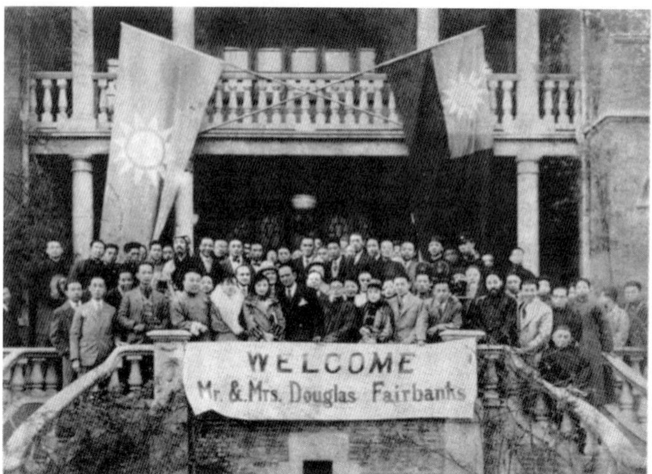

Figure 26.1 Mingxing Film Studio, Shanghai, 1938. Group photo from the memoirs of the Chinese actress Hu Die "Butterfly Wu" who is in the middle of the front row on the right of Douglas Fairbanks. Courtesy of Don Marion, Chinese Mirror.

In the same year that Romas opened his cinema, Hu Ruihua was born in Shanghai's Tilanqiao district, an area not far from Hongkou. This timely coincidence seemed to indicate that her life-long connection with films was predetermined by destiny. Hu spent her childhood moving between north and south China with her father, who worked in the railway industry. When she returned to Shanghai at the age of 16, the first thing she did was to apply to the Chinese Film School, which offered training programmes in acting. Perhaps dreaming of becoming a flying angel of art, she changed her name on the application to Hu Die, which means 'butterfly' in Chinese. Although she and her fellow students took classes every evening for a period of only half a year, they were among the first actors and actresses to receive professional training before undertaking roles for the big screen. There were 17 film schools of this kind in Shanghai during the 1920s, either simultaneously or successively. Nine years after her graduation from the film school, Hu Die was voted 'Queen of Film' by the public in a 1933 contest sponsored by the *Ming Xing Ribao* (Daily Star).

From the 1920s to the 1940s, about half of all Chinese films were produced in Shanghai. In 1927, according to available statistics, there were 175 film companies, both large and small, operating in China, of which 141 were based in Shanghai. During the ten-year period from 1921 to 1931 alone, studios in Shanghai produced more than 650 films. Apart from becoming the most advanced economy in China, with its high-level industrial and technical foundations essential for film-making and its massive scale of operations, Shanghai also projected its own vibrant urban culture in most films made during this period – another crucial reason behind this film boom. Multiple social forms existed in the dynamic lives of millions of Shanghai's citizens and in this prosperous, multi-layered society with its own blend of capitalism, feudalism and colonialism.

The popular themes of early Shanghai films were not as fresh as the films per se. Most of the stories described the countless ties between city and countryside and showed how the surrounding rural villages slowly converged to become part of the city. When people who were unwilling to endure the poverty and lagging development in villages actually moved to the city they failed to find the life they had been longing for – a life of freedom and new human relationships. Prior to the inevitable unhappy endings in their films, film-makers advocated their anti-feudalistic social ideas either in a melodramatic or ironic way, and, in a profoundly sympathetic manner, depicted the human foibles of the man in the street. From

The Difficult Couple (1913) to *Twin Sisters* (1934), films and other forms of art and literature at the time mirrored the value system and the emotional orientation of the generation who left the countryside for the cities.

The 1934 film *The Goddess* presents a vivid picture of the city, where restless chaos and sorrowful grief coexist. In old China, street girls were called 'Goddesses', a reference to the dual character of those women surviving at the bottom of society. In the film, a prostitute sells her body to support her son. Despite all the hardships and humiliations she endures day after day, she is unable to earn due respect for her son at school. When she makes up her mind to leave the city with her son, she finds that all her hard-earned money has been stolen and gambled away by the villain who owns her. The film ends with the mother's imprisonment for having murdered the villain in order to regain her dignity. This tragic yet heroic ending adds an angelic, motherly glow to this story of a lowly prostitute.

As the last important silent film in China, *The Goddess* represents the highest level of artistic achievements in Shanghai's film industry at the time. This was the first film by a talented director, Wu Yonggang, who was only 27 at the time. It showcased his distinctive artistic perspective and his intuitive sense of film narrative. Constrained by the supposed limitations of silent cinema, the 24-year-old actress Ruan Lingyu convincingly exuded the human dignity of a 'goddess' through subtle body expression based on a profound inner experience. Her performance made a memorable impression. In a memoir completed in his later years, Wu wrote, "... One day I bought a ticket and watched the film with an audience. As the film progressed, I was moved to tears, even forgetting that I was its screenwriter and director ..." The very last scene of the film was of the imprisoned mother gazing in darkness, overlaid by an image of her son's smiling face. Her gaze appeared to be one of expectation. Shortly after the completion of this film, however, Ruan Lingyu, one of the most beautiful actresses in the 20th century, sadly ended her life of 25 years. In the real world, she could no longer bear the insults experienced in a male-dominated society and the humiliation caused by slanderers. Because of this incident, the film left a notable mark in the history of Chinese film and even that of modern China.

24 Hours in Shanghai presents a vivid picture of the city, where excessive luxury and suffering coexist. By using a classical dramatic approach in this silent film, playwright Xia Yan and director Shen Xiling, two film masters of the 1930s, compressed amity and enmity between two families of opposing social classes into a time frame of one day and one night. The day does not begin in the morning. The director deliberately chooses four o'clock in the afternoon, because, in Shanghai, this was the hour when workers who laboured all day could finally clock out, and the wives of factory owners who indulged in nightlife were just getting up. A child labourer is injured by a machine on the factory floor, but his sister, a cotton mill worker, does not have a penny to take him to a hospital. She rushes for help to their elder brother, a peddler. He, in turn, goes to his wife, a maid working at the owner's house, to find a solution. However, misfortunes never come alone.

A sympathetic neighbour tries to help them. Instead, his efforts result in the elder brother being falsely sent to prison for reputedly having stolen money from the owner's house. This disastrous day passes. The elder brother, no longer a suspect, is eventually released from prison. At home, he finds his younger brother dead; and his sister is dismissed from her job.

As one of the last few important films of China's silent film tradition, *24 Hours in Shanghai* represents the artistic and technical achievements of Shanghai film-makers in the 1930s. There are two noteworthy footnotes to this film. First, audiences had their first opportunity to view a talented actor, Zhao Dan, who played leading roles in many subsequent films, such as *Street Angel, The Crow and the Sparrow, Life of Wu Xun and Lin Zexu*. Zhao became the most prominent Chinese actor in the period spanning the 1930s to 1960s. Secondly, the production year of the film had to be officially changed from 1933 to 1934 because government film censors, outraged at the incisive way in which the film unveiled social injustice – withheld it for one year. Only after it was re-edited more than ten times, did the film obtain release approval. This reflects the difficulties and hardships faced by progressive film-makers at the time.

While the storyline of *24 Hours in Shanghai* was arranged in 'time' sequence, the stories of the *Old and New Shanghai*, a sound comedy produced in 1936, occurred within a specified 'space'. In old Shanghai, many residents lived in alley houses typical of the local culture. Pedestrians walked through an exterior door, to find two or three stories of pigeonhole-like narrow spaces that housed multiple families. All equally poor, the neighbours occupied the lower rungs of the social ladder according to their professions and status. Each family had its own plight, and its own unique way of concealing it. In a mutually supportive environment, where people frequently bumped into one another, a mixture of pleasure, anger, sorrow and joy – unique to lives in those alley houses – took shape. Among the six families depicted in the film are a laid-off office worker who pretends to go to work everyday, a dance hostess who goes out in heavy make-up and returns home empty-handed, a furniture salesman who cannot find customers but who has had to take care of his sick wife and children, a landlady who worries everyday about not being able to collect rents to support her gambling-addicted son, an elementary schoolteacher who has not been paid his salary, and a driver whose daily job it is to take women on drives through the streets.

The comedy was one of a series created for the Ming Xing (Star) Film Studio by Hong Shen, a playwright who studied at Harvard and wrote China's first film script at the age of 20. By the time he was 42, Hong was respected as an 'old master' in the film and theatre communities. With his masterful writing of satiric comedy, he depicted, in a profound manner, the existence of those sympathetic but comical 'grey characters.' Compared with numerous more realistic films of the period which were particulary depressing, this comedy is of higher artistic value. The manner in which social conditions were exposed probably resulted in more reflection by its audience. Cheng Bugao, director of the *Old and New Shanghai*, was also one of the leading figures in Shanghai's film scene in the 1930s.

Cheng's masterpieces, *Spring Silkworm* (1933) and *Raging Current* (1933), have long been regarded as classics of early Chinese cinema.

From February to April 1982, film historians from ten European countries were lured to Torino, Italy, to review 135 Chinese films produced between 1925 and 1980. Among these films, most of those from the 1930s and 1940s were made in Shanghai. In terms of the number of films screened, this was an unprecedented exhibition of Chinese films held outside China. Some of the invited film historians suggested that these films displayed a 'New Realism' which pre-dated that to be found in Italian film-making. In local newspapers, critics and reviewers identified an unadorned simplicity in the Chinese films of the 1930s as compared with European and American films of the same period.

In fact, Europeans first experienced Chinese films and the depiction of Shanghai life on the silver screen 70 years ago. On 2 March 1935, *Fishing Light Song*, directed by Lai Chusheng in 1934, won international recognition at the Moscow International Film Festival, attended by 31 nations. The only actress in the Chinese film delegation was Hu Die, mentioned earlier, who arrived in Moscow ten days later after journeying along the lengthy Trans-Siberian railway. As the first Chinese film star on an official overseas visit, Hu and her producer, Zhou Jianyun, brought two of her films, *Twin Sisters* and *Lonely Orchid*. Over the next five months, they toured the Soviet Union, Germany, France, Britain, Switzerland and Italy. In those six countries European audiences as well as those involved in film-making had the chance to glimpse an unfamiliar nation through these films, and to become acquainted with a different film culture through their contact with this elegant, energetic actress from the Orient.

Twin Sisters again tells a story of two families of different social classes. The two leading characters in the film are twin sisters who were separated at a young age and never had the chance to reunite. The younger sister, Erbao, moves to the city with her father and is given to a wealthy family and becomes a concubine. More than a decade later, her elder sister, Dabao, migrating to the city from the countryside, as if by fate, becomes a wet-nurse of Erbao's baby. The dramatic conflict between the twin sisters, now mistress and servant, intensifies until an accidental death occurs. Eventually they reconcile after realising their true relationship. Family kinship has always been a pivot of Chinese culture. Zheng Zhengqiu, China's first film director, was seriously ill while making this film in which he managed to expand the pattern of tragedy – to which he devoted his entire career to exploring – and depicted family morality at its highest level. According to historical records, the film enjoyed a continuous run of more than 60 days in its first release in over 50 cities in China and South-East Asia, where overseas Chinese lived, setting a box office record in China.

Another factor, which should not be neglected, contributed to the unparalleled popularity of *Twin Sisters*. It had to do with the exceptional performance of Hu Die who played both sisters in the film. Adored by audiences, the 24-year-old star must have had a difficult task with this role, both in terms of make-up and having to perform two extremely contrasting roles often within the same temporal and spatial environment. When she travelled through Europe a few years later, Hu noticed the involvement of European audiences; they even applauded during showings. This experience made her more aware of the significance of her own performance. It is worth mentioning that Hu Die and the delegation brought both films to Berlin in 1934. However, their host had arranged for an official screening of only one of the films. The delegation asked the Chinese Embassy staff and students from China to preview both films and make a choice. As a result, German audiences only got to watch *The Lonely Orchid* but not *Twin Sisters*. Some 70 years have passed, and this film, a masterpiece of Chinese film-making in 1930s, will finally unveil its charms in Munich, having visited Germany once before but without being shown.

By the mid-1930s, when China was in a national crisis, the *Zeitgeist* inherent in Shanghai films became even more manifest. Voices of the Anti-Japanese and National Salvation Movement echoed on the big screen in films such as *In a Stormy Time* (1934). This film describes young exiles from north-eastern China who are active as anti-Japanese volunteers. Its solemn and inspiring theme song was later designated the national anthem of the People's Republic of China. Many films about urban lives in Shanghai were incorporated either directly or metaphorically in this surging tide. *Lian Hua Symphony*, released just before the July Seventh Incident in 1937, was a collective effort by a group of film-makers to propagate anti-Japanese sentiments.

Comprised of eight short features, *Lian Hua Symphony* united as never before key directors and actors of the time, including Sun Yu, Fei Mu, Lai Chusheng, Situ Huimin, Shen Fu, Zhu Shilin, and Zheng Junli. Anyone familiar with film-making in China knows that these people were the few giant pillars supporting almost the entire sky of China's film industry from that time until the 1950s. This film is therefore particularly valuable for researchers. Each story, with widely differing styles, stands alone. As Sun Yu stated in his comments published at the time, "We can discern the 'voices of each heart' through the eight short features. These voices are harmonious, and resonant in one direction, making a perfect symphony."

In people's minds, Shanghai is a city associated with daily changes, which makes people simultaneously excited and somewhat sentimental. That is one of the reasons why we wish to keep the city, as captured on film, for ever. For those who lived through those years, or those who now can only fantasise about them in their readings, a glimpse of a lively lane in a busy alleyway, a *zhongshan*, a bitter face or a joke, as captured in these films, is all they need.

In her later years, Hu Die lived in Vancouver as an ordinary citizen who did not want people to disturb her tranquility by talking about the past. One day on a bus, an old lady sitting next to her smiled at her and said, "I recognise you from your way of looking. I was a fan of yours." This chance encounter was the beginning of her memoir about Chinese films of the 1930s.

In October 2004, four Chinese films from the 1930s will arrive in Munich to be shown to audiences there. This encounter, I believe, will also leave behind some memorable "ways of looking".

27

The Storm Society *Manifesto* (October 1932)

Ni Yide, Pang Xunqin, *et al.**

The historical contexts for this 1932 manifesto are given by Ralph Croizier in the essay, "Post-Impressionists in Pre-War Shanghai: The Juelanshe (Storm Society) and the Fate of Modernism in Republican China," included in this volume. Written in 1932 and published by artists in Shanghai's Storm Society, "The Storm Society Manifesto" gave voice to the group's collective desire for innovation. Storm Society members included Ni Yide, Pang Xunqing, Yang Taiyang, and Zhou Duo, as well as Qiu Di (the only woman in the group) and Wang Jiyuan who joined later. Most were oil painters who had trained in Paris and Tokyo; all had access to books and magazines on Western modern art. Towards the end of their manifesto they refer to European artists and identify themselves with the Fauvists, Cubists, Dadaists, and Surrealists. Their most decisive statement was: "We detest all the old forms and colours, as well as all mediocre and rudimentary techniques. We will represent the spirit of a new era with new techniques." Artistic innovation was clearly valued above all else and they railed against conservatism. Although they were not the first artist group, society, or association to emerge in the 1920s (other well-known examples include the Heavenly Horse Society), the Storm Society was, however, one of the most radical. Their politics revolved around form and technique because they rejected the idea that their work should serve political purposes.

* Ni Yide, Pang Xunqin, *et al.* (2004 [1932]) "The Storm Society Manifesto" (*Art Trimonthly* [*Yishu xunkan*] 1(5), October, Shanghai). Reprinted in Jo-Anne Birnie Danzker, Ken Lum, and Zheng Shengtian (eds) *Shanghai Modern, 1919–1945* (exhibition catalog, p. 234). Ostfildern-Ruit, Germany: Hatje Cantz.

Modern Art in Africa, Asia, and Latin America: An Introduction to Global Modernisms, First Edition.
Edited by Elaine O'Brien, Everlyn Nicodemus, Melissa Chiu, Benjamin Genocchio, Mary K. Coffey, and Roberto Tejada.

Further Readings

Knight, Michael, Chan, Dany, and Berliner, Nancy (2010) *Shanghai: Art of the City*. San Francisco, CA: Asian Art Museum.

Roberts, Claire (2010) *Friendship in Art: Fou Lei and Huang Binhong*. Hong Kong: Hong Kong University Press.

The air around us is too still, as mediocrity and vulgarity continue to envelop us. Countless morons are writhing around and countless shallow minds are crying out.

Where are the creative talents of the past? Where are the glories of our history? Impotence and sickness are what prevail throughout the entire artistic community today.

No longer can we remain content in such a compromised environment.

No longer can we allow it to breathe feebly until it dies.

Let us rise up! With our raging passion and iron intellect, we will create a world interwoven with colour, line and form!

We acknowledge that painting is by no means an imitation of nature, nor a rigid replication of the human body. With our entire being, we will represent, unconcealed, our bold and daring spirit.

We believe that painting is by no means the slave of religion, nor a mere illustration of literature. We will freely, and cohesively, construct a world of pure shapes.

We detest all the old forms and colours, as well as all mediocre and rudimentary techniques. We will represent the spirit of a new era with new techniques.

Since the beginning of the 20th century, a new atmosphere has emerged in the European artistic community, comprised of the outcries of the Fauvists, the twists of the Cubists, the vehemence of the Dadaists and the cravings of the Surrealists …

It is time for a new atmosphere to emerge throughout the 20th-century artistic community of China.

Let us rise up! With our raging passion and iron intellect, we will create a world interwoven with colour, line and form!

Part III

Latin American Modern Art

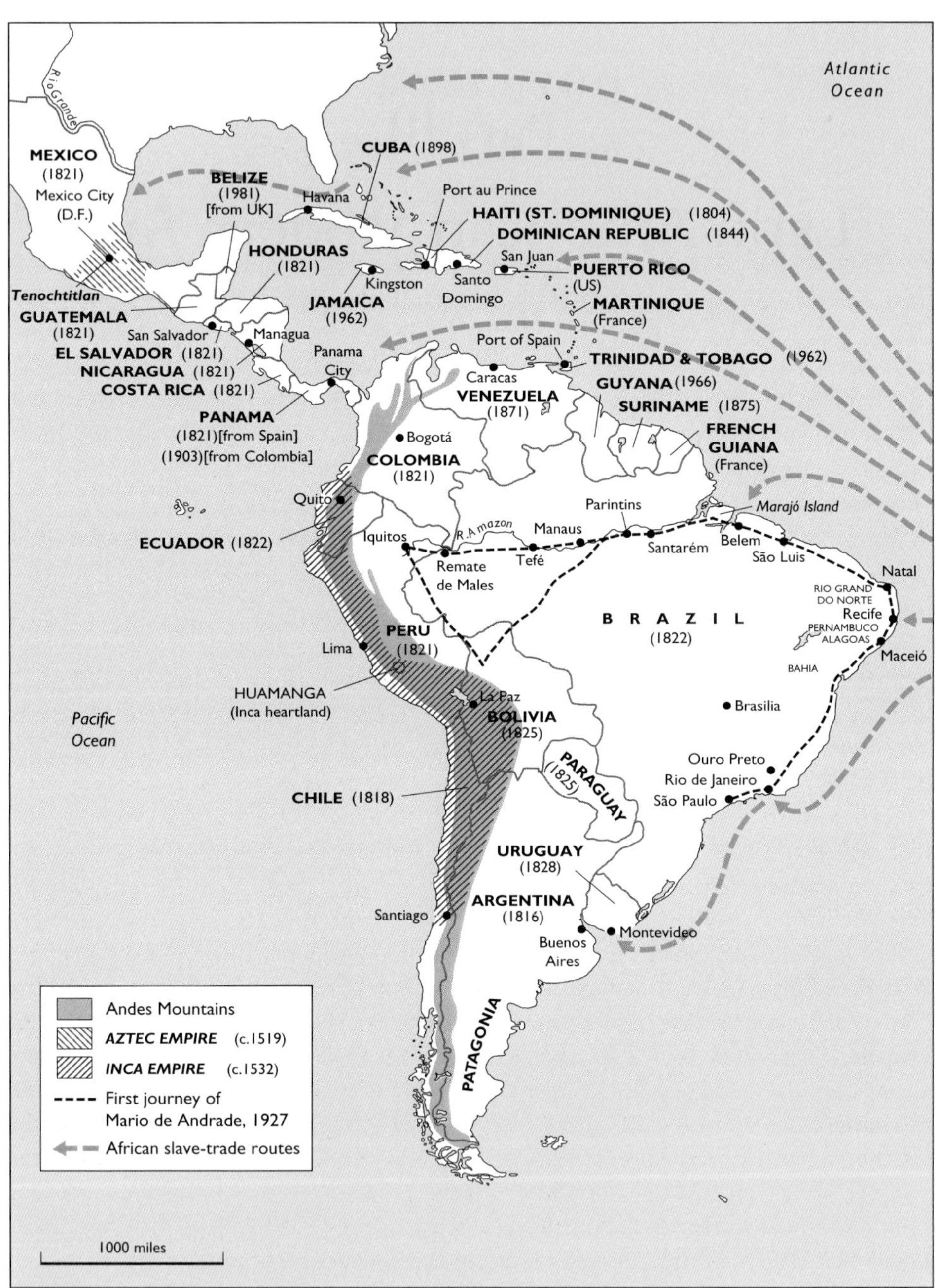

Map 3 Locations of Modern Art in Latin America.

Introduction

Modernism in Latin America: Strategic Vanguards

Mary K. Coffey and Roberto Tejada

In 2006 an anonymous telephone call set an auction house record at Sotheby's in New York City. The caller became the highest bidder on a small oil painting, a 1943 work by Mexican artist Frida Kahlo, entitled *Roots*, purchased for 5.6 million US dollars. Making news in recent years have been similar high-grossing sales of works by artists discussed in this section, including Brazil's Tarsila do Amaral, Uruguay's Joaquín Torres-García, and Cuba's Wifredo Lam. In 2008, a 1945 painting by another Mexican artist – Rufino Tamayo's *Trovador* – sold at Christie's for 7.2 million US dollars, further accelerating the value of modern Latin American art on the international market. As we write this in 2011, despite the uncertainty of a widening global economic recession, the art market's appetite for Latin American art has not waned. We begin, then, with one of several historical ironies that define the belated nature of the modern project. It takes a twenty-first-century marketplace to establish the symbolic value of Latin American vanguard art produced from 1920 to 1960.

The appeal of Latin American culture in the United States and Europe cannot be isolated from other social and historical factors. Over the last decade, while the United States and United Kingdom led war efforts in Iraq and Afghanistan, and the so-called "war on terror," important changes were taking place in the political and social life of Latin America. For example, starting with the 1994 neo-Zapatista movement in Mexico's Chiapas state, indigenous populations throughout the southern hemisphere have continued to organize so as to demand increased political sovereignty. While neoliberal policies throughout the 1990s led to dramatic financial boom and bust in countries like Mexico (1994) and Argentina (1999–2002), Brazil has since emerged as one of the world's leading economies, a member of the BRIC nations that also include Russia, India, and China. In the year 2000

Modern Art in Africa, Asia, and Latin America: An Introduction to Global Modernisms, First Edition.
Edited by Elaine O'Brien, Everlyn Nicodemus, Melissa Chiu, Benjamin Genocchio,
Mary K. Coffey, and Roberto Tejada.

presidential elections, after more than 70 years as Mexico's monolithic state system, the Partido Revolucionario Institucional (PRI) lost to the conservative challenger, Partido Acción Nacional (PAN). By contrast, citizens elsewhere have voted into office progressive reformers and controversial populists: Luiz Inácio Lula da Silva in Brazil, Hugo Chávez in Venezuela, and Evo Morales in Bolivia. In a region long ruled by violent despots and caudillos, there have been successful efforts, at the national and international level, to prosecute former military dictators, among them Augusto Pinochet of Chile and Jorge Rafael Videla of Argentina. While media accounts continue to expose the unspeakable serial murder of women in Ciudad Juárez and other sites along the US–Mexico border, a phenomenon tied to drug-traffic terror, women in Latin America have played an increasingly crucial role in politics. Since 2006 three women have held presidential office: Michelle Bachelet in Chile (2006–10), Cristina Fernández de Kirchner in Argentina (2007–), and Dilma Roussef in Brazil (2011–).

We highlight recent events to further underline the relationship of the present to the past. Modernism is the story of that connection to history and to the intertwining process of politics, economics, and culture. Latin America is no exception, even as the modernization meant to inaugurate new forms of human relations has yielded contrary results in the region's deeply unequal societies. We look at terms like "modernization," "modernity," and "modernism" as well as authors who consider Latin America a "problem" that has allowed artists and intellectuals to ask important questions about nationhood, identity, and modern life. What is the historical identity of Latin America? What are the cultural methods for fashioning a sense of local belonging in line also with modernity at large?

This part of the volume addresses critical questions as it presents Latin American art in the context of modern culture, society, and politics. It tells a story that begins with Cuban author Roberto Fernandez Retamar's "Our America and the West," which recounts the foundational violence that to this day inflects the narratives of countries in Latin America. The encounter between Europe and the "Indies," and the "subjection of one by the other, has been known throughout history by several names: invasion, migration or foundation." From the colonial period onward, a common pursuit linking the different cultures of Latin America has pointed back to conquest and colonization in order to make sense of history and of a people's place within it – a shared search for the recognition of complex regional identities.

The following chapters with selected texts locate Latin American modernism within the first five decades of the twentieth century. However, as each selection suggests, Latin American modernism, by necessity, engages with the effects of colonization and its contemporary legacies. This dialectic between past and present differs from the rhetorical rejection of the past that European modernists often proclaimed. Likewise, Latin American modernists recognized their "errancy" within the "West," simultaneously insiders and outsiders as a consequence of being settlers within colonized lands (see Esther Gabara, this volume). This sense of belonging and difference from the West often manifested itself in an ambivalent relationship with the United States – its contradictions as an open society ready to interfere in the political affairs of the southern hemisphere; a nation Latin Americans deemed the regional exemplar of modernity without an ethical project.

Modernization/Modernity/Modernism

Most countries in Latin America gained independence from Spain and Portugal in the period between 1810 and 1825. For nineteenth-century Latin American elites, the drive to consolidate bourgeois nations in the subcontinent fueled the desire to modernize: by the 1910s this included large-scale public works, factories, and industrial plants as well as the structural redesign of city centers for motorized transportation and laboring citizens. Many Latin American governments promoted foreign speculation and settlement as a means of modernizing, but the result was often beneficial only to a small fraction of the national populace. Latin American modernity, emerging from the social and cultural changes of modernized life, and with persistent residues of the region's former colonial status, entailed three stages: first, the determination to produce art and ideas on a par with those of metropolitan centers, chiefly those of Europe; second, a bold rejection of those models; and finally a third-stage integration of the regional and the cosmopolitan. In the late 1880s, Nicaraguan poet Rubén Darío coined the term *modernismo*, a first-stage effect of modernity, to account for the underbelly of bourgeois life. Darío wrote in a bold literary form of regional Spanish, and as with other *modernista* artists, he incorporated indigenous themes and national images particular to the American hemisphere. He upheld the value of art made by a cultural elite native to what he and others called "our America" as being superior to the technological and imperial advance of the United States, a nation that to this day uses the continent's name in reference only to itself (see Rubén Darío, this volume).

Art histories discuss the term modernism with definitions that are specific to the cultures of Europe and the United States. Subsequent to nineteenth-century *modernismo*, Latin America also underwent a second distinct period of intellectual innovation and creativity. With the exception of Brazil, where the use of the term "modernismo" is comparable to Euro-American modernism, in the early twentieth century a succession of art formations known more generally as *vanguardias* shared elective affinities with – while assuming a critical position toward – the "high" artistic modernisms of Europe and the technological modernization of the United States. Latin American *vanguardistas* viewed modernity as a process to which they belonged even as outsider-insiders. After World War I, the United States' cultural advances appeared increasingly utilitarian, especially in light of its insertion, often by military means, into the political and economic affairs of Latin America. This has led intellectual historians and literary critics

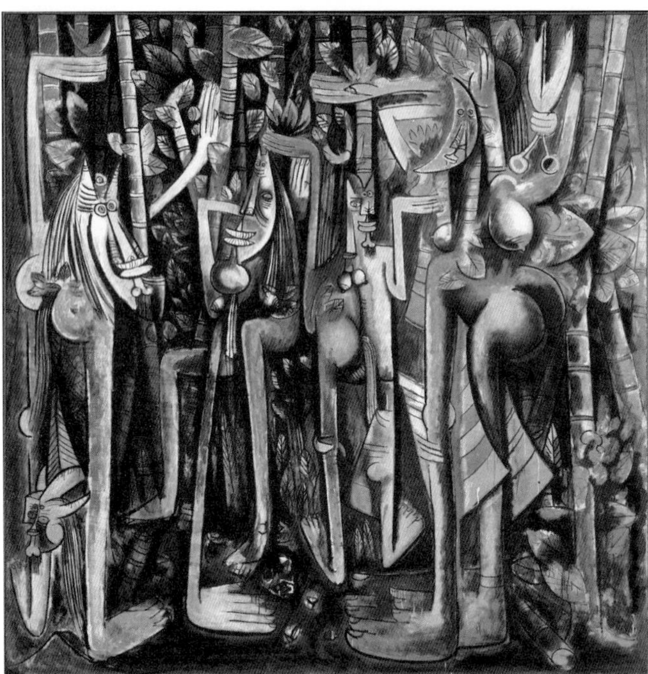

Figure I.3 Wifredo Lam, *La Jungla*, 1943, gouache on paper mounted on canvas, 239.5 × 229.75 cm / 94¼ × 90½ inches. The Museum of Modern Art (MoMA), New York, Inter-American Fund, 1945, © 2011. Digital image, The Museum of Modern Art, New York/Scala, Florence, © ADAGP, Paris and DACS, London 2011.

like Idelber Avelar to suggest a necessary link between "modernization and imperialism … in Latin American history. Hence the inseparability between aestheticism and Latin Americanism" (Avelar 1997: 125). Employing productive ambiguity in relation to the cultural ascendency of the "West," avant-garde artists from various regions in Latin America made conscious efforts to redirect aesthetic, philosophical, and geopolitical concerns neither as preordained effects of the dominant forms of modernity, nor as disavowals of the larger modern project. For example, James Holston's essay included here reveals Brasilia's debt to and difference from Le Corbusier's utopian city planning. By contrast, Clarice Lispector describes the sense of possibility and horror that this imposed feat of engineering on the Brazilian landscape generated within the country's social imaginary. Leonard Folgarait demonstrates Diego Rivera's engagement with cubism's semiotic challenge, while also revealing the muralist's collusion with Mexican state formation. And Mari Carmen Ramírez, in her discussion of the Latin American uptake of the tenets of concrete abstraction, surveys the myriad ways that artists, like Lygia Clark in her *Pintura Concreta* (*Concrete Painting*) and *Bicho* (*Critter*) of 1959–63, embraced the materiality of the modern while maintaining a utopian commitment to social change.

We employ Esther Gabara's discussion of "errancy" and Andrea Giunta's notion of strategies to capture the dynamic of elective affinity and critique that characterizes Latin American modernism. As Gabara argues in her discussion of Mario de Andrade's photography, formal stakes were inseparable from social ethics: a self-reflective questioning of the relationship between the dominant settler class and the ethnicized popular classes. Giunta's discussion of the strategic interventions of Tarsila do Amaral, Oswald de Andrade, Wifredo Lam, and Joaquín Torres-García reveals how different each unique response was to the specific sociopolitical concerns of discreet national and metropolitan realities.

The recognition of difference within the Latin American vanguards is important insofar as it resists the urge to collapse the region into a unified and essentialized ethno-geography. Corresponding with the Argentine theorist Walter Mignolo in *The Idea of Latin America*, rather than to view the region as a bounded place, we argue for the history of a "problem" that has pushed intellectuals and artists from Latin America to find ways to celebrate its complexity and grapple with its contradictions. Dubbed *l'Amérique Latine* by the French in the1860s during Louis-Napoléon Bonaparte's attempts to extend his empire, the region's intellectuals have endeavored to foreground national, regional, and local differences while at the same time embracing the symbolic possibilities of a culturally unified geopolitical block (Mignolo 2005). Similarly, Cuban critic Gerardo Mosquera argues that into the twenty-first century "the self-consciousness of belonging to a historical-cultural entity misnamed Latin America is maintained," and yet, he insists that as an "invention" Latin America has been and will continue to be "reinvented" in and through culture (Mosquera 2003: 74).

Race and Identity

Social realities that resulted from the ethnic mixing of indigenous populations with subsequent waves of European settlers and migrants, as well as with enslaved Africans and their descendants, prompted a search for regional differences, often centered around the visual circumstances of racial identity. In the cultural formations to emerge after the Mexican Revolution, philosopher José Vasconcelos published *The Cosmic Race*, a 1925 treatise whose argument was with Anglo-European and US American "exceptionalism." Vasconcelos sought to refute those attitudes that considered the Iberian Americas as some sort of "lesser new world." He turned to the conquest's foundational violence and the ensuing process of *mestizaje*, the sweeping integration of peoples and cultures from Europe with native peoples of Indo-America. In a very different cultural context, Oswald de Andrade sought to overturn the exotic image of his native Brazil by making European culture and the world at large a feast set out for modern (cannibalistic) Brazilian appetites. His 1928 "Cannibalist Manifesto" proposed a discerning taste that could incorporate foreign fodder into the national palate – an act of ingestion whereby eater and eaten are mutually transformed.

In Latin America, bodies have been the prime material for conveying notions about human subjects and institutions. Marked with meanings – skin color, dress code, class status, and sexual individuality – depictions of the human figure have had a deep impact on social categories, even as they frame the language used to connote nationhood, ethnicity, class identification, and gender roles. Gerardo Mosquera and Robert Stam relate how in the modern art of Latin America indigenous subjects, women, and peoples of African descent were often depicted as compulsory to national culture but estranged from modern life, or so generalized and idyllic as to be emptied of active historical meaning. Nonetheless, the presence of Africa in Latin America's visual art has allowed many twentieth-century and contemporary artists to "de-Westernize" Western culture from within. Mosquera describes how an African presence has carried over into modern

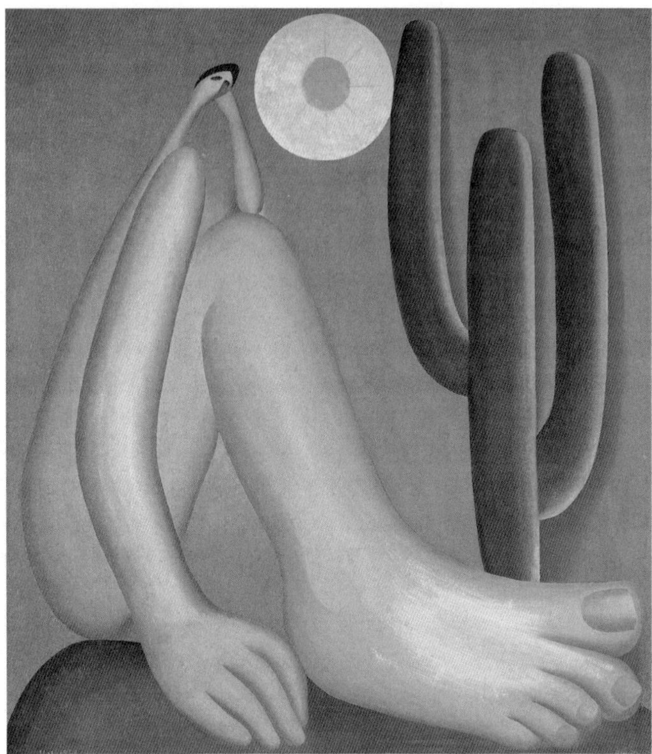

Figure I.4 Tarsila do Amaral, *Abaporú*, 1928, oil on canvas, 86.5 × 75.5 cm / 34 × 29¾ inches. Colección Malba, Fundación Constantini, Museo de Arte Latinoamericano de Buenos Aires.

and contemporary object-based art and performance to constitute *creolization*, or a greater Caribbean culture.

Language difference, local histories, and concrete settings determine the corporeal implication of race in Latin America. Thus, terms such as *creolization* and *criollo* may lead to some confusion. To clarify: the proper noun (*criollo*, *criolla*) refers to a person of European descent born in Latin America, and its adjectival form points to the culture of that particular class. By contrast, especially in a Caribbean context, the French-derived word *creolization* is a synonym for *mestizaje*: cultural and racial mixing. Moreover, in Portuguese, the term *crioulo* is meant to distinguish between African-born and Brazilian blacks; and in the nineteenth-century, throughout the Spanish-speaking Americas, *mestizo* chromatics varied to such a degree that some light-skinned *mestizos* identified as *criollo*. Today, writes anthropologist Lilia Moritz Schwarcz about Brazil, "You are what you describe yourself to be. Officially we have five different colors – black, white, yellow, indigenous, and *pardo* (meaning 'brown,' 'brownish,' or 'gray-brown'), but in reality, as research has demonstrated, we have more than 130 colors" (Darnton 2010).

Race is central to Latin American modernism in figurative traditions like those of Tarsila do Amaral in her oil on canvas entitled *Abaporú* of 1928. In Mexico, Frida Kahlo's *The Two Fridas* (1939) is a painting that disrupts the conventions of self-portraiture, even as it engages with regional identity and the legacies of conquest by means of the sitter's two dresses. Frida's twofold body depicts a divided self redoubled in the viewer's vision split between an indigenous Tehuana dress and European Victorian attire. Although the work is aligned with the French surrealist movement (André Breton famously exhibited the painting), its alliances are with the "magic real" – another name for the historical uncanny – rather than with the "surreal" (Carpentier 1995[1975]). As art historian Adriana Zavala has argued, Kahlo's art is rooted in the social reality it critiques: Latin America's racial discrimination, gender inequality, and the problematic ways in which women were incorporated into the modern project as symbols of modernity via their relationship to tradition (Zavala 2010). Race is a persistent question even when it is altogether ignored or sublimated into form. A turn to the "archaic culture of the Continent" allowed Torres-García, in a work such as *Constructivo con varillas sobrepuestas* (*Constructive with Attached Rods*), 1930, to synthesize a "cosmic" concept of humanity together with modern life, into a universal pictorial grammar proper to the Americas. Juxtaposed to metaphors of earth, ground, and rootedness were images of artifacts, architecture, and the cosmos. With these elements, Torres-García defied makers not to imitate but to adapt: to *construct*, in formal compositions, an analogous ethnos.

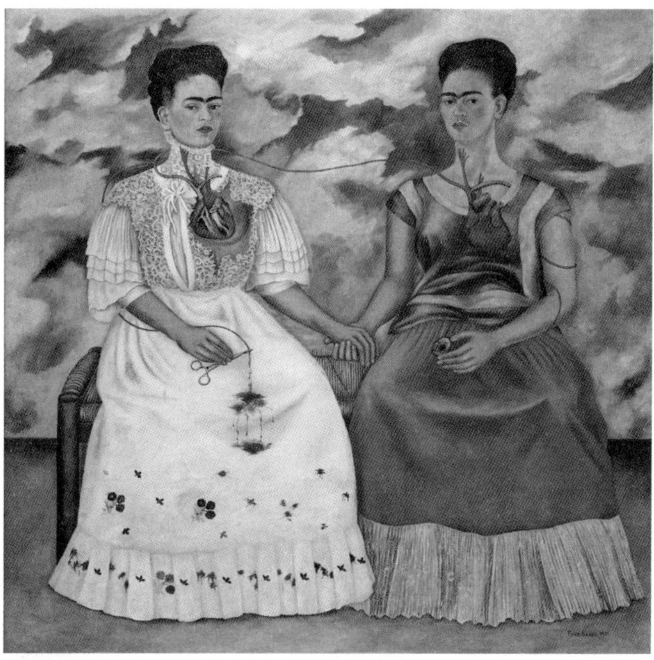

Figure I.5 Frida Kahlo, *The Two Fridas*, 1939, oil on canvas. Mexico, Museo de Arte Moderno, photo AKG Images, © 2011 Banco de México Diego Rivera, Frida Kahlo Museums Trust, Mexico, D.F. / DACS.

Most if not all of the authors in Part III of this volume deem inadequate the category of a "Latin American identity." However, disjunctive temporalities in the geography of modernism allow us to suggest relations between vastly different vanguards in Latin America. Leonard Folgarait demystifies Rivera's alleged "epic modernism," in the National Palace fresco *History of Mexico from the Conquest to the Future* (1929–30). The mural was political propaganda, not of Communism, as the artist famously asserted, but rather of a bureaucratic Mexican state: social change reduced to a "ritual" process. In a vastly different historic and geographical context, works by Gyula Kosice, Lygia Clark, and Hélio Oiticica produced experiences of art also as a kind of ritual. Mari Carmen Ramírez relates how these and other artists sought, in 1960s Brazil, to go beyond the object altogether. In a politics by other means, constructivist artists aspired to transform material, the self, and society from something inert into something alive.

In focusing on these nations and/or regions of Latin America, we have left out the Andean countries, much of the Caribbean and Central America, important centers of vanguard production, such as Venezuela, and the emerging 1960s art of the Latin American diaspora in the United States. Similarly, we emphasize work from cosmopolitan cities like Mexico City, São Paulo, Rio de Janeiro, Montevideo, or Havana produced in most – but not all – cases by an urban elite. However, by including essays on photography and film we have deliberately broadened the purview of modernist studies of the region to include the camera arts, printed media, and popular culture. And our inclusion of Darío, Vasconcelos, and Lispector highlights genres of modernist production beyond the artist's manifesto. The movements and artists we have selected are arguably

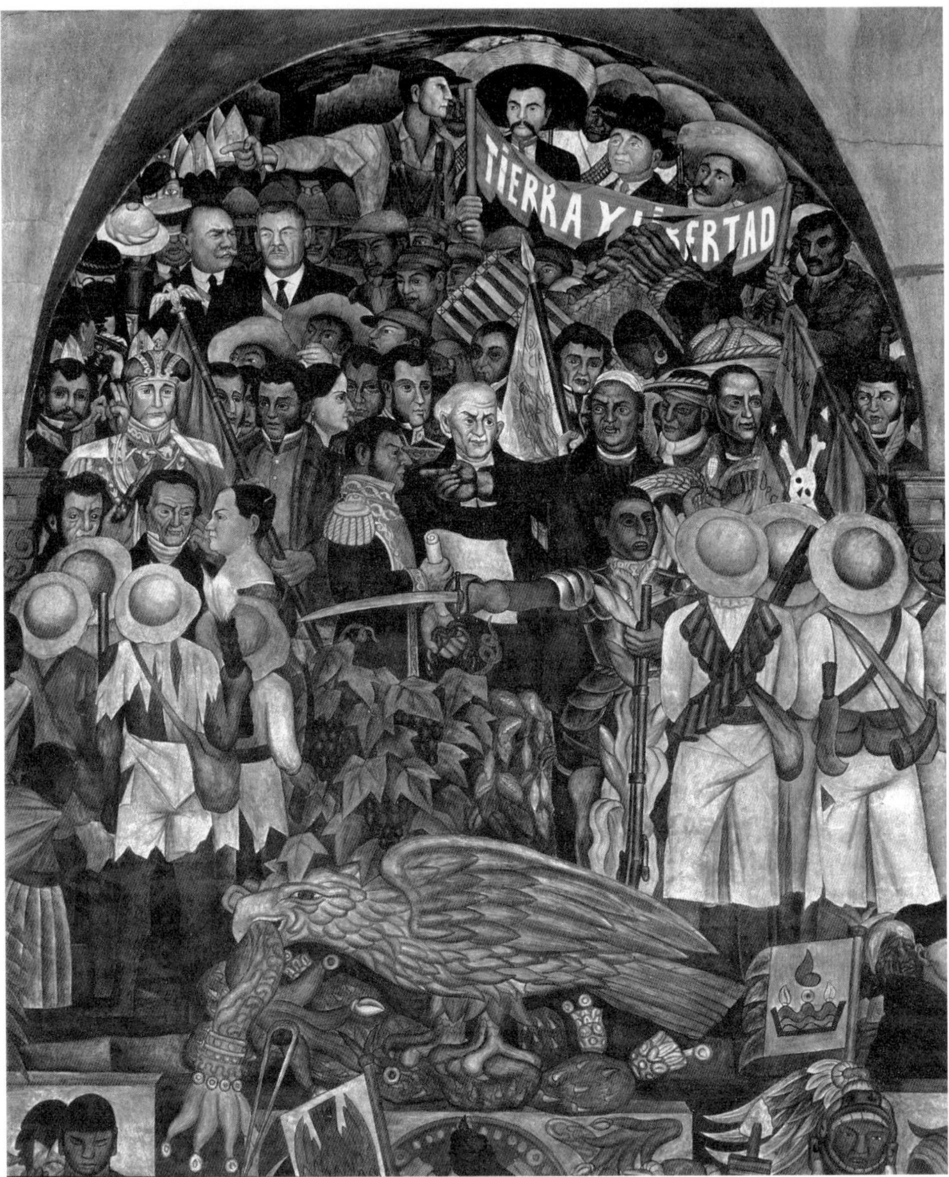

Figure I.6 Diego Rivera (1886–1957), *Legacy of Independence*, detail of central section from The Conquest to 1930. Mural, west wall. Mexico City, National Palace, © 2011. Photo Art Resource/ Bob Schalkwijk/Scala, Florence, © 2011 Banco de México Diego Rivera Frida Kahlo Museums Trust, Mexico, D.F./DACS.

among the most historically significant and influential, as well as the most documented and studied. This not only allows for rich pairings of primary and secondary literature, but also provides the reader with a deeper appreciation for the many approaches that scholars located within and outside of Latin America have brought to the study of its modern culture.

References

Avelar, Idelber (1997) "Toward a Genealogy of Latin Americanism." *Dispositio/n* 22(49): 121–33.

Carpentier, Alejo (1995[1975]) "The Baroque and the Marvelous Real." Reprinted in Lois Zamora and Wendy Faris (eds), *Magical Realism: Theory, History, Community* (pp. 89–108). Durham, NC: Duke University Press.

Darnton, Robert (2010) "Talking about Brazil with Lilia Schwarcz." The New York Review of Books Blog, www.nybooks.com/blogs/nyrblog/2010/aug/17/talking-about-brazil/ (accessed February 25, 2012).

Mignolo, Walter (2005) *The Idea of Latin America*. Oxford, England: Blackwell.

Mosquera, Gerardo (2003) "From Latin American Art to Art from Latin America." *ArtNexus* 48 (April–June): 74.

Zavala, Adriana (2010) *Becoming Modern, Becoming Tradition: Women, Gender, and Representation in Mexican Art*. University Park: The Pennsylvania State University Press.

28

Our America and the West

ROBERTO FERNÁNDEZ RETAMAR*

Roberto Fernández Retamar (Havana, b. 1930) is a poet and cultural critic. Like many other Latin American intellectuals not strictly aligned with the discipline of art history, he has written on visual culture, architecture, and design. In this essay the author historicizes how connections to cultural metropolises of Europe and the United States have had a vexed history across the globe; and that this link arguably constitutes the central issue surrounding modern art produced in the various geographic or cultural locations known as Latin America. As a term itself, "Latin America" is riddled with as many contradictions as the considerable diversity of peoples, environs, and histories it is meant to encompass. "Our America and the West" is a brief survey therefore of those conditions defining the region's major stakes in the modern project. Those features include a common history of conquest, colonization, independence struggle, the founding of constitutional republics and modern nations, at times interrupted by autocratic military rule, and the ever-encroaching prospect of foreign economic and cultural dominance.

In this essay a double account takes place to join two historical moments. When Fernández Retamar wrote this essay in the late 1970s, the Cuban Revolution had altered social and cultural relations on the island and polarized opinion throughout the continent. Fidel Castro's famous cautionary words in the early 1960s addressed to artists and intellectuals – "Within the revolution, everything; outside the revolution, nothing" – had been part of a context that included also a US economic embargo with the severing of diplomatic ties to the island, as well as hemispheric

* Roberto Fernández Retamar (1986) "Our America and the West." *Social Text* 15(Autumn): 1–25.

Modern Art in Africa, Asia, and Latin America: An Introduction to Global Modernisms, First Edition.
Edited by Elaine O'Brien, Everlyn Nicodemus, Melissa Chiu, Benjamin Genocchio,
Mary K. Coffey, and Roberto Tejada.

resistance to US military intervention and its cultural influence both high and low. Fernández Retamar retrieves the notion of "Our America" from the writings of Cuban poet and independence leader, José Martí (Cuba, 1853–95) who coined the phrase in a famous 1891 essay when he lived in New York City. United States expansionism in the nineteenth century had already led to conflicts that yielded the annexation of territories belonging to Mexico, and not long after Martí's essay, also the former Spanish colonies of the Philippines, Guam, and Puerto Rico. US American ascendancy had violently redrawn the geopolitical map of the western hemisphere and beyond, even as it continued to menace the region's cultural mood. The term "Our America" – used at the turn of the century, in the political climate of the 1970s, and even today – has meant to distinguish a cultural reality from that "other" America, the United States.

Fernández Retamar challenges his readers to examine the names that the West has given to such historical events as the foundational violence of the conquest. To speak from the position of "Our America" is to ask whether the arrival of Europeans in the American continent was a "discovery" at all, or rather a disastrous encounter in the name of mercantile and religious expansionism. To speak from the place of "Our America" is to equate the Western world and its culture with capitalism; and to ask whether Spain and Portugal were ever at the center of Europe's Enlightenment project, or if instead – on account of a heritage with cultural indebtedness to Islam and Judaism – they were at the perimeter of a Western ethos, something the author designates as "paleo-Western."

Who are the citizens of "Our America"? Coupled with Spain and Portugal's colonial governments and institutions, the cultural amalgamation that took place between Europeans, indigenous peoples, and African slaves (and the formerly enslaved) constituted a process referred to as *mestizaje*. American-born Europeans who formed part of the elite colonial classes – later the bourgeoisie or *criollo* sector of the nascent republics – saw themselves not as Europeans; however, a view from "Our America" is to see their sense of difference as having been at the expense of indigenous and African-descended populations. During the independence struggles symbolized by Simón Bolívar, support for the idea of a continental union of republics in "Our America" differed among the bourgeoisie and its ideologues in countries with an indigenous and *mestizo* constituency (Mexico, Peru), those with greater populations of African descent (Brazil, Cuba), and those in the Southern Cone (Argentina, Uruguay) where the labor force was supplied by subsequent waves of European immigrants. In some former colonies, intellectuals did not completely identify as unqualified Westerners, but rather identified as Westerners "with a difference"; in the Southern Cone and elsewhere the temptation was often to see themselves only as Westerners.

Citing authors before him in what constitutes a long-standing intellectual tradition, Fernández Retamar challenges the hubris of Western culture and its claims to a monopoly on a universal way of life – along with its restricted cultural and political forms. While some intellectuals in "Our America," like Domingo Faustino Sarmiento (Argentina, 1811–88), saw culture as a struggle between civilization and barbarism (namely, indigenous cultures), José Martí claimed that a native land contained every aspect of the human universe. José Enrique Rodó (Uruguay, 1872–1917), the philosopher and literary critic who in 1900 argued for the superiority of cultural and artistic refinement in Latin American countries as compared to the crude industrial materialism of US capitalist society. A powerful metaphor describing the symbolic relationship between Europe and "Our America" can be found as far back as William Shakespeare's *The Tempest* (1610–11). In 1900, Rodó had engaged the figure of Ariel as a symbol of Latin America's transcendent spirit. Seventy years later, Fernández Retamar himself turned to this European classic work, to the figure of the enslaved but rebellious Caliban as exemplary of a historically unique *mestizo* culture resistant to US cultural imperialism.

These positions form part of a debate whose cultural and philosophical implications over time have had demonstrable political consequences. Fernández Retamar provides the chronology of that problem with extended reference to authors who have wrestled with the following questions: What is the historical identity of Latin America? What is the historical identity of Western civilization, or of Eurocentric culture, without an account of the colonization that took place in the American hemisphere? What is the role of artists and intellectuals in "Our America"? How do they critically view the particularities of belonging to a region in the face of modernizing forces? What are their methods for fashioning a sense of cultural selfhood? How do the abstract generalizations from the centers of power and the knowledge of what others say *about* Latin America erase the differences in claims spoken from the various locations *within* Latin America? If "Latin America" is to have any legitimate meaning, perhaps it is at this confrontation of foreign expansionism and self-reflexive regionalism. In "Our America" these are all questions relevant to every aspect of its modern art and culture.

Further Readings

Bolivar, Simón (2003) *El Libertador: Writings of Simón Bolívar* (David Bushnell, ed., Fred Fornoff, trans.). New York, NY: Oxford University Press.

Martí, José (2002) "Our America." In Esther Allen (ed. and trans.), *José Martí: Selected Writings* (pp. 288–96). New York, NY: Penguin Classics.

Retamar, Roberto Fernández (1989) *Caliban and Other Essays* (Edward Baker, trans.). Minneapolis: University of Minnesota Press.

Zea, Leopoldo (1991) *The Role of the Americas in History* (Amy Oliver, ed., Sonja Karsen, trans.). Lanham, MD: Rowman & Littlefield Publishers.

What's in a Name

[...]

The task of defining historical parameters of Latin America [and] that of the so-called western world [...] is the topic of the pages that follow. [...]

[…] While it is true that the West refers to geographical boundaries, political empires, and religious schisms in a European context, its contemporary sense is […] only insinuated in Hegel's *Lectures on the Philosophy of History*, where the "heart of Europe," "European man," "European humanity," and even "the Germanic world" are preferred. By the middle of the 19th century, however, the Russians were speaking of westerners, that is, modernizers vis-à-vis feudal backwardness. In Our America, at about the same time, Andrés Bello used the West with an almost contemporary meaning. In western Europe the name was widely used by the second half of the 19th century, but only with the triumph of the October Revolution in our 20th century does it reach its apogee. […] The use of western culture, western world, or the West (vis-à-vis the Orient) [was also] a favorite weapon in the ideological arsenal of the bourgeoisie during the worst moments of the cold war.

Leopoldo Zea offers us a more serene and acceptable definition of the concept in 1955: "I use 'Western world' or 'the West' for that group of countries in Europe and America, particularly the United States of North America, which have attained the cultural and material ideals of Modernity discernible from the 16th century on." From the 16th century on? Marx writes in the first volume of *Capital* (1867) that "the first signs of the capitalist mode of production appear sporadically in some Mediterranean cities during the 14th and 15th centuries, although the *capitalist era* really begins in the 16th century." Zea will later equate the western world with capitalism.

[…]

Thus did the western world develop vertiginously, at the expense and indispensable exploitation of the rest of the world. In Europe itself, the furthest western regions (Spain and Portugal), which contributed most to capitalist development *in other countries*, would not know such development. Relegated to the margins of the West, which affected the destiny of their vast colonial empires, these backward countries might be called "paleowestern."

If metropolitan Spain and Portugal remained on the periphery of the West, it is not surprising that their American colonies should have had a similar fate. […] Our America was yoked to the multiple and rapacious capitalist exploitations which still afflict us. Such thinkers as Spengler may exclude us from the West, which fits with our condition in the capitalist world as exploited rather than exploiters. But for this very reason we are linked with western capitalism in a common history. Whether we accept it or not, whether we are oblivious of it, this link has been essential and permanent: it inheres in the reciprocal, dialectical constitution of what came to be the western world and Latin America from the 16th century on. It is absurd to trace the history of our countries without reference to the West. But, has it been equally clear that the West's history cannot be written without reference to our own? […]

Latin Americans' ideas on the relationship between Our America and the western world must be seen within this dramatic historical framework.

The First Visions

[...]

[In his 1891 essay, "Our America," José Martí wrote:] "The history of America, from the Incas to the present, must be taught thoroughly, even at the expense of dispensing with the Greek archons. Our own Greece is preferable, more necessary." There is, indeed, no serious way to assume our history other than to take its true roots as the point of departure. And the true roots of what came to be called America are, of course, the men who discovered it, populated it, and erected on its soil cultures as extraordinary as any others. But the smooth course of this history snags on an unfortunate term wittingly invented and propagated in self-interest. The encounter of two communities, and the subjection of one by the other, has been known throughout history by many names: invasion, migration or foundation. But the arrival of the paleowestern Europeans on these shores, an event which could have been variously designated (e.g., The Disaster), has been repeatedly referred to as a discovery, *The Discovery*.

Such a name, *per se*, is a complete falsification of history, a covering up of the true history. Thus are the people and cultures of these lands reified – ceasing to be subjects of history. Rather, they are "discovered," like landscape, flora and fauna, by Man. Moreover, the use of this name assumes the theoretical sanction of an even more lamentable practice. The frightful destruction of the indigenous populations of America at the hands of paleowesterners [...] is, according to Celso Furtado, "a demographic hecatomb without parallel in the history of mankind." [...]

That hecatomb, that cataclysm, was the first image, in these lands, of what would come to be known as the western world. [...] The little that has survived of this indigenous vision can be found in the kindly and energetic writings of men like Bernardo de Sahagún, in compilations such as the admirable *Visión de los vencidos* (1959) by Miguel León Portilla, or here and there in the archaeological materials of other American peoples. It is the image of dread and horror sown by those whom the besieged of Tenochtitlán called "*popolocas*," or barbarians in Father Garibay's translation.

Even more scandalous than Martí's reference to native Americans as our earliest ancestors is sure to be Alejandro Lipschutz's characterization of the African slaves brought to America as "imported 'natives'." In many regions of America they replaced the dwindling Indian population, "taking the character of enslaved natives." These other Latin American ancestors had a similar vision of the western world as that of the vanquished American Indians, but one even more poorly recorded in scant and scattered songs and prayers. [...]

[...] Indians and black Africans knew from the start that they were not western and came to form the ranks of American otherness. The descendants of Europeans, on the other hand, took much longer to feel that they were different, if not from Europeans in general, then at least from their metropolitan counterparts. Their distinguishing features, which emerged rather quickly, were understood from the perspective of colonialism. The American-born was distinguished from the European-born by his *criollo* ("creole") identity. This term, which appeared at the end of the 16th century, was initially used in Brazilian Portuguese (whence its dissemination to other languages) to refer to *American* rather than African blacks. Later the name came to include American-born whites, and eventually acquired almost exclusive reference to them.

The Latin American bourgeoisie, whose first inklings date from this period, does not perceive fully the stifling structures of the parasitic Iberian empires until well into the 18th century. That's when those who had no doubts about being Spaniards or Portuguese living abroad begin to adopt with pride their distinction as *criollos*. [...] To the dramatic otherness of the Indian and of the future-bound man who Martí characterized as "autochthonous mestizo," the *criollos* now add their relative otherness. It is just at this time, however, that the first concrete possibility of a break offers itself.

From First Independence to Neocolonialism

[...]

An anticolonialist and revolutionary war had just been fought against England in the other America, which resulted in independence for the thirteen colonies. [...] No wonder, then, that it also should have repercussions among the most progressive sectors in Our America, which, however, had neither the traits nor the conditions that made the struggle possible in the thirteen colonies. [...]

[...] Although a tempting, even admirable model for the nascent Latin American bourgeoisies, the United States only began to exert direct and substantial influence in the destiny of Our America at the end of the 19th century when it already had swallowed up half of Mexican territory, consolidated its monopoly capitalism, and embarked on its first imperialist adventures. These are the major western realities that affect the vast, complex, and still unfolding process of independence and attendant ideas in Our America.

Our independence, which has yet to be studied in depth, can be understood in three stages, with three respective ways of relating to the western world: the Haitian Revolution, between the end of the 18th and beginning of the 19th centuries; the actual separation of the Iberian colonies beginning in 1810; and Cuba's War of independence at the end of the 19th century. [...]

The Haitian Revolution, often forgotten as the beginning of Our America's independence, occurred under unique and extraordinary circumstances, which recurred, *mutatis mutandi*, in other American regions and colonized areas of the world. Let us recall that it was a victorious slave revolution and that Toussaint L'Ouverture wielded the West's most advanced and generous ideas (i.e., the egalitarianism, anticolonialism and antislavery of the French Revolution at its height) against the oppressive troops of Napoleon (the representative and direct heir of the bourgeois revolution) who sought to reinstate colonialism and slavery. In Our America, then, the contradictions between the admirable ideals and the deplorable practices of the West become evident.

[...]

Napoleon also played an important role in the second stage of Our America's independence. With the Iberian peninsula occupied by his troops [...] the Iberoamerican colonies began to break off, either violently as in Spanish America or gradually as in Brazil. [...]

[...] The great wars of independence [...] inspired dazzling though utopian ideas in men like the Liberator Bolívar. He never realized his grand project of preserving the unity which Spanish America had as a colony and which would have facilitated modernization and capitalist development. [...] Bolívar had understood that it was "necessary for our nation to resist successfully the aggressive ambitions of Europe; the power necessary to oppose the European colossus can only be attained by our own colossal union as Meridional America." Bolívar's project, based on unity and development, was also a call for American originality and autochthony, which did not ignore western values but refused to reproduce them. In 1815 Bolívar forcefully drew attention to our peculiarities: "We are a small human species ... neither Indian nor European, halfway between the legitimate owners of the country and the Spanish usurpers." And in 1819:

> Let's keep in mind that our people are neither European nor North American, more a composite of Africa and America than an outgrowth of Europe, for even Spain ceases to be European by its African bloodline, its institutions, its character. It is impossible to determine properly what human family we belong to. Most Indians have been annihilated; the European has mixed with Indians and Africans. Born in the same womb of foreign fathers differing by blood and origin, we also differ according to skin color. This difference has repercussions of transcendental proportions.
>
> [...]

On the Road to our Second Independence

[...] José Martí, commenting in 1889 on the First Panamerican Congress in Washington, wrote: "Spanish America was able to shake off Spanish tyranny; ... it must now be said, because it is true, that the time has arrived for Spanish America to declare its second independence." Martí had understood quite cleary the means by which "a nation of different interests, composition and awesome problems" tried to "wreak its system of colonization on free peoples." [...]

In good measure, to speak of Latin America from that period on, is to speak of our relationship with the United States. This nation, the first American nation to proclaim, in 1776, independence and to achieve a great anticolonial revolution, was, scarcely a century later, the new master of the other America. Having lived in the United States since 1880 and foreseen the imminent imperialist aggression, Martí wrote, in a letter to his friend Manual Mercado, on the eve of his death in battle (May 18, 1895) that his mission had been and would always be

> to prevent, with Cuba's independence, the expansion of the United States throughout the Antilles, swallowing up our American lands … to prevent the annexation of Our America, which we defend tooth and nail, to the ruthless and brutal North that disdains us… . I have lived in that monster and I am familiar with its entrails: but I've inherited David's slingshot.
>
> […]

In 1877, in Guatemala, Martí theorizes for the first time his conception of "Our America," which terms he coined. He explains that

> The conquest interrupted the natural and majestic evolution of American civilization, and with the coming of the Spaniards a strange society came into being. It wasn't Spanish because the new blood rejected the old bodies; it wasn't Indian because of the superimposition of a devastating civilization, two words which, in antagonism, constitute a process. A new people, *mestizo* in form, was created.
>
> […]

[…] During the first quarter of the 20th century, it was a bourgeois nationalist ideologue, Uruguayan José Enrique Rodó, who drew the widest audience in Our America. In response to Yankee intervention in Cuba's independence war of 1898 (feared by Martí, and seen by Lenin as the beginning of modern imperialism), Rodó published *Ariel* (1900), an essay in which he opposed the supposed spirituality of our countries to the crudest aspects of North American society. Wittingly or not, his was a censure of the greater development of the western world (North American capitalism, in particular). He also recommended that Latin America cultivate cultural forms proper to the capitalist countries of western Europe, which seemed less aggressive to him. (This criterion, of course, could not be shared by other colonized or semicolonized regions such as India, Indochina, the Arab world or black Africa.)

Rodó's ideas appealed to a diversity of social sectors in Our America: from true bourgeois nationalists with inevitable anti-imperialist sentiments, to those sectors which, momentarily subscribing to Rodoism, evolved toward socialism from an anti-imperialist position. It is worth comparing this new view of our relation with the West (Europe yes, United States no) to that held by the majority of liberal Latin American intellectuals throughout the 19th century: United States yes (they are, after all, part of America); down with Europe, which implied metropolitan domination or the most aggressive capitalism, both actualized in repeated invasions of and threats to Our America. We should also compare it with Martí's astute, realistic appraisal of the situation: "until we are strong enough to defend ourselves, our only salvation and guarantee of independence is that rival powers neutralize each other." This equilibrium ended shortly, as regards Our America, with the Yankee invasion of Cuba in 1898; as regards the whole world, it ended with WWI.

When WWI breaks out, democratization is already evident in Our America. The Mexican Revolution, which began in 1910 with the eventually defeated revolutionary democratic struggles of the likes of Ricardo Flores Magón and Emiliano Zapata, did, nevertheless, consolidate a national bourgeoisie sympathetic, unlike the 19th century bourgeoisie, to the distinctive traits of the popular classes. Our relationship with the West again becomes the topic of heated polemics. In his defiantly utopian writings, e.g., *The Cosmic Race: The Mission of the Iberoamerican Race* (1925) and *Indology: An Interpretation of Iberoamerican Culture* (1927), José Vasconcelos privileges the fusion of races in Our America over the brutal racism of the "civilizers." Yet, while he has the merit of extending his ideas to the entire continent (which explains their wide reception at the time), he nevertheless translates class struggle into an ontological unity which became the foundation for modern bourgeois thought in Mexico.

[…]

The idea that the true Latin Americans "are not European," that is, westerners, had already been maintained in this 20th century by spokespersons for such obviously nonwestern American communities as the descendants of Indians and Africans. The large indigenous enclaves of Our America ("national minorities" which in some countries are the real majority) did not need to argue this obvious point. They survived what Martí called a "devastating civilization," to become living proof of the barbaric intrusion of *another* civilization into theirs.

[…] In the 20th century, however, black Americans would no longer argue for their capacity to assimilate to western culture; they rejected it, on the contrary, as bearers of another culture, representatives of a different world. T. Albert Marrishow, another Anglo Antillean, anticipated Spengler's idea of the "decline of the West" in *Cycles of Civilization* (1917), with the added prediction, however, that the next cycle would be dominantly African. The most profound and the first of these Antillean intellectuals to attain universal recognition, Jamaican Marcus Garvey, rallied all blacks to return to Africa.

[…]

Blacks and Indians, far from extraneous nonwestern elements, are full fledged members of Our America, more so than the Europeanizing, disaffectionate "civilizers."

[…]

[…] Only a postwestern perspective which analyzes the problems of Latin America in a *worldwide* context can do justice to our reality.

Such a perspective has made it possible, even for those thinkers who assume it only partially, to discover our intellectual dependency concomitant with other dependences, and the subsidiary character of many of our ideas [remains]. This brings out our family resemblances to other colonized and semicolonized regions.

[…]

The impact of the Cuban Revolution, the most influential event in the history of Our America since independence, was decisive in the intellectual evolution and enrichment of these intellectuals.

[...]

[...] "We are a small human species," wrote Bolívar in 1815. But José Martí, the man whose thought best captured the difference of our reality, also wrote: "Native country is also humanity." He observed that beyond his times "of transformation," "a new universe, prepared by workers, is coming upon us." With the Cuban Revolution, Our America has taken its first steps in this new universe where "West" and "East" will turn out to be the most ancient cardinal points in the planetary (and now interplanetary) adventure of the total human subject.

29

Strategies of Modernity in Latin America

Andrea Giunta*

In this essay, Argentine art historian, critic, and curator Andrea Giunta, gives us an overview of Latin American modern art as strategies of encounter with the West. She recalls that from the first "encounter of two worlds" in the late fifteenth century to the modern era, European narratives had distorted Latin American reality and defined it as a cultural "other" to Europe. In opposition to the tendency to view Latin American modernists as "epigonal" imitators of European movements, Giunta shows how Latin American artists challenged Eurocentric assumptions underlying Western modernism.

She describes three distinct strategies – "swallowing," "inversion," and "re-appropriation" – associated with three episodes in the development of Latin American avant-gardes: Brazilian Oswald de Andrade's "Anthropophagite [Cannibalist] Manifesto" and the painting that inspired it, Tarsila do Amaral's *Abaporú*, both from 1928, which called for "swallowing" or cannibalizing the dominant discourse; Uruguayan Joaquín Torres-García's foundation of the School of the South in 1943 and his iconic *Inverted Map* (1935), which tactically reversed established hierarchies of Euro-US over Latin American art; and Cuban Wifredo Lam's painting, *The Jungle* (1943), which turned Western modernism's myth of originality inside out by a re-appropriation of primitivist appropriation. Oswald De Andrade's "Cannibalist Manifesto" (1928) and excerpts from Torres-García's essays, "The School of the South" (1935) and "The New Art of America" (1942), are

* Andrea Giunta (1995) "Strategies of Modernity in Latin America." In Gerardo Mosquera (ed.) *Beyond the Fantastic: Contemporary Art Criticism from Latin America* (pp. 53–66). London, England: The Institute of International Visual Arts.

Modern Art in Africa, Asia, and Latin America: An Introduction to Global Modernisms, First Edition.
Edited by Elaine O'Brien, Everlyn Nicodemus, Melissa Chiu, Benjamin Genocchio, Mary K. Coffey, and Roberto Tejada.

included in this volume. Wifredo Lam's Cuban modernism is discussed by Gerardo Mosquera in selections here from his essay, "Africa in the Art of Latin America"; and Mari Carmen Ramírez presents Torres-García's Universal Constructivism in "Vital Structures: The Constructive Nexus in South America."

The Brazilians, Giunta argues, rejected the avant-garde desire to erase the past and start from a blank page. Instead, they embraced their complex history, especially the violent experience of colonization, and its hybrid racial, social, and cultural legacies. Brazilian artists eschewed the search for something essential or authentic that preceded contemporary civilization, what in the European avant-gardes was often configured as a return to the innocence of childhood or to the nobility of the uncultured "savage." They celebrated cultural pollution and the messy hybridity of contemporary Brazilian reality: the mixing of European, African, and indigenous cultures; the coexistence of high (opera) and low (samba) art; Brazilians' simultaneous participation in Catholic catechism and carnival. Through tactics of bricolage, quotation, and assimilation, they willfully embraced their status as "bad savages" and cannibalized European modernism for their own ends.

Uruguayan Torres-García, on the other hand, pursued a universal expression founded upon the principles of concrete art (abstract work that rejects art's mimetic function by reducing expression to geometric principles and asserting the autonomy of color, line, and form from any descriptive role). Torres-García participated in the development of geometric abstraction during a 43-year sojourn in Europe. However, upon his transformative return to his native homeland, he discovered the unifying principles of structure, geometry, and abstract form in an American continental source, ancient Incan visual culture. Thus, rather than assert European avant-gardists Piet Mondrian or Le Corbusier as the originators of geometric abstraction, he argued that the principle of abstraction was universal, and that it emanated from the ancient past. His work foregrounded the American contributions to this universal impulse by drawing upon Incan iconography, design, and cosmology. In this way he repeated the strategy of his *Inverted Map*, refusing the North as his point of reference and taking his bearings, instead, from his location in South America.

Finally, Cuban artist Wifredo Lam exposed the relationship between artistic "primitivism" and European colonialism. By re-appropriating the "primitivized" forms of African culture in his art, he exposed the extent to which these aesthetic sources had been appropriated and decontextualized by Cubists and treated as universal signifiers of the irrational in Surrealist painting. In *The Jungle*, Lam retains the power of Afro-Cuban culture by integrating an iconography steeped in the secret rites of Santeria into the flattened composition and biomorphic forms associated with avant-garde painting. Like his European peers who appropriated "primitive" forms into their paintings, Lam sought to critique the prevailing values of Western culture. However, unlike his peers, Lam was a postcolonial subject of Congolese (and Chinese) descent and an initiate in the secret rites of Santeria. Therefore, according to Giunta, his strategic re-appropriation of African forms represents the radical assertion of Afro-Cuban identity against the European culture associated with both Christian colonization and artistic "primitivism."

In each case, Latin American artists worked with and against European modernism from their self-conscious position as its peripheral "other." Giunta's parable likewise partakes in the deconstructive strategies she surveys. For she notes that if the "deforming" encounter with the Americas was essential to the development of European modernity, we should not be surprised to find that a strategic deformation of European modernism has been essential to the construction of modern Latin American art and identity.

Giunta's paradigm of Latin American modern art is a useful way to map global modernisms overall. It is instructive to compare the strategies of Andrade, Torres-García, and Lam – "swallowing," "inversion," and "re-appropriation" – with the methods of engagement with Eurocentric modernity practiced by African and Asian modernists in this book. Négritude, for example, as defined by Aimé Césaire in the selection included here from *Discourse on Colonialism* (1955), and the syncretic vision Rabindranath Tagore presents in "Art and Tradition" (1926), are comparable strategies of modernity.

Further Readings

Amaral, Aracy (2009) *Tarsila do Amaral*. Madrid, Spain: Fundación Juan March.

Fletcher, Valerie (1992) *Crosscurrents of Modernism: Four Latin American Pioneers*. Washington, DC: Smithsonian Institution.

Ramírez, Mari Carmen (1992) *El Taller Torres-García: The School of the South and Its Legacy*. Austin: University of Texas Press.

Sims, Lowery Stokes (2002) *Wifredo Lam and the International Avant-Garde, 1923–1982*. Austin: University of Texas Press.

'It starts with a story, almost a parable.' (Mário de Andrade)

Around 1570 the *curacas* (chiefs of the 'ayllu' or Indian community) of Huamanga – a region in the heart of the old Inca Empire – surprisingly joined forces with other Andean chiefs to offer Philip II of Spain an enormous bribe to end the *encomienda* system.[1] Their offer was 100,000 ducados more than that of any of the Spanish *encomenderos* interested in maintaining the system.

This bribe was not the last strategy of the *curacas* during the first stage of the Conquest. Once the Inca Empire was dissolved in 1532 those communities freed from oppression chose to ally themselves with the Spanish in a series of negotiations between *encomenderos* and *curacas*. These negotiations show the Indians' capacity for developing strategies when faced with the devastating power of the Conquest, and their ability to adapt them as new situations arose. With the discovery of gold and silver in Atunsulla (1560) and mercury in Huancavelica (1563), Huamanga became an important mineral region, crucial to the colonial economy. Indians, either individually or collectively, found ways of making the most of new economic developments. They even proved to be aggressive entrepreneurs, sending representatives to open mines in the gold *sierras* abandoned by the Incas. But it was precisely mining and the devastating effect of the *mita*[2] that underlined the irreconcilable interests on which these initial agreements were based. *Curacas* refused to work in the mines and hostility increased. The final strategy was force. Huamanga burned in the epoch-making revolt of Taqui-Ongo.[3]

Them and Us

The 'encounter of two worlds' was marked by certain characteristics. In its first version the image of the New World was defined by its difference from the Old. The European *logos* was forced to stretch itself to cope with a new and diverse reality, which, not fitting the patterns, was inevitably distorted in this process. This was a conflict that affected, above all, language. In response to this, Alejo Carpentier [Alejo Carpentier (1904–80) was a leading Cuban literary figure. His historical novel, *EI Siglo de las Luces* (English title, *Explosion in a Cathedral*) explores the impact of modern European history on the Caribbean.] was to propose the use of localisms, even of exoticisms, as an answer to his question: 'Are we to suffer the anguish of Hernán Cortés when he complained to Charles V of not being able to describe certain great things in America "because I do not know the words by which they are known"?' The dispute between a reality and a language that tried to describe it is revealed in a graphic and eloquent manner by Carpentier in *El siglo de las luces*:

> Esteban was astonished as he realized how, in these islands, language had been forced to use agglutination, verbal amalgamation and metaphor to translate the formal ambiguity of things in which various essences were involved. Just as many trees were called 'acacia-bracelets', 'pineapple-porcelain', 'wood-rib', 'broom-ten', 'cousin-clover', 'pine-kernel-jug', 'tisane-cloud', 'branch-iguana', many marine creatures were given names that by trying to fix an image, created verbal errors, giving origin to a fantastic zoology of dog-fish, bull-fish, tiger-fish, snorers, blowers, flyers, red-coloured, striped, tattooed, tawnys...

Columbus arrived in America with a clear image of what he was going to find. Pierre d'Ailly's *Imago Mundi*, Pliny's *Historia Natural* (in its 1489 Italian version), Aeneas Sylvius's *Historiae Rerum Ubique Gestarunt*, and Marco Polo's *Voyages* (1485), were the sources from which he could select the images that would shape his perception of foreign worlds. Columbus did not discover, he verified and identified, mutilated and reduced. He started a long tradition of interpreting the reality of America through the reality of Europe, ignoring indigenous perceptions of it. Our image was made through a deforming mirror reflection. Our cultural development has been marked by being defined in terms of the 'other'.

Modernity is another great organizational discourse with symbolic and interpretative value (after the Conquest and along with nationality), and continues this tradition of 'relative to ...' definitions. Our most typical means of operation has been transgression of central discourse to communicate with a different reality.

Tactics and Strategies

The *curacas* of Huamanga demonstrated that they were not lacking in understanding. The intention and the fact of bribing are significant in many ways. First they prove that, faced with the appalling conditions created by the Conquest, the *curacas* could develop an economic strategy. It also shows that Indians – contrary to what one may tend to believe – understood the working of a monetary economy, even to the point of accumulating cash reserves. Finally, we can see that when the original alliances stopped working, they were able to change them. The *curacas* of Huamanga proved to be excellent strategists.

To speak of cultural strategies implies a conflict with something diverse and opposed. To develop a strategy it is essential to have previous knowledge of a situation in order to attack it through several tactics. It also implies finding weak spots that suggest ways to subvert an established order. Alternatively, it can be undermined through alliances, counter-discourses, value inversions, appropriations, mixtures, hybridizations, and even the practice of a certain clandestinity, creating a history of schemes and wit. One can borrow in order to develop one's own version, turn it upside down, deform, and selectively and intentionally assimilate.

Modernity in Latin America was a misappropriated and modified project. An educated and travelling intelligentsia built up alliances between a project born in the context of nascent capitalism in the nineteenth century and a discordant periphery. However, they soon realized the contradiction in singing the praises of technology and the machine age in countries where there were few cars (and those were imported) or roads on which to experience the heady excitement of speed.

Borges, Mariátegui and Vallejo all suggested an initial inversion of values. They coincided in criticizing the ideology of novelty. Peripheral strategies relativize the absolute truths of dominant discourse (be they of unlimited progress or 'the end of history'). By deconstructing this discourse they can find the relevant parts and rebuild it in relation to a diverse object. Latin American culture has worked in this way since it first gained independence. To formulate strategies and tactics requires an intelligent use of arms and tools, in this case cultural.

The Strategy of Swallowing

Few images are as successful as that of swallowing: eating the white man, devouring and digesting him. That which will nourish is selected and the negative parts are discarded. The swallowing metaphor was radically developed by the Brazilian avant-garde. Marked as an inaugural fact, it was also felt to be the start of a history that even required a new date-system, a chronological mark to vindicate the value of anthropophagy. [See Oswald de Andrade, "Cannibalist Manifesto" (1928), this volume.]

The revolt against the past born of the ideology of the new – an uprising marked in Latin America by Futurist discourse and by its iconoclastic choice, which was simultaneously foundational – was mixed with other elements from the very outset. Inaugural utopia arose in Brazil with a local rhythm that sought to establish differences from the beginning. The cult of the machine had a coffee aroma. In 'Atelier', Oswald de Andrade 'tropicalizes' the urban scenery from the tropicalized image of a Tarsila do Amaral, 'Caipirinha vestida por Poiret':

> Fords
> Viaducts
> Coffee aroma
> In a framed silence.[4]

From Amazonia to the big city, Macunaíma's migratory journey also superimposes scenes. Mário de Andrade also questions the belligerences of language that are now disputes translated into a *bricolage* of discourses, quotations and metanarratives.[5] It is a conflict that leaves Macunaíma for a week 'unable to eat, play or sleep just because he wanted to know the languages of the land.'[6]

São Paulo had a transformational impact that found montage to be the only way not to impoverish its description:

> … A new scale … A new form of industry, of aviation. Pylons. Petrol stations. Rails. Laboratories and technical workshops. Voices and clicking cables, and airwaves and flashing lights.[7]

It was a landscape ripe for Futurism that, in opposition to the substitutional break with the past beloved of the Italian movement, would propose a new image charged with localisms. It would vindicate invention and surprise from a culture that already existed 'in fact'; a complex reality, superimposed and impossible to abandon.

> The shacks of saffron and ochre among the greens of the hillside favelas, under cabraline blue, are aesthetic facts. The Carnival in Rio is the religious outpouring of our race. Pau-Brazil. Wagner yields to the samba school of Botafogo. Barbaric, but ours …
>
> The learned side. Fate of the first white colonizer, the political master of the virgin jungle. The graduate. We can't stop being learned. Doctors. Country of anonymous pain, anonymous doctors. The Empire was like that. We are all erudite …
>
> Language free of archaisms, free of erudition. Natural and neological. The millionfold contribution of error. How we speak. How we are.[8]

The battle for the new, which in the 1922 Week of Modern Art still lacked a distinctive visual aesthetic, would vindicate the option of also starting from what is given. From this reality Pau-Brazil inverted values and launched its export plan for a culture that assimilates all it can in a new creation:

> One lone battle – the battle for the way forward. Let us distinguish: imported poetry. And Pau-Brazil Poetry, for export.[9]

Markets, letters, industrial and telegraph towers, hillsides, fruits, cubes, are all filtered through an aesthetic that mixes Art Deco with Légeresque Cubism; Tarsila do Amaral's landscapes define the new in terms of the different. Nature is hot, rationalized, anthropomorphic and anthropophagite. In *Abaporu* the whole painting is filled with a man, naked, whose giant size is greater than nature. The anamorphic body extracts its meaning from the land on which it rests. The man-eating man is, for Oswald de Andrade, the Brazilian devourer of cultures, the creator of an existent culture that refounds, through each appropriation, its own culture:

> Tupy, or not Tupy, that is the question.
>
> Down with all catechisms. And down with the mother of Gracchi.
>
> The only things that interest me are those that are not mine. The laws of men.
>
> The laws of the anthropophagite … Justice became a code of vengeance and
>
> Science was transformed into magic. Anthropophagy. The permanent transformation of taboo into totem.[10]

The *Pau-Brazil Manifesto* (1924) and *Anthropophagite Manifesto* (1928) proposed the revaluation of (primitive) elements of nationality. Through a radical inversion of values, they searched for a new synthesis. Haroldo de Campos defined the anthropophagy of Pau-Brazil as: '… the theory of a critical swallowing of a universal cultural legacy, developed not from the passive and acceptable perspective of the "noble savage" … but rather from the uncompromising viewpoint of the "bad savage", the one that eats white men, the cannibal … Any past that is for us "other" should be ignored. In other words, it should be eaten and devoured. With this clarification: the cannibal is a "polemicist" (from the Greek *polemos*: fight, combat), but also an "anthologist": he only eats those enemies he considers to be brave, to eat their protein and marrow, to gain strength and renew their natural strengths.'[11]

The Inverted Map

In 1935 Joaquín Torres-García launched his text-manifesto *La Escuela del Sur* ('The School of the South'). Forceful and didactic, Torres translated into images what he may have thought as he saw the port of Montevideo from the ship in which he returned after forty-three years of absence, on 30 April 1934:

> Montevideo is unique. It has a character so peculiarly its own that it is unmistakable. It is apparent when you see the Cerro; and then its port; and it is perfectly fulfilled in the plazas, Independencia and Martriz. [See Torres-García, "The School of the South" (1935) this volume.]

With the foundation, with Michel Seuphor, of *Cercle et Carré* (1930), Torres-García had been a protagonist of the avant-garde in Europe. The development of his production connected successively to Mediterranean Classicism, Vibracionismo, Cubism, Fauvism; and the incorporation in his final Paris visit of the Golden Section and of a formal repertoire linked to pre-Columbian cultures had become by 1934 the form of a programme that Torres would redefine on arriving in Montevideo. The journey was a break for him. It is significant that *Historia de mi vida* (the autobiography that Torres narrates in the third person, from outside, as though it were about another person) ends precisely with his arrival in Uruguay, where he started a task of, first of all, recognition:

> The steamship enters into the port, looks for a place and ... over there a group of people. Torres-García has very fine eyesight and can already recognize them ... He is among his own! Now he recognizes it well! He breathes. Then he recognizes the houses and the paving stones, with little pieces of grass between them! That's them, the same ones! And for the rest about Torres-García, someone else will tell.[12]

What Torres did not find in the artistic field that he entered on his return he searched for in houses, colours, the air, the great River Plate, the special and different appearance of people (a type based simultaneously on the European, the Indian *mestizo* or the negro). It was a different city in which Torres denied precisely the distinguishing features of modernity visible in the new neighbourhoods, in as much as these traces of modernity were not his own ones. At this point Torres started to use his characteristic method of searching for a synthesis in opposed elements: dynamic syntheses that, in their contradictions, demonstrate the complex mixtures of a culture for which he wants to define a programme that is both sacrificial and integral.

Torres's concern is not with written or spoken language but with forms. His gesture takes on a graphic and visual form. To invert the map is a decontextualizing and resemanticizing operation. Once again it is the inaugural gesture of wanting to establish new parameters, which are now spatial:

> ... *Our north is the South*. There should be no north for us, except in opposition to our South.
>
> That is why we now turn the map upside down, and now we know what our true position is, and it is not the way the rest of the world would like to have it. From now on, the elongated tip of South America will point insistently at the South, our North. Our compass as well; it will incline irremediably and forever towards the South, towards our pole. When ships sail from here traveling north, they will be *travelling down, not up* as before. Because the North is now below. And as we face our South, the East is to our left.
>
> This is a necessary rectification; so that now we know where we are. [See Torres-García "The School of the South" (1935), this volume.]

The act of inversion implies a fundamentally ideological replacing; it marks a new stage, aiming for independence, for Latin American art. Torres's aesthetic programme, formed in a European context and led on by the interest in the exotic that fed the avant-garde of the central countries, would acquire a new dimension from its confrontation with a diverse reality in which currents of Latin Americanist thought circulated intensely.

Neither Mondrian nor all the theories on geometry and abstraction born in the European context can explain Torres's development in Montevideo. This development is not visible from a reading that interprets him as an epigonal figure. What is more, it was only in Montevideo that Torres could realize his original project. Thus these are the developments that follow a full understanding of his earlier itinerary in Europe and the USA.

While it is true that Torres always expressed his rejection of aestheticism, it was in the country to which he returned that his proposals to integrate art with life from the perspective of a retroactive utopia were received and accepted. It was also in Montevideo that Torres developed the corpus of his theories; it was there that he would launch a monumental didactic programme; and there, finally, that he would give form to his aspirations to create an anonymous, popular, monumental, metaphysical and ritual art.

Torres's intention was foundational. Thus he added a strategy of vacuum to the significant gesture of inverting the map. Considering Uruguay to be lacking in a strong local tradition, he proposed to use the universal tradition of art as a starting point, a constructive tradition to which the 'continental Inca civilization' also belonged:

> ... [for] we *rioplatenses*,[13] as regards *local tradition*, or one of our own, [it] is so short as not to warrant discussion. Habits and customs, folklore ... should be forgotten before they are remembered ...
>
> This is true as regards our immediate tradition because, on the other hand, can we not rely on the *civilization of our Continent?*
>
> ... if the ancient culture of this land can still be valid for us, it is because it is in line with the universal principles. For this reason, these cultures can incorporate themselves into the great tradition of knowledge of all ages.[14]

To not take a line or motif of Inca art, but instead to create with the ruler, with geometric order. The extreme austerity characteristic of Torres's work in the years following his return can be understood as the most radical expression of an art that, overcoming all temptation (pictorial, vanguard, realist), allows him to create an anonymous and monumental art. The abandoning of all sensual elements would become the pictorial expression of that stony and monumental art that was his ultimate aspiration.

Torres's utopia, simultaneously retrospective and foundational, synthesized the most extreme aspirations of European modernity. With his return journey to

Montevideo his original ideas would be submitted to a series of inversions that would allow him to reformulate his project and make America the measure of the Universe.

Appropriation of Appropriation

When Wifredo Lam created *The Jungle* (1942–3) in Cuba he repeated an act that the European avant-garde had done previously and which he now charged with a subversive content. Lam took the forms and structures of Cubism, which had itself appropriated the forms and structures of primitive art, in a movement that he himself described as intentional:

> Since my stay in Paris I had a fixed idea: to take African art and to make it operate in its own world, in Cuba. I needed to express in a work combative energy, the protest of my ancestors.[15]

However, rather than repeating a form of operation, Lam wanted a rebellion based on a vindication of cultural mixture. This mix has much more to do with his own pictorial formation than with ethnicity. His development also allows one to reconstruct a double itinerary: the consolidation process of the Latin American artistic field and that of the European avant-gardes.

On Lam's biographical 'journey' he stopped over at the best ports offered by Western culture at the time. From Cuba, Lam constructed his first imaginary map of Europe: Paris, the Louvre, Catalonia, Chardin, Anglada Camarasa.[16] He started his academic formation in San Alejandro, Havana, and completed it in the Prado with Fernando Alvarez de Sotomayor: José Ribera, Pedro Berruguete, Diego Velázquez, Goya, Zubarán, knowing Klee and Brancusi (which would take on another dimension when he met Picasso in Paris). This journey was also the confrontation of the magical world of his birth town (Sagua la Grande) with Spain's religious world.[17] And it gave him experience of an event that cut across the intellectual world of the 1930s: the Spanish Civil War. Subsequently, Paris, Picasso, Leiris, Marseille's Surrealism with his images for Breton's *Fata Morgana*, then the return to Cuba with a new starting point.

European modernity's appropriation of 'primitive' formal structures as food for a self-centred discourse was imitated and disarticulated as an operative system in Lam's work after his return to Cuba. He made the mechanisms of the centre evident, repeated them and charged them with a new meaning. He fed from their usurped forms. He expressed his 'otherness' in the central discourse so as to insert it, alive, into the universalizing discourses of modernity. Thus it was discovered that what, in European discourse, was a horizon of desires or the object of a laboratory experiment, in the Caribbean was the latent everyday, hidden and suppressed since the Conquest and slavery.

Lam, in common with other Latin American intellectuals, managed to establish an undoubtedly privileged position through his cultural travels. This was owing to his coexistence from childhood with America's cultural mix and because he also shared and participated in the European cultural and social laboratory. Lam did not observe the West from outside, he rather recognized himself and learnt. It is all this heritage that allowed him to undertake new researches upon his return. A knowledge of the decontextualizing operations of the European avant-gardes allowed him in turn to decontextualize the forms of the avant-garde to charge them with revolutionary and prophetic contents. And not only with the forms, but also with the utopian telos of modernity, allowing him to conceive his programme as the start of a different time. Lam repeated the pillaging gesture he had learnt, using whatever served his purpose of giving form to a different culture for which he had, through his journeys, developed a new vision that he now proposed as a recontextualizing programme.

> In *The Jungle*, the revenge of a small Caribbean country, Cuba, against the colonizers is plotted. I used the scissors as a symbol of a necessary cut against all foreign imposition in Cuba, against all colonization ... To paint *The Jungle*, I used to the maximum the lessons learned from a study of the classics ... I did my work like a ritual, based on experiences acquired in Spain and France.[18]

This inverted appropriation of the strategies of the centre by the periphery allowed Lam to refound Afro-Caribbean culture, along with Cubism and Surrealism. As Gerardo Mosquera has said: 'It is amazing how critics and art historians have not recognized Wifredo Lam as the first artist who presented a vision from the African in America in all the history of gallery visual arts.'[19]

Lam is a protagonist of the modern construction of Afro-American visuality. It is a construction in which, from the baroque aspects of Cubism, he discovered the sensual outlines of a nature that is simultaneously vegetable and religious. He wrote his own modern project taking advantage of the complex receptive constitution of European modernity and feeding it, in turn, with new components. Simultaneously, he interpreted his rereading as a cut: in America, culture is both summary and project; it gives new forms from difference.

To be Modern in America

The cultural responses artists made when faced with contexts that the transoceanic journey would necessarily redefine were, above all, visionary gazes towards the future. As an organizational discourse of experiences and expectations in which projective and reactive components germinated in a complex jumble of culture, modernity in the periphery was also an irritative, subversive and activist proposal. A response in which nationalism, cosmopolitanism, regionalism and internationalism coexisted and fought for hegemony. A proposal that was also articulated from research in existing lexicons and catalogues and which, when the conflict proposed by these doubts demanded a renunciation of all simulation, gave rise to a discourse that aimed at a rupture and subversion of the moral, spatial and temporal parameters in which it had initially moved.

This travelling backwards through the tracks of the conquistador towards a brief voluntary exile undertaken by a sector of the enlightened intelligentsia was fed by the fantasies provided by reading and fragmentary images and was also, for this reason, a voyage of self-discovery. A construction guided by diverse data, deposited in diverse times, and to which that which came from European political history (especially regarding wars and revolutions) was not alien and which, when faced with the reality of this land until the moment of the long-awaited journey, was inevitably modified. This was a modification that would also affect the vision of Latin America when it was time to come home.

The strategies used by Torres-García, Lam, Tarsila do Amaral or the Andrades to meditate on the cultural map of America were born of a kaleidoscopic game. Europe and America were reconfigured from shattered images, the fragments of which declared a battle to impose a new order.

Since the sixteenth century America had been an active element in the construction of European modernity: the 'encounter of two worlds' also forced a change in the conceptualization of the world. American modernity in turn absorbed differential characteristics that are not fully described by notions of copy, addition or epigonal development.

In the early twentieth century cultural proposals were born of strategies that implied, above all, an ideological inversion of values. To devour, mix, appropriate and reappropriate, invert, fragment and join, take central discourse, penetrate and cut through it until it becomes a useful tool for the search for and creation (plagued with achievements and failures) of our own subversive discourse: these are the exploratory ways in which some enlightened artists created their visual constructions as part of the programme of a liberational culture.

Notes

1 *Encomienda*: concession granted by the Spanish king for some Spanish colonists to receive tribute and labour from the Indians. The *encomendero* was supposed to look after the Indians financially and spiritually.

2 *Mita*: the system (originally of Indian origin) with which the Spanish controlled Indian labour. Indians were selected to work in the mines by drawing lots [translator's note].

3 *Taqui-Ongo*: name of the religious sect whose beliefs spread in the 1560s in the provinces of Central Peru as a way of confronting Christianity. [...]

4 Quoted by J. Schwartz, *Las vanguardias latino-americanas. Textos programáticosy criticos* (Madrid: Cátedra, 1991), p. 43.

5 See Raúl Antelo (ed), *Macunaíma o herói sem nenhum caráter* (Brasilia: edn Critica CNPq, 1988), pp. 255–65.

6 Mário de Andrade, *Maeunaíma o herói sem nenhum caráter, op. cit.*, p. 88.

7 Oswald de Andrade, 'Pau Brazil Poetry: Manifesto', in Dawn Ades, *Art in Latin America* (London: South Bank Centre, 1989), p. 310.

8 Ades, *op.cit.*

9 Ades, *op.cit.*

10 Oswald de Andrade, 'Anthropophagite Manifesto', in Dawn Ades, *op.cit.*, p. 312. [See Oswald de Andrade, "Cannibalist Manifest" (1928), this volume.]

11 Haroldo de Campos, 'Da razão antropofágica: diálogo e diferença na cultura brasileira', Boletim Bibliográfico Biblioteca Mário de Andrade 44

(January–December 1983), p. 107. Quoted by J. Schwartz, *op. cit.*, pp. 135–6.

12 Torres-García, *Historia de mi vidu* (Barcelona: Paidós), p. 234.

13 *Rioplatense*: literally 'of the River Plate', adjective used to characterize the shared culture of Buenos Aires and Montevideo [translator's note].

14 Torres-García, *Metafisica de la prehistoria indo-americana* (Montevideo. Asociación de Arte Constructivo, 1939). Original emphases.

15 In Antenio Nuhez Jimenez, *Wifredo Lam* (Havana: Editorial Letras Cubanas, 1982), p. 173.

16 *Ibid.*, p. 71.

17 *Ibid.*, p. 83.

18 *Ibid.*, pp. 173–5.

19 Gerardo Mosquera, 'Modernismo desde afroamérica: Wifredo Lam cambia el sentido', mimeograph, p. 6.

30

Revolution as Ritual

Diego Rivera's National Palace Mural

Leonard Folgarait*

In this essay, Leonard Folgarait, a US-based art historian, interprets Diego Rivera's epic mural chronicling Mexico's history in the central staircase of the National Palace in Mexico City, a massive colonial building that houses the offices of the president, as a ritual that the viewer performs. Folgarait argues that the viewer is at first ensconced in the action depicted along the base of the stairs. Here near life-size figures, seen at close range, engage in battle. However, when one completes the climb, he or she is offered a static view from a balcony removed from the action. This distanced vantage encourages *reading* through a flattened composition, copious display of text, and the depiction of figures seen from behind who model docile contemplation for the viewer.

For Folgarait these changes in the physical and thematic properties of the image enact a shift in the viewing subject from an active participant in history to a passive spectator of history as nationalist propaganda or "discourse" (political rhetoric, official history, legislation, etc.). He links this shift in the viewer's experience of the mural to the political shift in postrevolutionary Mexico in the late 1920s from strongman leaders, represented by Alvaro Obregon, to the "faceless" single party system orchestrated by Plutarco Elias Calles after Obregon's assassination. Noting that Rivera painted the central wall in 1929 at the beginning of Calles's rule-by-proxy (1929–34, a period known as the *Maximato*), Folgarait suggests that the compositional flatness, non-linear and synchronic presentation of figures and events, and collage-like use of text and the Mexican eagle symbol reflect the "political flatness" of an authoritarian state and the formation of a ruling party (the PNR) that cynically

* Leonard Folgarait (1991) "Revolution as Ritual: Diego Rivera's National Palace Mural." *Oxford Art Journal* 14(1): 18–33.

Modern Art in Africa, Asia, and Latin America: An Introduction to Global Modernisms, First Edition.
Edited by Elaine O'Brien, Everlyn Nicodemus, Melissa Chiu, Benjamin Genocchio,
Mary K. Coffey, and Roberto Tejada.

appealed to revolutionary nationalism to perpetuate its own power (Partido Nacional Revolucionario [National Revolutionary Party, or PNR], eventually the Partido Revolucionario Institucional [Institutional Revolutionary Party, or PRI], which governed Mexico for more than 70 years).

Folgarait, as a scholar who has also written about Picasso, is sensitive to Rivera's expert integration of Cubist visual techniques with the humanist figurative tradition initiated by Giotto. However, in his argument the hallmarks of formal modernism, such as flatness, simultaneity, or the anti-illusionistic use of collage and text, do not signal aesthetic progress, but rather the "domestication of figuration and its potential for describing action." What for other Marxist scholars like David Craven represent Rivera's "epic modernism," for Folgarait signal the repudiation of mural art's political mission (Craven 1997). Folgarait's interpretation also deviates from accounts of Mexican muralism that explore its artists' heroic allegiance to class politics and peasant movements (Rodríguez-Prampolini 1987; Hurlburt 1989; Rochfort 1993). He de-emphasizes Rivera's stated intentions and focuses instead on the image and its effects on the viewer.

Folgarait argues that Rivera was indeed a political propagandist, not of communism, as he famously asserted, but rather of the middle, bureaucratic, capitalist way promoted by the Calles regime. In this respect Rivera is no different than any master artist working for powerful patrons throughout history. Folgarait leaves it to the reader to determine why Rivera chose to represent the history of Mexico on the central wall in this way at this time. Was he capitulating to the Calles regime, and thereby functioning deliberately as a state propagandist? Or was he commenting critically on the regime's rhetoric and its conversion of revolutionary action into mere discourse?

References and Further Readings

Craven, David (1997) *Diego Rivera as Epic Modernist*. London, England: Prentice Hall International.

Hurlburt, Lawrence (1989) *The Mexican Painters in the United States*. Albuquerque: University of New Mexico Press.

Rochfort, Desmond (1993) *Mexican Muralists: Orozco, Rivera, Siqueiros*. San Francisco, CA: Chronical Books.

Rodríguez-Prampolini, Ida (1987) "Rivera's Concept of History." In Cynthia Newman Helms (ed.), *Diego Rivera: A Retrospective* (pp. 131–7). New York, NY: W. W. Norton.

The Mexican Revolution of 1910 was the event that projected its participants into the twentieth century. The very term *Revolución* was new on the minds and lips of those eager to transform their nation from a nineteenth-century dictatorship into a model of modern political and social organisation. [...] It was not clear until 1920, however, after a decade of bloody civil war between powerful generals, that the Revolution[1] had any chance for success or for the implementation of its principles. The 1920s marked the end of the military conflict and allowed for a consolidation of the Revolution under a stable government and social peace. The first presidents of this period encouraged and financed an educational and cultural programme, a strategy of propaganda directed at the urban and rural masses who were anxious to see how the new régime would serve their needs. In this context, the so-called Mexican mural movement started. Large surfaces of public walls were put to work bearing images of cultural and social progress.

Toward the end of the 1920s, the government began to re-programme its goals. It is within this context of a shift in the direction of the 'Revolutionary' state that I will examine a major mural project by Diego Rivera, the dominant Mexican painter of this time.

On July 18, 1928, President-elect Alvaro Obregón was assassinated by a Catholic fanatic. At the time of his death, Obregón was the most powerful and respected Mexican leader. Plutarco Elías Calles, president in 1924–8, thereupon became the Strong Man in Mexico, '*el jefe máximo de la revolución*' [the great chief of the Revolution], and for the next six years dominated three short-term puppet presidents.[2] That period is called '*el maximato*' in dubious honour to him.

Calles had already, during his own administration, redirected the course of state policy away from social reform based on satisfying workers' and peasants' demands for their share of the Revolutionary spoils and back toward a deliberately pro-capitalist development in favour of the presence of foreign capital in industry, and began a systematic co-optation of the masses.[3] In spite of this return to pre-Revolutionary statesmanship, the government still presented itself as authentically Revolutionary. The contradiction between behaviour and propaganda made it necessary for the scales to tip in favour of propaganda in order to legitimise policy.[4] At the very beginning of this period of ideological struggle, Rivera painted the history of Mexico for the régime on the walls of its central headquarters.[5]

In 1929,[6] Rivera began painting the vast walls in the large stairway of the National Palace in Mexico City, a massive structure that contained the offices of the President and the Cabinet, various government bureaucracies, and the Senate chambers.[7] The walls painted are the three that enclose this large stairway, leading from a central courtyard to the second floor.

In general (a detailed description follows below), the three walls present a comprehensive, panoramic history of Mexico. The right wall, *The Aztec World*,[8] starts a right-to-left visual narrative that continues with *From the Conquest to 1930* on the central wall (see Figure 1.6, this volume, p. 290), and concludes with *Mexico Today and Tomorrow* on the left wall. Dozens of historical portraits are included in scenes of pivotal importance from the Conquest, the colonial period, the Independence movement, the Revolution, and the present of the late 1920s and mid 1930s. Although there are some episodes of this history set in the deep spaces of the landscape, most of the scenes and figures are pressed up against the picture plane.

The viewer, on the walk up the stairs, encounters the mural first up-close to the walls, somewhat as a co-participant with the painted historical characters. Once on the second storey overlook, the now distant observer studies what she or he has just experienced, that having been an illusionistic immersion in the historical drama. The moment of this second-stage observation is therefore disinterested behaviour by definition, a stepping out of the flow of events in order to see, to assess, to control.

Something important has happened to the viewer in the course of this structured contact with the mural. The entire sequence of approach, arrival, participation, distancing and assessment makes for a total change in the quality of the experience, marking clear distinctions between its beginning and its ending. That the experience appears to be a ritual, a performance of some sort, will lead me into considerations of the mechanics of such, as well as to suggest its historically specific purposes and whose needs it was intended to satisfy.

A mural of such complexity as this needs a schematic description of the main events and persons it contains in advance of any analysis. What follows is not an exhaustive point-by-point inventory, but rather a focused selection of the most pertinent subjects.[9]

The subject of the mural is the history of Mexico, from its pre-Columbian times to an imagined future. Beginning with the right wall, the north wall, painted in 1929, also begins with the chronology of the subject of the mural. This is the world of the pre-Conquest, a panorama of cultural and social activities set in a volcanic landscape. The great light-skinned god, Quetzalcóatl (Feathered Serpent), appears in the upper centre holding an audience. To the right are examples of productive activities by farmers and artisans. To the left is a scene of the delivery of tribute, as bearers of subject tribes labour up the incline of a pyramid toward a costumed priest and warrior. Just behind the last bearer is a scene of dissent against the excesses of Aztec power, as a speaker before a small group gestures defiance toward the display of that power. Left of this scene is its narrative sequel, class warfare between the warriors of the régime and its slaves. In the distance, an erupting volcano propels the face of the Feathered Serpent out of its crater. This figure is seen again to the right as a stylised Aztec glyph, flying and bearing on its back its human form, Quetzalcóatl.

The central, west wall, painted in 1929–30, is so loaded with figures and events that it tends to flatten out at first into mere coloured patterning. Who the figures are and what they might mean seems, at first appearance, less important than that they simply occupy wall space without a particular order. To sort out this apparent confusion, I will follow the linear history as begun in and continued from the right wall.

The narrative on the central wall begins with the Conquest of 1521. At the lower right, Spanish soldiers load and fire muskets and a mortar. From that vantage point, all attention and energy are directed to the lower centre of the wall. Within this area, thirty-odd figures from both sides of the conflict tangle in close, hand-to-hand combat. Hernán Cortés is the major figure on horseback in the centre of the bottom level. He lifts a lance against a feather-costumed Indian standing before his horse. The immediate anticlimax to the Conquest, the colonial period, is shown in a narrow horizontal band running from above the firing soldiers on the right, continuing above the central battle scene (with the important exception of the area under the central arch occupied by a golden eagle), and continuing to the left on that same level to the bonfire. Next in historical order is the movement of Independence of 1810, when the Spanish colonial government was removed from power. This occurs under the central arch, above the eagle. The balding, white-haired priest is Hidalgo, great leader of the Independence, holding the broken chains of servitude.

Jumping in this historical progression to the far right arch, the Mexican-American war is represented, specifically the penetration of the US Army into Mexico City in 1847 and the armed resistance to it. In the next arch to the left, along the same horizontal line, one sees more episodes from the history of Independent Mexico. Presendent Benito Juárez holds up the 'CONSTITUTION' and 'LAWS OF REFORM' of 1857. Juárez is surrounded by important figures of the period. The historical narrative jumps next to the far left arch, which contains another moment of defense against foreign imperialism, this time French. In this case, the Mexicans are triumphant over Emperor Maximilian, shown in the far right with his split, spiral beard. He had been sent to Mexico in 1864 by Napoleon III and was executed in 1867 under orders of Juárez.

In the next arch to the right, figures from the Revolution of 1910 are depicted. Toward the left centre, in white plumed hat and moustache is Porfirio Díaz, dictator of Mexico from 1876–1910. It was against him and his policies that the Revolution was born. At the right centre, in formal clothes and presidential sash, is Francisco I. Madero, whose challenge removed Díaz and in turn elected him as first president of the Revolution. Madero is ringed by twenty or more figures representing every possible political position taken during the bloody years of 1910–17 and immediately after, some of these violently opposed to one another. Most important of the historical figures is Emiliano Zapata, at the top right with a large *sombrero*, radical agrarian leader of the South. Here also, to the far right centre, is Venustiano Carranza, president from 1916–20, the man who with his chief ideologue, Luis Cabrera, to the right, dominated the drafting of the Constitution of 1917. Carranza holds up the numbers of Articles of that document. And now a brief return to the central arch to point out Zapata again, at the top of the arch, behind the banner. The two grouped presidents to the left are, from the left, Obregón and Calles.

Finally, the eagle in the centre. The figure is copied from an Aztec stone carving.[10] As a symbol, it refers to a period before that pictured in the right wall, back to the very founding of the Aztec capital, Tenochtitlán, now Mexico City. As the Aztecs had migrated southward from unknown regions in search of a permanent home, they looked for an eagle perched on a cactus, holding a serpent in its mouth, as marking the site where they should settle, the place chosen by prophesy. Thus, this image of origins appears on the modern Mexican flag and has represented a nationalist ideology for over a century.[11] I shall return to remark on the reason for this particular version of the eagle holding not a serpent, but an Aztec war banner in its beak.[12]

The left, south wall, was painted in 1935. Its narrative quality is the same as that of the right wall, describing primarily one moment in history, rather than many scattered and mixed ones as does the central wall. The lower right contains scenes of intimidation and violence between armed and gasmasked defenders of the régime and their victims in both rural and urban settings. Directly above, a worker in overalls agitates a crowd, and Mexico City burns in class warfare in the distance. The central section at the bottom shows the teaching and reading of revolutionary texts, and continuing up the incline, various labourers in typical poses and actions. In the centre of the wall, Rivera divided the large space into distinct compartments and areas, creating a succession of staged actions. These include capitalists round a ticker tape machine; ex-President Calles flanked by evil advisors, one a general and the other a priest; and the rich and the Church in various conditions of decadence and debauchery. Above this piecemeal architecture of cells rises the dominant figure on this wall. Karl Marx holds a page from *The Communist Manifesto*, containing: 'THE HISTORY OF ALL HITHERTO EXISTING SOCIETY IS THE HISTORY OF CLASS STRUGGLE … IT IS NOT A MATTER OF REFORMING SOCIETY AS IT EXISTS, BUT RATHER OF FORMING A NEW ONE.' He addresses directly a trio of worker, soldier, and peasant and points to the left at a perfectly ordered society of the future, with rational cities and thriving agriculture, all in front of a rising sun.

With the National Palace mural, Rivera first tried his hand at narrative painting of a special sort. On three huge walls, meeting at two corners to extend one long, continuous surface of 275 square metres,[13] he set out to depict an entire national history. In none of his previous murals had the project been so simple and so complex at the same time.[14] The simplicity is that of having one story to tell on one large surface, the complexity is of pictorial organisation. In painting the history of Mexico, Rivera was behaving as a historian, faced with the same problems as that of a historian who writes, of how best to tell that history. […]

Rivera as the painter-historian encountered a problematic of a different order. Although the faces and events are painted one after another, in a specific order, the composition depends upon an instantaneity of vision as experienced by the viewer, the all-at-once, non-temporal quality of seeing the mural. Due to the crushing multitude of figures and their complex interaction, it registers at this level first as flat, generalised, coloured forms covering large wall surfaces, a sort of pluralism turned into a singularity, like the many words on a printed page becoming a unified visual field.

[…]

All of the examples of writing in the mural are about the imposition of order through legal systems. The words are sanctions and proof of power, of the sort to subject those in its legitimate because legal influence to follow its bidding. Thus, the events and people in the mural are not only the subjects of the painting, but are also subjects of (as subject to) the juridical power of the various texts.

It is in these terms that the details of the presentation of the central eagle can now be understood. The eagle on a cactus holding a serpent in its beak, as we know, is universally known in Mexico as its most explicit symbol of nationalism and of the myth of its origins. It is purely figurative in that it has no writing attached to it. The eagle in the mural perches on a cactus, but rather than a serpent, it holds Aztec war banners in its beak. This is important for several reasons. One is that any eagle on a cactus automatically begins a train of association leading to its identification as the founding, mythic, serpent eagle. This presumption is wrong here, and is corrected at the point of apprehending the banners rather than the expected serpent, but belongs to the first reading as an adjusted presumption. Another reason is that this war eagle *does* combine a form of 'writing' – the banners as graphic, coded information – with the figurative eagle, thereby doubly valent in its behaviour rather than singly as is its serpent-bearing counterpart.

[...] Whereas the serpent eagle is all action and drama, an end in itself in that its entire image is a message, this war eagle is but the standard bearer of a message, a means to an end. Rather than overpowering its prey, it is demoted to a mere illustration of the militant aggressions of the message. [...] The figure now serves the purposes of the juridical emblem and itself becomes flat, disembodied, and glyph-like. [...]

But why is the eagle in the centre of the composition? On the mural, the eagle escapes historical and spatial logic, yet has the ultimate power to occupy the centre of narrative and compositional gravity. All else revolves around it and yet does not take its notice. It is the unseen but always present determinant agent of their fate, a sort of empty fullness, an absent presence, and is the perfect device by which to anchor an at times drifting composition.

The eagle operates in the image field of the mural much as it does on the Mexican flag. The flag eagle is unrelated by any spatial logic to the white central panel it floats upon. It asserts the authority of the centre between the red and green panels to either side. The three-part (or panelled) National Palace mural is a huge flag, the breeze blowing it into an irregular contour, sometimes stiff and sharp-angled, at the bottom, elsewhere undulating in deep folds, producing scalloped edges, at the top. Because it is so full of events and faces, irregular on the middle wall as to narrative but formally unified by a flat, random logic, the wall surface becomes a smoothly unified visual field. Because the whole mural is lacking in deep or modulated space with but a few exceptions, relying mostly on simple and schematic overlapping, an even, planar sense of a screen is produced.

In its own absolute geometric abstraction, the flag contains and represents the same events and qualities of Mexican history as does the mural; they are both as full and as empty of meaning as each other. Another way of saying this is that such overbrimming fullness of history and meaning common to both mural and flag merges the contours of events and people into a generalised and unitary 'value' of their importance. Both mural and flag, as icons of nationalism, depend on the ultimate legitimising arbiter of meaning, the eagle marking the place of the myth of origins and of contemporary political power.

To press the point of the mural's 'smoothly unified visual field', by which I mean to connote a sense of 'flatness' to better fit the flag metaphor, I want to make more clear what I mean by the terms unified and flat.

I mean two things: the denial of deep space in most of the mural, but especially in the passages of the massing of faces, such as in the three central arches; and the evenness of attention across this sea of faces, an equality of presence which denies any single historical figure to stand out significantly from the others in these areas. The mural's exploitation of overlapping in the areas of most pronounced massing closes off any spatial development, as the figures are not so much in front or behind, but rather above, below, and beside each other, moving over the surface of the wall like a repeat in a wallpaper pattern. This second meaning depends upon a sense of *political* flatness, as these historical figures have political qualities over other kinds of qualities. That these two kinds of flatness matter in the painting is in the how of their becoming *one* kind; how an existing political condition in Mexico in the late 1920s could be best known and best told by this particular formal treatment. I want to stress now how the qualities of this mural painting and of politics at this time, qualities of flatness and discursivity, made for translations from one to the other possible, how the mural's formal characteristics found their 'best' subject, and how politics found its 'best' representation.

Mexico has always been the place where the Strong Man exerted the dominant political force, from pre-Conquest times to that of Calles.[15] And in their respective times, both Obregón and Calles ruled without qualification, the first in a highly personalised and visible manner, and the second with a hidden, behind-the-scenes approach. A great deal of Obregón's power came from an ability to humanise politics through charisma and face-to-face persuasiveness.[16] But with the death of Obregón, there appeared a curious condition in Mexico – it was, surprisingly and uncharacteristically, without a *caudillo*, or Strong Man, to mould the national political culture. […]

Beginning in mid-1928 and into the next handful of years, it was impossible for a frontline Strong Man to emerge. […] The success of Calles depended, to a large extent, upon projecting bland and unambitious men onto the front line of government. The resulting vacancy left by the departure of a Strong Man was filled by the crowded presence of undemanding and unrecognisable bureaucrats minding the Calles machine, the power concentrated in an institutionalised, rather than a personalised fashion. Calles spoke of the nation's need to 'pass, once and for all, from the historic condition of "the land of one man," to that "of institutions and laws … under a government institutional in nature"'.[17] Political 'flatness' serves well as a descriptive term for this condition, and 'abstraction' just as correctly for the quality of the centre of power supporting and organising it. Any representation of this condition would have to take account of these qualities, or as was claimed by a Calles backer at this time, 'the uniformity of the grand organism [the Calles machine]' would permit 'the uniformity of propaganda.'[18]

What Calles needed, and what he created and nurtured, was a crowd of generic politicians, effecting an evenness of presence and removing overtly personalised demands upon the system. And it was clear that a *system* should now take priority over personalistic leadership. The three presidents of the *maximato* were carefully chosen for their subservience to Calles.[19] […]

The formation of such a false-front political system began in late 1928, leading to Calles founding in 1929 the Partido Nacional Revolucionario (National Revolutionary Party), the PNR. It is no coincidence that the logo for the PNR was a circle banded vertically into three parts, coloured, in order from the left, red, white, and green, with the three initials PNR occupying one coloured band each. By taking the nation's flag as its logo, although freely changing its shape, the party assimilated the government and the ultimate sign of nationalism into its symbolic repertory of power.

An equivalence between these factors – the nation, the government, and the party – created yet another and complementary sort of political 'flatness' as I have been discussing, collapsing onto one plane and upon a single, ideologically homogeneous platform these previously distinct agents, now telescoped into an abstract, flat whole, efficient and absolute. [...]

What could remain constant in this fundamental shift in the behaviour of power was its spectacle, made up of the symbols of nationalism, especially the flag and the Constitution of 1917. In the face of such discontinuities of political practice, it was important to stress the continuity of the legitimacy of the nation's leaders by referring to static images of permanent values. Such changes in practice were masked in a remarkable manner by conflating Party leadership to populist nationalism and its symbols, even Calles to the flag itself: 'when one attacks General Calles, what is attacked is not his person but the flag of the Revolution; ... the very essence of our Revolutionary life.'[20] From 'person' to 'essence', from figure to discursive symbol. In this way, the flag came to legitimise the newly formed party by becoming its rubber stamp of propaganda, leaving its impression on the party logo and on the walls of the government's headquarters.

The ideological climate that made this representation of the government's new power structure not only possible, but necessary, was stated in the manifesto of the PNR, drafted in December of 1928, eight months before the mural was begun:

> Firmly convinced that now is the historic moment for the resurgence and formation of political parties of real principle and organizational strength, we address with great enthusiasm the nation's Revolutionaries, so that we may unite around our old flag, as we believe that if we succeed in organizing stable parties that will represent the distinct tendencies of the opinion of the nation, we will save the Republic from the anarchy created by purely personal ambitions and we will have established the bases for a new democracy.[21]

Terminology such as 'resurgence and formation', 'organisational strength', and 'represent the distinct tendencies', could be applied (and my argument is that they were) to the composition and content of the right and central walls of the mural (as the left wall was begun in 1935 under very different conditions, the demise of Calles for one) in ways that I have suggested. By representing all the political factions operative in Mexico in the late 1920s, post-Obregón, the mural images the words of the manifesto. As the PNR aimed to 'save the Republic from the anarchy created by purely personal ambitions', the central wall allows no single historical individual to assert dominance over another or over an entire group. Only the worker at the top of the central arch and the central eagle stand out as figures of authority and share an overscaled size. But as the eagle is not personalistic, neither is the worker, generically described to stand for an entire class, the proletariat, otherwise unrepresented in the central wall. His presence also satisfies the party's ambition at this time to be all-inclusive and '*no-clasista*'.[22]

And, of course, there is 'so that we may unite around our old flag'. The flag as metaphor for the anchor of organisational strategies of the PNR,[23] providing a united, or flat, field of support is confidently asserted here. [...] The emblematic display of the politically levelling power of the PNR since late 1928 found a smooth translation from manifesto to flag to Calles/PNR to party logo to painting, with all terms becoming one under the authority of a populist, nationalist Revolutionary ideology of abstract institutionalisation, managed by a 'government Party'.[24]

[...]

The three central arches of the large wall contain many written examples of the law of the land expressed in terms of liberty and equality. [...] The juridical system denies action on the part of the individuals-citizens, who in turn seem to exist for the purpose of representing a 'general will inside a "legal state",' rather than as agents of production or self-motivated political beings of any sort.

But there *are* agents of production in these sections, all along the bottom line of the three arches one sees, in order from the left: *campesinos* massed together, seen from the back, observing the historical figures as an audience to a mural painting would. Amidst general labour or armed readiness, some stop their activity to look at the massed portraits, at those who do nothing but merely 'are'. This difference between doing and 'being', between producing and posing, between audience and object, points to a fundamental division between producers and non-producers in a capitalist system.

[...]

It is clear that the peasants are gathered informally, almost casually pausing in their everyday routine, rather than organised and self-aware as a class. That we see them mostly from the back takes expression and will away from them. This also happens to viewers who 'assume' the place of the peasants by virtue of the automatic absorption of the viewer into figures facing the same direction and 'seeing' the same sights. Why then show this class at all if it plays such a diminished role? Well, perhaps because, according to Poulantzas:

> Popular sovereignty is identified with state sovereignty ... [and] the people are identified with the state only if they are *represented*.[25]

And if viewers become the peasants as I suggest, then they are also represented.

Let me get straight that what I am saying is that class differences are there in the mural, clearly pictured, in terms such as dress and activity, but that they are there in order to be *overcome* by the unifying force of the relationship under discussion.

Differences cannot be denied if they are not represented to begin with. As the PNR itself proclaimed at this time, the Party 'constitutes the site where radical, conservative, and moderate action can fit together,' and generally presented itself as non-ideological and all-inclusive.[26] Notice the strategy: naming the terms of difference before erasing the lines separating them.

All of which brings me back to the eagle, the symbol of the power of legality itself. For lack of a contemporary sign of such unifying power, the Calles years went to the ancient myth of origins, and to the legitimacy necessarily attached to it. It was not an unhappy coincidence that the Aztec stone monument bearing the image of the eagle copied by Rivera was found in the foundations of the National Palace. There was no other choice but the eagle, transformed from an agent of action to an emblem of the juridical levelling of differences, kept on its original site to retain its power.

Anthony Giddens claims that: 'it is around the intersection between discursive consciousness and "lived experience" that the ideological consequences of nationalism will cluster.'[27] I want to apply this insight to two of my previous observations. The first is about the behaviour of the viewer to the mural, in particular the difference between the 'participant' and 'observer' status as the viewer climbs first toward, then along the walls, arriving finally at the balcony overview. I mean to strike a parallel here between Giddens' 'intersection' and the one that occurs between the 'lived experience' of the viewer's first approach and the final 'discursive consciousness' of apprehending the mural from a static and uninvolved distance. That the viewer necessarily shifts from one behaviour to the other while consuming massive doses of visual nationalism speaks of a complementary purpose between the physical and thematic axes of the painting as it subjects its viewer into a special form of subjecthood.

The second point of application is to the figurative/discursive qualities of behaviour in the style itself, as there are those definite intersections between words and images. Again, that the mode of visual production can be thus described and that the subject depicted is a stressed form of nationalism, is no coincidence. These two points suggest that nationalism is a process in action in the workings of this mural. The 'cluster' dynamic in the mural works something like this: there are paired categories of behaviour on these walls, such as participant/observer and image/word, each member of a pair being other and discontinuous to its mate, but by virtue of being its mate, similar as being part of the same system. All of which suggests that I am talking about the mural in terms of nationalism according to Giddens, but also of nationalism-as-ritual.

Edmund Leach has written about ritual in precisely these terms. Rites of initiation, for instance, depend upon the discrete before and after states of the initiate, but also that by the nature of before eventually becoming after, these states are part of one continuum. Ritual is a way of both stating this bald paradox and then resolving it.[28]

I want to look at the central wall in these terms. We have seen that both side walls deal with distinct, dominant historical periods, the pre-Conquest on the right, and the present on the left. The central wall, however, includes scenes from all periods: before and through the Conquest; the colonial, Independence, Revolutionary, and present periods; and the perfected future. The two [side] walls, then, make up a system of differences in meaning (past vs. present) yet twins in function (in balancing the composition and the narrative). By definition the central wall is apparently not part of such a system and is not needed to produce the before–after ritual effect. But on the contrary, 'a boundary separates two zones of social space-time which are *normal, time bound, clear-cut,* ... but the spatial and temporal markers which actually serve as boundaries are themselves *abnormal, timeless, ambiguous, at the edge.*'[29]

The central wall, as slash mark and liminal space between discrete categories, explodes into huge dimensions to put this dynamic on explicit display. Yes, here all times *do* mix into a kind of timelessness, linear narrative ruptures its linked structure, the through-line of colonial history is broken by the central eagle, and nineteenth-century wars are thrown to opposite corners. In agreement with the blending of this one category, time, other sorts of blending are put on display. Classes lose their opposition, individuals are swallowed into groups, deep and shallow space coexist, and word and image are conjoined. To stress this synchronicity, the two great rituals of social change in Mexican history, the Conquest and the Revolution, share equal billing. All is levelled to a visual, historical, and conceptual flatness. This flatness controls the otherwise dangerous potentials for 'dimensionality' on the wall, the dimensionality of a real and fully formed present, of real class struggle and real social change, and reduces them to their formal role in the ritual process. 'The effect of ritual is to render continuous what is normally distinct. Within it, two opposed states become mutually accessible and the ideal order is expressed.'[30]

Let us remember that the blending of a Revolutionary past with a non-Revolutionary present was exactly the strategy upon which the entire success of the Calles 'ideal order' depended. And since this order was overtly capitalist, it is important to consider this blending of history as an example of 'the way in which capitalism constructs the past, in a massive totalization of human history ... as a moment of the present.'[31]

The central wall instructs the viewing of the entire mural in the semiotic terms developed above. The flattened 'dis'organisation of the central wall organises the whole system, another victory of discursivity over space and action and figuration. The one way in which this wall demonstrates linear narrative is in the central vertical axis leading upwards from the Conquest to the Worker, passing in order through the time of Independence, the Revolution, through the present and into the future. Whereas linear narrative is broken up on this wall across its undifferentiated expanse, it is joined and intact in the vertical axis, 'giving an ordered structure to what otherwise might have become *an overburdened form of representation.*'[32] It is important to remember that the bottom of this axis, the fighting of the Conquest, is the first section of the mural encountered by the viewer on the initial approach.

This vertical axis sets the major episodes and the sequence of the narrative for the rest of the mural at the 'beginning' of the viewer's path (another narrative), as a sort of table of contents, but at a cross direction to the general right-to-left horizontal sweep of the three walls. The instruction to shift to the horizontal comes in the 'cross piece' to this totem pole, that being the central eagle, belonging thus to both vertical and horizontal, but to neither completely. Out of scale with its vertical-axial neighbours and escaping their space, it hovers flat and emblem-like, pointing to the left and redirecting the flow of history and of sight. With this central, vertical, chronological axis that contains all the major historical periods depicted on the three walls, and with this cross form, this signal that determines the general narrative direction, the rest of the central wall can well afford to let go of linear narrative.

The three walls, then, are like the Mexican flag. Each side panel is of a specific and different period, as the side panels of the flag are each of a solid colour, but one green and the other red. The middle wall of the mural is dominated by the eagle, which, although belonging to the vertical axis at first, ultimately breaks away from its authority and floats freely in a historically mixed and spatially flat ground, an area as neutrally charged as the white central panel in the flag, which supports an eagle with a serpent in its mouth. The eagle in both cases belongs more to the side panels than to the central one, as only the sides and the eagle assert a visual presence, whereas the central panel recedes into a kind of absence. But it is the centre, in its liminal status, that has structurally allowed this to happen, that has served as stage for the ritual, allowed it its necessary space. [...]

There are ultimate rituals here: the mural becoming a flag, the history on the central wall changing from narrative incoherence to coherence with the application of a 'correct' viewing/reading, [...] and Revolutionary Mexico becoming a post-Revolutionary, capitalist state. The mural viewer becomes an initiate in this rite of passage, experiencing the mural in time. First as a participant, changing into an observer [...] and also first as a viewer, changing into a citizen, subject to and of the nationalist content of the mural. The ritual produced by the mural served the purpose of the capitalist state under a government party invoking the laws of the land in order to claim legitimacy and continuity in the face of induced and profound change.

Notes

1 When Revolution or Revolutionary appears with an upper case R, it refers to this specific event.

2 For the best account in English of the Calles years, see Cornelius, pp. 392–498. Includes an extensive bibliography.

3 See chapters I and II of L. Meyer, Segovia and Lajous; and Cornelius, pp. 395–408.

4 This had already started during Calles' own administration, as described in J. Meyer, Krauze and Reyes, especially chapters III and VII.

5 This essay does not consider the role of the artist in its deliberations, partly for lack of space, but mostly for reasons of methodology. I want to explain the look and content of the mural as produced by extra-personal forces. [...] I will simply say that in 1929, Rivera was as anxious as any other muralist to accept such a large and prestigious commission, regardless of his on and off again membership in the Mexican Communist Party (resigned in 1925, reinstated in 1926) and its

combative relations with the government. The opportunity to describe and make commentary upon all of Mexican history, with the freedom to press a Marxist line, presumably overrode any objections as to the collaborationist overtones of such a venture. In early 1929, Rivera had distanced himself from the Communist Party's vigorous attacks on the government, at the same time that the party was declared illegal. By August 18, when the painting began on the north, right wall of the National Palace stairway, Rivera had survived the general crackdown on communists.

[...]

6 There is a pencil sketch of 1926 for the south wall, reproduced as figure 189 in Helms, p. 90.

7 The building dates back to Aztec times and had been reconstructed several times since the days of Cortés to those of Calles. R. Casanova, in Acevedo, p. 117.

8 These titles are according to Stanton L. Catlin in his 'Mural Census,' in Helms, pp. 235–336. In general, I refer to the three walls as the National Palace stairway mural. Those paintings found on the walls of the second floor open-air corridor were painted by Rivera much later (1941–1951) and will not be considered here.

9 In this I depend on the descriptions by R. Casanova, pp. 117–22; A. Villagómez L., 'El Palacio Nacional', Reyero, pp. 140–55; and S. Catlin, 'Palacio Nacional', Helms, pp. 260–7.

10 From the rear of the so-called Moctezuma's Throne, or Temple of Sacred Warfare, discovered in 1926 under the southwest corner of the National Palace itself, English transcript of E. Umberger, 'El trono de Moctezuma', *Estudios de cultura Náhuatl*, 17, 1984, pp. 63–87. Umberger first shared this information with me in public discussion. Most probably, Rivera had seen Alfonso Caso's *El Teocalli de la Guerra Sagrada* (Mexico City, 1927). The title of Caso's work is one of the various names given to the Throne.

11 The account of this myth varies. Sometimes the vision is only of a cactus growing from a rock (Tenochtitlán means 'the place with the cactus in the rock'), or the eagle is holding a small bird or a human heart or nothing in its beak. The design of the flag as it looks today was determined by presidential decree in September of 1916, when Carranza called for a return to 'the Aztec eagle'. Although the general design of the flag has remained unchanged since 1823, Porfirio Díaz had decided that the eagle be upright and frontal. Since 1916, the eagle has been in profile, head lowered to attack the snake, and facing to the viewer's left W. Smith *Flags Through the Ages and Across the World* (New York, 1975), pp. 148–50.

12 It reads '*Atl Tlachinolli*'. Umberger (as in n. 7), explains this terminology as '*atl*-(water) *tlachinolli* (something burned), a metaphor for sacred warfare,' p. 4. The red (the symbol twisting toward the left in the mural) stands for fire, the blue for water. Villagómez L. (as in n.6), p. 150.

13 The side walls each measure 7.5 × 8.9 metres. The central wall is 8.6 × 12.9 metres.

14 In both the Preparatoria of 1922 and the 1923–8 Ministry of Education murals, both in Mexico City, circumstances of site and program had precluded these new categorical qualities. At the Preparatoria, the *Creation* mural is non-narrative, but rather depicts allegorical figures representing timeless cultural attributes. The series of paintings at the Ministry of Education does present explicit narratives, but the organisation of these is determined by the linear logic of the architectural setting, that being the wall surfaces of long corridors.

15 R. Hansen, *The Politics of Mexican Development* (Baltimore, 1971), pp. 133–45.

16 L. Hall, *Alvaro Obregón: Power and Revolution in Mexico, 1911–1920* (College Station, 1981).

17 Medin, p. 35. Calles was unquestionably in control of Mexico, but in the posture of calculated retreat, pulling the strings on a large cast of government men.

18 *El Nacional Revolucionario*, August 10, 1929.

19 The difficulties involved in maintaining this control are detailed in Medin.

20 Medin, p. 144.

21 Meyer, Segovia and Lajous, p. 37.

22 *Ibid.*, p. 88.

23 The Party was a coalition of generals and politicians, various state political organisations, and worker and peasant groups. The first declaration of the December 1928 manifesto was: 'To unite

all parties, groups, and political organizations of the Republic, of Revolutionary belief, and tendency; to unit and to form the National Revolutionary Party.' *Ibid.*, p. 36.

24 This is the term of Portes Gil, in *El Nacional Revolucionario*, May 3, 1930.

25 Poulantzas, p. 278.

26 Meyer, Segovia and Lajous, pp. 88–9.

27 Giddens, p. 220.

28 Leach, especially chapters 2, 3, 5, and 7.

29 *Ibid.*, p. 35.

30 This is C. Colley explaining the Leach theory in 'The function of art as 'iconic text': An alternative strategy for a semiotic of art,' *Semiotica*, 36, nos. 1/2, 1981, pp. 135–52, under the name A. C. Hasenmueller, p. 146. This essay introduced Leach to me and is, I think, groundbreaking for its topic.

31 This is a direction that deserves longer treatment than is possible here. The writer is J. Frow, *Marxism and Literary History* (Cambridge, Mass., 1986), p. 227.

32 R. Brilliant (my emphasis), on the organisational power of 'upright structure', in *Visual Narratives: Storytelling in Etruscan and Roman Art* (Ithaca and London, 1984), p. 96. He credits J. Brengelmann, 'Preference for Upright Structure in Memory-Traces,' *Psychologische Forschungen*, 30, 1967, pp. 273–80.

Bibliography

Acevedo, E., (ed.), *Guia de murales del centro histórico de la ciudad de México* (Mexico City, 1984).

Cornelius, W. A., 'Nation Building, Participation, and Distribution: The Politics of Social Reform Under Cárdenas,' Almond, G., Flanagan, S., and Mundt, R. (eds.), *Crisis, Choice, and Change: Historical Studies and Political Development* (Boston, 1973), pp. 392–498.

Giddens, A., *The Nation-State and Violence*, vol. 2 of *A Contemporary Critique of Historical Materialism* (Berkeley and Los Angeles, 1985).

Helms, C. (ed.), *Diego Rivera: A Retrospective* (New York and London, 1986).

Leach, E., *Culture and Communication: the logic by which symbols are connected – An introduction to the use of structuralist analysis in social anthropology* (Cambridge, 1976).

Medin, T., *El minimato presidencial: Historia politica del maximato, (1928–1935)* (Mexico City, 1982).

Meyer, J., with Krauze, E., and Reyes, C., *Estado y sociedad con Calles: Historia de la revolución mexicana, período 1924–1928* (Mexico City, 1977).

Meyer, L., with Segovia, R., and Lajous, A., *Los inicios de la institucionalización. La política del maximato: Historia de la revolucion mexicana, periodo 1928–1934* (Mexico City, 1978).

Poulantzas, N., *Political Power and Social Classes*, trans. by O'Horgan, T.; McLellan, D.; de Casparis, A.; and Grogan, B. (London, 1975).

Reyero, M. (ed.), *Diego Rivera* (Mexico City, 1983).

31

Africa in the Art of Latin America

Gerardo Mosquera*

Gerardo Mosquera (b. 1945) is a Cuban critic and art historian who publishes on modern and contemporary art. A cofounder of the Havana Biennial in 1984, his continued curatorial efforts have helped to situate Latin American art in a global context. He has worked as an advisor to international museums, and has served on the editorial board of key art journals. In this essay, Mosquera locates African imprints in an ethno-cultural renewal that has been at the historical core of Latin America. African expressive and symbolic traditions survive in constant transformation from the colonial period to the present day.

After 1492, the Spanish and Portuguese initiated a process of unprecedented violence on both sides of the Atlantic, on American soil and on the African continent. In an enterprise of entrepreneurial and religious expansion, the annihilation of native societies and the conquest of their lands resulted in further devastation: European colonizers enslaved Africans for exportation to the Americas where they were forced into labor. In a plantation economy that generated material wealth for Europe and its American settlements, the slave trade made possible the development of colonial societies in the New World. The atrocity of racial slavery marks the foundation of the early modern world, and it had profound effects for the history and culture of Latin America.

Even as African peoples integrated into colonial society and, after the abolition of slavery, into the narrative of postindependence nations, certain ethnic groups maintained a degree of coherence in terms of religious custom. Under domination, traditional religious practices were performed under cover; as a result, music, dance, songs, oral literature, and visual expressions all continued to convey elements pointing

* Gerardo Mosquera (1992) "Africa in the Art of Latin America." *Art Journal* 51(4): 30–8.

Modern Art in Africa, Asia, and Latin America: An Introduction to Global Modernisms, First Edition.
Edited by Elaine O'Brien, Everlyn Nicodemus, Melissa Chiu, Benjamin Genocchio,
Mary K. Coffey, and Roberto Tejada.

to original sources in Africa. But African spirituality also underwent *creolization*, an enduring creative integration that innovated by borrowing from colonial Catholicism. This involved "a dynamic adaptation to a different historical, cultural, and social context, achieved under strict conditions of domination."

Mosquera provides an overview of African religious practices uprooted in the Americas. *Creolization* reshaped spiritual iconographies, ceremonial objects, popular cultural expressions like those of carnival, and domestic altars – Mosquera calls these "the greatest expression of Afro-American aesthetics and ritual in the visual arts." The African presence in Latin America's visual production carried over into modern and contemporary object-based art and performance to constitute what Mosquera calls a greater "Caribbean" culture. In the broadest possible sense of the term, this creolized ethos stretches out from the Caribbean isles to include Colombia, Venezuela, Peru, Brazil and the countries of Central America.

For Mosquera, the presence of Africa in Latin America's visual art follows two distinct paths. One is marked by "an African consciousness" that may or may not reveal an immediate reference to, or identification with, the religious beliefs, mythological thought, and philosophies of Africa. The other path pictures African symbolic forms from the viewpoint of modern life. Many twentieth-century and contemporary artists are thereby able to "de-westernize" Western culture from within. The author relates the time he once interviewed the Cuban modernist Wifredo Lam (see Giunta) who referred to one of his works (containing visible African elements) as the product of a visual grounding indebted to such European artists as Poussin.

Questions for reading: According to Mosquera, how does this double dynamic inform recent examples of Latin American art? What are some of the stylistic elements and what is its cultural drive? What role did the dominant religion of Catholicism play in both creating and suppressing the presence of African expressive forms? Compare this essay with Michael Harris on the "Art of the African Diaspora" in this volume. How does art from Latin America's African legacy fit into a multi-located history of life and identity?

Further Reading

Mercer, Kobena (ed.) (2008) *Exiles, Diasporas & Strangers*. Cambridge, MA: Institute of International Visual Arts/MIT Press.

Africa's cultural presence in Latin America is different from that of the indigenous cultures. While both branches can be identified as dominated cultures that are part of the Latin American ethnogenetic soup cooked up by the West, there is an essential divergence: Africans were, to quote Alejandro Lipschütz, "imported aborigines." In another of its paradoxes, capitalism developed on the American plantations a mode of production based on slavery that displaced millions of Africans from their original lands in one of the largest and most brutal human migrations in history. […] Uprooted, reduced to slavery, their cultural and ethnic diversity homogenized under a racist construct (the appellation "Negro"), the Africans, who were employed as a means of production, were forced to occupy different geographical, social, and cultural environments. For Africans, unlike Indoamericans, acculturation meant the very loss of their communities, kinship structures, and social and cultural institutions, and an amalgamation that forced together men and women of diverse cultural backgrounds who had lived in Africa separated by thousands of kilometers.

In areas where they had considerable demographic weight, this uprooting resulted in the active participation of Africans and their descendants in the formative process of the new Latin American nationalities. [...] Emancipation and racial mixing, which often occurred in the Iberian colonies of the Americas, facilitated the process.

Nevertheless, cultural *mestizaje* (mixture) does not necessarily signify a balanced and harmonious fusion. What developed in America instead were new western cultures with a small dosage of nonwestern components that resulted from the separation and dispersion of the original ethnic groups, their *acriollamiento* (creolizing) and their *mestizaje*. This situation, however, was more marked in countries with a strong multiethnic indigenous presence in which diversity was disguised – and discriminated against – through the use of an integrative nationalist discourse. On the other hand, wherever a strong African presence existed, its cultural and idiosyncratic elements modified the national cultures of the western "*mestizo*" kind, by shaping, to a considerable extent, their particular accents.

Such is the case of the "Caribbean," a term that in practice goes beyond the purely geographic and refers to areas farther south and as far as the Pacific Ocean as a way of noting the internal presence in various cultures of distinctive features of African origin. In this sense, "Caribbean" becomes the reference to a general ethnoculture that includes several American groups: some constituted as nations (for example, Jamaica); others that are groups with their own specific characteristics within a nation (i.e., Barlovento in Venezuela); and still others, among them Martinique, which have nationalities without being nations. Anthropology has recently begun to use the adjective "Caribbean" to categorize an experience contrary to the monocultural narrative. The question of multinationalism, so masked by the integrationist designs of the Latin American creole bourgeoisie, is nonexistent in the case of the sub-Saharan presence in America simply because Africans were deprived of their nationalities when they were transplanted.

One can extend to all of the Caribbean Fernando Ortiz's famous metaphor defining Cuban culture as an *ajiaco*, a soup made with very diverse ingredients in which the broth that stays at the bottom represents an integrated nationality, the product of synthesis. We would then have to consider which ingredients were added by each group, and who got the biggest spoonful. In any case, the *ajiaco* is not an idyllic formula (as it is frequently considered today) removed from the original intentions of the Cuban anthropologist. And we would still have to point out that, beside the broth of synthesis, there are bones, gristle, and hard seeds that never fully dissolve, even after they have contributed their substance to the broth.

These undissolved ingredients are the survivals and recreations of African traditions within religious-cultural complexes, in addition to being the particular characteristics of blacks as subgroups within the "*mestizo*" ethnos that created the Latin American nations. Certain of these features were determined more by the sociohistorical situation than by the ethnocultural one. [...]

While it is true that blacks were active and integrated into Latin American nationalities, it is equally the case that they were able to develop religious-cultural complexes with clearly African roots. [...]

[...] While these religions experienced creolization, changes, and borrowings from each other and from popular Catholicism and Spiritualism, their essence, philosophy, structure, and liturgy remain very close to certain of their African roots. More than a case of syncretism – an emphasis found in discourses centered on *mestizaje* as the balanced and comprehensive solution for nationality – they constituted a paradigm for a dynamic adaptation to a different historical, cultural, and social context, achieved under strict conditions of domination.

The stress on syncretism derives from the narrative of hybridization (considered as a just and happy sharing of the integrated Latin American nation), while at the same time social and ethnic contradictions, as well as the hierarchical structure of the hybridization process conditioned by the dominant groups, remain concealed. Thus the term "syncretic cults," which has been officially imposed in Cuba, is both unacceptable and mistaken because it implies an unconscious discrimination. [...]

At the very least, the term "syncretic cults" is a post-colonial one disguised as erudition or ethnography. Outside the specialized group of scholars who study African culture or related topics in America, it is usual for researchers, critics, and essayists to place all of these diverse religions under one label, frequently attributed (with a shudder) to a Hollywoodesque exoticism known as "voodoo." In fact, this all-encompassing term comes from a lack of interest in acknowledging the rich cultural variety of black peoples; it is the historical result of contempt. This vulgar mistake, equivalent to putting in the same bag Anglican, Methodist, and Russian Orthodox churches, Jehovah's Witnesses, and even the Masons, can be found even in such erudite books as the 1984 catalogue published by the Museum of Modern Art in New York for its "Primitivism in 20th-Century Art" exhibition, when it refers to Wifredo Lam.

[...]

It is pertinent to compile a brief and very simplified listing of the main Afro-American religions and religious practices: Palo Monte (Cuba) and Macumba (Brazil), of Kongo origin; Shango (Trinidad), Santería (Cuba), Candomblé, Batuque, and Xangô (Brazil), derived from the Yoruba Orisha beliefs; the Arará Rule (Cuba), the House of Minas (Brazil), and the House of Rada (Trinidad), of Ewe-Fon origin; the Abakuá Secret Society (Cuba), the only re-creation in the whole diaspora of a male secret society, that of the Leopard-Men of Ejagham, Efik, and Efut, and of others from Calabar; Voodoo (Haiti), an Afro-American syncretic system with Ewe-Fon and Kongo foundations; the religion of the "Bush Negroes" (Guyanas), which is also syncretic and has a stronger Fanti-Ashanti and Ewe-Fon influence; the Umbanda (Brazil) and the cult of María Lionza (Venezuela), which are new creole religions of African inspiration and structure despite their open syncretism. The degree of "Africanism" differs in each case.

[...]

The cultural presence of Africa in America has three main manifestations. One is an internal, formative action synthesized in Caribbean ethnic or subethnic groups. Within these cultures, the western identity is modified by nonwestern elements of considerable weight in the shaping of idiosyncrasies, *cosmovisión* (or *Weltanschauung*), customs, and artistic practices, regardless of social class or skin color. A more evident manifestation lies in the sociocultural characteristics of the different black and mulatto classes within the social strata. Another, even more literal, is found in the features of African origin that have not disappeared and are still fully identifiable. Of course, there are overlappings and continuous exchanges between these three manifestations. Besides, it should be recalled that in the Caribbean, generally speaking, communication between social and cultural classes is relatively unobstructed.

[...]

African presence in the popular culture of Latin America follows two general lines: the Caribbean and the Afro-American. With the first, it acts internally upon several manifestations of "*mestizo*" folklore. In visual arts it can be seen in a number of handcrafts, and perhaps has its paradigm in the delirious visuality of the carnival. It is not by chance that the most inventive and exuberant visual expression is closely bonded to music and dance, given that in those zones there was a strong and extremely fecund African presence which manifested itself very early, while visual creation had a lesser place. [...] Because of the deformations of the slave system, any kind of manual work was considered improper for whites and was left to blacks as an inferior occupation. African traditions were destroyed not only by living and working conditions, but also by the imposition of European standards.

Afro-American development was also affected by colonial Catholicism, always ready to repress any creation of "idols." Ritual objects had to be disguised, and Catholic imagery was appropriated through syncretic representations of its saints and Virgins, who were then associated with the Yoruba and Ewe-Fon pantheons, a development coherent with the undercover polytheism of the devotion to Mary and the saints, a result of the expansion of primitive Christianity among the Old World "barbarians." [...]

African music, songs, and dances, on the other hand, were considered tolerable and even desirable entertainment, thus permitting the expansion of an activity that deeply affected both the ritual and the profane. In turn, this gave way to the strongest expression of African culture in America. In music and dance, the African presence manifested itself as richly in Afro-American religious practices as in bars, dance halls, and spectacles – to such a degree, in fact, as to make it apparent that these hybrid rhythms have been known since the sixteenth century.

Afro-American visual art is poor if compared to that of Africa, but is extremely fertile in creole inventiveness. Its main character consists of adapting the original canons and re-creating them under new circumstances with new materials, at times displaying a baroque style. [...] The numerous ritual objects constructed with clay, metal, wood, beads, fabric, and many other materials range from a quite strict formal relationship with their African ancestors to a reinvention that preserves only meanings and functions. Often they are also rearranged to serve new circumstances, and sometimes they are pure creole inventions, particularly in the syncretic religions. Many of these objects are part of the spectacular scenario of altars – perhaps the greatest expression of Afro-American aesthetics and ritual in the visual arts. Altars appear in diverse religious complexes and attain their finest display in Santería, Candomblé, and Umbanda. They are truly "post-modern" installations using a rich variety of objects. Some are custom-made; others are a kind of "readymade," in which meanings are freely rearranged to structure a very complex symbolic and aesthetic discourse – one where religious rules do not prevent a new vernacular creation that integrates the traditional and the contemporary.

[...]

In all of this imagery deriving from Africa, the original rules have been loosened; diverse elements and techniques have been assimilated, and personal fantasy has played a role. The tendency has been in the direction of naïve sculpture, like that made by popular artists. The same tendency can be found in certain personal creations such as Voodoo or Palo Monte mural paintings, or Abakuá illustrations, which are separated from the original typology but not from the traditional religious concepts they are trying to convey. In the syncretic religions of Umbanda and the cult of María Lionza, the profuse use of plaster, plastics, and clay is an example of contemporary fantasy deriving from African and other pantheons. Voodoo, a syncretic religion with pure African sources, also creates its own paraphernalia, such as embroidered flags, tin sculptures, and decorated bottles. Finally, circular houses with conical straw roofs and a floor plan similar to that of houses of the Mande of Mali are found in western Mexico's Costa Chica, a unique example of African architecture in America. With these houses, which traveled via memory from the Atlantic to the Pacific, I finish this rather incomplete list. The presence of Africa in popular Latin American visual art, unlike its presence in music, dance, mythology, and the religions of the diaspora, has still to be studied.

[...]

Within the diverse panorama offered by modern art in Latin America are artists in whose works the African presence serves as a primary one, as the conclusive factor of expression. I am not referring only to the thematic presence but also to the attempt to establish an important definition. Adding a mask or the figure of a drummer to a painting does not make a piece whose creative core is African. Many Latin American artists have casually drawn upon African themes, using these as formal or anecdotal motifs without making them an internal part of the work's conception. Nor is the African source a definitive agent when it is used as an attractive facade for an exotic vision. When Africa is forced to appear on the surface of a work, it seldom has profound resonance.

In my opinion there are two major directions – often mixed in diverse streams – in which the African presence as a conclusive factor in Latin American fine arts can be isolated. The first has to do with the predominance of general features typical of the African consciousness: its religious philosophies, cosmovisions, mythological and ethnopsychological thinking. Traces of this African consciousness, internalized and dissolved, must participate in the formation of the "Caribbean" sensibility and imaginary vision, with its particular symbolic world. Along this line, what is African functions from very deep within, like a backbone of works that may have no direct reference to their sources. [...] In this group we find both figurative and abstract artists such as the Cubans Wifredo Lam, Roberto Diago, Agustín Cárdenas, and Mateo Torriente; René Louise and Louis Laouchez of Martinique; Paul Giudicelli of the Dominican Republic; and Aubrey Williams of Guyana.

In the visual arts, this active presence of elements of African consciousness becomes evident in a diversity of shapes and contents: from languages and current preoccupations to ancient traditions. For example, it can be found in the fabulous view by Cuban artist Angel Acosta León of objects of daily life from marginal neighborhoods, where nothing comes directly from Africa but a great deal derives from the life of black people in big cities, though highly internalized by the artist. At times it is found in the details of an irreproachable "white" work, like the witty exchanges between objects made by Hervé Télémaque of Haiti, which remind one of the actual debates with kitchen utensils witnessed among black maids by Cuban folklorist Lydia Cabrera. It could also be germinally present in the paintings of Tarsila do Amaral and Antônio Henrique Amaral of Brazil and possibly in the violent fantasizing of Jean-Michel Basquiat (USA), studied by Robert Farris Thompson from the perspective of his discovery that New York is a "secretly African city."

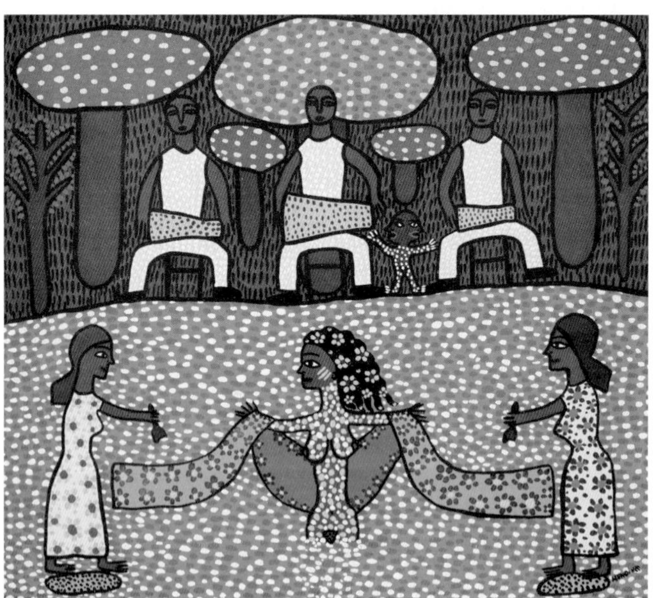

Figure 31.1 Manuel Mendive, *El Baño* (The Bath), c.1975, mixed media on cardboard, 38 × 41.9 cm/15 × 16½ inches, Cernude Arte, Florida.

On the side of tradition, the inner presence of African consciousness determines content, language, and direction in the work of very diverse artists, ranging from Lam (Cuba) to Mario Abreu (Venezuela). At its extreme, it is consubstantial with work entirely based on Afro-American tradition, as in the case of Manuel Mendive of Cuba. Both streams, with all their variations, are related because they share a common inner vision, not because of external myths or magic used as laboratory tools for an artistic search.

A number of Caribbean artists may use African forms taken from "outside," forms that do not specifically exist in their culture, and appropriate them naturally, without exoticism. An African mask, even if in a showcase in Paris, will be assimilated by someone who carries within something from Africa. But it will be reconstructed in terms of the artist's own originality, will be hybridized and "westernized" as it is transformed into an independent artistic sign for a museum or a gallery. At the same time, though, the artist will slightly "de-westernize" western culture – understood as the international culture of the contemporary world – by molding it according to nonwestern views, sensitivities, and contents. [...]

If along the first line I have tried to construct, the African presence comes from deep within, the second direction manifests itself on what we may call the phenomenal level. Works thus defined are based on the Afro-American tradition that makes an organic use of African shapes, themes, myths, practices, and conventions. [...] The spectrum of possibilities can be very wide. Within this paradigm are artists such as Helio de Souza Oliveira and Rubem Valentim (Brazil), Jorge Severino Contreras (Dominican Republic), Bertin Nivor (Martinique), Leandro Soto and Juan Francisco Elso (Cuba), whose work is integrated within a code that alludes to a general world vision; Carlos Zerpa (Venezuela), who makes collages that are usufructuary reconstructions in various techniques and from various sources taken directly from popular religions; and José Luis Rodríguez (Puerto Rico).

The "primitive" painters of Haiti and the intuitive Jamaican artists are spontaneous exponents of the two broad streams that I have tried to describe. Whether or not it is a case of works inspired directly by the Afro-American essence [...] there will always be, in general, a spirit of myth, a natural exuberance of fabulation. Such fabulation is not so much nourished by the magical real and the popular elements as *born* of them, giving this art a particular personality. One can observe a clear African stamp that, nevertheless, does not spring from the reuse of African forms or from the allusion to them, but from an original internal elaboration, fruit of a different reality.

[...] It is the opposite of the fashionable "otherness" that causes so much Latin American art to become "other" in order to satisfy the new occidental need for exoticism. Artists such as José Bédia, Juan Francisco Elso, Luis Gómez, Marta María Pérez, Ricardo Rodríguez Brey, and Santiago Rodríguez Olazábal have lifted traditions from their usual settings to produce work in an "educated" mode, to move a step toward a western culture transformed by nonwestern values and interests coming from the South.

In summary, we may distinguish the African presence in Latin American art on several levels. As a genetic part of "Caribbean" culture, it accents every work expressing this culture's specific identity. In folklore it has considerable weight in the composition of *mestizo* manifestations, and even more so in ceremonial visual art, less hybridized than that I have defined as Afro-American, where its structure of African origin will be conserved with greater purity. In "gallery" art, it appears as the defining agent in some creations. [...]

Five centuries after the *encontronazo* of cultures in America, it is useful to reflect that a number of the most important Latin American artists – and artistic manifestations – are those in whom African cultures have been a decisive agent for creation. And this is not a coincidence. Much of the richness and originality of Latin America derives from the nonoccidental, dominated, popular sides of our cultures. [...]

32

Vital Structures

The Constructive Nexus in South America

Mari Carmen Ramírez*

In this essay US-based art historian, critic, and curator Mari Carmen Ramírez provides an overview of the diverse constructive art movements that emerged over the course of the twentieth century in South America. (While Ramírez focuses on these paradigmatic groups, there were other important concrete art movements, most notably the parallel Argentine group Associación Arte Concreto-Invención [Buenos Aires], the Paris-based Visual Arts Research Group/GRAV, which included Argentine Julio Le Parc; the Ruptura group located in São Paulo; and the Venezuelan Kineticists, to name only a few.) She focuses her essay on three temporally and nationally distinct avant-garde artists: Uruguayan Joaquin Torres-García (both the work he executed in Europe and the United States in the 1920s and 1930s and his subsequent production upon his return to Montevideo in 1944); Rhod Rothfuss, Carmelo Arden Quin, and Gyula Kosice, who formed Arte Madí in Buenos Aires, Argentina in 1944; and Helio Oiticica and Lygia Clark, members of the Rio de Janeiro based group, Neoconcretismo, which broke from the São Paulo Ruptura group in 1959. Ramírez notes that apart from some Madí artists' contact with Torres-García's School of the South, these movements emerged independently and often without any knowledge of one another. For this reason she refers to these movements as a "nexus" (connected group) and emphasizes the distinct qualities of each, while also locating a shared, philosophical "nexus" (connection) that can explain the "paradoxical" inversions that constructivism underwent in South America.

* Mari Carmen Ramírez (2004) "Vital Structures: The Constructive Nexus in South America." In Mari Carmen Ramírez and Héctor Olea (eds) *Inverted Utopias: Avant-Garde in Latin America* (pp. 191–201). New Haven, CT: Yale University Press.

Modern Art in Africa, Asia, and Latin America: An Introduction to Global Modernisms, First Edition.
Edited by Elaine O'Brien, Everlyn Nicodemus, Melissa Chiu, Benjamin Genocchio,
Mary K. Coffey, and Roberto Tejada.

Ramírez begins by noting that the widespread interest in geometric and abstract concrete art in South America is of "indisputable European origin." Here she is referring to early twentieth-century European artists like Piet Mondrian or Vladimir Tatlin who attacked art's representational function and asserted the autonomy of line, plane, or color as objective entities in and of themselves. Within Europe, constructivism was an ideologically and formally broad, multinational movement with practitioners in the Netherlands, Russia, Germany, France, Eastern Europe, and beyond. Ramírez insists that the Latin American "nexus" be understood as part of an international "constructivist impulse," but not as a mere derivation of the European model. She distinguishes Latin American movements from these European precedents around a series of "progressions" or "ruptures" that she claims are unique to South American artists.

The overarching "rupture" Ramírez identifies as the "nexus" or root of Latin American constructivism is the shift from a "passive" to an "active" conception of structure. While European artists emphasized rational geometric form to assert the "objective" nature of the work of art, South American artists developed the "subjective" dimensions of the work of art by treating it as a "vital structure." Artists in South America viewed abstract form as animated by life, much in the way that the perfect geometry of the repeating chambers in a nautilus shell are produced by and therefore index the snail. From this fundamental rupture with constructivist precepts, Ramírez argues, a series of radical "progressions" followed that by the 1960s "dissolved art into a social act."

Ramírez elaborates on four aspects of "vital structure" within the South American nexus. First, she notes that Latin American constructivists treated the object as an "event" or an active presence that engages the space around it. She cites the Madí group's attack on the frame as an attempt to both resist the "window effect" of the plane and create "movement" in the object through the resultant play of mass and void. In this case the notched canvases or sculptural voids were treated not as absences, but rather as presences that define the work's form. Second, Latin American constructivists reasserted the human dimension of objective art, whether by integrating symbols in their grid formations (Torres-García) or by claiming an existential or therapeutic dimension to the interaction of an individual with the object (Neoconcretismo's "trans-objects").

Third, Latin American constructivists broke down the subject/object dichotomy by insisting upon the phenomenological relationship between the perceiving subject and the work of art. For example, Ramírez considers Torres-García's articulated toys or the jointed sculptures executed by Gyula Kosice or Lygia Clark, which must be manipulated by the viewer. In the case of the latter, it is the viewer's tactile and perceptual experience that determines the object, not the artist's act of creating it. Or, she discusses Oiticica's *Parangoles*, geometric environments created by the suspension of colored volumes that the viewer walks into or "inhabits." Finally, Ramírez notes that all of these artists arrived ultimately at a conception of art as a "form of ritual" that sought to transcend the object altogether in favor of the collective, whether understood as the "absolute" (Torres-García), society (Madí), or the cosmos (Neoconcretismo). This is related to the South American constructivist notion of the object as "magic" in its ability to transform material, the subject, or society from something inert into something alive.

Further Readings

Bois, Yves-Alain, Herkenhoff, Paulo, Jimenez, Ariel, and Perez Oramas, Luis Enrique (2001) *Geometric Abstraction: Latin American Art from the Patricia Phelps de Cisneros Collection.* Cambridge, MA: Harvard University Art Museums.

Martin, Susan and Ruiz, Alma (eds) (2000) *The Experimental Exercise of Freedom.* Los Angeles, CA: The Museum of Contemporary Art.

Pérez-Barriero, Gabriel (ed.) (2007) *The Geometry of Hope: Latin American Abstract Art from the Patricia Phelps de Cisneros Collection.* Austin, TX: Blanton Museum of Art and Fundación Cisneros.

> *What I try to find, above all, is one single thing: structure.... That is, the nexus between the vital and the abstract.*
>
> Joaquin Torres-Garcia, *Metafísica de la Prehistoria Americana*, 1939

> *In structures totally made by me, there is a wish to objectify a subjective structural conception, which only realizes itself upon becoming concrete in the "making of the work."*
>
> Helio Oiticica, *Bolides*, 1963

> *If man does not achieve a new expression within a new ethics, he will be lost. ... Form is already worn out in every sense. The plane has absolutely no interest whatsoever – what is left? New structures to discover. This is what is lacking in our times – structures that correspond absolutely to the needs of the artist to express himself or herself.*
>
> Lygia Clark, "Carta a Helio," ND

No artistic tendency illustrates more conclusively the theoretical scope and artistic originality of the Latin American avant-garde than that encompassed by the modes of geometric and concrete abstraction grounded in the international legacy of early twentieth-century Constructivism. Of indisputable European origin, these currents developed in South America during the post-World War II period, revealing the extent to which the assimilation – and, at times, inversion – of the "misplaced idea" of Constructivism took hold and manifested itself in highly innovative ways. The momentum that this widespread *constructive impulse* generated – both in its time and in subsequent decades – raises a number of questions. Is the work of these Latin American creators visually, conceptually, or ideologically linked to Russian and European Constructivism, beyond their common origins? Is it possible to identify a recurrent term or concept in these artists' essays, manifestoes, and pronouncements that reveals affinities? And, most important, given the paradoxes at stake, what is the benefit of locating these coincident fields of reference?

What follows is a detailed consideration of certain artists and works to reveal a series of formal and conceptual grounds that escape cursory notions such as "artistic influence" and outworn categories such as "style." [...]

[...] With the exception of the well-documented connections between Torres-García and several Madí artists, it is impossible to establish historical links between the South American Constructive groups, for they were separated both temporally and geographically. Similarly, interpretations based on the presumed origins of these links in a continental – or, in other words, "Latin American" – identity have all but lost their pertinence for a present that seriously mistrusts essentialism in any form. [...]

Leaving the pretensions of continuity, totality, and identity aside [...] this essay provides an initial overview of the similarities and divergences between the theoretical and practical propositions of [...] heterogeneous artistic groups. The more we delve into the problem of assessing affinities and dissimilarities, however, the more ungraspable it becomes. My aim, then, is not to arrive at a conclusive statement about Latin American geometric and constructive trends but [...] to objectify dialectically the *other* "possible orders" they suggest. In doing so, it is important to bear in mind that the constructive nexus between these works is not limited to one particular tendency or manifestation. Instead, it unfolds as a series of artistic problems and issues that range from the fundamental ideas of geometry and the concrete to the kinetic, optical, and haptic dimensions of Constructivism's rich legacy. [...]

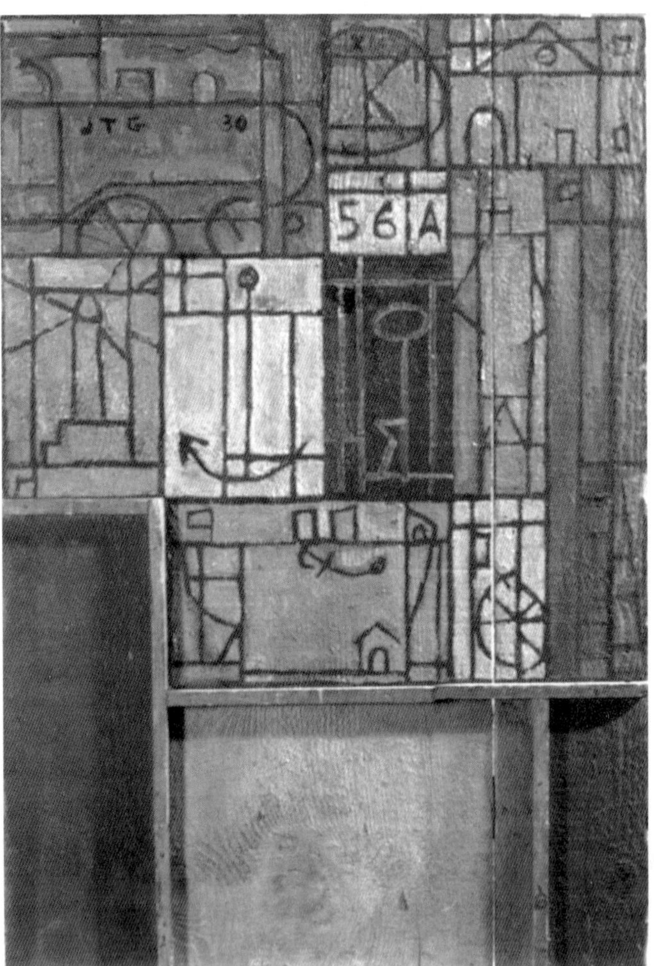

Figure 32.1 Joaquin Torres-García, *Constructivo con varillas sobrepuestas* (Constructive with attached rods), 1930, oil on wood, 60 × 42 cm/23½ × 16½ inches, Museo Torres-García, Montevideo. Courtesy of Cecilia de Torres, New York, © DACS 2011.

"Structure" – the concrete configuration of the artwork or artistic manifestation – is fertile conceptual ground on which to begin. Not only does this idea emerge as the nodal principle of Latin American constructive and geometric trends but it is also a discursive point in the European constructive movements. Therefore, structure is a versatile nexus for substantiating numerous practical and theoretical articulations between the New World artists and their Old World contemporaries and predecessors. This raises a pair of crucial questions: Is there a specificity to the notion of *structure* as it unfolds in these artists' production?

Without losing sight of the theoretical parameters established by pioneers such as Piet Mondrian, Theo Van Doesburg, Naum Gabo, and Vladimir Tatlin, how significant are the South American versions of this concept? What follows engages these questions from the perspective of three different cases: Torres-García, Madí, and Neoconcretismo. The traits, in turn, that these groups shared with each other find parallels in the work of the Venezuelan Cinéticos and the São Paulo Grupo ruptura.

Structural Nexus

"Structure" – described by Torres-García as the "cornerstone of Constructivism"[1] – originated when avant-garde artists definitively annulled representation and replaced it with the concrete, autonomous artistic entity. Instead of the "window effect" that had characterized art since the Renaissance, the structural principle was a self-referential construct in which line, plane, and color functioned with complete autonomy from the outside world. The terms "structure" and "construction" were used interchangeably,[2] and the theoretical and aesthetic postulates of the various constructive movements thus rested on divesting *structure* of the elements of the natural world. Mondrian, for example, wrote about *a culture of pure relationships* established by the plastic elements assembled inside the aseptic construct provided by the grid; Van Doesburg and Tatlin attempted to *structure* their work according to mechanical precision; while El Lissitzky equated *construction* with material production.

Working under different sociopolitical conditions, the South American constructive groups embraced the concrete notion of structure as the starting point for their nonrepresentational work. However, as their written statements and aesthetic production both reveal, this concept evolved from a "passive" (pure and objective) organizing principle to one that was "active" (contaminated and subjective). The result of this inversion is the extremely paradoxical – and ultimately subversive – "subjectiveness" that developed from the presumably "objective" constructive character of the work. That is to say, for Torres-García, Madí, and Neoconcretismo, the self-referential *structure* was more than an outward reflection of the work's internal order; it was also a concrete manifestation of its "vital" impulse. The structures of these works, then, were "alive," their life emanating from the unity and coherence of their internal elements, as well as from their relationship to a more encompassing totality, whether it be the Absolute (Torres-García), Society (Madí), or the Cosmos (Neoconcretismo). This also explains the *immanent* quality of these constructions and their intrinsic need for *transcendence* through, among others, the abolition of the plane or the negation of the duality between figure and ground. In my view, these two facets of the South American constructive proposal elucidate both the affinities between the disparate structures gathered in this constellation and the bewildering originality of their rupture. [...] The richness of such a contradictory starting point unfolds in at least three prolific, yet related, approaches to the *structure* of the artwork or artistic manifestation: idealist (Torres-García), material (Madí), and organic (Neoconcretismo).

In Torres-García's Neoplatonic framework, the structure was the reflection in the artwork of the order of the Universal Absolute. Outside of this structural wholeness, nothing existed but fragments.[3] Because the structure implied a re-creation (and not a representation) of the natural order in the work, Torres-García argued that "each work is an idea that has its development and its life, just like the different forms of life found in nature." From his earliest essays, it was clear to him that, beyond color and form, what the artist confronts is the "organism of the artwork, its structure."[4] The "life" of the structure was revealed in the transition from idea to matter.[5] The "movable" toys that the artist produced in the early 1920s exemplify this notion of the "animate" structure that grounds the work. Writing about one of these toys, Torres-García explained: "It has joints; it changes positions as do all living beings, as you do and I do, like a normal man."[6] Conceived in this way, the "animate" *structure* could be developed both in the plane and in three-dimensional space. One of Torres-García's most original contributions to the Constructivist legacy is the series of wood constructions that he created between 1929 and 1938. Neither painting nor sculpture, these works occupy an in-between zone, whose ambiguity endows them with material and animistic presence. For example, in *Formas sobre fondo blanco* (Forms on white background, 1924) and *Objet plastique* (Plastic object, 1931–4) – two pieces that clearly anticipate Madí's active constructions as well as Frank Stella's "shaped canvases" – Torres-García cut and mustered wood pieces into an irregular shape, thereby granting the *living structure* full autonomy.

Torres-García's structures, though conceived under the undeniable stigma of idealism, find their materialist counterparts in the theoretical and practical postulates of *Arturo* magazine (1944) and the Madí group represented by Rhod Rothfuss, Carmelo Arden Quin, and Gyula Kosice. These creators believed that "the visual object must be pure," but they also considered the factual "presence" of this object to be "an event" in its own right.[7] Nevertheless, for the members of Madí, the key to the work's structural organization was its *material* nature; that the work completely negated its connection to the natural world transformed it into a physical object and a new, dynamic presence. Following Torres-García's initial disruptive gesture, Madí emphasized this "materiality" by rupturing the regularity of the canvas and transforming the border, or frame, into an *active* – and therefore subjective – element of the picture. As Arden Quin explained, "By abandoning the four classic orthogonal angles – the square and the rectangle – as a basis for composition, we have increased the possibilities for invention of all kinds. We can create an infinite number of planar forms."[8] Rothfuss was the first to theorize the abolition of the traditional frame. He clearly understood that "unless the frame is *rigorously structured* according to the painting's composition,"[9] the painting would be unable to transcend the "window effect." The "structured" frame – as shown early by Arden Quin's *Plan vert* (Green plane,

1945) – individualizes Madí's painted constructions, establishing their difference, their particular rhythm, as well as their vital spark. Dynamism – rotation, energy, articulation – is at the core of these structures, which above all respond to the values of "plurality" and "playfulness" that Futurism promoted. In this regard, Madí's "animate" structures afforded unusual combinations of sculptural volume and space (Arden Quin); the active interplay between "mass" and "void" (Rothfuss); and the creation of actual movement by means of light and water (Kosice).[10]

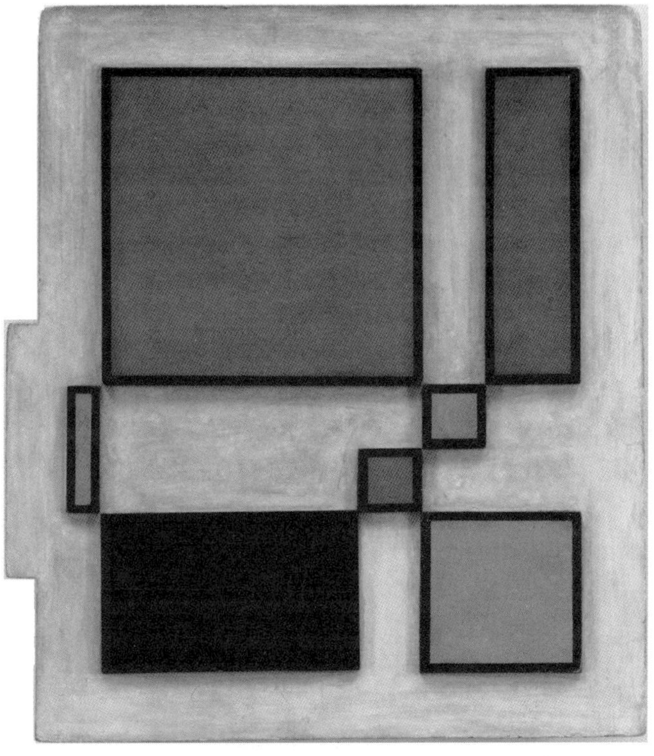

Figure 32.2 Rhod Rothfuss (1920–69), Uruguay, *Cuadrilongo Amarillo*, oil and synthetic paint on board, 37 × 33 cm/15 × 13 inches. Colección Patricia Phelps de Cisneros.

In contrast to Torres-García's idealism and the materialism of Madí, Neo-concretismo conceived the *structure* of the work in terms of a "quasi-corpus" or "living organism." In other words, as an entity "that amounts to more than the sum of its constituent elements" and whose being "can only be understood phenomenologically."[11] The Neo-Concrete term *não-objeto* (non-object) represents the most extreme subjective transformation of the self-referential structure. Echoing Torres-García's description of his movable toys, Clark referred to the series of flexible sculptures that she called *Bichos as* "organic entit[ies]," "living organism[s]" similar to the mollusk and close to the shell. Their parts, moreover, "like those of a true organism, are functionally related [to] and interdependent" of each other; thus, the *Bichos* brought into the world "a life of their own."[12] The "life" of these structures was revealed in the way they progressively abandoned the two-dimensional plane, projecting themselves as volumes into space. In Clark's work, this process follows a rigorous development that unfolds from the framed painting to the organic line of the *Modulated Spaces* to the *Bichos* to the *Casulos* and, in her late proposals, to the actual performance or therapeutic action based on corporeal interaction. Clark's manipulation of the surface/support into a living organism finds its counterpart in Oiticica's investigation of the nature and physicality of color. His well-known "chromatic structures" are, according to him, "organisms that stand apart from the physical world and from the space-world that surrounds us."[13] Thus, the color-liberation process begins with the *Metaesquemas* and reaches a climax with the *Nuclei*, structural labyrinths through which the viewer must walk in order to experience the prevailing specter of the work.

(a)

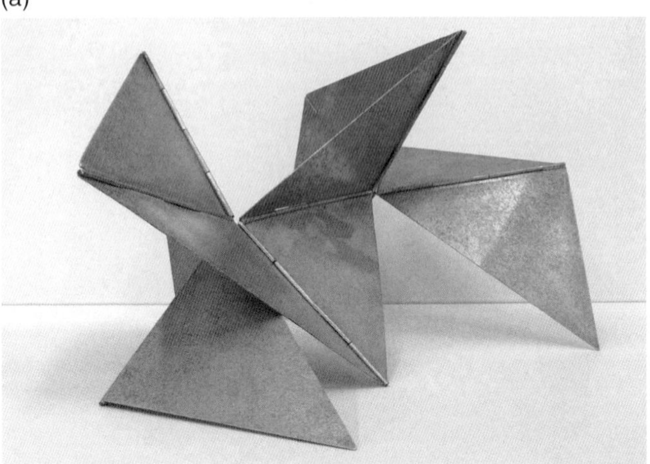

(b)

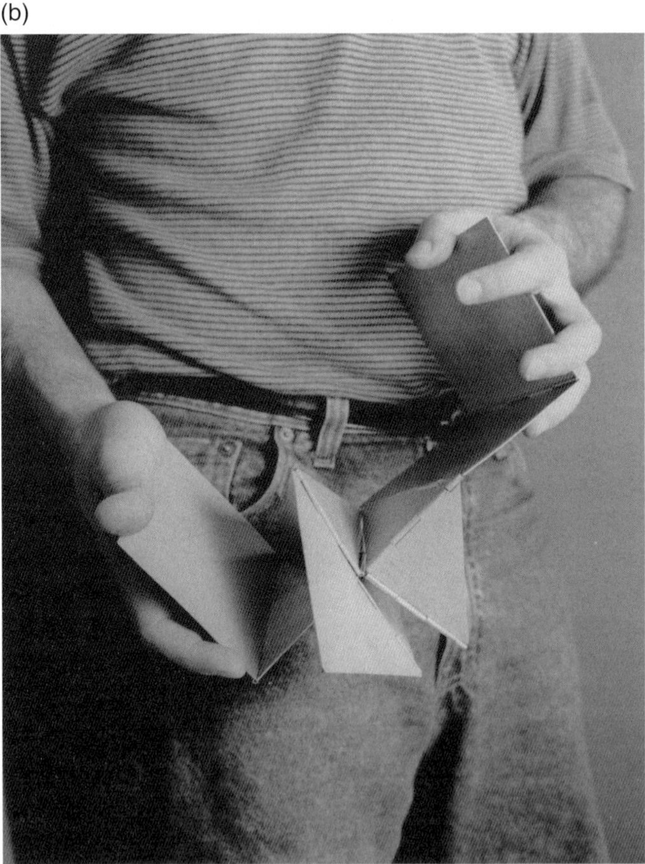

Figure 32.3 Lygia Clark (a) Bicho 1960 (showing multiple folds), (b) man holding Bicho, 1960, photograph by Michel Desjardins. Images courtesy of "The World of Lygia Clark" Cultural Association.

The subjective yet ungraspable dimension of these groups' proposals inevitably led to the recovery of the individual or humankind as either the kernel or the central receptor of the constructive work. Broadly speaking, all of these propositions took philosophical shape as humanism (Torres-García), dialectical materialism (Madí), or phenomenological existentialism and even animism (Neoconcretismo). For Torres-García, the idea that "man" was the measure of all things (MAN-UNIVERSE) justified the contamination of the Neo-Plasticist grid with paradigmatic symbols grounded in the human referent. The catalyst for the creation of Madí was a steady concern with the human being's existence in the world as, in the words of Kosice, an "interacting whole."[14] The Neo-Concrete proposal also focused on the individual; Clark, in turn, categorically asserted: "We reject any myth external to man."[15] The Neo-Concrete faith in humankind emerged from a profound existential approach to what was perceived as the reification of modern life. The need to overcome this state of alienation led the group to reconnect the "living object" or *structure* with the subject for whom it was intended. "When man plays with the *Bichos* he ... plays with life, he identifies himself with it. Feeling it in its wholeness, participating in a unique instant of totality, he exists."[16]

The reconnection of *subject* with *object* in the constructive proposal unfolded in a series of atypical structures that include the jointed structure, the magical structure, and the ritual structure. Taking their cue from Torres-García's toys, Madí developed the *jointed structure*, exemplified by Kosice's paradigmatic *Röyi* and Arden Quin's sculptures, articulated paintings, and hanging mobiles. The most outstanding feature of these movable structures is that they depend on a person to complete them. The participant-receptor must manipulate the *Röyi* in order to achieve each of its many possible forms; never static, these structures playfully reconstruct themselves with every shift and shape. Therefore, the real existence of this type of structure – beyond its status as an object – lies in the movement or action of its parts resulting from the subject's external stimulus. Clark's *Bichos* and *Trepantes*, as well as Oiticica's *Bólides* and *Parangolés*, although conceived twenty years after the *Röyi*, are also paradigmatic hinged structures. In the *Bichos*, the use of metal hinges instead of the less-flexible metal screws of the *Röyi* lends an extraordinary flexibility to the pieces, successfully communicating their "organic" quality. Pliability and suppleness also are intrinsic to the rubber structures that Clark used in the *Trepantes*. And Oiticica's *Parangolés* – color structures designed to be "inhabited" by individuals taking hold of the space through dance – change shape according to the movements of the participant's body.

These constructive proposals were also subjective in their immanent *transcendence*, which unfolded via two separate processes. First, through the exhaustion of the self-referential qualities of the symbol (Torres-García) or autonomous construction (Madí); and second, through the exaltation of the ready-made theorized by Oiticica and the Neo-Concrete artists in terms of the *Trans-objeto*. Torres-García explained: "Within the concrete, every form is both *symbolic* and magic. First, because *it represents itself;* and second, because what it conveys is not something intellectual (to be interpreted or read) but *what it really is*."[17] By expanding or manipulating the animistic potential of the concrete *structure* in these parameters, the artist could reject the modern-day materialism of the thing-in-itself (or commodity) and restore to art what was presumed to be its ancient, magical spirituality. Therefore, Torres-García urged artists to "return to this art, going from the *intellectual to the magic* symbol."[18] His idea of magic, however, had nothing to do with the occult, but rather with the work's capacity to connect to a network of universal symbols similar to those that characterized the art of primal societies; anchored in geometry, this goal explains his interest in pre-Columbian and other ancestral traditions. Torres-García's freestanding "totemic" constructions, exemplified by the trilogy *Pachamama, Father Inti*, and *Idea*, illustrate the implications of this expanded notion of the symbol.[19]

[...]

[...] Echoing Torres-García, Oiticica argued that the *Trans-objetos* were distinguished by their wholesale identification with the "universal idea." In other words, the idea of the object and its structure were *one and the same*: the transcendence of the structure was neither mystic nor esoteric, but instead emanated from the object and its need to overcome the subject-object opposition. Oiticica explained: "In the 'Trans-Objects,' there is the sudden identification of this subjective [structural] conception with the previously existing object as necessary to the structure of the work, which in its condition of object, opposed to the subject, already ceases to be opposed in the moment of identification because, in reality, it already existed implicitly in the idea."[20] In its extreme idealism, this statement underscores the striking affinities between the Uruguayan avant-garde, represented by Torres-García, and the Brazilian experimental movement of the 1960s, epitomized by Oiticica.

A further subjective dimension of these constructive proposals is their emphasis on art as a form of ritual. This *ritual structure* refers to the "act of doing" or "pure act," grounded in "the now," in the *hic et nunc*. Insofar as Clark is concerned with *the death of the plane*, she invites the other "to float in the cosmic reality as he does in his own innermost reality." Clark explained the dynamic of this process: "The spectator no longer projects himself and identifies himself in the work. [Instead] he lives the work and, in living out its nature he lives within himself,"[21] eliminating the subject/object duality and enacting the non-objective structure – or "direct action" – into the social space to produce magic.[22] In this context, the notion of *structure* expands beyond the organizing principle of the work to become what Torres-García described as the "nexus between the vital and the abstract."[23] Here, the *vital* refers to the energy – whether social or cosmic – that imbues the ritual structure or action with "life," and the *abstract* suggests the cultural and ethical values condensed in the ritual. This aspect of the abstract-constructive proposal evolved in different ways, taking on connotations that ranged from the religious (Torres-García) to the iconoclastic (Madí) to the environmental (Oiticica) or even to the therapeutic (Clark). The act of cutting a narrow Möbius strip out of paper – as in Clark's *Caminhando* (1963) – or the integration of Hélio's *Parangolés* into the popular dance and rhythm traditions of Rio de Janeiro's Escolas de Samba, epitomizes the dissolution of the self-referential structure into a collective dimension.

Paradoxically, in all of these manifestations, the exaltation of the subjectivity of the structure – in dynamic, magical, or ritual terms – does not imply an emphasis on the individuality of the artist or participant subject. Instead, each proposal aims at preferencing anonymity over ego. A recurrent idea in Clark's *Livro-obra* (Book-œuvre series) is that the artist vanishes within the world, and the spirit melds with the collective. Paradoxically, however, the self persists, for the type of *vital structure* that each of these groups proposed was contingent upon the hyper-activation of the artist's or subject's individual senses. Thrust into a labyrinth and open to tactile, olfactory, visual, or aural experiences [...] the work produces stimuli that can be satisfied only through the individual's direct experience.

New Primitives?

At its most extreme, the humanist component of these proposals paved the way for an organic version of Constructivism that ultimately dissolved art into a social act. Toward the end of his life, Torres-García arrived at a radical conclusion: "We can see as an astrologist [*sic*] with his lenses, the sketchy images of the cosmic plan: the micro-cosmic. The same is, in essence, Constructive Art. ... It can no longer be considered painting; not even art. ... Indeed, it goes beyond art. For this reason, I would call it a *human act*." In his view, the constructive undertaking "overflow[ed]" art's conventional parameters and was not to be "squandered in this or that wall or object"; instead, "it ha[d] a religious transcendence that must be respected."[24] To be sure, Torres-García's Neoplatonism – as well as the contradictions embedded in the delicate balance he established between idealism, humanism, and constructive art – prevented him from pursuing the full radical potential of these words. Yet, the transference from the *vital structure* to the *human act*, like many other theoretical propositions, remained a latent idea in his work.

It would take a new generation and a new set of social and cultural factors for this radical version of Constructivism to materialize into a viable proposition. As late as the 1950s, the Brazilian and Argentinean concrete art movements (whether in poetry or in the visual arts) remained locked in the most extreme forms of Constructivist orthodoxy. For this reason, the idea of a constructive art based on play, ritual, viewer reception, or phenomenological exploration could develop only in the fleeting context of the 1960s generation's profound formal and ideological artistic inquiry. Thus, a thorough exploration of the constructive proposal that Torres-García had envisioned over a decade earlier was left to the Neo-Concretists. "These days we have the action of making," Clark asserted, "the instant that transcends into the very meaning of pure action."[25] And Oiticica wrote, "The structure is brought to space, revolving 180 degrees around itself; that is the turning point to reach time in color. Henceforth, the spectator is not seeing a single side, deep in thought, but is impelled to action."[26] The "rituals" of both Clark's and Oiticica's works, moreover, were a consequence of these artists' risky attitudes about art's experimental nature. The ultimate consequence of this attitude was the obliteration of art and its simultaneous integration into life as a concrete – albeit subjective – reality.

Clearly, the organic versions of constructive art that these avant-garde groups either directly or indirectly pursued subverted the dehumanizing nature of the original Constructivist model, exemplified by Van Doesburg's machine-like aesthetics, Mondrian's relational grid, and El Lissitzky's productive materialism. Indeed, the publication of Torres-García's *Constructive Universalism* (1944) was an attempt to overcome what he perceived to be the extreme limitations of the Neo-Plasticist rational utopia. Similarly, implicit in Neoconcretismo's extreme *"toma de posição"* (positioning) with respect to the geometric tradition perpetuated in Neo-Plasticism, Constructivism, Suprematism, the Bauhaus, and Brazilian Concretismo was the rejection – and subsequent inversion – of the "rationalist suppression" that these movements had come to epitomize.[27] Yet, insofar as these proposals reintroduced the human element – the participant, actor, receptor – into the self-referential *structure* of the work, they also gave rise to a profound paradox: how could an objective structure reflect subjectivity in any form? And yet, it was precisely this suspension of the subject-object duality – present to varying degrees in the South American versions – that enabled international Constructivism to achieve its primary goal of integrating art and life. [...]

Also contradictory is the opposition between the progressive, modernizing impulse demonstrated in these South American movements and the type of regressive utopia that propelled their efforts. The European and Russian

Constructivists considered any attempt to reduce the artistic manifestation to a concrete *construct* based on the immutable laws of geometry to be symbolic of art's evolution into a superior stage of development. This hinted at cleansing the work of unnecessary external referents in order to project – in pure form – either the superior (or in other words, spiritual) order that underlies human creation and the scientific (objective) panacea to which a certain sector of Modernity aspired. Both views, however, are missing in the self-image and objectives of the [South American] groups [...]. For Torres-García, the idea of a "universal art" was synonymous with a *tabula rasa* of creation,[28] a new artistic beginning that implied "going back in a certain way to prehistoric times in order to consider once more what is essential to art." He speculated that this was the only way that artists could finally become authentic "primitives."[29] Echoing this view, Arden Quin proclaimed from the pages of *Arturo* that his generation was living, in both economy and art, "a new beginning, a primitive period" that, in turn, justified the modern artist's desire to get closer to indigenous art.[30] Furthermore, Madí's utopia went hand in hand with "the construction of a new classless society," as envisioned in dialectical materialism.[31] This reductive impulse was also evident in the radical "rediscovery of the world"[32] that Neoconcretismo proposed. As the critic Mário Pedrosa observed, this group's search for "the origins or the elementary grounds of art" situated them in "the prehistory of Brazilian art."[33] In fact, this excavation of the primeval nature of art led Oiticica to search for forms of "popular constructive primitivism" in the urban, suburban, and rural landscapes of the continent.[34] Clark summarized the regressive impulse at the core of Neoconcretismo when she declared: "We are the *new primitives* in a new era. So, we start again to revive the ritual, the expressive gesture, but now within a totally different concept to those from other periods."[35]

This antinomy between reality and irreality, materialism and animism, that justifies the *vital structure* corresponds to a primitivism that, far from being unique to South American abstract-constructive groups, existed at the core of the broader international avant-garde. One that was only fully developed in the psychologist brand of Surrealism that sought a return to the origins: a *degré zéro* of human experience. Nevertheless, the full implications of the momentum achieved by this particular reading of primitivism in this specific region are worth pondering. Whether understood in terms of a "healthy corrective" to the excesses of figuration and melodrama that characterized art on the continent, or as the embodiment of the successes and failures of developmentalism, this form of primitivism was directly related to the limitations and contradictions of the New World context. Torres-García mordantly asked: "Can we give something to Europe that was not produced there, and that is, at the same time its equivalent? What new and *original structures* have we created here?"[36] Regardless of the motivations behind this profound inversion of Constructivist principles, one fact remains clear: a significant part of their genuine contribution rested on their expanded notion of the *self-referential structure* of the work of art, artifact, or artistic manifestation.

To consider the notion of the *vital structure* as something that undermines Constructivism's inherent rationalism today lends flexibility to the plurality of readings that each of the interpretations of Constructivism [...] stimulates. Indeed, to reduce these works to one single proposal, history, or category is impossible. In order to follow the trajectories of these noncontinuous diachronic moments, it is necessary to overcome the reductive insulation of the pigeonholes and artificial continuities of current institutionalized art-historical accounts. Only then can we – as critics – resist the credulous debasement of art to discrete and unrelated histories: Geometric Abstraction, Constructive Universalism, Neo-concretismo, and so on.

Notes

1 Joaquin Torres-García, *Universalismo Constructivo; Contribución a la unificación del arte y la cultura de América* (Buenos Aires: Poseidón, 1944), 821.
2 Torres-García, *La recuperación del objeto* (Montevideo, 1952), 173–4.
3 Torres-García, *Estructura* (Montevideo: Ediciones La Regla de Oro, 1935), 17.
4 Torres-García, *Notes sobre art* (Gerona, 1917); quoted in *Joaquin Torres-García, escritos*, ed. Juan Fló (Montevideo: Arca, 1974), 69.
5 Torres-García, "Bases y fundamento del arte constructivo" (1934), in *Universalismo Constructivo*, 155–8.
6 Carmelo Arden Quin, "The Mobile," speech read at the home of the psychoanalyst Enrique Pichón-Rivière in 1945; reproduced in Yve-Alain Bois et al., *Geometric Abstraction: Latin American Art from the Patricia Phelps de Cisneros Collection* (Cambridge, MA and Caracas: Harvard University Art Museums and Fundación Cisneros, 2001), 142–3.
7 Arden Quin, "The Mobile," 142.
8 Ibid., 143.
9 Rhod Rothfuss, "El marco: Un problema de la plástica actual," Arturo 1, no. 1 (1944). [...]
10 Arden Quin, "The Mobile," 143.
11 Ferreira Gullar, "Manifesto neoconcreto," *Jornal do Brasil* (Rio de Janeiro), 22 March 1959; reprinted in *Projeto construtivo brasileiro na arte (1950–1962)*, ed. Aracy Amaral (Rio de Janeiro-São Paulo: MEC / FUNARTE / MAM / SCCTESP / Pinacoteca do Estado, 1977), 80–4.
12 Lygia Clark, "Bichos," in *Livro-obra* (Rio de Janeiro, 1983); reprinted in Manuel J. Borja-Villel, *Lygia Clark* (Barcelona: Fundació Antoni Tàpies, 1997), 121.
13 Hélio Oiticica, "Color, Time, and Structure" (21 November 1960), reprinted in *Hélio Oiticica* (Rotterdam: Witte de With Center for Contemporary Art, 1992), 34.
14 Gyula Kosice, *Arte Madí* (Buenos Aires: Ediciones de Arte Gaglianone, 1982), 13.
15 Lygia Clark, "Nós recusamos" (Rio de Janeiro, 1966).
16 Lygia Clark, "Sobre o ritual" (Rio de Janeiro, 1960); reprinted in Borja-Villel, *Lygia Clark*, 123.
17 Torres-García, *Estructura* (1935), cited in Fió, *Joaquin Torres-García, escritos*, 44. Emphasis added.
18 Ramírez, "Re-Positioning the South," 262.
19 This approach to the symbol would become the cornerstone of the mature contribution of the School of the South artists, boldly represented by Gonzalo Fonseca, Julio Alpuy, and Francisco Matto, among others. [...]
20 Oiticica, "Bólides" (October 29, 1963), in *Hélio Oiticica*, 67; previously published in *Aspiro ao grande labirinto (textos de Hélio Oiticica)*, ed. Luciano Figueiredo et al. (Rio de Janeiro: Edições Rocco, 1986).
21 Clark, "Sobre o ritual," 122.
22 Clark, "A propósito da magia do objeto," in *Livro-obra;* reprinted in Borja-Villel, *Lygia Clark*, 154.
23 Torres-García, *Metafisica de la prehistoria indo-americana* (Montevideo: Ediciones La Regla de Oro, 1939), 25.
24 Torres-García, *La recuperación del objeto*, 88–9.
25 Clark, "Um mito moderno: O instante como nostalgia do cosmos" (Rio de Janeiro, 1983); reprinted in *Lygia Clark* (Rio de Janeiro: FUNARTE, 1980), 29.
26 Oiticica, "Cor, tempo e estrutura," in *Hélio Oiticica*, 35.
27 Gullar, "Manifesto neoconcreto," 80.

28 See, for instance, the following passage from Torres-García's *Universalismo Constructivo* regarding a layman's reaction to the idea of a universal-constructive art: "I guess I understood your idea. In fact, what you want is to take very little or nothing of what has been produced in art lately. You want to begin anew, as if the world had collapsed. Isn't it? Exactly, I answered, that is my idea of a universal art." See *Universalismo Constructivo*, 666.

29 Torres-Garcia, *Mi opinión sobre la Exposición de Artistas Norteamericanos* (Montevideo: Ediciones La Regla de Oro, 1942), 18.

30 Arden Quin, "Invención," reprinted in *Heterotopías: Medio siglo sin lugar, 1918–1968*, by Mari Carmen Ramírez and Héctor Olea (Madrid: Museo Nacional Centro de Arte Reina Sofia, 2000), 500–1.

31 "Manifiesto Madí," in Kosice, *Arte Madí*, 36. The group handled very peculiar MAterialistic and DIalectic (ma-di) terms throughout their movement.

32 Gullar cited in Morais, "A vocação construtiva da arte latino-americana (mas o caos permanece)," in Pontual et al., *América Latina: Geometria Sensivel*, 24.

33 Mário Pedrosa cited in ibid.

34 Oiticica, "Bases fundamentais para uma definição do *Parangolé*" (1964), in *Hélio Oiticica*, 86.

35 Clark, "Sobre o ritual," 122.

36 Torres-García, "¿Qué es el arte constructivo?" (Montevideo, 1938); reprinted in *Continente Sul Sur*, 6:47.

33

Landscape

Errant Modernist Aesthetics in Brazil

Esther Gabara*

In this excerpt from her book on modern photography in Mexico and Brazil, US-based art and literary historian Esther Gabara focuses on Mario de Andrade's unpublished journals and the photographs he took while on two journeys through Brazil's interior between 1927 and 1929. Gabara asserts that these trips were essential to the development of Mario's theory of modernism in Brazil as necessarily "errado," meaning errant or erroneous, both lost and mistaken. She notes that Mario deliberately *errs* in his photographs of the Brazilian landscape through bad cropping, unaesthetic angles, poor focus, and overexposure. She links these errors to his awareness that travel writing, ethnography, folklore, and the genre of landscape have long been tools of empire within European colonies. As a light-skinned, urban intellectual taking pictures of an impoverished rural landscape and its largely dark-skinned populations, Mario identified with both the colonizer and the colonized. His errant position as both an insider and an outsider within Brazil recalls the race privilege and alienation of the settler class within Latin America's postcolonial nations. The paradox of being at once Brazilian (a specific nationality associated with an underdeveloped periphery) and modern (implicitly coded as European and therefore "universal") compelled an ethics of image making that moved, necessarily, beyond questions of aesthetics. How can the artist celebrate urban modernity without ignoring its relation to rural exploitation? Can the photographer address the legacies of colonialism and the slave trade without subjecting the racial "other" to a primitivizing or exoticizing gaze? Does abstraction sacrifice the referentiality necessary for a "critical modernism" capable of "facing"

* Esther Gabara (2008) "Landscape: Errant Modernist Aesthetics in Brazil." In *Errant Modernism: The Ethos of Photography in Mexico and Brazil* (pp. 36–50). Durham, NC: Duke University Press.

Modern Art in Africa, Asia, and Latin America: An Introduction to Global Modernisms, First Edition.
Edited by Elaine O'Brien, Everlyn Nicodemus, Melissa Chiu, Benjamin Genocchio, Mary K. Coffey, and Roberto Tejada.

(confronting/representing) rather than effacing (erasing/misrepresenting) Brazil and its place within international modernism?

Gabara elaborates Mario's modern ethic through a comparison with European artists who also distorted the landscape through abstraction. She argues that all modernist art partakes of one kind of errancy, that of correcting a perceived "error" in earlier representations of the subject. So, for example, by refusing landscape's traditional task of depicting (in an idealized form) a specific place modernist artists like Matisse, Gauguin, Munch, Kandinsky, or Mondrian, sacrificed naturalism in order to penetrate appearances and access a deeper "truth" that for them was trans-historical or "universal." Like his European peers, Mario deliberately distorts the Brazilian landscape through formal techniques that abstract it. However, Gabara argues that Mario engaged in a second kind of errancy that we do not find in the art of European modernists. Through photography's inherent capacity to index the real, Mario's images do refer to the Brazilian landscape; however, his deliberate formal "mistakes" appear to be "wrong" to the viewer. That is, they vacillate between abstraction and representation, between conjuring a specific locality and aspiring, via abstraction, to the status of the "universal," between being formally experimental images and "bad" photographs. For Gabara, Mario's photographs – "ethically engaged, but judged to be wrong" – exemplify the ethics of the theory of modernism he elaborated.

Further Readings

Dunn, Christopher (2001) *Brutality Garden: Tropicália and the Emergence of a Brazilian Counterculture*. Chapel Hill: University of North Carolina Press.

Schwartz, J. *et al.* (2000) *Brasil, 1920–1950: De la Antropofagia a Brasilia*. Valencia, Spain: IVAM Centro Julio González.

Sullivan, Edward (ed.) (2001) *Brazil: Body and Soul*. New York, NY: The Solomon R. Guggenheim Foundation.

Tejada, Roberto (2009) *National Camera: Photography and Mexico's Image Environment*. Minneapolis: University of Minnesota Press.

Setting off on a monthlong journey that will take him from bustling São Paulo to the farthest internal border of Brazil with Peru and Bolivia, his small Kodak camera in hand, Mário de Andrade panics: "My impression is that everything is wrong [*errado*]. I had an urge to fling all those people in the wagon, to stay on that eternally *Paulistana* platform, and to cry contently to my departing friends: 'Bye folks! Bon voyage! Have a lot of fun … Bon voyage!' "[1] Although Mário was one of the few modernists who never went to Europe, he was also one of the few who traveled throughout Brazil, complaining bitterly all the while. His two major journeys were the source for the manuscript *O turista aprendiz*, […] a parodic and inventive manuscript that combines tourist diary, ethnographic and folkloric collection, poetry, photographs, drawings, and fictions.

The crucial word in the opening passage of Mário's manuscript is *errado*, meaning both errant and erroneous, lost and mistaken. Each time the word *errar* appears, we must simultaneously picture a movement and an intentional mistake. Mário is not simply weary of the burden of the educated, civilized traveler setting off into the wilderness. He is certain that he is the wrong man for the job, or as we shall see, that he is the right man to do the job wrong. Mário even differentiates the serious and organized results of his "Portuguese error" from Oswald de Andrade's linguistic jokes, which he finds to be merely comic.[2] In a Brazilian modernist ethos everything must be "errado," which means that it is both local and out of place, ethically engaged but judged to be wrong, and, finally, abstract but referential. Mário composes this errant modernism in literary and photographic landscapes, simultaneously reproducing and parodying the genre natural to colonizers, naturalist explorers, and even members of the international avant-garde who visited Brazil, such as Blaise Cendrars and Filippo Marinetti.

Like any genre, landscape has its rules of conduct and a history in both the visual and literary arts. In the eighteenth century, cultured domestic landscapes showed smooth fields and shapely bushes, revealing no trace of the work done to create their views. […] Colonial landscapes served a very practical function in addition to their more subtle contribution to the colonial imagination: that of surveying the contents of the new possessions. […] Mário's photographs and texts contest this history and theory of the genre, foreground rather than erase the power relations implicit in the view, and insert modernist landscapes directly into the field of human life, politics, and ethics.

The title page of *O turista aprendiz* features a cartoonishly drawn parody of America with a tiny clownlike crown tipped on the side of her head, which mocks colonial engravings of America receiving European conquerors with a combination of seduction and deception […] Mário's preface expresses his fascination and difficulties with this inherited genre of the travel narrative:

> More a warning than a preface. During this journey through Amazonia, very resolved to write a modernist book, probably more resolved to write than to travel, I took a lot of notes, as you will see. Rapid notes, telegraphic many times. … But almost everything noted still without any intention of a work of art, reserved for future elaborations, *without the slightest intention to let others know about the land traveled*. And I never completed the definitive elaboration. I made a few attempts, I did. But I stopped right at the beginning, I don't know why, displeased.[3]

Mário's aborted travel narrative was never meant to represent Brazil to an uninitiated reader, and the knowledge refused blocks the easy acquisition of the natural resources contained in the vast interior of Brazil, as much as it interrupts the unifying, foundational promise of travel writing. His prefatory refusal to feed the appetite for an exotic Brazil is an early sign of the ethics of place contained in the landscapes that follow.

Yet apprentice tourism is based upon a paradox. While it would be tactically imprudent and unethical to reveal the riches contained in Brazil, Mário also reveals an urgent political need to locate the country accurately for all of its inhabitants. Nationalist sentiment – the desire to both promote and protect the nation – is thus at odds with itself when it comes to the creation and diffusion of knowledge in the postcolonial context. How is Mário to assert Brazil's place in the international sphere without revealing its secrets? [...] In response to this dilemma, we shall see that rather than attempt to capture the real, authentic place of Brazil, Mário created photographic landscapes that *err*. They paradoxically locate the nation and set the borders that define it into motion.

In the early decades of the twentieth century, landscape became a key genre for experiments with abstraction in mainstream modernism, and Mário's practice of errar produces a kind of abstraction that alters crucial aesthetic, ethical, and political characteristics generally associated with the genre. In the more familiar places of modernism such as Paris and Berlin, abstraction reinvented landscape in order to create a universal modernist aesthetic, such that the place these landscapes represented was the space of the two-dimensional representation itself. Effectively, the horizon of figurative landscapes is converted into an abstract line whose function is to divide the flat space of the canvas or print. [...] Once translated into abstraction, the horizon line no longer bears any relationship to the idea of a place contained in the original horizon. Modernist landscapes effectively lose their place in their achievement of this new aesthetic. However, when the landscape that the modernist artist reconfigures is a colonial landscape seen from within, the form and meaning of the resulting abstraction changes. Mário created landscapes that counter the trajectory of modernism, and of the genre itself. [...] Instead, these errant landscapes frame a photographic space that is always productively adulterated by the place of Brazil. This chapter examines how Mário used photography to alter the genre of landscape and thus created a modernist ethos that is simultaneously abstract and located in Brazil's colonial experience.

Modernist erring contains two movements: the first judgment locates an original error, which must be corrected by an intervening act; the second finds the first intervention to be already wrong and proclaims an aesthetic result of error itself. Mário emboldens the familiar avant-garde strategy of creating abstraction through formal distortion with his practice of errar. Distortion in mainstream modernism does not include the double ethical and aesthetic judgment inherent in errar. [...] The genre of landscape that provides mainstream modernism with the opportunity for abstract and universal truth contains something very different for Mário. The aesthetic pictured in landscapes on the periphery includes an ethical judgment about *how to live* in this particular, invented, and never quite representable place. Errant abstraction maintains the place of figurative landscape, even as it distorts its content and appearance.

It is important to note that photography presents a special challenge to the link between abstraction, landscape, and modernism. [...] The problem [...] is that the same medium-based abstraction that makes paintings modernist, and therefore isolated from the social, appears to defy photography's "natural" function of anecdotal mimeticism, its automatic figuration. While Euro-American modernists nevertheless are known for making photography produce a kind of abstraction in response to this dilemma, Mário instead focused on its resistance to these purer images.[4] Rather than make photography present abstract concepts of light and object, he made it *err*. Photography's special relationship to mimetic representation in fact reveals the intentional formal and conceptual errors that Mário made in his Brazilian landscapes. Due to the medium's ease of figurative representation, intentional errors are more obvious in photographs than in painting; while an error in a painting, especially a figurative one, may simply be taken as the sign of a bad painter, a "bad photograph" is rarely judged as such because it tried to reproduce a scene and failed. Mário made photographs look wrong, precisely because of their presumed mimetic function. "Accidental *desvairismo* / question of a boat [*lancha*] and/of *lunch* [English original]/June 7, 1927" shows a seated man and girl and does everything possible wrong: it decapitates both subjects, includes high-contrast blotches of light and shadow, turns the pictorial space at a forty-five-degree angle, and provides no context (no background) of the place in which the photograph was taken. These errors are the accidental encounter with "desvairismo," the titular concept of Mário's breakthrough poetry collection *Paulicéia desvairada* (*Hallucinated City*, 1922). This ode to modern São Paulo contains as its preface his first theory of modernism, which he read as a manifesto during the Week of Modern Art. So sought after in poetry, *desvairismo* is accidentally found in this photograph, as if by mistake. The landscapes included in *O turista aprendiz* constitute an ethos of modernist abstraction in photographs that references and exceeds the framing act of photography itself. They picture photography's invasive act of seeing and insistently populate even abstract landscapes by including figures as well as a corporealized photographer within the frame.

The ethical importance of this error lies precisely in its configuration of place, of the locale that remains inscribed in these photographs. The technical language and mechanics of photography reveal its intimate relationship to the determination of place: focal length, a basic setting of any standard single lens reflex camera of the kind that Mário was already using, is the distance from the lens of the camera to its point of focus. It is a measure of the space between the photographic machine (and generally the photographer) and the desired image. [...] Photographic language easily has entered common parlance and literary analysis, both of which link the focus of the camera with the position of the photographer in relation to his or her subject. Their proximity and the shared place it designates contribute to the conceptualization of the ethos of modernism, but as we shall see ultimately are not sufficient for its ethics. The errant photographs that Mário produced present neither strictly figurative nor entirely abstract images of the landscape of Brazil as they enact the ethical value of place in modernist aesthetics.

Mário began to photograph in earnest during the two journeys that make up the parodic and yet ethnographically detailed travel narratives of *O turista aprendiz*. During the first journey in 1927, Mário took 540 photographs; during the second,

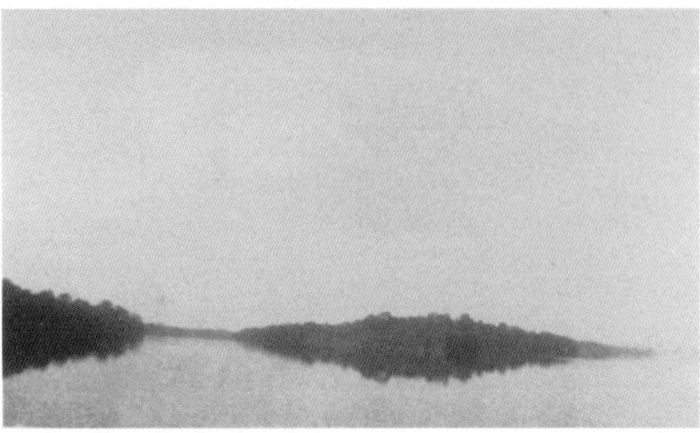

Figure 33.1 Mario de Andrade, "Entry of an Inlet, Madeira river, July 5, 1927, Island of Manicoré," Arquivo do Instituto de Estudos Brasileiros da Universidade de São Paulo – Fundo Mário de Andrade, código do documento: MA-F-0370.

between 1928 and 1929, he took 260. A very careful and interested photographer, Mário experimented with double-exposed images and frequently documented technical information about the images, noting the aperture and position of the sun in multiple photographs of the same subject. Nevertheless, his photographs are literally humble: printed small (most just 2 × 2 inches) and not exhibited publicly, they are like the tiny face of the cartoonish America seen above, who refuses to exaggerate her status. Kept with the unpublished manuscript, these modest photographs nonetheless prove to play a critical role in Mário's theory of modernism, which [...] is framed as a surprisingly humble sublime. Certain photographs, however, appeared to fascinate Mário; these he enlarged several times over, up to 8 × 11 inches. A photograph from the first trip, "Entry of an inlet [*paraná*] or inlet [*paranã*]/Madeira River/July 5, 1927 Island of Manicoré!" hints at the aesthetic possibilities and the ethical dilemmas Mário will elaborate during this extended journey of investigation. It shows an island dividing the brightness of the overexposed sky from similarly bright water; the island merges with its own dark reflection in a black oblong form. The horizon line of the landscape almost disappears into the reflection of island and sky, and the river that should lead into the heart of Brazil becomes a confusing mirror. The apprentice tourist's inviting path is confounded by the trompe l'oeil of horizon and river, yet the exclamation point ending the title reveals that Mário's enthusiasm is not dampened. The photograph shows what a landscape looks like when the foreign explorer of Brazil is replaced with a (disoriented) Brazilian modernist writer and photographer, who proclaims himself an apprentice but who has much to teach about the meaning of that disappearing horizon, of mirrors, and of place itself.

Ethos as Locale

The first and most colloquial definition of ethos connotes a habit or way of life. Embedded in this habit of living is the idea of living a particular way in a certain place. The word's etymological root in *ethêa*, meaning "haunts" or "hang outs," links ethos with a strange sort of home. [...] The particular knowledge of this ethos – between wandering and dwelling, subject and other – appears in Mário's configuration of the place of Brazil and the landscapes that compose it. The double meaning of ethos as a mobile home works through this modernist aesthetics and sets forth an ethical mode of living in the world.

This wandering locale appears in Mário's practice of errar, which makes possible a unique theory of the local that combines nationalism, far-ranging Americanism, and cosmopolitanism. Reshaping the form and content of the modern nation, it also connects Brazil with Spanish America. Mário develops a modernist aesthetics through the reconfiguration of the diverse geographical spaces of Brazil: from urban to rural, from the coastal areas to the border with Peru. In order to understand modernity's place, we find that we have to cover a great deal of territory, from city to interior, across the contested border with Peru and back to the city of São Paulo. The camera accompanies us to all of these places. In the early 1920s, Mário's representation of life in increasingly industrial São Paulo presents an ecstatic model of poetic production as a kind of modern machine, a type of lyrical camera. In the second half of the decade, Mário's journey north to Rio de Janeiro and west along the Amazon and Madeira rivers into the interior of the country led him to a careful examination of photographic technology and to a more complex view of modernist artistic production. During this second phase, Mário was most actively producing photographs himself, and the effects of this practice appear clearly in changes in his modernist poetics. Not satisfied with nineteenth-century, utopian nationalist representations of Brazilian natural phenomena nor convinced by Futurism's hyperbolic proclamations about the city, Mário combined experimental lyrics with photographic vision to create a modernist ethos. His concept of the local nature of modernism works through the tradition of landscape – in both image and word – and its relationship to forms of abstraction.

Errar, Part 1: Writing Brazilian

From his early writings until his death, Mário phonetically transcribed the colloquialisms of Brazilian Portuguese in texts replete with orthographic and grammatical "mistakes." He even worked on a kind of textbook of "Brazilian" grammar that formalized these errors.[5] While he carried out research into indigenous cultures throughout his life, [...] Mário does not dream of a Brazil in which the national language would revert to the major indigenous-language group, Tupi. Instead, his vision of national expression takes the form of an incorrect Portuguese reinvented in Brazil. Mário reconfigures a modernist lyric voice as part of a broader epistemological claim that emerges out of the traumatic legacy of colonialism in Brazil, revealed in the pressure to write in Portuguese even though he speaks Brazilian. He conceives of a language that is flawed, disfigured, by its place of inscription as much as utterance.[6] Modernist lyricism becomes not simply a question of poetic stylistic conventions, but also an epistemological proposal for writing and speaking "Brazilian": a poetically self-conscious, abstract metalanguage that articulates an ethics and an aesthetics.

[...]

Errar, Part 2: Cities out of Place

[…] As much as Mário sought to liberate Brazilian aesthetics from its colonial past, he was also painfully aware of a similar dynamic between center and periphery that governed the city of São Paulo's relationship with its rural populations. In the early 1920s, the city was the site of contact between its longtime inhabitants, Afro-Brazilian and indigenous rural populations arriving in search of relief from poverty, and a variety of European (especially Italian and Polish) and Japanese immigrants. Mário's vision of this contact was less celebratory than Oswald de Andrade's famous "Anthropophagist Manifesto," and the tension between the imagination of the modern nation as urban and the overwhelming historical and literary associations of Brazilian identity with its rural interior permeates his theory of modernism. The beginnings of Brazilian modernism are located in major shifts in the landscape of the city, but loyal to the ethos of erring, it immediately begins to wander through Brazil.[7]

[…]

Concern for that rural Brazil led Mário to make the two journeys into the interior between 1927 and 1929, traveling with his camera in hand. These trips are the source for much of his writing during the next decade […]. Immediately following these journeys in 1929, Mário explains his concern with incorporating the rural into his nationalist modernism: "A concern for cities is dominant. They seek to synthesize a civilization and progress that do not correspond to the national reality. There is established therefore, a disequilibrium between these centers and the rest of the country. … And when we remember that the fascination with the cities is at the cost of that immense mass of Brazilians … we find a point for profound meditations."[8] He finds that he must represent a modern Brazil that is simultaneously made up of this "massa immensa," the settled *paulistas*, and the increasing movement of these groups from one place to another.

Mário pictures a tense and errant place of the modern Latin American intellectual: rooted in São Paulo, looking both at Paris and toward the interior of Brazil, he creates an aesthetics self-consciously located at the intersection of West and non-West. Thus, despite his loathing of travel, Mário must set off on a journey, producing landscapes that reflect on the awkward relationship of proximity and distance between city and country. Travel brings him closer to the rural space that he named "Brazil with its arms crossed," yet he will also struggle against the history of representing these places. He experiments with photographs and text in order to reconfigure the genre of landscape and to create a Brazilian modernist ethos in which the aesthetic and ethical concerns of picturing place are equally urgent and intertwined. This ethos ultimately makes possible what Mário terms "critical nationalism," a bridge between this ethical and aesthetic union and its political promise.

[…]

Notes

1 De Andrade, *O turista aprendiz*, 201: "Minha impressão é que está tudo *errado*. Tive ímpeto de botar toda aquela gentarada no vagão, ficar na plataforma eternamente paulistana e berrar contente pros amigos partindo: – Adeus, gente! Boa viagem! Divirtam bastante … Boa Viagem!" Henceforth cited as *TA*.

2 See Schwartz, *Las vanguardias latinoamericanas*, 64.

3 *TA*, 49, emphasis added. […]

4 Canonical exemplars of modernist photography took straight photographs that nonetheless displayed abstracted images of the medium's own tools: light, perspective, and focalization. Edward Weston, Man Ray, and Henri Cartier-Bresson produced "abstracted" images not through any manipulation of photographic negative or print, but rather in their use of close-ups, cropping, and lighting. These photographers are best known for their compositions of light and shadow, paper forms, and everyday objects made abstract. Mainstream modernist photography is thus declaredly about the use of light and lens, a "true" photography that despite its capture of an image from the world is able to present an abstract, formal essence.

5 This was a project he announced, but never published, a "Gramatiquinha da Fala Brasileira" ("Little Grammar of Brazilian Speech").

6 Similar linguistic play appeared in Latin American avant-garde movements from Peru to Cuba, many of which responded to the desire to write national literatures in the language of former colonial powers. […]

7 There were many modernist writers and artists outside of São Paulo and Rio de Janeiro, many of whom corresponded with Mário. […]

8 "E o Interior," 3. […]

Bibliography

Andrade, Mário de. *Amar, verbo intransitivo: Idilio*. 1927. São Paulo: Livraria Martins Editora, 1955.

Andrade, Mário de. "E o Interior," *Movimento* 1, no. 2 (1929): 3.

Andrade, Mário de. *O turista aprendiz*. Edited by Telê Ancona Lopez. São Paulo: Livraria Duas Cidades, 1978.

Schwartz, Jorge. *Las vanguardias latinoamericanas: Textos programáticos y críticos*. Portuguese translated by Estela dos Santos. Madrid: Catedra, 1991.

34

The Spirit of Brasília

Modernity as Experiment and Risk

James Holston*

In this essay US-based social cultural anthropologist James Holston examines the building of Brazil's capital city in the late 1950s as "stagecraft" for a charismatic state. Unlike other studies of Brasília that focus exclusively on the principles of urban planning and modernist architecture exemplified by its built environment, Holston emphasizes the tensions between the city's utopian and totalizing plan and the contingency design and improvisation undertaken by the laborers charged with building it and by the inhabitants who ultimately lived there (see Valerie Fraser's essay on Brasília in *Building the New World: Studies in the Modern Architecture of Latin America, 1930–1960*). Holston notes that before Brasília was built it existed as a massive public relations campaign for the modernizing will of the national government. He characterizes this will as "millenarian" insofar as it "proposed to transform an unwanted present (the rest of Brazil) by means of a future imagined as radically different." In that future Brasília's streamlined modernity would inoculate the rest of the country against the legacies of colonization, namely underdevelopment, racial inequality, class stratification, and persistent poverty.

In order to appreciate fully Holston's discussion of the "millenarian modern" it is helpful to understand the origins of Brasília as a state project. While there were proposals to create a federal district by relocating the capital to the central plateau as early as 1891 (the first decade of Brazil's independence from Portugal), the initiative was not enacted until 1955 with the election of the progressive visionary and patron of modern art Jucelino Kubitschek to the presidency. As part of his broad national program for rapid industrialization, Kubitschek formed a development corporation

* James Holston (2001) "The Spirit of Brasília: Modernity as Experiment and Risk." In Edward J. Sullivan (ed.) *Brazil Body and Soul* (pp. 540–57), New York, NY: Guggenheim Museum.

Modern Art in Africa, Asia, and Latin America: An Introduction to Global Modernisms, First Edition.
Edited by Elaine O'Brien, Everlyn Nicodemus, Melissa Chiu, Benjamin Genocchio,
Mary K. Coffey, and Roberto Tejada.

(Companhia Urbanizadora da Nova Capital do Brasil/NOVACAP), headed by his long-time friend and collaborator the architect Oscar Niemeyer, to organize and jury a competition for the design of the city with the goal of completing the project during his presidency. The building of Brasília in just three and a half years stands as but one of Kubitschek's accomplishments.

NOVACAP selected a plan submitted by Lúcio Costa, known as the "plano piloto" (or pilot plan) that modeled the city layout according to the principles of modern city planning elaborated by Le Corbusier and promoted internationally by the Congrés Internationaux d'Architecture Moderne (CIAM). Whereas Holston argues that Brasília is the "most complete example of CIAM tenets ever constructed," he insists that it is not a mere copy. Rather, he describes it as "generative and original" insofar as the Kubitschek state recognized that the value of the urban design promoted by CIAM was its emblematic claim to represent modernity. In adopting this paradigm for the new capital, the state theatrically rejected architectural styles and urban plans associated with Brazil's colonial past (namely the Baroque and the Neoclassical) and demonstrated its capacity not only to be modern itself, but also to modernize the country through "spectacular public works."

As Holston notes, CIAM design imposed totalizing measures to reorganize both public and private space. Brasília's plan did away with the "spatial logic" of preindustrial cities by eliminating sidewalks, corners, and "corridor streets." It attempted to homogenize social classes and eradicate slums by creating identical "collective dwelling" units stripped of traditional features. While Holston argues that these methods were "brutally effective," they were also challenged immediately by an insurgent reality that no totalizing plan could completely control. Holston focuses on the tensions between the plan's utopian logic and the errant desires of the workers, bureaucrats, and entrepreneurs who pioneered and populated Brasília. To this day, he argues, the evolution of Brasília is marked by the development of insurgent modifications that deform the original plan. Ironically, the state's ongoing attempts to "entomb" the city in its original form militate against the spirit of improvisation and risk that brought Brasília into being.

For a deeper understanding of the generative tensions of modern art in Latin America, Holston's discussion of Brasília can be considered alongside other discussions of modern art in this book. How does the "millenarian modern" as a solution to Brazil's social and regional inequities differ from Mario de Andrade's theory of modernism on the periphery? Can Folgarait's analysis of Rivera's National Palace mural as propaganda for the *Maximato* in postrevolutionary Mexico be applied to the relationship between Costa's plan or Niemeyer's architecture and the Kubitschek state? How does Holsten's discussion of Brasília as an "original copy" of the CIAM's model city relate to Ramirez's arguments about the constructivist impulse in South America? You can read in the African modern art section of this book about the modern town of New Gourna created in the 1940s from the ground up by Egyptian architect and urban designer Hassan Fathy. How does Fathy's design for New Gourna compare with the Costa and Niemeyer designs for Brasília in the 1950s? What were the motives of the architects and the governments that commissioned them? What dilemmas characterize the confrontation between modern and traditional architecture and city planning in Egypt and Brazil?

Further Readings

Fraser, Valerie (2000) *Building the New World: Modern Architecture in Latin America.* London, England: Verso.

Holsten, James (1989) *The Modernist City: An Anthropological Critique of Brasilia.* Chicago, IL: University of Chicago Press.

Underwood, David Kendrick (1994) *Oscar Niemeyer and Brazilian Free-Form Modernism.* New York, NY: George Braziller.

Travelers usually experience Brasília as a city removed from the rest of Brazil. This sense of separation derives in part from Brasília's great distance from the Atlantic coast [...]. By road or by air, travelers must cross this distance to reach the city. They traverse a limbo not of jungle, as outsiders sometimes imagine, but of two million square kilometers of highland *cerrado*, dry and stunted, that is the desolate Central Plateau of Brazil. At the approximate center of this flatland, Brasília comes into view as an exclamation mark on the horizon, like an idea, heroic and romantic, the acropolis of an enormous empty expanse. Once swept inside the city on its superspeedways, travelers confront a more complex separation, that of Modernist Brasília from the familiar Brazil: they encounter an entire city of detached rectangular boxes, the transparencies of a world of glass facades, automobile traffic flowing uninhibited in all directions, vast spaces seemingly empty without the social life of streets and squares, and serial order, clean, quiet, and efficient. In short, they find modernity, regulation, and progress on display.

Yet if this urbanism appears incongruously Brazilian, for those who know Brazil, Brasília's history expresses at the same time a remarkably Brazilian way of doing things. By history, I refer to the processes of building the city and structuring its society. Although their result may appear the opposite today, these processes also exemplify that knack for improvisation for which Brazil is famous. I mean that sense of invention found in so many facets of Brazilian life, from soccer and samba to *telenovelas*, from theories of modernity (such as *Antropofagia*) to everyday race mixing, from "autoconstructed" (self-built) housing in the urban peripheries to federal initiatives in the treatment of AIDS. It is improvisation by design, a desire to overcome by leaping, an instinct for the advantages of play. It is the need to be modern that views a lack of resources as an opportunity for innovation. After all, Brazilians built Brasília in just three and a half years. They turned a spot in the middle of nowhere, marked by an "x" on the ground, not only into an inhabitable city in record time but also into one that presented to the whole world of 1960 the most modern form of urbanism. To do so, they employed the tactics of bricolage, and they experimented in all fields. Thus, they reproduced in pioneering Brasília Brazil's distinctive style of inventing its own modernity.

In specific ways, therefore, Brasília is both radically separate from and part of the "rest of Brazil." Examples of this contradiction abound. For example, Brasília's Master Plan prohibited the development of an urban periphery for the city's poor, typical of other Brazilian cities. As the national capital, Brasília had to be different, and its planners aimed to preclude unwanted characteristics of the rest of Brazil. Yet, as I explain later, government policy created an impoverished periphery of Satellite Cities even before the capital's inauguration in 1960, "Brazilianizing" its foundations. Therefore both the Plano Piloto (as the privileged Modernist city is called) and the Satellite Cities constitute Brasília, which must be understood as a regional city from the beginning. The city that resulted, however, does not simply reproduce the rest of Brazil around it that planners wanted to deny. In its combination of the radically new and the familiar, Brasília remains distinct in the constellation of Brazilian cities.

This special quality derives not so much from the city's identity as a capital of capitals, but from Brasília's founding conception as an experiment in urbanism to risk something new. It is precisely this daring to embrace the modern as a field for experiment and risk that the city's pioneers called the "spirit of Brasília." This spirit of innovation structured Brasília at many levels. It motivated planners to make Brasília different, not for the sake of exoticism but to establish an arena of experimentation in which to solve important national problems. In some aspects, Brasília's experiments succeeded; in others they failed. But both successes and failures derive from the same source, as both possibilities accompany genuine experiments.

If the spirit of Brasília is, therefore, that of experiment, is it not strange that this city of total design and improvisation, of innovation and contradiction, is now frozen in time? That is, the entire urban area of the Plano Piloto is legally preserved – entombed or *tombado*, as Brazilians call this preservation of patrimony – by local, national, and international layers of legal protection. If this experimental city has thus become a memorial, what memory does it record? To memorialize is never to tell the whole story. It is rather to select certain conditions that the memorializers want to preserve and ignore others. Thus, the spirit of a place – what the Romans called its *genius loci* – consists of what is both emplaced and displaced in memoriam. In these terms, what is the genius of Brasília, constructed in the backlands of Brazil in the late 1950s, and has its spirit been compromised by preservation? In what follows, I address these questions in turn.

Statecraft and Stagecraft

The Plano Piloto's basic residential units are all equal [...]

As for the apartments themselves, some are larger and some are smaller in number of rooms. They are distributed, respectively, to families on the basis of the number of dependents they have. And because of this distribution and the nonexistence of social class discrimination, the residents of a superquadra are forced to live as if in the sphere of one big family, in perfect social coexistence [...]

This description of "perfect social coexistence" [...] is taken from the periodical of the state corporation (Novacap) that planned, built, and administered Brasília – from a "report" on living conditions in the new capital three years after its inauguration. Nevertheless, it presents the fundamentally utopian premise that the design and organization of Brasília were meant to transform Brazilian society. Moreover, it does so according to conventions of utopian discourse: by an implicit comparison with and negation of existing social conditions. In this case, the subtext is the rest of Brazil, where society is perniciously stratified into social classes, where access to city services and facilities is differentially distributed by wealth and race, and where residential organization and architecture are primary markers of social standing. Brasília is put forth not merely as the antithesis of this stratification, but also as its antidote, as the "cradle of a new civilization." Furthermore, planners assume what they wish to prove, namely, that the unequal distribution of advantage that orders urban life elsewhere in Brazil is already negated in Brasília.

This thesis of negation and invention is the premise that structures Brasília's foundation. It is at the core of what Brazilians meant when they referred to the spirit or idea of Brasília, epithets widely used during the pioneering phase of the city. As such, this idea crystallizes an important paradigm of Modernity. It proposes that the state, as a national government, can change society and manage the social by imposing an alternative future embodied in plans – in effect, that it can make a new people according to plan. Moreover, as a Modernist plan, this idea is millenarian. It proposes to transform an unwanted present (the rest of Brazil) by means of a future imagined as radically different. This millenarian modern exemplifies a kind of stagecraft that has come to define the statecraft of modern nation-building: modern states use planned public works to promote new forms of collective association and personal habit that constitute their projected nation.[1]

Brasília's Modernism is exemplary of this statecraft. [...]

[...] Brasília's founders envisioned it as more than the symbol of a new age. They also intended Brasília's Modernist design and construction as the means to create that new age by transforming Brazilian society. They saw it as the means to invent a new nation for a new capital – a new nation to which this radically different city would then "logically belong" as Costa claimed.[2]

This project of transformation redefines Brazilian society according to the assumptions of a particular narrative of the Modern, that of the Modernist city proposed in the manifestos of CIAM (Congrès Internationaux d'Architecture Moderne). In Brasília, this model is most clearly expressed in Costa's Master Plan and in the architecture of Oscar Niemeyer, the city's principal architect. But it is also embodied in many other aspects of the city's organization. From the 1920s until the 1970s (and in many places, until today), CIAM established a worldwide consensus among architects and planners on problems confronting the modern city. This consensus was especially shaped by the visionary architect Le Corbusier, whose writing framed its themes and whose urban design became its dominant grammar. As interpreted with world-renowned clarity by Costa and Niemeyer in the 1950s, Brasília is the most complete example of CIAM tenets ever constructed.

[...] As is universally acknowledged, the project of Brasília is a blueprint-perfect embodiment of the CIAM model city. Moreover, its design is a brilliant reproduction of Le Corbusier's version of that model.[3] The point I want to make, however, is not that Brasília is merely a copy. Rather, it is that as a Brazilian rendition of CIAM's

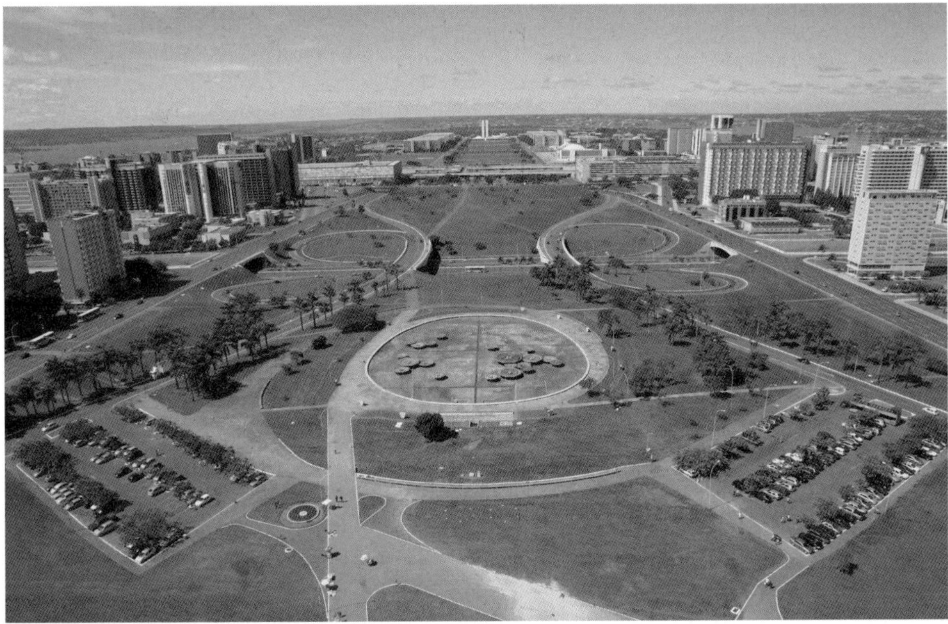

Figure 34.1 Aerial view of Brasilia's South Wing, showing residential superquadras and row houses. Ton Koene, © Picture Contact BV, Alamy Images.

global Modernism, its copy is generative and original. [...] Brasília is a CIAM city inserted into what was the margins of modernity in the 1950s, inserted into the Modernist ambitions of a postcolony. In this context, the very purpose of the project was to capture the spirit of the modern by means of its likeness, its copy. It is this homeopathic relation to the model, brilliantly executed to be sure, that gives the copy its transformative power. [...] This display of an "original copy" constitutes the stagecraft that I referred to earlier as statecraft. It is the state in its theatrical form, in the sense of constructing itself by putting on spectacular public works. Under Kubitschek, Brazil showed itself to be modern by staging it. As the centers of decisive political, economic, and cultural power remained elsewhere in Brazil for at least a decade, Brasília's initial mission was above all gestural: to display modern architecture as the index of Brazil's own modernity as a new nation, establishing an elective affinity between the two.

[...]

Innovation by Design

Brasília was designed to mirror to the rest of Brazil the modern nation it would become. [...] Brasília [was to be] a civilizing agent, the missionary of a new sense of national space, time, and purpose, colonizing the whole into which it has been inserted.

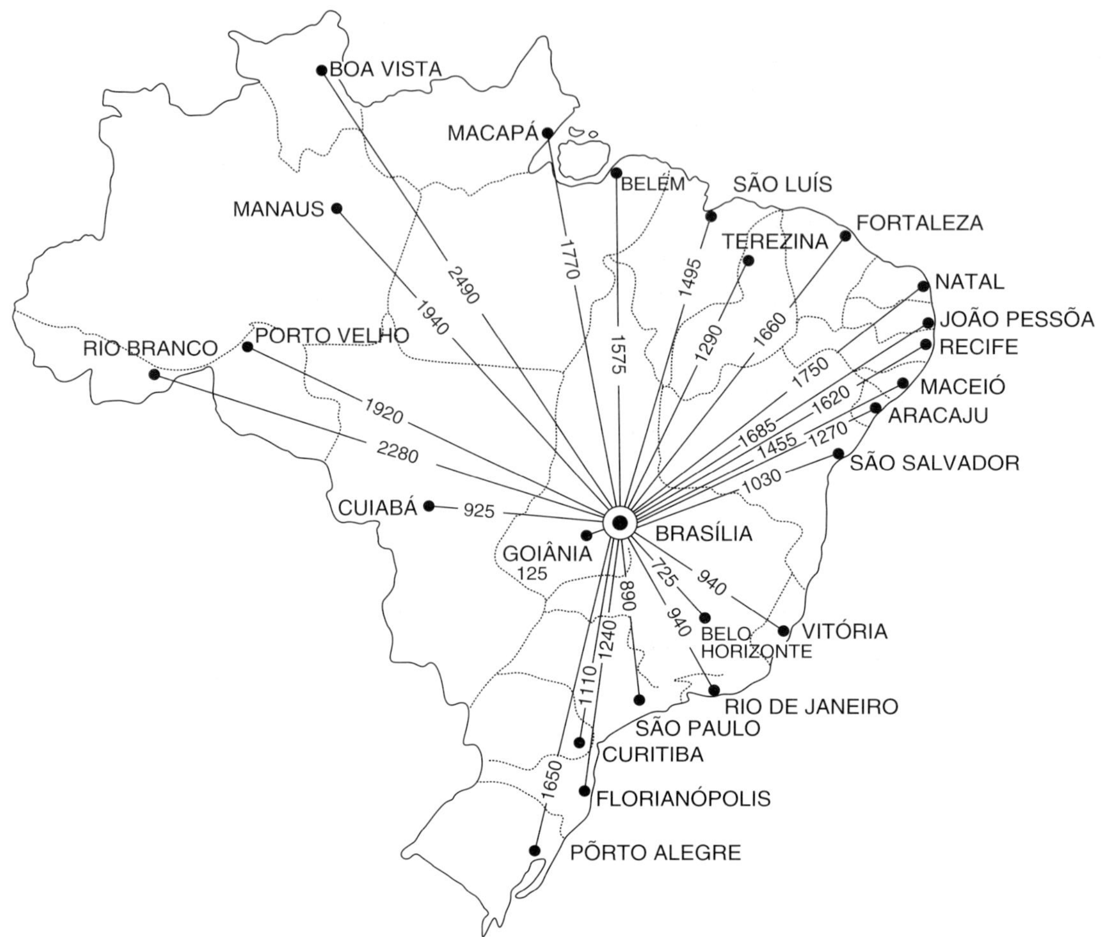

Figure 34.2 Map from an elementary school textbook used to illustrate the idea of Brasilia as the hub of national development. From James Holston, *A Modernist City: An Anthropological Critique of Brazilia*, map 1.2, page 19, 1989. University of Chicago Press, All Rights Reserved.

[…]

[...] Brasília's Modernism signified Brazil's emergence as a modern nation because it simultaneously broke with the colonial legacies of underdevelopment as it posited an industrial modernity. The new architecture and planning attacked the styles of the past – the Iberian Baroque and the Neoclassical – that constituted one of the most visible symbols of a legacy the government sought to supersede. Literally, Modernism stripped these styles from building facades and city plans, demanding instead industrial-age building materials and an industrial aesthetic appropriate to "the new age." In planning, it privileged the automobile and the aesthetic of speed at a time when Brazil was embarking on a program of industrialization especially focused on the automobile industry. It also required centralized planning and the exercise of state power that appealed to the statist interests of the political elite.

In these terms of erasure and reinscription, the idea of Brasília proposes the possibility of an inversion in development: a radically new city would produce a new society to which it would then belong. The first premise of this inversion is that the plan for a new city can create a social order based on the values that motivate its design. The second premise projects the first as a blueprint for change in the context of national development. Both premises promised a new and modern agency of innovation for Brazil, and both motivated the building of Brasília. In what follows, I suggest that these premises generated two modes of planning and design in Brasília, and that these modes are fundamentally at odds. One is total design and master planning; the other is contingency design and improvisation. The latter is experimental by nature; the former was an experiment when tried in Brasília that soon overwhelmed and negated the other. Moreover, it engendered a set of social processes that paradoxically subverted the planners' utopian intentions.

Total Design

To create a new kind of society, Brasília redefines what its Master Plan calls the key functions of urban life, namely work, residence, recreation, and traffic. It directs this redefinition according to the tenets of the CIAM model city. CIAM manifestos call for national states to assert the priority of collective interests over private. They promote state planning over what they call the "ruthless rule of capitalism," by imposing on the chaos of existing cities a new type of urbanism based on CIAM master plans. CIAM's overarching strategy for change is totalization: CIAM its model city imposes a totality of new urban conditions that dissolves any conflict between the imagined new society and the existing one in the imposed coherence of total order. Precisely because of its emphasis on the state as supreme planning power, state-building elites of every political persuasion have embraced the CIAM model of urban development, as its phenomenal spread around the world attests.

[…]

In its critique of the cities and society of European capitalism, CIAM Modernism proposed the elimination of the corridor street as a prerequisite for modern urban organization – a plan of attack Le Corbusier labeled "the death of the street" in 1929. CIAM vilifies the street as a place of disease and criminality and as a structure of private property that impedes modern development. More consequentially, however, Modernist architecture attacks the street because it constitutes an architectural organization of the public and private domains of social life that it seeks to overturn.

[…]

[…] In the Modernist city, vast areas of continuous space without exception form the perceptual ground against which the solids of buildings emerge as sculptural figures. There is no relief from this absolute division of architectural labor: Space is always treated as continuous and never as figural; buildings always as sculptural and never as background. The consequences of this total inversion are profound. By asserting the primacy of open space, volumetric clarity, pure form, and geometric abstraction, Modernism not only initiates a new vocabulary of form. More radically, it inverts the entire mode of perceiving architecture, turning it inside out – as if the figural solids of the Modernist city have been produced in the mold of the figural voids of preindustrial urbanism. [...] Modernism has imposed a total and totalizing new urban order.

[...]

Brasília's Modernist Master Planning is a comprehensive approach to restructuring urban life precisely because it advances proposals aimed at both the public and the private domains of society. Its proposal for the private realm centers on a new type of domestic architecture and residential unit that organizes residence into homogeneous sectors, structured by a concept of "collective" dwelling. [...]

In sum, Brasília's Modernist design achieves a similiar kind of defamiliarization of public and private values in both the civic and the residential realms. On the one hand, it restructures the city's public life by eliminating the street. On the other, it restructures the residential by reducing the social space of the private apartment in favor of a new type of residential collectivity in which the role of the individual is symbolically minimized. Together, these strategies constitute a profound estrangement of residential life as Brazilians know it.

[...]

Contingency Design

I suggested earlier that the project of Brasília generated two modes of design and planning. Although both were experimental and innovative, they were fundamentally at odds. One is Modernist total design. As I have shown, this mode attempts to overcome the contingency of modern experience by totalizing it, that is, by fixing the present as a totally conceived plan based on an imagined future. [...]

The second mode of design and planning is based on contingency itself. It improvises and experiments as a means of dealing with the uncertainty of present conditions. Contingency design works with plans that are always incomplete. Its means are suggested by present possibilities for an alternative future, not by an imagined and already scripted future. It is a mode of design based on imperfect knowledge, incomplete control, and lack of resources, which incorporates ongoing conflict and contradiction as constitutive elements. In this sense, it has a significant insurgent aspect. I will illustrate contingency planning with three examples from the construction period of Brasília. The first concerns the worker himself as *bricoleur*; the second, the contrast between the totally regulated construction zone and the market city that developed on its fringes; and the third, the development of illegal settlements as a reaction to the government's planned occupation.

In late 1956, Novacap divided the area of the future Federal District into two zones of planned but temporary occupation based on a spatial organization of work. One zone was reserved for construction camps that would build the city and one for commercial establishments that would provide services and supplies to the work force. The need to build Brasília quickly and the lack of skilled labor created a work regime of improvisation and ingenuity in both zones. In this regime, Brasília's workers became famous as *quebra-galhos* ("trouble-shooters, handymen"), a type of *bricoleur* ready to tackle any job with great ingenuity but limited resources; or, as one *candango* joked, "ready to undertake tasks for which he has not been sufficiently prepared." Moreover, the shortage of skilled laborers meant that unskilled workers could move into a category of skilled labor and higher pay with relative ease. Nearly every *candango* I interviewed told the same story of unlimited hours of work, rapid advancement based on audacity, and learning on the job.

As Novacap was constructing the Plano Piloto to accommodate the government and its civil servants transferred from Rio de Janeiro, it wanted to preclude the possibility that this labor force might take root in shanties on the site. Therefore, with statelike authority and its own security force, Novacap strictly controlled access to and accommodations within the construction zone. However, if the construction zone was marshaled like a boot camp, Novacap established a commercial zone for private initiative at its edge that grew as its opposite under a laissez-faire policy. This site became known as the Free City (Cidade Livre), though officially called the Provisional Pioneer Nucleus or Núcleo Bandeirante. The government encouraged entrepreneurs to supply the construction effort at their own risk and profit, and, after the city's inauguration, to become its commercial and service population. To that end, it offered entrepreneurs two incentives: free land and no taxes for four years. The combination of laissez-faire governance and temporary wooden buildings turned the Free City into a veritable frontier town of abundant cash and ambition. However, Novacap's commercial contracts stipulated that at the end of the four-year period it had the right to raze the entire city to the ground. With a turn of phrase still famous in the Free City, the president of Novacap declared, "In April 1960, I will send the tractors to flatten everything."

Thus, in classic imperial fashion, Novacap created a kind of bazaar at the gates of its noncommercial capital. On the one hand, those whom it recruited for jobs in construction were billeted in regimented camps as the work crews of a public building project. On the other, those recruited for their capital investments in all activities except construction populated the Free City and dominated its capitalist economy. It was called a Free City precisely because it grew in an area free of regulations that applied elsewhere. In contrast to the construction zone, it was immediately accessible to all: to those just off the bus, to those awaiting documentation for construction work, to those rags-to-riches dreamers seeking their frontier Eldorado, to those whose husbands and fathers were laboring in the camps. All could enter the Free City freely to find a place to live and work – freely meaning, of course, in accordance with individual means. The Free City was thus a capitalist city, organized around contingency and risk, on the fringes of a totally planned economy.

[...]

Brazilianization

Built Brasília thus resulted from the interaction of both modes of planning: the total and totalizing, the contingent and insurgent. In most cases, however, the former soon overwhelmed the latter. I will use the example of the illegal periphery to demonstrate. The government planned to recruit a labor force to build the capital, but to deny it residential rights in the city it built for the civil servants from Rio. By 1958, however, it became clear that many workers intended to remain and that almost 30 percent of them had already rebelled against their planned exclusion by becoming squatters in illegal settlements. Yet the government did not incorporate the *candangos* into the Plano Piloto, even though it was nearly empty at inauguration. The government found this solution unacceptable because inclusion would have violated the preconceived model. [...] Rather, under mounting pressure of the *candango* rebellion, and in contradiction of the Master Plan, the administration decided to create legal Satellite Cities, in which *candangos* of modest means would have the right to acquire lots and to which Novacap would remove all squatters [...] In authorizing the creation of these Satellite Cities, the government was in each case giving legal foundation to what had in fact already been usurped: the initially denied residential rights that *candangos* appropriated by forming squatter settlements. Thus, Brasília's legal periphery has a subversive origin in land seizures and contingency planning.

To remain faithful to their model, the planners could not let the legal periphery develop autonomously. They had to counter contingency, in other words, by organizing the periphery on the model of the center. [...] That model had two principal objectives: to keep civil servants in the center and others in the periphery, and to maintain a "climate of tranquillity" that eliminated the turbulence of political mobilization. Given these objectives, the planners had little choice but to use the mechanisms of social stratification and repression that are constitutive of the rest of Brazil they sought to exclude. [...] Through this combination of political subordination and preferential recruitment, of disenfranchisement and disprivilege, planners created a dual social order that was both legally and spatially segregated. Ironically, it was this stratification and repression and not the illegal actions of the squatters that more profoundly Brazilianized Brasília.

[...] A striking illustration of the perpetuation of Brasília's contradictory development is that, even today, the Plano Piloto remains more than half empty while only containing 14 percent of the Federal District's total population. This comparison strongly suggests that the government continues to expand the legal periphery rather than incorporate poor migrants into the Plano Piloto.[4]

[...]

[...] [M]any among Brasília's elite (including city planners and officials) rejected the residential concept of the superquadra altogether. They moved out of their Plano Piloto apartments and created their own neighborhoods of individual houses and private clubs on the other side of the lake. [...] The existence of these elite neighborhoods repudiates the aims of the Master Plan to achieve social change by instituting a new type of residential organization. Whereas the superquadra concretizes a set of egalitarian prescriptions, especially through standardization, the houses of these elite neighborhoods often compete with each other in ostentation, using a bricolage of historical styles. While significant in its own right as a counterstyle, this display fractures every tenet of the Modernist aesthetic and social program of the Master Plan. [...]

Entombment

We have seen that the history of Brasília's development is one of interaction between its total and contingent planning. Mostly, however, the total overwhelmed the contingent, as planners insist on reiterating the original model in the face of insurgent developments. In a few cases, such as the front/back reversal of stores and the settlement of the periphery, contingency planning made lasting changes to the Master Plan. However, even these insurgent alternatives were retotalized, as planners either neutralized their significance by isolating them (the first case) or subsumed them into the whole by organizing their development according to original principles and objectives (the second).

With these conclusions in mind, we can return to a question posed at the beginning: If the spirit of Brasília is that of innovation, experiment, and risk, is this insistence on totalizing the contingent – that is, on perpetuating one experimental moment at the expense of all others – a betrayal of that spirit? Even though planners may think they are furthering the project of Brasília through this insistence, are they misguided in imposing one model that was experimental in the 1950s but that now prevents subsequent generations of Brazilians from using Brasília as *their* field of experimentation? [...]

Brasília is today preserved by various levels of law. What is "entombed" is the original urban conception of Costa's Master Plan (1957), including the Plano Piloto and the Lake Districts but not the periphery. Indeed, Brasília was born preserved when the Master Plan became law with the city's inauguration (Article 38 of Law 3751, April 1960). Since then, it has been protected by three additional levels of law.

[...]

I prefer to conclude by noting that there is no mention in the pronouncements about Brasília's preservation of what is to my mind the most important of its "essential characteristics," namely, its spirit of invention. If that spirit is essential, and if preservation is intended to protect the essential, then at the very least *tombamento* should preserve Brasília as a field of experimentation, indeed of continuous innovation. It should preserve the city as special place in Brazil where that kind of risk is possible. Freezing Brasília at one moment betrays that spirit and turns it into a ghost.

[...]

At the very least, memorializing Brasília must mean re-presenting its premises as they developed through both total and contingent/insurgent modes of design. Presenting that dialogue between the modes of Brasília's design is a challenge worthy of a memorial to the real history of the city. [...] As it is now, Brasília's preservation tells only part of the story, that of the elite planners and architects but not that of the workers who built the city but who rebelled against their exclusion. It also neglects the story of the officials who developed new but not architectural proposals for urban life. And it preserves an exaggerated, state-sponsored social and spatial stratification. [...]

In the 1950s, Brasília dared to be an innovation in urbanism. Like most significant experiments, it took the risk of submitting itself to public evaluation. That I criticize aspects of its development does not diminish my admiration for its foundation. To the contrary, I have argued that it is important to commemorate the particular experiment of its founders, but only in the context of memorializing that greater idea of modernity as experiment and risk that is the spirit of Brasília.

Notes

1 For an extensive discussion of this Modernist political and planning project, see my study of Brasília, on which I rely for various passages of this essay. This study was based on several years of fieldwork in Brasília. James Holston, *The Modernist City: An Anthropological Critique of Brasília* (Chicago: University of Chicago Press, 1989).

2 Lúcio Costa, "Razões da nova arquitetura," *Arte em Revista* 4 (1980), p. 15.

3 See Holston, *The Modernist City*, pp. 31–58 for proof and discussion of the Le Corbusian derivation.

4 The Plano Piloto was planned for a maximum population of 500,000. As of 1996, the date of the most recent findings, it has a population of 199,000. If we include the Lake districts, we add another 54,000 residents, for a total that is still just half Brasília's planned population. Moreover, the demographic imbalance between center and periphery has only worsened with time. At inauguration, the Plano Piloto had 48 percent of the total District population and the periphery (both Satellite Cities and rural settlements) had 52 percent. In 1970, the distribution was 29 percent to 71 percent; in 1980, 25 percent to 75 percent; in 1990, 16 percent to 84 percent; and in 1996, 14 percent to 86 percent. IBGE 1996.

35

Carmen Miranda, Grande Otelo, and the *Chanchada*, 1929–1949

Robert Stam*

In his "Cannibalist Manifesto," Brazilian Oswald de Andrade exalts "Carnaval" over the Catholic "Catechism" and proclaims, "American movies will inform us" (see Chapter 39, this volume). Esther Gabara characterizes these gestures toward Afro-Brazilian culture and American cinema as part of the "ethos" of Brazilian modernism that entails a "sense of ethical responsibility to sectors of society that were increasingly defining modernity [the ethnographic, the folk, and popular classes] and an aesthetic that reflects its formulation through disciplines and discourses not proper to high art" (Gabara 2008: 9). Taking up this claim in his history of Brazilian cinema, *Tropical Multiculturalism: A Comparative History of Race in Brazilian Cinema and Culture*, Robert Stam explores the gap between the rhetoric and practice of racial ethics in Brazil's modern film industry.

As a US-based scholar of cinema studies, Stam endeavors to familiarize Brazilian culture for US readers through comparisons with parallel developments within the US film industry. For he notes in the introduction to his book that the two countries have much in common: both are the largest nations in their respective continents; both experienced colonization; both have populations descended from not only Europeans and Indigenous Americans but also Africans, forced immigrants of the slave trade, and multiple subsequent waves of immigrants from all over the world; and both countries forged independent national identities by symbolically embracing Indigenous culture. These similarities notwithstanding, Stam also points out that the racial discourse in the two countries developed quite differently. US national identity,

* Robert Stam (1997) "Carmen Miranda, Grande Otelo, and the *Chanchada* 1929–1949." In *Tropical Multiculturalism: A Comparative History of Race in Brazilian Cinema and Culture* (pp. 79–105). Durham, NC: Duke University Press.

Modern Art in Africa, Asia, and Latin America: An Introduction to Global Modernisms, First Edition.
Edited by Elaine O'Brien, Everlyn Nicodemus, Melissa Chiu, Benjamin Genocchio, Mary K. Coffey, and Roberto Tejada.

he argues, has been organized around a normative "whiteness," due to the segregationist politics of US British settlers and the negative attitudes of the dominant classes toward miscegenation. Brazilian national identity, on the other hand, extols *mestiçagem* (interracial mixing) as a consequence of the widespread intermarriage between peoples of European, Indigenous, and African decent necessitated by the militaristic and largely male demographics of Portuguese colonization. The multiculturalism of both countries suggests, Stam argues, not only that their respective film histories are comparable but also that they should be studied within the context of evolving race relations.

Stam's focus in this excerpt is on the *chanchada* or musical comedy, a popular genre with roots in US and Brazilian musical theater as well as radio that emerged with the advent of sound filmmaking in the 1930s and dominated Brazilian cinema until the 1950s. Unlike the silent films from the preceding decades, the *chanchadas* embraced Afro-Brazilian culture, and in particular the "cultural universe" of carnival and the famed samba schools from Rio's *favelas* (shanty towns). As a hybrid phenomenon, the *chanchada* exemplifies the ethos of modernism that Oswald de Andrade hailed in his "Cannibalist Manifesto." However, as Stam notes, while "black culture" was celebrated for its authenticity and modernity (its links to radio and cinema), blacks, themselves, were systematically discriminated against, as the genre tended to focus on white protagonists with black characters, musicians, and dancers relegated to the "background."

To demonstrate both the inroads and limits of "racial democracy" in modern Brazilian cinema, Stam compares the persona and fate of the two most prominent *chanchada* performers: Carmen Miranda and *Grande Otelo*. Miranda was a light-skinned woman from the bohemian neighborhood of "Lapa" in Rio, who adopted and exaggerated the costume of the *baiana* (the women who sell traditional African foods in the streets) in a parodic performance of "blackness" that was not only wildly popular in Brazil but also embraced by Hollywood as the ultimate expression of Latin exoticism. *Grande Otelo* (Sebastião Bernardes Souza Prata) was a dark-skinned man from the provinces who became one of Brazil's most celebrated comic actors. Despite his long and prolific career, *Grand Otelo* encountered a "glass ceiling" that restricted his acting ambitions to comic roles, and separated him from other black performers as an "exemplary" but ultimately "lone representative of black Brazil."

It is important to note that in forging this comparison Stam is not demonizing Miranda or "whiteness" in favor of *Grande Otelo* and "blackness," but rather demonstrating the ways that performances could be coded as culturally black even as "epidermically" white actors enacted them. Moreover, he is sensitive to the ways that this "blackness" did or did not read abroad. In the case of Miranda, her ethnic drag, while apparent to Brazilian audiences familiar with carnival, samba, and the *baianas*, was misread by US audiences, who understood her performance to be an authentic, if slightly outrageous, demonstration of the sultry Latina stereotype. For *Grande Otelo*, his blackness blocked entry into the international film arena as elites in both Brazil and the US found it impossible to imagine that "black stars from Brazil" could be exported successfully.

Stam notes that *Grande Otelo*'s talents *were* appreciated by Orson Welles, who came to Brazil in the 1940s to film *It's All True,* in which the actor was to have a staring role. The beginning of a "Hollywood interlude," Welles's failed film marked a new stage in Brazilian cinema wherein foreign directors collaborated with Brazilian studios and emphasized Afro-Brazilian culture to make art films – both essentializing and progressive – for the international market. Chief among these was Marcel Camus's *Black Orpheus,* which won the Cannes Film Festival's *Palme d'Or* in 1946. For many, within and outside of Brazil, *Black Orpheus* represents the emergence of a distinctly "national" cinema. The international recognition of black Brazil within the medium of film would ultimately inform the emergence of *Cinema Novo* in the 1950s and 1960s, an avant-garde style of cinema that returned to Andrade's cannibalist ethos by critiquing colonialism and foregrounding racial inequality, only this time from an explicitly "third world" political point of view.

Further Readings

Carmen Miranda: Bananas Is My Business (1998) [documentary film]. Fox Lorber.

Elena, Alberto and Díaz López, Marina (eds) *The Cinema of Latin America.* London, England: Wallflower Press.

Gabara, Esther (2008) *Errant Modernism: The Ethos of Photography in Mexico and Brazil.* Durham, NC: Duke University Press.

Johnson, Randal and Stam, Robert (eds) (1995) *Brazilian Cinema* (expanded edn). New York, NY: Columbia University Press.

In the 1930s, the situation of blacks improved somewhat as immigration declined and ideological winds shifted. The 1930s were the era of the Afro-Brazilian Congresses in Recife (1934) and Bahia (1937) and of the Black Brazilian Conference (1940).[1] It was in 1934 that Article 113 of the Brazilian Constitution declared that "All are equal before the law" and that "there will be no privileges or distinctions by reason of birth, sex, race, profession, country, social class, wealth, religious belief or political ideas." It was also in the 1930s that Afro Brazilians in São Paulo formed A Frente Negra Brasileira (The Black Brazilian Front) to protest precisely the same discriminations based on race, wealth, and social class presumably prohibited by the Constitution, in a movement that mobilized thousands of blacks before it was banned by the populist dictator Vargas in 1938.

At the same time, anthropologist Gilberto Freyre, a student of the anti-racist Franz Boas, formulated the theory of "racial democracy" in his 1933 *Casa Grande e Senzala* (literally, "Big House and the Slave Quarters" but translated as "The Masters and the Slaves"). Rather than see Afro Brazilians as the cause of Brazil's "inferiority," Freyre emphasized the many-faceted contribution of blacks and Indians to Brazil's cultural mix. In the patriarchal system typical of Brazilian slavery, according to Freyre, African influences, "carried" by black cooks and mammies, allowed for a certain cultural democracy. Unlike other multiracial societies in the Americas, Brazilian social life was characterized by exceptional familiarity between the races. The tropics softened everything, including racial relations. Freyre's Luso-Tropicalism, as Emília Viotti da Costa points out, discarded two pillars of European racist theories: the innateness of racial difference and the degeneracy of mixed blood.[2] But Freyre's vision of a "slaveholding utopia" was sentimental and, ultimately, colonialist.[3] A Brazilian variant of what Michael Hanchard calls "the Iberian model of racial exceptionalism," it traces its roots to the nineteenth century, when antiabolitionist Brazilian elites "began concocting favorable representations of Brazilian slavery for foreign consumption."[4] Freyre's rosy picture of rampant interracial mating in tropical hammocks ignored the asymmetrical power relations within which such mating took place. The black contribution to Brazilian culture, furthermore, was reduced to the picturesque and the folkloric, more a matter of dance and cuisine than of fundamental political or economic achievements. (The cinema, as we shall see, often recapitulates this paternalistic culturalism.)

The 1930s also witnessed the resurgence of racist thought. The Integralist Party, a Brazilian variant of fascism especially strong in the European-dominated South of the country, grew rapidly after its founding in 1932. [...] Anti-Semitic and implicitly antiblack and Aryanist, Integralism provoked well-known intellectuals such as Roquete Pinto, Artur Ramos, and Gilberto Freyre to sound an alarm in their "Manifesto against Racial Prejudice," published in 1935, warning against "the transplantation of racist ideas, and especially their social and political corollaries" as a grave risk for a country like Brazil, "whose ethnic formation was decidedly heterogenous."[5]

The 1930s also witness the transformation of "ethnic" practices – samba, carnival, capoeira – into national symbols. Although the cinema cannot be seen as reflecting in any direct way the thinking of ideological elites, the 1930s do bring a changed atmosphere and altered conceptualizations of the Afro Brazilian presence. And if Brazilian cinema of the silent period was symbolically "white," the cinema of the ensuing decades might be called *moreno* (Freyre's ideal) or even "light mulatto." As in the United States, the advent of sound brought new possibilities for black participation; black sounds opened the way for black images. Blacks became a significant presence within the musical review films and later in the *chanchadas*, which dominated production from the 1930s through the late 1950s. Partially modeled on American musicals, and particularly on the "radio broadcast" musicals, the Brazilian musical film had roots as well in popular "review" theater and in Brazilian radio. The "Alô" in Adhemar Gonzaga's *Alô Alô Brasil* (1935) and *Alô Alô Carnaval* (1936), for example, derived from the annual radio salutes to carnival revelers. Both films feature Carmen Miranda, already famous from radio and records. The 1930s films generally favored white stars and a white aesthetic, while featuring occasional blacks and mulattoes in minor or background roles, such as the black drummer with the Simon Boutman orchestra accompanying Carmen Miranda in *Alô Alô Brasil*. [...]

It was also in the 1930s that cinema first began to examine the favelas of Rio, the place of origins of the *samba de morro* (samba of the hills). The favelas were created when the poorer population of Rio was pushed out onto the hills by the real-estate boom created by the construction of Avenida Central (now Rio Branco) at the turn of the century. Rio's samba was born in the homes of elderly Bahian matriarchs, or *tias* (aunts), like Tia Ciata, who lived in Praça Onze, and where musicians such as Pixinguinha, Donga, and Sinho gathered to create music. The first song officially recorded as a samba ("Pelo Telefone" [By Telephone]), was composed at Tia Ciata's house and released in 1917. In the early decades of the twentieth century, samba was socially despised and even repressed. [...] But as Samba slowly became disseminated through musical recording – the first was the "Isto É Bom" in 1902 – and through radio beginning in the 1920s, its popularity gradually spread to other classes of Brazilians. Samba took a number of forms, from the grittier favela versions themselves to the more "sophisticated" orchestrations of singers like Carmen Miranda and Linda Batista. It was thus in the poor milieus that we find the origins of the Afro-inflected popular music of the diaspora and ultimately even of the "world music" now disseminated by multinational companies, as largely poor and discriminated black people – whether in Chicago, New York, or New Orleans, Havana or Rio de Janeiro – created their music, amidst generally hostile populations that only slowly learned to appreciate the musical gifts.

The advent of sound happened to coincide with the social emergence of "samba schools," previously known to the inhabitants of the *morros* (hills) but unfamiliar to Rio's elite. The samba schools amalgamated preexisting traditions like the *entrudo* (carnivalesque slapstick pranks), masked balls, and *cordões* (carnival groupings) into a new and dynamic formation. The name of the first samba school in 1928 – Deixa Falar (Let Us Speak) – evokes a preexisting repression and the finding of voice.

[...]

Although the *chanchada* has its origins in the *filmes cantantes* (sung films) of the silent period, the genre only "took off" in the 1930s. The musical films were intimately linked to the cultural universe of carnival, in that they were timed to be released around the carnival, featured carnival songs, and had an imaginary deeply imbued with carnivalesque values. [...] Although immensely popular with the public, the *chanchadas* were the object of all sorts of critical scorn. [...]

The first film to anticipate the *chanchada*'s typical mixture of carnival music and comedy was Wallace Downey's *Coisas Nossas* (Our Things, 1930), modeled after the "all-singing" studio musicals then arriving from Hollywood. [...] Most of the musicals use blacks largely as background and foil for the love intrigues of white stars like Eliane Macedo and Cyl Farney. Although samba was fundamentally an Afro Brazilian creation, the product of the primarily black *morros* of Rio, film after film gave the impression that samba was a white cultural product.[6] The exclusion of black performers from the Brazilian musical seems especially anomalous in those musicals that exploit Afro Brazilian music and dance. The veiled presence of Afro Brazilian music and dance in numerous films paradoxically marks Afro Brazilian *absence* from the screen.[7] [...]

In this sense, the epidermically white performer Carmen Miranda, a star in many of the 1930s musicals, plays a highly ambiguous role. For North Americans,

Miranda is the "Brazilian bombshell," a zany emblem of pan-*latinidad*, as well as a gay camp icon. In American musicals, Miranda performed extravagantly flamboyant numbers involving swaying hips, exaggerated facial expressions, kitschy sexy costumes, and "think-big" style props. Her final idealized image as fertility goddess in *The Gang's All Here* (1943) reverberates textually in the opening of the number where raw materials from the South are unloaded in the United States; the North here celebrates the tropical South as the fecund feminine principle that gives birth to the raw materials that the North consumes. The bananas in Miranda's song not only enact the agricultural reductionism of Brazil's monocultural products but also form phallic symbols, here raised by voluptuous latinas over circular, quasi-vaginal forms.[8] Miranda's "excessive" performances allowed her to undercut and parody stereotypical roles, but did little to gain her substantive power.

Whereas for non-Brazilian audiences, the ethnicity of the Miranda persona was submerged, invisible, dissolved into that of a generic *latina*, within a Brazilian context her music and performance style can be seen to be deeply indebted to Afro Brazilian culture. This debt is multidimensional, having to do with her body language and kinetics, with her samba dance steps, with the use of her voice as an instrument, with her percussive approach to tongue-twisting lyrics (a distant cousin to "scat" singing), with her talking-style singing (as in blues), and with her capacity for improvisation. [...] Miranda grew up in Rio's bohemian district, called "Lapa," where she absorbed Afro Brazilian slang and musical styles. She drew on the repertory of songs by the best samba composers, most of them of African ancestry – Ismael Silva, Ary Barroso, Assis Valente, Dorival Caymmi – and she benefited from the arrangements of an important black composer-performer: Pixinguinha.

Miranda's famous "tutti-fruti" costume, furthermore, stylized and even hyperbolized the already stylized costume of the *baianas* – the female figures dressed in white who sell ritual African foods like *acarajé* (bean fritters with shrimp fried in palm oil) in the streets of Salvador, who became absorbed into Rio's carnival and into Carioca burlesque theater in the early decades of this twentieth century and who are even today an obligatory presence in the Carioca samba pageants. Like the typical *baiana* costume, Miranda's outfit comprises turban, necklaces, bracelets, and *balangandas* (jewelry, ornaments). Aloísio Oliveira, one of the members of Carmen's band originally brought by Sudanese slaves of Islamic faith relates that Miranda originally fashioned the costume to illustrate the Doryval Caymmi song "O Que É Que a Baiana Tem?" Broadway producer Lee Shubert saw the performance and brought Miranda to the United States.

[...]

The figure of Miranda was subsequently reinvoiced by the tropicalists of the 1960s, affectionately valued by them as an object for artistic recycling. As she was the first "export-quality" Brazilian star to enjoy international success, she prepared the way for the subsequent successes of bossa nova, samba, and *axé* music. [...]

The most important black star of this period was Sebastião Bernardes Souza Prata, or "Grande Otelo." If artistic prestige were distributed more fairly, Grande Otelo would be as well known as Charlie Chaplin, Buster Keaton, or James Earl

Jones. One of Brazil's finest and most versatile actors, Grande Otelo was described by Orson Welles as "the greatest comic actor of the 20th century" and by novelist Jorge Amado as "the epitome of Brazil."[9] [...] Born in 1915, Otelo reportedly got his name because as a child some adults took him to be a future tenor who "would make a good Othello" in the Verdi opera. Grande Otelo's multiple talents included composing, singing, dancing, acting, and screenwriting. He performed in over 100 Brazilian feature films, participating in virtually all phases of Brazilian Cinema and television, from the *chanchada* through Cinema Novo, the Underground of the 1960s, and the telenovelas of the 1970s and 1980s, working tirelessly up until 1994, when he died just after arriving in Paris for a French retrospective of his work at the Three Continents Festival. [...]

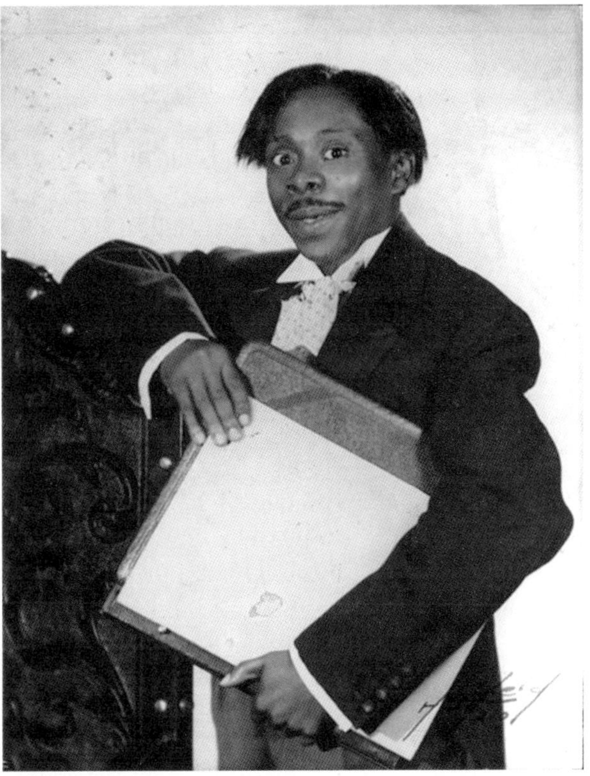

Figure 35.1 Grande Otelo, c.1940, photo Themistocles Halfeld, Wikimedia Commons.

At the time of his first cameo in *Noites Cariocas* (Carioca Nights, 1935), Grande Otelo was already well known as an actor in comic theater and vaudeville. He began work as an artist at the age of eight, in a circus in the provincial town of Uberlândia, in a sketch in which he appeared in drag. After running away from home, Otelo was adopted by a rich white Paulista family, thus gaining access to some of the best schools in São Paulo. The first theatrical company for black actors and musicians – the Companhia Negra de Revista (The Black Theatrical Review Company) hired Grande Otelo, then only nine, in 1924. It was during one of the troupe's performances that Otelo met the Brazilian novelist Mário de Andrade, the author of the novel *Macunaíma*, in the adaptation of which Grande Otelo would star over 40 years later. [...]

Grande Otelo was reportedly inspired to work in film by the presence of a black boy (Farina) in the American "Our Gang" series; Otelo wanted to be the black boy in a Brazilian equivalent series. In the early period, Grande Otelo polished his musical and linguistic talents, learning to speak English, French, Italian, and Spanish, even singing *Tosca* and dancing the minuet, and distinguishing himself generally by his improvisatory talents. Grande Otelo became a star in the world of Rio Casinos such as the Urca, where Orson Welles was to see him perform when he went to Brazil to make *It's All True*. At the time, the Urca Casino had a policy of allowing blacks to perform on stage but not be patrons in the casino, a policy analogous to that which allowed African American stars like Lena Horne to sing at New York's Savoy Hotel, for example, but not to stay as guests. Even before having performed in the Welles film, Grande Otelo was famous enough to be invited to Hollywood. Walt Disney expressed interest in having Otelo provide the voice for his cartoon character Zé Carioca, and in 1940, he was invited to join Carmen Miranda in Hollywood. (Otelo ultimately did not go only because he was tied down by an exploitative contract that obliged him to remit 50 percent of his earnings to the Urca Casino.) [...]

It would be difficult to summarize all of Grande Otelo's innumerable film roles.[10] [...] Also in 1943, he starred in *Moleque Tião* (Street Kid Tião), the premiere film of the Rio film studio Atlântida. Founded in 1941, Atlântida hoped to create a socially conscious cinema. Its self-declared goals were to create a "Carioca cinematic experience," and "to explore social problems which had up to that point been absent from national cinema."[11] [...]

Directed by José Carlos Burle and scripted by Alinor Azevedo, *Moleque Tião* offered a fictionalized version of Grande Otelo's own life. At the time it was considered a very risky enterprise to feature a black actor in the leading role for a studio's first film, especially since Grande Otelo was not yet a star. The film tells the tale of a young black man from the back country of Minas Gerais, who, inspired by newspaper reports about the successes of a black theatrical company, does all in his power to go to Rio. Once there, he learns that the company is about to break up, but he shows his dramatic talents to the theater director anyway. After getting a job as an errand boy, he is interned in an orphanage, but he manages to escape. Finally he gets his break, and he is a tremendous success. To complete his happiness, his mother arrives from Minas to applaud his theatrical apotheosis. *Moleque Tião* tells the formulaic tale of the artist who suffers setbacks before achieving his goals. [...] Extremely popular with the public, *Moleque Tião* guaranteed Grande Otelo's future as a star performer.

[...]

Tristezas Não Pagam Dívidas was the first film in which Grande Otelo joined in a duo comprising himself and another famous comic actor – Oscarito. (The two had acted together in earlier films, such as *Noites Cariocas*, but not as a pair.) Like most comic duos – the slender Laurel and the obese Hardy, the elegant Bing Crosby and the clumsy Bob Hope, the smooth-voiced white Jack Benny and the rough-voiced black Rochester – the Oscarito–Grande Otelo pair plays with oxymoronic contrasts. Paired with Oscarito, and later with Ankito, Otelo became the "king of the *chanchadas*." Unlike the servant-master pattern that prevailed in the black-white friendships in Hollywood films of the same period (e.g., Jack Benny and his valet Rochester), there was a rough equality between Otelo and his white costars, although Otelo was perhaps more likely to suffer from injustice outside of the friendship. Within the friendship, however, Oscarito's characters tended to be more vulnerable. At the same time, a sense of physical ease reigns between Grande Otelo and Oscarito. *Matar ou Correr* (To Kill or to Run, 1954) ends with a parodic "final kiss" between the two actors, a kiss that probably would have provoked paroxysms of racialized homophobia in the Hollywood of the same period.

[...]

According to Sérgio Augusto, Grande Otelo complained of his subordinate status in relation to Oscarito, in the sense that although Oscarito's character was more vulnerable, Otelo's role was always to save him rather than to take the lead in the first place.[12] Otelo also resented earning less than his partner because he thought of himself as a more complete actor,[13] and indeed Otelo did deploy a vast arsenal of postures, faces, and gestures for comic, dramatic, and distancing effects. For Otelo, Oscarito was an "eccentric" whereas Otelo "tried to valorize the dialogue and the interpretation, always looking for the right tone. ... Oscarito was a 'type,' while ... [Otelo] was an actor."[14] Otelo's first films were written for him to be the "straight man" for Oscarito, but Otelo subverted that arrangement through his diabolically creative improvisions. His resentment is given narrative form in Carlos Manga's *A Dupla do Barulho* (A Great Pair, 1953), a film that treats, in a displaced semibiographical manner, the lives of the two greatest stars of Atlântida. In this sentimental melodrama, Otelo and Oscarito are both circus artists, who separate when Otelo begins to drink. Otelo is badly treated, both as a black man and as an alcoholic, but in the end he is restored to well-being and applauded in his return to circus performance. In one sequence, a drunken Tião (Otelo) complains about his partner Tônico (Oscarito): "Tônico and Tião! Why not Tião and Tônico? I'm tired of being a ladder to someone else's success." (In Portuguese, *escada* [ladder] means "straight man.") Oscarito himself collaborated with this critical portrayal and even gave some of his better lines to Otelo. The director, meanwhile, a self-described man of the left, had the explicit intention of "questioning the subaltern position of blacks."[15]

Parenthetically, it was this same hatred for racial prejudice that led Carlos Manga to give support to a mulatto artist named José Cajado Filho, who had made a career for himself as a set designer in film and theater. Manga, in one of the rare direct testimonies to the effects of racism in the world of Brazilian cinema, describes Cajado Filho as a resentful person but one who had every reason to be resentful: "Cajado was an eternal victim of racial prejudice. They didn't let him into the School of Fine Arts, even though he won First Prize in the contest they offered. We, the whites of the Atlântida Studio, were highlighted; he wasn't. But all of us directors – myself, Macedo, Burle, Roberto Farias – were paying the price of losing his enormous talent. He knew how to do everything – decor, script, gags, directing. For me, Cajado was the real father of the chanchada."[16]

Vinícius de Moraes, author of the source play for *Black Orpheus*, described Grande Otelo as "an especially rich person in human terms, with a formidable capacity for pathos and an extreme tenderness, all hidden behind irony and verve."[17] Given this emotional range, it is fortunate that not all of Grande Otelo's roles were comic. Apart from his role in *Moleque Tião*, Otelo also played in the first Brazilian film to confront the problem of contemporary racial discrimination – José Carlos Burle's symptomatically titled *Também Somos Irmãos* (We Are Also Brothers, 1949). The film was a Brazilian example of the "problem film" genre then popular in Hollywood, that is, the socially conscious reformist films of the late 1940s that examine specific problems such as antiblack racism (*Pinky* [1949]), or anti-Semitism (*Gentleman's Agreement* [1947]).

[...]

Grande Otelo also played a key role in the Brazilian *chanchada* parodies of North American films, a tradition that goes all the way back to *O Babão* (The Baboon, 1930), a spoof of Roman Novarro's *The Pagan* (1929; in Portuguese, *O Pagão*), and which continues as late as a parody of Spielberg's *Jaws* (1975) – entitled *Bacalhau* (Codfish, 1976).[18] The Brazilian parodies must be set against the backdrop of the elitism dominating the critical scene in Brazil. In the 1950s a critic from the *Revista Anhembi* denounced the *chanchadas* for "exploiting the bad taste of the masses, feeding its primitive instincts, confusing and deluding the masses, lowering the cinema for the public rather than raising the public to the level of cinema."[19] For elite critics, then, the *chanchadas* were distinctly uncivilized, too full of sambas and *baianas*. At times the implicitly anti-African spirit of these critiques becomes explicit.

[…]

Speaking generally, what can we say about the role of blacks in the comic musical films of this period? First, given their Brazilian origins, their Rio de Janeiro setting, and their samba subject, the musicals shockingly underrepresent the black presence. Apart from Vera Regina, Colé, Chocolate, Blecaute, Otelo, and occasional singers, dancers, and musicians, blacks are not a strong presence. […] Second, the musicals do manifest the strong presence of black cultural forms, as if Brazilian producers, not unlike their Hollywood counterparts, wanted to have black culture without dealing with the people who produced it. Third, we must note the virtually complete absence of black women as major players. […] Fourth, although we do see musicians and dancers of color in the background of the films, they are there to support the white stars, with blacks serving to visually "set off" the beauty and elegance of the white elite, in a slightly less binaristic version of the racial "foil effect" so well analyzed by James Snead.[20] […]

The privileging of the figure of Grande Otelo as the key black actor, and his pairing with white costars, had the effect of isolating him from his black brothers and sisters. As a lone representative of black Brazil, he was made to bear a heavy "burden of representation." At the same time, it would be a mistake to always correlate specific traits of the Otelo character with race, given his extremely variegated roles and the fact that he often plays figures such as the *malandro* who transcend racial definition, constituting archetypes incarnated as well by other, nonblack actors. The Carioca *malandro* was always viewed with a mixture of sincere admiration and class condescension, considered lower-class but also a gifted trickster or shape-shifter loved for his survival skills and for his antiauthoritarian stance. The audience generally laughed with the *malandro* figure rather than at him. As an actor, Otelo tended to incarnate a popularesque type in the grand comic tradition, characterized by broad gestures, exaggerated facial expressions, and acrobatic corporality. At the same time, he was generally treated as comically asexual; his role was to help along the amorous intrigues of his white partners (Oscarito, Zé Trindade) a desexualizing pattern that Donald Bogle has noted about the North American black-white buddy films. Indeed, Otelo's persona has something of the smart child, bright but somehow presexual, infantilized, as if the middle-class white audience might have trouble accepting a sexually assertive black male.

In real life, pressured by the black community and by activists such as Abdias do Nascimento, Otelo progressively came to affirm his blackness. He retroactively described his 1940s persona as that of the *enfant gâté* of Carioca high society, blithely unaware of the racist policies that prevented blacks from entering the Casino da Urca as patrons.[21] Although Otelo was hardly what in North America would be called a "race man," it is nevertheless significant that he repeatedly chose to work in acting companies led by black men like Oduvaldo Viana and Chocolate. Over the years, he showed an increasing identification with his Afro Brazilian roots, attributing his strength as an actor, for example, to an "ancestral heritage very linked with the formation of my race."[22] [...]

Grande Otelo was not the only black actor who gained fame in the 1940s and 1950s; among the others were Nilo Chagas, Chocolate, Blackout, Príncipe Pretinho (Little Black Prince), and Colé. Interestingly, the names of many of the black performers, like that of Grande Otelo, call attention to their blackness, evidence perhaps of a relatively unembarrassed color-consciousness or perhaps of objectification: they could not simply be seen as actors but rather only as *black* actors. These "comic" names reflect as well, perhaps, a kind of generic glass ceiling, a difficulty in moving beyond comedy, in taking black people seriously, as if by their mere presence blacks connoted instant humor and gratification for white audiences.

[...]

A newspaper report from February 11, 1942, reveals the nuances of Brazilian-style racism. Entitled "From the Favela to Hollywood," the article concerns two Afro Brazilian radio stars, Henricão and Carmen Costa, who have been contracted by an American impresario to work in Hollywood. Unlike similar reports about Hollywood-bound performers such as Carmen Miranda, the report is framed by a patronizing preface, which speaks of "almost-perfect" white civilizations and the "retardation of black civilizations." The report begrudgingly acknowledges a white debt to blacks for having "aided us when the domination of the aboriginal element became difficult." At the same time, the article speaks of "our great pride" in the "black stars from Brazil."[23] The paternalistic tone conveys a sense of astonishment that Hollywood might be interested in "our" blacks. The article was published, ironically, just three days after the arrival in Brazil of Orson Welles, a director who, it turned out, was very much interested in black Brazil.

Notes

1 For Abdias do Nascimento, these fora were dominated by the "pomp and circumstance of white scholars and scientists." See Abdias do Nascimento and Elisa Larkin Nascimento, *Africans in Brazil*, (Trenton, NJ: Africa World Press, 1992), p. 37.

2 Emília Viotti da Costa, *Brazilian Empire: Myths and Histories* (Chicago: University of Chicago Press, 1985), p. 239.

3 Clóvis Moura is quoted in Martiniano J. Silva, *Racismo à Brasileira* (Brasília: Thesaurus, 1987), p. 180.

4 Hanchard, *Orpheus and Power*, (Princeton, NJ: Princeton University Press, 1994) pp. 43, 47.

5 Thomas E. Skidmore, *Preto no Branco: Raça e Nacionalidade no Pensamento Brasíleiro* (Rio de Janeiro: Paz e Terra, 1989), p. 225.

6 It is interesting to compare other 1930s musical films from the other countries of the Americas in terms of their racial representations. The Argentinean film *Tango* (1933) features one black woman dancing in a crowd of tango dancers. The Cuban film *El Romance del Palmar* (1938), the product of a multiracial society very much like Brazil's, features whites in leading roles but also includes black musicians.

7 Henry Louis Gates Jr. notes the iconographic links between blackness, the harlequin, and the minstrel figure, whereby the "inherent nobility of Harlequin the Black Clown [became] transformed by degrees into the ignoble black minstrel figure." See Gates, *Figures in Black* (New York: Oxford University Press, 1987), pp. 51–3.

8 My discussion here is indebted to Ella Shohat's analysis, first published in her essay "Gender and the Culture of Empire" and subsequently included in our coauthored *Unthinking Eurocentrism*.

9 The characterization by Jorge Amado is part of a series of homages to Grande Otelo after his death and included in *Écrans d'Afrique* (3rd–4th trimester, 1993), p. 34.

10 The only biography of Grande Otelo is Roberto Moura's thoroughly researched and insightful *Grande Otelo* (Rio de Janeiro: Relume/Dumara, 1996). Otelo worked with Moura on a script about the *gafieiras* (club elite) and also performed in Moura's *Katharsys: História dos Anos 80* (Katharsys: Tales from the 1980s, 1994).

11 Quoted in Rosángela de Oliveira Dias, *O Mundo como Chanchada: Cinema e Imaginário das Classes Populares na Década de 50*, (Rio de Janeiro: Dumara, 1993), p. 9.

12 See Augusto, *Este Mundo É um Pandeiro: A Chanchada de Getúlio a JK* (São Paulo: Cinemateca Brasileira Companhia das Letras) (1989), p. 192.

13 See ibid., p. 130.

14 Interview with Grande Otelo, *Positif*, no. 314 (April 1987), p. 48.

15 Quoted in Augusto, *Este Mundo É um Pandeiro*, p. 131.

16 Quoted in ibid., p. 132.

17 Vinícius de Moraes, *O Cinema de Meus Olhos* (São Paulo: Companhia das Letras, 1991), p. 264.

18 For an incisive discussion of the Brazilian parodies, see João Luiz Vieira, *Hegemony and Resistance: Carnival and Parody in Brazilian Cinema*, PhD diss., NYU, 1982.

19 "Cinema Brasileiro Entre Aspas," *Revista Anhembi* (São Paulo), 20, no. 58 (September 1955).

20 See James Snead, *White Screen/Black Images* (London: Routledge, 1993).

21 Otelo makes remarks to this effect in the BBC documentary about *It's All True*.

22 In interviews, Otelo called for a kind of black capitalism and mutual support: "I think that we should shake up those blacks who rise on the social ladder and come to occupy key positions and who, whether out of fear or because they already suffered too much, decide to hide or wash their hands. In the final analysis, every ethnic group in Brazil has organized." Otelo seems ambivalent about Brazilian racism, arguing on the one hand that there is less racism in Brazil because all Brazilians have partial black ancestry – "I only believe that a Brazilian is really white when I've seen photos of all his grandparents" – and lamenting on the other the fact that he has always had to struggle harder than a white actor would have. He was rarely paid the money due him, he says, and expresses the common complaint of black performers throughout the diaspora that blacks have to work twice as hard to get what whites get as a matter of course. He has also insisted in interviews on the importance of black celebrities' marrying black women, rather than the white women who seek out black celebrities. Quotations here are taken from an interview with Grande Otelo in *O Estado de São Paulo* (June 10, 1978).

23 When asked why it was only in the 1960s that he became concerned about black issues, Otelo answered that he had always been concerned but that it was only recently that the black community began to pressure him to make a more vocal commitment. Otelo contrasted his own attitude with that of another black celebrity – Pelé. "I want to unite the blacks of Brazil, including those who are abroad like Pelé. I would like Pelé to feel black and join with his people in this struggle." Nestor de Holanda, "Da Favela para Hollywood," *A Cena Muda* (February 11, 1942).

36

To Roosevelt

RUBÉN DARÍO*

Hispano-American *modernismo* can trace its origins to Nicaragua and the writings of poet Félix Rubén García Sarmiento, known by his literary name Rubén Darío (1867–1916). Darío's writing turned away from the outmoded lexicon and literary gestures of Romantic poetry in Spain. His verse and prose poetry looked instead to trends in France and the United States: the Parnassian poets, Stéphane Mallarmé, and Charles Baulelaire, as well as Edgar Allan Poe and Walt Whitman. Broadly speaking, all these poets wrote from a common historic perspective. Capitalist ambitions and industrialized life increasingly alienated individuals from expressive values. With the rise of mass culture, artists felt caught in a conflict: even as they viewed themselves as the rightful arbiters of meaning, there was little room for what they could contribute in a society whose aspirations were more inclined to material ends.

Marginalized in this way, the poets of *modernismo* turned to the underbelly of bourgeois life: to decadence, madness, melancholy, the macabre, cosmopolitan reality, and the ineffable core of artistic expression. They also depicted fanciful incidents driven by nocturnal forces; scenes filled with swans and marble statues. Darío and other Latin American *modernistas* wrote in the Spanish not of Spain but of "Our America," and they incorporated indigenous themes and images particular to the American hemisphere. Darío understood the role of art as something on the side not only of subject matter when he wrote: "I pursue a shape that my style cannot uncover [Yo persigo una forma que no encuentra mi estilo]."

Historians tend to consider *modernismo* primarily a literary movement. The interaction of text and images in literary magazines and other print media reveals it to have been a boldly visual movement as well. Related to *Jugendstil* in Germany and

* Rubén Darío (2004 [1876]) "To Roosevelt" (translated by Gabriel Gudding). *Mandorla* 7: 108–9.

Modern Art in Africa, Asia, and Latin America: An Introduction to Global Modernisms, First Edition.
Edited by Elaine O'Brien, Everlyn Nicodemus, Melissa Chiu, Benjamin Genocchio,
Mary K. Coffey, and Roberto Tejada.

Art Nouveau in France, the "print culture" associated with *modernismo* made use of highly stylized design elements and illustrations that were curvilinear, floral, with references often to physical demise and the eroticized female body. These magazines circulated widely in different countries and helped to fashion a feeling of Latin American artistic identity.

When he wrote the poem "To Roosevelt" in 1905, Darío was considered the most important poet of the Spanish language. Artists and writers in Latin America had long demonstrated a distrustful admiration of the United States, albeit praising its democratic principles and technological advances. Darío was no exception. Added to this was the fact that Central America's history, including that of Nicaragua, had been one of repeated armed interventions from the United States government and US American soldiers of fortune.

President Theodore Roosevelt had been responsible for one such incursion that, in 1903, led to the US annexation of territory destined for the Panama Canal. A year later, Roosevelt had so amended the Monroe Doctrine as to authorize continued US military actions in Latin America. In the poem, Roosevelt personifies the "powerful and huge" United States, and the poem critiques aggression in Latin America as an ongoing futurist project: "into whatever bones you shoot, you hit the future."

Gabriel Gudding's admirable translation employs US American vernacular expressions – the word "whackjobs," or the phrase "if you are to snick us" – to convey the forms by which Darío inflected regional usage of the Spanish language. Consider the many references in this poem to actual historic or mythical figures. What is the point the poet wished to make by employing such a grand rhetorical style? What does it mean for Darío to both deify Roosevelt and at the same time claim that he lacks "the one thing needed," that is, the Almighty?

Further Readings

Avelar, Idelber (1997) "Toward a Genealogy of Latin Americanism" (The Cultural Practice of Latin Americanism I). *Dispositio/n: American Journal of Cultural Histories and Theories* 49: 121–34.

Langley , Lester D. (1988) "Anti-Americanism in Central America" (Anti-Americanism: Origins and Context). *Annals of the American Academy of Political and Social Science* 497: 77–88

Martí, José (2002) "Our America." In Esther Allen (ed. and trans.), *José Martí: Selected Writings* (pp. 288–96). New York, NY: Penguin Classics.

Rodó, José Enrique (1988) *Ariel* (Margaret Sayers Peden, trans.). Austin: University of Texas Press.

It is with the voice of the Bible, or the verse of Walt Whitman
that I advance upon you now, Hunter!
Primitive and modern, sensible and complicated,
with something of Washington and a dash of Nimrod.
You are the United States,

you are the future invader
of all that's innocent in America and its Indian blood,
blood that still says Jesus Christ and speaks in Spanish.

You are a superb and strapping specimen of your people;
you are cultured and capable; you oppose Tolstoy.
You are a horse-whisperer, an assassinator of tigers,
you are Alexander-Nebuchadnezzer.
(You are a Professor of Energy
as the whackjobs among us now say.)

You think that life is a fire,
that progress is eruption
and into whatever bones you shoot,
you hit the future.

No.

The United States is powerful and huge.
And when it shakes itself a deep temblor
runs down the enormous vertebrae of the Andes.
If it yells, its voice is like the ripping boom of the lion.
It is just as Hugo said to Grant: "The stars are yours."
(Glinting wanly, it raises itself, the Argentine sun,
and the star of Chile rises too ...) You are rich –
you join the cult of Hercules with the cult of Mammon;
and illuminating the way of easy conquest,
"Freedom" has found its torch in New York.

But our America, which has had poets
from the ancient times of [Nezahualcóyotl],
which has kept walking in the footprints of the great Bacchus
(who had learned the Panic alphabet at one glance);
which has consulted the stars, which has known Atlantis,
(whose name comes down drumming to us in Plato),
which has lived since the old times on the very light of this world,
on the life of its fire, its perfume, its love,
the America of the great Moctezuma, of the Inca,
our America smelling of Christopher Columbus,
our Catholic America, our Spanish America,
the America in which the noble Cuauhtemoc said:
"I am in no bed of roses": that same America
which tumbles in the hurricanes and lives for Love,
it lives, you men of Saxon eyes and Barbarian souls.
And it dreams. And it loves, and it vibrates; and she is the daughter of the Sun.
Be very careful. Long live this Spanish America!
The Spanish Lion has loosed a thousand cubs today: they are at large, Roosevelt,

and if you are to snick us, outlunged and awed,
in your claws of iron, you must become God himself, the alarming
Rifleman and the hardened Hunter.

And though you count on everything, you lack
the one thing needed:
God.

37

Essays on Latin American Art

Joaquín Torres-García*

Joaquín Torres-García (Uruguay, 1874–1949) understood that geographic factors and localized histories determine viewpoint. In 1935, when this modernist painter and sculptor returned home to Uruguay, after years spent living in Europe and New York, he discovered, now at the seasoned age of 51, that his native city of Montevideo had been radically transformed. Social life and the built environment showed signs of industrial modernity of the kind he had experienced in Spain, France, and the United States, but Uruguayan standards conveyed anxieties about local culture in relation to foreign lifestyles and art forms.

Upon his return, Torres-García established the Association of Constructive Art in an effort to advance the order of aesthetic production in Uruguay and to transform the understanding of art through instruction, publishing, exhibitions, and public lectures. He wrote treatises, like the two presented here, to articulate his program for change. Manifestos commonly outline a method; they locate values and desires, and posit a design for the future. This is true of the unique logic and rhetorical style in "The School of the South" (1935), originally presented as a lecture, and "The New Art of America" (1942). Consistent with his visual thinking, Torres-García structures his arguments so as to resemble the grid work of his paintings – paragraph upon paragraph, his language reiterates claims and attitudes patterned with differences in example or image.

* Joaquín Torres-García (1992 [1935]) "The School of the South." In Mari Carmen Ramirez (ed.) *El Taller Torres-García: The School of the South and Its Legacy* (trans. Anne Twitty, pp. 53–7). Austin, TX: University of Texas Press.

Joaquín Torres-García (2004) "The New Art of America." In Mari Carmen Ramírez and Héctor Olea (eds) *Inverted Utopias: Avant-Garde in Latin America* (pp. 472–5). New Haven, CT: Yale University Press.

Modern Art in Africa, Asia, and Latin America: An Introduction to Global Modernisms, First Edition.
Edited by Elaine O'Brien, Everlyn Nicodemus, Melissa Chiu, Benjamin Genocchio, Mary K. Coffey, and Roberto Tejada.

In order for a unique school of art to flourish – in Uruguay, and more generally throughout the southern countries of Latin America – Torres-García challenged writers, artists, and composers to invert the global map, upending former symbolic relations between north and south; that is, between the so-called centers and margins of cultural authority. To privilege things foreign was to live the present as a kind of dependency, as the "past of a future" whose arrival is never guaranteed. Imported culture was tantamount to misguided artifice, perhaps even an invasion meant to prompt a specific kind of cultural consumption. However, backward glances in search of authenticity or of a "retrospective typicality" were gestures as disingenuous as looking only to Europe.

Use a search engine on a computer to find a present-day map of Montevideo, the capital of Uruguay, and you will see that the city does in fact protrude like a peninsula: in Torres-García's vivid image, it seeks "to spearhead the continent, to be the vanguard." Torres-García wanted readers to appreciate what was unique to Montevideo: the physical design of the river-city, the quality of light, and the human patterns combining peoples of European, Indigenous, and African descent. These appeals to his Uruguayan readership implored not to replace local forms with overseas culture, but to integrate only that which suited the texture of everyday life and the city habitat.

Like many participants in Latin America's avant-garde, Torres-García was ambivalent about modernity. He saw innovation not exceptionally in modern architecture or imported consumer items (these latter a form of "bastard culture"), but rather in those cultural manifestations that managed to render foreign influence unsuccessful. This "distinct character," however, was not in the name of some preordained authenticity. He wanted modern expressions to be consistent with regional temperament. In this line of reasoning, distinctiveness separated society, whereas a common identity and universal laws – "form and what it expresses" – had the capacity to unite men and women. For this reason he called for a vindication of pre-conquest civilizations in a modern search for that which was native to location.

A turn to the "archaic culture of the Continent" allowed Torres-García to synthesize a "cosmic" concept of humanity together with modern life (as did José Vasconcelos before him in Mexico), into a universal pictorial grammar proper to the Americas. In both these treatises, Torres-García sets into motion a dynamics of depth and surface. Juxtaposed to metaphors of earth, ground, and rootedness were images of artifacts, architecture, and the cosmos. To overcome anxieties prompted by a Euro-American monopoly on innovation – that is, to overturn the notion that art in Latin America was a second-order copy of a first-order original – Torres-García defied makers not to imitate but to adapt: to *construct* an analogous universe in formal structures.

As you read Torres-García's idiosyncratic vocabulary, what are the differences between artistic "renewal" and "construction"? How can we distinguish "decorative meaning" (closely linked to architecture) from "socially functional art"? What questions does the author mean to pose by pitting the human scale to a universal order or measure?

The School of the South

A great School of Art ought to arise here in our country. I say it without hesitation: *here in our country*. And I have my reasons for affirming this.

I have said School of the South; because in reality, *our North is the South*. There should be no North for us, except in opposition to our South.

That is why we now turn the map upside down, and now we know what our true position is, and it is not the way the rest of the world would like to have it. From now on, the elongated tip of South America will point insistently at the South, our North. Our compass as well; it will incline irremediably and forever toward the South, toward our pole. When ships sail from here traveling north, they will be *traveling down, not up* as before. Because the North is now below. And as we face our South, the East is to the left.

This is a necessary rectification; so that now we know where we are.

Also our city, the one we live in, has nothing to do with any other. *Montevideo is unique*. It has a character so peculiarly its own that it is unmistakable. It is apparent when you see the Cerro; and then its port; and it is perfectly fulfilled in the plazas, Independencia and Matriz. It's a shame that a few moles disfigure it!

The houses of our country force us to consider where we are. Particularly where they are still low, contrasting with the width of the streets. And this provides an abundance of light that is not found elsewhere. Besides, it is white (without fear of pleonasm I call it *luminous light*), and its angle is also peculiar to it; it can fit perfectly into an orthogonal ordering. The tall, narrow doors and windows of the houses should not be forgotten, for they lend a special and characteristic proportion.

The composition of the air also pertains to it: an air that corrodes the walls and covers them with a sort of greenish slime. This must undoubtedly be due to our great River. Because this water, which to us seems like an ocean on account of its enormous breadth, and which can be seen from most of the streets in Montevideo, confuses us; for it seems that it must be an ocean, but we have to think of it only as a river: our great Rio de la Plata, also unique. To it, as we all know, many of our streets slope down vertiginously, for these streets are continuously rising and falling; and this is something else peculiar to our city.

All right, now, looking closely, we discover the inner character of everything. Because our people are not like those of any other city, either; they have as much character as the city itself. And it isn't easy for them to realize what character they have, or to understand that it is generally different from that of other nations. It is not that there is a uniform type; on the contrary, it is extremely heterogeneous. Its particular physiognomy results from a characteristic expression rather than from facial features in themselves. For we have many types of features – one based on the European, another on the mestizo of Indian and Negro blood, and others that are almost pure Indian or Negro. And that is why our people, as a group, are extremely varied in appearance.

If we move on to what we could call *expression*, ways of gesturing, choice of words, the angle from which things are seen, etc., we also find ourselves in the presence of something very marked and particular. So that just by listening to people talk, we begin to penetrate into the idiosyncratic nature of this population. And – strangely enough – we do not find this character we are speaking of in the tango or in local street slang. That would be like looking for it in the *fashionable stores and shops*, or in modern architecture, for it is just there that our character is diluted. To such a point that our own typical city, although it exists everywhere, is less evident and almost nonexistent in certain new or modernized neighborhoods. This doesn't mean that it shouldn't be changed or modernized, for that should happen; but in accord with our character: a very subtle nuance, which needs to be *explicitly designated*, so that everyone can become conscious of it. The fact is, that by accentuating certain customs and sayings that are held to be very much our own, an artificial and detestably bland character is being created. And in numerous things. For example, what does *soccer* have to do with us? And if we examine what that game contributes to our country, not only in terms of its character, but in any other way, we will see that it gives 0. But let us abandon this touchy subject.

In certain places in Montevideo, one wonders if one is really here: there are so many imported things around. People will say: hasn't modern life brought them here? I say: not at all; it is commerce and industry from other countries that have already invaded this country. And there are neighborhoods *in which this has not been able to exterminate the native atmosphere*, despite the fact that the necessities of modern life are dispensed and sold there. That atmosphere is due to the people who live there, who are more rooted in their native soil and less frivolous, less spendthrift, and less inclined to cultivate frivolities. Such a street, with its tall, narrow doorways and its stained-glass transoms in the shape of a fan, with that sort of tree (not a plane tree), and with that sort of general store or other business, and with those types of men and women, could only exist in Montevideo. But I repeat; the character of the city is to be found everywhere within it. Consequently, the elegant young girl with her European pretensions to be French or English is Uruguayan! whether she likes it or not, and if she doesn't like it, she is on the wrong road. And this character does not reside in *mate*, or the poncho, or in song; it is something subtler that saturates everything and has the same clarity, the same white light as the city. And the man in this city is as unique as the city itself, with those ten letters in a row, neither rising nor falling, equal in size, and disquieting in their pure lack of expression: MONTEVIDEO. It had to be like that. Even the name is unique.

And here we are, the eye of all those whirling winds of these regions that perturb minds and bodies on this singular bank of the Great River: a quasipeninsula, *as if it wanted to forge ahead in the continent to march in the vanguard*. Our geographical position, then, indicates our destiny. And we are responsible for it.

So I say, careful about getting out of line! and I say also: we can *do everything* (now I'm referring to the vital things, those we could call telluric, that give the right aspect to everything); and then, *not exchange what belongs to us for the foreign* (which is unpardonable *snobbery*) but, on the contrary, convert the foreign into our *own substance*. Because I believe that the epoch of colonialism and importation is over (I am now referring to culture more than anything else), and so, away! with anyone who uses any other language than *ours*, for literature (and I don't mean the criollo language), whether he is writing, painting, or composing music. If he didn't learn a lesson from Europe at the right time, so much the worse for him, for that moment has passed. But if he believes that the other, folkloric, way is better, he is deceiving himself; it is worse, unbearably worse. Besides, that too is out of date. And didn't he realize that?

Present reality is different. Made by men who are not asleep, men who are within the present moment of things. Attached to life and molded by it. And therefore, *Uruguayans of today*.

And that is what I wanted to get to: *to the Uruguayan women of today, to the Uruguayan men of today*. Or rather: our own nuance, in things of today. I do not use the word *European* here, but simply say *that which time brought to us*. And that is why so much becomes paralyzed or reverts *to that*, both the man who follows *folkloric styles that are no longer viable*, and the one who follows European trends, which today are equally unviable. Because things of today are *more real* than all that, something that uplifts the spirit of our people, a spirit that no longer inhabits a *past* or a *future*, but a *present*. Uruguay, then, of the XXth Century – affirming its own personality and constructing.

Yes, *constructing everything*. And if there has been too much haste in pursuing novelty, today construction will continue in a more positive way, in a slower and surer rhythm. Many things will have to be reconsidered and redone to rectify them.

All right, today's Uruguayan must say: we have to move toward our *own positive originality*, positive in that it is candid and natural, produced by those who are neither *dreamers* nor *apprentices*, but men who are at long last *conscious*, who work in a frankly *realistic* way. And then, that same man will say: Down with imitation, down with theater, down with the senseless, the illogical, whatever lacks a true reason for being, for the age of *rehearsals* is over! Because today we are moving toward concrete and well-defined things. In a word: we want to construct with *art* (which means with knowledge), and with *our own materials*. For we are now *adults*.

Things are moving, and faster than we think. We didn't realize it, but the platform has already changed; today's rhythm is accelerated. And, fortunately, we are keeping pace with it.

Yes, things are moving. And this is hardly even the time for *renovation*; due to the conditions I have described, it is now the time for *construction*. And consider this: even the man who hasn't yet realized it is *working in that direction*.

In all nations, there are two factors that constitute the axis around which everything else turns: *the political factor and the economic, industrial, and commercial factors*. Well then, if we examine the condition of those factors here and now, in comparison to the way they used to be, we will see an enormous difference. And that difference already indicates another concept of things, and forms a man with a different mentality: *the Uruguayan of today*.

Let us explain, if only very rapidly, what this difference consists of. It is the following: that a local problem transcends that definition and is transformed into a *national problem*; and, naturally, without losing sight of the local. That is what gives a new character to the problem. That is why I said that things are moving.

The perspective determined by this fact is new and inconceivably vast. So man departs from his small base and has to launch himself into the world.

Well then, what is the artist to do and what is he doing? He must do the same: he must remain conscious of the world without forgetting what is close at hand. And thus, what is nearby will acquire a different character. It will become larger in concept, on a larger scale, and the space in which he must move will be limitless. He will be working in a grand ensemble. And this will not only form a new vision for him, but also provide him equally with new themes he would never have thought of. Besides, he will know that the tone must be raised. Isn't he working, from now on, with other masters from other lands? Then he will have to come up to their level and be in harmony with them.

The Uruguayan of today *is changing in the respects that we have just mentioned*. And therefore the artist, whether musician, painter, poet, architect, or writer, is changing too. The rest are behind: like something old, that used to be, something that cannot be joined to this or influence it; and being captive to the quotidian, is made and unmade every day.

Already the artist of today, who prefers to go to our port (and not for its picturesque qualities), salutes the great transatlantic liner, observes the cranes, the piles of merchandise, and the man who is working there … and, if you prefer, he doesn't even notice the picturesque touch of the sun or its reflections on the water. He sees the huge chimney of the steamer, the ladders, the ropes, the winches and the portholes, the enormous mass of the ship. He sees the hangars, the letters and numbers; and other signs and the passing locomotive. … He sees all this as something ideal, because he is contemplating *forms and not things*; and their architecture.

What does all this mean?: It means that the romantic age of the picturesque is over and that we are faced with *the Doric age of form*. And now one doesn't even know what country he is in, for he is in the universal. And will therefore be more Uruguayan than ever. Uruguayan of the XXth Century. Well then, from that position to *constructing* is only a step, and he will take that step. He will construct with *form* and *hue* and only then will he *paint* and realize that what he was doing before was literature.

And then look at his work: it is universal, but it is from here. Let's leave that aside for the moment. Let's move on to something else.

We began by saying that a great School of Art should be erected here. Great, not because of its organization, its ornate building, or the resources at its disposal, and thousands of other things; no, great *because of its robust life*, which is *real and effective* because it corresponds to a *real necessity*.

In art, as in everything else, *necessity* has always been the great spur. And I use the word *art* here in its *highest* sense: of constructing well, of using the rules wisely.

And then, we see that this *necessity*, in determining an art (in this case, visual), will reside *as it always has at all times and in all countries* in *decorative* expression. But here the decorative will not be an ornament: it will be an art that definitely has a *social function*. Meaning, *an art with a real, authentic base*.

An art that is not naturalistic (for naturalistic art is always subjective, based on personality and ephemeral emotion), but strongly *linked to the city*: commenting on it and singing of its life; emphasizing it, displaying it, and even, in a way, guiding it.

And if I have said *decorative*, it is only to make myself understood: for in reality such an art is a *monumental* art, planar and bidimensional, *schematic and synthetic*; an art of large rhythms and one that is closely tied to architecture.

All right then: if by way of all this we arrive at a *truth*, and not a partial, unilateral truth but a *total truth*; a truth *in all senses*, we will undoubtedly arrive at our particular tone, and then the *work of today* will be inescapably linked to *the work of yesterday*.

It seems to me that that is the nature and function of the School of the South that should arise on this eastern bank of the Río de la Plata.

If we paint any aspect of the city – a street, a park, etc., or a stretch of beach or a corner of the port, making the work as veristic as possible, we will have only barely suggested the already intense life of the city, its thousands of varied intellectual, moral, artistic, and industrial mechanisms; and also the contradictory aspects of it, and beyond that, of the *idea* we have of its importance. For, through such a *fragmentary* approach, we will never be able to give a full and diverse impression of the city, and even less of the concept we have of it. That is the *raison d'être* of a schematic and *symbolic* art. An art that, removed from the imitative and descriptive naturalistic aspect, corresponds perfectly to the contemporary spirit of synthesis, and can provide us with all of that within new rhythms. Symbolically, the River, the vibration of the factory or the streets, the moral tone of its people, the geographical situation, their aspirations, its marvelous light, the character of its inhabitants, their games and art – in short, everything.

With such an aim, then, and conscious of the magnitude of such an art, whether expressed in a small object or on a wall; such an art, I say, has to enter into the rhythm, that is, not only into the fixed and eternal laws of art, but also into the system of proportions, so that, through *measure*, it arrives at unity, which means harmony. Then each artist (whether visual artist or musician), *independently* but in reality linked to the rest through the law of the *Harmonic Rule*, will lend to the panorama of our art a unity that it presently lacks, a unity that has always been the sign of great art through all the ages and in all countries. That is to say: a style. That would really demonstrate *a true comprehension of artistic problems* and a *higher level*, which we should now achieve.

The New Art of America

The artist of today understands that art cannot be separated from the human problem. Therefore, he must select what each period requires but, in my opinion, only what it requires, in a universal sense, to unite men rather than separate them.

In this regard, art must preserve not only its purely plastic and nondescriptive qualities – the plastic act belonging to the universal order, since it is based on universal laws – and there will no longer be any disparity between the form and what it expresses, because everything will go together in perfect unity. Perhaps the artist has misunderstood something when trying to approach human life by believing that what is human is only anecdotal; but we who don't believe this have resolved the problem in a different way. Thus, we have entered fully into the great universal tradition that demands, as we do, that man's life and aspirations, as well as those of art, be founded on the pure laws of thought, thereby establishing an objective law that would raise man above the level of his individuality. This individuality is what separates men while the universal law is what unites them.

On our continent, many centuries ago, a perfect and astounding culture was founded on these principles. Which is why we should not search far afield for something that we already have close at hand and that is more appropriate to our world. As vestiges of those generations, there are still arts and men who believe in these principles, and who struggle to reestablish them by fighting off the avalanche of conquerors who tried to annihilate them. This is the idea of a people founded on *the universal and cosmic concept of man*. A concept that today arises anew from the relics of those ancient and noble races, surrounded by a motley crowd of the sometimes rude and ignorant invaders who are impelled only by corrupt ambition. And we, who lack those coats of arms, but who similarly interpret the ancient and honored law, should we be indifferent to such noble aspirations?

Today, a great desire for unification has risen from the Americas. And, although some may interpret it in a narrow political way, we ought to contribute to this movement without losing sight of what is most important by distancing ourselves completely. We must explore the depths, disregarding what is purely material. Faced with the problems of other countries, which must surely interest us because they concern human nature (always in the universal order). Without being selfish, we should be even more involved in our own problems. Here we have been given land to cultivate, and we should fulfill our duty. Which is why we had already inverted the map, indicating that the South was our aim, and in a way severing our ties to the spiritual tyranny of Europe. Let us, then, reintegrate into the great Native American family.

What we are proposing is not Pan-Americanism, but a spiritual union based on a profound relationship that goes beyond the concept of states. We need an objective in order to direct our production and to serve as a base from which to launch it. Not only for defining ourselves before our own eyes, but also before others. So that, under the sign of Native America, we can march in perfect unison, basing ourselves on something real, since the artist, too, must take from the earth. We must, then, be artists of the Americas. …

Our generation should be new, and should attempt to relate to this land by penetrating into its depths. For this reason we should disregard or repudiate the superficial, which is a dead element because it has no roots, and which signifies everything foreign. We should also reject the family of colonialism, of the invader, and of the pseudo-culture it created: a bitter drink brewed from the worst kinds of alcohol. To be precise, if we want to find stature, nobility, measure, order – what should be called culture – we can find it in the archaic culture of the Continent. Everything that could elevate, regenerate, cleanse us. Purify us of vulgarity and tastelessness (our gaucho ways), and of the heritage of intrigue and the pettifoggery whose underhanded procedures give rise to the customs, feelings, and character of *the native* we now are. And should cease to be. In other countries in South America, all of this is being shaken off. The native is being vindicated because the strength of the race is being discovered under the avalanche, and it is no longer a compound substance, but a pure native state. Whatever we may be, pure or mixed (of native blood or not), by the mere fact of being born here, our motto should be – whether we are from Chile or from Mexico, from the River Plate region or from Brazil – to search for America. This means to delve into the living bowel of the earth, to take root in it forever. To grow, to exist for this soil, without European whims. To build. To form ourselves. To create. A true culture must replace what is often referred to here as culture. Not, then, an amalgam of different kinds of knowledge and principles, incoherent and random, but rather something mature, unified: a *structure*. Something integral, based on a main idea, on harmonious conjunction.

Thus, during these past few years, we have taken a first step. The idea of structure, of construction, has been launched, and plastic works have been created accordingly. The geometric principle has appeared, and already this is a reintegration into the archaic culture. Also the idea of the cosmos, of universality. And, since these ideas did not previously exist among us, we can say that the return to the tradition of the Continent begins now. Not by way of archaeological studies, as in other parts of America, but through the essence of that tradition. In this way, not by imitation, but by wanting only to perpetuate this tradition in order to adapt it, with another form and expression, to our present spiritual needs. Yes, now our works of art – which we believe can still show traces of European culture (for that is from whence we started – already contain the entire essence of their qualitative tone and own structure. With greater affirmation, this is sustained by the concept of *analogous universe*. A very humble beginning, but a beginning nonetheless.

The fact that we want to give our art a very concrete path in this regard does not mean that we have to make a mold in order to develop it by thinking; to fabricate it, as they say. Not at all. To think, yes, and a great deal; to meditate on all of this; to adjust our behavior: to live in that great thought of the Americas – that, yes. But then, when we begin to work on our art, to forget everything! To try, as always, to make a structure, only a structure, guided by our feelings. Then, this tone of the Americas will show itself through color, through an arabesque or a type of composition, and through symbols, according to each particular temperament. And everything will belong to this nuance of the Americas. A tone that we can barely perceive, precisely because it is ours, because it is natural. But it could be perceived, as it already was in Paris – in the works shown in our exhibition; for, according to a critic from the journal *Beaux Arts*, these works had a Native American character. And this, I repeat, will be achieved only when we stop worrying about it. Because by worrying about it, something extremely dangerous could happen: we could fall into the archaeological, into making South American pastiches. And this has to be avoided at all costs. This is what everyone who has tried to make indigenous art has fallen into: Chileans, Mexicans, Peruvians, etc., including figures such as Diego Rivera. The other, equally dangerous, stumbling block is to descend into the picturesque or the folkloric. For now we have freed ourselves from such a fall, and I am sure that we will continue in that vein. So we are untouched by the values and qualities of European art (which we have studied so devotedly). May [Paul] Cézanne and [Pablo] Picasso, [Henri] Matisse and [Pierre-Auguste] Renoir stay over there. May Cubism and Neo-Plasticism stay over there. And even the masters of all the other schools. And why not Egypt and Greece, and Byzantium, since we have an art that is just as strong and profound as theirs? It is more important that we study our own art in order to penetrate its essence.

Our attitude will have to be better interpreted for the public, so that they can see where we come from and where we are going. … Then maybe the reason for this schematic art could be understood, as well as its symbolism, still incomprehensible to so many, and its logic. But it will take great effort to show that we are not in this tradition in order to plagiarize it, but because we have realized that it is part of the great universal tradition of the centuries: La tradición del hombre abstracto (Abstract tradition throughout time). …

We are in need of a true renaissance. We will surely contribute to it, but in conjunction with archaeologists and historians, artists and poets, in order to exhume, with true enthusiasm, the buried America. A strong and complete civilization is already visible, complete in every sense.

Now then, what do we discover by delving into its essence? The Truth, which is always the same, and which we will find wherever man has thought deeply. Does this mean that it doesn't differ from any other culture? Yes and no. It does not differ (nor could it be different in essence, for it would not be true and certain). But it does differ in appearance, modality, and form. It has its own structure, mythology, arts, and details, according to a corresponding medium. And it is perfect, complete. This is one fundamental reason for severing our ties to Europe, as an attempt both to perpetuate the native culture and to repudiate the bastard culture that has taken hold of our continent. We must go deeper. And this does not mean, as some have thought, that we should reject the knowledge of the world. Well, I will not insist on this. The lack of character of these South American peoples is only apparent, for underneath the European veneer our own character lies dormant. The problem is that the former does not allow the latter to thrive. But with a different consciousness of the situation, it can grow and develop as it should. This true character is also threatened by the bastard culture to which I have referred, and which is a sort of scab that has formed, leaving no outlet for the genuine. We live in this shadow, ignoring a reality whose hour has come. Above all, the exaltation of the adventurer and his grotesque manifestations should already have ceased. Because the Native was a geometer. And this means culture. Because this is a manifestation of

Universal Man. We can understand the Native (and one can hardly speak of the contemporary indigenous population). His monuments, his cosmic concept of the world which determined his social system, his calendar, mythology, and art, all speak to us eloquently. But these, so similar to those of other countries, are stamped with their own particular structure and qualities. Therefore, we must follow the great Tradition of Man, but within this Native American modality.

38

The Cosmic Race

José Vasconcelos*

In Mexico, a confluence of armed revolts succeeded in toppling the prolonged autocratic presidency of Porfirio Diaz who fled the country in 1911. Comprising a series of violent upsurges in the battle for political power, the Mexican Revolution lasted more than a decade thereafter. During those turbulent years, cultural philosopher José Vasconcelos (1882–1959) had campaigned for Francisco Madero, the democratically elected head of state, assassinated within two years of his term during a 1913 *coup d'état* staged by General Victoriano Huerta. Vasconcelos was forced to seek exile in France and, later at odds with Venustiano Carranza's presidency, sought refuge in the United States. Eventually in 1920, under the presidency of General Álvaro Obregón, the nation was now prepared to begin a material, ideological, and cultural reconstruction. Vasconcelos had returned to Mexico as rector of the National University of Mexico, and later as Minister of Public Education (1921–4). In that capacity, he gathered artists and intellectuals to contribute to the emerging revolutionary culture: a progressive agenda aimed to provide social welfare, widespread literacy, and art for the people. The muralist movement in Mexican art flourished thanks to the support of Vasconcelos who commissioned painters to cover walls of public buildings with nationalist content.

José Vasconcelos and the muralist painters sought to reverse the aesthetic and intellectual dependency of Mexico on foreign models by firmly grounding art and culture in native tradition. *Indigenismo*, that is, a renewed attention to Mexico's ancient civilizations and indigenous culture, linked art to the nation-building project,

* José Vasconcelos (1997 [1925]) *The Cosmic Race* (trans. Didier T. Jaén, pp. 7–40). Baltimore, MD: The Johns Hopkins University Press.

Modern Art in Africa, Asia, and Latin America: An Introduction to Global Modernisms, First Edition.
Edited by Elaine O'Brien, Everlyn Nicodemus, Melissa Chiu, Benjamin Genocchio,
Mary K. Coffey, and Roberto Tejada.

even as indigenous subjects could be portrayed emptied of active historical participation and meaning. Mexico was forging an image of itself by foregrounding the value of its Indian ethnicity, its ancient ruins, its manual arts, the country's long history and volcanic landscape, and with mythologies old and new.

Vasconcelos published *La raza cósmica* [*The Cosmic Race*] in 1925. It is a dense piece of rhetoric filled with internal contradictions and ambivalent motives. Just as science fiction is otherwise known as speculative literature, one might consider *The Cosmic Race* a speculative ethnography. Its argument is with Anglo-European and US American "exceptionalism," even as it makes special claims of its own. Vasconcelos sought to refute those attitudes that considered the Iberian Americas as some sort of "lesser new world." To this end, he found recourse in the ancient civilizations of Mesoamerica and the Andes, along with that unique phenomenon resulting from the conquest's foundational violence: namely, *mestizaje*, the sweeping integration over time of peoples and cultures from Europe (above all Spain and Portugal) with native peoples of Indo-America. A diagnostic and a philosophy of the future, *The Cosmic Race* submits *mestizaje* as "the moral and material basis for the union of all men into a fifth universal race, the fruit of all the previous ones and amelioration of everything past."

The Cosmic Race may strike readers today as alarmingly racialist or utterly outlandish. It is important to recall the unifying nationalist goals of Mexico's new state formation at the time this was written, as well as the audience to which the essay was directed – namely, the cultural elites of "Our America" (see Roberto Fernández Retamar on José Martí, this volume). Vasconcelos opposes the notion that there can be anything resembling an impartial empirical history. Instead, he offers what Fernández Retamar refers to as a "vast comprehensive theory" grounded in experimental intuition. For Vasconcelos, Europe's expansionist project had served as "a bridge" uniting the "four racial trunks: the Black, the Indian, the Mongol, and the White." An overarching cultural difference remained between the dominant colonizers of the modern period, Spain and England, but more precisely, between "Latinism" and "Anglo-Saxonism." As a child, Vasconcelos had grown up on the US–Mexico border and attended school in Eagle Pass, Texas. Having experienced the United States first hand, he would claim that, "ideologically, the Anglos continue to conquer us."

In a 1932 issue of a US journal Vasconcelos later came to his own defense against those who depicted him as an "anti-foreigner" or as "a racial patriot overzealous for the interests of Mexico and Spanish America." He did not object to the United States, he clarified; he opposed its "political influence in Mexico because it has always been exercised for the benefit of the big business interests, and for the behoof of a few Mexican traitors whose conduct is that of despots and military dictators."

Despite the prevailing *indigenismo* of Mexico's cultural renaissance, Vasconcelos did not disavow the cultural heritage of Spain. On the contrary he values the Spanish over the Anglo-Saxon precisely because of the former's capacity to assimilate "a mixture of dissimilar races." He writes: "Spanish colonization created mixed races [whereas] the English kept on mixing only with the whites and annihilated the natives." It is in Iberian America whence there will emerge a future – as remote as Atlantis stands in relation to the past – for "the definitive race, the synthetical race, the integral race, made up of the genius and the blood of all peoples and, for that reason, more capable of true brotherhood and of a truly universal vision."

A racial thinker, Vasconcelos was not exempt from his own period-based racism, especially with regard to peoples of African and Asian descent. *The Cosmic Race*, however, was not meant as a prescriptive text submitting a form of eugenics. It was not a plan for improving the human species. Rather, it proposes an ethics that views complexity as an aesthetic value, and benevolence capable of producing a more dignified humanity: "Procreation by love is already a good antecedent for a healthy progeny, but it is necessary that love itself be a work of art, and not the last resort of desperate people." Equally important as his writings are those works he commissioned from José Clemente Orozco, David Alfaro Siqueiros, and Diego Rivera. The latter's murals at the National Palace are discussed by Leonard Forgarait in this volume. Rivera also produced an ambitious series of narrative murals in the Palace of Public Education in Mexico City. There, Vasconcelos had allegories carved to represent "Spain, Mexico, Greece, and India [Africa and the rest of Asia are glaring omissions], the four particular civilizations that have most to contribute to the formation of Latin America."

Consider Leonard Folgarait's analysis of Diego Rivera's murals at Mexico City's National Palace. What were the pitfalls of *mestizaje* as employed in the ideological service of Mexico's revolutionary regime? Who does this vision exclude? How does Vasconcelos's biological model of utopian advancement account for the place of women or that of alternate sexualities? Does Vasconcelos argue for the eventual disappearance of racial difference? Or does he rehearse compelling language to cast doubt altogether on the term "race" as a methodically quantifiable category? How is *mestizaje* in *The Cosmic Race* of 1925 comparable to the Brazilian metaphor of consumption in Oswald de Andrade's 1928 "Cannibalist Manifesto"? How are these two essays a response to the racial beliefs associated with Eurocentrism? Compare Vasconcelos's racialism with commentary by Frantz Fanon, Aimé Césaire, and Ousmane Sembène in the African modernism section.

Further Readings

Brenner, Anita (1943) *The Wind That Swept Mexico: The History of the Mexican Revolution, 1910–1942*. New York, NY: Harper & Brothers.

Brenner, Anita (2002[1929]) *Idols Behind Altars: Modern Mexican Art and Its Cultural Roots*. New York, NY: Dover Publications.

Hedrick, Tace (2003) *Mestizo Modernism: Race, Nation, and Identity in Latin American Culture, 1900–1940*. New Brunswick, NY: Rutgers University Press.

Knight, Alan (1990) "Racism, Revolution, and Indigenismo: Mexico, 1910–1940." In Richard Graham (ed.), *The Idea of Race in Latin America, 1870–1940* (pp. 71–113). Austin, TX: University of Texas Press.

Vasconcelos, José (1932) "Why I Became a Magazine Editor." *Books Abroad* 6(1): 6–9.

Mestizaje

I

In the opinion of respectable geologists, the American continent includes some of the most ancient regions of the world. The Andes are, undoubtedly, as old as any other mountain range on earth. And while the land itself is ancient, the traces of life and human culture also go back in time beyond any calculations. The architectural ruins of legendary Mayans, Quechuas, and Toltecs are testimony of civilized life previous to the oldest foundations of towns in the Orient and Europe.

[...]

If we are, then, geologically ancient, as well as in respect to the tradition, how can we still continue to accept the fiction, invented by our European fathers, of the novelty of a continent that existed before the appearance of the land from where the discoverers and conquerors came?

The question has paramount importance to those who insist in looking for a plan in History.

[...]

Greece laid the foundations of Western or European civilization; the white civilization that, upon expanding, reached the forgotten shores of the American continent in order to consummate the task of re-civilization and re-population. Thus we have the four stages and the four racial trunks: the Black, the Indian, the Mongol, and the White. The latter, after organizing itself in Europe, has become the invader of the world, and has considered itself destined to rule, as did each of the previous races during their time of power. It is clear that domination by the whites will also be temporary, but their mission is to serve as a bridge. The white race has brought the world to a state in which all human types and cultures will be able to fuse with each other. The civilization developed and organized in our times by the whites has set the moral and material basis for the union of all men into a fifth universal race, the fruit of all the previous ones and amelioration of everything past.

White culture is migratory, yet it was not Europe as a whole that was in charge of initiating the reintegration of the red world into the modality of preuniversal culture, which had been represented for many centuries by the white man. The transcendental mission fell upon the two most daring branches of the European family, the strongest and most different human types: the Spanish and the English.

[...]

Our age became, and continues to be, a conflict of Latinism against Anglo-Saxonism; a conflict of institutions, aims and ideals. [...] Not only were we defeated in combat; ideologically, the Anglos continue to conquer us. The greatest battle was lost on the day that each one of the Iberian republics went forth alone, to live her own life apart from her sisters, concerting treaties and receiving false benefits, without tending to the common interests of the race. [...] We keep ourselves jealously independent from each other, yet one way or another we submit to, or ally ourselves with, the Anglo-Saxon union.

[…]

So that we shall not be forced to deny our own fatherland, it is necessary that we live according to the highest interests of the race, even though this may not be yet in the highest interest of humanity. It is true that the heart is not satisfied with less than a full-fledged internationalism, but given the present world conditions, internationalism would only serve to consummate the triumph of the strongest nations; it would only serve the aims of the English. Even the Russians, with their two hundred million population, have had to postpone their theoretical internationalism, in order to devote themselves to the support of oppressed nationalities such as India and Egypt. At the same time, they have strengthened their own nationalism in order to defend themselves against a disintegration which could only favor the great imperialist states. It would, then, be puerile for weak countries like ours, to start denying what is rightfully theirs in the name of aims that could not crystalize in reality. The present state of civilization still imposes patriotism on us as a necessity for the defense of material and moral interests; but it is indispensable for this patriotism to seek vast and transcendental aims. Its mission was cut short, in a sense, with independence. Now it is necessary to bring it back to the flow of its universal historical destiny.

The first stage of the profound conflict was decided in Europe and we lost. Afterwards, when all the advantages were on our side in the New World, since Spain had conquered America, the Napoleonic stupidity gave Louisiana away to the Englishmen from this side of the ocean, to the Yankees; this decided the fate of the New World in favor of the Anglo-Saxons. […] Napoleon, in his foolishness, was not able to surmise that the destiny of the European races was going to be decided in the New World. When, in the most thoughtless manner, he destroyed French power in America, he also weakened the Spaniards. He betrayed us and placed us at the mercy of the common enemy. Without Napoleon, the United States would not exist as a world empire, and Louisiana, still French, would have to be part of the Latin American Confederation.

[…]

Should one talk to the most exalted Indianist of the convenience of adapting ourselves to Latinism, he will raise no questions; but tell him that our culture is Spanish and he will immediately bring up counter arguments. The stain from the spilled blood still remains. It is an accursed stain that centuries have not erased, but which the common danger must annul. There is no other recourse. Even the pure Indians are Hispanized, they are Latinized, just as the environment itself is Latinized. Say what one may, the red men, the illustrious Atlanteans from whom Indians derive, went to sleep millions of years ago, never to awaken. There is no going back in History, for it is all transformation and novelty. No race returns. Each one states its mission, accomplishes it, and passes away. This truth rules in Biblical times as well as in our times; all the ancient historians have formulated it. The days of the pure whites, the victors of today, are as numbered as were the days of their predecessors. Having fulfilled their destiny of mechanizing the world, they themselves have set, without knowing it, the basis for a new period: The period of the fusion and mixing of all peoples. The Indian has no other door to the future but the door of modern culture, nor any other road but the road already cleared by Latin civilization. The white man, as well, will have to depose his pride and look for progress and ulterior redemption in the souls of his brothers from other castes. He will have to diffuse and perfect himself in each of the superior varieties of the species, in each of the modalities that multiply revelation and make genius more powerful.

[...] It seems as if God Himself guided the steps of the Anglo-Saxon cause, while we kill each other on account of dogma or declare ourselves atheists. How those mighty empire builders must laugh at our groundless arrogance and Latin vanity! They do not clutter their mind with the Ciceronian weight of phraseology, nor have they in their blood the contradictory instincts of a mixture of dissimilar races, *but they committed the sin of destroying those races, while we assimilated them, and this gives us new rights and hopes for a mission without precedent in History.*

For this reason, adverse obstacles do not move us to surrender, for we vaguely feel that they will help us to discover our way. Precisely in our differences, we find the way. If we simply imitate, we lose. If we discover and create, we shall overcome. The advantage of our tradition is that it has greater facility of sympathy towards strangers. This implies that our civilization, with all defects, may be the chosen one to assimilate and to transform mankind into a new type; that within our civilization, the warp, the multiple and rich plasma of future humanity is thus being prepared. This mandate from History is first noticed in that abundance of love that allowed the Spaniard to create a new race with the Indian and the Black, profusely spreading white ancestry through the soldier who begat a native family, and Occidental culture through the doctrine and example of the missionaries who placed the Indians in condition to enter into the new stage, the stage of world One. Spanish colonization created mixed races, this signals its character, fixes its responsibility, and defines its future. The English kept on mixing only with the whites and annihilated the natives. Even today, they continue to annihilate them in a sordid and economic fight, more efficient yet than armed conquest. This proves their limitation and is indication of their decadence. [...] To build an English world and to exterminate the red man, so that Northern Europe could be renovated all over an America made up with pure whites, is no more than a repetition of the triumphant process of a conquering race. This was already attempted by the red man and by all strong and homogeneous races, but it does not solve the human problem. America was not kept in reserve for five thousand years for such a petty goal. The purpose of the new and ancient continent is much more important. Its predestination obeys the design of constituting the cradle of a fifth race into which all nations will fuse with each other to replace the four races that have been forging History apart from each other. The dispersion will come to an end on American soil; unity will be consummated there by the triumph of fecund love and the improvement of all the human races. In this fashion, the synthetic race that shall gather all the treasures of History in order to give expression to universal desire shall be created.

The so-called Latin peoples, because they have been more faithful to their divine mission in America, are the ones called upon to consummate this mission. Such fidelity to the occult design is the guarantee of our triumph.

[...]

[...] In Latin America, the repulsion of one blood that confronts another strange blood also exists, but infinitely more attenuated. There, a thousand bridges are available for the sincere and cordial fusion of all races. The ethnic barricading of those to the north in contrast to the much more open sympathy of those to the south is the most important factor, and at the same time, the most favorable to us, if one reflects even superficially upon the future, because it will be seen immediately that we belong to tomorrow, while the Anglo-Saxons are gradually becoming more a part of yesterday. The Yankees will end up building the last great empire of a single race, the final empire of White supremacy. Meanwhile, we will continue to suffer the vast chaos of an ethnic stock in formation, contaminated by the fermentation of all types, but secure of the avatar into a better race. In Spanish America, Nature will no longer repeat one of her partial attempts. This time, the race that will come out of the forgotten Atlantis will no longer be a race of a single color or of particular features. The future race will not be a fifth, or a sixth race, destined to prevail over its ancestors. What is going to emerge out there is the definitive race, the synthetical race, the integral race, made up of the genius and the blood of all peoples and, for that reason, more capable of true brotherhood and of a truly universal vision.

[...]

[...] So many races that have come and others that will come. In this manner, a sensitive and ample heart will be taking shape within us; a heart that embraces and contains everything and is moved with sympathy, but, full of vigor, imposes new laws upon the world. And we foresee something like another head that will dispose of all angles in order to fulfill the miracle of surpassing the sphere.

II

After examining the close and the remote possibilities of the mixed race that inhabits the Ibero-American continent, as well as the destiny that drives it to become the first synthetic race of the earth, it is necessary to inquire if the physical milieu within which this human stock is being developed corresponds to the ends determined by its bionomy. [...] The climate, it will be said, is adverse to the new race, because the greatest part of the available land is located in the hottest region of the earth. However, this is precisely the advantage and the secret of the future. The great civilizations began in the Tropics and the final civilization will return to the Tropics. The new race will begin to fulfill its destiny as new means are invented to combat the heat insofar as it is adverse to man, yet leaving intact its benefic power for the production of life. The triumph of the Whites began with the conquest of snow and cold. The basis of white civilization is fuel. First, it served as a protection against the long winters. Then, it was discovered that its power could be used not only for warmth, but also for work; and the motor was born. And so it is that, from the hearth and the stove proceed all the machinery that is transforming the world.

[...]

At the beginning, the Whites will try to take advantage of their inventions for their own benefit, but since science is no longer esoteric, it is not likely that they will succeed. They will be absorbed in the avalanche of all the other races, and, finally, deposing their pride, they will combine with the rest to make the new racial synthesis, the fifth race of the future.

The conquest of the Tropics will transform all aspects of life. Architecture will abandon the Gothic arch, the vault, and, in general, the roof, which answers to the need for shelter. The pyramid will again develop. Colonnades and perhaps spiral constructions will be raised in useless ostentation of beauty, because the new aesthetics will try to adapt itself to the endless curve of the spiral, which represents the freedom of desire and the triumph of Being in the conquest of infinity. The landscape, brimming with colors and rhythms, will communicate its wealth to the emotions. Reality will be like fantasy. The aesthetics of cloudiness and grays will be seen as the sickly art of the past. A refined and intense civilization will answer to the splendors of a Nature swollen with potency, habitually generous, and shining with clarity. The panorama of present day Rio de Janeiro, or Santos, with the city and the bay, can give us an idea of what the future emporium of the integral race that is to come will be like.

[...] With the resources from such region – the richest on earth, filled with all kinds of treasures – the synthetic race will be able to consolidate its culture. The world of the future will belong to whoever conquers the Amazon region. Universopolis will rise by the great river, and from there the preaching, the squadrons, and the airplanes propagandizing the good news will set forth. If the Amazon becomes English, the world metropolis would not be called Universopolis, but Anglotown, and the armies would come out of there to impose upon the other continents the harsh law of domination by the blond-haired Whites and the extinction of their dark rivals. On the other hand, if the fifth race takes ownership of the axis of the future world, then airplanes and armies will travel all over the planet educating the people for their entry into wisdom. Life, founded on love, will come to be expressed in forms of beauty. Naturally, the fifth race will not pretend to exclude the Whites, just as it does not propose to exclude any of the other races. [...] Latin America owes what it is to the white European, and is not going to deny him. To the North Americans themselves, Latin America owes a great part of her railroads, bridges, and enterprises. By the same token, it needs [all of] the other races. However, we accept the superior ideals of the Whites but not their arrogance. We want to offer them, as well as to all other peoples, a free country where they will find a home and a refuge, but not a continuation of their conquests. The Whites themselves, unhappy with the materialism and social injustice in which their race, the fourth race, has fallen, will come to us for help in this conquest of freedom.

Perhaps the traits of the white race will predominate among the characteristics of the fifth race, but such a supremacy must be [a] result of the free choice of personal taste, and not the fruit of violence or economic pressure. The superior traits of culture and nature will have to triumph, but that triumph will be stable only if it is based on the voluntary acceptance by conscience and on the free choice of fantasy. Up to this date, life has received its character from man's lower faculties; the fifth branch will be the fruit of the superior faculties. The fifth race does not exclude but accumulates life. For this reason, the exclusion of the Yankee, like the exclusion of any other human type, would be equivalent to an anticipated mutilation, more deadly even than a later cut. If we do not want to exclude even the races that might be considered inferior, it would be much less sensible to keep from our enterprise a race full of vigor and solid social virtues.

[…]

III

[…]

If we acknowledge that Humanity is gradually approaching the third period of its destiny, we shall see that the work of racial fusion is going to take place in the Ibero-American continent according to a law derived from the fruition of the highest faculties. The laws of emotion, beauty, and happiness will determine the selection of a mate with infinitely superior results than that of a eugenics grounded on scientific reason, which never sees beyond the less important portion of the love act. […] The entire species will change its physical makeup and temperament. Superior instincts will prevail and, in a happy synthesis, the elements of beauty apportioned today among different races will endure.

[…]

A mixture of races accomplished according to the laws of social well-being, sympathy, and beauty, will lead to the creation of a type infinitely superior to all that have previously existed. […]

No contemporary race can present itself alone as the finished model that all the others should imitate. The mestizo, the Indian, and even the Black are superior to the White in a countless number of properly spiritual capacities. Neither in antiquity, nor in the present, have we a race capable of forging civilization by itself. The most illustrious epochs of humanity have been, precisely, those in which several different peoples have come into contact and mixed with each other. India, Greece, Alexandria, Rome are but examples that only a geographic and ethnic universality is capable of giving the fruits of civilization. […] The truth is that vigor is renewed with graftings, and that the soul itself looks for diversity in order to enrich the monotony of its own contents. Only a long lasting experience will be able to show the results of a mixture no longer accomplished by violence, nor by reason of necessity, but by the selection founded on the dazzling produced by beauty and confirmed by the *pathos* of love.

[…]

The doctrine of sociological and biological formation we propose in these pages is not a simple ideological effort to raise the spirits of a depressed race by offering it a thesis that contradicts the doctrine with which its rivals wanted to condemn it. What happens is that, as we discover the falsity of the scientific premise upon which the domination of contemporary power rests, we also foresee, in experimental science itself, orientations that point the way, no longer for the triumph of a single race, but for the redemption of all men.

[...]

[...] [I]n the new order, by its own law, the permanent elements will not support themselves on violence but on taste, and, for that reason, the selection will be spontaneous, as it is done by the artist when, from all the colors, he takes only those that are convenient to his work.

If in order to constitute the fifth race we should proceed according to the law of the second period, then a contest of craftiness would ensue, in which the astute ones and those lacking in scruples would win the game over the dreamers and the kind at heart.

[...] The joy-creating faculty is contained in the law of the third period, which is a feeling for beauty and a love so refined that it becomes identified with divine revelation. [...] Its dynamism is contagious, it moves the emotions and transforms everything, even destiny itself. The race best qualified to discover and to impose such a law upon life and material things will be the matrix race of the new civilization. Fortunately, such a gift, necessary to the fifth race, is possessed in a great degree by the mestizo people of the Ibero-American continent, people for whom beauty is the main reason for everything. A fine aesthetic sensitivity and a profound love of beauty, away from any illegitimate interests and free from formal ties, are necessary for the third period, which is impregnated with a Christian aestheticism that puts upon ugliness itself the redemptive touch of pity which lights a halo around everything created.

We have, then, in the continent all the elements for the new Humanity: A law that will gradually select elements for the creation of predominant types; a law that will not operate according to a national criterion, as would be the case with a single conquering race. [...]

The people that Hispanic America is forming in a somewhat disorderly manner, yet free of spirit and with intense longings on account of the vast unexplored regions, can still repeat the feats of the Castilian and Portuguese conquerors. The Hispanic race, in general, still has ahead of it this mission of discovering new regions of the spirit, now that all lands have already been explored.

Only the Iberian part of the continent possesses the spiritual factors, the race, and the territory necessary for the great enterprise of initiating the new universal era of Humanity. All the races that are to provide their contribution are already there: The Nordic man, who is today the master of action but who had humble beginnings and seemed inferior in an epoch in which already great cultures had appeared and decayed; the black man, as a reservoir of potentialities that began in the remote days of Lemuria; the Indian, who saw Atlantis perish but still keeps a quiet mystery in the conscience. We have all the races and all the aptitudes. The only thing lacking is for true love to organize and set in march the law of History.

Many obstacles are opposed to the plan of the spirit, but they are obstacles common to all progress. Of course, some people may object, saying that how are the different races going to come to an accord, when not even the children of the same stock can live in peace and happiness within the economic and social regime that oppresses man today. But such a state of mind will have to change rapidly. All the tendencies of the future are intertwined in the present: Mendelianism in biology, socialism in government, growing sympathy among the souls, generalized progress, and the emergence of the fifth race that will fill the planet with the triumphs of the first truly universal, truly cosmic culture.

If we view the process panoramically, we shall find the three stages of the law of the three states of society, each one vivified with the contribution of the four fundamental races that accomplish their mission and, then, disappear in order to create a fifth superior ethnic specimen. This gives us five races and three stages, that is, the number eight which in the Pythagorean gnosis represents the ideal of the equality of all men. Such coincidences are surprising when discovered, although later they may seem trivial.

In order to express all these ideas that today I am trying to expound in a rapid synthesis, I tried, some years ago, when they were not yet well defined, to assign them symbols in the new Palace of Public Education in Mexico. Lacking sufficient elements to do exactly what I wished, I had to be satisfied with a Spanish renaissance building, with two courtyards, archways, and passages that give somewhat the impression of a bird's wing. On the panels at the four corners of the first patio, I had them carve allegories representing Spain, Mexico, Greece, and India, the four particular civilizations that have most to contribute to the formation of Latin America. Immediately below these four allegories, four stone statues should have been raised, representing the four great contemporary races: The white, the red, the black, and the yellow, to indicate that America is home to all and needs all of them. Finally, in the center, a monument should have been raised that in some way would symbolize the law of the three states: The material, the intellectual and the aesthetic. All this was to indicate that through the exercise of the triple law, we in America shall arrive, before any other part of the world, at the creation of a new race fashioned out of the treasures of all the previous ones: The final race, the cosmic race.

39

Cannibalist Manifesto[1]

Oswald de Andrade*

In the early decades of the twentieth century, economic growth and technological development transformed the city of São Paulo into a site of financial, intellectual, and political ferment that had a wide-ranging impact on Brazilian culture and its links to the globe. Brazil's national and local governments had encouraged waves of immigration, primarily from Europe, to satisfy industrialization's labor demands in the city of São Paulo and for a prosperous coffee industry in the interior of the state. Subsequent to the belated abolition of slavery in 1888, predominant racial beliefs drove immigration policies that sought to "whiten" the nation, even as an influx of chiefly Afro-Brazilian migrants from the Northeastern states arrived in São Paulo. In the 1920s, the material facts and demographics of modern life were visible in a city that bustled with crowds and automobiles, punctuated with new structures like the 14-storey Sampaio Moreira Building built in 1924, and the 28-storey Martinelli Building constructed in 1929.

Artists and intellectuals found venues for political and cultural debate at salons and other informal gatherings of friends and associates. In discussing the relevance of European artistic trends – Fauvism, Cubism, Surrealism, Dada – this creative class was not blind to the predicaments of an avant-garde in developing countries like Brazil where modernization and modern life were often the privilege of a socioeconomic elite that had access to education and travel abroad. In an effort to address those contradictions, Brazilian modernists turned to journalism and the printed information media (newspapers, magazines) so as to prompt public debate in the form of editorials, short articles, and other idiosyncratic news items. They also staged highly

* Oswald de Andrade (1991) "Cannibalist Manifesto" (translated by Leslie Bary). *Latin American Literary Review* 19(38): 38–47.

Modern Art in Africa, Asia, and Latin America: An Introduction to Global Modernisms, First Edition.
Edited by Elaine O'Brien, Everlyn Nicodemus, Melissa Chiu, Benjamin Genocchio,
Mary K. Coffey, and Roberto Tejada.

publicized events such as the Semana da Arte Moderna [Week of Modern Art], a series of exhibitions, conferences, and literary readings that startled São Paulo's cultural life in February 1922.

In line with avant-garde magazines such as *Klaxon* (May 1922–January 1923) edited by artists and writers who had organized the Week of Modern Art, another journal appeared in May 1928, published by journalist Antônio de Alcântara Machado and poet Raul Bopp. In the first of the magazine's two issues, the pages of *Revista de Antropofagia* featured writing by literary experimentalists like Carlos Drummond de Andrade, Manuel Bandeira, Oswald de Andrade, and Mário de Andrade (no relation). The irreverent tone of the magazine's title, *Revista de Antropofagia* [*The Cannibalist Review*] was compatible with its bold graphic design and provocative content. The cover reproduced a woodcut by sixteenth-century German artist Hans Staden (1525–79), one of many illustrations that supplemented a written account describing his captivity among the Tupinambá peoples of Brazil who, he claimed, practiced cannibalism. One of many similar images that transfixed the imagination of Europe during the Renaissance and thereafter, the woodcut depicts Tupinambá men detaining European intruders, roasting severed body parts on a spit, and devouring human flesh.

The modernist poet Oswald de Andrade (1890–1954) published his "Cannibalist Manifesto" in that inaugural issue of *Revista de Antropofagia*. Its opening lines were deliberately meant to incite reaction: "Cannibalism alone unites us. Socially. Economically. Philosophically." What follows is a droll performance written in a series of eccentric statements and counterstatements that stage – with added visual irony in Staden's woodcut on the journal's cover – a dilemma that fueled Brazilian *modernismo*: How does one write Brazilian culture into a universal history overdetermined by Europe and its systems of representation and as defined by the colonial enterprise? To that question Oswald de Andrade replies unapologetically, poker-faced, and with tongue firmly planted in cheek. He playfully attacks assumptions about history (that it possesses a preordained logic) and about cultural influence (that it is one-directional). The manifesto enacts a theory about the laws of culture: sound historic claims are always threatened by the opposing principle of randomness. This brief uncontainable text satirizes a Western ontology that sees itself as singular and universal. Shakespeare's existential lines articulated by Hamlet transpose into a question about the status of the native Tupinambá peoples in the project of modernity: "Tupi or not Tupi, that is the question."

To the degree that the eating of human flesh has been culturally proscribed, Oswald de Andrade sought to overturn modern-day taboos that dictate what is forbidden or dangerous. He viewed the pageantry of European culture, and of the world at large, as a feast set out for modern (cannibalistic) Brazilian appetites: "I am only concerned with what is not mine. Law of Man. Law of the cannibal." It is, however, a discriminating taste that does not passively accept; rather, it selectively chooses among the offerings, and in eating it incorporates the foreign into the national palate. This national selfhood by means of consumption is a defiance achieved using parody to redefine originality; it critiques the modern idolatry of innovation by seizing opportunity. "I asked a man what the Law was. He answered that it was the guarantee of the exercise of possibility. That man was named Galli Mathias [a word play here for 'gibberish']. I ate him." The manifesto creatively blurs the line between punch lines, allegations, and nonsense. In a joke about psychoanalysis, with its interest in prelinguistic functions of the mouth, the manifesto appears even to eat its own words.

Mimicking the style of high-speed communication, Oswald de Andrade adopts a telegraphic structural device to convey end-line urgency: "The stop of thought that is dynamic." Similarly, he prefers anecdote to sweeping historic analysis. His sign-off dates the text in relation to the first year of Brazilian history: the year Brazilian Indians ate the Bishop Sardinha. The route back and forth between that definitive occasion and the present-day is a travel log for so remapping the place of Brazil in history as to make the standard narratives as unreliable as many of the manifesto's outrageous claims.

The editors of *Revista de Antropofagia* typeset "Cannibalist Manifesto" around a drawing by the leading modernist painter Tarsila do Amaral, to whom Oswald de Andrade was married. The sketch, *O antropófago* [*Cannibal*], relates to a canvas completed in January, *Abaporú* (see Figure I.4, this volume, p. 288), the Tupi-Guarani word for "man who eats." Over time, the manifesto has come to encapsulate the cultural contradictions of Brazilian *modernismo*. In the act of ingestion, both eater and eaten are mutually transformed; a digestive metaphor that poet Haroldo de Campos later referred to as the "unrestrainable metabolism of difference."

How are opposite terms set into play in "Cannibalist Manifesto" – for instance, civilization versus barbarism, cosmopolitan versus primitive, and original versus copy? In the act of "devouring" European culture, how does Oswald de Andrade incorporate the native self? What is the role of former African slaves in this worldview?

Further Readings

De Andrade, Oswald (1995) "Anthropophagist Manifesto" (Alfred MacAdams, trans.). *Latin American Literature and Arts* 51.

Tapscott, Stephen (1996) *Twentieth Century Latin American Poetry*. Austin: University of Texas Press.

Vicuña, Cecilia and Livon-Grosman, Ernesto (eds) (2009) *The Oxford book of Latin American poetry: a bilingual anthology*. New York, NY: Oxford University Press.

Staden, Hans (2008[1557]) *True History an Account of Cannibal Captivity in Brazil* (Neil L. Whitehead, ed., Michael Harbsmeier, trans.). Durham, NC: Duke University Press.

Cannibalism alone unites us. Socially. Economically. Philosophically.

* * *

The world's single law. Disguised expression of all individualism, of all collectivisms. Of all religions. Of all peace treaties.

* * *

Tupi or not tupi, that is the question.[2]

* * *

Down with every catechism. And down with the Gracchi's mother.[3]

* * *

I am only concerned with what is not mine. Law of Man. Law of the cannibal.

* * *

We're tired of all the suspicious Catholic husbands who've been given starring roles. Freud put an end to the mystery of Woman and to other horrors of printed psychology.

* * *

What clashed with the truth was clothing, that raincoat placed between the inner and outer worlds. The reaction against the dressed man. American movies will inform us.

* * *

Children of the sun, mother of the living. Discovered and loved ferociously with all the hypocrisy of *saudade*,[4] by the immigrants, by slaves and by the *touristes*. In the land of the Great Snake.[5]

* * *

It was because we never had grammars, nor collections of old plants. And we never knew what urban, suburban, frontier and continental were. Lazy in the *mapamundi* of Brazil.[6]

A participatory consciousness, a religious rhythmics.[7]

* * *

Down with all the importers of canned consciousness. The palpable existence of life. And the pre-logical mentality for Mr. Lévy-Bruhl to study.[8]

* * *

We want the Carib Revolution. Greater than the French Revolution. The unification of all productive revolts for the progress of humanity. Without us, Europe wouldn't even have its meager declaration of the rights of man.[9]

The Golden Age heralded by America. The Golden Age. And all the *girls*.

* * *

Heritage. Contact with the Carib side of Brazil. *Où Villegaignon print terre.*[10] Montaigne. Natural man. Rousseau. From the French Revolution to Romanticism, to the Bolshevik Revolution, to the Surrealist Revolution and Keyserling's technicized barbarian.[11] We push onward.

* * *

We were never catechized. We live by a somnambulistic law. We made Christ to be born in Bahia. Or in Belém do Pará.[12]

* * *

But we never permitted the birth of logic among us.

* * *

Down with Father Vieira.[13] Author of our first loan, to make a commission. The illiterate king had told him: put that on paper, but without a lot of lip. The loan was made. Brazilian sugar was signed away. Vieira left the money in Portugal and brought us the lip.

⋆ ⋆ ⋆

The spirit refuses to conceive a spirit without a body. Anthropomorphism. Need for the cannibalistic vaccine. To maintain our equilibrium, against meridian religions.[14] And against outside inquisitions.

⋆ ⋆ ⋆

We can attend only to the orecular world.

⋆ ⋆ ⋆

We already had justice, the codification of vengeance. Science, the codification of Magic. Cannibalism. The permanent transformation of the [Tatoo] into a totem.[15]

⋆ ⋆ ⋆

Down with the reversible world, and against objectified ideas. Cadaverized. The stop of thought that is dynamic. The individual as victim of the system. Source of classical injustices. Of romantic injustices. And the forgetting of inner conquests.

⋆ ⋆ ⋆

Routes. Routes. Routes. Routes. Routes. Routes. Routes.[16]

⋆ ⋆ ⋆

The Carib instinct.

⋆ ⋆ ⋆

Death and life of all hypotheses. From the equation "Self, part of the Cosmos" to the axiom "Cosmos, part of the Self." Subsistence. Experience. Cannibalism.

⋆ ⋆ ⋆

Down with the vegetable elites. In communication with the soil.

⋆ ⋆ ⋆

We were never catechized. What we really made was Carnaval. The Indian dressed as senator of the Empire. Making believe he's Pitt.[17] Or performing in Alencar's operas,[18] full of worthy Portuguese sentiments.

⋆ ⋆ ⋆

We already had communism. We already had Surrealist language. The Golden Age.

⋆ ⋆ ⋆

Catiti Catiti
Imara Notiá
Notiá Imara
Ipejú.[19]

⋆ ⋆ ⋆

Magic and life. We had the description and allocation of tangible goods, moral goods, and royal goods.[20] And we knew how to transpose mystery and death with the help of a few grammatical forms.

⋆ ⋆ ⋆

I asked a man what the Law was. He answered that it was the guarantee of the exercise of possibility. That man was named Galli Mathias.[21] I ate him.

⋆ ⋆ ⋆

Only where there is mystery is there no determinism. But what does that have to do with us?

⋆ ⋆ ⋆

Down with the histories of Man that begin at Cape Finisterre. The undated world. Unrubrified. Without Napoleon. Without Caesar.

⋆ ⋆ ⋆

The determination of progress by catalogues and television sets. Only machinery. And blood transfusers.

⋆ ⋆ ⋆

Down with the antagonistic sublimations. Brought here in caravels.

⋆ ⋆ ⋆

Down with the truth of missionary peoples, defined by the sagacity of a cannibal, the Viscount of Cairu:[22] – It's a lie told again and again.

⋆ ⋆ ⋆

But those who came here weren't crusaders. They were fugitives from a civilization we are eating, because we are strong and vindictive like the Jabuti.[23]

⋆ ⋆ ⋆

If God is the consciousness of the Uncreated Universe, Guaraci is the mother of the living.[24] Jaci is the mother of plants.[25]

⋆ ⋆ ⋆

We never had speculation. But we had divination. We had Politics, which is the science of distribution. And a social system in harmony with the planet.

⋆ ⋆ ⋆

The migrations. The flight from tedious states. Against urban scleroses. Against the Conservatories and speculative tedium.

⋆ ⋆ ⋆

From William James and Voronoff.[26] The transfiguration of the Taboo into a totem. Cannibalism.

⋆ ⋆ ⋆

The paterfamilias and the creation of the Morality of the Stork: Real ignorance of things + lack of imagination + sense of authority in the face of curious offspring.

⋆ ⋆ ⋆

One must depart from a profound atheism in order to arrive at the idea of God. But the Carib didn't need to. Because he had Guaraci.

* * *

The created object reacts like the Fallen Angels. Next, Moses day-dreams. What do we have to do with that?

* * *

Before the Portuguese discovered Brazil, Brazil had discovered happiness.

* * *

Down with the torch-bearing Indian. The Indian son of Mary, the stepson of Catherine of Medici and the godson of Dom Antonio de Mariz.[27]

* * *

Joy is the proof of nines.

* * *

In the matriarchy of Pindorama.[28]

* * *

Down with Memory as a source of custom. The renewal of personal experience.

* * *

We are concretists. Ideas take charge, react, and burn people in public squares. Let's get rid of ideas and other paralyses. By means of routes. Believe in signs; believe in sextants and in stars.

* * *

Down with Goethe, the Gracchi's mother, and the court of Dom João VI.[29]

* * *

Joy is the proof by nines.

* * *

The struggle between what we might call the Uncreated and the Creation – illustrated by the permanent contradiction between Man and his Taboo. Everyday love and the capitalist way of life. Cannibalism. Absorption of the sacred enemy. To transform him into a totem. The human adventure. The earthly goal. Even so, only the pure elites managed to realize carnal cannibalism, which carries within itself the highest meaning of life and avoids all the ills identified by Freud – catechist ills. What result is not a sublimation of the sexual instinct. It is the thermometrical scale of the cannibal instinct. Carnal at first, this instinct becomes elective, and creates friendship. When it is affective, it creates love. When it is speculative, it creates science. It takes detours and moves around. At times it is degraded. Low cannibalism, agglomerated with the sins of catechism – envy, usury, calumny, murder. We are acting against this plague of a supposedly cultured and Christianized peoples. Cannibals.

* * *

Down with Anchieta singing of the eleven thousand virgins of Heaven,[30] in the land of Iracema[31] – the patriarch João Ramalho, founder of São Paulo.[32]

* * *

Our independence has not yet been proclaimed. An expression typical of Dom João VI: "My son, put this crown on your head, before some adventurer puts it on his!"[33] We expelled the dynasty. We must still expel the Bragantine spirit,[34] the decrees and the snuff-box of Maria da Fonte.[35]

* * *

Down with the dressed and oppressive social reality registered by Freud – reality without complexes, without madness, without prostitutions and without penitentiaries, in the matriarchy of Pindorama.

Oswald de Andrade
In Piratininga, in the 374th Year
of the Swallowing of Bishop Sardinha.[36]

Notes (by Leslie Bary, translator)

1 Translation of Oswald de Andrade's "Manifesto Antropófago," *Revista de Antropofagia* 1:1 (São Paulo, May 1928). I want to thank Margaret Abel-Quintero, Wilton Azevedo, Aloísio Gomes Barbosa, José Niraldo de Farias, Dalila Machado, Sonia Ramos, and Lisa Fedorka-Carhuaslla at *Latin American Literary Review*, who read and commented on earlier versions of this translation.

2 In English in original. *Tupi* is the popular, generic name for the Native Americans of Brazil and also for their language, *nheengatu*.

3 A student of Greek and Latin literature, Cornelia is said to have been virtuous, austere, and extremely devoted to her sons. In the *Manifesto* she is the bad mother who (in contrast to the mother-goddesses Jaci and Guaraci) brings her children up as subjects of a "civilized" culture.

4 *Saudade* or yearning, homesickness, nostalgia, is a sentiment traditionally associated with the Portuguese national character.

5 In his annotated French translation of the *Manifesto*, Benedito Nunes points out that the sun is a maternal deity here. As Nunes points out as well, The "Great Snake" (*Cobra Grande*) is a water spirit in Amazonian mythology, and is the theme of Raul Bopp's poem *Cobra Norato* (1928). See Oswald de Andrade, "Le manifeste anthropophage," trans. Nunes, *Surréalisme périphérique*, ed. Luis de Moura Sobral (Montréal: Université de Montréal, 1984) 180–92, esp. 181, n. 3.

6 Nunes writes, "Oswald establishes an analogy between the absence of grammatical discipline and the absence of a split between Nature and Culture [in Brazil]. [As they were] so close to nature, [Brazilians] did not need to gather herbs (collections of old plants) as Rousseau and Goethe did" ("Le manifeste anthropophage" 182, n. 4). "Old plants" (*velhos vegetais*) also seems to allude to the entrenched, inactive, vegetative attitude of the Brazilian literary and cultural establishment Oswald wants to displace.

7 References to the work of Lévy-Bruhl on the structure of "primitive" thought. See below, n. 8.

8 Lucien Lévy-Bruhl, French philosopher and ethnologist (1857–1939). Among his publications are *Les fonctions mentales dans les sociétés inférieures* (1910), *La mentalité primitive* (1927), and *La mythologie primitive* (1935). The "primitive" mentality, according to Lévy-Bruhl, is not a deformation of the "civilized" one, but rather a completely different structure of thought. The primitive mind is mystical, collective and pre-logical.

9 Neil Larsen writes, "The *Manifesto* itself plays ironically on the 'theory' that the Enlightenment discourse of natural right, leading from Locke through Rousseau and ultimately to the *Declaration of the Rights of Man* and the Bourgeois Revolution as such, has its origins in Montaigne's 'noble savage,' based on the first reports from Brazil of 'cannibalism' among members of the Tupinamba tribal

aggregate." *Modernism and Hegemony* (Minneapolis: University of Minnesota Press, 1990) 80.

10 In Montaigne's essay "Des cannibales," "où Villegaignon print terre" is Antarctic France (the French mission in Brazil). Montaigne argues in this essay that ritual cannibalism is far less barbaric than many "civilized" European customs.

11 Count Herman Keyserling, German philosopher, world traveller and Orientalist, (1880–1946). His works propose the (Spenglerian) ideas that the Western world must be compenetrated with Eastern philosophy and that Latin America will rise as a world power while Europe declines. Nunes informs us that Keyserling, whose "visit to São Paulo in 1929 was welcomed by the *Revista de antropofagia*, set forth the idea of *technical barbarism* in his book *Die neuentstehende Welt*" ("Anthropophagisme et surréalisme," *Surréalisme périphérique*, ed. Luis de Moura Sobral, Montréal: Université de Montréal, (1984), 159–79, esp. 173, n. 15). Oswald inverts Keyserling's idea that a soulless "technical barbarism" is the sign of the modern world. In Oswald's utopia, primitive man enjoys the fruits of modernization.

12 The Brazilian city of Belém, or Bethlehem (state of Pará). Christ is thus not *brought* to the New World in Oswald's text, but born in His own Bethlehem.

13 Antonio Vieira (1608–97), Portuguese Jesuit instrumental in the colonization of Brazil. He came to be known as "the Judas of Brazil." In the war between Portugal and Holland over Pernambuco, Vieira negotiated a peace treaty by which Pernambuco was given to Holland so that Portugal would not have to pay Holland to end the war (with money made in Brazil). A noted orator and writer, Vieira is associated with formal, elegant rhetoric – a language directly opposed to the poetic idiom Oswald is forging for Brazil. Nunes writes that Vieira "is for Oswald the strongest of all emblems of Brazilian intellectual culture. … Oswald refers to Vieira's 1649 proposition to organize a company to exploit the sugar produced in the state of Maranhão" ("Le manifeste anthropophage" 183, n. 11).

14 According to Nunes, "meridian" religions are religions of salvation. See "Antropofagia ao Alcance de Todos," in Oswald de Andrade, *Do Pau-Brasil á Antropofagia e às Utopias* (1972); Rio de Janeiro: Civilização Brasileira, (1978) xxxi. *Meridian* as a dividing line seems, in the context of the *Manifesto*, to connote the divisions body/soul, native/foreign, and so on, which Oswald is attempting to dismantle.

15 In *Totem and Taboo* (1913, tr. 1918), Freud argues that the shift from "totemistic" to "taboo" systems of morality and religion consolidated paternal authority as the cornerstone of culture. Subjects of the taboo system are "civilized" because they have internalized the paternal rule. Oswald's advocacy of totemistic cannibalism, then, constitutes a rejection of patriarchy and the culture of the (Portuguese) "fathers." See also Nunes' more detailed explanation in "Anthropophagisme et surréalisme," 169–70.

16 The original *roteiros* (from *rotear*, to navigate) can also signify ships' logbooks or pilots' directions. Oswald can thus be construed here as referring to a rediscovery of America.

17 William Pitt, (1759–1806), British statesman influential in the formation of colonial policy for India.

18 José de Alencar, Brazilian writer and conservative politician, (1829–77). His Indianist novel *O Guarani* (1857) was turned into an opera, with music by Carlos Gomes (1836–96), which opened in the Teatro Scala, Milan, 2 December 1870. Nunes points out that "Peri, the hero of *O Guarani*, [has] civilized manners, imitating the great Portuguese lords" ("Le manifeste anthropophage" 186, n. 18).

19 In a footnote, Oswald provides a Portuguese translation of this Tupi text, running "New moon, oh new moon, blow memories of me into [the man I want]." The note gives the source of this text as *O Selvagem*, an anthropological work by Couto Magalhães, the politician and anthropologist (1836–98). Nunes quotes Couto de Magalhães' complete translation of the Tupi text: "Lua Nova, ó lua Nova! assoprai em … lembranças de mim; eisme aqui, estou em vossa presença; fazei com que eu tão somente ocupe seu coração." [New moon, oh new moon! Blow memories of me into …; I stand here before you; let me and no other fill his heart. "Le manifeste anthropophage" 186, n. 19].

20 The original here reads "dos bens físicos, dos bens morais, dos bens dignários." Oswald is playing with legal terms for various kinds of property, so as to ridicule "civilized" European institutions and show that they are superfluous to Brazilian culture. *Bens físicos* are probably the land and natural resources of Brazil, and *bens morais* the native culture. *Bens dignários*, property granted by the king, suggests both the aspects of Brazilian culture held in common with Portugal and also property "granted" by the Portuguese king that was in fact originally Brazilian.

21 "Galli Mathias" is a pun on *galimatias*, or nonsense.

22 José de Silva Lisboa, Viscount of Cairu (1756–1835), Brazilian politician. After Dom João VI established his court in Rio de Janeiro (1808) in the wake of Napoleon's invasion of Portugal, the Viscount of Cairu convinced him to open Brazilian ports to "all nations friendly to Portugal."

23 Tortoise of northern Brazil; in the popular culture of the Indians, he is a trickster figure. The jabuti is astute, active, comical, and combative.

24 Tupi sun goddess, mother of all men.

25 Tupi moon goddess, creator of plants.

26 William James, American philosopher (1842–1910), is the author of *Principles of Psychology* (1890), *The Varieties of Religious Experience* (1902), and *A Pluralistic Universe* (1909). Serge Voronoff, Russian-born biologist (1866–1951), is the author of *Etude sur la vieillesse et la rajeunissement par la greffe* (1926) and *La conquête de la vie* (1928), a method of rejuvenation by the grafting of genital glands. James' demystifying interpretation of religion can be contrasted to the *catachesis* Oswald rejects, and Voronoff's interest in grafting, as well as the return to youth and defiance of death, has affinities with Oswald's project. Nunes writes that "one could consider [Voronoff] to represent a biological pragmatism, towards which the *Anthropophagy Manifesto* leans" ("Le manifeste anthropophage" 188–9, n. 26).

27 Nunes writes that this is a "[s]uperimposition of three images: that of the sculpted Indians of the chandeliers of certain Baroque churches, that of the Indian Paraguassu, who went to France in the 16th century, accompanied by her husband, the Portuguese Diogo Alvares Correia, and [that of] D[om] Antonio de Mariz, the noble rural lord, father of Ceci, with whom Peri falls in love, in *O Guarani*. Paraguassu was baptized as Saint-Malo. A false version [of the story], spread through schoolbooks, made Catherine of Medici the godmother of this native" ("Le manifeste anthropophage" 189–90, n. 28).

28 *Pindorama* is the name of Brazil in the Tupi language. It may mean "country or region of palm trees."

29 Dom João VI, King of Portugal (reigned 1816–26). As Prince Regent, he fled the Napoleonic invasion of Portugal (1807) and installed the Portuguese court in Rio de Janeiro (1808–21). He made Brazil a kingdom (1815), equal in status to Portugal, and was Brazil's last colonial monarch before independence (1822).

30 Father Anchieta, (1534–97), Jesuit missionary among Indians; known as "The Apostle of Brazil" and generally considered to be the first Brazilian writer. He helped found São Paulo in 1554, after founding a Jesuit school at Piratininga (São Vicente). Anchieta is the author of a long Latin poem to the Virgin Mary, which he composed and committed to memory while a captive of the Indians, and a dramatic poem in Portuguese about the arrival of a relic of the Eleven Thousand Virgins (legendary companions of St. Ursula, martyred at Cologne in the early 4th century, after whom the Virgin Islands are named) in Brazil. Anchieta thus embodies the catachesis, importation of culture, and inscription of Brazil as colony that Oswald rejects.

31 Indian heroine in Alencar's novel of the same name (1865).

32 João Ramalho was one of the first Portuguese colonizers of Brazil. Shipwrecked off the coast near São Paulo in 1512, he made friends with the Tamoia Indians, married the daughter of a chief, had many children by her and other Tamoias, and created a small empire. He founded what is now Santo André and also the village of Piratininga. He was opposed to the Jesuits' founding of São Paulo, and organized the Indians' resistance against the missionaries.

33 Dom João VI's son, Dom Pedro I, became Emperor of Brazil when Independence was declared in 1822. According to tradition Dom João, already sensing that Brazil would separate itself from Portugal, had given Dom Pedro the directions Oswald quotes here before returning to Lisbon in 1821.

34 The Portuguese kings of the period were of the Bragança dynasty.

35 The legendary figure Maria da Fonte became the symbol of a popular rebellion in the Minho (1846) against higher taxation to finance the improvement of roads and reforms in public health. The uprising strengthened conservative forces in Portugal, associated with absolution and colonialism. In the context of the *M A*, Maria da Fonte is an emblem of allegiance to Portuguese tradition and a patriarchal woman, parallel to the Gracchi's mother and opposed to Jaci and Guaraci.

36 Sardinha was Bishop of Bahia from 1552 to 1556, when he was killed and apparently eaten by the Caltis Indians, into whose hands he fell when the ship that was taking him back to Lisbon sank in the São Francisco River. Sardinha had favored punishing Portuguese settlers who, enraged at the Jesuits' opposition to the enslavement of Indians, attacked the school at Piratininga in 1554.

40

Brasília

Clarice Lispector*

Elsewhere in Part III of this volume (Chapter 34), James Holston discusses the history of Brazil's capital and its peculiar place in national life. Brasília was meant to embody the nation while remaining altogether distinct from the "rest of Brazil." Its history, then, has been one of contradictions. Written in 1962, a few years after the city was finished, the following pages offer a ground level view of Brasília's monumental scale: its built environs rendered in such writing as to convey the unprecedented form of human experience identified with the new capital. In addition, it was written by a woman whose biography tells us something distinct about the varieties of Brazilian citizenship. The third and youngest daughter of Eastern European Jewish émigrés, she was born in Chechelnik, Ukraine. The newborn's family was en route to Brazil where "Chaya" eventually became Clarice Lispector (1920–77), one of Brazil's most important writers of the twentieth century. Her short fiction, novels, and journalism take up questions of national belonging, "foreignness," variable identity, and "self-fashioning" – all concerns that inform her idiosyncratic writing style.

It becomes readily apparent to a reader that "Brasília" is neither a short story, nor an essay. This first-person reflection published in the Rio de Janeiro newspaper *Jornal do Brasil* is – like the city of Brasília – both instantly identifiable and altogether uncanny. Like everything Lispector wrote, the prose in "Brasília" is a slippery surface that gives way to delirium. An impressionistic account, this daydream submits repeated shifts in tone, attention, and intensity. Lispector's subject here is the future world that

* Clarice Lispector (2000 [1962]) "Brasília." In *Brasil de la Antropofagia a Brasília, 1920–1950* (trans. Elizabeth Power, Génese Andrade, Karel Clapshaw, Lucia Wataghin, Marianne Fischer, Regina Salgado Campos and Stella O. Tagnin, pp. 629–30). Valencia, Spain: IVAM Institut Valencia d'Art Modern, VEGAP.

Modern Art in Africa, Asia, and Latin America: An Introduction to Global Modernisms, First Edition.
Edited by Elaine O'Brien, Everlyn Nicodemus, Melissa Chiu, Benjamin Genocchio, Mary K. Coffey, and Roberto Tejada.

Lúcio Costa and Oscar Niemeyer created in the desolate Central Plateau of Brazil – in architecture Holston nominates as "millenarian modern." The chronicle's persona is an elusive identity and her attitudes are indefinable. The account begins with an overblown anthropological myth about a race of peoples who inhabited Brasília in the fourth century BC – "very tall, fair-haired men and women who were not Americans or Swedes and who sparkled in the sunlight." It surreptitiously devolves into a tale of gothic horror: "I waited for the night like someone waiting for the shadows so as to be able to slip away. When night came I saw with horror that ... it was built without anywhere for rats. A whole part of us, the worst part, the part that is afraid of rats, that part has no place in Brasília."

With abrupt turns, while juxtaposing the possible and improbable, Lispector's aim is to produce critical readers better equipped to account for the contradictory nature of the nation's capital. In this experimental prose, as in Brasília itself, "contingency design" undercuts "total design" (Holston, this volume). Lispector renders Brasília's reality as a disconnected sequence of incidents or "rhythms" – often using a long dash to mark a rupture, but also to visualize the bar that separates words from lived experience. She refers both to the constructed environs of Brasília and her own writing when she concludes: "This is the place where space most resembles time ... slowness and silence, which is also my idea of eternity."

In relation to James Holston's article on Brasília, how does Lispector articulate the notions of statecraft versus stagecraft? How are the ominous and playful tones Lispector rehearses in this written account similar to strategies found in modern Latin American artworks described elsewhere in this volume? How are the tonal shifts in this chronicle comparable to those in Oswald de Andrade's "Cannibal Manifesto"? How does the writing shape and frustrate reader expectations – and to what effect? If the construction of a city determines the structure of its society, how do the descriptive powers of language and viewpoint so assemble as to also produce social "spaces"?

Further Readings

Lispector, Clarice (1989) *The Stream of Life* (Elizabeth Lowe and Earl Fitz, trans.). Minneapolis: University of Minnesota Press.

Lispector, Clarice (1992) *The Hour of the Star* (Giovanni Pontiero, trans.). New York, NY: New Directions.

Lispector, Clarice (1996) *Selected Cronicas* (Giovanni Pontiero, trans.). New York, NY: New Directions.

Waldemer, Thomas P. (2008) "Imperfect Harmony: Coca-Cola and the Cannibal Metaphor in *Beba Coca Cola, Sangue de Coca Cola* and *a Hora da Estrela*." *Hispanofilia* 153 (16–18): 97–108.

Brasília is built along the line of the horizon. Brasília is artificial. As artificial as the world must have been when it was created. When the world was created, a man had to be created especially for that world. We are all deformed by adaptation to God's freedom. We do not know what we would be like if we had been created first and then the world deformed to our needs. Brasília does not yet have the man of Brasília. If I were to say that Brasília is beautiful they would see immediately that I like the city. But if I say that Brasília is the image of my insomnia they see an accusation in it. But my insomnia is neither attractive nor ugly, my insomnia is me, it is lived, it is my fear. It is a semi-colon. The two architects were not thinking about constructing beauty, that would be easy: they built unexplained fear. The enactment is not an understanding, it is a new mystery. When I died, one day I opened my eyes and there was Brasília. I was alone in the world, There was a taxi standing there. Without a driver. What a scare. – Lúcio Costa and Oscar Niemeyer, two solitary men. – I see Brasília as I see Rome: Brasília began with a final simplification of ruins. The ivy has not yet grown. Apart from the wind there is something else that blows. It is only recognised by the supernatural tension of the lake. Wherever a child stands it may fall, and fall out of the world. Brasília is on the edge. – If I lived here I would let my hair grow down to the ground. – Brasília had a splendid past that no longer exists. That kind of civilisation disappeared thousands of years ago. In the fourth century BC it was inhabited by very tall, fair-haired men and women who were not Americans or Swedes and who sparkled in the sunlight. They were all blind. And that is why there is nothing to bump into in Brasília. The people of Brasília dressed in white gold. The race died out because too few male children were born. The more beautiful the people of Brasília were, the more blind and pure and sparkling they became, and the fewer male children were born. The people of Brasília used to live for nearly three hundred years. There was no reason to die. Thousands of years later it was discovered by a band of outlaws who would not be received in any other place: they had nothing to lose. There they lit their fires, pitched their tents, gradually they excavated the sand in which the city was buried. They were shorter, dark-skinned men and women, with aloof, restless eyes, and, because they were fugitives and desperate, they had a reason for living and dying. They lived in the ruined houses and multiplied, creating a very contemplative human race. – I waited for the night like someone waiting for the shadows so as to be able to slip away. When night came I saw with horror that it was no use: wherever I was I would be seen. What frightens me is: seen by whom? – It was built without anywhere for rats. A whole part of us, the worst part, the very part that is afraid of rats, that part has no place in Brasília. They wanted to deny that people are not suitable. Construction with space calculated for clouds. Hell understands me better. But rats are invading, all very big ones. That is an invisible headline in the newspapers. – Here I am afraid. – The construction of Brazil: that of a totalitarian State. – This great visual silence that I love. My insomnia would also have created this peace of a never-never world. I, too, would meditate in that desert, like those two who are monks. Where there is no place for temptations. But in the distance I see vultures flying overhead. Good heavens, what can be dying? – I have never wept in Brasília. There was no place for it. – It is a beach without the sea. – In Brasília there is no way in and there is no way out. – Mummy, it's nice to see you standing there with that white cloak flying. (It's because I have died, my child.) – A prison in the open air. In any case, there would be nowhere to escape to. Anyone who escaped would probably go to Brasília. – They captured me in freedom. But freedom is only what is conquered. When they give me it, they are ordering me to be free. – A whole aspect of human coldness that I have, I find in myself here in Brasília, and it flourishes, icy, powerful, a frozen force of Nature. This is the place where my crimes (not the worst ones, but the ones that I will not understand in myself), where my icy crimes have a space. I am going away. Here my crimes would not be crimes of love. I am going away for my other crimes, those that God and I understand. But I know that I will return. I am drawn here by what frightens me in myself. – I have never seen anything like it in the world. But I recognise this city in the very depths of my dreams. The deepest level of my dreams is a kind of lucidity. – Well, as I was saying, Flash Gordon ... – If they took a full-length portrait of me in Brasília, when they developed the photograph only the landscape would be visible. – Where are the giraffes in Brasília? – A certain tension of mine and certain silences make my son say: wow, you adults are far out. It's urgent. If it is not populated, or rather, overpopulated, it will be too late: there will be no place for people. They will feel themselves tacitly expelled. – Here the soul does not cast a shadow on the ground. – During the first days I was not hungry. It seemed to me that everything was going to be airline food. – At night I thrust my face into the silence. I know that there is an unknown time when manna descends and moistens the land of Brasília. – However close one may be, everything here is seen from far away. I did not find a way of touching. But at least there is this advantage in my favour: before arriving here I already knew how to touch from far away. I never despaired greatly: from far away I touched. I had a great deal, but not even what I touched, you know. A rich woman is like that. She is pure Brasília. – The city of Brasília lies outside the city. – *Boys, boys come here, will you, look who is coming on the street all dressed up in modernistic style. It ain't nobody but ... (Aunt Hagar's Blues, Ted Lewis and his Band*, with Jimmy Dorsey on the clarinet.) – That startling beauty, this city, traced in the air. – For the time being, samba cannot be created in Brasília. – Brasília does not let me become tired. It pesters me a little. Well disposed, well-disposed, well-disposed, I feel good. And after all, I always cultivated my tiredness, as my richest passivity. – All that barely exists now God alone knows what will happen in Brasília. For here chance is abrupt. – Brasília is badly shadowed. It is the motionless profile of something. – In my insomnia I look out of the hotel window at three o'clock in the morning. Brasília is the landscape of insomnia. It never falls asleep. – Here an organic creature does not deteriorate. It petrifies. – I wanted to see five hundred thousand eagles of the blackest onyx scattered throughout Brasília – Brasília is sexless. – The first moment of seeing is like a certain moment of drunkenness: your feet don't touch the ground. – How deeply people breathe in Brasília. One who breathes begins to want. And wanting cannot be. It does not exist. Will it exist? But I cannot see where. – I would not be astonished to meet Arabs in the street. Ancient, dead Arabs. – Here my passion dies. And I achieve a lucidity that makes me great for no reason. I am fabulous and useless, I am pure gold. And almost mediumistic. – If there is some crime that humanity has not yet committed, that new crime will be inaugurated here. And with so little secrecy, so well adapted to the plateau, that nobody will ever know. – This is the place where space most resembles time. – I am sure that this is the right place for me. But the land has depraved me too much. I have grown used to bad ways of living. – Erosion is going to strip Brasília to the bone. – The religious air that I felt from the very first, and that I denied. This city was achieved by prayer. Two men beatified by solitude created me standing here, restless, lonely, exposed to the wind. – What is really needed is white horses set loose in Brasília. At night they would be green in the moonlight. – I know what those two wanted: slowness and silence, which is also my idea of eternity. The two of them created a portrait of an eternal city. – There is something here that makes me afraid. When I discover what frightens me, I will also know what I love here. Fear always guided me to what I love. And because I love, I am afraid. Often it was fear that took me by the hand and led me. Fear leads me to danger. And all that I love is hazardous. – The craters of the Moon are in Brasília. – The beauty of Brasília is its invisible statues.

Credits and Sources

The editors and publisher gratefully acknowledge the following for permission to reproduce copyright material:

Chika Okeke-Agulu, "Modern African Art," *The Short Century: Independence and Liberation Movements in Africa 1945–1994*, Okwui Enwezor, ed., © 2001 by Chika Okeke-Agulu, pp. 29–34, 36. Reprinted with the kind permission of the author.

Steven Sack, "From Country to City: The Development of an Urban Art," *Catalogue: Ten Years of Collecting (1979–1989)*, Anitra Nettleton and David Hammond-Tooke, eds, pp. 54–7. Published by the University of the Witwatersrand, Johannesburg, South Africa, Art Galleries 1989. Reprinted with permission of the author.

Elza Miles, *Nomfanekiso Who Paints at Night: The Art of Gladys Mgudlandlu*, © 2002, Elza Miles, p. 7–8, 10, 13, 37–8, 90–1. Published by Fernwood Press, © 2002 Fernwood Press, an imprint of Random House Struik (Pty) Ltd, Cape Town, South Africa (www.randomstruik.co.za).

Okwui Enwezor and Octavio Zaya, "Negritude, Pan-Africanism, and Postcolonial African Identity: African Portrait Photography," Selection from "Colonial Imaginary, Tropes of Disruption: History, Culture, and Representation in the Works of African Photographers," Okwui Enwezor and Octavio Zaya, *In/sight: African Photographers, 1940 to the Present*, © 1996, The Solomon R. Guggenheim Foundation, pp. 26–35, 46–7. Reprinted with permission of The Guggenheim Foundation.

Modern Art in Africa, Asia, and Latin America: An Introduction to Global Modernisms, First Edition.
Edited by Elaine O'Brien, Everlyn Nicodemus, Melissa Chiu, Benjamin Genocchio,
Mary K. Coffey, and Roberto Tejada.

Okwui Enwezor, "A Critical Presence: *Drum* Magazine in Context," *In/sight: African Photographers, 1940 to the Present*, © 1996, The Solomon R. Guggenheim Foundation, pp. 179–91. Reprinted with permission of The Guggenheim Foundation.

Michael Harris, "Art of the African Diaspora," *A History of Art in Africa*, Monica Blackmun Visonà, Robin Poynor, Herbert M. Cole and Michael D. Harris, © 2001, Harry N. Abrams, Inc., pp. 500–1, 504–10, 512–14.

Hassan Fathy, "Chorale: Man, Society, and Technology: An Experiment in Rural Egypt" (1973 [1969]), *Architecture for the Poor: An Experiment in Rural Egypt*, © 1973, The University of Chicago Press, pp. 24–6, 37–8, 43–6. Reprinted with permission of University of Chicago Press.

Nwachukwu Frank Ukadike, "Oral Tradition and the Aesthetics of Black African Cinema," *Black African Cinema*, Nwachukwu Frank Ukadike, © 1994, the Regents of the University of California, pp. 70–2, 201–4, 207, 210–11, 213–16, 322, 334–5. Published by University of California Press. Reprinted with permission of University of California Press.

Frantz Fanon, "On National Culture," *The Damned* (or *The Wretched of the Earth*), trans. Constance Farrington, © 1963, Presence Africaine, pp. 180–1. Originally published by Editions François Maspero, Paris under the title *Les Damnés de la Terre*, © 1967, Penguin Books UK.

Aimé Césaire, *Discourse on Colonialism*, trans. Joan Pinkham, © 1972, Monthly Review Press, pp. 75–6. Originally published as *Discours sur le colonialisme* by Présence Africaine, © 1955 by Editions Présence Africaine.

Uche Okeke, "Natural Synthesis" (1960), *Seven Stories about Modern Art in Africa*, Whitechapel Art Gallery, London, pp. 208–9. Paris, New York: Flammarion, 1995. Reprinted with permission of Whitechapel Art Gallery and Uche Okeke.

Jean Rouch and Ousmane Sembène, "A Historic Confrontation between Jean Rouch and Ousmane Sembène in 1965: 'You Look at Us as if We Were Insects,'" transcribed by Albert Cervoni and translated by Muna El Fituri, *The Short Century: Independence and Liberation Movements in Africa 1945–1994*, Okwui Enwezor, ed., published by Prestel, pp. 440–1. Reprinted with kind permission of the translator Muna El Fituri.

Jim Supangkat, "Multiculturism/Multimodernism," *Contemporary Art in Asia: Traditions/Tensions* (exhibition catalog), pp. 76–8. New York: Asia Society Galleries, 1996. Copyright © Asia Society Galleries. Reprinted with permission.

Ahmad Mashadi, "Negotiating Modernities: Encounters with Cubism in Asian Art," *Cubism in Asia: Unbounded Dialogues*, K. Miwa, K. Suzuki and T. Matsumoto, eds, © 2006, Singapore Art Museum, pp. 215–18.

Geeta Kapur, "When Was Modernism in Indian Art?" *When Was Modernism: Essays on Contemporary Cultural Practice in India*, © 2000, Geeta Kapur, pp. 297–303, 307, 309, 313–14, 317, 323–4 (with cuts). Published by Tulika Books. Reprinted with kind permission of the publisher and the author.

Partha Mitter, "The Formalist Prelude," *The Triumph of Modernism: Indian Artists and the Avant Garde 1922–1947*, © 2007, Partha Mitter, pp. 15–27, 230–2. Published by Reaktion Books.

Osman Jamal, "E. B. Havell and Rabindranath Tagore: Nationalism, Modernity and Art," *Third Text*, 53, Winter 2000–1, pp. 19–30. Reprinted with permission of Taylor & Francis.

Rabindranath Tagore, "Art and Tradition" (1926), *On Art and Aesthetics: A Selection of Lectures, Essays and Letters*, © 1961, Inter-National Cultural Centre, New Delhi, pp. 58–64, Published by Orient Longman, India.

Gennifer Weisenfeld, "Western Style Painting in Japan: Mimesis, Individualism and Japanese Nationhood," *Mavo: Japanese Artists and the Avant-Garde 1905–1931*, © 2002, the Regents of the University of California, pp. 11–27, 270–3. Published by University of California Press. Reprinted with permission of University of California Press.

John Clark, "Artistic Subjectivity in the Taishō and Early Shōwa Avant-Garde," *Japanese Art after 1945: Scream against the Sky*, Alexandra Munroe, ed., © 1985, Alexandra Munroe, pp. 41–53. Published by Harry N. Abrams, Inc.

Joe Takeba, "The Age of Modernism: From Visualization to Socialization," *The History of Japanese Photography* (exhibition catalog), © 2003, The Museum of Fine Arts, Houston, pp. 142–57. Reprinted courtesy of the Museum of Fine Arts, Houston.

Jonathan M. Reynolds, "The Architectural Profession in Japan, 1850–1930," *Maekawa Kunio and the Emergence of Japanese Modernist Architecture*, © 2001, the Regents of the University of California, pp. 9–19, 21–37, 256–61. Published by University of California Press. Reprinted with permission of University of California Press.

Takahashi Shinkichi, *Dangen wa Dadaisuto* (Assertion Is Dadaist) [1923], *Buddhist Elements in Dada: A Comparison of Tristan Tzara, Takahashi Shinkichi, and*

Their Fellow Poets, Ko Won, © 1977, New York University Press, pp. 31–4. Reprinted with permission of New York University Press.

Eugene Y. Wang, excerpted from "Sketch conceptualism as modernist contingency," *Chinese Art: Modern Expressions*, M. Hearn and J. G. Smith, eds, © 2001, The Metropolitan Museum of Art, New York, pp. 103–21, 127–34, 140–53, 156–61. Reprinted by permission.

Ralph Croizier, "Post-Impressionists in Pre-War Shanghai: The Juelanshe (Storm Society) and the Fate of Modernism in Republican China," *Modernity in Asian Art*, J. Clark, ed., © 1993, Wild Peony, pp. 135–53. Reprinted with permission of Wild Peony Pty Ltd.

Zheng Dongtian, "Films and Shanghai," *Shanghai Modern 1919–1945* (exhibition catalog), Jo-Anne Birnie Danzker, Ken Lum and Zheng Shengtian, eds, © 2004, Museum Villa Stuck, Hatje Cantz Verlag, Ostfildern-Ruit, and the authors, pp. 298, 300–2, 304–6. Published by Hatje Cantz Verlag. Translated by Michael Fei.

Ni Yide, Pang Xunqin, *et al.*, "The Storm Society Manifesto," *Art Trimonthly* [*Yishu xunkan*], 1(5), October 1932, Shanghai, reprinted in *Shanghai Modern 1919–1945* (exhibition catalog), Jo-Anne Birnie Danzker, Ken Lum, and Zheng Shengtian, eds, © 2004, Museum Villa Stuck, Hatje Cantz Verlag, Ostfildern-Ruit, and the authors, p. 234. Published by Hatje Cantz Verlag. Translated by Michael Fei.

Roberto Fernández Retamar, "Our America and the West," *Social Text*, 15 (autumn), © 1986, Durham: Duke University Press, pp. 1–8, 12–20, 23. Copyright © 1986 Duke University Press. All rights reserved. Reprinted with permission of the publisher.

Andrea Giunta, "Strategies of Modernity in Latin America," *Beyond the Fantastic*, Gerardo Mosquera, ed., 1995, London: inIVA, pp. 53–66, © Andrea Giunta. Reprinted with kind permission of the author.

Leonard Folgarait, "Revolution as Ritual: Diego Rivera's National Palace Mural," *Oxford Art Journal*, 14(1), © 1991, pp. 18–33.

Gerardo Mosquera, "Africa in the Art of Latin America," *Art Journal*, 51(4), © 1992, Latin American Art, pp. 30–8. © Gerardo Mosquera. Reprinted with kind permission of the author.

Mari Carmen Ramírez, "Vital Structures: The Constructive Nexus in South America," *Inverted Utopias: Avant-Garde Art in Latin America*, Mari Carmen Ramírez and Héctor Olea, eds, © 2004, New Haven: Yale University Press, pp. 191–201. Reprinted with the kind permission of the author.

Esther Gabara, "Landscape: Errant Modernism and Aesthetics in Brazil," *Errant Modernism: The Ethos of Photography in Mexico and Brazil*, © 2008, Durham: Duke University Press, pp. 36–50, all rights reserved. Reprinted with permission of the publishers.

James Holston, "The Spirit of Brasília: Modernity as Experiment and Risk," *Brazil Body and Soul*, Edward J. Sullivan, ed., © 2001, New York City: Solomon R. Guggenheim Foundation, pp. 540–57, all rights reserved. Used with permission.

Robert Stam, "Carmen Miranda, Grande Otelo, and the *Chanchada*, 1929–1949," *Tropical Multiculturalism: A Comparative History of Race in Brazilian Cinema and Culture*, © 1997, Durham: Duke University Press, pp. 79–105, all rights reserved. Reprinted with permission of the publisher.

Rubén Darío, "To Roosevelt" (1876, poem) trans. Gabriel Gudding, *Mandorla*, 7, (Spring), © 2004, Normal: Illinois State University; San Diego: UCSD, pp. 108–9. Reprinted with kind permission of the translator and Mandorla.

Joaquín Torres-García, "The School of the South" trans. Anne Twitty, from *El Taller Torres-García: The School Of The South And Its Legacy*, Mari Carmen Ramírez, ed.; Cecilia Buzio de Torres, Mari Carmen Ramírez, curators, © 1992. By permission of the University of Texas Press.

Joaquín Torres-García, "The New Art of America" (1942), *Inverted Utopias: Avant-Garde Art in Latin America*, Mari Carmen Ramírez and Héctor Olea, eds, © 2004, New Haven: Yale University Press, p. 470. Reprinted with permission of Yale University Press.

José Vasconcelos, *The Cosmic Race* (1925), Didier T. Jaén, trans. and annotated, first bilingual edition originally published by the Department of Chicano Studies, California State University, 1979 © 1979 California State University (English Edition) afterword, © 1997, Baltimore: Johns Hopkins University Press. Reprinted with permission of the Department of Chicano Studies.

Oswald de Andrade, "Cannibalist Manifesto" (1928) trans. Leslie Bary, *Latin American Literary Review*, 19(38) (July–Dec. 1999), pp. 38–47. Reprinted with permission of Latin American Literary Review.

Clarice Lispector, "Brasília" (1962), *Brasil de la Antropofagia a Brasilia, 1920–1950*, © 2000, Valencia: IVAM Institut Valencià d'Art Modern, VEGAP, pp. 629–30.

Index

Italic type indicates pages with illustrations.

Modern Art in Africa, Asia, and Latin America: An Introduction to Global Modernisms, First Edition.
Edited by Elaine O'Brien, Everlyn Nicodemus, Melissa Chiu, Benjamin Genocchio, Mary K. Coffey, and Roberto Tejada.